D1413586

Brazil:
A Handbook of
Historical Statistics

A
Reference
Publication
in
International
Historical
Statistics

Oliver Pollak
Editor

Brazil:
A Handbook of
Historical Statistics

BOWLING GREEN STATE UNIVERSITY DISCARDED LIBRARY

ARMIN K. LUDWIG

G.K.HALL &CO.

70 LINCOLN STREET, BOSTON, MASS.

JEROME LIBRARY–BOWLING GREEN STATE UNIVERSITY

All Rights Reserved
Copyright © 1985 by Armin K. Ludwig

Library of Congress Cataloging in Publication Data

Ludwig, Armin K.
  Brazil : a handbook of historical statistics.

  (A Reference publication in international historical statistics)
  Includes index.
  1. Brazil—Statistics—History—Handbooks, manuals,
etc. I. Title. II. Series.
  HA984.L83 1985   318.1   85-21849
  ISBN 0-8161-8188-8

This publication is printed on permanent/durable acid-free paper
MANUFACTURED IN THE UNITED STATES OF AMERICA

*For Kirk, Erik and Deborah who know Brazil
and David and Kathy who would like to*

Contents

Contents

About the Author

Dr. Armin K. Ludwig is the emblem-heraldic specialist of the United States Air Force and is attached to the Air Force Historical Research Center at Maxwell Air Force Base, Montgomery, Alabama. He has previously served as chairman of the Geography Department and the Foreign Area Studies Program at Colgate University, Hamilton, New York, as senior research associate at the Center for Applied Urban Research, University of Nebraska at Omaha, and as consultant to the University of Texas Coordinating Board and the Agency for International Development (AID). He has taught at Colgate University, Ball State University, City University of New York, University of Nebraska at Omaha, University of Massachusetts--Amherst, and in both the United States and Germany for the Air Force. He holds a doctorate in geography from the University of Illinois--Champaign.

Dr. Ludwig began his research in Brazil in 1956 with soil studies in the region of the new capital, Brasília, before the city was built. In 1963 and 1964 he returned to Brasília under a grant from the Social Science Research Council and based on this research published "The Planning and Creation of Brasília: Toward a New and Unique Brazilian Regional Environment?" in New Perspectives of Brazil (Nashville: Vanderbilt University Press, 1966). His Brazilian field research in 1967, supported by the Social Science Research Council and the Agricultural Development Council, led to publication of Brazil's New Agrarian Reform: An Evaluation of Its Property Classification and Tax Systems (New York: Frederick A. Praeger, 1969); Harry Taylor was the joint author. In 1980 the International Area Studies Programs at the University of Massachusetts at Amherst published Dr. Ludwig's monograph entitled Brasília's First Decade: A Study of Its Urban Morphology and Urban Support Systems.

Series Preface

International Historical Statistics is a descriptive and explanatory reference series. It includes national and thematic volumes depicting historical, economic, social, and political development in statistical terms. The series is designed for use in university, college, junior college, high school, and public library settings as well as by United States and foreign government departments, corporations, and scholars. The compilers are noted for their expertise in chosen areas, necessary language skills, access to pertinent primary source materials, and ability to present quantitative data to a diverse audience. The series includes volumes by country and sourcebooks on topics such as statistical bibliography, archives, stock prices over an extended period, and other cohesive statistically-oriented topics.

Oliver B. Pollak
Series Editor

List of Tables

List of Tables

List of Tables

List of Tables

List of Tables

List of Tables

List of Tables

List of Tables

List of Maps

List of Maps

Sources of Data for Tables and Maps

Owing to space limitations the sources for tables and maps were either abbreviated or given only partial citations. The following are more complete citations for those table and map sources that were not dealt with in the text and therefore were not covered by footnotes or references at the end of each chapter.

AN =
   Anuário estatístico do Brasil. Volumes have been published for 1908-12, 1936, 1937, 1939-40, 1941-45, and annually to date (1981) from 1946.

Baer 1965 =
   Werner Baer, Industrialization and Economic Development of Brazil, a publication of the Economic Growth Center, Yale University (Homewood, Ill.: Richard D. Irwin, 1965).

Brasil 1966 =
   Brasil 1966, Resources and Possibilities (Brasília: Administration Department of the Ministry of Foreign Relations, 1966).

BT (1931) =
   Brazil of Today (Rio de Janeiro: Ministry of Labor, Industry, and Commerce, 1931).

CEB 1925, 1932, 1919-23, 1930-36, Resumo Mensal jan-dez 1949-50 =
   Commercio exterior do Brasil, resumo por mercadorias (Rio de Janeiro: Directoria de Estatística Commercial, Ministério da Fazenda). Translation: Brazilian Foreign Trade, Commodity Summary (Rio de Janeiro: Directorate of Commercial Statistics, Ministry of Finance). Note: the pre-1930 volumes use the double "m" in Commercio and the "c" in Directoria, both of which were dropped after 1930. Resumo Mensal = Monthly Summary.

Enciclopédia Delta Universal =
Enciclopédia Delta Universal (Rio de Janeiro: Editora Universal, 2d edition, 15 volumes, 8,592 pages, 1980).

Ferrovias do Brasil =
Ferrovias do Brasil (Rio de Janeiro: IBGE, Conselho Nacional de Estatística, 1956). Translation: Railroads of Brazil.

Lombardi =
Mary Lombardi, Brazilian Serial Documents: Selective and Annotated Guide (Bloomington: Indiana University Press, 1974).

Ports, Rivers and Navigation of Brazil =
Ports, Rivers and Navigation of Brazil, published in English by the National Department of Ports and Navigation for the New York World's Fair, 1939.

Present Situation of Graduate Studies in Brazil, 1975 =
Present Situation of Graduate Studies in Brazil, 1975 (Brasília: Department of University Affairs, Ministry of Education and Culture, no date given).

RE 1872 =
Census of 1872 (Recenseamento de população do império de Brasil a que se procedeu no dia 1 de agôsto de 1872).

RE 1890 =
Census of 1890 (Recenseamento geral da República dos Estados Unidos do Brazil em 31 de dezembro de 1890).
    RE 1890A   Rio de Janeiro
    RE 1890B   Synopsis
    RE 1890C   Sex, Race, Marital State, Nationality, Religion, Literacy
    RE 1890D   Age

RE 1920 =
Census of 1920 (Recenseamento do Brasil realizado em 1 setembro de 1920).
    RE 1920A   Introduction, Volume I
    RE 1920B1   Rio de Janeiro, Vital Statistics, Volume II, Part 1
    RE 1920B2   Rio de Janeiro, Agriculture, Volume II, Part 2
    RE 1920B3   Rio de Janeiro, Housing, Volume II, Part 3
    RE 1920C1   Agriculture, Volume III, Part 1
    RE 1920C2   Agriculture, Volume III, Part 2
    RE 1920C3   Agriculture, Volume III, Part 3
    RE 1920D1   Population Characteristics for States, Municipios, Distritos: Sex Civil State, National-

ity, Physical Defects, Education, Occupation,
Dwellings, and Buildings, Volume IV,
Parts 1-6
    RE 1920E1 Industry and Salaries

RE 1940 =
  Census of 1940 (Recenseamento geral do Brasil-1 de
  setembro de 1940).
    RE 1940A1 Introduction to Brazilian Culture, Tomo I
    RE 1940A2 Population and Habitation, Tomo II
    RE 1940A3 Agriculture, Tomo III
    RE 1940A4 Industry, Tomo III
    RE 1940A5 Retail/Wholesale and Service
    RE 1940B   Regional Series, Population, Habitation,
               Agriculture, Industry, Retail/Wholesale,
               Service, Tomos 1-22

RE 1950 =
  Census of 1950 (IV recenseamento do Brasil, 1950).
    RE 1950A1 Demographics, Volume I
    RE 1950A2 Agriculture, Volume II
    RE 1950A3 Industrial, Volume III, Tomo 1
    RE 1950A4 Retail/Wholesale and Services, Volume III,
               Tomo 2
    RE 1950A5 Transportation and Communication, Volume IV
    RE 1950B1 Regional Series, Population, Habitation,
               Agriculture, Industry, Retail/Wholesale,
               Services, Volumes VI-XXX (volume V was not
               published)

RE 1960 =
  Census of 1960 (VII recenseamento geral do Brasil, 1960).
    RE 1960A1 National Series - Demographic Census
    RE 1960B1 Regional Series - Demographic Census,
               Volumes I-XVIII
    RE 1960C1 Agriculture, both national and regional
    RE 1960D1 Industrial, both national and regional

RE 1970 =
  Census of 1970 (VIII recenseamento geral do Brasil, 1970).
    RE 1970A1 National Series - Demographic Census
    RE 1970B1 Regional Series - Demographic Census

RS 1924 =
  Summary of Various Financial and Economic Statistics
  (Resumo de Várias Estatísticas-Financeiras (Rio de
  Janeiro: Directoria Geral de Estatística, Ministério da
  Agricultura Indústria e Commércio, 1924).

SI 1940 =
  Synopses of the 1940 Census

SI 1940A   Synopsis of the Demographic Census
SI 1940B   Synopsis of the Industrial Census
SI 1940C   Synopsis of the Census of Personal Service
SI 1940D1   Synopsis of the Retail/Wholesale Census
SI 1940D2   Synopsis of the Business Service Census

SI 1970A =
Synopsis of the 1970 Census (Sinopse preliminar do censo demográfico, VIII recenseamento geral, 1970).

SI 1980 =
Synopsis of the 1980 Census (Sinopse preliminar do censo demográfico, IX recenseamento geral do Brasil, 1980).

UN 1982 =
Yearbook of National Accounts Statistics, 1980, Volume I, Part 1, "Individual Country Data" (New York: United Nations, 1982).

Glossary of Brazilian Government Agencies Originating Data

Associação Brasileira para o Desenvolvimento das Indústrias
de Base (ADIB)
  Brazilian Association for the Development of Basic
  Industry

Associação Brasileiro de Industria de Álcalis e Cloro
Derivados
  Brazilian Association of the Alkali and Chlorine Deriva-
  tive Industry

Associação Nacional dos Fabricantes de Papel
  National Association of Paper Manufacturers

Balanços Financeiros dos Estados
  Financial Balances of the States

Banco do Brasil
  Bank of Brazil

Banco do Brasil, Carteira de Comércio Exterior (CACEX)
  Bank of Brazil, External Trade Section

Banco Central do Brasil
  Central Bank of Brazil

Bôlsa de Mercadorias do Rio de Janeiro
  Rio de Janeiro Commodities Market

Bôlsa Oficial de Valores de São Paulo
  Official Stock Market of Sao Paulo

Bôlsa de Valores, Rio de Janeiro, Recife, Paraná, Vitória e
Santos
  Stock Markets of Rio de Janeiro, Recife, Paraná, Vitória
  and Santos

Caixa de Amortização, Banco do Brasil
  Amortization Section, Bank of Brazil

Caixa Economica Federal
  Federal Savings Bank

Caixa de Estabilização
  Stabilization Bank

Câmara Sindical de Bôlsas de Valores, Rio de Janeiro
  Chamber of Syndicates of the Rio de Janeiro Stock Market

Camara Sindical dos Corretores, Bôlsa de Fundos Públicos
  Chamber of Syndicates of Brokers in the Public Funds
  Markets

Campanha Nacional de Álcalis
  National Campaign for the Development of the Alkali
  Industry

Companhia Pernambucana de Borracha Sintética (COPERBO)
  Pernambuco Synthetic Rubber Corporation

Carteira Estatística de Minas Gerais
  Minas Gerais Statistical Section

Censo do Servidor Público Federal
  Census of Federal Public Servants

Centro de Informações Econômicos Fiscais (CIEF)
  Center for Fiscal/Economic Information

Comissão Censitária Nacional
  National Census Commission

Comissão Executivo de Defesa da Borracha
  Executive Commission for Development of the Rubber
  Industry

Comissão de Marinha Mercante
  Merchant Marine Commission

Comisão de Plano de Classificação de Cargos
  Commission for the Employment Classification Plan

Conselho de Desenvolvimento Indústrial - Grupo Setorial VI
  Sixth Sectoral Group of the Industrial Development Council

Conselho Nacional de Águas e Energia Elétrica
  National Council of Waters and Electrical Energy

Conselho Nacional de Petróleo
  National Petroleum Council

Conselho Superior das Caixas Econômicas Federais
  Supreme Council of Federal Savings Banks

Conselho Técnico de Economia e Finanças
  Technical Council for Economics and Finances

Contadoria Geral da República
  General Accounts Department of the Republic

Departamento Administrativo do Serviço Público (DASP)
  Administrative Department of Public Service

Departamento dos Correios e Telégrafos
  Postal and Telegraph Department

Departamento Estadual de Estatística de Estado de São Paulo
  São Paulo State Department of Statistics

Departamento de Geografia e Estatística de Estado da
Guanabara
  Geography and Statistics Department of Guanabara State

Departamento de Estradas de Rodagem do Distrito Federal
  Highway Department of the Federal District

Departamento Nacional de Águas e Energia Elétrica
  National Department of Waters and Electrical Energy

Departamento Nacional de Endêmias Rurais
  National Department of Endemic Rural Diseases

Departamento Nacional de Endêmias Rurais, Divisão de
Profiláxia
  National Department of Endemic Rural Diseases, Division
  of Prevention and Protection

Departamento Nacional de Estatística of the Ministério do
Trabalho, Indústria e Commércio
  National Department of Statistics of the Ministry of
  Labor, Industry and Commerce

Departamento Nacional de Estradas de Ferro
  National Department of Railroads

Departamento Nacional de Estradas de Rodagem (DNER)
  National Highway Department

Departamento Nacional de Imigração
  National Immigration Department

Departamento Nacional de Mão-de-Obra, Divisão de Migração

Division of Migration, National Department of Hand Labor

Departamento Nacional de Obras Contra as Sêcas
National Department for Public Works Against Droughts

Departamento Nacional de Pôrtas e Navegação
National Department of Ports and Navigation

Departamento Nacional de Pôrtos, Rios e Canais
National Department of Ports, Rivers and Canals

Departamento Nacional de Pôrtas e Vias Navegáveis
National Department of Ports and Navigable Waterways

Departamento Nacional de Previdência Social
National Department of Social Welfare

Departamento Nacional do Produção Mineral
National Department of Mineral Production

Departamento Nacional de Saúde
National Health Department

Diretoria Geral de Communicações e Estatística, Polícia
Civil, Distrito Federal
General Directorate for Communications and Statistics of
the Civil Police of the Federal District

Diretoria Geral de Estatística
General Directorate of Statistics

Diretoria de Levantamentos Estatísticos, IBGE
Directorate for Statistical Surveys of the Brazilian
Institute of Geography and Statistics

Divisão de Caça e Pesca, Distrito Federal
Division of Hunting and Fishing of the Federal District

Divisão de Caça e Pesca, Guanabara
Division of Hunting and Fishing, State of Guanabara

Divisão de Estatística e Documentação Social da Prefeitura de
São Paulo
Division of Statistics and Social Documentation of the
city of São Paulo

Divisão de Estatística da Secretaria Geral do Justiça
Statistical Division of the General Secretariat of
Justice

Divisão de Estatística de Secretaria Geral, Ministério da

Justiça
  Statistical Division of the General Secretariat of the
  Ministry of Justice

Divisão de Águas do Departamento Nacional da Produçao Mineral
  Water Division of the National Department of Mineral
  Production

Divisão Nacional de Epidemiologia e Estatística da Saúde
  National Division of Epidemiology and Health Statistics

Divisão Nacional de Saúde Mental
  National Mental Health Division

Divisão Nacional de Tuberculose
  National Tuberculosis Division

Emprêsa Brasileira de Aeronaútica (EMBRAER)
  Brazilian Aeronautical Corporation

Emprêsa Brasileira de Correios e Telégrafos
  Brazilian Postal and Telegraph Corporation

Emprêsa Brasileira de Turismo (EMBRATUR)
  Brazilian Tourist Corporation

Emprêsa Pública Caixa Economica Federal
  Public Corporation of Federal Savings Banks

Emprêsa de Pôrtos do Brasil
  Ports Corporation of Brazil

Equipe Técnico de Estatística Agropecuaria
  Technical Team for Farming and Ranching Statistics

Escritório de Estatística do Ministério da Agriculture
  Office of Statistics of the Ministry of Agriculture

Federal de Seguros, S.A.
  Federal Insurance Corporation   S.A. = Sociedade Anônima,
  a Corporation equivalent

Fundo de Assistência e Previdência do Trabalhador Rural
  Fund for Rural Worker Welfare and Assistance

Fundação Getúlio Vargas
  Getúlio Vargas Foundation

Fundaçao IBGE - (FIBGE)
  Foundation - Brazilian Institute of Geography and
  Statistics

Gabinete Técnico do Serviço Nacional de Recenseamento
  Special Technical Group of the National Census Bureau

Grupo Executivo da Indústria Automobilística (GEIA)
  Executive Group for the Development of the Automobile
  Industry

Grupo Executivo da Indústria de Construção Naval (GEICON)
  Executive Group for Development of the Naval Construction
  Industry

Grupo Executivo da Indústria Mecánica Pesada (GEIMAPE)
  Executive Group for the Development of the Heavy
  Machinery Industry

Grupo de Trabalho da Indústria de Material Ferroviário
  Working Group for the Development of the Railroad Equipment Industry

IBGE, Laboratório de Estatística
  Brazilian Institute of Geography and Statistics,
  Laboratory of Statistics

IBGE, Serviço Nacional de Recenseamento
  Brazilian Institute of Geography and Statistics,
  National Census Service

Inspectoria das Estradas da Ministério da Viação e Obras
Públicas
  Inspectorate of Roads of the Ministry of Transport and
  Public Works

Inspectoria Federal de Obras Contra as Sêcas
  Federal Inspectorate for Public Works Against Droughts

Inspectoria Geral de Finanças
  General Inspectorate of Finances

Inspectoria Geral de Finanças, Ministério da Fazenda
  General Inspectorate of Finances of the Ministry of
  Finance

Inspectoria Regionais de Estatística Municipal, CNE
  Regional Inspectorate of Municipal Statistics of the
  National Statistics Council

Instituto do Açucar e do Alcool
  Sugar and Alcohol Institute

Instituto Brasileiro de Café
  Brazilian Coffee Institute

Instituto Brasileiro de Economia
  Brazilian Economics Institute

Instituto Brasileiro de Estatística
  Brazilian Statistics Institute

Instituto Brasileiro de Geografia e Estatística - IBGE
  Brazilian Institute of Geography and Statistics

Instituto Brasileiro de Siderúrgia
  Brazilian Steel Institute

Instituto Nacional de Colonização e Reforma Agrária (INCRA),
Divisão de Cooperativismo
  National Institute of Colonization and Agrarian Reform,
  Division of Cooperatives

Instituto Nacional de Imigraçao e Colonização
  National Institute for Immigration and Colonization

Instituto Nacional de Previdência Social (INPS)
  National Institute of Social Welfare

Instituto Nacional de Siderúrgia
  National Steel Institute

Instituto de Pesquisas Econômicas da Universidade de São
Paulo
  Institute for Economic Research, University of São Paulo

Instituto de Previdência e Assistência do Servidor do Estado
(IPASE)
  Institute for Welfare and Assistance to State Employees

Instituto de Resseguros do Brasil
  Brazilian Reinsurance Institute

Laboratório de Estatística do Conselho Nacional de
Estatística
  Statistics Laboratory of the National Statistics Council

Laboratório de Estatística - IBGE
  Laboratory of Statistics - Brazilian Institute of
  Geography and Statistics

Ministério da Agriculture
  Ministry of Agriculture

Ministério da Agriculture, Superintendência do Desenvolvimento da Pesca, Secretaria de Planajamento e Orçamento
  Secretariat of Planning and the Budget, Superintendency

for the Development of Fishing, Ministry of Agriculture

Ministério da Fazenda
  Ministry of Finance

Ministério de Justiça, Secretaria de Documentação e Infor-
mática, Divisão de Estatística
  Ministry of Justice, Secretariat for Documentation and
  Information, Statistics Division

Ministério da Justiça, Secretaria de Planejamento, Divisão de
Estatística, Secretaria de Documentação e Informática
  Secretariat of Documentation and Information, Statistical
  Division, Secretariat of Planning, Ministry of Justice

Ministério das Minas e Energia
  Ministry of Mines and Energy

Orçamento Geral da União
  General Federal Budget

Orgãos Regionais de Estatística e Directoria de Levantamentos
Estatísticos, IBGE
  Regional Statistical Organs and Statistical Development
  Directorate, Brazilian Institute of Geography and
  Statistics

Orgãos Regionais do Sistema Estatística Nacional
  Regional Organs of the National Statistical System

Petróleo Brasileiro S.A. (Petrobrás)
  Brazilian Petroleum Company. The national petroleum
  monopoly usually referred to as Petrobrás. S.A. stands
  for Sociedade Anônima, similar to Incorporated.

Prefeitura Municipal de São Paulo Capital
  Mayoral Office of the City of São Paulo

Rêde Ferroviária Federal, S.A.
  Federal Railway System. The government railroad corporation. S.A. stands for Sociedade Anônima, which is
  tantamount to incorporation.

Secção de Diretoria de Correios do Departmento dos Correios e
Telégrafos
  Postal Directorate Section of the Postal and Telegraph
Department

Secretaria de Economia e Finanças
  Secretariat of Economics and Finances

Secretaria de Economia e Finanças, Ministério da Fazenda
  Secretariat of Economics and Finances, Ministry of Finance

Secretaria Geral do Conselho Nacional de Estatística
  General Secretariat of the National Statistics Council

Secretaria Técnica do Grupo da Indústria Automobilística
  Technical Secretariat of the Executive Group for the
  Development of the Automobile Industry

Secretaria do Tribunal Superior Eleitoral
  Secretariat of the Supreme Electoral Court

Serviço de Economia Rural do Ministério da Agricultura
  Rural Economic Service of the Ministry of Agriculture

Serviço de Emplacamento do Estado da Guanabara
  Auto License Service of the State of Guanabara

Serviço de Estatística Demografica, Moral e Política
  Service for Demographic, Cultural and Political
  Statistics

Servico de Estatística do Departamento Nacional de Águas e
Energia Elétrica
  Statistical Service of the National Department of Waters
  and Electrical Energy

Serviço Estatística Econômica e Financeira (SEEF)
  Economic and Financial Statistics Service

Servico de Estatística da Educação e Cultura, Conselho da
Economia e Finanças, Ministério da Fazenda
  Educational and Cultural Statistics Service of the
  Economic and Technical Council of the Ministry of Finance

Serviço de Estatística da Educação e Saúde
  Statistical Service of Education and Health

Serviço de Estatística de Previdência e Trabalho
  Statistical Service of Welfare and Labor

Serviço de Estatística da Produção
  Production Statistics Service

Serviço de Estatística da Saúde
  Health Statistics Service

Serviço de Expansão de Trigo
  Service for the Expansion of Wheat

Serviço Nacional de Doenças Mentais
  National Mental Health Service

Serviço Nacional de Febre Amarela
  National Yellow Fever Service

Serviço Nacional de Lepra
  National Leprosy Service

Servico Nacional de Malária
  National Malaria Service

Serviço Nacional de Peste
  National Plague Service

Serviço Nacional da Produção
  National Production Service

Serviço Nacional de Tuberculose
  National Tuberculosis Service

Serviço Social da Indústria
  Social Service for Industry

Serviço Social aos Servidores Economiários
  Social Service for Administrators

Serviço de Saúde Publica (SESP)
  Public Health Service

Setor de documentação do Departamento de Assuntos Univer-
sitários
  Documentation Sector of the Department of University
  Subjects

Sindicato da Indústria de Adubos e Colas
  Syndicate for the Fertilizer and Glue Industry

Sindicato da Indústria de Matérias Primas para Inseticídas e
Fertilizantes no Estado de São Paulo
  Syndicate of the Industry Producing Raw Materials for
  Insecticides and Fertilizers in the State of São Paulo

Sindicato da Indústria do Papel
  Syndicate of the Paper Industry

Sindicato Nacional de Cimento
  National Cement Syndicate

Sistema Regional e Secção de Sistematização da Secretaria
Geral do IBGE
  Regional Network and Section for Systematization of the
  General Secretariat of the Brazilian Institute of
  Geography and Statistics

Sistema Regional e Serviço de Inquéritos da Secretaria Geral
do IBGE
  Regional System and Investigatory Service of the General
  Secretary of the Brazilian Institute of Geography and
  Statistics

Subsecretaria de Economia e Finanças
  Subsecretariat of Economics and Finances

Superintendência da Borracha
  Superintendency for Rubber

Superintendência de Campanhas de Saúde Pública
  Superintendency of Public Health Campaigns

Superintendência do Desenvolvimento da Pesca
  Superintendency for the Development of Fishing

Superintendência da Campanha de Erradicação da Variola
  Superintendency of the Measles Eradication Campaign

Superintendência da Moeda e Crédito
  Superintendency of Currency and Credit

Superintendência Nacional de Marinha Mercante
  National Superintendency of the Merchant Marine

Superintendência da Política Agrária
  Superintendency of Agrarian Policy

List of Standard Abbreviations for Brazilian Political Subdivisions

AC	Acre
AL	Alagoas
AM	Amazonas
AP	Amapá
BA	Bahia
CE	Ceará
DF	Distrito Federal
GB	Guanabara
GO	Goiás
ES	Espírito Santo
FN	Fernando de Noronha
MA	Maranhão
MG	Minas Gerais
MS	Mato Grosso do Sul
MT	Mato Grosso
PA	Pará
PB	Paraíba
PE	Pernambuco
PI	Piauí
PR	Paraná
RJ	Rio de Janeiro
RN	Rio Grande do Norte
RO	Rondônia
RR	Roraíma
RS	Rio Grande do Sul
SC	Santa Catarina
SE	Sergipe
SP	São Paulo

On all tables in this book the names and spellings of the
political subdivisions are those that were in use in 1970.

Introduction

The title historical statistics when applied to a work on Brazil approximates a contradiction in terms, for whatever the Portuguese interest in this huge land mass it was not in the counting of people or things. From 1500 to 1800 this numerical lack of interest pervaded all levels of society and, in fact, was encouraged by policies at the highest level. Early Portuguese colonists were apt to be illiterate while black slaves who made up a very large minority of the country's early population were not motivated to maintain counts of things around them, although many could have done so, being literate in Arabic in keeping with their Koranic tradition. The sheer magnitude of the country and the difficulty of travel over its dissected and forest-covered terrain virtually precluded any kind of systematic counts of things Brazilian even if the Portuguese crown had been interested in doing so. James Lang[1] points out that Brazil's sugar and tobacco exports went first to Portugal, where they could be taxed. The crown was thus able to profit from the colony's development without establishing an elaborate bureaucracy in Brazil, and bureaucracies, whatever else they do, count the things over which they have jurisdiction. By contrast, Lang notes, the Spanish colonies had the most comprehensive bureaucracy in the New World. The size and pervasiveness of the Roman Catholic Church in Brazil paralleled that of the Portuguese colonial bureaucracy, with the result that the Church was not a large repository of information about things Brazilian.

In the nineteenth century, literate travelers and scientists, the latter including Spix, Martius, and Darwin, visited Brazil. Their purposes, however, related principally to flora and fauna and did not countenance systematic counts of humans and their works. After Brazil's independence from Portugal in 1822 interest grew in enumerating the people who occupied Brazil and some of their activities but these attempts were sporadic. Most were undertaken by gentleman scholars or ecclesiastics. The federal government showed little interest in even these attempts, but the presidents of the provinces did often include bits of statistical data in

1

their annual reports. Ann Graham Harkness[2] has prepared a guide to the statistical materials in these reports. Various other kinds of data, albeit with very limited longitudinality, have been collected in the French volume L'Histoire quantitative du Brésil de 1800 à 1930.[3]

The late nineteenth century saw changes in the official attitude toward systematic enumeration of Brazil's population and its characteristics. The nation's first national census was taken in 1872. It was followed by others in 1890 and 1900 but progress was desultory: part of the 1900 census was taken in 1906 and no census at all was taken in 1910. The published 1920 national census contained 8,861 pages, a considerable portion of which, however, was devoted to a history of attempts to count population, to flora and fauna, and to analysis and explanation of the data collected. No census was taken in 1930, a year of political instability, but with the advent of the first Vargas regime (1930-45) and its emphasis on government-directed social and economic change the need for information became acute. The 1940 census contained 12,405 published pages, nearly all of which reported raw data in tabular form. Each of the four subsequent dicennial censuses expanded the types of data collected, sharpened data definitions, and improved the clarity and parsimony of presentation.

Brazil's Ministry of Agriculture, Industry, and Commerce published the first Anuário estatístico do Brasil[4] in 1917. It covered the years 1908 through 1912. The Instituto Brasileiro de Geografia e Estatística (IBGE: Brazilian Institute of Geography and Statistics) was founded in 1936 and beginning with that year, with the exception of 1938, has published an Anuário estatístico do Brasil to cover every subsequent year to date. These statistical yearbooks of Brazil present a wide variety of data, much of it gleaned from the operations of government agencies, and cover material which until recently was ignored by the dicennial censuses. The Anuários quickly became large: the one for 1939-40 contained over 1,000 pages of contemporary data and some 400 pages of historical data in tabular form. Their quality and size did, however, fluctuate with the economic and political status of the country. Reflecting the troubled early 1960s, the 1962 Anuário contained only 384 pages. Since then these publications have been expanded to cover more data and have been improved in clarity and sophistication. Over the years nearly 150 government agencies have supplied data to the Anuários. Any agency that served as the origin for data used on a table or map in this book is reported in the text exactly as it was named in the Anuário. These agencies come and go and their names change frequently. To dispel some of the confusion regarding these agencies a glossary/translation of those recorded in the text precedes the introduction. Following the glossary is a list of standard abbreviations used in this book for the names of Brazil's political subdivisions.

Both the census and the government agencies responsible for providing data to the Anuários have through the years added, deleted, and redefined some of the variables with which they have worked. The result has been to put a strain on the neatness of the longitudinality of the published data. The prime rationale for this book is to preserve the longitudinality of comparable variables. Every effort has been made to present well-defined sets of data for as many consecutive years as possible. Alas, there are gaps. Most of them result from the fact that Brazilian data totals are usually the sums of totals for the states, territories, and the Federal District (the major political subdivisions) and that some of these subdivisions may fail to report data for a given year.

This book was long in the making and in the course of its completion Patricia Ludwig contributed immensely to the typing and editing of tables. She also created the first map in the work. The Latin American Library of the University of Texas at Austin was the prime location for source materials used in this book. Pauline Collins of the library of the University of Massachusetts at Amherst provided the author with a microformed set of early Anuários. Some of the older historical data were found in the Library of Congress; John Hébert of that institution was helpful in this search. In Rio de Janeiro the staffs of the IBGE offices and the library at the American consulate were helpful in filling in some of the data gaps. At one time or another Gregory Schroeder, Richard Wilkie, Oriol Pi-Sunyer, Delta Best, Diana Schroeder, and Dennis and Judy Endicott were able to provide significant help in moving the work along. Several libraries aided by sending publications on interlibrary loan or by photocopying and forwarding data. Among these were the libraries at Texas Christian University, the State University of Iowa, Northwestern University, the University of Chicago, and, in Washington, those at the United States Department of Labor, the Organization of American States, and the Pan American Union.

References

1. James Lang, Portuguese Brazil: The Kings Plantation (New York: Academic Press, 1979).

2. Ann Graham Harkness, Subject Guide to Statistics in the Presidential Reports of the Brazilian Provinces, 1830-

1889 (Austin: Institute of Latin American Studies, The University of Texas at Austin, 1977).

3. <u>L'Histoire quantitative du Brésil de 1800 à 1930</u>, No. 543, Colloques Internationaux du Centre National de la Recherche Scientifique, Octobre 11-15, 1971 (Paris: Editions du Centre National de la Recherche Scientifique, 1973).

4. The spelling of many Brazilian Portuguese words was formally changed in 1930. Most readily apparent among others in this book is the change to one "n" from two in Anuário and the change to "s" from "z" in Brasil.

Chapter I. The Political and Physical Base

Table I-1 documents the changes in names and administrative status of Brazil and its major political subdivisions and their capital cities from 1808 to 1980. The year 1808 marked the arrival of the Portuguese court in Rio de Janeiro after its flight from Lisbon to escape Napoleon's invading armies. Pedro Álvares Cabral took possession of Brazil for Portugal in 1500, the first Portuguese settlement was established in 1532, and from 1534 to 1549 a scheme of privately administered colonies was the principal means by which the crown sought to populate and control Brazil. From 1549 to 1714 Brazil was ruled by governors-general appointed by the king (see Table XXII-4) and from 1714 to 1808 was under regally appointed viceroys.

The political/administrative patterns of Brazil in 1534 and after 1549 are presented on Maps I-1A and I-1B, respectively. They were developed by Patricia Ludwig from those in the Atlas histórico e geográfico brasileiro.[1] In 1494 the pope promulgated the Treaty of Tordesillas and drew a line of the same name through what proved to be the continent of South America (its existence was not even known at the time) dividing it into a western, Spanish sphere and an eastern, Portuguese sphere. The latter incorporated about 40 percent of present-day Brazil. Brazil contained neither the easily plucked wealth nor the population to exploit it that the Spanish found in the highlands from Mexico to Peru. To settle Brazil, to make it de facto Portuguese and to make it pay, the Portuguese crown offered hereditary land grants (capitânias hereditárias) to Portuguese nobles (donatários) whose charge it was to develop agricultural bases to create wealth for the crown. The hereditary grants shown on Map I-1A were all at least nominally apportioned by 1534, two years after the first Portuguese settlement in Brazil at São Vicente (present state of São Paulo coast) on January 22, 1532. Very few were successful. According to Boxer[2] the grants originally numbered 15, but he does not list them; Atlas histórico shows only 14 by name.

5

Map I-1B shows the political subdivisions of Brazil in the late 1500s, after a governor-general was installed in Bahia and the Portuguese crown had assumed direct control of some existing hereditary captaincies and created some new royal captaincies. From 1621 to 1626, according to Boxer[3] the crown created the State of Maranhão comprised of Grão-Pará, Maranhão, and Ceará. Ceará was rejoined to Brazil in 1656 but Grão-Pará and the Maranhão remained a separately administered state until 1774.

By 1630 Boxer[4] notes the existence of the Sergipe captaincy where the state of the same name is now located. He does not show Santana as a captaincy in what was to become the state of Santa Catarina. He does, however, show the Ilha de Santa Catarina (Santa Catarina Island) without indicating it as a captaincy.

Every coastal state that existed in Brazil in 1980 had an established political core in the 1630 captaincies with the exception of Piauí, Alagoas, Paraná, Rio Grande do Sul, and Santa Catarina. São Vicente and Santo Amaro became parts of São Paulo state.

In 1808 Brazil's change of political status was profound as it went from an isolated colony to the functional (and later formal) seat of the Portuguese Empire. Nearly all the states existing in 1980 were in place as provinces in 1808. Those on the coast were cored in the hereditary land grants, but many of those in the interior owed their existence to the frontiersmen known as bandeirantes. The great, roving, semi-military columns (bandeiras) emanating from São Paulo carried these tough backwoodsmen well beyond the Tordesillas line during the seventeenth and eighteenth centuries in their search for gold and slaves. Their discovery of gold brought population and the eventual establishment of administrative structures to form the cores of such inland provinces as Minas Gerais, Goiás, and Mato Grosso.

All of the places noted on Table I-1 are also shown on Map I-2. In 1808, however, the full formal name of Alagoas's capital city was Santa Maria Madelena da Alagoa do Sul. According to Grande Região centro-oeste,[5] the decree to move the Goiás capital from Goiás Velho to a new city to be called Goiânia was signed in 1933. Construction was begun in 1935. Some government elements were built and occupied that year, and the transfer was completed in 1937. The territories of Iguaçu and Ponta Porã were created in 1943 and dissolved in 1946, the areas being returned to the states from which they were taken by Article 8 of the Transitory Provisions of the 1946 Constitution.

All of the areas in square miles and square kilometers include internal water bodies. The area of Fernando de Noronha includes the small island specks of Rocas, São Pedro, and São Paulo in the mid-Atlantic Ocean. The area of Espírito Santo includes the islands of Trindade and Martim Vaz in the Atlantic Ocean.

Map I-2 shows the present and past political subdivisions and their capitals, which are described in Table I-1. The map also locates the 35 largest urbanized areas whose 1950 to 1980 populations are presented on Table II-4.

Map I-3 depicts the landforms of Brazil. Its creator, Guy-Harold Smith, located cities by means of hollow dots but did not name them. The author of this work has added names where they do not obscure the landform pattern.

Map I-4 shows land elevation in Brazil. The highest points are named and elevations given in meters (one meter = 3.280 feet). Pico da Neblina in Amazonas state is Brazil's highest point at 3,014 meters or 9,886 feet.

Map I-5 shows the landforms of the southeastern part of the country. The map was created for James[6] by Erwin Raisz. The title has been changed by the author of this work.

On Map I-6 the landforms of south Brazil were depicted, without labeling, by Maria Francisca T.C. Cardoso of the Instituto Brasileiro de Geografia e Estatística. The author of this work added the place names. The salient feature on this map is the Great Escarpment, which rises in most places more than 2,000 feet and forms the eastern edge of the Brazilian plateau overlooking the Atlantic Ocean from Rio de Janeiro state to Rio Grande do Sul. North of central Rio Grande do Sul the regional slope of this plateau is westward so nearly every river flows inland away from the Escarpment. A great basaltic lava plateau covers the western halves of the states shown on this map. Its east-facing escarpment is shown clearly in São Paulo and Paraná states. It comes to the Atlantic Ocean on the Santa Catarina-Rio Grande do Sul border, then turns westward and faces south in central Rio Grande do Sul. Between these two escarpments lies a narrow strip of sedimentary rocks known in São Paulo state as the Inner Lowland. These beds protrude out from under the basalt cap along the face of the Great Escarpment in southern Santa Catarina and in Rio Grande do Sul state and here are Brazil's only sources of bituminous coal.

Table I-2 notes climatic data for 23 well-distributed Brazilian stations. The data were presented by Ratisbona,[7] the Brazilian meteorologist/climatologist, who notes that they are for the years 1912-1942 but that some stations have incomplete records. The data were originally presented in Celsius and converted by the author of this work to Fahrenheit. Two decimal places were left to make reconversion more accurate. The daily mean = the high for the day (+) the low for the day (÷) 2. The daily mean for the month = the sum of daily means ÷ days in the month. Because the data are confined to the 1912-42 period the extreme temperatures shown on the table have probably been exceeded.

On Table I-2 and Map I-7 the climatic types shown are derived from a modified Köppen system, which is based principally on vegetative responses to temperature and rainfall conditions. The following is an outline of this system as it applies to Brazil.

A = All months have a mean temperature greater than 64.4° (18°C)

    f = There is no dry season.

    m = A dry season which is not reflected by the vegetation because it is compensated by heavy monsoon rainfall in the long rainy season.

    w = A dry season in the low-sun (winter) period to which the vegetation responds principally by losing its leaves.

    s = A dry season in the high-sun (summer) period to which the vegetation responds.

B = Potential evaporation exceeds precipitation.

    S = Potential evaporation exceeds precipitation by enough to produce a semi-arid or steppe-type vegetation but not by enough to create a desertic plant cover.

C = Mean temperature of the coldest month is below 64.4° (18°C) but above 32° (0°C).

    f = There is no dry season.

    w = A dry season occurs in the low-sun (winter) season and the vegetation responds.

    a = Warmest month of high-sun (summer) season is greater than 71.6° (22°C).

    b = Warmest month of high-sun (summer) season is less than 71.6° (22°C) but at least 4 months have means over 50° (10°C).

Note: a and b can be used with both Cf and Cw.

The Af climate is generally referred to as the tropical rainforest climate, the Am as the monsoon climate, the Aw as the savanna climate, and the BS as the steppe climate. In Brazil the Cwa is simply an Aw/savanna climate at higher elevations. There are probably also some Cwb climatic stations at the highest elevations but Ratisbona included none in his study. The Cfa climate is referred to as humid subtropical and at higher elevations in the south of Brazil the cooler winter temperatures produce a Cfb climate. Except for the southern tip of Florida, which is Aw, no A climates occur in the United States. BS climates occur in the western Great Plains along the front of Rocky Mountains. No Cw climates occur because the United States north of southern Florida is beyond the air mass systems that produce rainy summers and winter droughts. Most of the southeastern United States is under a Cfa/humid subtropical climate and higher elevations as in the Appalachians produce a Cfb climate.

Map I-8 depicts the vegetation pattern of Brazil. The map was created for James[8] by David J. de Laubenfels. Vegetation refers to noncultivated plants and is used without the term "natural" because human activities over long periods of time have in places altered what might have been originally a natural vegetation cover. This map, as well as recent Brazilian counterparts, brings the tropical rain forest cover, which usually forms under an Af/Am climate, well south into the region of Aw/savanna climates whose principal diagnostic (see text for Table I-2 and Map I-7) is a winter dry season to which the vegetation responds, generally by losing its leaves. Despite the distinct dry season the presence of rain forests as far south as 12° South indicates either that the heavy rains of the rainy season provide compensatory moisture for most of the plants (in which case the climate should be labeled Am) or that plant species respond differentially and for only a short period to the drought, thus maintaining a general rainforest physiognomy.

Seasonal or deciduous forest, generally on slopes, and woodland savanna, generally on flatter surfaces such as those around Brasília, alternate in the central plateaus of Brazil under the Aw climate. The woodland/brush, characterized by the thorn forests known as caatinga, predominate in the BS/steppe climatic region and its margins in the interior of northeastern Brazil. The patch of savanna vegetation surrounded by seasonal forest in São Paulo state is associated with the sedimentary rocks of the Inner Lowland, which provide poor parent material for soils under this type of climate. The grassland patches grade from sparse covers of coarse tropical grasses in central Brazil to the more succulent, more mid-latitude pampa types on the open plains of southern Rio Grande do Sul state.

Map I-9 shows the soils in Brazil, which are defined by the first three levels of classification: orders, suborders, and great soil groups. Soil Taxonomy[9] served as the source for descriptions of the soils shown on the map.

Alfisols are marked by an argillic horizon (a layer in the soil made up of silicate clays which have filtered down from above), by a medium to high supply of bases, and by the availability of water to plants for more than three consecutive months during a warm season.

Ustalfs are mostly reddish Alfisols of warm humid to semi-arid regions. They usually have a warm rainy season and moisture moves through the soil to deeper layers only in occasional years. The dry seasons are pronounced enough that trees are often xerophytic (drought-tolerant). Ustalfs tend to form between the Aridisols of the warm dry regions and the Ultisols, Oxisols, and Inceptisols of warm humid regions.

Natrustalfs are Ustalfs that have a natric horizon. This is an argillic horizon (see Alfisols), which is rich in sodium (hence the Na in the name) or sometimes calcium salts. These soils occupy the drought polygon of northeastern Brazil. In the United States their area is the southern Great Plains.

Entisols are characterized by the absence of marks in the soil of any major set of soil-forming processes.

Psamments are Entisols in well-sorted sands with low water-holding capacities. In Brazil they occur in Ceará and Piauí states, in the São Francisco Valley in Bahia, and in the southern Pará/northern Goiás region. In the United States they occur in the Sand Hills of Nebraska.

Troposamments are Psamments that have an udic (humid) moisture regime. In most years the soil moisture control section is not dry in any part for as long as ninety days cumulative.

Inceptisols are characterized by water availability to plants during more than half the year or more than three consecutive months during a warm season, a texture finer than loamy sand and a moderate to high capacity of the clays to retain bases. They form in almost any but an arid climate and are found in both polar and tropical regions. They commonly have rock at a shallow depth and form on relatively young geomorphic surfaces. The alluvial soils of the Amazon basin and the lower Mississippi River valley are predominately Inceptisols.

Aquepts are wet Inceptisols whose internal drainage is poor and whose groundwater may stand at the surface.

Cryaquepts are Aquepts that have a cryic temperature regime, that is, one in which the mean annual soil temperature is above 32° (0°C) but below 47° (8°C). In Brazil they occur principally on the great barrier strand on the coast of Rio Grande do Sul state.

Andaquepts are Aquepts that in the Amazon basin are formed of alluvium and which have a nearly black surface rich in organic carbon. In the 1938 United States classification they were considered Humic-Gley soils.

Tropepts are brownish or reddish, more or less freely
drained Inceptisols on moderate to steep slopes. In Brazil
they lie on the hilly to mountainous seaward margin of the
Brazilian plateau in eastern São Paulo, Rio de Janeiro,
southern Minas Gerais, and Espírito Santo, where they have
long been associated with shifting cultivation. Their soil
moisture is high most of the year but where there is a dry
season moisture is present at the time of plant growth.
Where Tropepts are wet, broadleaf evergreen forests
develop; where they have a wet/dry regime deciduous forests
or savanna develop. In Brazil most Tropepts have a warm
mean annual temperature which ranges between 59° (15°C) and
72° (22°C).

   Sombritopepts are Tropepts that have a sombric horizon,
   that is, a layer in the soil composed of humus filtered
   down from above.

Oxisols are characterized by extreme weathering of most
minerals, other than quartz, to kaolin (white clay) and free
oxides, by very low mobility of clays in the soil, and by a
loamy or clayey texture. They occur in tropical regions on
land surfaces that have been stable for a long time.

   Orthox are yellowish to reddish Oxisols that develop under
   a short dry season or none at all. They occur in the
   Amazon basin under a rain forest cover. Many have an oxic
   horizon at least twelve inches thick. This is a subsurface
   horizon composed of hydrated oxides of iron and aluminum
   and contains few or no primary minerals that can weather to
   release bases.

      Gibbsiorthox are Orthox that have cemented sheets of
      Gibbsite or gravel-size cemented aggregates that are rich
      in Gibbsite. This suborder predominates in Amazon basin.

   Ustox are mostly red Oxisols that are dry in all parts of
   the moisture control sector for extended periods but that
   are moist for at least a ninety-day rainy season. Their
   vegetation is savanna and they predominate in western Minas
   Gerais, Goiás, and the Distrito Federal around Brasília.

      Acrustox are red to dark red Ustox that have virtually no
      ability to retain bases in their mineral fraction. At
      present they are extremely unproductive. The vegetation
      cover is sparse and much of the surface between the
      scattered plants is bare. In Goiás, where their
      well-developed oxic horizons (see Orthox) occur in gravel
      form, they have been used as road metal. Where these
      horizons occur as solid masses they have been quarried
      for bridge abutments.

Ultisols all have argillic horizons (see Alfisols) and are
intensively leached of their bases. Without fertilizer they
can be used only for shifting cultivation but because they
are relatively warm and moist they can be made highly
productive if fertilizers are used.

11

Aquults are gray or olive Ultisols of wet places whose ground water is very close to the surface during most of each year.

Fragiaquults are Aquults that have a fragipan, which is a loamy subsurface horizon low in organic content and seemingly cemented when dry but brittle and easily cracked when wet. These soils occur in Acre state.

Paleaquults are Aquults of old land surfaces, probably mid-Pleistocene or older. They were called Low Humic-Gleys in the 1938 soil classification. They are found in northeastern Mato Grosso state.

Humults are dark-colored, freely drained Ultisols that occur on steeply sloping uplands that have high annual rainfalls. Despite this precipitation they do have a moisture deficit at some season. They are often formed from rocks that are chemically basic. In the mid latitudes their vegetation is coniferous forest, and at low latitudes rain forest. In Brazil they occur on the hilly uplands of southern Paraná, Santa Catarina, and northern Rio Grande do Sul, which are composed of basaltic lava flows. The Paraná pine is the predominant vegetation on the uplands but rain forest is found along the coast.

Sombrihumults are Humults with a sombric horizon (see Sombritropepts) within one meter of the surface.

Udults are more or less freely drained, humus-poor, light-colored Ultisols that occur in warm humid climates with a well-distributed annual rainfall. Many are cultivated in a system in which they are cropped for a very few years then returned to forest to allow the trees to regain in their tissues a small supply of nutrients. Most of these soils have had a forest cover but now some have a savanna that is probably man-created.

Tropudults are more or less freely drained Udults in tropical regions. They are similar to but have a greater supply of nitrogen than the mid-latitude Hapudults. They usually had an evergreen forest cover so where savanna occurs as in Mato Grosso do Sul state it is probably man-engendered. In the 1938 classification they were called Red and Yellow Podzolic and Reddish Brown Laterite soils.

Hapudults are Udults with a brown to yellowish argillic horizon (see Alfisols). They are warm soils which were generally formed from acid rocks. In the 1938 soil classification they were categorized as Red and Yellow Podzolics in the warmer climates of the southeastern United States and as Gray Brown Podzolics in the colder climate of the eastern Midwest. In Brazil they occur along the northeast coast from Pernambuco to southern Bahia, the sugar cane, slavocratic culture hearth of Brazil, and in the northern Mato Grosso-southern Pará region.

Ustults are humus-poor, light-colored Ultisols that occur in warm humid climates with high annual rainfalls but pronounced dry seasons (Aw climates).

Rhodustults are freely drained Ustults with a dark red or dusky red argillic horizon (see Alfisols). They have formed from basic rocks and as a consequence have more total phosphorous than most Ustults. They predominate across central Mato Grosso and in southwestern Goiás.

Mollisols are mainly the very dark colored, humus- and base-rich soils of the steppes. Many have an argillic horizon (see Alfisols), a natric horizon (see Natrustalfs), or a calcic (calcium-rich) horizon.

Albolls are Mollisols that have an albic horizon, that is, a white layer in the soil from which clay and free iron oxides have been removed or isolated in small pockets leaving the original light-colored sand or silt particles to dominate the color of the horizon.

Natralbolls are Albolls with a natric horizon (see Natrustalfs) that occur only in a small corner of northwestern Rio Grande do Sul.

Udolls are more or less freely drained Mollisols of humid climates with definite winter cool seasons. In the United States they formed under the tall-grass prairies of Illinois and Iowa; in Brazil under the pampalike grasses of southern Rio Grande do Sul state.

Vermudolls are Udolls that have been intensively mixed by earthworms and their predators. Although they predominate in Southern Rio Grande do Sul they do not occur in significant areas of the United States.

References

1. *Atlas histórico e geográfico brasileiro*, historical text and maps by Manoel Maurício de Albuquerque, geographic text by Antônio Pedro Souza Campos, Programa de Emergência, Ministério da Educação e Cultura (no date given but circa 1962; no location given but probably Rio de Janeiro).

2. C.R. Boxer, *The Dutch in Brazil, 1624 - 1654* (Oxford: Clarendon Press, 1957), p. 17.

3. C.R. Boxer, *Race Relations in the Portuguese Colonial Empire, 1415-1825* (Oxford: Clarendon Press, 1963), p. 93 footnote.

4. Boxer, *Dutch in Brazil*, map 1.

5. Maria Magdalena Vieira Pinto, "Núcleos Urbanos," chapter 10 in <u>Grande região centro-oeste</u>, vol. 2, ser. A of <u>Geografia do Brasil</u> (Rio de Janeiro: Conselho Nacional de Geografia of the Instituto Brasileiro de Geografia, 1960).

6. Preston, James, <u>Latin America</u>, rev. ed. (New York: Odyssey Press, 1950), p. 401.

7. L.R. Ratisbona, "The Climate of Brazil," pp. 219-93 in <u>World Survey of Climatology</u>, vol. 12, <u>Climates of Central and South America</u>, ed. Werner Schwertfeger (Amsterdam, Oxford, and New York: Elsevier Scientific Publishing Co., 1975).

8. Preston, James, <u>Latin America</u>, 4th ed. (New York: Odyssey Press, 1969), p. 35.

9. <u>Soil Taxonomy, A Basic System of Soil Classification for Making and Interpreting Soil Surveys</u>, Agricultural Handbook no. 436, by the Soil Survey Staff (Washington, D.C.: Soil Conservation Service, United States Department of Agriculture, December 1975).

Table I-1. Administrative Status, Capital Cities, and Areas of Brazil. Its Major Regions and Its Major Political Subdivisions, 1808–1980

1980 Region Political Subdivision Capital City	1808 Administrative Status	Changes in Administrative Status and In Names	1980 Administrative Status	1979 Total Area Square Miles	1979 Total Area Square Kilometers	Areas of Pre-1980 Subdivisions Square Miles	Square Kilometers
Brazil	Colony of Portugal	a) 1808, State of Brazil in Kingdom of Portugal and Algarve; b) 1821, Kingdom of Brazil; c) 1822, First Empire of Brazil; d) 1831, Second Empire of Brazil; e) 1891, Republica dos Estados Unidos do Brasil; f) 1967, Republica do Brasil; g) 1969, Republica Federativa do Brasil	Federated Republic	3,285,930	8,511,965	—	—
North				2,223,913	3,581,180	—	—
Acre	Part of Bolivia	a) 1903, Bolivia to Territory of Brazil, b) became a State	State	94,758	152,589	—	—
Pôrto Velho	None		State Capital			—	—
Amapá	Part of Pará/Northern 80% Claimed by French for Guiana	a) 1900, Guiana boundary fixed by international arbitration	Territory	87,112	140,276	—	—
Macapá	None		Territorial Capital			—	—
Amazonas	Province		State	971,520	1,564,445	—	—
Manaus	Provincial Capital		State Capital			—	—
Pará	Province	a) 1800's (early), known as Grão-Pará	State	775,034	1,248,042	—	—
Belém	Provincial Capital		State Capital			—	—
Rondônia	Part of Amazonas & Mato Grosso	a) 1943, created as Guaporé Territory, b) 1956 became Rondônia	Territory	150,930	243,044	—	—
Rio Branco	None		Territorial Capital			—	—
Roraima	Part of Amazonas	a) 1943, created as Territory of Rio Branco, b) 1962, became Roraima	Territory	142,895	230,104	—	—
Boa Vista	None		Territorial Capital			—	—
Amazonas/Pará Zone	None		In Litigation	1,664	2,680	—	—
Northeast				961,725	1,548,672	—	—
Alagoas	Province		State	17,221	27,731	—	—
Alagoa do Sul	Provincial Capital	a) 1839, lost capital functions to Maceió	None			—	—
Maceió	None	b) 1839, became provincial capital	State Capital			—	—
Bahia	Province		State	348,397	561,026	—	—
Salvador	Provincial Capital		State Capital			—	—
Ceará	Province		State	91,918	148,016	—	—
Fortaleza	Provincial Capital		State Capital			—	—
Fernando de Noronha	None	a) 1942, created as a Territory	Territory	16	26	—	—
Maranhão	Province		State	204,100	328,663	—	—
São Luís	Provincial Capital		State Capital			—	—
Paraíba	Province		State	35,007	56,372	—	—
João Pessoa	Provincial Capital		State Capital			—	—
Pernambuco	Province		State	61,033	98,281	—	—
Recife	Provincial Capital		State Capital			—	—
Piauí	Province		State	155,830	250,934	—	—
Oeiras	Provincial Capital	a) 1852, lost capital functions to newly-built Teresina	Município Seat			—	—
Teresina	None	a) 1852, newly-planned & constructed city became province capital	State Capital			—	—
Rio Grande do Norte	Province		State	32,922	53,015	—	—
Natal	Provincial Capital		State Capital			—	—
Sergipe	Province		State	13,658	21,994	—	—
São Cristovão	Provincial Capital	a) 1855, lost capital functions to Aracaju	Município Seat			—	—
Aracaju	None	a) 1855, became capital of province	State Capital			—	—
Piauí/Ceará Zone	None		In Litigation	1,623	2,614	—	—

Table I-1 (continued)

Administrative Status, Capital Cities and Areas of Brazil, Its Major Regions and Its Major Political Subdivisions, 1808–1980

1980 Region Political Subdivision Capital City	1808 Administrative Status	Changes in Administrative Status and In Names	1980 Administrative Status	1979 Total Area		Areas of Pre-1980 Subdivisions	
				Square Miles	Square Kilometers	Square Miles	Square Kilometers
Southeast				574,385	924,935	–	–
Espírito Santo	Province		State	28,316	45,597	–	–
Vitória	Provincial Capital		State Capital	–	–	–	–
Guanabara	Part of Rio de Janeiro Province	a) 1834, became Neutral Municipio, seat of Imperial Regency b) 1889, Neutral Municipio to Distrito Federal under new Republic c) 1960, Distrito Federal became State of Guanabara as capital moved to Brasília d) 1975, (under 1974 law) absorbed by Rio de Janeiro State	Municipio Seat	–	–	–	–
Rio de Janeiro	National Capital	a) 1960, became capital of State of Guanabara as national capital was moved to Brasília b) 1975, (under 1974 law) became capital of Rio de Janeiro State	State Capital	–	–	–	–
Minas Gerais	Province		State	364,634	587,172	–	–
Ouro Preto	Provincial Capital	a) 1899, lost capital functions to newly-created Belo Horizonte	Municipio Seat	–	–	–	–
Belo Horizonte	None	b) 1899, became state capital as planned city	State Capital	–	–	–	–
Rio de Janeiro	Province	a) 1834, lost Neutral Municipio which in 1889 became the Distrito Federal, and which in 1960 became State of Guanabara b) 1975, (under 1974 law) regained Guanabara	State	27,490	44,268	–	–
Niterói	Provincial Capital	a) 1975, (under 1974 law) lost capital functions to Rio de Janeiro	Municipio Seat	–	–	–	–
Rio de Janeiro	National Capital	a) 1960, became capital of State of Guanabara as national capital moved to Brasília b) 1975, (under 1974 law) became capital of State of Rio de Janeiro	State Capital	–	–	–	–
São Paulo	Province		State	153,945	247,898	–	–
São Paulo	Provincial Capital		State Capital	–	–	–	–
Serra dos Aimores	None	a) 1940–1965, area in litigation between Minas Gerais and Espírito Santo States	None	–	–	–	–
South				358,766	577,723	–	–
Iguaçu	None	a) 1943, created as a Territory from Paraná & Santa Catarina States	None	–	–	40,392	65,044
Paraná	None	a) 1853, created as a State	State	123,923	199,554	–	–
Curitiba	None		State Capital	–	–	–	–
Santa Catarina	Province		State	59,607	95,985	–	–
Florianópolis	Provincial Capital	a) 1800's (early) known as Destêrro	State Capital	–	–	–	–
Rio Grande do Sul	Province		State	175,236	282,184	–	–
Pôrto Alegre	Provincial Capital	a) 1800's (early) known as São Pedro do Rio Grande do Sul	State Capital	–	–	–	–
Center West				1,167,141	1,879,455	–	–
Distrito Federal	Part of Goiás Province	a) 1955, separated from State of Goiás to house newly-created national capital city of Brasília	Federal District	3,610	5,814	–	–
Brasília	None	a) 1960, (April 1) became national capital as planned city	National Capital	–	–	–	–
Goiás	Province		State	398,739	642,092	–	–
Goiás Velho	Provincial Capital	a) 1937, lost capital functions to newly-created city of Goiânia	Municipio Seat	–	–	–	–
Goiânia	None	a) 1937, became state capital as newly planned city	State Capital	–	–	–	–
Mato Grosso	Province		State	547,102	881,001	–	–
Cuiabá	Provincial Capital		State Capital	–	–	–	–
Mato Grosso do Sul	None	a) 1979, (January 1) created as state from southern part of Mato Grosso State	State	217,690	350,548	67,619	108,888
Campo Grande	None	a) 1979, became capital of new state of Mato Grosso do Sul	State Capital	–	–	–	–
Ponta Porã	None	a) 1943, created as a Territory from the southern part of Mato Grosso state (which in 1980 was Mato Grosso do Sul State) b) 1946, dissolved	None	–	–	–	–

Sources: Lombardi, p. 3; Atlas Histórico, pp. 26–27; AN 1941-45, pp. 5–6; AN 1956, p. 5; AN 1979, p. 28; Enciclopédia Delta Universal, Vol. 1, pp. 52 & 348; Vol. 2, p. 596; Vol. 9, p. 4,948; Vol. 13, pp. 6,948, 7,047 & 7,052; Vol 14, p. 7,625.

Map 1-1. Brazil's Hereditary Land Grants 1534, and Brazil Under the Governors-General, 1549-

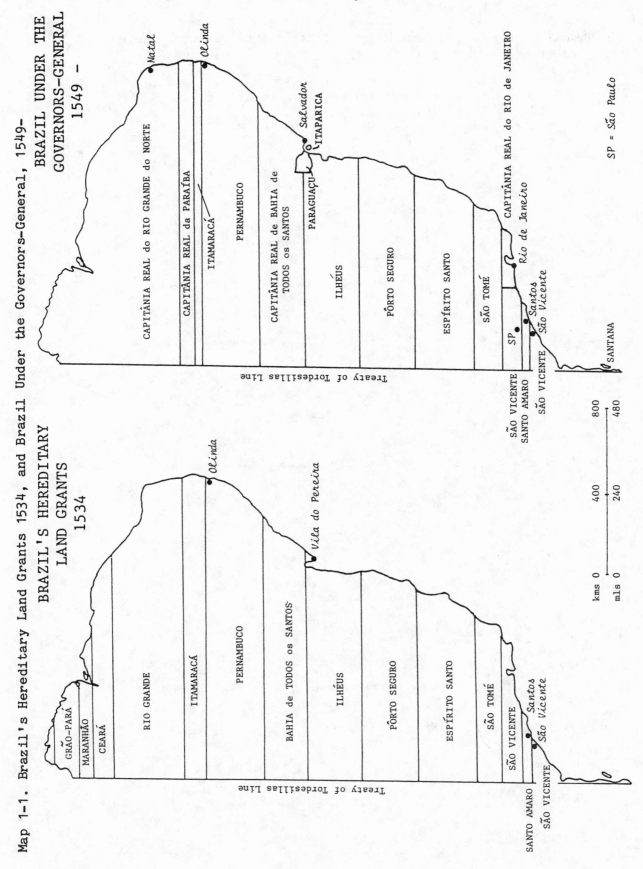

BRAZIL UNDER THE GOVERNORS-GENERAL 1549 –

CAPITÂNIA REAL do RIO GRANDE do NORTE

CAPITÂNIA REAL da PARAÍBA

ITAMARACÁ

PERNAMBUCO

CAPITÂNIA REAL de BAHIA de TODOS os SANTOS

PARAGUAÇU

ILHÉUS

PÔRTO SEGURO

ESPÍRITO SANTO

SÃO TOMÉ

CAPITÂNIA REAL do RIO de JANEIRO

Natal

Olinda

Salvador
ITAPARICA

Rio de Janeiro

SP
Santos
São Vicente

SANTANA

Treaty of Tordesillas Line

SÃO VICENTE
SANTO AMARO
SÃO VICENTE

SP = São Paulo

Patrícia Ludwig

BRAZIL'S HEREDITARY LAND GRANTS 1534

GRÃO-PARÁ
MARANHÃO
CEARÁ

RIO GRANDE

ITAMARACÁ

PERNAMBUCO

BAHIA de TODOS os SANTOS

ILHÉUS

PÔRTO SEGURO

ESPÍRITO SANTO

SÃO TOMÉ

SÃO VICENTE

Olinda

Vila do Pereira

Santos
São Vicente

Treaty of Tordesillas Line

SANTO AMARO
SÃO VICENTE

kms 0   400   800
mls 0   240   480

Source: Atlas Histórico e Geográfico Brasileiro

17

Map I-2. Brazil's Present and Past Major Political Subdivisions, Their Present and Past Capitals and the 35 Largest Urbanized Areas, 1980

BRAZIL'S PRESENT AND PAST
MAJOR POLITICAL SUBDIVISIONS,
THEIR PRESENT AND PAST CAPITALS AND
THE 35 LARGEST URBANIZED AREAS, 1980

AMAPÁ

Macapá

Belém

São Luís

AMAZONAS

PARÁ

Fortaleza

FERNANDO
de
NORONHA

MARANHÃO

CEARÁ

Teresina

RIO
GRANDE
do NORTE

Natal

Oeiras

PARAÍBA Campina
Grande

João
Pessoa

PIAUÍ

PERNAMBUCO

Recife

ALAGOAS

Maceió
Alagoa do Sul

SERGIPE

São Cristovão

Aracaju

MATO GROSSO

GOIÁS

BAHIA

Feira de Santana

Salvador

Cuiabá

DISTRITO
FEDERAL

Itabuna

Goiás
Velho

Brasília

MINAS GERAIS

Goiânia

Bolivia

SERRA
dos
AIMORES

ESPÍRITO
SANTO

MATO GROSSO do SUL

Belo Horizonte

Campo Grande

Ouro
Preto

Vitória

PONTA PORÃ

Ribeirão Prêto

Juiz de Fora

Volta
Redonda

Campos

SÃO PAULO

RIO de JANEIRO

Campinas

Jundiaí

Paraguay

Sorocaba

SJ

Niterói

Londrina

São Paulo

DF/GB Rio de Janeiro

Santos

PARANÁ

IGUAÇU

Curitiba

DF/GB = DISTRITO FEDERAL/
GUANABARA

Argentina

SANTA CATARINA

SJ = São José dos Campos

Florianópolis

RIO GRANDE do SUL

Pôrto
Alegre

Uruguay

Pelotas

Ludwig

Boa
Vista

RORAÍMA

Manaus

AMAZONAS

ACRE

Rio
Branco

Pôrto
Velho

RONDÔNIA

18

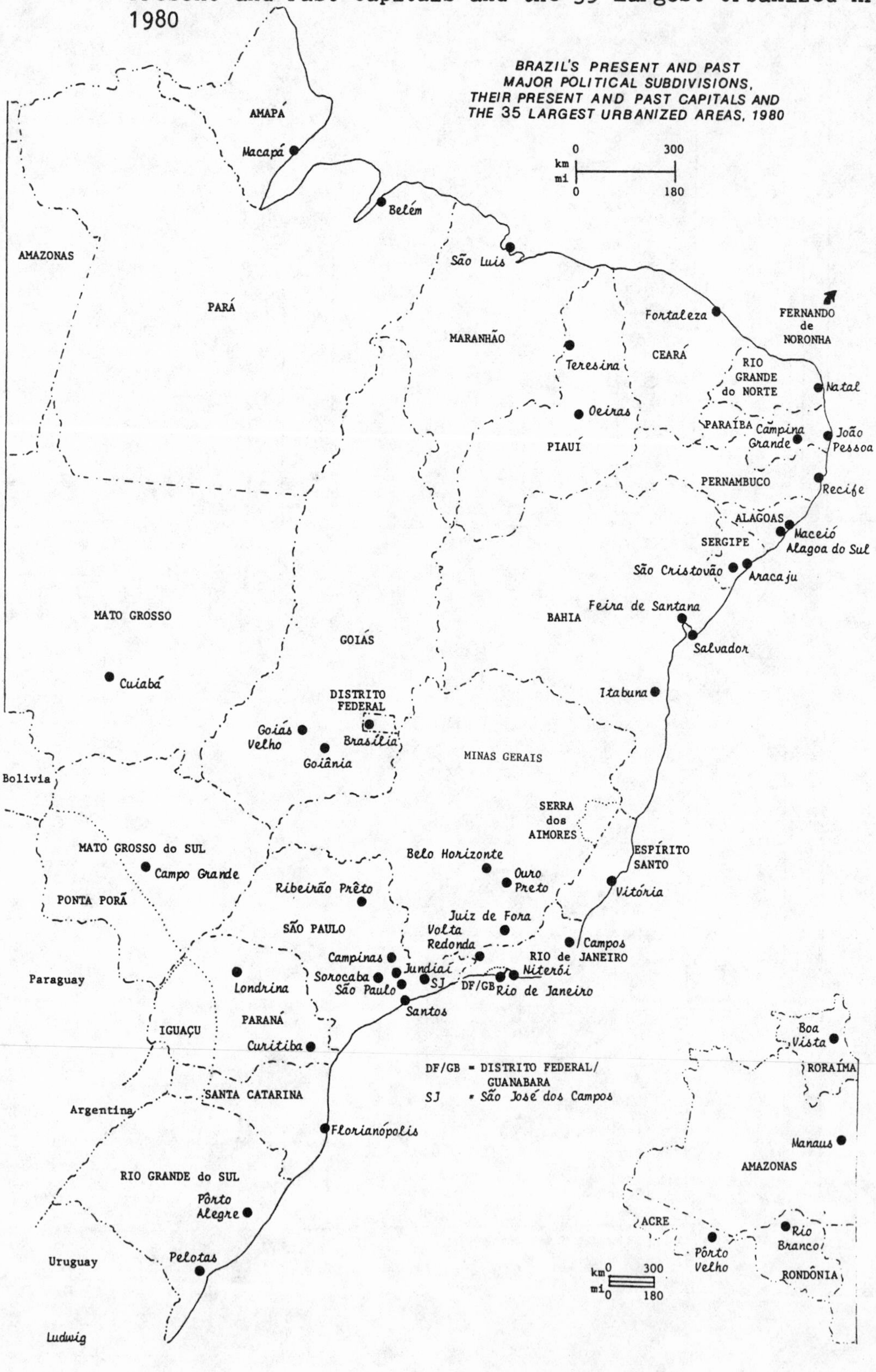

Map I-3. Landforms of Brazil

LANDFORMS of BRAZIL

| 0 | mi | 600 |
| 0 | km | 1000 |

Map I-4. Land Elevation in Brazil

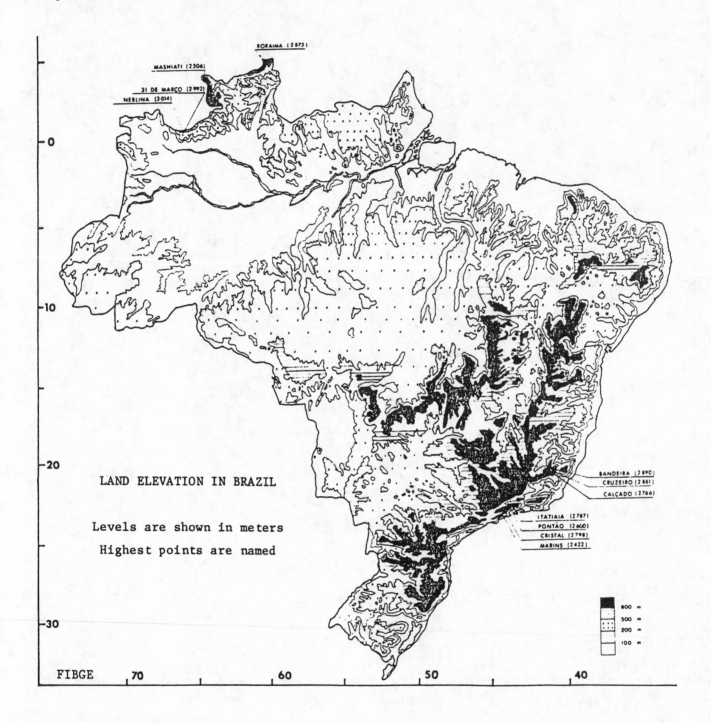

LAND ELEVATION IN BRAZIL

Levels are shown in meters

Highest points are named

Map I-5. Landforms of Southeastern Brazil

Map I-6. Landforms of South Brazil

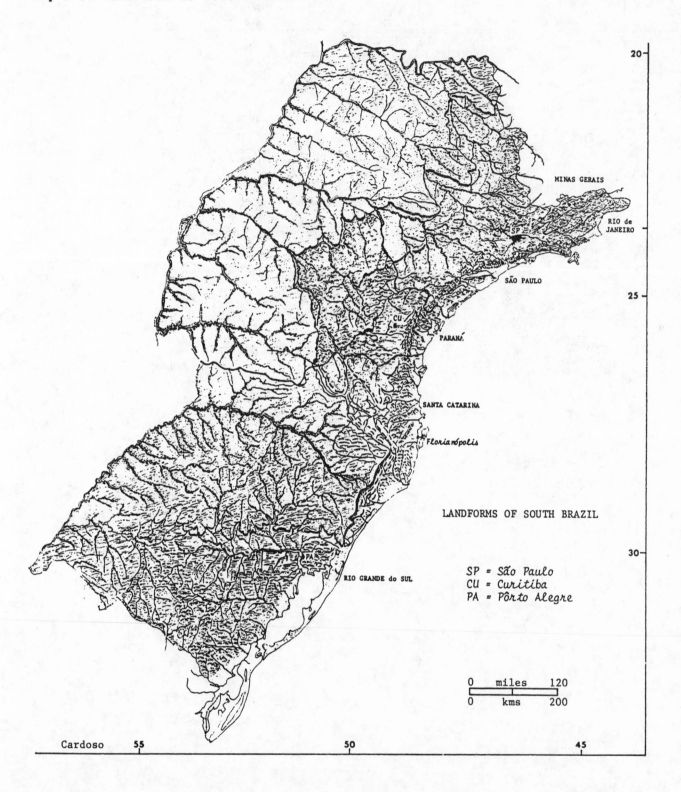

LANDFORMS OF SOUTH BRAZIL

SP = São Paulo
CU = Curitiba
PA = Pôrto Alegre

Table I-2. Climatic Data: Temperatures in Fahrenheit and Precipitation in Inches Recorded at Twenty-Three Brazilian Climatic Stations

Climatic Station	Climatic Type	Altitude in Feet	Latitude of Station	Longitude of Station		Jan.	Feb.	Mar.	Apr.	May	Jun.	Jul.	Aug.	Sep.	Oct.	Nov.	Dec.	Year	Temp. Extreme High	Temp. Extreme Low
Alegrete RS	Cfa	341.2	29°46'S	55°47'W	T	76.46	75.20	72.14	64.40	59.00	56.66	55.22	57.56	60.08	63.68	69.62	74.30	65.48	102.90	23.00
					P	6.15	4.91	5.81	7.53	6.75	4.30	4.31	4.44	5.52	6.52	4.82	5.15	66.21		
Barra da Corda MA	Aw	265.7	5°30'S	45°16'W	T	77.90	77.72	77.72	78.08	77.36	76.28	75.56	77.72	80.96	81.32	80.60	79.16	78.44	102.90	53.60
					P	7.48	8.20	8.42	5.69	2.37	.65	.28	.28	.89	1.61	2.76	4.59	43.22		
Belém PA	Af	78.7	1°28'S	48°27'W	T	77.36	77.00	77.18	77.90	78.44	78.44	78.44	78.62	78.44	78.98	79.34	78.62	78.26	95.72	65.30
					P	13.36	16.04	17.16	13.52	11.33	6.88	5.71	4.98	4.67	3.62	3.39	6.90	107.56		
Belo Horizonte MG	Cw	3,002.1	19°56'S	43°56'W	T	72.50	73.04	71.42	70.34	66.56	63.86	62.96	66.02	68.90	70.52	71.06	71.42	69.08	95.90	36.32
					P	12.57	7.93	6.19	3.12	.80	.33	.33	.72	1.66	5.33	8.87	13.60	61.45		
Campinas SP	Cfa	2,175.3	22°53'S	47°05'W	T	72.32	72.14	71.42	68.00	63.50	60.98	61.16	62.60	65.84	68.18	71.42	71.78	67.46	98.06	29.30
					P	9.47	7.82	5.84	2.39	2.21	2.07	1.13	1.40	2.96	4.77	6.29	8.47	54.82		
Caetité BA	Aw	2,880.7	14°03'S	42°37'W	T	72.68	72.50	72.68	71.60	69.80	67.10	66.02	68.00	70.70	72.86	72.32	72.14	70.52	98.42	45.68
					P	4.71	4.60	3.83	2.07	.62	.35	.35	.41	.64	2.42	5.80	5.97	51.77		
Corumbá MS	Aw	452.8	19°00'S	57°39'W	T	80.06	79.70	78.78	75.74	72.68	70.16	69.80	73.58	76.64	78.26	79.88	80.24	76.28	107.24	33.44
					P	6.99	5.77	4.67	3.28	2.62	1.26	.70	.95	2.60	4.07	4.82	6.41	44.14		
Cuiabá MT	Aw	561.1	15°35'S	56°06'W	T	79.52	79.16	79.16	78.62	75.74	73.40	72.50	76.64	79.88	80.60	80.24	79.70	77.90	107.96	34.16
					P	8.38	7.88	8.75	4.17	1.82	.54	.35	1.05	1.90	4.89	6.36	8.17	54.26		
Curitiba PR	Cfb	3,113.7	25°26'S	49°16'W	T	68.18	68.18	66.56	62.78	57.74	55.22	53.78	56.30	58.10	60.62	63.86	66.74	61.54	93.92	20.66
					P	7.19	5.86	4.15	2.97	3.47	3.33	2.72	3.33	4.87	4.80	4.72	5.44	53.62		
Formosa GO	Aw	2,992.3	15°32'S	47°18'W	T	71.06	71.24	71.24	70.70	68.18	66.20	65.66	69.26	72.86	72.86	71.24	70.70	70.16	96.44	41.18
					P	10.72	8.95	7.65	3.91	.74	.17	.16	.35	1.77	5.44	9.16	13.76	62.78		
Manaus AM	Aw	157.5	3°08'S	60°01'W	T	79.16	79.16	79.52	79.16	79.34	79.88	80.24	81.50	82.22	82.04	81.68	80.24	80.42	104.48	63.68
					P	10.45	9.71	10.60	10.51	7.63	3.94	2.51	1.48	2.35	4.90	5.97	8.52	78.57		
Olinda (Recife) PE	As	187.0	8°01'S	34°51'W	T	80.78	80.78	80.60	79.88	78.62	77.00	75.74	75.92	77.54	79.16	79.88	80.42	78.80	93.02	64.04
					P	1.84	4.28	6.16	8.88	10.25	10.10	7.33	4.58	2.06	1.19	1.09	1.31	59.07		
Pôrto Alegre RS	Cfa	32.8	30°02'S	51°13'W	T	76.46	75.74	73.40	67.96	62.78	58.64	57.74	59.18	61.70	65.48	69.80	74.48	67.10	104.72	28.40
					P	3.65	3.56	3.59	4.27	4.91	5.03	5.02	4.83	5.26	4.22	3.36	3.39	51.09		
Pôrto Nacional GO	Aw	777.6	10°31'S	48°43'W	T	77.36	76.82	77.36	78.26	78.08	76.28	75.74	78.98	81.68	80.06	78.44	77.54	78.08	109.04	49.10
					P	11.73	11.42	11.49	5.99	1.72	.01	.11	.35	1.66	3.16	9.52	11.50	71.39		
Quixeramobim CE	BS	649.6	5°12'S	39°18'W	T	83.48	82.04	80.78	80.24	79.70	79.16	79.52	81.14	82.40	83.12	83.30	83.84	81.50	98.06	65.12
					P	2.63	4.25	7.39	6.65	4.36	2.13	1.01	.35	.12	.09	.22	.82	30.02		
Remanso BA	BS	1,348.5	9°41'S	42°04'W	T	80.96	78.62	80.78	81.14	80.06	79.16	78.26	79.16	80.96	82.40	82.22	80.96	80.24	103.00	49.64
					P	3.07	3.25	3.46	1.36	.86	.40	.40	.00	.30	.54	2.19	3.61	19.44		
Rio de Janeiro GB	Aw	100.1	22°54'S	43°10'W	T	77.18	78.08	75.74	74.48	71.78	69.98	68.36	69.44	69.80	71.24	73.22	72.32	72.86	102.38	50.36
					P	6.17	4.91	5.29	4.00	2.49	2.22	2.00	1.56	2.50	1.84	3.63	5.11	43.04		
Salvador BA	Af	147.6	12°55'S	38°41'W	T	78.98	79.34	79.16	78.44	76.64	74.84	73.40	73.58	74.84	76.28	77.18	78.08	76.64	95.36	62.24
					P	2.89	4.56	6.51	10.96	11.67	8.84	8.02	4.55	3.85	4.00	4.58	4.89	75.32		
Sena Madureira AC	Af	442.9	9°08'S	68°40'W	T	77.72	77.54	77.36	78.44	78.08	76.28	73.22	75.05	76.82	77.90	77.90	77.90	76.46	101.84	45.14
					P	12.46	11.24	10.49	9.10	4.93	2.60	1.42	1.79	4.97	6.82	7.61	10.78	84.21		
Taperinha PA (Santarem)	Aw	65.6	2°25'S	54°42'W	T	78.26	77.54	77.54	77.72	77.54	77.18	77.18	78.80	79.88	80.42	80.42	77.72	78.44	98.78	65.30
					P	6.60	10.64	13.04	13.22	11.25	7.38	3.96	1.70	1.41	1.84	2.37	4.28	77.69		
Três Lagoas MS	Aw	1,023.7	20°47'S	51°42'W	T	77.72	77.18	77.18	74.84	69.44	67.10	66.56	69.08	72.68	75.38	77.00	77.54	73.58	105.80	30.56
					P	7.94	6.63	5.06	3.56	2.44	1.95	.81	1.39	2.89	4.30	5.78	7.86	50.61		
Uaupés AM	Af	278.9	0°08'S	67°05'W	T	77.90	78.44	78.08	77.72	76.46	75.74	75.74	77.00	78.44	78.44	78.98	78.26	77.72	102.20	60.80
					P	11.17	10.28	11.16	10.35	12.95	9.62	9.22	7.33	6.31	6.45	7.48	10.63	112.95		
Vitória ES	Af	101.7	20°19'S	40°20'W	T	77.54	78.08	77.54	75.56	72.68	70.70	68.90	69.80	71.42	72.86	74.48	76.28	73.76	99.14	48.74
					P	5.94	4.63	5.92	5.11	3.54	2.61	2.83	1.88	3.33	5.32	6.65	7.53	55.29		

Sources: Ratisbona/Schwertfeger, pp. 219-293.

Map I-7. Brazilian Climatic Regions and Climatic Stations

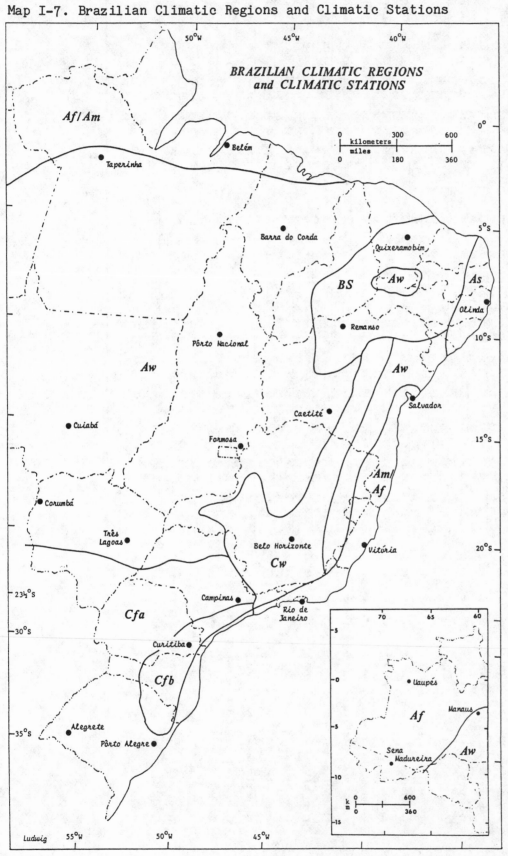

BRAZILIAN CLIMATIC REGIONS
and CLIMATIC STATIONS

Af/Am

Belém

Taperinha

Barra do Corda

Quixeramobim

BS

Aw

As

Olinda

Remanso

Pôrto Nacional

Aw

Aw

Caetité

Salvador

Cuiabá

Formosa

Aml/Af

Corumbá

Três Lagoas

Belo Horizonte

Vitória

Cw

Campinas

Rio de Janeiro

Cfa

Curitiba

Cfb

Alegrete

Porto Alegre

Uaupés

Manaus

Af

Sena Madureira

Aw

Ludwig

Map I-8. Vegetation of Brazil

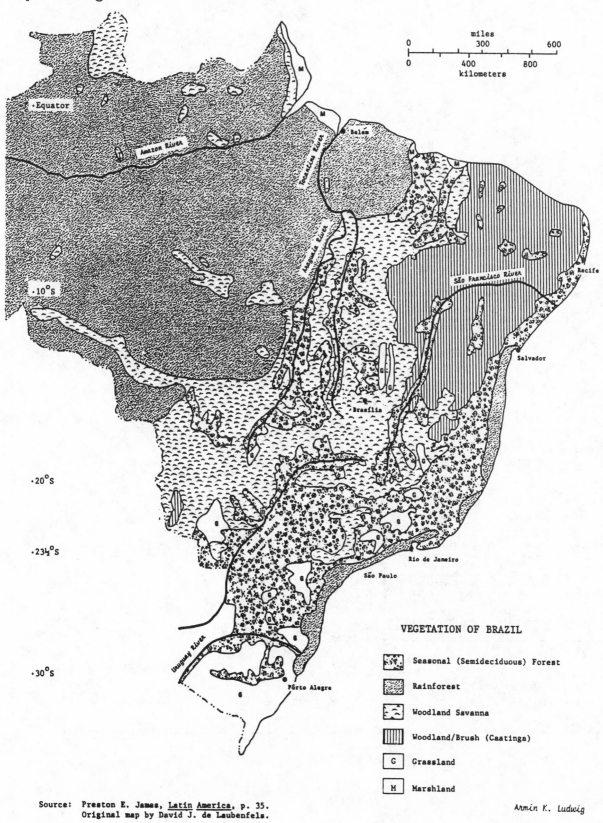

VEGETATION OF BRAZIL

- Seasonal (Semideciduous) Forest
- Rainforest
- Woodland Savanna
- Woodland/Brush (Caatinga)
- G Grassland
- M Marshland

Source: Preston E. James, <u>Latin America</u>, p. 35.
         Original map by David J. de Laubenfels.

Armin K. Ludwig

Map I-9. Soils of Brazil. Orders, Suborders, Great Soil Groups

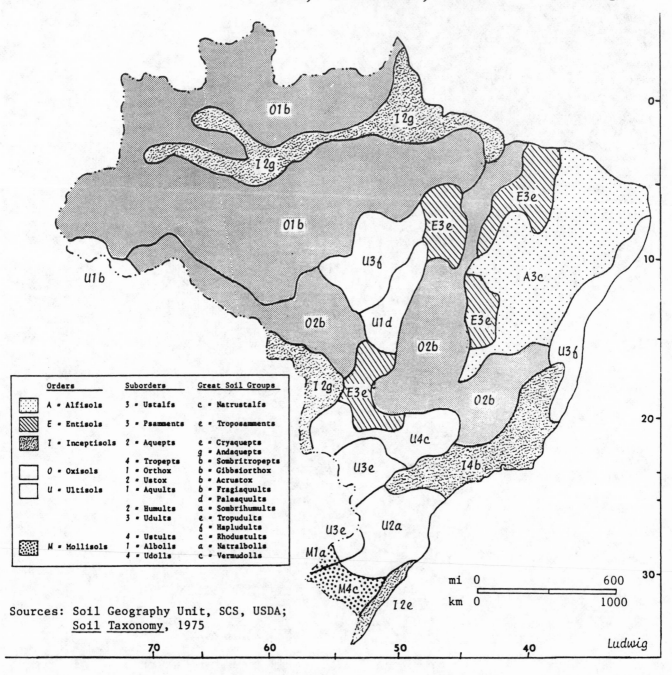

SOILS of BRAZIL
Orders, Suborders, Great Soil Groups

Orders	Suborders	Great Soil Groups
A = Alfisols	3 = Ustalfs	c = Natrustalfs
E = Entisols	3 = Psamments	e = Troposamments
I = Inceptisols	2 = Aquepts	e = Cryaquepts
		g = Andaquepts
	4 = Tropepts	b = Sombritropepts
O = Oxisols	1 = Orthox	b = Gibbsiorthox
	2 = Ustox	b = Acrustox
U = Ultisols	1 = Aquults	b = Fragiaquults
		d = Paleaquults
	2 = Humults	a = Sombrihumults
	3 = Udults	e = Tropudults
		f = Hapludults
	4 = Ustults	c = Rhodustults
M = Mollisols	1 = Albolls	a = Natralbolls
	4 = Udolls	c = Vermudolls

Sources: Soil Geography Unit, SCS, USDA;
<u>Soil</u> Taxonomy, 1975

Ludwig

Chapter II. The Human Base

Table II-1 shows the population of Brazil and its major political subdivisions from 1776 to 1980. The accuracy of the figures on this table may have improved through time but the 1872 census certainly raised this accuracy to a new level. Detailed descriptions of the pre-1872 counts in the _Resumo histórico_ indicate that at worst they were guesses and at best they were unsystematically taken.[1] The 1776 count resulted from Abbott Correa da Serra's order to his ecclesiastics to enumerate the populations of their jurisdictions. The 1808 figure appeared in an obscure Brazilian historical journal in 1829. Although its author is unknown, it is the first to enumerate population by provinces and by condition of servitude, the detail of the latter suggesting that the author had access to government documents for the year 1808. In 1819 Judge Velloso, charged with improving the administration of justice in Brazil, "corrected" a count he had had taken in 1815. The latter was taken in the field by parish priests, royal judges, and police magistrates. It distinguished free and slave population in Brazil's seven archbishoprics, but failed to count military personnel and children under the age of seven. Velloso "corrected" for these and guessed at the Indian population to produce the 1819 figures. Later, Joaquim Norberto reorganized the Velloso figures within the framework of the Brazilian provinces as they existed in 1870, assigning to each its proportion of free and slave population. An 1823 count, also by an unknown author and also appearing in the same obscure journal as the 1808 count, provided slave/free figures for the provinces. In 1830 Malte-Brun estimated Brazil's population by province and by race, but not by condition of servitude. The 1854 count was developed by the Imperial Minister of Commerce, who asked the president of each province to supply him province population figures. No record exists as to how these figures were gathered.

In January 1871 an imperial decree established the Bureau of General Statistics, which was to take the census every ten years. Under the Bureau's control Brazil's first population enumeration to merit the designation census was

taken on August 1, 1872. The process, however, was delayed
in three provinces. The dicennial rhythm did not begin until
1890, but even after it began no census was taken in the
years 1910 and 1930.

On Table II-1 population figures for 1930 were estimates
by the Instituto Brasileiro de Geografia e Estatística (since
1967 called Fundação IBGE). Figures for 1872 through 1960
record population present, which is also referred to as
population de facto. This is a count of all persons in a
locale at the time of the census regardless of their
permanent residences. The figures for 1970 and 1980 record
population resident (also called population de jure). This
count assigns to a locale all persons who reside there
regardless of their whereabouts at the time of the census.
The 1970 census records population by political subdivision
only for population resident.

The names, statuses, and spellings of Brazil's major
political subdivisions have changed considerably since 1776.
On this and all subsequent tables the names and spellings of
the political subdivisions are those that were in use in
1970. The figures for 1808 through 1854 for the province
(called state in 1970) of Rio de Janeiro included the
population of the city of Rio de Janeiro, the national
capital in that period. The state of Guanabara existed only
during the 1960 and 1970 censuses. From the census of 1872
through that of 1950 Guanabara was the Distrito Federal
(Federal District) which contained the city of Rio de
Janeiro, the national capital in that period. Guanabara came
into being when the city of Brasília, surrounded by the new
Distrito Federal, became the national capital. After the
1970 census, the state of Guanabara became part of the state
of Rio de Janeiro. The subdivision referred to on Table II-1
as the Distrito Federal is the new Federal District
surrounding Brasília. As of 1980 Rondônia (formerly
Guaporé), Amapá, Fernando de Noronha, and Roraíma (formerly
Rio Branco) were territories. Serra dos Aimores was an area
of 10,137 square kilometers (3,914 square miles) in
litigation between the states of Minas Gerais and Espírito
Santo. The case was settled in 1963. The state of Mato
Grosso do Sul was separated from Mato Grosso state on January
1, 1979, in accordance with Lei Complementar No. 31 of
October 11, 1977.

Population changes in Brazil's major political
subdivisions have reflected the regional and historical
components of the country's settlement and economic
development. Preston James,[2] Rollie Poppino,[3] and Richard
Momsen[4] have described both the historical and contemporary
man/land relationships affecting differential settlement and

development patterns. Charles Wagley[5] fleshes out Brazil's regional cultural characteristics, and T. Lynn Smith[6] describes in detail the demographic, institutional, and life-style characteristics accompanying settlement of the country. João Calogeras[7] puts settlement in a general political framework and economic analyses of settlement patterns are provided by Caio Prado,[8] Roberto Simonsen,[9] Celso Furtado,[10] and Thomas Merrick.[11]

The slave-based, sugar economy established in the 1500s on the northeast coast (the first new culture hearth in the New World) supported the population of the states Pernambuco and Bahia. This culture hearth is the subject of two works by Gilberto Freyre.[12] The discovery of gold brought an influx of people to Minas Gerais state after 1698, many from Pernambuco and Bahia. Charles Boxer[13] describes this "golden age" of Brazil. In Minas Gerais, a loss of population accompanied the decline of easily mined gold. Despite these losses, Minas Gerais continued to support the country's largest population until 1920. It was based on subsistence agriculture, which was accompanied by the development of sugar, then coffee, plantations, and finally by the grazing of cattle on the vast plateau that was denuded of trees in the processing of sugar and alcohol. In the 1800s a slave-based coffee economy was added to the earlier slave-based sugar economy to sustain a growing population in the state of Rio de Janeiro. The slave-coffee period is documented by Stanley Stein.[14]

In the late 1800s São Paulo state's population began to burgeon. Early growth was based on exports of coffee from plantations worked by free European immigrant labor; later growth on heavy industrialization. By 1940 São Paulo had passed Minas Gerais to become Brazil's most populous state. In the early 1900s large numbers of European immigrants were occupying small, general farms in Rio Grande do Sul to swell that state's population. Later in this century enough Brazilians together with European and Japanese immigrants had settled small coffee farms in Paraná state to make it Brazil's sixth most populous by 1980.

Map II-1 is a three-dimensional choropleth map of the 1980 population of Brazil's major political subdivisions. A choropleth map is one in which the value assigned to a subdivision, in this case the population of the subdivision, is applied to the entire area of that subdivision without reflecting any variations within it. The map was created by T. Gallagher and Richard Wilkie in 1981 at the Geography Cartographic Laboratory of the University of Massachusetts at Amherst using the SYMVU program of the Harvard University Center for Computer Graphics. Map II-2 is a cartogram of

Brazil's 1980 population by political subdivision. In a cartogram the area of each political subdivision and city (shaded) reflects its population. M. Voutselas, A. Paine, R. Hynes, and Richard Wilkie created the map in the Laboratory noted above. Map II-3 is a three-dimensional choropleth map of population change by percent in Brazil's major political subdivisions between 1970 and 1980. Its origins are the same as those for Map II-1. Map II-4 is a three-dimensional choropleth map of total population by major political subdivisions in 1970. It was produced in the Laboratory noted for Map II-1 above by S. Kocur, T. Gallagher, and Richard Wilkie. Map II-5 is a cartogram of Brazil's 1970 population by major political subdivisions, and was created in the Geography Cartographic Laboratory by R. Hynes and A. Paine. Map II-6 is a three-dimensional choropleth map of population change by percent in Brazil's major political subdivisions between 1960 and 1970.

Table II-2 presents the slave/free population counts for the years 1819 and 1872. In each year Rio de Janeiro includes both the city and province of Rio de Janeiro. Paraná and Amazonas were not in existence as political subdivisions in 1819 but the national figures for 1819 were distributed by Velloso (see text for Table II-1) to those provinces that were in existence in 1870. The 1872 slave/free total for Brazil was 9,930,478 out of a total censused population of 10,112,161. Slave/free enumeration was lower than the total population in each of six political subdivisions: Maranhão, Minas Gerais, Piauí, Rio de Janeiro, Rio Grande do Sul, and Sergipe.

The total number of slaves in an 1823 count (1,147,515) was similar to that for 1819, but for some political subdivisions they differ sharply from one another. The total slave counts by political subdivisions for 1867 (1,400,000) and 1869 (1,690,000) closely paralleled the 1872 census total, but again the internal distributions differed sharply. In the interests of parsimony only the earliest (1819) and latest (1872) figures are shown on Table II-2, although the accuracy of the 1819 count may be no greater than that for 1823. The abolition of slavery in 1888 preceded the census of 1890, so 1872 is the only formal Brazilian census to enumerate slaves.

Slaves were originally concentrated on the coastal sugar plantations (<u>engenhos</u>) of Pernambuco and Bahia. Large numbers also worked the canefields of Rio de Janeiro and Alagoas. They moved with their masters to mine gold and diamonds in Minas Gerais and gold in Goiás. Slaves eventually came to reside in every province of Brazil and in many locales in the seventeenth century outnumbered the

Human Base

Portuguese. By 1819 the slave proportion of the Brazilian population was only 30.8 percent.

Between 1819 and 1872 only two provinces had absolute gains in the number of slaves reported: Maranhão, a traditional plantation province on the north coast, and Rio Grande do Sul, a nonplantation province, which ironically, by the late nineteenth century was a region of heavy yeoman farmer immigration from Europe. In most provinces the decline in absolute numbers of slaves between 1819 and 1872 was accompanied by sharp declines in the percentages of slaves in the total population. This proportionate decline can be attributed to several conditions which are described by João Calogeras. They include the very effective Queiroz Law of 1850, which virtually eliminated slave importation, the growth of the native white population, and the influx of European immigrants. Only the province and city of Rio de Janeiro reported an increase in the proportion of slaves between 1819 and 1872. In part, this occurred because the capital city was the major slave market in the first half of the nineteenth century. In addition, slaves were in demand on the expanding coffee plantations (fazendas) of Rio de Janeiro province. The demand for slaves in Rio was, in fact, so great that between 1870 and 1880 more than 200,000 were purchased and transported by sea from the agriculturally depressed and drought-ridden northeast.[15]

On Table II-3 the areal base used to record the population for each year is the county, that is, the município. This is done to preserve the historical continuity of the data since prior to 1940 Brazilian censuses did not distinguish between urban and rural populations in counties. As a consequence the population given for a city was actually that for the county in which the city was located. Despite this attempt at longitudinal uniformity, comparability through the years is still not achieved because Brazilian counties have been undergoing constant, though in most cases small, boundary changes.

The table traces the populations of only the twenty-five largest counties in 1980. A dash indicates either that a county was not in existence at the time the census was taken or that its early existence is hidden by a previous name. A population decline between censuses in some counties may be more apparent than real since it may be a product of a new county being carved out of an older one. Brazilian sources use figures from the 1906 municipal census for the 1900 population of Rio de Janeiro. The 1930 figures are IBGE estimates which were made only for the Federal District and those counties surrounding state capitals. For 1970 and 1980 the municípios of São Paulo, Santo André, Guarulhos, Osasco,

31

and São Bernardo do Campo were all part of the São Paulo metropolitan region. For these same census years the municípios of Rio de Janeiro, Nova Iguaçu, São Gonçalo, Duque de Caxias, and Niterói were all part of the Rio de Janeiro metropolitan region.

On Table II-3 there are three exceptions to the use of the county as the areal base for population. In 1950 Osasco, Sao Paulo, was a distrito (township) of the município of São Paulo. It became a município in 1959. The source does not specify whether Osasco's population in both 1950 and 1960 was present or resident or in some other form. The other two exceptions involve the use of the entire Federal District as the Rio de Janeiro population base prior to 1960 and as the Brasilia population base for 1960 and after. As a consequence of using the District base some of the early figures included sizeable rural populations. In 1906, for example, 23 percent of Rio de Janeiro's population was rural. Many of the late-developing counties were essentially satellites of larger, nearby cities and were characterized by small core cities surrounded by industrial-residential sprawl. Nova Iguaçu, Duque de Caxias, and São Gonçalo (although it had a long nonindustrial history) around the city of Rio de Janeiro and Santo André, São Bernardo do Campo, Guarulhos, and Osasco around the city of São Paulo are examples of this pattern.

Figures for 1872 through 1920 and for 1940, 1950, and 1960 report population present, or population de facto, that is, all persons at the site of the enumeration regardless of their permanent residences. Figures for 1930 and 1975 (both columns) are estimates by the Instituto Brasileiro de Geografia e Estatística (now called Fundação IBGE). The 1970 figures are for population resident, or population de jure. This system reports all residents at the enumeration site regardless of their whereabouts.

Urban growth closely paralleled the regional/historical changes in the country's overall population. In the north-east the cities of Recife and Salvador were already flourishing in the 1600s, but did not attain one million inhabitants until 1970. A major impetus for Rio de Janeiro's urban growth came in 1763 when the colonial capital was transferred from Salvador to control the outflow of Minas Gerais gold bullion. Rio received a further impetus in 1808 when the Portuguese court fled Lisbon in the face of Napoleon's advance and made Rio the capital of the entire Portuguese empire. Rio, however, did not attain one million inhabitants until 1920, fully 355 years after its founding. In the late 1800s Brazilian capital earned by the coffee planters of São Paulo state was contributing to the development of the city of São Paulo. In the early part of this century São Paulo added to its economy a sizable manufacturing sector (comprised principally of cotton textile plants), the precursor of the huge and varied complex that by mid-century was to make the city the industrial metropolis of the southern hemisphere. Warren Dean[16] and Stanley Stein[17] describe the early stages of this process. In 1960 São Paulo passed Rio de Janeiro to become Brazil's largest urban center, and its remarkable growth has continued unabated into the 1980s. During the past ninety years Brazil's urban network has been by design extended into the interior. In 1896 the planned city of Belo Horizonte became the state capital of Minas Gerais. The planned city of Goiânia became the state capital of Goiás in 1935, and in 1960 the new city of Brasília was inaugurated as the national capital. Goiânia's development is dealt with in detail by Aroldo de Azevedo,[18] and Brasília's by Armin K. Ludwig[19] and Willy Staubli.[20] By 1980 these three cities numbered among the twelve largest in Brazil.

Table II-4 shows the populations from 1950 to 1980 for the twenty-five largest urbanized areas in Brazil in 1980. It also shows the 1970 and 1980 populations of Brazil's nine metropolitan regions. Until recently the concept "urbanized area" has not been applied to Brazilian population figures. In a 1975 publication, Robert W. Fox, drawing upon basic spatial work by Dr. Speridião Faissol of Fundação IBGE, developed the populations of Brazilian urbanized areas for 1950, 1960, and 1970 and projected 1980 figures by assuming a 2.7 percent growth rate for each urbanized area.[21] The thirty-five largest urbanized areas by descending order of their 1970 populations are shown on Table II-4. An urbanized area is comprised of the central city (political city), contiguous built-up areas, and some noncontinguous built-up areas that are functionally tied to the central city or to one of the built-up areas contiguous to the central city. The most obvious functional tie is measured by the number of commuters to the central city. The metropolitan regions are made up of contiguous <u>municípios</u> (counties) surrounding the central <u>município</u> in which the central city is located.

The metropolitan region of São Paulo consists of the following thirty-seven <u>municípios</u>: São Paulo, Arujá, Barueri, Biritiba Mirim, Caieiras, Cajamar, Carapicuiba, Cotia, Diadema, Embu, Embu-Guaçu, Ferraz de Vasconcellos, Francisco Morato, Franco da Rocha, Guararema, Guarulhos, Itapecerica da Serra, Itapevi, Itaquaquecetuba, Jandira, Juquitiba, Mairiporã, Mauá, Mogi das Cruzes, Osasco, Pirapora do Bom Jesus, Poá, Ribeirão Pires, Rio Grande da Serra, Salesópolis, Santa Isabel, Santana de Parnaíba, Santo André, São Bernardo do Campo, São Caetano do Sul, Susano, and Taboão da Serra.

Rio de Janeiro's metropolitan region includes these fourteen _municípios_: Rio de Janeiro, Duque de Caxias, Itaboraí, Itaguaí, Magé, Mangaratiba, Maricá, Nilópolis, Niterói, Nova Iguaçu, Paracambi, Petrópolis, São Gonçalo, and São João de Meriti.

The metropolitan region of Recife incorporates nine _municípios_: Recife, Cabo, Igaraçu, Itamaracá, Jaboatão, Moreno, Olinda, Paulista, and São Lourenco da Mata. Belo Horizonte's metropolitan region is composed of these fourteen _municípios_: Belo Horizonte, Betim, Caeté, Contagem, Ibirité, Lagoa Santa, Nova Lima, Pedro Leopoldo, Raposos, Ribeirão das Neves, Rio Acima, Sabará, Santa Luzia, and Vespasiano. The Pôrto Alegre metropolitan region is made up of fourteen _municípios_ including: Pôrto Alegre, Alvorada, Cachoeirinha, Campo Bom, Canoas, Estância Velha, Esteio, Gravataí, Guaíba, Novo Hamburgo, São Leopoldo, Sapiranga, Sapucaia do Sul, and Viamão.

Salvador's metropolitan region includes these eight _municípios_: Salvador, Camaçari, Candeias, Itaparica, Lauro de Freitas, São Francisco do Conde, Simões Filho, and Vera Cruz. The metropolitan region of Fortaleza is made up of five _municípios_: Fortaleza, Aquiraz, Caucaia, Maranguape, and Pacatuba. Curitiba's metropolitan region contains fourteen _municípios_: Curitiba, Almirante Tamandare, Araucária, Balsa Nova, Bocaiúva do Sul, Campina Grande do Sul, Campo Largo, Colombo, Contenda, Mandirituba, Piraquara, Quatro Barras, Rio Branco do Sul, and São José dos Pinhais. Belém's metropolitan region consists of the _municípios_ of Belém and Ananindeua.

The urban/rural population of Brazil and its major political subdivisions are shown on Table II-5. The Brazilian definition of urban depends upon the political status and dwelling density of a given place. According to Decree Law 311 of March 2, 1938, a place is urban if it is a _sede municipal_ (the seat of a _município_--Brazil's county) and has at least 200 dwellings clustered closely together. Such places are referred to as _cidades_ (cities). Subunits of counties are called _distritos_ (districts) and their seats are classed as urban if they are comprised of at least thirty closely clustered dwellings. These places are referred to as _vilas_, the best translation for which would seem to be towns or villages. In the American idiom, however, towns and villages take on a size relationship in comparison with cities that is not always the case in the Brazilian situation. In 1950, for example, Brazil had fifteen _vilas_ with populations greater than 10,000, the largest of which, Neves, Rio de Janeiro state, contained 52,424 inhabitants.

Many of the larger vilas were located in the state of Rio de Janeiro, and many were on the fringes of the city of Rio de Janeiro where new industrial plants attracted a large residential population. Volta Redonda, Rio de Janeiro state, although not in the Rio city periphery, was the site of Brazil's huge national steel mill, built during World War II. By 1950 it was the country's second largest vila with a population of 32,143. As new municípios were formed old vilas became new cidades. All of Brazil's area outside cidades and vilas is considered rural.

When a set of data is published in the Brazilian censuses for cidade and vila locations separately, the two subgroups are referred to as urban and suburban, respectively. This subgrouping is limited in Brazilian censuses to population counts and housing characteristics. In 1940 3,690,447 persons, 8.9 percent of the total Brazilian population, lived in vilas, that is, were suburban. In 1950 the number rose to 5,825,348, 11.2 percent of the population of the country. By 1970 the number of vila residents had declined to 2,169,033, a figure that represented only 2.3 percent of the Brazilian population. The urban and rural figures for 1940, 1950, and 1960 are for population present; those for 1970 and 1980 are for population resident.

The proportion of Brazil's population that was urban fell during the decade of the 1940s from 26.5 percent in 1940 to 25.0 percent in 1950. High rural fecundity and the wide distribution of simple but effective government-sponsored public health measures during World War II contributed to the expansion of a rural population, which had not yet begun to move to cities in large numbers. In only one political subdivision, Guanabara (comprised mostly of the city of Rio de Janeiro and called the Distrito Federal at the time), was the urban population greater than 50 percent in 1940. In twelve other subdivisions the urban population made up less than 20 percent of the population. By 1950 Guanabara was still the only subdivision with an urban population of more than 50 percent and in eighteen subdivisions (three were added in the late 1940s) the urban population was still below 20 percent.

During the 1950s rural to urban migration had begun to change this pattern and Brazil's urban population rose to 45.1 percent of the total. In six subdivisions the urban population was greater than 50 percent and in only one, Maranhão, was it less than 20 percent. In the Planalto Central (Central Plateau) and the Amazon region population growth in and around urban centers more than kept pace with new rural settlement.

By 1970 the urban proportion of Brazil's population had risen to 56 percent. In ten subdivisions the urban population was greater than 50 percent of the total and in every subdivision the urban population exceeded 20 percent. Maranhão continued to be the country's most rural state with only 25.1 percent of the population urban.

In 1980 Brazil's population was 67.6 percent urban. With the exception of Maranhão, whose population was only 31.4 percent urban, the urban proportion in every other political subdivision in Brazil exceeded 40 percent.

Table II-6 indicates that in each of the censuses from 1940 to 1970 women outnumbered men in urban areas and men outnumbered women in rural areas. In absolute numbers these differentials have steadily increased during the thirty-year period. In 1940 in urban areas there were 551,236 more women than men. This differential increased to 840,555 in 1950, to 1,154,259 in 1960, and to 1,629,334 in 1970. Conversely, in rural areas there were 543,097 more men than women in 1940, 666,170 in 1950, 1,081,981 in 1960, and 1,152,983 in 1970.

To a large degree these figures reflected the fact that Brazil's vast undeveloped interior has long been and continues to be the purview of the single male. This pattern held among the <u>bandeirantes</u> of the 1600s, who set out from São Paulo in quasi-military organizations to scour the interior for gold, diamonds, and slaves and continues today among the cowboys (<u>vaqueiros</u>), the diamond- and gold-panners (<u>garimpeiros</u>), and the road builders and agriculturists who fell the Amazon forest.

Table II-7 presents the sex/age distribution of Brazil's population from 1872 to 1970. All of these data must be regarded as suspect. Whipple's Index, which classifies world census age information, places Brazil's 1950 and 1970 census figures in category IV, that of rough data. There is no reason to believe that earlier censuses attained any higher level of accuracy. This age-data caveat certainly applies to the 1872 census which included the slave population. The 1872 through 1960 figures are for <u>de jure</u> population, that is, population present. The 1970 figures are for <u>de facto</u> population, population resident. The latter are used here because only resident population figures provided the "under 1" and "80 and over" age categories.

Brazil's support ratio, or dependency ratio, has remained high since 1940. This ratio is derived by dividing the "worker" population, aged 15-64, into the rest of the population, the dependent population. In 1940 this ratio stood at .82, then fell slightly to .80 in 1950. In both

1960 and 1970 it stood at .83. Vaz da Costa warns that the dependency ratio is less reliable for Brazil than for most industrialized countries.[22] Although he makes use of it as a rough comparative tool, he points out that "many Brazilians under 15 years of age work, especially in the rural areas, while many in the 15-64 age group are idle or underemployed."

There is no check on the veracity of the sex data. Despite the Brazilian tendency to sequester women, a residual of the colonial past and a practice that could lead to their being undercounted in the early censuses, there is no evidence that such an undercounting took place. The figures probably present a fair picture of the sex differentials in the Brazilian population at the time the censuses were taken. The high male ratio in the total population in 1872 seems to reflect the emphasis on male slaves as field laborers (although slave importation was effectively cut off some twenty years earlier), for among the slave population this ratio is even higher. In the 1872 free population, however, females outnumbered males in the 5-15 year age group even though in all other age groups males outnumbered females. In each of the succeeding censuses males outnumbered females up to the age of 14, but females then outnumbered males in the next three or four age groups despite the fact these age groups encompass the principal child-bearing years. In the 1920, 1940, and 1950 censuses males began to outnumber females in the 30-39 year age group, but in the 1960 and 1970 censuses this pattern was pushed back to the 40-49 year age group. These high male ratios continued in all but the 1940 census through the 60-69 year age group, beyond which females again outnumbered males.

The number of adherents to major religions is reported on Table II-8. The 1872 figures included 1,510,806 slaves, all of whom were considered Roman Catholic. According to Emilio Willems[23] the three largest non-Catholic movements in recent Brazilian history have been Pentecostalism, a Protestant sect, Spiritualism, and Umbanda, the latter classed by the census as Roman Catholic. The validity of the data on Table II-8 is certainly questionable if the statistical histories of these movements are any indication. The first Pentecostal sects were founded in 1910 and, although early Pentecostalists were reluctant to count their followers, the movement began to gain momentum after World War II. By 1958, the Evangelical Federation of Brazil counted 1.5 million members in two Pentecostal bodies. This number accounted for 55 percent of the Federation's total Protestant count of 2,697,273.

Organized Spiritualism first appeared in Brazil in 1873 and in its most sophisticated version follows the teachings of Allan Kardec. By 1920 it had reached the proportions of a religious mass movement. Umbanda is rooted in <u>macumba</u> (also referred to as <u>candomblê</u>), a syncretism of Catholicism and Afro and Indian fetishistic beliefs, which might cautiously be described as Brazilian voodoo. Onto this some teachings of Spiritualism have been grafted. Umbanda, however, is not recognized by the census as a separate denomination, and, because Kardecist Spiritualists do not tolerate Umbanda Spiritualists declaring themselves to be Spiritualists, Umbandistas are officially listed as Roman Catholics.

Most of those classed as Buddhists are probably Japanese immigrants or descendants of Japanese who are, in fact, Shintoists. Why their numbers increased between 1940 and 1960 is not clear, particularly in light of the fact that Japanese colonists tend to claim to be Catholics soon after their arrival in Brazil. Standiford[24] points out that among those Japanese who emigrated to the Amazon a concern for upward mobility and accumulation of wealth reduced their interest in the ancestor-oriented religion of their homeland. Brazilian officials have discouraged the transplanting of organized Japanese religion to Brazil by refusing entry to Buddhist monks. No Shinto shrine is to be found in the colony of Tomé Açu, Pará, although two Japanese-funded Catholic churches were constructed there in the 1960s. Valente,[25] referring to Japanese agricultural settlements in the northeast, notes the public conversion of many Japanese-Brazilians to Catholicism. Nevertheless, many who consider themselves Catholic maintain a Shinto shrine in the home. This domestic religion, however, cut off as it is from its natural base--the Japanese land and culture--has not been a stumbling block to conversion. What they tell the census-taker regarding their religion is another matter.

Hebrew numbers in Brazil have never been large, but their involvement with the country is as old as Brazil itself. In 1503, according to Serebrenick,[26] a consortium led by Fernando de Noronha, a <u>novo</u> <u>cristão</u> (new Christian or converted Jew), was granted a royal charter to settle and trade in Brazil. Jews were instrumental in the development of the sugar cane industry on the Atlantic islands of Madeira and São Tomé. When this industry was transplanted to Brazil (1515-30) Serebrenick suggests that Jews had to have predominated in the process. A prohibition on Jewish emigration from Portugal to Brazil in the late 1500s kept their numbers low. In 1630, however, Jews who had fled Portugal for Holland came to Brazil under the aegis of the Dutch West India Company, which had conquered the Pernambuco sugar lands. A Jewish community of some 700 flourished in Recife during the Dutch occupation. When the Portuguese retook the city in 1654 many Jews chose to leave for Dutch

Guiana or various Caribbean islands and twenty-three came to New Amsterdam (New York) to found what was to become the first Jewish community in the United States. In the face of subsequent persecutions, including the Portuguese Inquisition, few Jews came to Brazil until the country declared independence from Portugal in 1822 and the new Brazilian constitution of 1824 guaranteed religious freedom. Non-Iberian Jews then began to arrive in Brazil. In 1828 Moroccan Jews founded a community and synagogue in Belém, Pará. Through the nineteenth century small numbers of Jews arrived from north Africa and western Europe. These numbers were augmented by Jews from the eastern Mediterranean (Greece, Turkey, Syria, Lebanon, and Palestine) and from eastern Europe. Their total number, however, remained small.

The census of 1900 was the earliest to record the Jewish (Hebrew) population of Brazil. In that year they numbered only 1,021, with 60 percent of this total divided nearly equally among São Paulo state, the Distrito Federal (the city of Rio de Janeiro), and the state of Pará. By 1950, 38 percent of Brazil's Jewish population resided in São Paulo state, 36 percent in the Distrito Federal, and 12 percent in Rio Grande do Sul state.

In the early twentieth century, according to Lipiner,[27] Baron Hirsch's World Jewish Colonization organization developed two rural colonies in Rio Grande do Sul state, but these faltered as colonists drifted to the nearby small towns and to Pôrto Alegre the state capital. The turmoil of World War I brought some 7,000 Jews to Brazil and small flows of immigrants continued to Brazilian cities until 1930. Jewish immigration has been minimal since then.

Those researchers who estimated the numbers of Brazilian Indians arrived at their widely varying conclusions by widely varying assumptions and methods. The results of their efforts are presented on Table II-9. Most of the authors are cited in Red Gold by John Hemming,[28] who proceeds to explain the means by which each researcher divined his Indian count.

Alfred L. Kroeber, "Cultural and Natural Areas of Native North America," University of California Publications in American Archeology and Ethnology 38 (1939). Kroeber's modest estimate was, according to Hemming, rooted in his suspicion of Indian population claims by soldiers and missionaries, which he took to be greatly exaggerated. Kroeber ignored the effects of disease as a population suppressant following Indian contact with Europeans, but he did think the introduction of metal tools tended to increase the numbers of Brazilian Indians.

Angel Rosenblatt, <u>La población indígena de América desde 1492 hasta la actualidad</u> (Buenos Aires, 1945). According to Hemming, "Rosenblatt made accurate calculations by working through colonial records, but he was more interested in Spanish South America where census records were better than in the Portuguese Empire." Rosenblatt's rather low estimate is based on his assumption that all Brazilian Indians were hunters and gatherers. He ignored the fact that many groups, the Guarani and Tupi, for example, were agriculturists.

Julian H. Steward, "The Native Population of South America," <u>Handbook of South American Indians</u>, ed. Julian H. Steward (Washington, D.C.: Smithsonian Institution, Bureau of American Ethnology, 1949), 5:655-88. Hemming says Steward estimated populations for tribes or groups of tribes by calculating the area occupied by them and then applying an assumed population density.

John Hemming, <u>Red Gold</u> (London: Macmillan, 1978), pp. 487-501. Hemming developed population figures for 239 tribes. He based his estimates on eyewitness accounts of these tribes, on the recorded efforts to subdue each one, on the sizes of early missions, and on the fertility of the regions occupied by the tribes.

Karl Sapper, "Die Zahl und Volksdichte der indianischen Bevölkerung in Amerika von der Conquista und in der Gegenwart," in <u>International Congress of Americanists</u> (The Hague, 1924), pp. 95-104. Sapper, a geographer, based his population estimates on assumed land use according to the fertility of each region, says Hemming.

William Denevan, "The Aboriginal Population of Amazonia," in William Denevan, ed., <u>The Native Population of South America in 1492</u> (Madison, Wis., 1977), pp. 205-34. Denevan, says Hemming, developed population figures only for the Amazon basin. He assumed population densities of twenty-eight persons per square kilometer on the flood plains and 1.2 per square kilometer for the forest upland and reduced his final figure by 25 percent to account for unoccupied buffers between warring tribes.

Pierre Clastres, "Éléments de démographie amérindienne," <u>L'Homme</u> 13, no. 1-2 (1973). Clastres, reports Hemming, used Hans Staden's observations of Tamoio settlement patterns (coastal Rio de Janeiro state) to arrive at a population density of 400 persons per 100 square kilometers (4 persons per square kilometer). He then applied this to all of Brazil's land area, 8,511,965 square kilometers. This yielded the rather high figure of 34,047,860 aboriginal people. Clastres further believed that the native population of the Americas was as high as 80-100 million, one-quarter of the earth's population at the time.

Antonio Rodrigues Velloso de Oliveira. This was part of a work entitled "A Igreja do Brazil" published by Velloso on June 28, 1819. He was charged by the Royal Court to undertake a study of the redistricting of the old bishoprics in Brazil and the creation of new ones. Presumably among his respondents were priest and church officials who possessed some information about native peoples.

Thomaz Pompeu de Souza Brazil. Souza appended a population table to his geographic compendium on Brazil in 1869. No information is available regarding how he arrived at any of his populations, slave, free, or Indian.

Carlos Alberto Dória and Carlos Alberto Ricardo, "Populations indigenes du Brésil: perspectives de survie dans la région dite 'Amazonie légale,'" Bulletin de la Société Suisse des Américanistes 36 (1972):19-35. Hemming lists their estimates of the population of each of seventy-four tribes.

Darcy Ribeiro, "Culturas e linguas indígenas do Brasil," Educação e Ciências Sociais 2, no. 6 (1957), translated in Janice Hopper, ed., Indians of Brazil in the Twentieth Century (Washington, D.C., 1967), pp. 77-165. Dale W. Kietzman, "Indians and Culture Areas of Twentieth Century Brazil," in Hopper, ed., Indians of Brazil in the Twentieth Century, pp. 1-51. Hemming combines the population estimates by these authors for each of ninety-nine tribes.

The ninety-eight year record of Brazil's housing stock and occupancy ratios is presented on Table II-10. Data for the years 1940, 1950, 1970 and 1980 are for private domiciles and the number of persons occupying them. Group quarters and unoccupied dwelling units are not included. There is some confusion in the 1940 census. In RE 1940A2, Table 1 on page 6 shows the number of private domiciles occupied to be 7,897,769 and this agrees with the sum of the figures on Table 6, page 170. Table 6 also shows that 41,566,407 persons occupied these private domiciles, and this figure divided by the 7,897,769 domiciles yields a 5.26 occupancy ratio. Table 1, however, indicates an occupancy ratio of only 5.2 which results from the census assumption that the 41,566,407 residents occupied all domiciles, not only those that were private but also those that were collective, which together totaled 7,949,768. For no better reason than that the data on Table 6 are more detailed than those on Table 1, the author reports the data on Table 6.

41

The 1960 data include only permanent private domiciles, excluding 6,802 improvised private dwelling units. Data for 1900 and 1920 include not only private domiciles but also collective dwelling units such as asylums and barracks. The 1872 figures are for households (fogões), which, in fact, occupied only 1,330,210 dwelling units.

Brazil's housing stock grew more rapidly than the country's population during the eighteen years from 1872 to 1900, when the person/domicile ratio improved from 7.58 to 5.87. The next twenty years included World War I, which may have contributed to the housing stock's not keeping pace with population growth. By 1920 the 7.73 occupancy ratio was higher than that of 1872. The ratio reached 5.26 in 1940 and continued to improve slowly in successive decades.

Most of this improvement occurred with very little official aid until the 1960s, when by means of Brasília's construction the government did add directly, albeit minimally, to the country's stock of housing. A major step was taken in 1964 when the federal government set up the National Housing Bank (Banco Nacional de Habitação) to finance the construction of dwelling units as a part of overall urban development. In 1971 BNH became a public corporation capitalized at one billion cruzeiros. In 1973 agencies of BNH embarked on a huge program of low income housing construction. In many Brazilian cities the aggregate effects of BNH programs has been to create whole new subcities, most of them on the margins of established urban centers. According to the BNH Information Office,[29] at the end of 1973 the Bank and its agencies had funded one million housing units in 809 Brazilian counties. The effects of these activities is apparent in the sharp decline in the 1980 person-per-domicile ratio.

The marital status of Brazilians is shown on Table II-11. The data manifest the Brazilian pattern of female marriage at an early age to males somewhat older than their brides. In the 15-19-year age group from 1950 to 1970 nearly ten times as many females as males were married. (The 1940 figures are not comparable in this regard because the "marriage" age group in this census extends from 10 to 19 years.) The differential continued, although considerably abated, as the cohorts moved into the 20-29-year age group. In all three census years, in the 30-39-year age group there were actually more married men than married women as the effects of early male death created sizable numbers of widows. In the 15-19-year age group the percentage of married females peaked in 1950 and declined steadily to 1970; in the 20-29-year age group the married female percentage peaked in 1960 and dropped sharply by 1970. These declines can be attributed in part to a greater number of opportunities outside marriage offered young women by a rapidly modernizing society. In part, they can be attributed to the larger number of "divorced" women than "divorced" men.

The term divorce is used advisedly on the table, for an amendment permitting legal divorce did not become part of the Brazilian constitution until June 28, 1977, and did not become law until December 26, 1977. These acts are detailed by Oliveira and Acquaviva.[30] Prior to this a kind of legal separation called a desquite was available but was used primarily by middle and upper income Brazilians. It did not permit legal remarriage since it was not a legal divorce. Among lower-income Brazilians, however, common-law marriages, amasiado relationships, were prevalent, as were religious marriages without legal sanction. Charles Wagley[31] and Harry Hutchinson[32] deal with these arrangements in their studies of Brazilian communities. Given these arrangements it was possible for a man to "divorce" a common-law wife or a wife bound to him only by a religious ceremony and to "remarry" in either a common law or a civil ceremony. Women were less apt to remarry either way, thus providing an explanation for the larger number of divorced women than men on Table II-11. According to Levenhagen,[33] a constitutional amendment, No. 1 of October 17, 1969, established that a religious marriage must be publicly registered thereby making it equivalent to a civil (legal) marriage.

Despite all these possibilities there are no apparent reasons why there were more married men than women in Brazil in 1872, 1890, 1920, and 1970, and more married women than men in the country in 1940, 1950, and 1960.

References

1. Directoria Geral de Estatística, "Resumo Histórico dos Inquéritos Censitários Realizados no Brazil," in Introducção, vol. 1, Recenseamento do Brazil realizado em 1 Setembro de 1920 (Rio de Janeiro, 1922).

2. Preston E. James, Latin America (New York: Odyssey Press, 1969).

3. Rollie E. Poppino, Brazil, the Land and People (New York: Oxford University Press, 1968).

4. Richard P. Momsen, Brazil: A Giant Stirs (Princeton, N.J.: Van Nostrand, 1969).

5. Charles Wagley, An Introduction to Brazil (New York: Columbia University Press, 1971).

6. T. Lynn Smith, <u>Brazil: People and Institutions</u> (Baton Rouge: Louisiana State University Press, 1972).

7. João Pandía Calogeras, <u>A History of Brazil</u>, translated by Percy Alvin Martin (New York: Russell & Russell, 1963).

8. Caio Prado, Jr., <u>The Colonial Background of Modern Brazil</u>, translated by Suzette Macedo (Berkeley: University of California Press, 1967).

9. Roberto Simonsen, <u>História econômica do Brasil, 1500-1820</u> (São Paulo: Companhia Editora Nacional).

10. Celso Furtado, <u>The Economic Growth of Brazil from Colonial to Modern Times</u>, translated by Ricardo Aguiar and Eric Drysdale (Berkeley: University of California Press, 1963).

11. Thomas W. Merrick and Douglas H. Graham, <u>Population and Economic Development in Brazil, 1800 to the Present</u> (Baltimore: Johns Hopkins University Press, 1969).

12. Gilberto Freyre, <u>The Masters and the Slaves</u>, translated by Samuel Putnam (New York: Alfred A. Knopf, 1956). Gilberto Freyre, <u>The Mansions and the Shanties</u>, translated by Harriet de Onís (New York: Alfred A. Knopf, 1963).

13. Charles R. Boxer, <u>The Golden Age of Brazil, 1695-1750</u> (Berkeley: University of California Press, 1962).

14. Stanley Stein, <u>Vassouras: A Brazilian Coffee County, 1850-1900</u> (Cambridge: Harvard University Press, 1957).

15. Nicolas Sanchez-Albornoz, <u>The Population of Latin America</u>, translated by W. A. R. Richardson (Berkeley: University of California Press, 1974).

16. Warren Dean, <u>The Industrialization of São Paulo, 1880-1945</u> (Austin: University of Texas Press, 1969).

17. Stanley Stein, <u>The Brazilian Cotton Manufacture: Textile Enterprise in an Underdeveloped Area</u> (Cambridge: Harvard University Press, 1957).

18. Aroldo de Azevedo, "Goiânia: uma cidade 'criada,'" <u>Revista Brasileira de Geografia</u> 3, no. 1 (1941).

19. Armin K. Ludwig, "The Planning and Creation of Brasília: Toward a New and Unique Regional Environment?" in <u>New</u>

Perspectives of Brazil (Nashville: Vanderbilt University Press, 1966).

Armin K. Ludwig, Brasília's First Decade: A Study of Its Urban Morphology and Urban Support Systems. Program in Latin American Studies, Occasional Papers no. 11, International Area Studies Programs, University of Massachusetts-Amherst, 1980.

20. Willi Staubli, Brasília (Stuttgart: Verlagsanstalt Alexander Koch, no date).

21. Robert W. Fox, Urban Population Growth Trends in Latin America (Washington, D.C.: Inter-American Development Bank, 1975).

22. Rubens Vaz da Costa, "Population and Development: The Brazilian Case," Population Bulletin 25, no. 4 (September 1969).

23. Emilio Willems, "Religious Mass Movements and Social Change in Brazil," in New Perspectives of Brazil (Nashville: Vanderbilt University Press, 1966).

24. Philip Standiford, Pioneers in the Tropics: The Political Organization of Japanese in an Immigrant Community in Brazil (New York: Athlone Press, 1973).

25. Waldemar Valente, O Japonês no nordeste agrário: aspectos sócio-culturais e antropológicos (Recife: Ministério da Educação e Cultura-Instituto Joaquim Nabuco de Pesquisas Sociais, Série Estudos e Pesquisas 8, 1978).

26. Salomão Serebrenick, "Quatro séculos de vida judaica no Brasil (1500-1900)," in Breve história dos Judeus no Brasil (Rio de Janeiro: Edições Biblios, 1962).

27. Elias Lipiner, "A nova immigração judaica no Brasil," in Breve história dos Judeus no Brasil (Rio de Janeiro: Edicões Biblios, 1962).

28. John Hemming, Red Gold: The Conquest of the Brazilian Indians, 1500-1760 (Cambridge: Harvard University Press, 1978).

29. Assessoria de Planejamento e Coordenação, BNH: avaliação e perspectivas (Rio de Janeiro: Secretaria de Divulgação do BNH, 1974).

30. Juarez de Oliveira and Marcus Cláudio Acquaviva, Casamento e divórcio (Edição Saraiva, 1978).

31. Charles Wagley, <u>Amazon Town: A Study of Man in the Tropics</u> (New York: Macmillan, 1953).

32. Harry William Hutchinson, <u>Village and Plantation Life in Northeastern Brazil</u> (Seattle: University of Washington Press, 1957).

33. Antonio José de Souza Levenhagen, <u>Do casamento ao divórcio</u> (São Paulo: Editôra Atlas, S.A., 1978).

Table II-1. Population of Brazil and Its Major Political Subdivisions

Political Subdivisions	1776	1808	1819	1823	1830	1854	1872	1890	1900
Brazil	1,900,000	2,419,406	3,596,132	3,960,860	5,340,000	7,677,800	9,930,478	14,333,915	17,438,434
São Paulo SP	–	200,408	238,323	280,000	600,000	500,000	837,354	1,384,753	2,282,279
Minas Gerais MG	–	350,000	631,885	640,000	930,000	1,300,000	2,039,735	3,184,099	3,594,471
Rio de Janeiro RJ	–	235,079	510,000	451,648	591,000	1,200,000	782,724	876,884	926,035
Bahia BA	–	335,961	477,912	671,922	560,000	1,100,000	1,379,616	1,919,802	2,117,956
Rio Grande do Sul RS	–	87,167	92,180	150,000	170,000	201,300	434,813	897,455	1,149,070
Paraná PR	–	–	59,942	–	–	72,400	126,722	249,491	327,136
Pernambuco PE	–	244,277	368,465	480,000	602,000	950,000	841,539	1,030,224	1,178,150
Ceará CE	–	160,000	201,170	200,000	273,000	385,300	721,686	805,687	849,127
Guanabara GB	–	–	–	–	–	–	274,972	522,651	811,443
Maranhão MA	–	120,000	200,000	164,836	183,000	360,000	359,040	430,854	499,308
Goiás GO	–	50,365	63,168	61,000	150,000	180,000	160,395	227,572	255,284
Santa Catarina SC	–	38,687	44,031	50,000	50,000	105,000	159,802	283,769	320,289
Pará PA	–	96,000	123,901	128,000	190,000	207,400	275,237	328,455	445,356
Paraíba PB	–	95,182	96,448	122,407	246,000	209,000	376,226	457,232	490,784
Piauí PI	–	70,000	61,226	90,000	46,000	150,000	202,222	267,609	334,328
Espírito Santo ES	–	70,219	72,845	120,000	74,000	51,300	82,137	135,997	209,783
Alagoas AL	–	116,000	111,973	130,000	257,000	204,000	348,009	511,440	649,273
Rio Grande do Norte RN	–	50,000	70,921	71,053	69,000	190,000	233,979	268,273	274,317
Amazonas AM	–	–	19,350	–	–	42,600	57,610	147,915	249,756
Mato Grosso do Sul MS	–	–	–	–	–	–	–	–	–
Distrito Federal DF	–	–	–	–	–	–	–	–	–
Sergipe SE	–	75,061	114,996	120,000	267,000	183,600	176,243	310,926	356,264
Mato Grosso MT	–	25,000	37,396	30,000	82,000	85,000	60,417	92,827	118,025

Political Subdivisions	1920	1930	1940	1950	1960	1970	1980
Brazil	30,635,605	37,625,436	41,236,315	51,944,397	70,191,370	93,139,037	119,098,992
São Paulo SP	4,592,188	5,882,554	7,180,316	9,134,423	12,823,806	17,771,948	25,040,698
Minas Gerais MG	5,888,174	6,991,564	6,736,416	7,717,792	9,698,118	11,487,415	13,390,805
Rio de Janeiro RJ	1,559,371	1,870,253	1,847,857	2,297,194	3,367,738	4,742,884	11,297,327
Bahia BA	3,334,465	3,902,861	3,918,112	4,834,575	5,918,872	7,493,470	9,474,263
Rio Grande do Sul RS	2,182,713	2,736,600	3,320,689	4,164,821	5,388,659	6,664,891	7,777,212
Paraná PR	685,711	892,011	1,236,276	2,115,547	4,263,721	6,929,868	7,630,466
Pernambuco PE	2,154,835	2,664,026	2,688,240	3,395,185	4,080,601	5,160,640	6,147,102
Ceará CE	1,319,228	1,536,738	2,091,032	2,695,450	3,289,595	4,361,603	5,294,876
Guanabara GB	1,157,873	1,505,595	1,764,143	2,377,451	3,281,908	4,251,918	–
Maranhão MA	874,377	1,063,758	1,235,169	1,583,248	2,477,371	2,992,686	4,002,599
Goiás GO	511,919	654,931	826,414	1,214,921	1,917,460	2,938,677	3,865,482
Santa Catarina SC	668,743	868,653	1,178,340	1,560,502	2,129,252	2,901,734	3,628,751
Pará PA	983,507	1,304,912	944,644	1,123,273	1,538,193	2,167,018	3,411,868
Paraíba PB	961,106	1,218,676	1,422,282	1,713,259	1,991,145	2,382,617	2,772,600
Piauí PI	609,003	751,782	817,601	1,045,696	1,249,200	1,680,573	2,140,066
Espírito Santo ES	457,328	603,390	750,107	861,562	1,169,553	1,599,333	2,023,821
Alagoas AL	978,748	1,127,840	951,300	1,093,137	1,256,159	1,588,109	1,987,581
Rio Grande do Norte RN	537,135	681,095	786,018	967,921	1,140,823	1,550,244	1,899,720
Amazonas AM	363,166	413,138	438,008	514,099	714,774	955,235	1,432,066
Mato Grosso do Sul MS	–	–	–	–	–	–	1,370,333
Distrito Federal DF	–	–	–	–	139,796	537,492	1,177,393
Sergipe SE	477,064	527,130	542,326	644,361	751,778	900,744	1,141,834
Mato Grosso MT	246,612	320,418	432,265	522,044	892,233	1,597,090	1,141,661
Rondônia RO	–	–	–	35,935	70,232	111,064	942,810
Acre AC	92,379	107,511	79,768	114,755	158,852	215,299	301,605
Amapá AP	–	–	–	37,477	68,520	114,359	175,634
Roraíma RR	–	–	–	18,116	28,871	40,885	79,153
Fernando de Noronha FN	–	–	–	581	1,346	1,241	1,266
Serra dos Aimores	–	–	66,994	160,072	382,794	–	–

Sources: RE 1920A, pp. 403–405, 407 and 409; AN 1936 p. 62; AN 1956, p. 47; RE 1960A1, p. 85; AN 1974, p. 47; AN 1977, pp. 76 and 85; SI 1980, pp. 36–93.

Map II-1. Population of Brazil's Major Political Subdivisions, 1980

POPULATION OF BRAZIL'S MAJOR
POLITICAL SUBDIVISIONS, 1980

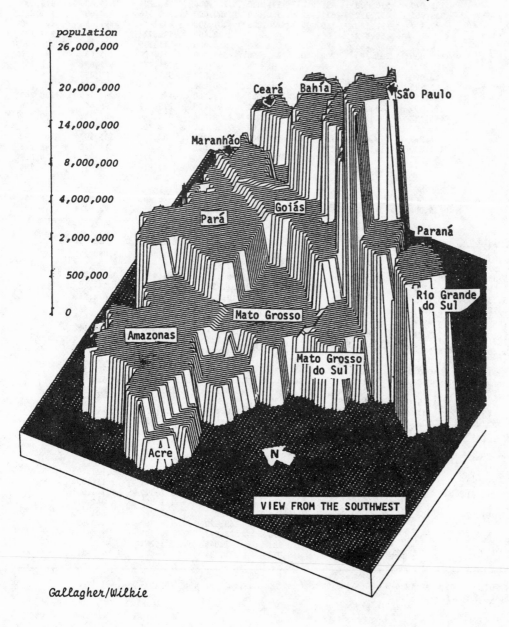

Gallagher/Wilkie

Map II-2. Cartogram of the Population of Brazil's Major Political
          Subdivisions, 1980

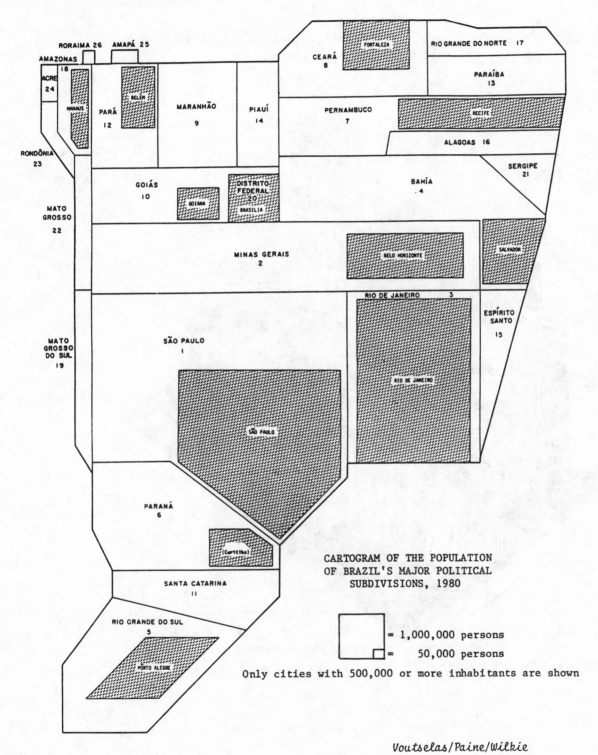

RORAIMA 26   AMAPÁ 25

AMAZONAS
18

ACRE
24

MANAUS

PARÁ
12

BELÉM

MARANHÃO
9

PIAUÍ
14

CEARÁ
8

FORTALEZA

RIO GRANDE DO NORTE 17

PARAÍBA
13

PERNAMBUCO
7

RECIFE

ALAGOAS 16

RONDÔNIA
23

MATO
GROSSO
22

GOIÁS
10

GOIANA

DISTRITO
FEDERAL
20
BRASILIA

BAHÍA
4

SERGIPE
21

MINAS GERAIS
2

BELO HORIZONTE

SALVADOR

MATO
GROSSO
DO SUL
19

SÃO PAULO
1

SÃO PAULO

RIO DE JANEIRO   3

RIO DE JANEIRO

ESPÍRITO
SANTO
15

PARANÁ
6

(Curitiba)

SANTA CATARINA
11

RIO GRANDE DO SUL
5

PORTO ALEGRE

CARTOGRAM OF THE POPULATION
OF BRAZIL'S MAJOR POLITICAL
SUBDIVISIONS, 1980

☐ = 1,000,000 persons
□ =   50,000 persons

Only cities with 500,000 or more inhabitants are shown

Voutselas/Paine/Wilkie

49

Map II-3. Percent of Population Change in Brazil's Major Political
        Subdivisions, 1970-80

PERCENT OF POPULATION CHANGE IN BRAZIL'S MAJOR POLITICAL SUBDIVISIONS, 1970-1980

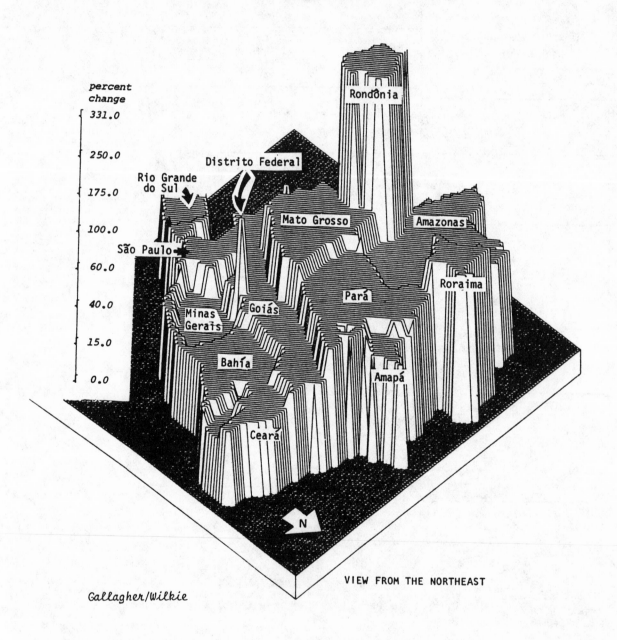

Gallagher/Wilkie

VIEW FROM THE NORTHEAST

Map II-4. Population of Brazil's Major Political Subdivisions, 1970

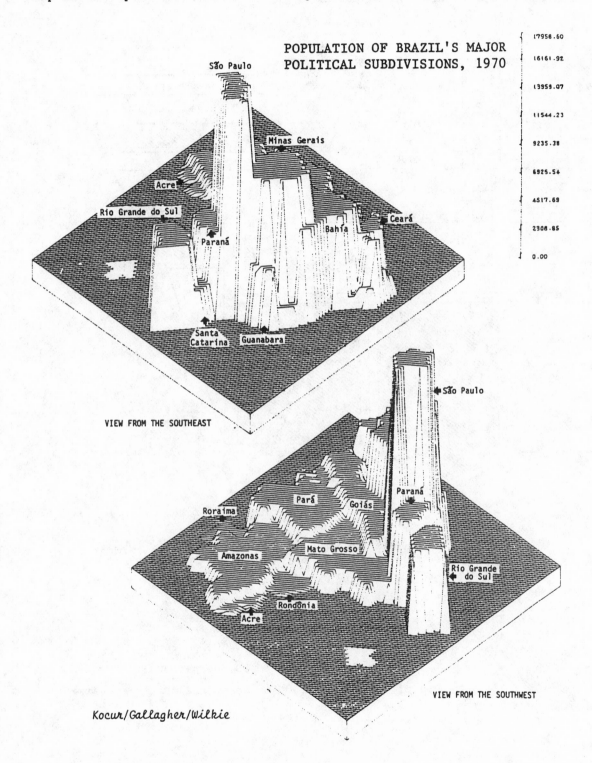

POPULATION OF BRAZIL'S MAJOR
POLITICAL SUBDIVISIONS, 1970

Kocur/Gallagher/Wilkie

Map II-5. Cartogram of the Population of Brazil's Major Political

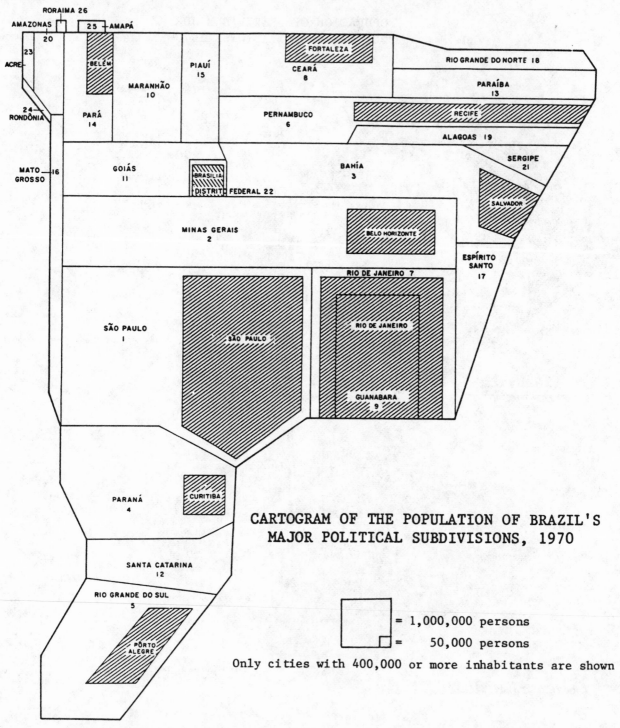

CARTOGRAM OF THE POPULATION OF BRAZIL'S
MAJOR POLITICAL SUBDIVISIONS, 1970

☐ = 1,000,000 persons

= 50,000 persons

Only cities with 400,000 or more inhabitants are shown

Hynes/Paine

Map II-6. Percent of Population Change in Brazil's Major Political
        Subdivisions, 1960-70

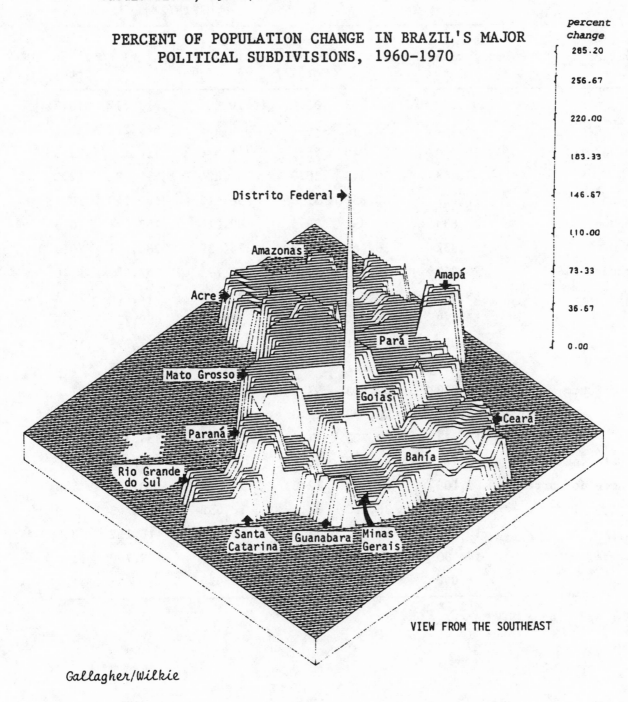

PERCENT OF POPULATION CHANGE IN BRAZIL'S MAJOR
POLITICAL SUBDIVISIONS, 1960-1970

Gallagher/Wilkie

53

Table II-2. Slave and Free Populations in Brazil, 1819 and 1872

Political Subdivision	1819			1872		
	Slave Population	Free Population	Slave % of Total	Slave Population	Free Population	Slave % of Total
Brazil	1,107,389	2,488,743	30.8	1,510,806	8,419,672	15.2
Minas Gerais	168,543	463,342	26.7	370,459	1,669,276	18.2
Rio de Janeiro	146,060	363,940	28.6	341,576	716,120	32.3
Bahia	147,263	330,649	30.8	167,824	1,211,792	12.2
São Paulo	77,667	160,656	32.6	156,612	680,742	18.7
Pernambuco	97,633	270,832	26.5	89,028	752,511	10.6
Maranhão	133,332	66,668	66.7	74,939	284,101	20.9
Rio Grande do Sul	28,253	63,927	30.6	67,791	367,022	15.6
Alagoas	69,094	42,879	61.7	35,741	312,268	10.3
Ceará	55,439	145,731	27.6	31,913	689,733	4.4
Pará	33,000	90,901	26.6	27,458	247,779	10.0
Piauí	12,405	48,821	20.2	23,795	178,427	11.8
Espírito Santo	20,272	52,573	27.8	22,659	59,478	27.6
Sergipe	26,213	88,783	22.8	22,623	153,620	12.8
Paraíba	16,723	79,725	17.3	21,526	354,700	5.7
Santa Catarina	9,172	34,859	20.7	14,984	144,818	9.4
Rio Grande do Norte	9,109	61,812	12.8	13,020	220,959	5.6
Goiás	26,800	36,368	42.4	10,652	149,743	6.6
Paraná	10,191	49,751	17.0	10,560	116,162	8.3
Mato Grosso	14,180	23,216	37.9	6,667	53,750	11.0
Amazonas	6,040	13,310	31.2	979	56,631	1.7

Sources: RE, 1920A, pp. 405 and 414.

Table II-3. Brazilian Population Centers, 1872-1980

County	1872	1890	1900	1920	1930	1940	1950	1960	1970	1980
São Paulo SP	31,385	64,934	239,820	579,033	887,810	1,326,261	2,198,096	3,781,446	5,921,796	8,493,598
Rio de Janeiro RJ	274,972	522,651	811,443	1,157,873	1,505,595	1,764,141	2,377,451	3,281,908	4,252,009	5,093,232
Belo Horizonte MG	-	-	13,472	55,563	116,981	211,377	352,724	683,908	1,235,001	1,781,924
Salvador BA	129,109	174,412	205,813	283,422	335,309	290,443	417,235	649,453	1,007,744	1,506,602
Fortaleza CE	42,458	40,902	48,369	78,536	126,666	180,185	270,169	507,108	859,135	1,308,919
Recife PE	116,671	111,556	113,106	238,843	390,942	348,424	524,682	788,336	1,060,752	1,204,738
Brasília DF	-	-	-	-	-	-	-	139,796	538,351	1,177,393
Pôrto Alegre RS	43,998	52,421	73,674	179,263	256,550	272,232	394,151	635,125	885,564	1,125,901
Nova Iguaçu RJ	-	-	-	-	-	140,606	145,649	356,645	727,674	1,094,650
Curitiba PR	12,651	24,553	49,755	78,986	102,173	140,656	180,575	356,830	608,417	1,025,979
Belém PA	61,977	50,064	96,560	236,402	284,549	206,331	254,949	399,222	633,749	934,322
Goiânia GO	-	-	-	-	-	48,166	53,389	151,013	381,055	717,948
Campinas SP	31,325	33,921	-	115,602	-	129,940	152,547	217,219	376,497	664,356
Manaus AM	29,334	38,720	50,300	75,704	84,646	106,399	139,620	173,703	312,160	634,659
São Gonçalo RJ	8,176	17,811	-	47,019	-	89,528	127,276	244,617	430,349	614,688
Duque de Caxias RJ	-	-	-	-	-	-	92,459	241,026	431,345	575,533
Santo André SP	-	-	-	-	-	89,874	127,032	242,920	418,578	552,797
Guarulhos SP	-	-	-	5,961	-	13,439	34,683	100,760	236,865	532,908
Osasco SP	-	-	-	-	-	-	43,427	116,240	283,203	473,856
São Luís MA	31,604	29,308	36,798	52,929	64,069	85,583	119,785	158,292	265,595	449,877
São Bernardo do Campo SP	-	-	-	-	-	-	29,295	82,411	201,462	425,780
Natal RN	20,392	13,725	16,056	30,696	43,149	54,836	103,215	160,235	264,567	416,906
Santos SP	9,191	13,012	-	102,589	-	165,568	203,562	262,997	346,096	416,784
Niterói RJ	47,548	34,269	53,433	86,238	110,898	142,407	186,309	243,188	324,367	400,140
Maceió AL	27,703	31,498	36,427	74,166	107,756	90,253	120,980	168,055	263,583	400,041

Sources: RE 1872 (microfilm), pp. 353-354, 427 and 429; SY 1922, p. 39; AN 1936, p. 39; AN 1947, pp. 63-66; AN 1956, pp. 50-57; RE 1960 BI, Vols. 1-18; SP 1961, p. 31; SI 1970A, pp. 85 and 106-244; SI 1980, pp. 36-93.

Table II-4. Population of Brazilian Urbanized Areas, 1950-80, and
         Metropolitan Regions, 1970-80

| | Urbanized Areas | | | | Metropolitan Regions | |
	1950	1960	1970	1980	1970	1980
São Paulo SP	2,336,000	3,950,000	7,838,000	12,273,000	8,137,410	12,588,439
Rio de Janeiro GB	3,044,000	4,574,000	6,847,000	9,619,000	7,082,404	9,018,637
Recife PE	647,000	1,028,000	1,630,000	2,307,000	1,792,688	2,348,362
Belo Horizonte MG	409,000	778,000	1,505,000	2,279,000	1,605,663	2,541,788
Pôrto Alegre RS	464,000	749,000	1,409,000	2,133,000	1,531,168	2,231,370
Salvador BA	396,000	652,000	1,067,000	1,563,000	1,148,828	1,772,018
Fortaleza CE	251,000	490,000	864,000	1,340,000	1,038,041	1,581,588
Curitiba PN	157,000	381,000	647,000	1,093,000	820,766	1,441,743
Belém PA	242,000	377,000	606,000	909,000	656,351	1,000,349
Santos SP	242,000	381,000	588,000	848,000	-	-
Brasília DF	-	140,000	538,000	1,082,000	-	-
Goiânia GO	40,000	131,000	362,000	723,000	-	-
Campinas SP	105,000	191,000	356,000	572,000	-	-
Vitória ES	79,000	163,000	323,000	505,000	-	-
Manaus AM	96,000	161,000	243,000	346,000	-	-
João Pessoa PB	119,000	182,000	292,000	409,000	-	-
Natal RN	98,000	159,000	268,000	401,000	-	-
Pelotas RS	146,000	209,000	259,000	324,000	-	-
Maceió AL	99,000	151,000	243,000	346,000	-	-
Juiz de Fora MG	85,000	123,000	219,000	317,000	-	-
Volta Redonda RJ	56,000	134,000	201,000	314,000	-	-
Sorocaba SP	76,000	118,000	193,000	285,000	-	-
Ribeirão Prêto SP	63,000	115,000	191,000	294,000	-	-
Aracajú SE	68,000	114,000	183,000	259,000	-	-
Teresina PI	51,000	99,000	181,000	286,000	-	-
São Luís MA	80,000	123,000	168,000	-	-	-
Campina Grande PB	73,000	115,000	163,000	220,000	-	-
Jundiaí SP	39,000	82,000	161,000	269,000	-	-
Itabuna BA	54,000	109,000	161,000	236,000	-	-
Londrina PN	33,000	73,000	157,000	291,000	-	-
Campos RJ	62,000	89,000	153,000	230,000	-	-
Florianópolis SC	54,000	80,000	151,000	239,000	-	-
Campo Grande MT	32,000	64,000	131,000	233,000	-	-
São Jose dos Campos SP	26,000	55,000	130,000	228,000	-	-
Feira de Santana BA	27,000	61,000	127,000	208,000	-	-

Sources: Robert W. Fox, <u>Urban Population Growth Trends in Latin America</u>, IADB, 1975, pp. 63-69;
           SI 1980, pp. 14-16.

Table II-5. Urban and Rural Population of Brazil and Its Major Political Subdivisions, 1940-80

Political Subdivisions	1940 Urban Population Number	%	1940 Rural Population Number	%	1950 Urban Population Number	%	1950 Rural Population Number	%	1960 Urban Population Number	%	1960 Rural Population Number	%
Brazil	12,880,182	31.2	28,356,133	68.8	18,782,891	36.2	33,161,506	63.8	31,533,681	44.9	38,657,689	55.1
São Paulo	3,168,111	44.1	4,012,205	55.9	4,804,211	52.6	4,330,212	47.4	8,044,377	62.7	4,779,429	37.3
Minas Gerais	1,693,040	25.1	5,043,376	74.9	2,320,054	30.1	5,397,738	69.9	3,880,388	40.0	5,817,730	60.0
Rio de Janeiro	693,201	37.5	1,154,565	62.5	1,091,359	47.5	1,205,835	52.5	2,054,040	61.0	1,313,698	39.0
Bahia	937,571	23.9	2,980,541	76.1	1,250,507	25.9	3,584,068	74.1	2,049,124	34.6	3,869,748	65.4
Rio Grande do Sul	1,034,486	31.2	2,286,203	68.8	1,421,980	34.1	2,742,841	65.9	2,412,279	44.8	2,976,380	55.2
Paraná	302,272	24.5	934,004	75.5	528,288	25.0	1,587,259	75.0	1,310,967	30.7	2,952,752	69.3
Pernambuco	787,808	29.3	1,900,432	70.7	1,167,400	34.4	2,227,785	65.6	1,828,426	44.8	2,252,175	55.2
Ceará	475,028	22.7	1,616,004	77.3	679,604	25.2	2,015,846	74.8	1,103,436	33.5	2,186,159	66.5
Guanabara	1,519,010	86.1	245,131	13.9	2,303,063	96.9	74,388	3.1	3,198,591	97.5	83,317	2.5
Maranhão	185,552	15.0	1,049,617	85.0	274,288	17.3	1,308,960	82.7	442,995	17.9	2,034,376	82.1
Goiás	142,110	17.2	684,304	82.8	245,667	20.2	969,254	79.8	580,518	30.3	1,366,942	69.7
Santa Catarina	253,717	21.5	924,623	78.5	362,717	23.2	1,197,785	76.8	688,358	32.3	1,440,894	67.7
Pará	286,865	30.4	657,779	69.6	389,011	34.6	734,262	65.4	623,816	40.6	914,377	59.4
Paraíba	311,402	21.9	1,110,880	78.1	456,716	26.7	1,256,543	73.3	695,232	34.9	1,295,913	65.1
Piauí	124,197	15.2	693,404	84.2	170,584	16.3	875,112	83.7	292,422	23.4	956,778	76.6
Espírito Santo	157,008	20.9	593,009	79.1	194,935	22.6	666,627	77.4	370,075	31.7	799,478	68.3
Alagoas	229,126	24.1	722,174	75.9	286,379	26.2	806,758	73.8	421,148	33.5	835,011	66.5
Rio Grande do Norte	164,248	21.4	603,770	78.6	253,765	26.2	714,156	73.8	427,543	37.5	713,280	47.6
Amazonas	104,789	23.9	333,219	76.1	137,736	26.8	376,363	73.2	236,654	33.1	478,120	66.9
Mato Grosso do Sul	-	-	-	-	-	-	-	-	-	-	-	-
Distrito Federal	-	-	-	-	-	-	-	-	88,295	63.3	51,501	36.7
Sergipe	166,241	30.6	376,085	69.4	204,984	31.8	439,377	68.2	291,109	38.7	460,669	61.3
Mato Grosso	128,727	29.8	303,538	70.2	177,830	34.1	344,214	65.9	346,922	38.9	545,311	61.1
Rondônia	-	-	-	-	13,816	37.4	23,119	62.6	30,626	43.6	39,606	56.4
Acre	14,138	17.7	65,630	82.3	21,272	18.5	93,483	81.5	33,534	20.9	125,318	79.1
Amapá	-	-	-	-	13,900	37.1	23,577	62.9	35,241	51.5	33,279	48.5
Roraíma	-	-	-	-	5,123	28.3	12,984	71.7	12,460	43.2	16,411	56.8
Fernando de Noronha	-	-	-	-	581	100.0	-	-	1,346	100.0	-	-
Serra dos Aimores	1,535	2.3	65,459	97.7	7,112	4.4	152,960	95.6	33,757	8.8	349,037	91.2

Table II-5 (continued)

Political Subdivisions	1970 Urban Population Number	%	1970 Rural Population Number	%	1980 Urban Population Number	%	1980 Rural Population Number	%
Brazil	52,084,984	55.9	41,054,053	44.1	80,479,448	67.6	38,619,544	32.4
São Paulo	14,276,429	80.3	3,495,709	19.7	22,195,330	88.6	2,845,368	11.4
Minas Gerais	6,060,300	52.8	5,427,115	47.2	8,986,266	67.1	4,404,539	32.9
Rio de Janeiro	3,654,228	77.0	1,088,656	23.0	10,373,300	91.8	924,027	8.2
Bahia	3,085,483	41.2	4,407,987	58.8	4,667,247	49.3	4,807,016	50.7
Rio Grande do Sul	3,553,006	53.3	3,111,885	46.7	5,252,465	67.5	2,524,747	32.5
Paraná	2,504,378	36.1	4,425,490	63.9	4,473,541	58.6	3,156,925	41.4
Pernambuco	2,810,843	54.5	2,349,797	45.5	3,785,697	52.2	2,361,405	47.8
Ceará	1,780,093	40.8	2,581,510	59.2	2,814,235	53.2	2,480,641	46.8
Guanabara	4,251,918	100.0	-	-	-	-	-	-
Maranhão	752,027	25.1	2,240,659	74.8	1,257,109	31.4	2,745,490	68.6
Goiás	1,237,108	42.1	1,701,569	57.9	2,403,234	62.2	1,462,248	37.8
Santa Catarina	1,246,043	42.9	1,655,691	57.1	2,154,527	59.4	1,474,224	40.6
Pará	1,021,966	47.2	1,145,052	52.8	1,669,662	48.9	1,742,206	51.1
Paraíba	1,002,156	42.1	1,380,461	57.9	1,450,346	52.3	1,322,254	47.7
Piauí	536,612	31.9	1,143,961	68.1	897,993	42.0	1,242,073	58.0
Espírito Santo	721,916,	45.1	877,417	54.9	1,293,334	63.9	730,487	36.1
Alagoas	631,739	39.8	956,370	60.2	978,597	49.2	1,008,984	50.8
Rio Grande do Norte	737,368	47.6	812,876	52.4	1,115,630	58.7	784,090	41.3
Amazonas	405,831	42.5	549,404	57.5	858,181	59.9	573,885	40.1
Mato Grosso do Sul	-	-	-	-	918,865	67.0	451,468	33.0
Distrito Federal	516,082	96.0	21,410	4.0	1,139,480	96.8	37,913	3.2
Sergipe	415,415	46.1	485,329	53.9	618,344	54.2	523,490	45.8
Mato Grosso	648,189	42.8	912,901	57.2	656,513	57.5	485,148	42.5
Rondônia	59,564	53.6	51,500	46.4	233,301	47.3	259,509	52.7
Acre	59,307	27.5	155,992	72.5	132,174	43.8	169,431	56.2
Amapá	62,451	54.6	51,908	45.4	103,926	59.2	71,708	40.8
Roraíma	17,481	42.8	23,404	57.2	48,885	61.8	30,268	39.2
Fernando de Noronha	1,241	100.0	-	-	1,266	100.0	-	-

Sources: RE 1940, Regional Series; RE 1950A1, pp. 260-261; RE 1960, Regional Series;
RE 1970, Regional Series; SI 1980, p. 26.

Table II-6. Urban and Rural Population of Brazil by Sex, 1940-80

1940

	Urban	%	Rural	%	Total	%
Male	6,164,473	47.9	14,449,615	51.0	20,614,088	50.0
Female	6,715,709	52.1	13,906,518	49.0	20,622,227	50.0
Total	12,880,182	100.0	28,356,133	100.0	41,236,315	100.0

1950

	Urban	%	Rural	%	Total	%
Male	8,971,163	47.8	16,913,838	51.0	25,885,001	49.8
Female	9,811,728	52.2	16,247,668	49.0	26,059,396	50.2
Total	18,782,891	100.0	33,161,506	100.0	51,944,397	100.0

1960

	Urban	%	Rural	%	Total	%
Male	15,189,711	48.2	19,869,835	51.4	35,059,546	49.9
Female	16,343,970	51.8	18,787,854	48.6	35,131,824	50.1
Total	31,533,681	100.0	38,657,689	100.0	70,191,370	100.0

1970

	Urban	%	Rural	%	Total	%
Male	25,227,825	48.4	21,103,518	51.4	46,331,343	49.7
Female	26,857,159	51.6	19,950,535	48.6	46,807,694	50.3
Total	52,084,984	100.0	41,054,053	100.0	93,139,037	100.0

1980

	Urban	%	Rural	%	Total	%
Male	39,238,730	48.8	19,914,174	51.6	59,152,904	49.7
Female	41,240,718	51.2	18,705,370	48.4	59,946,088	50.3
Total	80,479,448	100.0	38,619,544	100.0	119,098,992	100.0

Sources: RE 1950A1, pp. 260-261; RE 1960A1, p. 2; RE 1970A1, pp. 4-5; SI 1980, p. 26.

Table II-7. Brazilian Sex/Age Distribution, 1872-1980

1872
Free and Slave

Age In Years	Total	Male	Female	Male/Female Ratio
Under 1	343,719	178,035	165,684	107.4
1-4	731,985	376,751	355,234	106.1
5-10	1,256,995	634,814	622,181	102.0
11-15	1,126,828	564,798	562,030	100.5
16-20	1,102,159	565,422	536,737	105.3
21-25	1,004,396	527,643	476,753	110.7
26-30	1,085,241	570,032	515,209	110.6
31-40	1,103,081	568,612	534,469	106.4
41-50	748,102	391,802	366,300	107.0
51-60	593,622	315,826	277,796	113.7
61-70	416,796	376,488	40,308	934.0
71 & Over	407,377	364,695	42,682	854.4
Age Unknown	10,177	5,689	4,488	126.7
Total	9,930,478	5,123,869	4,806,609	106.6

1872
Free

Age In Years	Total	Male	Female	Male/Female Ratio
Under 1	343,457	177,915	165,542	107.5
1-4	557,247	284,686	272,561	104.4
5-10	1,066,056	531,093	534,963	99.3
11-15	985,678	487,255	498,423	97.8
16-20	922,999	468,005	454,994	102.9
21-25	800,255	418,989	381,266	109.9
26-30	869,639	455,080	414,559	109.8
31-40	901,193	464,264	436,929	106.3
41-50	682,826	347,813	335,013	103.8
51-60	542,458	289,033	253,425	114.1
61-70	220,229	199,295	21,004	948.8
71 & Over	214,046	191,570	22,476	852.3
Age Unknown	6,681	3,601	3,080	116.9
Total	8,419,672	4,318,699	4,100,973	105.3

1872
Slave

Total	Male	Female	Male/Female Ratio
162	120	42	285.7
174,738	92,065	82,673	111.4
190,939	103,721	87,218	118.9
141,150	77,543	63,607	121.9
179,160	97,417	81,743	119.2
204,141	108,654	95,487	113.8
215,602	114,952	100,650	114.2
201,888	104,348	97,540	107.0
65,276	33,989	31,287	108.6
51,164	26,793	24,371	109.9
196,497	177,193	19,304	917.9
193,431	173,125	20,306	856.8
3,496	2,088	1,408	148.2
1,510,806	805,170	705,636	114.1

Table II-7 (continued)

1890

Age In Years	Total	Male	Female	Male/Female Ratio
Under 1	366,237			
1-4	1,756,531			
5-9	2,069,569			
10-14	1,710,856			
15-19	1,400,910			
20-24	1,353,179			
25-29	1,182,886			
30-39	1,802,682			
40-49	1,231,197			
50-59	730,753			
60-69	426,826			
70-79	157,472			
80 & Over	84,240			
Age Unknown	58,577			
Total	14,333,915	7,237,932	7,095,983	102.0

1920

Age In Years	Total	Male	Female	Male/Female Ratio
Under 1	830,354	417,542	412,812	101.1
1-4	3,762,809	1,900,693	1,862,116	102.1
5-9	4,575,530	2,326,092	2,249,438	103.4
10-14	3,909,630	1,989,290	1,920,340	103.6
15-19	3,374,432	1,597,410	1,777,022	89.9
20-24	2,982,849	1,468,770	1,514,079	97.0
25-29	2,487,431	1,231,455	1,255,976	98.0
30-39	3,560,225	1,847,248	1,712,977	107.8
40-49	2,401,200	1,263,057	1,138,143	111.0
50-59	1,451,319	753,364	697,955	107.9
60-69	800,866	408,107	392,759	103.9
70-79	308,243	147,849	160,394	92.2
80 & Over	125,067	53,905	71,162	75.7
Age Unknown	65,650	39,036	26,614	146.7
Total	30,635,605	15,443,818	15,191,787	101.7

Table II-7 (continued)

1940

Age In Years	Total	Male	Female	Male/Female Ratio
Under 1	1,370,530	693,479	677,051	102.4
1-4	5,069,120	2,562,022	2,507,098	102.2
5-9	5,758,816	2,923,976	2,834,840	103.1
10-14	5,328,080	2,682,254	2,645,826	101.4
15-19	4,443,923	2,157,630	2,286,293	94.4
20-24	3,813,355	1,835,847	1,977,508	92.8
25-29	3,356,370	1,649,306	1,707,064	96.6
30-39	4,901,682	2,466,499	2,435,183	101.3
40-49	3,441,727	1,789,582	1,652,145	108.3
50-59	2,044,907	1,053,453	991,454	106.3
60-69	1,076,139	524,655	551,484	95.1
70-79	427,684	193,026	234,658	82.3
80 & Over	171,711	67,690	104,021	65.1
Age Unknown	32,271	14,669	17,602	83.3
Total	41,236,315	20,614,088	20,622,227	100.0

1950

Age In Years	Total	Male	Female	Male/Female Ratio
Under 1	1,915,760	969,785	945,975	102.5
1-4	6,455,120	3,266,091	3,189,029	102.4
5-9	7,015,527	3,560,850	3,454,677	103.1
10-14	6,308,567	3,164,704	3,143,863	100.7
15-19	5,502,315	2,644,531	2,857,784	92.5
20-24	4,991,139	2,384,460	2,606,679	91.5
25-29	4,132,271	2,030,312	1,101,959	96.5
30-39	6,286,052	3,145,715	3,140,337	100.2
40-49	4,365,359	2,246,107	2,119,252	106.0
50-59	2,650,314	1,363,580	1,289,734	105.5
60-69	1,451,468	728,802	722,666	100.8
70-79	545,170	247,755	297,415	83.3
80 & Over	208,703	81,432	127,271	64.0
Age Unknown	116,632	53,877	62,755	85.9
Total	51,944,397	25,885,001	26,059,396	99.3

Table II-7 (continued)

1960

Age In Years	Total	Male	Female	Male/Female Ratio
Under 1	2,186,020	1,107,194	1,078,826	102.6
1-4	9,007,369	4,580,318	4,427,051	103.5
5-9	10,158,423	5,170,579	4,987,844	103.7
10-14	8,560,956	4,297,589	4,263,367	100.8
15-19	7,174,811	3,452,198	3,722,613	92.7
20-24	6,237,920	2,993,680	3,244,240	92.3
25-29	5,245,848	2,545,283	2,700,565	94.3
30-39	8,486,378	4,228,185	4,258,193	99.3
40-49	5,950,688	3,051,078	2,899,610	105.2
50-59	3,752,967	1,933,852	1,819,115	106.3
60-69	2,190,638	1,120,329	1,070,309	104.7
70-79	849,717	411,028	438,689	93.7
80 & Over	290,641	119,717	170,924	70.0
Age Unknown	98,994	48,516	50,478	96.1
Total	70,191,370	35,059,546	35,131,824	99.8

1970

Age In Years	Total	Male	Female	Male/Female Ratio
Under 1	2,798,798	1,413,307	1,385,491	102.0
1-4	11,013,008	5,556,638	5,456,370	101.8
5-9	13,459,508	6,799,972	6,659,536	102.1
10-14	11,859,119	5,934,189	5,924,930	100.2
15-19	10,253,283	4,995,432	5,257,851	95.0
20-24	8,285,805	4,037,135	4,248,670	95.0
25-29	6,504,069	3,173,285	3,330,784	95.3
30-39	10,754,252	5,302,780	5,451,472	97.3
40-49	8,082,277	4,083,291	3,998,986	102.1
50-59	5,228,732	2,646,519	2,582,213	102.5
60-69	3,007,637	1,508,003	1,499,634	100.6
70-79	1,224,100	584,131	639,969	91.3
80 & Over	484,471	203,857	280,614	72.6
Age Unknown	183,978	92,804	91,174	101.8
Total	93,139,037	46,331,343	46,807,694	99.0

Table II-7 (continued)

1980 LOW ESTIMATE

Age In Years	Total	Male	Female	Male/Female Ratio
0-4	18,431,197	9,340,711	9,090,486	102.8
5-9	16,798,560	8,489,796	8,308,764	102.2
10-14	13,913,066	7,005,216	6,907,850	101.4
15-19	13,170,560	6,645,932	6,524,628	101.9
20-24	11,556,990	5,771,049	5,785,941	99.7
25-29	9,929,116	4,822,805	5,106,311	94.4
30-39	14,233,687	6,916,402	7,317,285	94.5
40-49	10,181,413	4,993,535	5,187,878	96.3
50-59	7,351,972	3,661,000	3,690,972	99.2
60-69	4,288,852	2,101,470	2,187,382	96.1
70-79	1,907,457	903,799	1,003,658	90.1
80 & Over	439,860	186,373	253,487	73.5
Total	122,202,730	60,838,088	61,364,642	99.1

1980 HIGH ESTIMATE

Age In Years	Total	Male	Female	Male/Female Ratio
0-4	19,800,780	10,034,798	9,765,982	102.8
5-9	17,458,250	8,823,195	8,635,055	102.2
10-14	13,913,066	7,005,216	6,907,850	101.4
15-19	13,170,560	6,645,932	6,524,628	101.9
20-24	11,556,990	5,771,049	5,785,941	99.7
25-29	9,929,116	4,822,805	5,106,311	94.4
30-39	14,233,687	6,916,402	7,317,285	94.5
40-49	10,181,413	4,993,535	5,187,878	96.3
50-59	7,351,972	3,661,000	3,690,972	99.2
60-69	4,288,852	2,101,470	2,187,382	96.1
70-79	1,907,457	903,799	1,003,658	90.1
80 & Over	439,860	186,373	253,487	73.5
Total	124,232,003	61,865,574	62,366,429	99.2

Sources: RE 1872; RE 1890, pp. 2-7; RE 1920D2, p. 3;   RE 1940A2, pp. 2-3;
RE 1950A1, pp. 2-3;   RE 1970A1, pp. 4 & 10;   AN 1978, pp. 69-71.

Table II-8. Adherents to Major Religious Groups in Brazil, 1872-1970

Group	1872 Number	%	1890 Number	%	1940 Number	%	1950 Number	%	1960 Number	%	1970 Number	%
Roman Catholic	9,902,712	99.7	14,179,615	98.9	39,177,880	95.0	48,558,854	93.5	65,329,520	93.1	85,472,022	91.8
Protestant			143,743	1.0	1,074,857	2.6	1,741,430	3.4	2,824,775	4.0	4,814,728	5.2
Spiritualist					463,400	1.1	824,553	1.6	977,561	1.4	1,178,293	1.3
Buddhist					123,353	.3	152,572	.3	179,464	.3		
Hebrew					55,666	.1	69,957	.1	96,199	.1		
Other Religions	27,766	.3	3,300	negl	151,855	.4	184,989	.3	395,725	.6	954,747	1.0
No Religion			7,257	negl	87,330	.2	274,236	.5	353,607	.5	701,701	.7
No Declaration					101,974	.3	137,806	.3	34,519	negl	13,355	negl
Total	9,930,478	100.0	14,333,915	100.00	41,236,315	100.00	51,944,397	100.00	70,191,370	100.00	93,134,846	100.0

Source: RE 1872, (microfilm); RE 1890C, p.297; SI 1940A, p.2; RE 1950A1, p.8; RE 1960A1, pp.8-9; RE 1970A1, pp.10-11

Table II-9. Indigenous (Indian) Population of Brazil, Pre-1500-1972

A. Pre Conquest (Pre-1500) Native Population of Brazil

Estimators	Date of Estimate	Population Estimated
Alfred Kroeber	1939	< 1,000,000
Angel Rosenblatt	1945	1,400,000
Julian Steward	1949	1,500,000
John Hemming	1978	2,341,000
Karl Sapper	1924	2-3,000,000
William Denevan	1977	3,625,000
Pierre Clastres	1973	34,000,000

B. Nineteenth Century Native Population of Brazil

Estimators	Date of Estimate	Population Estimated
Velloso de Oliveira	1819	800,000
Souza Brazil	1869	215,000

C. Modern Brazilian Indian Population

Estimators	Date of Estimate	Population Estimated High	Low
Carlos Alberto Dória & Carlos Alberto Ricardo	1972	70,200	61,800
Darcy Ribeiro	1957	81,300	65,300
Dale W. Kietzman	1967		

Sources: John Hemming, Red Gold, The Conquest of the Brazilian Indians, 1500-1760, pp.487-501; RE 1920A, pp. 405-411.

Table II-10. Domiciles Occupied and Persons Per Domicile in Brazil,
1872-1980

Year	Number of Domiciles Occupied	Number of Persons Occupying Domiciles	Persons Per Occupied Domicile
1872	1,332,274	10,103,920	7.58
1900	2,969,288	17,432,326	5.87
1920	3,962,585	30,625,331	7.73
1940	7,897,769	41,566,407	5.26
1950	10,046,199	51,584,665	5.13
1960	13,497,823	69,222,849	5.12
1970	17,643,387	90,020,290	5.10
1980	25,352,739	-	4.70

Sources: RE 1920D6, p. VIII-X;   RE 1940A2, pp. 167, 170-171;   RE 1950A1,
p. 293; RE 1960A1, p. 125; RE 1970A1, pp. 262-263; SI 1980, p. 27.

Table II-11. Marital Status of Brazilians, 1872–1970

1872

	Free		Slave		Total	
	Number	%	Number	%	Number	%
Male						
Single	2,975,449	68.9	711,869	88.4	3,687,315	72.0
Married	1,165,866	27.0	73,079	9.1	1,238,945	24.2
Widowed	177,387	4.1	20,222	2.5	197,609	3.8
Total	4,318,699	100.0	805,170	100.0	5,123,869	100.0
Female						
Single	2,752,582	67.1	622,804	88.3	3,375,386	70.2
Married	1,121,000	27.3	63,016	8.9	1,184,016	24.6
Widowed	227,391	5.6	19,816	2.8	247,207	5.2
Total	4,100,973	100.0	705,636	100.0	4,806,609	100.0

1890 / 1920

	1890 Total		1920 Total	
	Number	%	Number	%
Male				
Single	5,154,991	71.2	11,023,060	71.5
Married	1,892,866	26.2	3,998,743	26.0
Divorced	9,896	.1	-	-
Widowed	180,159	2.5	386,959	2.5
Total	7,237,932	100.0	15,408,762	100.0
Female				
Single	4,832,022	68.1	10,294,327	68.3
Married	1,853,983	26.1	3,885,084	25.8
Divorced	11,417	.2	-	-
Widowed	398,561	5.6	896,251	5.9
Total	7,095,983	100.0	15,075,662	100.0

Table II-11 (continued)

	15-19		20-29		30-39		40-49		50-59		60-69		70 & Over		All Ages	
	Number	%	Number	%	Number	%	Number	%	Number	%	Number	%	Number	%	Number	%
1940																
Male																
Single	4,811,714	99.5	2,084,743	59.8	54,660	2.8	248,025	13.9	119,383	11.2	52,815	10.1	25,537	9.8	7,881,877	54.7
Married	24,653	.5	1,374,215	39.5	1,859,086	94.0	1,436,397	80.3	829,393	78.9	383,684	73.2	156,483	60.1	6,063,911	42.1
Divorced	78	negl.	2,971	.1	6,527	.3	7,211	.4	5,219	.5	2,644	.5	1,082	.4	25,732	.2
Widowed	370	negl.	20,448	.6	57,874	2.9	96,186	5.4	99,405	9.4	84,955	16.2	77,289	29.7	436,527	3.0
Total	4,836,815	100.0	3,482,377	100.0	1,978,147	100.0	1,787,819	100.0	1,052,400	100.0	524,098	100.00	260,391	100.0	14,408,047	100.0
Female																
Single	4,597,404	93.3	1,448,101	39.4	492,978	20.3	266,979	16.2	145,176	14.7	77,000	14.0	51,402	15.2	7,079,040	48.6
Married	327,231	6.6	2,160,737	58.7	1,771,483	72.9	1,109,352	67.3	536,513	54.2	197,530	35.9	59,557	17.5	6,162,367	42.3
Divorced	1,116	negl.	9,854	.3	12,291	.5	10,021	.6	5,392	.5	1,994	.3	626	.2	41,294	.3
Widowed	3,223	negl.	59,927	1.6	153,567	6.3	262,517	15.9	302,652	30.6	273,982	49.8	227,421	67.1	1,282,289	8.8
Total	4,928,974	100.0	3,678,619	100.0	2,430,319	100.0	1,648,869	100.0	989,733	100.0	550,506	100.0	338,970	100.0	14,564,990	100.0
1950																
Male																
Single	2,604,600	98.5	2,571,147	58.4	622,748	19.9	277,645	12.4	129,236	9.5	63,119	8.3	28,336	8.6	6,296,831	42.4
Married	38,340	1.5	1,815,611	41.2	2,458,988	78.3	1,863,994	83.1	1,116,517	82.2	557,566	76.6	206,393	62.9	8,057,408	54.3
Divorced	23	negl.	1,220	negl.	4,222	.1	5,324	.2	3,686	.3	1,930	.3	629	.2	11,034	.1
Widowed	573	negl.	17,866	.4	54,087	1.7	95,249	4.3	108,669	8.0	104,768	14.4	92,914	28.3	474,156	3.2
Total	2,643,536	100.0	4,405,844	100.0	3,140,045	100.0	2,242,212	100.0	1,358,108	100.0	727,383	100.0	328,301	100.0	14,845,429	100.0
Female																
Single	2,429,677	85.1	1,811,304	38.6	575,156	18.4	303,813	14.4	164,959	12.8	94,082	13.0	59,537	14.1	5,438,528	35.7
Married	422,520	14.8	2,826,450	60.2	2,390,260	76.3	1,504,866	71.2	752,172	58.5	284,958	39.6	78,334	18.5	8,259,560	54.2
Divorced	267	negl.	3,755	.1	7,440	.2	6,508	.3	3,414	.3	1,325	.2	314	.1	23,023	.2
Widowed	3,040	.1	55,267	1.1	159,007	5.1	298,358	14.1	365,691	28.4	340,091	47.2	284,842	67.3	1,506,296	9.9
Total	2,855,504	100.0	4,696,776	100.0	3,131,863	100.0	2,113,545	100.0	1,286,236	100.0	720,456	100.0	423,027	100.0	15,227,407	100.0
1960																
Male																
Single	3,405,288	98.7	3,026,380	54.7	590,330	14.0	222,272	7.3	108,725	5.6	54,828	4.9	25,728	4.8	7,433,551	37.5
Married	42,829	1.2	2,431,128	43.9	3,513,259	83.2	2,677,153	87.9	1,664,590	86.2	901,411	80.6	350,859	66.2	11,581,229	58.4
Divorced	3,409	.1	63,189	1.2	80,347	1.9	71,571	2.3	54,033	2.8	33,504	3.1	16,387	3.1	322,440	1.6
Widowed	431	negl.	13,758	.2	38,775	.9	75,694	2.5	103,714	5.4	129,066	11.5	137,124	25.9	498,502	2.5
Total	3,451,957	100.0	5,534,455	100.0	4,222,711	100.0	3,046,690	100.0	1,931,062	100.0	1,118,749	100.0	530,098	100.0	19,835,722	100.0
Female																
Single	3,172,342	85.2	1,996,604	33.6	513,690	12.1	257,558	8.9	156,445	8.6	93,360	8.8	58,766	9.6	6,248,765	30.8
Married	519,963	14.0	3,726,173	62.8	3,439,222	80.9	2,208,088	76.2	1,144,039	63.0	462,035	43.2	119,783	19.7	11,619,303	57.2
Divorced	27,445	.7	172,938	2.9	166,854	3.9	138,561	4.8	89,547	4.9	44,096	4.1	15,744	2.6	655,185	3.2
Widowed	2,164	.1	43,870	.7	133,602	3.1	291,896	10.1	427,006	23.5	469,652	43.9	414,724	68.1	1,782,914	8.8
Total	3,721,914	100.0	5,939,585	100.0	4,253,369	100.0	2,896,103	100.0	1,817,037	100.0	1,069,143	100.0	609,017	100.0	20,306,167	100.0
1970																
Male																
Single	4,937,898	98.5	4,228,434	58.5	801,865	15.2	323,599	8.0	161,613	6.1	83,242	5.4	40,978	5.3	10,577,629	39.9
Married	69,804	1.4	2,912,949	40.3	4,356,397	82.3	3,550,845	87.7	2,293,283	86.5	1,245,422	81.4	523,568	67.2	14,952,268	56.3
Divorced	4,706	.1	69,579	1.0	98,434	1.9	102,085	2.5	83,259	3.2	54,802	3.6	28,186	3.6	441,051	1.7
Widowed	782	negl.	11,488	.2	34,182	.6	71,893	1.8	111,905	4.2	146,592	9.6	186,657	23.9	563,499	2.1
Total	5,013,190	100.0	7,222,450	100.0	5,290,878	100.0	4,048,422	100.0	2,650,060	100.0	1,530,058	100.0	779,389	100.0	26,534,447	100.0
Female																
Single	4,636,581	87.4	2,996,671	39.6	698,685	12.9	366,685	9.3	223,743	8.7	134,045	8.8	87,069	9.5	9,143,479	33.5
Married	636,364	12.0	4,344,438	57.4	4,352,467	80.1	3,007,596	76.2	1,656,620	63.7	683,867	44.8	192,502	20.9	14,873,854	54.5
Divorced	29,316	.5	183,065	2.4	224,451	4.1	219,264	5.6	158,533	6.1	84,501	5.5	36,790	4.0	935,920	3.4
Widowed	2,928	.1	44,885	.6	158,815	2.9	350,612	8.9	552,442	21.3	624,111	40.9	603,152	65.6	2,336,945	8.6
Total	5,305,189	100.0	7,569,059	100.0	5,434,157	100.0	3,944,157	100.0	2,591,338	100.0	1,526,524	100.0	919,513	100.0	27,290,198	100.0

Sources: RE 1872 (microfilmed), p. 4; RE 1890C, pp. 2-3; RE 1920D2, pp. 4-5; RE 1940A1, pp. 6-7; RE 1950A1, p. 5; RE 1960A1, pp. 6-7; RE 1970A1, pp.

Chapter III. Vital Statistics

Brazil's live birth rates, death rates, and resulting natural population increases are reported on Table III-1. Data for the years 1872 through 1960 were taken from Rubens Vaz da Costa[1] who in turn relied heavily on IBGE sources. Nicolas Sanchez Albornoz[2] supplied the 1965-70 figures. These he drew from the Boletin demográfico, no. 8, of CELADE, the United Nations Regional Center for Demographic Training and Research. The figures for 1975, 1976, and 1977 were taken directly from the Anuário estatistico do Brasil, 1977, in which the birth rates are FIBGE estimates. The 1975 death rates were calculated by the author using FIBGE population estimates for the seven urban municípios for which death figures were available. They included Manaus, Amazonas; Belém, Pará; Teresina, Piauí; Belo Horizonte, Minas Gerais; Vitória, Espírito Santo; Curitiba, Paraná; and Brasília, D.F. These municípios are moderately well scattered through the country, but the largest cities and the south are not well represented.

The rate of natural population increase rose steadily decade by decade between 1872 and 1960, principally as a function of declining death rates. The rate of population increase was expected to continue to climb in the ensuing decade. Vaz da Costa[3] noted in 1969 that "the population census of 1970 may hold some surprises for Brazil. . . . Rather than a slightly lower overall growth rate as projected by the country's Strategical Planning and Development Program, the census may show an acceleration in this rate in the 1960s. If so, the cause will again be the same: a continued decline in death rates--principally in infant mortality--not totally offset by a slow reduction in birth rates." The Program planners were, however, on target as the 1960-70 rate of population increase fell to 2.82. The post-1970 annual birth rates shown on Table III-1 fluctuated widely and offer virtually no basis for predicting the 1970-80 natural increase in Brazil's population.

If in the post-1970 era the rate of natural population increase in Brazil had, indeed, begun to level off, then the country may have entered the third phase of the so-called "demographic transition," which is marked by falling birth rates. Industrialization and a population's participation in the amenities of urban life are assumed to be instrumental in the reduction of the birth rate. If that is the case then the birth and death rates for São Paulo, Brazil's most industrialized city and state, may hold a clue to the future population structure of the country. In 1961, the município of São Paulo had a birth rate of 31.9 per 1,000, and the rest of the state of São Paulo a rate of 34.1. These rates were calculated from figures presented in the Anuário, 1961,[4] published by the state of São Paulo. This same source yields a município death rate of 8.3 and a death rate for the remainder of the state of 9.10.

Table III-2 shows the number of deaths in the first year of life per 1,000 live births in some of Brazil's urban municipíos. The data for 1920 were taken from the census, and those for the 1939-41 and 1948-50 periods were developed by the IBGE Laboratório de Estatística. The 1970 and post-1970 figures were reported by the Divisão Nacional de Epidemiologia e Estatística da Saúde. Figures for rural areas and for the nation as a whole were not available. Indeed, the wide fluctuations among urban municipíos for the same years suggest that a national figure would not be a very meaningful measure of Brazil's infant mortality. For Fortaleza in 1948-50 the actual period is 1947-49. For São Paulo and Rio de Janeiro in 1948-50 the actual period is 1949-51. For Natal, Fortaleza, Goiânia, Belo Horizonte Brasília, Salvador Curitiba, São Luis, and Pôrto Alegre in 1970 and for João Pessoa, Fortaleza, Florianópolis, Salvador, São Luis, Rio de Janeiro, and Pôrto Alegre in the post-1970 period the rate is for 1,000 persons under one year of age. For São Paulo and Rio de Janeiro in 1970 the actual year is 1969.

A regional pattern barely manifests itself in the data and in addition there is no evidence of a steady decline in infant mortality over time. Clearly, local and temporal incidences of child-killing diseases have dominated regional and historical trends. In 1970 some of the cities in the poor Northeast--Recife PE, Natal RN, Joao Pessoa PB, Fortaleza CE, and Maceió AL--had higher infant mortality rates than some of the central and southern cities such as Niterói RJ, Rio de Janeiro GB, and Pôrto Alegre RS. Nevertheless, the northeastern city of Aracajú SE had the lowest infant mortality rate in 1970. In 1920, in a reversal of their 1970 positions, Recife PE had the lowest rate and Pôrto Alegre RS was among those places with very high infant mortality rates. Such figures, however, may say more about public access to medical facilities, whose administrators report infant deaths, than about infant mortality per se.

Table III-3 presents Brazilian life expectancy data developed by Arriaga.[5] The 1870 figure was interpolated from a near life table value, that is, the 1872 census. The figures for 1880, 1910, and 1930 were interpolated between two life table values, that is, the censuses bracketing these respective years. All other figures are life tables based on the census of the year shown.

Brazilian life tables could not be constructed using any of the usual methods because of the incompleteness of death data. As a consequence Arriaga employed a technique based on "the stable population theory; [and] . . . with it only the proportional age group distribution of the population aged 10-59 and an estimate of the natural growth rate. . . ."[6] Brazil's constant fertility for so many years aided in the use of this technique.

Immigration and underenumeration posed other problems. Arriaga, however, points out that information on the foreign-born population is available for most years thus permitting some corrections in the distortion of age structure due to international migration. He concludes that all pre-1960 censuses were underenumerated, especially those of 1900 and earlier, but that the underenumeration was distributed evenly through all age groups, thus not affecting the proportional age group distribution. One serious irregularity in this assumed pattern for which Arriaga had to make a correction was the severe underenumeration of the under-20 age group in 1872.

Brazilian life expectancy stood at an abysmal 27.3 years in 1870 and by 1940 had improved by only 9.4 years to 36.7. During the decade of World War II (1940-50) another 6.3 years was added to the country's life expectancy bringing it to 43.0 years. This sharp gain was owed principally to Brazil's very effective Serviço de Saúde Pública (SESP), which was abetted by the United States in support of the latter's military personnel in Brazil and which focused on vaccinating the populace and eradicating disease-carrying insects. After the war programs aimed at ridding rural water supplies of infant-killing bacteria were added to these activities. In the 1950-60 decade the life expectancy increase doubled that of the previous decade, rising by 12.5 years to 55.5 years.

Brazil's leading causes of death are shown on Table III-4. The figures for 1922 appear in a 1931 publication of the Departamento Nacional de Saúde Pública which is presumably the source of the information as well. The 1939-41 data were generated by the Gabinete Técnico do

Serviço Nacional de Recenseamento. The 1956 information originated in <u>Pesquisas sôbre a mortalidade no Brasil</u>, Second Series, 1956, published by IBGE's Laboratório de Estatístico. Figures for 1959 were developed by the Departamento de Geografia e Estatística de Estado da Guanabara and the Departamento Estadual de Estatística de Estado de São Paulo. The 1969 and 1975 data are from the Divisão Nacional de Epidemiologia e Estatística de Saúde.

The accuracy of these data is not known. They were recorded for only a few of Brazil's urban areas, some of which were quite small, and cannot be developed into a national picture. The area of Rio de Janeiro is the old Distrito Federal, and that of São Paulo is the <u>município</u> (county) of which the city is the seat. The nine urban <u>municípios</u> from which the 1939-41 data came were Recife PE, Salvador BA, Pôrto Alegre RS, Belo Horizonte MG, Belém PA, Fortaleza CE, Niterói RJ, Curitiba PR, and Manaus AM. The 1969 data were from the following nineteen urban <u>municípios</u>: Manaus AM, Belém PA, São Luis MA, Teresina PI, Fortaleza CE, Natal RN, João Pessao PB, Recife PE, Maceió AL, Aracajú SE, Salvador BA, Belo Horizonte MG, Vitória ES, Niterói RJ, Rio de Janeiro GB, Curitiba PR, Pôrto Alegre RS, Goiânia GO, and Brasília DF. Perinatal causes were not included in the 1922 data but were included in the congenital and pregnancy categories in the 1939-41 data. Except for the 1922 data, Brazilian sources distributed indeterminate causes proportionately among the "other" categories in calculating mortality rates per 100,000 persons.

On Table III-4 the more numerous categories of causes of death for the early years were regrouped to conform to the fewer and more general categories used in the 1969 and 1975 data. The rates per 100,000 persons for 1922 are based on a 1922 population calculated from the 1920-30 population growth curve. The 1939-41 and 1952 rates were originally presented by IBGE with the data. The former rates presumably involved the 1940 population, but the latter rates do not conform to any set of published population data. The 1959 and 1969 rates were based on 1960 and 1970 populations principally because it was not feasible to establish intercensal populations of the <u>município</u> parts of these data. The 1975 rates are based on IBGE estimates of 1975 populations of the eight urban <u>municípios</u>.

Table III-5 shows the rates and causes of suicides in Brazil and in selected political subdivisions from 1908 to 1979. The 1908 and 1937 figures originated with the <u>Relatório</u> of the Diretoria Geral de Estatística, anos 1922 and 1929, and with the <u>Anuário estatístico do Brasil, ano III and ano IV</u>. The 1938 and 1939 data for Guanabara (then the

Distrito Federal) originated with the Diretoria Geral de Comunicações e Estatística of the Policia Civil of the Distrito Federal. Figures from 1942 to 1978 were originated by the Serviço de Estatística Demografia, Moral e Política, while all later figures were generated by the Divisão de Estatístico of the Minísterio da Justiça. To establish suicide rates per 100,000 persons it was necessary to estimate the intercensal population of Brazil and its political subdivisions. This was done by the author using the straight-line method which assumes the annual increment to be constant between two census years. This annual increment was obtained by dividing the difference between two census years by 10. The age group 45-59 on the table was reported by the sources as 45-65 for the 1958-62 period, as 45-64 in the 1963-69 period and as 45-59 from 1970 on.

For 1942 the sex of the suicide victim was not reported by the source in twenty-eight cases. Also in 1942 the data for the municípios of the capital cities of Maranhão and Bahia were for 1941. For the same year the data for Amazonas and Paraíba states were for 1941. The 1950 data excluded the município of Recife in Pernambuco state and ten municípios in São Paulo state. For 1953 the Amazonas state data included twenty-nine suicides in Manaus some of which may have been only attempted suicides. In the state of Rio de Janeiro forty-eight suicides in the municípios of Campos and Duque de Caxias may have been only attempts and in Rio Grande do Sul state in 1953, thirty-eight suicides in the municípios of Erechim and São Luis Gonzaga may have been only attempts. For 1955 the data were subject to rectification but no such recitification appeared in subsequent sources. For 1957, data for the capital cities of Paraíba and Pernambuco were missing.

The 1954 peak may or may not have been affected by the suicide of President Getúlio Vargas that year. The seven political subdivisions with the highest number of suicides in 1954, 1969, and 1978 are listed in descending order on Table III-5. Although the country's most populous subdivisions tended to have the largest number of suicides, Rio Grande do Sul, which has never ranked higher than fourth in population, has the highest suicide rate among the seven subdivisions for these years. Victims have with increasing regularity tended to use methods other than poison, gas, firearms, or hanging to commit suicide.

The number and rates of marriages and marriage dissolutions for selected years are shown on Table III-6. Brazil had no divorce law until December 26, 1977, so all marriage dissolutions on the table refer to desquites, or formal separations. Dissolution figures for 1958 through

1974 are for suits initiated. To establish the rates per 100,000 persons intercensal populations were calculated on a straight-line basis from one census year to another. The 1950 figures were for the twenty-five urban <u>municípios</u> (counties) in which national, state or territorial capitals were located. Their populations totaled 8,321,346. Figures for 1960 are for the same twenty-five urban <u>municípios</u>, which together had a population of 13,238,856 inhabitants.

The pre-1977 data were originated by the Serviço de Estatística Demografia, Moral e Política. Data for 1977 and later were collected by FIBGE. The validity of these figures cannot be established, but the number of informal marriages and marriage dissolutions in Brazil makes these formal data somewhat less than representative of the country as a whole. Detailed descriptions of the social and legal structures of Brazilian marriages and marriage dissolutions, including divorce and <u>desquite</u>, are presented in the text for Table II-11.

Table III-7 records the number and specialization of hospital beds, and beds per person for selected years in Brazil. The data include all beds operated by public, quasi-public, and private agencies. Bed-per-person rates for intercensal years are based on straight-line population projections between the census years. Data for 1940 through 1961 originated with the Serviço de Estatística da Saúde. Those for 1968 and later were from the Divisão Nacional de Epidemiologia e Estatística da Saúde. The Psychiatric Specialization for 1954, 1961, and 1968 included neurologic disorders.

Brazil's first hospitals according to Campos and Campos[7] were Santas Casas founded and operated by the Misericórdia order from Portugal. A Santa Casa was built in Santos by Bráz Cubas in 1543. By the end of the century São Paulo had such an institution and Olinda, Recife's neighbor in Pernambuco, had constructed a community hospital. Hospitals subsequently proliferated over Brazil but they were entirely private and community operations, the state having no formal interest in them. These conditions prevailed for the next several hundred years. Neither independence from Portugal (1822) nor the formation of a republican government in 1890 altered them. In the early 1930s Dr. Odair Pedroso surveyed hospitals and their conditions in São Paulo state. In 1938 Brazilian hospitals were classified and placed in a hierarchy according to their physical plants, equipment, and organization, but the results of this survey, presumably done by the federal government, were incomplete and hampered by the lack of a well-defined system of classification. When the Clinical Hospital of the University of São Paulo and the new Santa Casa Hospital in Santos were completed Dr. Pedroso coordinated their operations and pioneered Brazil's first rational hospital administration system. In 1951, under the auspices of Professor Horácio de Paula Souza and the Kellogg Foundation, Brazil's first graduate program in hospital administration was set up at the University of São Paulo.

Brazil's first hospital census was taken in 1965 and reported 2,833 hospitals, only thirty-two of which were full service institutions. As late as 1974, 80 percent of the country's hospitals were privately operated.

Table III-8 traces the numbers and types of medical personnel in Brazil since 1872. The dicennial censuses are the sources for all the information on the table. Surgeons and other specialists are not set apart by the censuses but are included in the "physician" category. The 1872 census does not separate "licensed" from "practical" pharmacists. In this table they have all been listed as "practical pharmacists." The "x-ray technician" category in 1960 also included "practical orthopedists" but other censuses did not specify in which category this latter group was included.

In 1872 there was one physician in Brazil for every 5,049 persons but by 1950 this ratio was nearly halved to 1:2,361. The supply of physicians, however, barely kept pace with population growth during the ensuing two decades and by 1970 the ratio had been reduced only slightly to one physician for every 2,070 persons. The supply of practical nurses, a highly valued occupation in areas unserved by physicians, more than kept pace, improving from a 1960 ratio of 1:985 to a 1970 ratio of 1:684. The total number of medical personnel in the country relative to the total population stood at 1:480 in 1960 but improved to 1:322 by 1970.

Table III-9 presents data on communicable diseases in Brazil since 1938, and shows the numbers of new cases reported, numbers of persons treated and numbers of persons vaccinated against these diseases. The data are spotty since the reporting net was very coarse. It is made up principally of government programs directed at specific diseases in limited parts of the country. The table reports data for every other year since 1938 and in so doing catches much of the high annual variability of communicable disease incidences while at the same time making the table of manageable proportions. The data all relate to human incidence, treatment, and vaccination and do not deal with the various specific vector (carrier) erradication campaigns mounted in Brazil during the last forty years.

Sources for the data were Brazil's major governmental health agencies and included the Departamento Nacional de Saúde (Health), the Serviço Nacional de Lepra (Leprosy), de Febre Amarela (Yellow Fever), de Tuberculose (Tuberculosis), de Malária and de Peste (Plague), and the Divisão Nacional de Tuberclose. They also included the Departamento Nacional de Endêmias Rurais (Rural Endemic Diseases) and its Divisão de Profiláxia (Prevention), the Superintêndencia da Campanha de Erradicação da Variola (Smallpox), the Divisão Nacional de Epidemiologia e Estatística da Saúde, and the Superin-tendência de Campanhas de Saúde Pública.

The category of "New Cases" on Table III-9 refers to cases confirmed. This condition applies to all diseases for the years 1968 through 1976 except leprosy. The leprosy figures are for persons fichado (registered as lepers) during a given year. Prior to 1968 the figures for ancylostoma and schistosomiasis refer to the number of positive fecal examinations, those for filariasis and malaria to the number of positive blood examinations, and those for trachoma to the number of persons discovered with the disease in rural areas. The figures in the category of "Persons Receiving Treatment" refer to persons being medicated for the given disease and not to doses of medication administered. The category includes persons confined to leprosaria, adults and children with tuberculosis who are occupying hospital beds, and persons with trachoma who are matriculado, presumably meaning being referred for specific treatment. From 1938 through 1966 the figures in the "Persons Vaccinated" category have no age specificity. In 1968 this is also true for influenza and smallpox, but the tuberculosis figures are for persons 0-1 years of age and those for all other diseases are for persons 0-14 years of age. In 1974 yellow fever vaccination figures are not age specific, but those for tuberculosis are for persons 0-1 years of age, those for typhoid/paratyphoid are for persons 1-14 years of age, and all others are for persons 0-14 years of age. Figures for yellow fever vaccinations in 1976 are not age specific.

Illnesses caused by parasites have long dominated the Brazilian pattern of communicable diseases. The following descriptions of some of these diseases were supplied by Dr. H. McFadden of the University of Nebraska Medical School[8] and from the Pequeno diccionário brasileiro da língua portu-guêsa.[9] Ancyclostoma is caused by intestinal hookworm ancylostoma duodenale and can lead to a form of anemia. Necatoriasis is a closely related disease caused by the intestinal hookworm Necator americanus. Bouba is an infectious disease akin to syphilis that is caused by the spirochete bacterium Treponema pertenue Castel. Chagas is akin to sleeping sickness and is caused by protozoans (genus

<u>Trypanosoma</u>) which are transmitted by large flies (<u>barbeiros</u>). Filariasis has its origin in a roundworm (genus <u>Filaria</u>), which is parasitic in vertebrate blood and tissue. A larval form of the flatworm genus <u>Echinococcus</u> produces Hydatid in humans. This disease, also called echinococcous, is characterized by cysts in the human male and female sex organs. Leishmaniasis stems from the protozoan genus <u>Leishmania</u>, which produces lesions and sores of the skin and mucuous membrane but which can also attack internal organs. There is a canine form of this disease and Brazilian health agencies track and eliminate dogs who carry it. Schistosomiasis results from shistosomes infesting the bloodstream. The latter are hosted by fresh-water mollusks.

Beginning in the 1940s the various branches of Brazil's public health services concentrated on eliminating the vectors (carriers) of such diseases as yellow fever and malaria and on diagnosing and isolating cases of leprosy and tuberculosis. Early vaccination campaigns were mounted against yellow fever and later additional campaigns, sporadic in time, place and target age group, sought to immunize the population against tuberculosis, smallpox, and poliomyelitis and various childhood diseases. The numbers of persons receiving treatment reflected the public health agencies' programs of diagnosis and treatment undertaken in limited parts of the country where given diseases are prevalent.

The diagnoses of cases admitted to Brazil's psychiatric hospitals are shown on Table III-10. Some totals include small numbers of foreign nationals: 1,739 in 1954, 905 in 1961, and 1,339 in 1969. In 1975 8,195 of the cases admitted for "alcoholism" were classified as "alcoholic-psychotic." The Serviço Nacional de Doenças Mentais was the origin of the 1954 and 1961 data. The Divisão Nacional de Saúde Mental originated the figures for 1969 and 1975.

The sharp rise in the number of cases per 100,000 persons that occurred between 1961 and 1969 probably reflected an increase in the number of mental hospitals in Brazil. Nevertheless, stresses associated with a rapidly changing and urbanizing society may have contributed to an actual increase in the number of mental cases in the country. Argandoña and Kiev[10] point out that "the value of psychiatry to the process of development has not been recognized," but that it "can assist governments in understanding the affects of social turmoil on the individual, his family and his community." They identify the "dependency wish," that is, a desire to earn personal protection through loyalty, as an important Latin American value. This value is rooted in a preindustrial society which is being disrupted by concentrations of population, modernization of preexisting urban patterns, and by diffusion of modern urban patterns to the whole population. Rising proportions of Latin American populations are undergoing new and distressing socioeconomic changes whose concomitants are the breakdown of the security of religion and ancestral loyalties.

Table III-11 shows the food sources of calories per capita for the years 1960[11] and 1975. The principal food consumed in each food group is shown in parentheses. In 1960 eggs were included in the Meat/Fish Group. The 1975 data were reported in the Anuário estatístico do Brasil, 1977. They resulted from a week-long survey (the year was not given) of 55,000 Brazilian family units by IBGE in its Pesquisa nacional por amostra de domicílios (a sampling of the nation's households) following the United Nations Food and Agriculture Organization's guidelines. The results were reported for each of seven regions in the country but not for the country as a whole. Table III-11 shows data for two regions: the South, with the highest per capita calorie consumption, is comprised of the states of Paraná, Santa Catarina, and Rio Grande do Sul; the Northeast, made up of the states of Maranhão, Piauí, Ceará, Rio Grande do Norte, Paraíba, Pernambuco, Alagoas, Sergipe, and Bahia, was near the lower end of the per capita calorie intake scale. Per capita calorie consumption was actually lower in the Amazon/Central West states (1,925.87) than in the Northeast, but the rural part of this sample was not reported by IBGE.

In the 1975 study a "family unit" was defined as a group of persons, related or not, residing in a private domicile and consuming food from the same stock. "Consumption" was defined as the food entering the domicile plus the foodstock on hand at the beginning of the study minus the foodstock on hand at the end of the study. Per capita calorie intake was derived by dividing the number of those sharing the foodstock during the week of the study into the amount of food "consumed" during that week. On Table III-11 the totals report the calories in the food "consumed" (as defined above) but some of this was given to other families or to animals. The calories so dispersed were not reported by food group. In the South a total of 58.15 calories was dispersed in this way making the human "consumption" in the domicile 2,360.83 calories per capita. In the Northeast, a total of 32.01 calories was so dispersed, lowering the human "consumption" level to 1,898.56 calories per capita.

The two Brazilian regions shown are known to be strikingly different in nearly all physical, cultural, and economic characteristics and the same holds true for alimentation. The northeastern diet was heavy with beans and mandioca and although fresh milk was the dominant food in the

Dairy Products/Oils/Fats group it provided only 47.6 calories per person per day. The southern diet was heavy with cereals and animal fats. Calories derived from fresh milk total 97.0 calories per capita per day. Despite the Northeast's long involvement with sugar cane the southern diet included higher consumption levels of sugar. The South's consumption of calories through alcoholic beverages led all other Brazilian regions.

Food groups in the 1960 surveys are only roughly correspondent to those in the 1975 studies. The 1960 data were reported for the country as a whole without regard to region. Legumes and vegetables were not reported, but they may have been included in the cereals group. Eggs were included in the Meat/Fish group. Beverages were not included in the survey.

References

1. Rubens Vaz da Costa, "Population and Development: The Brazilian Case," Population Bulletin 25, no. 4 (September 1969).

2. Nicolas Sanchez Albornoz, The Population of Latin America (Berkeley: University of California Press, 1974).

3. Vaz da Costa, "Population and Development."

4. Departamento de Estatística do Estado de São Paulo, Govêrno do Estado de São Paulo, Anuário, 1961 (São Paulo, 1963).

5. Eduardo Arriaga, New Life Tables for Latin American Populations in the Nineteenth and Twentieth Centuries, Population Monograph Series, no. 3, Institute of International Studies (Berkeley: University of California Press, 1968).

6. Arriaga, New Life Tables.

7. Juarez de Queiroz Campos and José de Queiroz Campos, O hospital a lei e a ética (São Paulo: LTR Editôra Limitada, 1976).

8. Personal communication with Dr. McFadden, Microbiology Department, University of Nebraska Medical School, Omaha, Nebraska.

9. Pequeno diccionário brasileiro da língua portuguêsa, 10th ed., ed. Aurelio Buarque de Hollanda Ferreira (Rio

de Janeiro: Editôra Civilização Brasileira, S.A., 1961).

10. Mario Argandoña and Ari Kiev, <u>Mental Health in the De-veloping World: A Case Study in Latin America</u> (New York: Free Press, 1972).

11. <u>Food Consumption in Brazil: Family Budget Surveys in the Early 1960's</u>, Brazilian Institute of Economics, The Getúlio Vargas Foundation, published for the United States Department of Agriculture Economic Research Service, by the Israel Program for Scientific Translation, November 1970.

Vital Statistics

Table III-1. Brazilian Birth and Death Rates and Natural Population
Increase, 1872-1977

Period	Live Births Per 1,000 Persons	Deaths Per 1,000 Persons	Natural Increase Per 100 Persons
1872-1890	47.0	30.0	1.70
1890-1900	46.0	28.0	1.80
1900-1920	45.0	26.0	1.90
1920-1940	44.0	25.0	1.90
1940-1950	44.0	20.0	2.40
1950-1960	42.0	12.0	3.00
1965-1970	37.7	9.5	2.82
1975	39.6	9.4	3.02
1976	51.5	-	-
1977	39.6	-	-

Sources: Vaz da Costa, p. 92;   Sanchez Albornoz, p. 189;   AN 1977, p. 127.

83

Brazil: A Handbook of Historical Statistics

Table III-2. Infant Mortality in Brazil's Urban Counties, 1920-75

Number of Deaths in the First Year of Life Per 1,000 Live Births

Urban County	1920	1939-41	1948-50	1970	Post 1970	Year
Recife PE	107.7	272.3	243.6	205.7	256.4	1974
Natal RN	271.0			166.1	104.4	1974
João Pessoa PB	217.1			156.0	169.2	1973
Fortaleza CE	317.1		236.2	152.0	140.2	1974
Maceió AL	318.2			141.0	100.4	1974
Goiânia GO				123.1	98.8	1973
Vitória ES				121.9	101.5	1975
Belo Horizonte MG	183.1	160.9		107.7	115.6	1975
Brasília DF				96.3	55.0	1975
Florianópolis SC	193.2				97.8	1971
Salvador BA	209.8	206.3	162.6	88.5	99.1	1975
Curitiba PR	138.3			83.9	71.5	1975
São Paulo SP	174.2	137.8	93.4	83.8		
São Luis MA				82.7	88.4	1973
Manaus AM				80.4	58.3	1975
Teresina PI				79.5	90.6	1975
Cuiabá MT				70.2	86.0	1971
Niterói RJ	185.7			64.0		
Belém PA	143.8	150.5	111.0	60.3	60.7	1975
Rio de Janeiro GB	154.3	159.3	97.2	52.9	79.5	1972
Pôrto Alegre RS	231.6	180.2	107.3	39.1	54.8	1973
Aracajú SE				32.3	40.2	1973

84

Table III-3. Brazilian Life Expectancy at Birth, 1870-1960

	Male	Female	Both Sexes
1870	27.1	27.6	27.3
1880	27.3	27.9	27.6
1890	27.5	28.2	27.8
1900	29.1	29.7	29.4
1910	30.1	31.1	30.6
1920	31.4	32.5	32.0
1930	33.4	34.6	34.0
1940	36.1	37.3	35.7
1950	42.1	43.9	43.0
1960	54.0	57.0	55.5

Source: Arriaga, p. 2.

Table III-4. Leading Causes of Death, and Mortality Rates, in Selected
Brazilian Municipíos, 1922-75

	1922		1939-1941						1952	
	Rio de Janeiro		Rio de Janeiro		São Paulo		Nine Urban Municipios		Rio de Janeiro	Sao Paulo
Causes	Number	Rate Per 100,000	Number	Rate Per 100,000	Number	Rate Per 100,000	Number	Rate Per 100,000	Rate Per 100,000	Rate Per 100,000
Infections/Parasitic Diseases	8,557	697	29,195	557	11,703	295	40,614	709	68	43
Circulatory Diseases	2,649	216	15,268	292	8,668	218	15,660	278	214	198
Accidents/Violence/ Poisoning	749	59	4,103	78	2,252	57	3,335	59	81	56
Respiratory Diseases	2,690	219	11,011	210	6,847	172	11,245	200	247	125
Perinatal Diseases									68	75
Neoplasms (malignant and non-malignant)	535	44	3,778	72	3,604	91	3,779	65	87	102
Digestive Diseases	5,673	462	15,541	297	10,777	272	27,235	481	148	116
Nervous System Diseases	1,121	91	3,711	71	2,889	73	3,852	68	58	57
Congenital Diseases	888	72	2,751	53	2,488	63	4,669	83	19	23
Urinary/Genital Diseases	1,503	122	6,112	117	3,975	100	8,071	131	50	29
Pregnancy/Birth- Related Diseases	199	16	855	16	476	12	1,035	19	10	6
Other Causes	504	41	1,160	22	483	12	1,458	14	139	97
Cause Indeterminate	416	34	1,006		136		6,156			
Total	25,484	2,073	94,491	1,785	54,298	1,365	127,109	2,118	1,189	927

	1959				1969				1975	
	Rio de Janeiro		São Paulo		Rio de Janeiro		19 Urban Municipios		Eight Urban Municipios	
Causes	Number	Rate Per 100,000	Number	Rate Per 100,000	Number	Rate Per 100,000	Number	Rate Per 100,000	Number	Rate Per 100,000
Infections/Parasitic Diseases	1,614	49	1,709	45	3,961	96	23,070	172	9,106	192
Circulatory Diseases	7,249	219	5,803	152	13,000	316	29,924	224	8,876	187
Accidents/Violence Poisoning	2,771	84	2,062	54	3,697	89	10,039	75	4,460	94
Respiratory Diseases	5,491	166	3,598	94	3,432	83	11,395	85	4,268	90
Perinatal Diseases	2,028	61	3,003	79	1,578	38	9,413	70	4,172	88
Neoplasms (malignant and non-malignant)	3,296	100	3,770	99	4,885	119	12,073	90	3,682	77
Digestive Diseases	4,356	132	2,932	77	927	23	3,531	26	1,082	23
Nervous System Diseases	2,686	81	2,251	59	198	5	1,068	8	735	15
Congenital Diseases	523	16	1,279	33	491	12	1,535	12	539	11
Urinary/Genital Diseases	611	18	603	16	274	7	1,458	11	479	10
Pregnancy/Birth- Related Diseases	212	6	104	3	104	3	412	3	184	4
Other Causes	3,172	96	2,724	71	434	10	10,039	76	7,165	151
Cause Indeterminate										
Total	34,009	1,028	29,838	780	32,981	801	114,025	852	44,748	942

Sources: ANN 1922, pp. 59-60; AN 1947, p. 76; AN 1956, p. 68; AN 1961, pp. 49-50; AN 1971, pp. 86-89; AN 1977, pp. 199-204.

Table III-5. Numbers, Rates, and Characteristics of Suicides by
Political Subdivisions with the Largest Numbers, 1908-79

	1908	1909	1910	1911	1912	1913	1914	1915	1916	1917	1918	1919	1920
Number	348	604	551	757	744	693	936	944	765	743	691	734	739
Rate/100,000	1.53	2.59	2.30	3.07	2.94	2.67	3.51	3.46	2.73	2.59	2.36	2.45	2.41
Sex Male	257	433	371	497	486	448	572	610	516	502	465	504	500

	1921	1922	1923	1924	1925	1926	1927	1928	1934	1935	1936	1937
Number	683	682	497	528	524	558	776	964	1,232	1,185	1,345	1,643
Rate/100,000	2.18	2.13	1.52	1.58	1.53	1.60	2.18	2.66	3.15	3.00	3.38	4.09
Sex Male	480	458	339	334	344	370	503	623	783	796	872	1,085

	1938	1939	1942	1949	1950	1951	1952	1953	1954	1955	1956
Number	-	-	1,986	2,835	2,594	2,775	3,065	3,132	3,353	3,859	4,155
Rate/100,000	-	-	4.58	5.57	4.99	5.16	5.15	5.45	5.66	6.31	6.61
Sex Male	-	-	1,291	-	-	-	-	1,925	2,156	2,504	2,742
Age 0-14	-	-	-	-	-	-	-	-	-	-	-
15-24	-	-	-	-	-	-	-	-	-	-	-
25-44	-	-	-	-	-	-	-	-	-	-	-
45-59	-	-	-	-	-	-	-	-	-	-	-
60+	-	-	-	-	-	-	-	-	-	-	-
Marital Status Single	-	-	-	-	-	-	-	1,472	1,703	1,891	2,032
Married	-	-						1,216	1,251	1,586	1,698
Schooling Illiterate	-	-	-	-	-	-	-	1,507	568	593	684
Primary	-	-	-	-	-	-	-	505		2,193	2,197
Secondary/College	-	-	-	-	-	-	-				101
Means Used (P = poison)	-	-	-	-	-	-	-	P 1,892	P 2,156	P 2,405	P 2,611
(F = firearms)	-	-	-	-	-	-	-	F 347	H 367	H 441	F 474
(H = hanging)	-	-	-	-	-	-	-	H 292	F 354	F 421	H 443
Political Subdivisions Number	GB 256	GB 269	SP 691	SP 913	-	SP 989	SP 1,069	SP 1,168	SP 1,166	SP 1,481	SP 1,435
Rate	14.95	15.48	12.06	10.21	-	10.41	10.82	11.41	10.99	13.49	12.64
Number	-	-	RS 308	RS 415	-	RS 419	RS 435	RS 493	RS 516	RS 524	RS 657
Rate	-	-	8.82	11.61	-	9.77	9.87	10.88	11.09	1,097	13.41
Number	-	-	GB 259	MG 391	-	MG 277	GB 300	MG 249	MG 300	MG 426	MG 427
Rate	-	-	14.19	5.13	-	3.41	11.73	3.00	3.53	4.89	4.80
Number	-	-	MG 206	GB 228	-	GB 271	MG 275	GB 234	GB 263	GB 289	GB 301
Rate	-	-	2.97	9.84	-	10.99	3.39	8.84	9.60	10.22	10.31
Number	-	-	BA 209	RJ 177	-	RJ 237	RJ 182	RJ 216	RJ 253	BA 202	RJ 284
Rate	-	-	5.10	7.85	-	9.87	7.25	8.25	9.28	3.76	9.66

Table III-5 (continued)

	1957	1958	1959	1960	1961	1962	1963	1964	1965	1966	1967
Number	3,914	3,993	3,608	3,366	3,151	3,075	3,474	2,697	2,959	3,051	3,236
Rate/100,000	6,05	6.00	5.28	4.80	4.35	4.11	4.51	3.40	3.62	3.63	3.75
Sex											
Male	2,642	2,664	2,452	2,338	2,179	2,046	2,426	1,890	2,100	2,131	2,343
Age											
0-14	–	54	60	170	51	41	46	39	43	47	40
15-24	–	1,146	1,002	887	786	930	890	967	704	755	787
25-44	–	1,699	1,569	1,433	1,336	1,285	1,524	1,086	1,174	1,189	1,287
45-59	–	718	616	581	531	529	669	521	582	670	703
60+	–	196	169	157	152	146	169	133	214	165	208
Marital Status											
Single	1,889	1,892	1,621	1,526	1,406	1,488	1,586	1,178	1,262	1,317	1,322
Married	1,637	1,722	1,557	1,435	1,305	1,300	1,551	1,229	1,318	1,403	1,520
Schooling											
Illiterate	702	701	538	522	537	524	544	445	551	482	530
Primary	2,371	2,256	1,802	1,786	1,654	1,903	1,960	1,485	1,468	1,654	1,719
Secondary/College	128	171	98	181	124	168	160	146	162	165	170
Means Used											
(P = poison)	P 2,399	P 2,470	P 2,057	P 1,926	P 1,667	P 1,564	P 1,505	P 885	F 802	F 863	F 992
(F = firearms)	F 449	F 487	F 496	F 479	F 514	F 485	F 699	F 676	P 800	P 752	P 775
(H = hanging)	H 428	H 401	H 441	H 418	H 398	H 439	H 530	H 495	H 631	H 694	H 707
Political Subdivisions											
Number	SP 1,401	SP 1,365	SP 1,111	SP 1,066	SP 881	SP 828	SP 1,365	SP 809	SP 958	SP 899	SP 981
Rate	11.95	11.29	8.92	8.31	6.62	5.99	9.54	5.46	6.26	5.69	6.02
Number	RS 528	RS 527	RS 547	RS 506	RS 484	RS 434	RS 404	RS 416	RS 395	RS 437	RS 451
Rate	10.52	10.25	10.39	9.39	8.77	7.69	7.16	7.05	6.55	7.12	7.18
Number	MG 418	GB 466	GB 422	GB 362	MG 362	MG 348	GB 345	MG 291	MG 395	MG 314	MG 378
Rate	4.59	15.03	13.22	12.58	3.67	3.46	9.66	2.79	3.73	2.92	3.45
Number	GB 311	MG 426	MG 400	MG 377	GB 363	GB 330	MG 322	GB 278	GB 196	GB 234	PR 226
Rate	10.33	4.58	4.21	3.89	10.74	9.49	3.15	7.57	5.20	5.70	3.69
Number	RJ 248	RJ 289	RJ 229	RJ 207	PR 163	RJ 214	RJ 190	RJ 149	PR 163	PR 190	GB 207
Rate	8.14	9.17	7.02	6.15	3.60	5.87	5.03	3.80	2.91	3.24	5.23

	1968	1969	1971	1972	1973	1974	1975	1976	1977	1978	1979
Number	3,021	3,105	3,541	3,463	3,761	4,086	3,430	3,157	3,839	4,125	4,167
Rate/100,000	3.41	3.42	3.70	3.52	3.73	3.93	3.23	2.90	3.45	3.62	3.50
Sex											
Male	2,175	2,209	2,512	2,407	2,632	2,670	2,349	2,118	2,725	2,832	2,898
Age											
0-14	34	43	76	77	48	72	53	61	90	110	132
15-24	711	810	879	836	935	1,122	856	837	1,029	1,131	1,152
25-44	1,190	1,217	1,410	1,377	1,488	1,569	1,331	1,299	1,483	1,646	1,608
45-59	695	582	662	590	648	658	584	474	643	627	605
60+	164	255	347	376	374	403	332	279	369	360	359
Marital Status											
Single	1,217	1,333	1,408	1,371	1,489	1,689	1,400	1,296	1,537	1,801	1,782
Married	1,447	1,443	1,647	1,589	1,692	1,784	1,512	1,370	1,750	1,728	1,719
Schooling											
Illiterate	442	478	478	449	477	449	386	301	429	425	424
Primary	1,687	1,687	1,758	1,541	1,525	1,917	1,496	1,477	1,886	1,622	1,577
Secondary/College	168	205	354	319	358	364	335	331	407	363	452
Means Used											
(P = poison)	F 1,002	F 1,027	F 1,101	F 1,026	F 1,074	F 1,128	F 919	H 860	H 1,121	H 1,114	H 1,114
(F = firearms)	H 707	H 710	H 931	H 923	H 1,042	H 1,014	H 897	P 698	F 963	P 949	F 1,040
(H = hanging)	P 659	P 671	P 700	P 685	P 725	P 797	P 724	F 797	P 793	F 984	P 956
Political Subdivisions											
Number	SP 911	SP 923	SP 932	SP 867	SP 962	SP 1,244	SP 932	SP 948	SP 1,014	SP 661	SP 898
Rate	5.42	5.34	5.04	4.51	4.82	6.06	4.35	4.28	4.44	2.80	5.61
Number	RS 514	RS 502	RS 597	RS 588	RS 642	RS 655	RS 620	RS 634	RS 692	RS 491	RS 692
Rate	8.02	7.68	8.81	8.54	9.17	9.35	8.58	8.64	9.30	6.41	9.02
Number	MG 225	MG 360	MG 428	MG 416	MG 407	MG 491	RJ 388	RJ 429	MG 429	MG 347	RJ 500
Rate	2.02	3.18	3.67	3.56	3.38	4.01	3.33	4.13	3.35	2.67	4.52
Number	PR 211	PR 222	PR 244	PR 245	PR 281	RS 401	MG 334	MG 368	RJ 406	RJ 306	MG 476
Rate	3.30	3.33	3.49	3.94	3.94	5.64	2.69	2.91	3.83	2.82	3.60
Number	GB 204	RJ 167	GB 212	GB 211	GB 211	PR 299	PR 293	PR 243	PR 325	PR 259	PR 331
Rate	5.03	3.62	–	–	–	4.14	4.02	3.31	4.38	3.46	4.38

Sources: AN 1939-40, p. 1,408 and 1,179; AN 1941-45, p. 463; AN 1951, p. 478; AN 1952, p. 493; AN 1953, p. 420; AN 1954, p. 455; AN 1955, pp. 510-511; AN 1956, pp. 393-395; AN 1957, p. 439; AN 1958, pp. 434-435; AN 1959, pp. 420-421; AN 1960, pp. 361-363; AN 1961, pp. 404-406; AN 1962, pp. 326-328; AN 1963, pp. 338-430; AN 1964, pp. 317-119; AN 1965, pp. 380-382; AN 1966, pp. 385-387; AN 1967, 520-522; AN 1968, p. 489; AN 1969, 592-594; AN 1970, pp. 638-640; AN 1972, pp. 677-679; AN 1973, pp. 729-731; AN 1974, pp. 727-729; AN 1975, pp. 755-757; AN 1977, pp. 290-292; AN 1978, pp. 310-312; AN 1979, pp. 288-290; AN 1980, pp. 298-299; AN 1981, pp. 282-283.

Table III-6. Numbers and Rates of Marriages and Marriage Dissolutions in Brazil, 1936-77

	Marriages		Marriage Dissolutions	
Year	Number	Rate Per 100,000 Persons	Number	Rate Per 100,000 Persons
1936	155,110	366.0	-	-
1937	143,534	332.0	-	-
1938	132,404	300.0	-	-
1946	-	-	1,101	2.3
1947	-	-	1,773	3.6
1948	-	-	1,267	2.5
1949	-	-	1,346	2.6
1950	63,284	760.5	-	-
1958	-	-	3,087	4.6
1959	-	-	3,429	5.0
1960	77,426	584.0	3,422	4.9
1967	342,368	397.0	5,626	6.5
1968	382,719	432.0	6,603	7.4
1969	415,967	458.0	7,684	8.5
1974	-	-	21,958	21.2
1975	841,216	792.8	-	-
1976	891,158	819.9	-	-
1977	881,955	792.5	-	-

Sources: AN 1939-40, pp. 107-108; AN 1951, pp. 52 & 474; AN 1963,pp. 33 & 36
       AN 1971, pp. 84 & 110; AN 1977, p. 130.

Table III-7. Number and Specialization of Hospital Beds and Beds per Person in Brazil, 1940-74

Specialization	1940	Number of Hospital Beds			
		1954	1961	1968	1974
General Clinical Medicine		83,653	56,452	88,560	103,542
Psychiatric		40,090	32,508	74,551	87,832
Pediatric		4,067	13,188	21,869	41,803
Surgery		–	24,574	33,742	41,451
Obstetric		5,344	21,315	31,933	40,713
Tuberculosis		18,095	21,146	25,794	22,076
Leprosy		18,297	16,554	18,204	15,839
Injury & Orthopedic		–	6,866	6,747	8,181
Communicable Diseases		–	3,852	3,441	5,251
Cardiology		–	–	–	3,487
Cancer		–	2,014	2,953	3,343
Neurologic		–	–	–	3,187
Other		22,023	12,403	13,713	14,433
Total	114,808	191,569	210,872	321,507	391,138
Beds Per 1,000 Persons	2.78	3.24	2.91	3.59	3.78

Sources: AN 1947, pp. 377-378; AN 1956, p. 306; AN 1963, p.296; AN 1971, p. 548; AN 1977, p. 154.

Table III-8. Medical Personnel in Brazil, 1871-1970

	1872 Total	1872 Male	1872 Female	1890 Total	1890 Male	1890 Female	1920 Total	1920 Male	1920 Female	1940 Total	1940 Male	1940 Female
Physicians	1,967	1,967	0	-	-	-	-	-	-	-	-	-
Dentists	-	-	-	-	-	-	-	-	-	-	-	-
Midwives	1,197	50	1,147	-	-	-	-	-	-	-	-	-
Registered Nurses	-	-	-	-	-	-	-	-	-	-	-	-
Practical Nurses	-	-	-	-	-	-	-	-	-	-	-	-
Physiotherapists	-	-	-	-	-	-	-	-	-	-	-	-
Prostheticians	-	-	-	-	-	-	-	-	-	-	-	-
X-Ray Technicians	-	-	-	-	-	-	-	-	-	-	-	-
Licensed Pharmacists	-	-	-	-	-	-	-	-	-	-	-	-
Practical Pharmacists	1,392	1,392	-	-	-	-	-	-	-	-	-	-
Laboratory Technicians	-	-	-	-	-	-	-	-	-	-	-	-
Total	4,556	3,409	1,147	-	-	-	37,142	29,954	7,188	34,188	27,417	6,771

	1950 Total	1950 Male	1950 Female	1960 Total	1960 Male	1960 Female	1970 Total	1970 Male	1970 Female
Physicians	22,002	21,215	787	34,269	31,920	2,349	44,984	40,468	4,516
Dentists	18,445	17,265	1,180	28,553	26,190	2,363	32,566	28,358	4,208
Midwives	3,549	14	3,535	3,292	148	3,144	4,588	133	4,455
Registered Nurses	39,782	12,401	27,381	71,229	20,710	50,519	5,520	339	5,181
Practical Nurses	-	-	-	-	-	-	136,246	28,340	107,906
Physiotherapists	-	-	-	-	-	-	3,117	1,198	1,919
Prostheticians	3,123	2,969	154	7,385	6,980	405	7,393	7,019	374
X-Ray Technicians	-	-	-	1,353	1,025	328	4,095	2,504	1,591
Licensed Pharmacists	-	-	-	-	-	-	3,966	2,530	1,436
Practical Pharmacists	-	-	-	-	-	-	7,971	7,067	904
Laboratory Technicians	8,125	4,868	3,257	-	-	-	38,978	28,568	10,410
Total	95,026	58,732	36,294	146,081	86,973	59,108	289,424	146,524	142,900

Sources: RE 1920D5, p. VIII & XII; RE 1940A2, p. 41; RE 1950A1, p. 36; RE 1960A1, p. 34; RE 1970A1, p. 50.

Table III-9. Communicable Diseases in Brazil, 1938-76; Numbers of New Cases, Persons Receiving Treatment and Persons Vaccinated

NUMBERS OF NEW CASES

	1938	1940	1942	1944	1946	1948	1950	1952	1954	1956	1958	1960
Ancylostoma	-	-	-	-	-	-	-	-	-	56,409	166,207	231,826
Chagas	-	-	-	-	-	-	-	-	-	-	-	-
Chicken Pox	-	-	-	-	-	-	-	-	-	-	-	-
Diphtheria	-	-	-	-	-	-	-	-	-	-	-	-
Dysentery	-	-	-	-	-	-	-	-	-	-	-	-
Filariasis	-	-	-	-	-	-	-	-	-	4,146	20,530	18,709
Hydatid	-	-	-	-	-	-	-	-	-	-	16	7
Influenza	-	-	-	-	-	-	-	-	-	-	-	-
Leishmaniasis	-	-	-	-	-	-	-	-	-	-	287	262
Leprosy	-	-	-	-	-	-	-	5,128	4,875	4,659	7,070	6,667
Malaria	-	-	-	-	100,514	70,516	6,905	5,435	7,589	17,979	22,906	36,627
Measles	-	-	-	-	-	-	-	-	-	-	-	-
Meningitis	-	-	-	-	-	-	-	-	-	-	-	-
Necatoriasis	-	-	-	-	-	-	-	-	-	-	-	-
Plague	255	35	-	154	338	386	59	65	-	4	25	28
Poliomyelitis	-	-	-	-	-	-	-	-	-	-	-	-
Schistosomiasis	-	-	-	-	-	-	-	-	-	20,007	46,850	49,412
Smallpox	-	-	-	-	-	-	-	-	-	-	-	-
Syphilis	-	-	-	-	-	-	-	-	-	-	-	-
Trachoma	-	-	-	-	-	-	-	-	-	13,244	182,363	129,688
Tuberculosis	-	-	-	-	-	-	-	-	-	-	-	-
Typhoid/Para-T.	-	-	-	-	-	-	-	-	-	-	-	-
Undulant Fever	-	-	-	-	-	-	-	-	-	-	222	461
Whooping Cough	-	-	-	-	-	-	-	-	-	-	-	-
Yellow Fever	262	-	-	-	1	3	4	220	-	2	25	1

Table III-9 (continued)

	1962	1964	1966	1968	1970	1972	1974	1976
Ancylostoma	218,476	329,527	534,590	774,011	910,281	476,294	187,832	215,820
Chagas	-	-	-	11,800	20,120	-	-	-
Chicken Pox	-	-	-	20,497	25,422	-	17,500	-
Diphtheria	-	-	-	19,169	10,496	-	7,531	-
Dysentery	-	-	-	493,612	636,347	-	-	-
Filariasis	14,125	17,104	8,826	8,657	4,411	12,636	7,362	8,024
Hydatid	4	2	1	1	-	-	-	-
Influenza	-	-	-	855,492	963,148	-	-	-
Leishmaniasis	107	373	2,005	1,593	2,690	3,202	3,248	-
Leprosy	5,542	5,324	4,563	5,568	5,313	6,411	8,199	-
Malaria	2,087	508	106,890	52,985	46,151	84,191	65,306	88,244
Measles	-	-	-	116,959	109,125	-	72,719	-
Meningitis	-	-	-	772	1,923	-	41,057	-
Necatoriasis	-	-	-	222,713	274,498	-	-	-
Plague	36	285	48	285	375	169	290	97
Poliomyelitis	-	-	-	22,812	11,545	-	6,063	-
Schistosomiasis	36,974	50,699	56,875	100,564	167,642	56,300	54,847	51,718
Smallpox	-	-	-	18,341	5,752	-	-	-
Syphilis	-	-	-	41,238	65,388	-	43,452	-
Trachoma	228,205	202,679	320,874	102,019	90,054	30,160	17,493	12,752
Tuberculosis	-	-	-	76,161	111,945	-	11,600	-
Typhoid/ParaT.	-	-	-	13,929	11,243	-	-	-
Undulant Fever	17	-	-	-	-	-	-	-
Whooping Cough	1	-	-	99,615	81,014	-	67,085	-
Yellow Fever	-	12	22	-	39,702	9	13	-

Table III-9 (continued)

PERSONS RECEIVING TREATMENT

	1938	1940	1942	1944	1946	1948	1950	1952	1954	1956	1958	1960	1962
Ancylostoma	-	-	-	-	-	-	-	-	-	137,879	79,810	29,338	44,303
Bouba	-	-	-	-	-	-	-	-	-	3,353	16,080	21,407	21,102
Filariasis	-	-	-	-	-	-	-	-	-	22,273	19,104	18,283	18,231
Leprosy	-	-	-	20,531	20,004	21,546	22,929	23,136	22,099	-	-	-	-
Malaria	-	-	-	-	164,111	1,201,228	1,025,069	1,070,369	1,312,782	1,033,416	911,773	1,555,746	146,681
Schistosomiasis	-	-	-	-	-	-	-	-	4,053	10,867	11,634	12,030	7,842
Trachoma	-	-	-	-	-	-	-	-	-	31,919	53,457	39,559	196,656
Tuberculosis	-	-	-	-	-	-	-	-	-	-	-	-	-
Undulant Fever	-	-	-	-	-	-	-	-	-	-	-	45	-

	1964	1966	1968	1970	1972	1974	1976
Ancylostoma	-	-	-	-	905,945	314,566	165,443
Bouba	21,962	-	7,421	3,217	1,124	118	-
Filariasis	21,899	10,393	15,083	8,644	12,892	7,901	10,434
Leprosy	16,690	18,600	17,151	16,188	16,406	15,462	-
Malaria	3,150	-	-	-	-	-	-
Schistosomiasis	11,344	12,383	9,208	5,600	4,685	11,824	8,670
Trachoma	193,514	-	-	-	-	-	-
Tuberculosis	-	-	25,244	26,993	25,256	-	-
Undulant Fever	-	-	-	-	-	-	-

PERSONS VACCINATED

	1938	1940	1942	1944	1946	1948	1950	1952	1954	1956	1958	1960	1962
Diphtheria	-	-	-	-	-	-	-	-	-	-	-	-	-
Influenza	-	-	-	-	-	-	-	-	-	-	-	1,853	-
Measles	-	-	-	-	-	-	-	-	-	-	-	-	-
Plague	-	-	-	-	-	-	-	-	-	-	2,573	2,084	10,486
Poliomyelitis	-	-	-	-	-	-	-	-	-	-	-	4,032	-
Smallpox	-	-	-	-	-	-	-	-	-	-	149,435	788,238	259,480
Tuberculosis	-	-	-	-	-	-	249,546	233,321	1,248,540	2,686,746	2,657,172	3,033,835	482,299
Typhoid/ParaT.	-	-	-	-	-	-	-	-	-	-	-	77,051	19,672
Whooping Cough	-	-	-	-	-	-	-	-	-	-	-	-	-
Yellow Fever	-	-	-	-	-	-	514,669	4,812,393	3,767,157	1,461,654	1,689,921	843,669	567,418

	1964	1966	1968	1970	1972	1974	1976
Diphtheria	223,909	780,368	501,948	1,059,328	2,434,531	2,621,416	3,083,133
Influenza	-	-	-	-	-	-	-
Measles	-	-	53,884	212,941	1,878,313	-	-
Plague	-	-	-	-	-	-	-
Poliomyelitis	-	-	-	-	-	6,846,377	6,042,677
Smallpox	243,535	5,894,320	21,405,020	36,936,613	13,882,924	4,702,857	-
Tuberculosis	81,515	134,393	472,584	435,603	-	4,304,582	-
Typhoid/ParaT.	-	-	746,574	875,721	844,034	1,375,610	-
Whooping Cough	-	-	2,370,274	2,931,827	3,425,145	-	-
Yellow Fever	833,496	3,540,658	1,682,158	1,153,589	1,168,820	3,074,350	2,004,392

Sources: AN 1941/45, pp. 358-9; AN 1946, p. 395; AN 1947, p. 380; AN 1948, p. 448;
AN 1950, pp. 364-6; AN 1951, p. 365; AN 1952, p. 390; AN 1953, pp. 359-363;
AN 1955, pp. 387-395; AN 1956, pp.314-19; AN 1957, pp. 319-20; AN 1959, pp.
312-26; AN 1960, pp. 253-9; AN 1961, pp. 318-334; AN 1963, pp. 310-26;
AN 1965, pp. 349-64; AN 1967, pp. 487-98; AN 1969, pp. 553-562; AN 1971,
pp. 567-97; AN 1971, pp. 578-84; AN 1973, pp. 675-699; AN 1974, p. 679;
AN 1975, pp. 705-20; AN 1978, pp. 193-203.

Table III-10. Diagnoses of Cases Admitted to Psychiatric Hospitals in
              Brazil, 1954-75

Diagnoses	Number of Cases			
	1954	1961	1969	1975
Psychoses	18,439	22,011	55,636	66,487
Alcoholism	3,297	5,116	19,152	25,900
Neuroses	1,583	2,797	13,585	17,918
Mental Deficiency	2,040	1,937	6,306	7,343
Drug Dependency	–	–	–	1,859
Other	1,754	1,852	7,057	10,249
Not Classified	3,792	5,666	7,940	1,079
Total	30,905	39,379	109,676	130,835
Total Rate per 100,000 Inhabitants	5.92	5.43	12.07	12.33

Sources: AN 1956, pp. 311-312; AN 1963, pp. 321-322; AN 1971, p. 590;
         AN 1977, p. 194.

95

Table III-11. Average Brazilian Daily Calorie Intake per Person by Foods
Consumed, 1960 and 1975

Food Group	1960 Calories	%	1975 South Calories	%	1975 Northeast Calories	%
Cereals	1,160	45.2	990.74 (rice)	41.0	517.91 (rice)	26.8
Root Crops	329	12.8	143.07 (mandioca)	5.9	495.92 (mandioca)	25.7
Sugars	302	11.8	313.26	13.0	210.60	10.9
Legumes	–	–	212.31 (beans)	8.8	324.26 (beans)	16.8
Vegetables	–	–	22.71 (squash)	.9	10.18 (squash)	.5
Fruits	107	4.2	36.51 (bananas)	1.5	35.10 (bananas)	1.8
Meat/Fish	215	8.4	204.68 (beef)	8.5	178.45 (beef)	9.3
Eggs	–	–	25.40	1.0	9.98	.5
Dairy Products/ Oils/Fats	453	17.6	445.33 (lard)	18.4	137.88 (milk)	7.2
Beverages	–	–	24.97 (alcoholic)	1.0	10.29 (coffee)	.5
Total	2,566	100.0	2,418.98	100.0	1,930.57	100.0

Sources: Food Consumption in Brazil, Family Budget Surveys in the Early 1960's,
Table 14, p. 23; AN 1977, p. 208.

Chapter IV. Immigration and Internal Migration

Table IV-1 documents voluntary (as opposed to slave) immigration to Brazil from 1820 to 1975. The data originated with the Boletim comemorativo da Exposição nacional de 1908, the Departamento Nacional de Imigração, the Instituto Nacional de Imigração e Colonizacão, the Departamento Nacional de Mão-de-Obra/Divisão de Migraçao, and the Superintendência da Política Agrária. Although all the immigration reported on this table was voluntary (as opposed to slave immigration) not all of it was what the Brazilian authorities called spontaneous. Immigration organized in the homeland on either a private group to Brazilian government basis or a government to Brazilian government basis characterized some of the early German and nearly all the Japanese immigration. For some years the sources distinguished permanent from temporary immigrants. In these cases only permanent immigrants were recorded on this table. For most years the sources did not specify whether immigrants were permanent or not, but they did supply enough information to suggest that when immigrants were not characterized they were, in fact, permanent.

The terms Turk/Arab were initially applied to immigrants coming from the Ottoman Empire among whom were probably many from national groups other than Turkish. Later sources dropped the term Arab. Many of the Russian immigrants were actually German-speaking Volga-Deutsch who had lived along the middle Volga River since the time of Catherine the Great. As early as 1904 the Brazilian authorities distinguished between Austrians and Hungarians even though they were citizens of the Austro-Hungarian Empire. Egyptian and Syrian immigrants were distinguished by the sources during most of the time these two countries formed the United Arab Republic. After 1945 all Germans were from West Germany. The sources did not indicate the political unit from which immigrants of Chinese nationality came.

Voluntary immigration to Brazil had begun in the early 1500s but numbers were small prompting Celso Furtado's[1] remark that no more than 30,000 Portuguese were to be found along the coast of Brazil by the end of the century, that is, 1600. During the period when Portugal was under Spanish rule (1580-1640) some Spaniards immigrated to the extreme southern part of Brazil, an area in dispute between the two Iberian nations. A few Dutch came to stay during Netherlands occupation of the northeast coast (1624-54), an occupation that was determined by Brazilian action alone, without outside help. In 1720, at the height of the Brazilian gold rush, the Portuguese government forbade Portuguese emigration to the Minas Gerais gold fields. Despite this, Boxer[2] estimates that between 1705 an 1750 as many as 3,000 to 4,000 persons per year left Portugal for Brazil. Between 1808 and 1817 more than 50,000 Portuguese came to Brazil, mostly to Rio de Janeiro, during the Brazilian stay of the exiled Portuguese court; few returned.

In 1808 Brazil proclaimed an "open door" policy regarding non-Luso (non-Portuguese) immigration from Europe. The results of the policy, however, were sporadic during the first half of the nineteenth century. As early as 1812 a German colony was established in the mountainous interior of Espírito Santo province, and in 1824 Germans founded São Leopoldo on the plateau of northern Rio Grande do Sul province. In 1818 Swiss settled Nova Friburgo in the mountains of Rio de Janeiro province. Brazilians, however, were uninterested in either free labor or yeoman farmers and thought only in terms of slave labor to work the large fazendas. Between 1820 and 1840, according to Calogeras,[3] only 12,000 non-Luso immigrants came to Brazil.

In 1840 Senator Vergueiro personally inaugurated a system (the parceria) under which Europeans were staked to passage and living expenses that were to be paid back by labor on the expanding coffee fazendas of São Paulo province. By 1850, 60,000 Europeans, a large number of whom were Italian, had come to São Paulo; many had paid off their debts and had begun to purchase coffee lands of their own. The Queiroz Law (1850) effectively truncated the slave trade and the government fully recognized the need to populate the southern province with colonists loyal to Brazil. In the last quarter of the nineteenth century these factors together with the huge growth in Brazilian coffee exports and economic stagnation in Italy contributed to an upsurge in European immigration to Brazil.

During the last eight years of the 1870s, 176,000 immigrants reached Brazilian shores. By the decade of the 1890s, Brazil's peak immigration period, this number had increased to nearly 1.2 million. This period was characterized by the movement of Italians to São Paulo, while Germans, eastern Europeans, and smaller numbers of Italians colonized the lands of the southern plateau in Paraná, Santa Catarina, and Rio Grande do Sul. Italian immigration fell sharply after reaching the 1890-99 peak and continued to decline through the twentieth century. The flow of colonizing immigrants from countries other than Italy, however, increased through the early years of the century. By the 1920-29 decade immigrants from Germany, Japan and a variety of other countries such as Poland, Russia (mostly Volga-Deutsch), and Syria, accounted for 42 percent of all immigrants to Brazil. Japanese immigration peaked in the 1930-39 decade when, with the support of both the Japanese and Brazilian governments, nearly 100,000 Japanese came to Brazil.

The 1934 constitution promulgated by Getúlio Vargas nearly closed the "open door." Annual immigration limits were set at 2 percent of the total number of persons of each nationality who entered Brazil during the preceding fifty years (1883-1933). Quotas were set as follows: Italian, 27,000; Portuguese, 23,000; Spanish, 12,000; Japanese, 3,500; Germans, 3,100. The Japanese, under Brazilian government dispensation, exceeded the quota set for them.

As early as the 1550s numbers of black slaves had begun to arrive in Brazil. This was the beginning of a veritable flood of black humanity, which was wrenched from African homelands and which is documented from 1600 to 1860 on Table IV-2. These involuntary migrations continued for more than three hundred years and came to constitute one of the largest international migration streams in history. Philip Curtin[4] estimates that between 1600 and 1860 more than 3.33 million slaves reached Brazil alive. If between 12 and 30 percent died enroute, as various sources indicate, the total leaving African shores for Brazil was very likely well over four million.

During the sixteenth and seventeenth centuries, slaves were brought to work the sugar engenhos of Bahia and Pernambuco where the Portuguese were emulating their experience of the late 1400s with the same crop in the Madeira Islands. Bahia was the early chief port of entry. The plantation provinces of Maranhão and Alagoas also received large numbers of Africans. Brazilian slave immigration rose sharply in the decade 1821-30 when the need for labor in the gold and diamond fields of Minas Gerais reached its peak. Because of Rio de Janeiro's proximity to these fields, that city became Brazil's new principal port of entry. In the 1840s, expanding coffee production in the province of Rio de Janeiro created a demand for slaves and produced Brazil's peak decade of slave imports, all of which were illegal under the country's weak and unenforceable slavery laws. The strong Queiroz Law of 1850 effectively ended this dolesome trans-Atlantic migration. Rollie Poppino[5] and João Calogeras[6] document the economic and political background of Brazil's slave period. Stanley Stein[7] adds the social and life-style detail in his treatment of the last decade of slavery importation. Nicolas Sanchez-Albornoz[8] describes the demographic significance of Brazilian slave populations.

Slave sources shifted during the three hundred years of importation. Sudanese, valued for their stamina and vigor, were preferred by the Portuguese in the early years, but by 1750 this Guinea Coast source (centered in present-day Ghana) had shifted southward. Africans referred to as Bantu (reputed to be more docile than Sudanese) and Mozambique replaced Sudanese as the focus of embarkation shifted to Angola and Mozambique.

Brazil's net gains from immigration are shown on Table IV-3. They are based on figures from Jansen[9] and Merrick and Graham[10]. During the three decades between 1880 and 1909 Brazil's new population gain from immigration averaged only 54.8 percent. This period was dominated by immigration of Italians, a national group which was particularly fluid in the late nineteenth century. Many came to Brazil on short-term labor contracts (as they had to Argentina) and chose to return after their contracts expired.

During the last half of the decade 1910-19 there was little incentive for immigrants to return to a Europe enmeshed in World War I and as a consequence Brazil's immigrant-retention rate rose to 85.9 percent. The rate remained about 90 percent in the next twenty years. Virtually none of the Japanese who came to Brazil in large numbers during this period returned to their homeland and this helped to keep the retention rate high. During the first half of the 1940-49 decade, World War II severely reduced international migration and during the postwar period Europe was not an attraction for migrants from Brazil.

Table IV-4 presents in detail the exchanges of population among Brazil's political subdivisions from 1940 to 1970. These details are generalized on Map IV-1, which portrays graphically at least five significant migration patterns. The dominant pattern is created by the heavy flows of migrants from the poor northeastern states and Minas Gerais to the more prosperous southern states of São Paulo, Paraná, and Guanabara (the city of Rio de Janeiro). A second major migrant stream flows westward and is targeted on Goiás and Mato Grosso states and the Distrito Federal (Brasília). Again the northeastern states and Minas Gerais state are the principal origins of the flows to Goiás and Brasília. São

Paulo state is the prime origin of migrants to Mato Grosso. Migrants from the northeast who resided for a time in Minas Gerais and São Paulo make up a significant portion of the westward movement from both these latter states.

Migrants from the northeast have been moving intermittently into the Amazon for nearly a century. In the early years they came to gather rubber and Brazil nuts. Later they came to build the trans-Amazon highways and to populate the new agricultural settlements along these routes. None of these activities, however, has made permanent settlers of the peripatetic northeasterners. A fourth migration pattern is that from a rural to an urban environment. Although this has long been a major component of the general north to south flow it is reflected at the local level in the movements of population from the deficit state of Rio de Janeiro to the state of Guanabara (the city of Rio de Janeiro) in 1940 and 1950. By 1960 the city of Rio had sprawled beyond the Guanabara state boundaries spawning new urban nucleii in the surrounding state of Rio de Janeiro. These urban areas in the state of Rio de Janeiro then became targets of migrants from the same origins that had earlier supplied migrants to the city of Rio de Janeiro.

A fifth, and more or less local, flow originated in the prosperous southern state of Rio Grande do Sul. Migrants from this state's overpopulated small farms (minifúndios) moved northward to the newly cleared forest lands of western Santa Catarina state. In both 1950 and 1960 Santa Catarina gained population at Rio Grande do Sul's expense but by 1960 both states were losing population to the newly opened lands of western Paraná state.

All these patterns are closely related to and to a great extent products of the economic and cultural geography of Brazil which are treated either regionally or nationally by many of the authors cited in Chapter II. In his population oriented geographic study of Brazil James[11] touches upon most of these migration patterns. The results of migration to cities are dealt with by a number of authors, among whom Leeds[12] and Pearse[13] treat Rio de Janeiro and Epstein,[14] Brasilia. Ludwig[15] focuses on specific migration patterns to and from Brasilia, and Ludwig and Taylor[16] and Kluck[17] document the rural population pressure leading to the out-migration from Rio Grande do Sul state.

References

1. Celso Furtado (see Chapter II).

2. Charles R. Boxer (see Chapter II).

3. João Pandia Calogeras (see Chapter II).

4. Philip Curtin, <u>The Atlantic Slave Trade: A Census</u> (Madison: University of Wisconsin Press, 1969).

5. Rollie Poppino (see Chapter II).

6. Calogeras (see Chapter II).

7. Stanley Stein, <u>Vassouras, A Brazilian Coffee County, 1850-1900</u> (Cambridge: Harvard University Press, 1957).

8. Nicolas Sanchez-Albornoz (see Chapter II).

9. Clifford J. Jansen, <u>Readings in the Sociology of Migration</u> (Oxford, N.Y.: Pergamon Press, 1970).

10. Thomas W. Merrick and Douglas H. Graham (see Chapter II).

11. Preston E. James (see Chapter II).

12. Anthony Leeds and Elizabeth Leeds, "Brazil and the Myth of Urban Reality: Urban Experience, Work and Values in 'Squatments' of Rio de Janeiro and Lima." Paper presented at the Conference on Work and Urbanization in Modernizing Societies, St. Thomas, Virgin Islands, November 2-4, 1967.

13. Andrew Pearse, "Some Characteristics of Urbanization in the City of Rio de Janeiro," in Philip Hauser, ed., <u>Urbanization in Latin America</u> (New York: International Documents Service, 1961).

14. David G. Epstein, <u>Brasília, Plan and Reality: A Study of Planned and Spontaneous Urban Settlement</u> (Berkeley: University of California Press, 1973).

15. Armin K. Ludwig, 1980 (see Chapter II).

16. Armin K. Ludwig and Harry W. Taylor, <u>Brazil's New Agrarian Reform: An Evaluation of Its Property, Classification and Tax Systems</u> (New York: Frederick A. Praeger, 1969).

17. Patricia Ann Kluck, "Decision Making among Descendants of German Immigrant Farmers in Rio Grande do Sul, Brazil" (Ph.D. diss., Cornell University, 1975).

Table IV-1. Immigrants to Brazil by Nationality, 1820-1975

	1820/ 1883	1872/ 1879	1880/ 1883	1884/ 1893	1884	1885	1886	1887	1888	1889	1890	1891
Total	427,046	176,337	105,507	883,668	23,574	34,724	32,650	54,932	132,070	65,165	106,819	215,239
Portuguese	221,536	55,027	38,375	170,621	8 683	7,611	6,287	10,205	18,289	15,240	25,174	32,349
Italian	96,018	45,467	43,793	510,533	10,502	21,765	20,430	40,157	104,353	36,124	31,275	132,326
Spanish	15,537	3,392	10,573	103,116	710	952	1,617	1,766	4,736	9,712	12,008	22,146
German	59,674	14,325	8,388	22,778	1,719	2,848	2,114	1,147	782	1,903	4,812	5,285
Japanese	-	-	-	-	-	-	-	-	-	-	-	-
Russian	8,835	-	-	40,589	457	275	146	197	259	-	27,125	11,817

	1892	1893	1894/ 1903	1894	1895	1896	1897	1898	1899	1900	1901	1902
Total	85,906	132,589	862,110	60,182	164,831	157,423	144,866	76,862	53,610	37,807	83,116	50,472
Portuguese	17,797	28,986	157,542	17,041	36,055	22,299	13,558	15,105	10,989	8,250	11,261	11,606
Italian	55,049	58,552	537,784	34,872	97,344	96,505	104,510	49,086	30,846	19,671	59,869	32,111
Spanish	10,471	38,998	102,142	5,986	17,641	24,154	19,466	8,024	5,399	4,834	212	3,588
German	800	1,368	6,698	790	973	1,070	930	535	521	217	166	265
Japanese	-	-	-	-	-	-	-	-	-	-	-	-
Russian	158	155	2,886	57	275	592	567	258	412	147	99	108

	1903	1904/ 1913	1904	1905	1906	1907	1908	1909	1910	1911	1912	1913
Total	32,941	1,006,617	44,706	68,488	72,332	57,919	90,536	84,090	86,751	133,575	177,887	190,333
Portuguese	11,378	384,672	17,318	20,181	21,706	25,681	37,628	30,577	30,857	47,493	76,630	76,701
Italian	12,970	196,521	12,857	17,360	20,777	18,238	13,873	13,668	14,163	22,914	31,785	30,886
Spanish	4,466	224,672	10,046	25,329	24,441	9,235	14,862	16,219	20,843	27,141	35,492	41,064
German	1,231	33,859	797	650	1,333	845	2,931	5,413	3,902	4,251	5,733	8,004
Japanese	-	11,868	-	-	-	-	830	31	948	28	2,909	7,122
Russian	371	48,100	287	996	,751	703	5,781	5,663	2,462	14,013	9,193	8,251

	1914/ 1923	1914	1915	1916	1917	1918	1919	1920	1921	1922	1923	1924/ 1933
Total	503,981	79,232	30,333	31,245	30,277	19,793	36,027	69,042	58,476	65,007	84,549	737,233
Portuguese	201,252	27,935	15,118	11,981	6,817	7,981	17,068	33,883	19,981	28,622	31,866	233,650
Italian	86,320	15,542	5,779	5,340	5,478	1,050	5,231	10,005	10,779	11,277	15,839	70,177
Spanish	94,779	18,945	5,895	10,306	11,113	4,225	6,627	9,136	9,523	8,869	10,140	52,405
German	29,339	2,811	169	364	201	1	466	4,120	7,915	5,038	8,254	61,728
Japanese	20,398	3,675	65	165	3,899	5,599	3,022	1,013	840	1,225	895	110,191
Russian	8,096	2,958	640	616	644	181	330	245	1,526	279	777	7,953

	1924	1925	1926	1927	1928	1929	1930	1931	1932	1933
Total	96,052	82,547	118,686	97,974	78,128	96,186	62,610	27,465	31,494	46,081
Portuguese	23,267	21,508	38,791	31,236	33,882	38,872	18,740	8,152	8,499	10,695
Italian	13,844	9,846	11,977	12,487	11,169	16,648	14,076	5,632	11,678	24,494
Spanish	7,238	10,062	8,892	9,070	4,436	4,565	3,218	1,784	1,447	1,693
German	22,168	7,175	7,674	4,874	4,228	4,351	4,180	2,621	2,273	2,180
Japanese	2,673	6,330	8,407	9,084	11,169	16,648	14,076	5,632	11,678	24,494
Russian	559	756	751	616	823	839	2,699	370	461	79

Table IV-1 (continued)

	1820/1883	1884/1893	1894/1903	1904/1913	1924/1933	1914/1923	1934	1935	1936	1937	1938	1939
Total	427,046	883,868	862,110	1,006,617	503,981	737,223	46,027	29,585	12,773	34,677	19,388	22,668
Portuguese	221,536	170,621	157,621	384,672	201,252	233,650	8,730	9,327	4,626	11,417	4,735	15,120
Italian	96,018	510,533	537,784	196,521	86,320	70,177	2,507	2,127	462	2,946	1,882	1,004
Spanish	15,537	103,116	102,142	224,672	94,779	52,405	1,429	1,206	355	1,150	290	174
German	59,674	22,778	6,698	33,859	29,339	61,728	3,629	2,423	1,226	4,642	2,348	1,975
Japanese	-	-	-	11,868	20,398	110,191	21,930	9,611	3,306	4,557	2,524	1,414
Russian	8,835	40,589	2,886	48,100	8,096	7,953	114	291	19	52	19	2
Argentine	-	1,225	2,523	4,013	3,136	6,540	948	325	49	138	1,199	95
Austrian	1,404	13,684	32,456	22,961	6,285	8,814	580	301	89	493	115	12
Belgian	800	2,657	171	1,128	981	742	52	56	14	91	51	66
British (UK)	6,687	2,870	825	6,710	3,964	5,829	490	342	33	1,835	538	309
Dutch	-	1,026	1,044	3,456	842	1,111	142	98	15	244	112	110
French	8,012	7,977	2,517	8,572	5,392	5,609	359	328	82	1,029	322	186
Hungarian	-	-	-	1,699	1,221	4,954	154	112	60	154	67	134
Lithuanian	-	-	-	-	1,931	26,077	160	166	179	73	55	24
North American (USA)	-	649	2,664	2,949	1,898	2,556	233	146	13	558	487	508
Polish	-	370	1,050	-	3,073	33,957	2,380	1,428	1,743	2,540	612	612
Rumanian	-	-	-	248	4,396	33,404	362	216	113	229	52	93
Syrian	-	93	602	3,826	1,145	14,264	158	152	31	109	110	17
Swedish	1,266	2,469	128	1,681	211	327	28	9	3	55	16	20
Swiss	7,181	1,385	607	1,852	2,581	2,585	170	120	109	473	200	178
Turk/Arab	96	3	8,522	42,177	19,255	10,227	120	51	17	47	24	12
Uruguayan	-	477	1,527	1,785	1,336	2,556	307	152	4	250	299	54
Yugoslav	-	-	-	-	905	21,661	74	27	10	63	34	64

	1940	1941	1942	1943	1944	1945	1946	1947	1948	1949	1950	1951
Total	18,449	9,938	2,425	1,308	1,593	3,168	13,039	18,753	21,568	23,844	35,492	62,594
Portuguese	11,373	5,777	1,317	146	419	1,414	6,342	8,921	2,751	6,780	14,739	28,731
Italian	411	89	3	1	3	180	1,059	3,284	4,437	6,352	7,342	8,285
Spanish	409	125	37	9	30	74	203	653	965	2,197	3,808	9,636
German	1,155	453	9	2	-	22	174	561	2,308	2,123	2,725	2,858
Japanese	1,268	1,548	-	-	-	-	6	1	1	4	33	106
Russian	17	23	-	-	20	2	28	18	1,342	36	-	-
Argentine	225	160	67	71	66	99	79	52	50	68	121	172
Austrian	-	-	-	-	-	-	-	-	598	275	201	382
Belgian	99	62	12	1	4	9	163	134	158	148	107	227
Bolivian	4	3	4	6	4	16	17	4	10	4	19	18
British (UK)	273	72	45	36	49	78	524	328	281	355	417	421
Canadian	-	-	-	-	-	-	-	-	48	60	79	56
Chilean	24	18	5	10	16	20	11	12	16	19	23	63
Czech	199	102	3	2	3	7	116	99	170	195	93	326
Danish	-	-	-	-	-	-	-	-	64	5	51	85
Dutch	63	49	7	2	2	12	242	267	229	485	645	464
French	169	147	64	17	18	53	577	437	477	489	536	755
Greek	-	-	-	-	-	4	82	299	198	89	64	485
Hungarian	126	43	-	-	-	3	219	216	567	479	392	404
Lebanese	-	-	-	-	-	4	155	581	925	850	658	1,865
North American (USA)	830	612	650	891	812	788	975	732	633	825	913	1,310
Paraguayan	47	35	25	11	23	64	27	6	19	11	8	14
Polish	513	280	8	6	2	44	706	561	2,439	360	188	269
Rumanian	74	8	-	-	3	6	45	82	326	347	74	139
Syrian	-	-	-	-	-	5	42	139	413	237	249	-
Swedish	-	-	-	-	-	-	-	-	39	69	107	129
Swiss	154	89	75	5	8	33	106	153	144	195	199	286
Turk/Arab	-	-	-	-	-	-	-	-	-	-	-	-
Uruguayan	129	69	47	47	31	80	53	27	52	29	48	52
Yugoslav	-	-	-	-	-	-	-	-	509	66	90	283

Table IV-1 (continued)

	1952	1953	1954	1955	1956	1957	1958	1959	1960	1961	1962	1963
Total	88,150	80,242	72,248	55,166	44,806	53,613	49,839	44,520	40,507	43,589	31,138	23,859
Portuguese	42,815	33,735	30,062	21,264	16,803	19,471	21,928	17,345	13,105	15,819	13,713	11,585
Italian	15,207	15,543	13,408	8,945	6,069	7,197	4,819	4,233	3,431	2,493	1,900	867
Spanish	14,898	13,677	11,338	10,738	7,921	7,680	5,768	6,712	7,662	9,813	4,968	2,436
German	2,364	2,305	1,952	1,122	844	952	825	890	842	703	651	601
Japanese	261	1,928	3,119	4,051	4,912	6,147	6,586	7,123	7,746	6,824	3,257	2,124
Russian	–	193	20	2	–	–	–	–	–	–	–	–
Argentine	–	–	485	345	288	267	317	247	295	–	–	–
Austrian	–	–	831	248	132	120	71	69	80	–	–	–
Belgian	–	–	89	86	54	69	46	63	52	–	–	–
Bolivian	–	–	17	115	64	65	95	78	104	–	–	–
British (UK)	–	–	380	315	304	446	409	431	367	–	–	–
Canadian	–	–	51	63	67	103	104	83	97	–	–	–
Chilean	–	–	37	65	57	–	–	–	–	–	–	–
Chinese	–	–	265	206	282	308	530	537	422	–	–	–
Czech	–	–	–	–	–	–	–	–	–	–	–	–
Danish	–	–	–	–	–	–	–	–	–	–	–	–
Dutch	–	–	669	852	356	264	329	255	325	–	–	–
Egyptian	–	–	–	621	84	42	42	–	–	–	–	–
French	–	–	659	435	628	805	457	475	348	–	–	–
Greek	–	–	1,850	1,049	641	1,220	831	751	687	725	595	340
Hungarian	–	–	–	–	–	2,017	162	34	18	–	–	–
Iranian	–	–	24	74	109	74	55	56	53	–	–	–
Israeli	–	–	1,011	400	616	782	1,036	493	228	–	–	–
Jordan	–	–	289	510	257	375	284	402	415	–	–	–
Lebanese	–	–	1,186	1,518	1,481	900	629	1,061	653	734	642	547
Lithuanian	–	–	–	–	–	–	–	–	–	–	–	–
Moroccan	–	–	11	10	207	67	8	11	34	–	–	–
North American (USA)	–	–	1,236	966	1,168	1,361	1,905	1,462	1,184	1,208	973	971
Paraguayan	–	–	55	50	48	–	–	–	–	–	–	–
Polish	–	–	–	–	–	124	195	120	158	–	–	–
Rumanian	–	–	–	–	–	–	–	–	–	–	–	–
Syrian	–	–	372	378	231	241	127	103	64	–	–	–
Swedish	–	–	114	85	62	84	113	72	85	–	–	–
Swiss	–	–	302	250	171	219	184	157	180	–	–	–
Turk/Arab	–	–	21	30	78	143	57	15	25	–	–	–
Uruguayan	–	–	54	70	107	80	101	101	118	–	–	–
Yugoslav	–	–	–	–	–	92	92	61	43	–	–	–

Table IV-1 (continued)

	1964	1965	1966	1967	1968	1969	1970	1971	1972	1973	1974	1975
Total	9,995	9,838	8,175	11,352	12,521	6,613	6,887	6,378	8,767	5,931	6,766	11,566
Portuguese	4,249	3,262	2,708	3,838	3,917	1,933	1,773	807	1,095	581	426	959
Italian	476	642	643	747	738	477	357	254	535	402	478	1,356
Spanish	616	550	469	572	743	568	546	281	470	225	244	410
German	323	365	377	550	723	524	535	354	635	404	641	1,248
Japanese	1,138	903	937	1,070	597	496	435	260	472	25	75	111
Russian	93	52	41	38	32	23	5	6	8	–	27	–
Argentine	203	138	132	182	232	97	270	276	370	628	775	1,095
Austria	30	57	17	29	32	22	29	49	29	36	14	121
Belgian	71	88	65	53	117	89	104	63	83	36	93	164
Bolivian	36	41	78	44	49	45	103	94	143	46	115	–
British (UK)	328	322	143	241	240	171	281	233	301	262	320	536
Canadian	75	109	87	111	140	58	34	29	78	43	–	118
Chilean	49	47	27	21	43	32	71	224	305	860	700	1,203
Chinese	253	402	232	766	1,066	432	444	226	897	358	319	198
Czech	5	2	7	2	24	10	5	5	2	1	–	–
Danish	14	18	15	9	55	38	24	14	44	57	–	–
Dutch	119	192	179	167	163	18	128	69	143	77	109	239
Egyptian	80	59	–	45	257	16	15	15	13	16	–	–
Finnish	8	10	6	2	11	7	7	2	4	–	–	–
French	146	121	109	189	122	62	71	34	101	72	146	175
Greek	103	58	32	33	32	3	3	8	10	13	5	–
Hungarian	7	38	4	11	–	–	2	–	3	1	1	–
Indian	–	–	–	–	–	–	–	26	26	31	–	–
Iranian	–	–	–	–	–	–	–	–	–	–	–	–
Irish	–	–	–	–	–	–	–	–	11	13	–	–
Israeli	14	40	33	41	–	6	6	14	15	21	14	–
Jordanian	–	–	–	142	373	3	20	14	17	37	9	–
Korean	–	–	–	–	–	–	–	1,895	1,190	204	–	–
Lebanese	202	188	178	360	299	11	9	9	7	46	1	–
Lithuanian	–	–	–	–	–	–	–	–	–	–	–	–
Moroccan	–	–	–	–	–	–	–	–	–	–	–	–
North American (USA)	764	979	823	1,261	1,537	406	810	675	1,068	874	1,014	1,414
Norwegian	23	12	18	15	20	27	20	11	24	4	–	–
Panamanian	–	–	–	–	–	–	–	–	8	9	–	–
Paraguayan	72	57	60	67	54	29	77	65	83	48	19	–
Peruvian	12	19	34	12	17	26	21	19	32	17	–	–
Polish	38	49	33	19	–	9	14	36	26	18	10	–
Rumanian	37	14	3	1	–	–	1	8	3	5	7	–
South African	–	–	–	–	–	–	–	2	24	18	–	–
Syrian	–	41	27	40	74	7	1	2	4	–	–	–
Swedish	64	46	50	99	116	15	67	59	69	85	–	199
Swiss	37	130	122	103	134	19	86	62	91	88	185	325
Turk/Arab	3	2	6	11	–	6	–	–	2	–	–	–
Uruguayan	171	192	125	108	165	283	202	110	203	165	274	469
Venezuelan	29	21	60	28	37	31	25	13	19	9	–	–
Yugoslav	13	6	18	20	12	11	25	10	11	10	3	–

Sources: AN 1939-1940, pp. 42, 1,307; AN 1949, pp. 70-71; AN 1951, pp. 53-54; AN 1952, pp. 67-68, AN 1956, pp. 480-481; AN 1957 p. 54; AN 1959, p. 39; AN 1961, p. 52; AN 1962, p. 40; AN 1963, p. 38; AN 1964, p. 48; AN 1969, p. 111; AN 1970, p. 83; AN 1973, p. 134; AN 1974, p. 133; AN 1975, p. 107; AN 1976, p. 142.

Table IV-2. Black African Immigration (Slave Importation) to Brazil, 1600-1860

Period	Number
1600-1650	200,000
1651-1700	100,000
1701-1710	153,700
1711-1720	139,000
1721-1730	146,300
1731-1740	166,100
1741-1750	185,100
1751-1760	169,400
1761-1770	164,600
1771-1780	161,300
1781-1790	178,100
1791-1800	221,600
1801-1810	206,200
1811-1820	266,800
1821-1830	325,000
1831-1840	212,000
1841-1850	338,300
1851-1860	3,300
Total	3,336,800

Source: Philip Curtin, quoted in Sánchez-
        Albornoz, pp.74, 97-98, 126.

Table IV-3. Brazilian Immigration and Emigration, 1880-1949

Period	Immigration	Emigration	Net Gain	Net Gain as % of Immigration
1880-1889	448,622	205,100	243,522	54.3
1890-1899	1,198,327	479,900	718,427	60.0
1900-1909	622,407	311,500	310,907	50.0
1910-1919	815,453	115,200	700,253	85.9
1920-1929	846,647	84,500	762,147	90.0
1930-1939	332,768	13,600	319,168	96.0
1940-1949	114,085	16,500	97,585	85.5
Total	4,378,309	1,226,300	3,152,009	72.0

Sources: Clifford J. Jansen; Merrick and Graham

Immigration

Table IV-4. Net Internal Migration by Brazilian Political Subdivisions, 1940-70

Subdivision	Net Migrant Exchange With All Other Subdivisions			
	1940	1950	1960	1970
Paraná	+151,598	+ 590,146	+555,230	+1,096,270
São Paulo	+495,162	+ 556,761	+325,558	+ 412,079
Goiás	+119,466	+ 244,101	+134,740	+ 246,831
Guanabara	+551,300	+ 787,793	+154,451	+ 170,153
Rio de Janeiro	-229,439	- 138,374	+ 8,440	+ 134,136
Mato Grosso	+ 54,317	+ 42,036	+ 17,022	+ 96,020
Maranhão	+ 53,825	+ 60,928	+ 35,439	+ 62,802
Distrito Federal	-	-	+ 3,549	+ 15,210
Pará	+ 35,385	- 9,662	+ 2,016	+ 7,576
Rondônia	-	+ 28,762	+ 2,003	+ 4,030
Amapá	-	+ 29,946	+ 2,059	+ 1,965
Roraíma	-	+ 13,728	+ 1,639	+ 735
Fernando de Noronha	-	+ 493	+ 2,400	- 651
Acre	+ 12,931	+ 15,996	+ 1,019	- 692
Amazonas	+ 28,492	- 3,773	+ 1,087	- 1,895
Espírito Santo	+ 38,611	- 55,067	- 2,894	- 23,406
Santa Catarina	+ 46,400	+ 32,903	- 11,901	- 33,888
Rio Grande do Norte	- 10,009	- 26,381	- 26,591	- 52,201
Sergipe	- 42,111	- 71,309	- 41,417	- 75,488
Piauí	- 47,770	- 58,616	- 36,300	- 76,393
Paraíba	- 54,572	- 146,621	- 64,013	- 123,145
Alagoas	- 74,773	- 140,575	- 83,718	- 127,202
Rio Grande do Sul	- 92,774	- 161,141	- 50,916	- 143,103
Ceará	-116,043	- 160,948	-102,410	- 172,208
Pernambuco	-113,255	- 103,828	-116,760	- 202,457
Bahia	-233,963	- 289,323	-248,404	- 368,983
Minas Gerais	-633,729	-1,156,371	-462,075	- 846,095
Serra dos Aimores	+ 60,951	+ 118,396	+ 747	-

Sources: AN1956, p. 80; RE1960Al, pp. 72-77; RE1970Al, pp. 141-146.

Map IV-1. General Migration Flows in Brazil, 1940-70

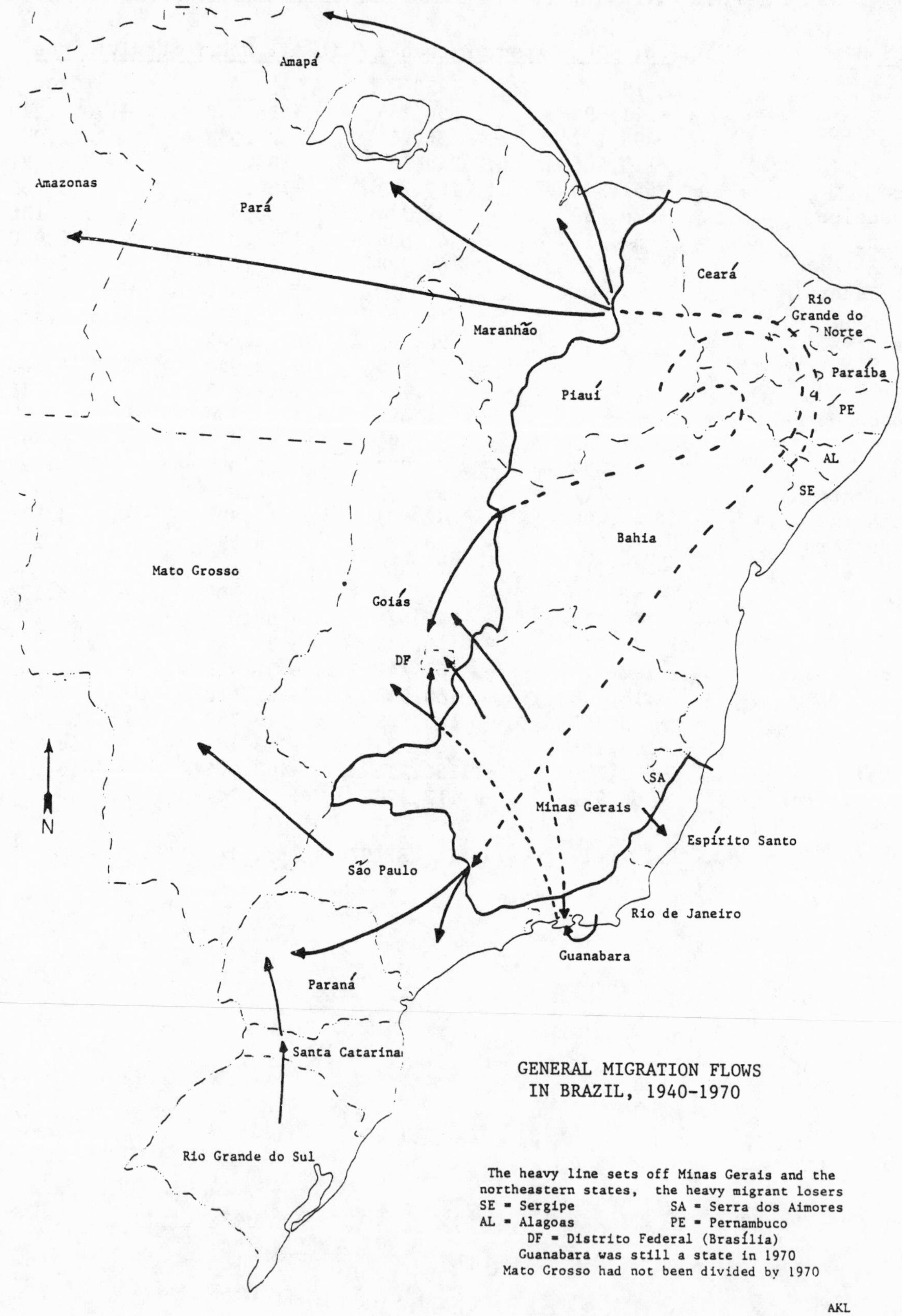

Amapá

Amazonas

Pará

Ceará

Rio Grande do Norte

Maranhão

Paraíba

Piauí

PE

AL

SE

Bahia

Mato Grosso

Goiás

DF

SA

Minas Gerais

Espírito Santo

N

São Paulo

Rio de Janeiro

Guanabara

Paraná

Santa Catarina

GENERAL MIGRATION FLOWS
IN BRAZIL, 1940-1970

Rio Grande do Sul

The heavy line sets off Minas Gerais and the
northeastern states, the heavy migrant losers
SE = Sergipe   SA = Serra dos Aimores
AL = Alagoas   PE = Pernambuco
        DF = Distrito Federal (Brasília)
     Guanabara was still a state in 1970
  Mato Grosso had not been divided by 1970

AKL

Chapter V. Education

The historical phases in the development of the Brazilian educational system are capsulized nicely by Haussmann and Haar,[1] who note that the state manifested virtually no interest in education in an early Brazil characterized by an agrarian-slavocratic society dominated by a rural aristo-cracy. For more than 200 years after their arrival in 1549 the Jesuits dominated the educational scene providing a humanistic, literary, and abstract schooling that cor-responded closely with the cultural value of the elite. The Jesuits were expelled in 1759 by Portuguese Prime Minister Pombal, who replaced them with lay teachers, expanded the basic curricula to include some scientific and technical subjects, and developed advanced schools for training military officers and public administrators. During the Empire (1822-89) postsecondary professional schools were established in a variety of scientific and technical fields as well as in the arts and humanities. Law schools became the elite training grounds, according to Haussmann and Haar. Primary schooling was expanded and, although most basic schooling was preparatory to admission to the professional schools, agricultural, teacher-training and vocational-technical schools were also established.

The Republican Constitution of 1891 produced a dual educational system: a primary, secondary and higher system operated by the states, and a secondary and higher system controlled by the federal government. The positivist influences in the new government ironically had more impact on the state than on the federal system. State curricula came to include more sciences and mathematics and focused on skill development and the acquisition and analysis of knowledge. The federal system, however, focused on classical subjects in the French lycée model and was dedicated to preparation for higher education.

In the early years of the first Vargas era (1930-45) education was to provide a mechanism for social and economic change. In 1931 Francisco Campos, minister of education and health, created a two-level secondary educational system. It was comprised of a five-year basic course and a two-year preparatory course for professional study.

The 1946 Constitution authorized a new national educational plan, major elements of which were embodied in a bill presented to Congress in 1948. After thirteen years of debate, compromise, and revision the Law of Directives and Bases of National Education was passed in 1961. It paid little attention to higher education and, as Haussmann and Haar note, only modified the existing educational system. It entitled Brazilian children between the ages of seven and fourteen to eight years of free and compulsory first-level schooling, but even where such public facilities were made available many children had to work and were unable to take advantage of the educational opportunities offered. The academic-specialized dichotomy at the senior high school (colégio) level remained. Despite this two-track system nearly all colégio graduates, whether from the academic or specialized track, desired admission to the small number of university places available. The number of universities expanded sharply through the 1960s and growth reached a peak in the early 1970s. Nevertheless, the number of places in them was not sufficient to accommodate those who sought entrance.

In August of 1971 Law No. 5,692 was passed to reform the entire Brazilian educational system. It increased the free and compulsory educational period, providing for a first level made up of the old primário and ginásio levels (these corresponded to the American primary and junior high schools). The new second level replaced the old colégio, which corresponded to the American senior high school. The curriculum of grades five through eight was enriched with compulsory vocational training courses. At the second level the academic curriculum was complemented by work-oriented special studies, a rather popular and cumbersome system.

The numbers of Brazilian school units, teachers, and students from 1871 through 1970 are presented in Table V-1. The 1871, 1872, and 1920 figures originated with the 1872 and 1920 censuses. Those for all other pre-1940 years are from two publications of the Directoria Geral de Estatística--the Estatística do instrucção and the Relatório, ano 1922--and from the Anuários estatísticos do Brasil, numbers III, IV, and V. All other figures were generated by the Serviço de Estatística da Educação e Cultura.

Prior to 1970 the term "school unit" was not defined by the Brazilian sources but presumably it referred to a school per se. For 1970 the term referred to the number of study tracks (<u>cursos</u>). A given school might have offered more than one track and thus have been recorded as being more than one unit. From 1871 through 1960 teaching staffs were presumably reported according to the numbers of individuals on a staff. In 1970 "teaching staff" was defined in terms of "professor/cursos." Thus, one teacher teaching in two separate tracks equaled two teachers. The 1872 teaching staff figures were from an occupational table in the 1872 census, which reported "<u>profesores e homens de letras</u>" (teachers and men of letters). None of the sources specified whether teaching staff totals included part-time staff members as well.

From 1871 through 1960 the numbers of students matriculated were based on <u>matricula geral</u> (general matriculation), which is not defined but which presumably counted initial matriculation in a given year without regard to no-shows and early dropouts. The latter were certainly taken into account in the reporting of effective matriculation and obviously accounted for in the numbers matriculated at the end of the school year, which data sets, however, were not available for all years. The use of general matriculation figures not only retains longitudinal continuity in Table V-1 but also better reflects the numbers of Brazilians seeking educational opportunities. From 1871 through 1960 the numbers of students graduated referred to the numbers completing a track (<u>conclusões de cursos</u>). The 1970 figures referred to the numbers of students passing exams (<u>aprovações</u>) at the end of a track.

Most of the information shown on Table V-1 refers to the formal Brazilian educational system. Its pre- and post-1971 structure as laid out by the Ministry of Education and Culture and reported in Haussmann and Haar is presented graphically on the next page in modified form. The nation's educational system also includes supplementary schools, mostly public, outside this formal pattern. These schools are geared principally to young persons who have not kept up with their age groups in the formal system. Adult literacy schools are also part of this system.

Figures on primary schools for the period 1871 through 1960 included data for pre-primary schools as well. From 1907 through 1950 the figures on junior and senior high specialized schools included some data for specialized schools that existed at the primary level in that period. The postsecondary figures for 1960 included graduate schools, but sources for figures prior to 1960 did not indicate whether graduate school data were included. From 1907 through 1950 the major "Other" category included supple- mentary schools and might have incorporated a few types of

113

specialized schools. No figures for either of these two classes of schools were available for 1960 so no major "Other" category appears. For 1970 the major "Other" category includes data on supplementary primary schools and on junior high vocational training courses (ginásios orientados para o trabalho) outside the formal specialized courses. All these figures are actually for the year 1969 but are included to show the magnitude of supplementary schooling in the Brazilian educational system.

	Pre-1971		Post-1971	Age
		Apprentice Training		— 18
LEVEL EDUCATION	SENIOR HIGH SCHOOL (colégio)	ACADEMIC Classical Scientific Other	SECOND-LEVEL SCHOOLING	— 17 — 16 — 15
		SPECIALIZED Industrial Commercial Agricultural Nursing Artistic Other		
		PEDAGOGICAL		
MIDDLE	JUNIOR HIGH SCHOOL (ginásio)	ACADEMIC COMMERCIAL INDUSTRIAL AGRICULTURAL PEDAGOGICAL	FIRST-LEVEL SCHOOLING	— 14 — 13 — 12 — 11 — 10
	PRIMARY EDUCATION			9 8 7

Brazil's early reliance upon the private educational sector continued into the mid-twentieth century. As late as 1955 more than two-thirds of all junior and senior high academic units shown on Table V-1 were privately administered, but this proportion had begun to decline by 1970. The greatest increase in public sector units after 1960 occurred among supplemental primary and university units.

During the twentieth century, increases in school enrollments have exceeded the national population increases by considerable amounts. From 1907 to 1930 enrollments increased by 226.4 percent, the population by 71.0 percent. Between 1930 and 1940 these respective figures were 63.4 and 9.6 percent. From 1940 to 1950 they were 66.6 and 26.0 percent, and from 1950 to 1970 enrollments increased by 206.9

percent as compared to a population increase of 79.3 percent. The 1970 figures on Table V-1 are not totaled since the major "Other" category does not include middle-level supplemental schools. The percent increase would be even larger with these schools counted.

Table V-2 reports the numbers of undergraduate fields of study, faculty, female faculty, students matriculated, and students graduated for each university by name and location for 1955 and 1970. It also reports the number of graduate offerings at the masters and doctoral levels in each university and isolated establishment by name for 1975. The undergraduate data originated with the Serviço de Estatística da Educação e Cultura and in Ensino superior, legislação e jurisprudência[2] by Guido de Carvalho who drew upon data supplied by the Setor de Documentação e Informação do Departamento de Assuntos Universitários.

Sources differ regarding the founding dates of Brazilian universities shown on Table V-2 but the problem may be one of definition of a university. Haussmann and Haar note that "Brazil's first university, the University of Rio de Janeiro, was not created until 1920." Carvalho, however, refers to the Universidade Federal de Paraná in Curitiba, founded in 1912, as Brazil's first university. Haussmann and Haar report that "to be a university an educational institution must comprise five or more institutes," but they do not indicate whether the rule operated as early as 1912. Isolated, single-purpose colleges unaffiliated with a university or consortium have long dominated the Brazilian higher educational system, and for the mid-1970s (exact year not specified) Haussmann and Haar report 786 such institutions. Table V-2 reports 1,077 fields of study in isolated establishments in 1970. Probably many fewer than 1,077 establishments existed in 1970 because several offered more than one course of study. Carvalho lists sixty-eight Brazilian universities in existence by 1972, although he provides no dates of founding for six of these. Of the sixty-two whose dates of founding are shown on Table V-2, thirty-two were created in the decade 1960-69.

Table V-3 shows the numbers of undergraduate students by sex and the numbers of students graduated by major fields of study in Brazilian institutions of higher education from 1956 to 1970. The data originated with the Serviço de Estatística da Educação e Cultura. Students listed as graduating in 1956 actually graduated at the end of the 1955 school year. Sources for the 1956 figures did not specify whether they included graduate students, but if they did, judging by 1960 graduate student figures, the 1956 graduate student numbers were not large and probably do not distort comparisons with

1960 or 1970 figures. From 1955 to 1960 the numbers of undergraduates grew by 33 percent and from 1960 to 1970 by 324 percent. Between 1956 and 1970 several fields increased their proportions of the total university student body. The philosophy, science, and letters fields led by letters, education, mathematics, sciences, history, and geography, nearly doubled the proportion of the total number of students enrolled. The proportion of students studying administration also rose sharply while student proportions declined in the fields of law, medicine, engineering, dentistry, and the arts.

Graduate school matriculates and degrees conferred by fields in 1960, 1969, and 1970 are presented on Table V-4. The figures originated with the Serviço de Estatística da Educação e Cultura. From 1960 to 1970 the numbers of graduate students matriculated increased by 89.7 percent, but the numbers of degrees conferred (1960-69) grew by only 42.1 percent. The proportion of total graduate students in the philosophy, science, and letters fields rose sharply from 1960 to 1970. Proportions fell in the fields of law, nursing, and the arts.

Table V-5 reports the expenditures for public education in Brazil from 1901 through 1976. The origins of the figures for 1901 through 1907 and for 1931 are not given by the respective sources: The Brazilian Yearbook, 1909 and Brazil of Today (1931). The 1919 figures originated with the census of 1920. The 1942 figures were originated by the Serviço de Estatística da Educação e Saúde of the conselho Técnico de Economia e Finanças of the Ministério da Fazenda and by the Balanços Financeiros dos Estados. The 1950 and 1960 figures originated with the Contadoria Geral da República and the Conselho Técnico de Economia e Finanças. The 1969 figures were originated by the Subsecretaria de Economia e Finanças, the Inspetoria Geral de Finanças, and the Conselho Técnico de Economia e Finanças. The Orçamento Geral de União and the Secretaria de Economia e Finanças originated the 1976 figures.

The 1901 state figures were for only four political subdivisions: Alagoas, Bahia, Espírito Santo, and Piauí. The 1902 state figures were for all political subdivisions except Mato Grosso, Maranhão, Pará, Pernambuco, and the Distrito Federal (later Guanabara). The state figures for 1903, 1904, and 1905 were for all political subdivisions except Mato Grosso; those for 1906 for all but Bahia and Maranhão; those for 1907 for all but Alagoas, Amazonas, Bahia, Espírito Santo, Maranhão, Pará, Pernambuco, and Piauí. The state figures for 1908 were for the Distrito Federal (later Guanabara) only. State educational budgets for Pará,

Paraná, and Pernambuco were for split calendar years, for example, 1901/1902. The author added these figures to the first year appearing in the split year budgets. Thus, the 1901/1902 educational budget for Pará was added to other state educational budgets for the year 1901.

The author used the budget of the Ministry of Education and Culture as the federal education budget for 1960 and 1969. Educational expenditures in 1976 at the county level included only those counties in which were located the capital cities of the political subdivisions. The Distrito Federal was also included with these counties. In 1976 the total federal budget included transfers to the political subdivisions, some of which may have been used for education.

Table V-5, where feasible, shows each government level's percent of the total Brazilian expenditure for education. It also shows the percent of each level's budget spent on education. In 1901, for example, the Cr$ 1,814,000 spent by the states on education (excluding Alagoas, Bahia, Espírito Santo and Piauí) represented 7.8 percent of the aggregate budgets for all but these four states.

In Brazil since 1902 the burden of educational expenditures has fallen on the states whose proportions have ranged from one-half to more than two-thirds of the country's total outlays for education. The educational portion of the states' budgets increased steadily between 1942 and 1976, rising from 12.6 to 18.5 percent of the total. The federal outlays for education remained below 5.0 percent until after 1942, although any given year not shown on Table V-5 may yield a higher proportion. From 1950 on, Table V-5 shows that the proportion of the federal budget dedicated to education rose sharply, peaking with outlays in 1969 for federal universities. Since then it has fallen considerably in the years reported.

Table V-6 presents the levels of educational attainment among persons ten years of age and older in Brazil from 1940 through 1970. All the data are from the respective dicennial censuses. In 1940 only 5.4 percent of the population ten years of age and older had completed elementary schooling. This proportion rose sharply to 14.7 percent in 1950, to 20.6 percent in 1960, and then leveled off somewhat, reaching 22.5 percent in 1970. The proportion of Brazilians twenty years of age and older who had completed high school was only 2.2 percent in 1960 but had doubled to 4.5 percent by 1970.

The numbers of college-level graduates in the Brazilian population are shown by fields of study for the years 1940 through 1970 on Table V-7. All these data originated with the national censuses for the given years. Among Brazilians twenty-four years of age and older only 0.7 percent had attained postsecondary degrees in 1940 and this figure rose to only 0.8 percent by 1950. In 1960 it was 1.1 percent and by 1970 1.5 percent of the population twenty-four and over had earned a college-level degree. The professions, law, engineering, medicine, dentistry, and the military, dominated the fields represented in all four censuses, but by 1960 liberal arts and economics/accounting fields had begun to rival them.

Literacy in Brazil, as reported in the censuses from 1872 to 1970, is shown on Table V-8. Only persons five years of age and older were censused. A "yes" to the question "can you read and write" was tantamount to a respondent's being literate. The literate proportion of the Brazilian population decreased slightly between 1872 and 1890 and again between 1900 and 1920, but then increased progressively and steeply to 60.3 percent in 1970.

References

1. Fay Haussmann and Jerry Haar, <u>Education in Brazil</u> (Hamden, Conn.: Archon Books, 1978).

2. Guido Ivan de Carvalho, <u>Ensino superior, legislação e jurisprudência</u>, 4th ed., revista e atualizada, 1973.

Table V-1. The Brazilian School System 1871–1970: By School Types; Number of Public and Private Units; Teachers, Matriculates, and Graduates by Sex; and Student/Teacher Ratios

Year / School Type	Units Total	Units No. of Private	Units % Private	Teaching Staff Total	Teaching No. Male	Teaching % Male	Matriculated Total	Matric. No. Male	Matric. % Male	Graduated Total	Grad. No. Male	Grad. % Male	Student/Faculty Ratio
1871 Primary	4,096	—	—	—	—	—	138,232	—	—	—	—	—	—
1872 Primary	4,552	—	—	—	—	—	139,321	—	—	—	—	—	—
Jr/Sr High Academic	—	—	—	—	—	—	181,428	—	—	—	—	—	—
1882 Primary	6,395	—	—	3,525	—	—	320,749	—	—	—	—	—	91.0
Total	—	—	—	—	—	—	—	—	—	—	—	—	—
1888/1889	8,157	—	—	—	—	—	209,374	—	—	—	—	—	—
1907 Primary	12,448	—	—	15,586	6,082	39.0	638,378	355,150	55.7	22,399	12,628	56.4	41.0
Jr/Sr High Academic	373	—	—	2,306	—	—	30,426	—	—	—	—	—	13.2
Jr/Sr High Specialized	44	—	—	—	—	—	—	—	—	—	—	—	—
Pedagogical	177	—	—	510	—	—	5,020	—	—	—	—	—	9.8
Other	25	—	—	1,500	—	—	20,501	—	—	—	—	—	13.7
Post-Secondary	—	—	—	688	—	—	5,795	—	—	—	—	—	8.4
Total	13,067	—	—	20,590	—	—	700,120	—	—	—	—	—	34.0
1920 Primary	21,789	—	—	—	—	—	1,250,729	678,029	54.2	—	—	—	—
1930 Primary	33,049	—	—	53,110	12,768	24.0	2,084,954	1,136,394	54.5	—	—	—	39.3
Jr/Sr High Academic	1,145	—	—	7,436	—	—	72,541	—	—	—	—	—	9.8
Jr/Sr High Specialized	211	—	—	3,312	—	—	29,168	—	—	—	—	—	8.8
Pedagogical	943	—	—	7,816	—	—	84,525	—	—	—	—	—	10.8
Other	87	—	—	1,881	—	—	13,695	—	—	—	—	—	7.3
Post-Secondary	35,435	—	—	73,555	—	—	2,284,883	—	—	—	—	—	31.1
1932 Primary	27,662	—	—	56,320	10,201	18.1	2,071,437	1,087,892	52.5	121,379	59,947	49.4	36.8
Jr/Sr High Academic	394	—	—	5,173	—	—	56,208	—	—	—	—	—	10.9
Jr/Sr High Specialized	258	—	—	3,056	—	—	27,243	—	—	—	—	—	8.9
Pedagogical	1,444	—	—	8,638	—	—	97,799	—	—	—	—	—	11.3
Other	190	—	—	2,838	—	—	21,526	—	—	—	—	—	7.6
Post-Secondary	29,948	8,678	29.0	76,025	—	—	2,274,213	—	—	—	—	—	29.9
Total	38,829	—	—	74,527	10,320	13.8	2,910,441	1,514,686	52.0	203,345	102,224	50.3	39.1
1937 Primary	629	—	—	9,276	—	—	123,590	—	—	—	—	—	13.3
Jr/Sr High Academic	445	—	—	4,242	—	—	30,603	—	—	—	—	—	7.2
Jr/Sr High Specialized	2,507	—	—	11,539	—	—	160,201	—	—	—	—	—	13.9
Pedagogical	217	—	—	3,506	—	—	25,461	—	—	—	—	—	7.3
Other	42,627	11,618	27.3	103,090	—	—	3,250,296	—	—	—	—	—	31.5
Post-Secondary	41,670	—	—	80,920	—	—	3,302,857	—	—	240,383	—	—	40.8
Total	821	—	—	12,026	—	—	170,057	—	—	19,828	—	—	14.1
1940 Primary	616	—	—	4,663	—	—	52,454	—	—	10,517	—	—	11.2
Jr/Sr High Academic	825	—	—	2,380	—	—	43,085	—	—	11,304	—	—	18.1
Jr/Sr High Specialized	381	—	—	3,697	—	—	25,151	—	—	8,589	—	—	6.8
Commercial	159	—	—	1,438	—	—	16,978	—	—	1,992	—	—	11.8
Domestic	610	—	—	1,520	—	—	12,251	—	—	2,873	—	—	8.1
Pedagogical	1,243	—	—	5,720	—	—	90,028	—	—	—	—	—	17.1
Industrial	258	—	—	3,922	—	—	20,017	—	—	4,223	—	—	5.1
Artistic	46,583	14,292	30.7	115,836	—	—	3,732,878	—	—	322,355	—	—	32.2

120

Table V-1 (continued)

Year	Category	Units Total	Units No. of Private	Units % Private	Teaching Staff Total	Teaching Staff No. Male	Teaching Staff % Male	Students Matriculated Total	Students Matriculated No. Male	Students Matriculated % Male	Students Graduated Total	Students Graduated No. Male	Students Graduated % Male	Student/Faculty Ratio
1950	Primary	77,625	-	-	137,526	-	-	5,240,142	-	-	427,340	-	-	38.1
	Jr/Sr High Academic	2,072	-	-	25,610	-	-	406,920	-	-	60,048	-	-	14.2
	Jr/Sr High Specialized	-	-	-	-	-	-	-	-	-	-	-	-	-
	Commercial	874	-	-	8,953	-	-	85,905	-	-	18,649	-	-	9.6
	Pedagogical	768	-	-	6,973	-	-	40,415	-	-	15,680	-	-	5.8
	Industrial	2,359	-	-	9,333	-	-	109,904	-	-	27,459	-	-	11.8
	Agricultural	139	-	-	1,335	-	-	11,239	-	-	1,685	-	-	8.4
	Artistic	1,228	-	-	3,297	-	-	31,468	-	-	6,161	-	-	9.5
	Other	2,468	-	-	9,439	-	-	247,924	-	-	77,001	-	-	26.3
	Post-Secondary	437	-	-	7,097	-	-	44,097	-	-	7,120	-	-	6.2
	Total	87,970	-	-	210,563	-	-	6,218,014	-	-	641,143	-	-	29.5
1955	Junior High Academic	1,850	1,395	75.4	27,607	14,867	53.7	495,832	253,350	50.1	-	-	-	17.9
	Senior High Academic	739	507	68.6	11,404	8,267	72.5	77,932	58,646	75.3	-	-	-	6.8
	Post-Secondary	715	-	-	12,768	-	-	72,652	-	-	14,316	-	-	5.7
1960	Primary	95,938	9,265	9.7	255,569	13,989	6.2	7,458,002	3,798,467	50.9	549,634	269,455	49.0	33.1
	Junior High Academic	2,921	-	-	45,618	-	-	785,705	-	-	97,306	-	-	17.2
	Senior High Academic	939	-	-	15,326	-	-	118,547	-	-	23,319	-	-	7.7
	Jr/Sr High Specialized	-	-	-	-	-	-	-	-	-	-	-	-	-
	Commercial	1,393	-	-	15,764	-	-	194,158	-	-	29,746	-	-	12.3
	Pedagogical	1,408	-	-	14,517	-	-	97,457	-	-	24,817	-	-	6.7
	Industrial	442	-	-	7,460	-	-	27,327	-	-	3,708	-	-	3.7
	Agricultural	99	-	-	1,183	-	-	6,852	-	-	1,916	-	-	5.8
	Artistic	440	-	-	1,206	-	-	5,902	-	-	1,794	-	-	4.9
	Nursing	56	-	-	638	-	-	2,237	-	-	1,068	-	-	3.5
	Other	383	-	-	3,458	-	-	43,328	-	-	3,697	-	-	12.5
	Post-Secondary	1,571	-	-	24,517	-	-	102,971	-	-	19,432	-	-	4.2
1970	Primary	146,136	9,312	6.4	457,406	-	-	12,812,029	6,443,116	50.3	1,324,565	-	-	28.0
	Junior High Academic	8,745	4,803	54.9	196,347	84,377	43.0	3,080,201	1,545,138	50.2	406,236	191,461	47.1	15.7
	Senior High Academic	6,034	3,679	61.0	112,205	59,718	53.2	1,003,385	476,523	47.5	225,913	96,265	42.6	8.9
	Junior High Specialized	-	-	-	-	-	-	-	-	-	-	-	-	-
	Commercial	1,061	926	87.3	15,534	8,568	55.2	234,873	131,759	56.1	31,603	17,513	55.4	15.1
	Pedagogical	412	108	26.2	5,980	1,589	26.6	85,183	37,543	44.1	8,324	2,450	29.4	14.2
	Industrial	220	64	29.1	9,141	4,641	50.8	113,207	71,915	63.5	12,570	7,765	61.8	12.4
	Agricultrual	98	15	15.3	1,309	849	64.9	11,730	10,016	85.4	1,883	1,747	92.8	9.0
	Artistic	5	3	60.0	114	23	20.2	429	74	17.2	18	-	-	3.8
	Nursing	26	17	65.4	296	55	18.6	1,292	117	9.1	26	24	92.3	4.4
	Other	132	70	53.0	3,069	1,312	42.8	42,598	21,039	49.4	7,918	3,638	45.9	13.4
	Senior High Specialized	-	-	-	-	-	-	-	-	-	-	-	-	-
	Commercial	1,611	1,266	78.6	21,832	15,963	73.1	219,101	138,578	63.2	46,710	31,157	66.7	10.0
	Pedagogical	2,248	1,346	59.9	33,443	9,660	28.9	262,690	21,275	8.1	89,089	7,151	8.0	7.9
	Industrial	155	91	58.7	7,762	6,282	80.9	49,522	45,068	91.0	7,129	6,187	86.8	6.3
	Agricultural	76	7	9.2	1,202	905	75.3	8,146	7,585	93.1	1,525	1,457	95.5	6.8
	Artistic	5	3	60.0	114	18	15.9	300	57	19.0	33	10	30.3	2.6
	Nursing	6	6	100.0	65	29	44.6	171	39	22.8	-	-	-	2.6
	Other	17	9	52.9	379	106	28.0	1,089	72	6.6	312	-	-	2.9
	Other	7,769	1,027	13.2	25,558	1,811	7.1	719,688	415,065	57.8	395,112	227,694	57.6	28.2
	Post-Secondary Undergrad.	2,221	-	-	42,968	34,070	79.3	430,473	265,305	61.6	64,049	-	-	10.0
	Post-Secondary Graduate	55	-	-	-	-	-	4,995	2,992	59.9	-	-	-	-

Sources: RE 1872; RE 1920D4, pp. VI & VII; AN 1939-40, pp. 1393 & 1397; AN 1941-45, p. 384; AN 1955, pp. 432, 444, 450-460; AN 1956, p. 338; AN 1962, pp. 281-288; AN 1972, pp. 698-831.

Table V-2. Brazilian Universities by Dates of Founding, Administrative
Jurisdictions, Locations, Numbers of Undergraduate Fields of
Study, Faculty (by Sex), Students, and Student/Faculty
Ratios, 1955 and 1970, and Graduate Programs Offered, 1975

Date of Founding	Admin. Jurisdict.	University	City	PS	1970 No. of Fields	1970 No. of Faculty	1970 No. of Female Faculty
1912	F	U. Federal do Paraná	Curitiba	PR	33	895	100
1920	F	U. Federal do Rio de Janeiro	Rio de Janeiro	GB	75	2,315	253
1927	F	U. Federal de Minas Gerais	Belo Horizonte	MG	45	1,665	279
1934	S	U. de São Paulo	São Paulo	SP	65	2,295	412
1936	F	U. Federal do Rio Grande do Sul	Pôrto Alegre	RS	42	1,474	238
1944	F	U. Federal Rural do Rio de Janeiro	Kilometer 47	RJ	13	204	32
1946	F	U. Federal da Bahia	Salvador	BA	54	1,047	278
1946	F	U. Federal de Pernambuco	Recife	PE	54	1,204	211
1946	P	Pontifícia U. Católica de São Paulo	São Paulo	SP	14	338	118
1946	P	Pontifícia U. Católica do Rio de Janeiro	Rio de Janeiro	GB	22	376	72
1948	P	Pontifícia U. Católica do Rio Grande do Sol	Pôrto Alegre	RS	24	685	68
1951	P	U. Católica de Pernambuco	Recife	PE	14	196	50
1951	S	U. do Estado da Guanabara (Rio de Janeiro	Rio de Janeiro	GB	27	535	87
1952	F	Fundação U. do Maranhão	São Luís	MA	15	220	85
1952	P	Universidade Mackensie	São Paulo	SP	19	392	33
1954	F	U. Federal Rural de Pernambuco	Recife	PE	2	59	5
1954	P	U. Mineira de Arte	Belo Horizonte	MG	-	-	-
1955	F	U. Federal do Ceará	Fortaleza	CE	24	749	81
1955	P	U. Católica de Campinas	Campinas	SP	20	307	53
1955	F	U. Federal de Paraíba	João Pessoa	PB	30	567	100
1957	F	U. Federal do Pará	Belém	PA	30	541	95
1958	F	U. Federal do Rio Grande do Norte	Natal	RN	16	235	59
1958	P	U. Católica de Minas Gerais	Belo Horizonte	MG	22	439	125
1959	P	U. Católica de Goiás	Goiânia	GO	16	155	32
1960	F	U. Federal de Santa Catarina	Florianópolis	SC	22	665	103
1960	F	U. Federal de Goiás	Goiânia	GO	22	484	101
1960	P	U. Católica do Paraná	Curitiba	PR	15	275	26
1960	P	U. Católica de Pelotas	Pelotas	RS	31	433	122
1960	F	U. Federal de Juiz de Fora	Juiz de Fora	MG	18	370	40
1961	F	U. Federal Fluminense	Niterói	RJ	32	1,038	173
1961	P	U. Católica de Petrópolis	Petrópolis	RJ	11	140	20
1961	P	U. Católica de Salvador	Salvador	BA	22	286	140
1961	F	U. Federal do Espirito Santo	Vitória	GO	20	424	73
1961	F	U. Federal de Santa Maria	Santa Maria	RS	24	569	146
1961	F	U. Federal de Alagoas	Maceió	AL	20	239	30
1964	S	U. Estadual de Campinas	Campinas	SP	12	386	53
1965	F	U. de Amazonas	Manaus	AM	19	350	62
1965	S	U. para o Desenvolvimento do Estado de Santa Catarina	Florianópolis	SC	3	94	8
1965	S	U. Norte Mineira	Montes Claros	MG	9	115	40
1966	S	U. de Itaúna	Itaúna	MG	9	112	19
1966	F	Fundação U. de Brasília	Brasília	DF	26	519	102
1966	M	U. Regional do Nordeste	Campina Grande	PB	6	77	12
1967	M	U. Municipal de Taubaté	Taubaté	SP	17	233	37
1967	F	U. Federal de Sergipe	Aracaju	SE	12	198	58
1967	M	U. Regional do Rio Grande do Norte	Mossoró	RN	7	91	23
1967	P	U. de Caxias do Sul	Caxias do Sul	RS	19	220	45
1968	M	Fundaçao U. Regional de Blumenau	Blumenau	SC	9	112	8
1968	P	U. de Passo Fundo	Passo Fundo	RS	17	252	85
1969	P	U. do Vale do Rio do Sinos	São Leopoldo	RS	15	193	21
1969	F	U. Federal de São Carlos	São Carlos	SP	2	11	1
1969	P	U. de Uberlândia	Uberlândia	MG	13	101	28

Table V-2 (continued)

1970 No. of Students	1970 Student/ Faculty Ratio	1970 No. of Students Graduated	1955 No. of Fields	1955 No. of Faculty	1955 No. of Female Faculty	1955 No. of Students	1955 No. of Students Graduated	No. of Graduate Programs Offered, 1975		
								Masters	Doctorate	Total
7,776	7.9	1,288	29	375	-	3,000	742	12	2	14
16,585	7.2	2,735	60	1,773	-	8,218	2,819	58	29	87
11,941	7.2	1,603	38	655	-	3,118	464	26	8	34
24,061	10.5	2,776	33	623	-	7,486	1,016	133	94	227
8,882	6.0	1,275	41	933	-	3,323	620	26	3	29
1,627	8.0	239	2	85	-	314	79	2	-	2
8,848	8.5	1,190	29	426	-	2,161	486	13	1	14
8,783	7.3	1,718	38	582	-	3,118	647	21	-	21
3,493	10.3	775	39	644	-	2,712	505	13	-	13
3,942	10.5	501	28	672	-	1,604	337	21	6	27
6,088	8.9	1,035	26	340	-	1,783	421	7	-	7
3,227	16.5	657	12	170	-	857	115	-	-	-
5,847	10.9	958	25	418	-	3,967	808	5	-	5
2,143	9.7	314	-	-	-	-	-	-	-	-
6,416	16.4	1,327	10	157	-	2,061	247	1	1	2
378	6.4	88	2	70	-	229	37	-	-	-
-	-	11	-	-	-	-	-	-	-	-
6,694	8.9	1,272	21	231	-	1,016	225	5	-	5
4,056	13.2	604	19	209	-	1,664	360	2	-	2
3,504	6.2	633	9	128	-	411	63	6	-	6
5,044	9.3	679	-	-	-	-	-	1	1	2
2,016	8.6	483	-	-	-	-	-	-	-	-
5,058	11.5	868	-	-	-	-	-	-	-	-
1,963	12.6	252	-	-	-	-	-	-	-	-
3,104	4.5	508	-	-	-	-	-	7	-	7
4,644	9.6	442	-	-	-	-	-	3	-	3
2,436	8.9	532	-	-	-	-	-	-	-	-
3,178	7.3	211	-	-	-	-	-	-	-	-
2,642	7.1	395	-	-	-	-	-	-	-	-
12,547	12.1	1,704	-	-	-	-	-	16	1	17
1,280	9.1	134	-	-	-	-	-	-	-	-
3,623	12.7	257	-	-	-	-	-	-	-	-
3,198	7.5	509	-	-	-	-	-	-	-	-
3,298	5.8	503	-	-	-	-	-	10	-	10
2,561	10.7	512	-	-	-	-	-	-	-	-
1,540	4.0	96	-	-	-	-	-	18	7	25
2,920	8.3	282	-	-	-	-	-	-	-	-
465	4.9	106	-	-	-	-	-	-	-	-
719	6.3	61	-	-	-	-	-	-	-	-
1,039	9.3	155	-	-	-	-	-	-	-	-
3,269	6.3	477	-	-	-	-	-	13	2	15
731	9.5	110	-	-	-	-	-	-	-	-
4,913	21.1	542	-	-	-	-	-	-	-	-
1,225	6.2	130	-	-	-	-	-	-	-	-
354	3.9	58	-	-	-	-	-	-	-	-
2,188	9.5	287	-	-	-	-	-	-	-	-
739	6.6	-	-	-	-	-	-	-	-	-
2,472	9.8	328	-	-	-	-	-	-	-	-
2,858	14.8	224	-	-	-	-	-	-	-	-
100	9.1	-	-	-	-	-	-	-	-	-
2,210	21.9	308	-	-	-	-	-	-	-	-

Table V-2 (continued)

Date of Founding	Admin. Jurisdict.	University	City	PS	1970 No. of Fields	1970 No. of Faculty	1970 No. of Female Faculty
1969	F	U. Federal de Ouro Preto	Ouro Preto	MG	8	111	–
1969	F	U. Federal de Viçosa	Viçosa	MG	4	193	26
1969	F	U. Federal de Pelotas	Pelotas	RS	2	78	18
1969	F	U. Federal do Piauí	Teresina	PI	1	22	–
1970	F	U. do Rio Grande	Rio Grande	RS	1	25	1
1970	F	U. Federal de Mato Grosso	Cuiabá	MT	–	–	–
1970	S	U. Estadual de Mato Grosso	Campo Grande	MT	–	–	–
1970	S	Fundação U. de Minas Gerais	Belo Horizonte	MG	2	68	1
1971	S	U. Estadual do Acre	Rio Branco	AC	–	–	–
–	S	U. Estadual de Ponta Grossa	Ponta Grossa	PR	–	–	–
–	–	U. do Sul de Minas	–	MG	4	31	14
–	–	U. de Nordeste de Minas	–	MG	5	27	6
–	S	U. de Maringá	Maringá	PR	–	–	–
–	F	U. de Itajubá	–	MG	4	31	18
–	–	U. Presidente Antônio Carlos	–	MG	5	56	12
–	F	Instituto de Pesquisas da Amazônia	–	AM	–	–	–
–	P	Faculdade de Odontologia de Pernambuco	–	PE	–	–	–
1972	P	U. Gama Filho	–	RJ	–	–	–
–	F	Instituto Militar de Engenharia	–	RJ	–	–	–
–	F	Instituto de Matemática Pura e Aplicada	–	RJ	–	–	–
–	F	Instituto Brasileiro de Bibliografia e Documentação	–	RJ	–	–	–
–	F	Centro Brasileiro de Pesquisas Físicas	–	RJ	–	–	–
–	P	Fundação Getúlio Vargas (Rio de Janeiro)	–	RJ	–	–	–
–	P	Inst. Universitário de Pesquisas do Rio de Janeiro	–	RJ	–	–	–
–	F	Escola Superior de Agricultura de Lavras	–	MG	–	–	–
–	F	Escola Paulista de Medicina	–	SP	–	–	–
–	P	Instituto de Física Teórica	–	SP	–	–	–
–	P	Instituto Brasileiro de Estudos e Pesquisas em Gastroenterologia	–	SP	–	–	–
–	P	Fundação Escola de Sociologia e Política	–	SP	–	–	–
–	P	Fundação Getúlio Vargas (São Paulo)	–	SP	–	–	–
–	P	Universidade Metodista Piracicaba	–	SP	–	–	–
–	F	Instituto de Pesquisas Espaciais	–	SP	–	–	–
–	F	Instituto Tecnológico da Aeronáutica	–	SP	–	–	–
–	S	Faculdade de Ciências Medicas e Biológicas de Botucatu	–	SP	–	–	–
–	P	Faculdade de Filosofia, Ciência e Letras "Sagrado Coração de Jesus" – Bauru	–	SP	–	–	–
–	P	Faculdade de Filosofia, Ciências e Letras "Barao de Mauá" – Ribeirão Preto	–	SP	–	–	–

Total:	Universities 1970 and 1955			1,144	25,522	4,838
Total:	Isolated Establishments 1970 and 1955			1,077	17,446	4,060
Total:	Post-Secondary System 1970 and 1955			2,221	42,968	8,898
Total:	Graduate Programs Offered 1975					

Sources: AN 1956, pp. 358-359; AN 1971, p. 713; AN 1972, pp. 824-826; Ensino superior, pp. 651-657; Present Situation of Graduate Studies in Brazil, 1975, pp. 6-8.

124

Table V-2 (continued)

1970 No. of Students	1970 Student/ Faculty Ratio	1970 No. of Students Graduated	1955 No. of Fields	1955 No. of Faculty	1955 No. of Female Faculty	1955 No. of Students	1955 No. of Students Graduated	Number of Graduate Programs Offered, 1975		
								Masters	Doctorate	Total
615	5.5	149	-	-	-	-	-	-	-	-
789	4.1	147	3	78	-	195	49	9	3	12
527	6.8	173	-	-	-	-	-	4	-	4
216	9.8	87	-	-	-	-	-	-	-	-
161	6.4	139	-	-	-	-	-	-	-	-
-	-	69	-	-	-	-	-	-	-	-
-	-	24	-	-	-	-	-	-	-	-
666	9.8	198	-	-	-	-	-	-	-	-
-	-	59	-	-	-	-	-	-	-	-
-	-	207	-	-	-	-	-	-	-	-
667	21.5	-	-	-	-	-	-	-	-	-
650	24.1	-	-	-	-	-	-	-	-	-
-	-	172	-	-	-	-	-	-	-	-
438	14.1	51	-	-	-	-	-	2	-	2
462	8.3	56	-	-	-	-	-	-	-	-
-	-	-	-	-	-	-	-	1	-	1
-	-	-	-	-	-	-	-	1	-	1
-	-	-	-	-	-	-	-	1	-	1
-	-	-	-	-	-	-	-	6	1	7
-	-	-	-	-	-	-	-	1	1	2
-	-	-	-	-	-	-	-	1	-	1
-	-	-	-	-	-	-	-	1	1	2
-	-	-	-	-	-	-	-	4	1	5
-	-	-	-	-	-	-	-	2	-	2
-	-	-	-	-	-	-	-	2	-	2
-	-	-	-	-	-	-	-	11	9	20
-	-	-	-	-	-	-	-	1	1	2
-	-	-	-	-	-	-	-	1	-	1
-	-	-	-	-	-	-	-	1	1	2
-	-	-	-	-	-	-	-	1	-	1
-	-	-	-	-	-	-	-	2	-	2
-	-	-	-	-	-	-	-	6	3	9
-	-	-	-	-	-	-	-	6	6	12
-	-	-	-	-	-	-	-	1	1	2
-	-	-	-	-	-	-	-	3	-	3
-	-	-	-	-	-	-	-	2	-	2
223,726	8.8	33,683	454	8,569	-	47,237	10,400	-	-	-
206,747	11.9	30,366	350	5,019	-	28,187	4,276	-	-	-
430,473	10.0	64,049	804	13,588	1,843	75,424	14,316	-	-	-
-	-	-	-	-	-	-	-	489	183	572

Table V-3. Numbers of Undergraduate Students by Sex and Number Graduated by Major Fields of Study in Brazilian Institutions of Higher Education, 1956-70

	1956			1960		1970			
	Number of Students Matriculated	% of Students Matriculated	Number of Students Graduated	Number of Students Matriculated	Number of Students Graduated	Number of Students Matriculated	% of Students Matriculated	Female Students Matriculated	Students Graduated
Philosophy/Science/Letters	13,071	17.3	2,974	20,741	5,353	123,384	34.5	85,582	23,631
Letters	3,868	5.1	773	—	—	34,499	9.6	25,868	6,405
Education	3,196	4.2	1,272	—	—	21,816	6.1	18,463	5,443
Mathematics	904	1.2	138	—	—	10,050	2.8	4,119	1,636
Sciences	212	-	42	—	—	9,947	2.8	5,455	1,623
History	2,002	2.7	341	—	—	9,160	2.5	6,620	1,909
Geography	(2,002)	(2.7)	(341)	—	—	6,302	1.8	4,543	1,349
Social Sciences	507	-	35	—	—	6,985	2.0	4,930	1,094
Philosophy	1,012	1.3	187	—	—	4,943	1.4	2,787	1,321
Psychology	-	-	-	—	—	4,866	1.4	4,100	942
Natural History	976	1.3	131	—	—	3,602	1.0	2,270	646
Physics	394	-	55	—	—	3,530	-	704	275
Other	-	-	-	—	—	7,684	2.1	5,723	998
Law	18,835	25.0	2,273	22,835	3,228	71,236	19.9	17,441	8,959
Engineering	7,171	9.5	1,026	11,192	1,550	29,213	8.2	894	6,417
Civil	4,594	6.1	676	—	—	12,914	3.6	413	2,679
Mechanical	357	-	37	—	—	4,723	1.3	32	1,462
Electrical	803	1.1	111	—	—	4,605	1.3	99	961
Chemical	311	-	74	—	—	2,242	-	263	436
Electronic	107	-	14	—	—	665	-	11	153
Industrial	245	-	5	—	—	-	-	-	200
Metallurgical	43	-	3	—	—	453	-	3	182
Mining	182	-	29	—	—	183	-	-	53
Other	529	-	77	—	—	3,428	-	73	291
Economics	4,367	5.8	528	8,073	1,088	19,790	5.5	2,362	4,298
Accounting	1,382	1.8	271	957	122	4,371	1.2	651	1,218
Administration	605	-	29	—	—	15,359	4.3	1,602	3,344
Medicine	12,650	16.8	2,747	10,503	1,540	32,287	9.0	7,095	4,270
Dentistry	4,808	6.4	1,322	5,522	1,320	9,254	2.6	3,089	1,806
Agriculture	1,274	1.7	274	1,930	332	6,371	1.8	440	1,200
Social Service	1,194	1.6	277	1,371	247	6,201	1.7	5,784	780
Arts	2,309	3.0	602	4,947	1,440	4,900	1.4	3,879	782
Music	1,071	1.4	426	—	—	3,113	-	2,588	437
Other	1,238	1.6	176	—	—	1,787	-	1,291	345
Physical Education	586	-	245	665	242	4,651	1.3	2,146	882
Operations Engineering	-	-	-	—	—	4,570	1.3	115	871
Architecture/Urban Planning	1,713	2.3	328	1,699	326	4,527	1.3	1,452	519
Pharmacy	1,621	2.1	487	1,806	366	3,955	-	1,961	1,078
Veterinary Medicine	730	-	146	821	140	2,830	-	339	724
Nursing	1,592	2.1	392	1,523	318	2,726	-	2,606	851
Journalism	461	-	71	503	92	2,181	-	1,303	570
Library Science	170	-	102	270	99	2,164	-	2,010	498
Other	885	-	216	3,980	819	7,926	2.2	3,602	1,351
Total By Major Field	75,424	100.0	14,316	100,338	18,622	357,896	100.0	144,353	64,049
Basic Courses (No Field Yet)	-	-	-	-	-	67,582	-	15,820	-
Total	75,424		14,316	100,338	18,622	425,478		160,173	64,049

Sources: AN 1956, pp. 359-360; AN 1962, p. 287; AN 1972, pp. 830-833.

Table V-4. Graduate School Matriculation by Sex and Degrees Conferred by Field, 1960-70

Major Field	1960 Students Matriculated	1960 Students Graduated	1969 Students Matriculated	1969 Female Students Matriculted	1969 Students Graduated	1970 Students Matriculated	1970 Female Students Matriculated
Philosophy/Science/Letters	567	226	1,891	1,177	110	2,729	1,677
Mathematics	–	–	–	–	–	657	194
Education	–	–	512	313	67	304	254
Psychology	–	–	151	109	35	153	146
Hist/Geog/Soc/Poli Sci	–	–	15	6	8	17	4
Other	–	–	1,213	749	–	1,598	1,079
Administration/Economics	–	–	96	29	44	637	52
Hygiene/Public Health	211	124	307	135	576	452	–
Pharmacy	7	2	17	10	–	–	–
Other	204	122	290	125	576	452	–
Engineering	186	118	396	14	16	274	9
Agriculture	–	–	185	28	163	449	112
Architecture/Urban Planning	114	19	160	45	69	116	25
Law	807	88	635	179	74	154	52
Medicine	23	6	85	11	27	60	7
Nursing	164	72	37	37	25	50	50
Construction Sciences	–	–	–	–	–	32	11
Dentistry	–	–	40	5	4	26	2
Nutrition	–	–	18	4	13	10	6
Art	214	44	15	15	15	6	–
Physical Education	137	74	29	7	–	–	–
Veterinary Medicine	–	–	11	–	15	–	–
Bio-Sciences	–	–	33	11	15	–	–
Biochemistry	–	–	20	8	4	–	–
Other	–	–	13	3	11	–	–
Other	210	39	–	–	–	–	–
Total	2,633	810	3,938	1,697	1,151	4,995	2,003

Sources: AN 1962, pp. 287-288; AN 1971, p. 739.

Table V-5. Expenditures for Public Education in Brazil, 1901-76

Government Level	1901 Cr$ 1000	1901 % of Brazil Total	1901 % of Govt. Level	1902 Cr$ 1000	1902 % of Brazil Total	1902 % of Govt. Level	1903 Cr$ 1000	1903 % of Brazil Total	1903 % of Govt. Level	1904 Cr$ 1000	1904 % of Brazil Total	1904 % of Govt. Level	1905 Cr$ 1000	1905 % of Brazil Total	1905 % of Govt. Level
Federal	3,439	-	1.1	3,547	-	1.3	3,568	-	1.1	3,758	-	.9	3,903	-	1.1
State	1,814	-	7.8	16,592	-	11.2	24,250	-	11.8	23,911	-	11.1	23,618	-	8.4
County	-	-	-	-	-	-	-	-	-	-	-	-	-	-	-
Brazil Total	-	-	-	-	-	-	-	-	-	-	-	-	-	-	-

Government Level	1906 Cr$ 1000	1906 % of Brazil Total	1906 % of Govt. Level	1907 Cr$ 1000	1907 % of Brazil Total	1907 % of Govt. Level	1919 Cr$ 1000	1919 % of Brazil Total	1919 % of Govt. Level	1931 Cr$ 1000	1931 % of Brazil Total	1931 % of Govt. Level	1942 Cr$ 1000	1942 % of Brazil Total	1942 % of Govt. Level
Federal	4,117	-	1.1	4,909	-	-	-	-	-	70,392	-	4.8	162,711	23.7	2.8
State	24,546	-	7.5	-	-	12.6	-	-	12.8	-	-	-	467,926	68.3	12.6
County	-	-	-	-	-	-	16,086	-	9.4	-	-	-	54,788	8.0	5.4
Brazil Total	-	-	-	-	-	-	-	-	-	-	-	-	685,425	100.0	-

Government Level	1950 Cr$ 1000	1950 % of Brazil Total	1950 % of Govt. Level	1960 Cr$ 1000	1960 % of Brazil Total	1960 % of Govt. Level	1969 Cr$ 1000	1969 % of Brazil Total	1969 % of Govt. Level	1976 Cr$ 1000	1976 % of Brazil Total	1976 % of Govt. Level
Federal	2,497,474	47.1	10.6	18,029,848	33.1	6.8	1,150,053	26.2	6.2	8,351,037	-	4.4
State	2,632,809	49.7	14.2	32,158,332	59.0	14.5	2,769,138	63.0	17.4	21,667,933	-	18.5
County	170,598	3.2	4.2	4,335,524	7.9	9.4	473,314	10.8	11.5	-	-	-
Brazil Total	5,300,881	100.0	-	54,523,704	100.0	-	4,392,505	100.0	-	-	-	-

Sources: BY 1909, pp. 366-7, 368-9, 371-412; RE 1920D4, p. VI; BOT, p. 185; AN 1946, p. 451; AN 1952, pp. 504, 525, 539; AN 1961, p. 435; AN 1962, pp. 344, 350; AN 1970, pp. 725, 728; AN 1972, pp. 940-1; AN 1977, p. 726; AN 1978, p. 754.

Education

Table V-6. Level of Elementary or Secondary Education Completed and Subjects Studied by Persons in Brazil Ten Years of Age and Older, 1940-70

1940	Elementary Level				Junior & Senior High Level			
Subjects:	Male	Female	Total	% of Total	Male	Female	Total	% of Total
General Academic	753,964	740,474	1,494,438	95.7	100,857	85,649	186,506	52.0
Teacher Training	111	1,176	1,287	.1	4,874	57,871	62,745	17.5
Commercial	1,506	690	2,196	.1	46,018	8,885	54,903	15.3
Industrial	2,607	288	2,895	.2	2,072	234	2,306	.7
Military	1,243	-	1,243	.1	684	-	684	.2
Agricultural	304	106	410	negl.	771	91	862	.2
Nursing	-	-	-	-	-	-	-	-
Domestic Arts	297	10,289	10,586	.7	240	1,730	1,970	.5
Other Specialized	23,445	25,010	48,455	3.1	30,580	18,130	48,710	13.6
Total	783,477	778,033	1,561,510	100.0	186,096	172,590	358,686	100.0
1950								
Subjects:								
General Academic	2,701,891	2,682,103	5,383,994	99.9	358,282	270,521	628,803	63.7
Teacher Training	-	-	-	-	11,300	166,429	177,729	18.0
Commercial	361	533	894	negl.	105,288	42,371	147,659	15.0
Industrial	715	674	1,389	negl.	9,466	2,700	12,166	1.2
Military	1,140	-	1,140	negl.	2,899	-	2,899	.3
Agricultural	229	105	334	negl.	2,024	81	2,105	.2
Nursing	131	238	369	negl.	1,533	6,817	8,350	.8
Domestic Arts	-	-	-	-	-	-	-	-
Other Specialized	369	206	575	negl.	5,118	2,319	7,437	.8
Total	2,704,836	2,683,859	5,388,695	100.0	495,910	491,238	987,148	100.0

129

Table V-6 (continued)

	Elementary Level				Junior High Level				Senior High Level			
	Male	Female	Total	% of Total	Male	Female	Total	% of Total	Male	Female	Total	% of Total
1960												
Subjects:												
General Academic	5,054,336	5,015,743	10,070,079	99.9	613,436	577,620	1,191,056	90.1	199,740	101,539	301,279	41.5
Teacher Training	-	-	-	-	12,125	104,646	116,771	8.8	20,514	198,543	219,057	30.2
Commercial	80	53	133	negl.	2,258	1,338	3,596	.3	151,235	50,578	210,813	27.8
Industrial	165	67	232	negl.	984	372	1,356	.1	1,961	321	2,282	.3
Military	481	12	493	negl.	5,022	28	5,050	.4	411	46	457	.1
Agricultural	47	19	66	negl.	169	21	190	negl.	346	8	354	negl.
Nursing	-	-	-	-	-	-	-	-	-	-	-	-
Domestic Arts	-	-	-	-	-	-	-	-	-	-	-	-
Other Specialized	1,364	1,181	2,545	negl	1,086	2,907	3,993	.3	157	127	284	negl.
Total	5,056,473	5,017,075	10,073,548	100.0	635,080	686,932	1,322,012	100.0	374,364	351,162	725,526	100.0
1970												
Subjects:												
General Academic	7,388,734	7,395,524	14,784,258	99.9	1,314,543	1,268,218	2,582,761	98.1	564,577	276,294	840,871	42.6
Teacher Training	173	542	715	negl.	2,577	18,506	21,083	.8	37,925	676,196	714,121	36.2
Commercial	621	602	1,223	negl.	10,144	8,244	18,388	.7	263,809	106,292	370,101	18.7
Industrial	1,970	637	2,607	negl.	4,063	975	5,038	.2	19,259	2,555	21,814	1.1
Military	520	73	593	negl.	1,054	39	1,093	negl.	2,597	126	2,723	.1
Agricultural	170	117	287	negl.	443	41	484	negl.	4,125	184	4,309	.2
Nursing	-	-	-	-	279	1,220	1,499	negl.	402	2,943	3,345	.2
Domestic Arts	-	-	-	-	-	-	-	-	-	-	-	-
Other Specialized	139	95	234	negl.	1,562	1,060	2,622	.1	11,627	5,454	17,081	.9
Total	7,392,327	7,397,590	14,789,917	100.0	1,334,665	1,298,303	2,632,968	100.0	904,321	1,070,674	1,974,995	100.0

Sources: RE 1940A2, p. 32; RE 1950A1, p. 25; RE 1960A1, p. 22; RE 1970A1, p. 36.

Table V-7. Persons in Brazil with Postsecondary Degrees by Major Fields
of Study, 1940-70

| Subject Field | 1940 | | | | 1950 | | | |
	Male	Female	Total	% of Total	Male	Female	Total	% of Total
Law	20,145	482	20,627	20.5	30,254	1,048	31,302	19.8
Liberal Arts	-	-	-	-	-	-	-	-
Engineering	13,912	96	14,008	13.9	20,256	183	20,439	12.9
Medicine	18,042	543	18,585	18.4	24,718	1,093	25,811	16.3
Economics/Accounting	1,735	158	1,893	1.9	5,150	371	5,521	3.5
Dentistry	10,817	1,225	12,042	11.9	15,291	2,027	17,318	11.0
Military	5,089	-	5,089	5.1	13,612	-	13,612	8.6
Pharmacology/Bio-chemistry	8,242	1,841	10,083	10.0	8,685	2,560	11,245	7.1
Agronomy/Agriculture	3,652	47	3,699	3.7	5,735	79	5,814	3.7
Religion	4,598	86	4,684	4.6	8,535	-	8,535	5.4
Nursing	-	-	-	-	-	-	-	-
Industrial Chemistry	1,558	125	1,683	1.7	3,095	401	3,496	2.2
Administration	-	-	-	-	-	-	-	-
Architecture	-	-	-	-	1,560	78	1,638	1.0
Social Work	-	-	-	-	-	-	-	-
Veterinary Medicine	1,250	34	1,284	1.3	1,632	35	1,667	1.1
Physical Education	249	87	336	.3	450	465	915	.6
Fine Arts	1,037	2,835	3,872	3.8	-	-	-	-
Psychology	-	-	-	-	-	-	-	-
Statistics	-	-	-	-	-	-	-	-
Other	2,473	455	2,928	2.9	5,260	5,497	10,757	6.8
Total	92,799	8,014	100,813	100.0	144,233	13,837	158,070	100.0

| Subject Field | 1960 | | | | 1970 | | | |
	Male	Female	Total	% of Total	Male	Female	Total	% of Total
Law	51,768	3,845	55,613	19.3	79,673	11,459	91,132	16.8
Liberal Arts	15,992	17,477	33,469	11.6	26,024	55,704	81,728	15.1
Engineering	39,314	692	40,006	13.9	67,452	1,267	68,719	12.7
Medicine	36,925	3,232	40,157	13.9	48,316	5,786	54,102	10.0
Economics/Accounting	12,141	1,269	13,410	4.7	44,893	6,262	51,155	9.5
Dentistry	24,623	3,801	28,424	9.9	29,941	6,476	36,417	6.7
Military	22,030	19	22,049	7.7	18,002	46	18,048	3.3
Pharmacology/Bio-chemistry	11,207	4,485	15,692	5.5	10,469	4,933	15,402	2.8
Agronomy/Agriculture	9,056	217	9,273	3.2	12,857	474	13,331	2.5
Religion	9,471	338	9,809	3.4	12,073	907	12,980	2.4
Nursing	-	-	-	-	586	8,233	8,819	1.6
Industrial Chemistry	4,082	380	4,462	1.5	7,502	1,227	8,729	1.6
Administration	-	-	-	-	6,325	1,154	7,479	1.4
Architecture	3,504	402	3,906	1.4	5,905	1,186	7,091	1.3
Social Work	-	-	-	-	575	5,120	5,695	1.1
Veterinary Medicine	3,172	289	3,461	1.2	4,558	280	4,838	.9
Physical Education	453	465	918	.3	2,138	2,586	4,724	.9
Fine Arts	461	537	998	.3	1,257	3,120	4,377	.8
Psychology	-	-	-	-	844	1,980	2,824	.5
Statistics	410	97	507	.2	574	108	682	.1
Other	2,146	3,654	5,800	2.0	22,895	20,188	43,083	8.0
Total	246,755	41,199	287,954	100.00	402,852	138,496	541,348	100.0

Sources: RE 1940A2, p. 32; RE 1950A1, p. 25; RE 1960A1, p. 22; RE 1970A1, p. 37

Brazil: A Handbook of Historical Statistics

Table V-8. Literacy in Brazil, 1872-1970

	Male	%	Female	%	Total	% of Total
1872						
Literate	1,013,055	19.8	551,426	11.5	1,564,481	15.8
Illiterate	4,110,814	80.2	4,255,183	88.5	8,365,997	84.2
Total	5,123,869	100.0	4,806,609	100.0	9,930,478	100.0
1890						
Literate	1,385,854	19.1	734,705	10.4	2,120,559	14.8
Illiterate	5,852,078	80.9	6,361,278	89.6	12,213,356	85.2
Total	7,237,932	100.0	7,095,983	100.0	14,333,915	100.0
1900						
Literate	2,767,621	31.1	1,701,060	19.9	4,468,681	25.6
Illiterate	6,132,905	68.9	6,836,848	80.1	12,969,753	74.4
Total	8,900,526	100.0	8,537,908	100.0	17,438,434	100.0
1920						
Literate	4,470,068	28.9	3,023,289	19.9	7,493,357	24.5
Illiterate	10,973,750	71.1	12,168,498	80.0	23,142,248	75.5
Total	15,443,818	100.0	15,191,787	100.0	30,635,605	100.0
1940						
Literate	7,344,772	42.3	5,947,833	34.1	13,292,605	38.2
Illiterate	9,908,255	57.1	11,387,235	65.3	21,295,490	61.2
Not Known	105,560	.6	103,010	.6	208,570	.6
Total	17,358,587	100.0	17,438,078	100.0	34,796,665	100.0
1950						
Literate	9,966,382	46.0	8,622,340	39.3	18,588,722	42.6
Illiterate	11,645,573	53.8	13,262,023	60.5	24,907,596	57.2
Not Known	37,170	.2	40,029	.2	77,199	.2
Total	21,649,125	100.0	21,924,392	100.0	43,573,517	100.0
1960						
Literate	16,362,285	55.7	15,000,498	50.6	31,362,783	53.2
Illiterate	12,978,840	44.2	14,600,131	49.3	27,578,971	46.7
Not Known	30,909	.1	25,318	.1	56,227	.1
Total	29,372,034	100.0	29,625,947	100.0	58,997,981	100.0
1970						
Literate	24,402,668	62.0	23,461,863	58.7	47,864,531	60.3
Illiterate	14,592,133	37.1	16,126,464	40.4	30,718,597	38.7
Not Known	366,597	.9	377,506	.9	744,103	1.0
Total	39,361,398	100.0	39,965,833	100.0	79,327,231	100.0

Sources: RE 1872; RE 1890C, p. 373; RE 1920D4,p. XVI; RE 1920A2, p. 28; RE 1950A1, p. 18; RE 1960A1, p. 16; RE 1970A1, p. 22.

Chapter VI. Work Force:
Categories of Employment

Table VI-1 presents figures on employment by industry group in Brazil from 1872 to 1970. The data originated with the Brazilian censuses, which from 1872 (a census that included slaves) through 1920 included persons of all ages in their employment figures but which from 1940 through 1970 included only persons ten years of age and older. The 1960 and 1970 data are for "all persons," meaning a respondent could report more than one economic activity. These data are in sufficient industry group detail to permit a reorganization of the categories to conform to United States census groupings and to provide longitudinal consistency in industry groups on Table VI-1. In the 1940 and 1950 censuses, however, only industry groups reported according to "principal activity" (meaning one activity per person) were detailed enough to permit the reorganization of these groups and the maintenance of longitudinal consistency. The 1960 and 1970 censuses sharply reduced this discrepancy between "all persons" and "principal activity." Based on calculations dealing with figures on Table VI-2 later in this chapter the 1960 census had reduced this differential to 10,904, and in the 1970 census only 5,604 more activities were calculated to be in the "all persons" than in the "principal activity" count.

In 1872 and 1890 the Brazilian labor force figures reflected the classic dichotomy between agriculture and personal/business service activities that marked and has continued to mark so many third world countries. By 1920, following the industrial boomlet during World War I, employment in Brazilian manufacturing industries had risen to take second place among the industry groups shown on Table VI-1. The year 1920 also saw agricultural employment attain the highest percentage (63.9) of any industry group in the ninety-eight-year period covered by Table VI-1. From 1950 to 1970 the proportion of the labor force in agriculture declined steadily while the proportion in personal/business services rose steadily. The proportion in manufacturing fell slightly from 1950 to 1960 and rose between 1960 and 1970. Several of the smaller industry groups increased their proportions of the Brazilian labor force between 1950 and 1970. Among these were the social service, public administration, retail/wholesale, and finance/insurance/real-estate groups.

The economically active and noneconomically active populations in Brazil from 1872 to 1970 are presented on Table VI-2. The 1900 figures did not include persons in the Distrito Federal because the census was not completed in this political subdivision in that year. For 1960 the economically active population ten years of age and older and the noneconomically active population ten and older (from Table 18, RE 1960A1) were added together and this sum was subtracted from the total 1960 Brazilian population (70,191,370). This yielded the value for the category "other noneconomically active," which totaled 21,362,716 but overstated the Brazilian population under ten years of age (21,351,812) shown on Table II-7 in this work. The discrepancy of 10,904 is the difference between the "all persons" and "principal activity" counts reported in the Brazilian censuses. Reporting by "all persons" allows an individual to state more than one economic activity. In the male "other economically active" category there are 8,532 more persons than there are persons ten years of age and older, and in the female category there are 2,372 more. This same condition prevails in the 1970 figures. Among the 27,276,918 persons in the "other noneconomically active" category (from Table 20, RE 1970A1) only 27,271,314 are ten years of age and under according to Table II-7 in this work. This is a discrepancy of 5,604 persons. Among the males in this category the differential is 4,937 and among females 667. The urban-rural figures show reversed differentials. There are 9,444 more persons under ten in urban areas than the "other noneconomically active" category shows and 15,048 fewer persons under ten in rural areas than are shown in the category. The discrepancy remains at 5,604 (15,048 minus 9,444).

The 1940 and 1950 figures are for the principal activity of persons ten years of age and older. The censuses for 1872, 1900, and 1920 did not specify whether their counts were for "all persons" or for "principal activity," but they included persons of all ages, not just those ten and older. The 1872 figures included slaves.

Figures on Table VI-2 document some very sharp shifts in the dependency ratio during the ninety-eight years covered. This ratio is the quotient derived by dividing the number of economically active persons into the number of non-economically active persons. Normally the dependency ratio is based on age groups, the 15-64 age group being a surrogate

for the economically active group and the 0-14 and 65 and
older groups being surrogates for the noneconomically active
group (see the text for Table II-7). The dependency ratio
calculated here is based on whether a person tells the census
taker that he or she is employed rather than on the age
distribution surrogates. In 1872 this ratio stood at 0.72
(4,172,114 noneconomically active persons divided by
5,758,364 economically active persons), and meant that every
100 workers supported themselves and 72 other persons. By
1900 the ratio had fallen to 0.66, and then by 1920 had risen
to a ninety-eight year high of 2.19 (21,027,993 nonactive
divided by only 9,607,612 active). Among the nonactive
persons were 12,631,575 fourteen years of age and under,
2,754,600 from fifteen to twenty years of age, and 5,641,818
twenty-one years of age and older. In 1940 the dependency
ratio was down to 1.35 but by 1950 had risen to 2.03. In
1960 it was 2.09 and by 1970 the dependency ratio had
attained a value of 2.15.

Free and slave employment by occupation/industry group
for 1872 is presented on Table VI-3. The data are taken from
the 1872 census. More than 70 percent of all slaves were
engaged in agricultural pursuits and most of the remainder
were active in domestic service or as daily wage workers.
Some 40,000 slaves (3.5 percent of the total slave work
force), all females, were employed as seamstresses and
another 13,000 (1.1 percent of the total slave work force)
worked in textile mills. Although their numbers were not
large more than 1,800 slaves worked as artists (artistas), an
occupation that the 1872 census classed as a liberal
profession and which probably included artisans and crafts-
men.

Table VI-4 shows the occupational structure of the
Brazilian work force by sex in 1950, 1960, and 1970. The
data are from the Brazilian censuses of those years. The
list of occupations specified by name includes every
occupation whose share of the national total was 0.10 percent
or larger in any one of the three years reported on the
table. To meet this criteria a minimum of 18,117 persons had
to be employed in a given occupation in 1950, or 22,750 in
1960 or 29,557 in 1970. Veterinarians were the only exception to these minima. Each census did not report every
occupation separately. One census grouped several occupations while another distinguished them. When two or more
occupations on the table were grouped for any given year they
were also grouped for all years. The numbers of occupations
reported in the censuses increased with time, and as a
consequence occupations appeared by name in the 1970 census
that did not appear at all in the 1950 or 1960 censuses.
These were carefully matched with occupational groups

reported in earlier censuses and combined with them.

From 1950 to 1970, among those occupations that doubled their proportions of the Brazilian work force, private household employees showed the greatest increase (4.04 percentage points). This was followed by teachers/professors (1.56), truck drivers (1.40), and hod carriers (0.90). Truck farm laborers, nurses, electricians, tellers, and tractor drivers also showed significant increases in their proportions of the Brazilian work force between 1950 and 1970. In the same period the proportion of farm laborers declined by 12.45 percentage points, cooks by 1.75, and farm owners by 1.10. Other significant declines in the proportion of the Brazilian work force were registered by carters/mule drivers, loom operators, rubber gatherers, fiber spinners, and shoemakers.

Table VI-5 presents the distribution by industry group of the work forces in the states of São Paulo and Guanabara and for the rest of Brazil from 1940 to 1970. The data are from the dicennial censuses. The figures for 1940 were for "principal activity" (see text for Table VI-1). They do match the totals on Tables VI-1 and VI-2. If the economically active population on Table VI-5, which sums to 14,655,551 (the industry group categories are not summed on the table), is subtracted from the Total Economically Active on Tables VI-1 and VI-2 (17,580,382), the remainder (2,924,831) is the economically active portion of the 14,382,298 persons shown on Table VI-5 for 1940. When this remainder is subtracted from the 14,382,298 it yields the noneconomically active population on Table VI-2, or 11,457,467. The 1960 and 1970 figures were for "all persons" (see text for Table VI-1), thus permitting data comparability across Tables VI-1, VI-2, and VI-5. The figures for 1950 were for "all persons" since this was the only way the work forces in the political subdivisions were reported in that census. As a consequence the totals for the country as a whole in 1950 do not match those reported on Tables VI-1 and VI-2, for which principal activity is shown. All industry groups are not comparable for all years shown on Table VI-6, thus impairing comparisons across the entire 1940-70 period. Nevertheless, some longitudinal comparisons can be made for some industry groups across the period covered by the table and comparisons between similar categories can be made for several of the years shown on the table.

Table VI-1. Employment by Industry Group of Economically Active Persons
in Brazil by Sex, 1872-1970, and by Sex and Urban/Rural
Residence in 1970

1872

	Total		Male		Female	
	Number	%	Number	%	Number	%
Agriculture/Silviculture	3,037,466	52.7	2,131,830	67.9	905,636	34.6
Ranching	206,132	3.6	147,443	4.7	58,689	2.2
Vegetal Extraction	–		–		–	
Hunting/Fishing	17,742	.3	17,742	.6	–	
Mining	4,332	.1	4,332	.1	–	
Manufacturing	257,010	4.4	118,750	3.8	138,260	5.3
Construction	20,960	.4	20,960	.7	–	
Utilities	–		–		–	
Retail/Wholesale	102,133	1.8	93,577	3.0	8,556	.3
Finance/Insurance/Real Estate	–		–		–	
Personal/Business Services	1,552,065	26.9	196,784	6.2	1,355,281	51.8
Transport/Communication/Warehousing	21,703	.4	21,703	.7	–	
Social Services	6,143	.1	3,639	.1	2,504	.1
Liberal Professions	50,130	.9	44,686	1.4	5,444	.2
Public Administration	13,297	.2	13,297	.4	–	
Public Security/National Defense	27,716	.5	27,716	.9	–	
Other/Mal-Defined/No Declaration	441,535	7.7	297,357	9.5	144,178	5.5
Total Economically Active	5,758,364	100.0	3,139,816	100.0	2,618,548	100.0

Table VI-1 (continued)

1900

	Total		Male		Female	
	Number	%	Number	%	Number	%
Agriculture/Silviculture	4,868,686	48.7	3,828,608	68.8	1,040,078	23.5
Ranching	152,984	1.5	128,501	2.3	24,483	.6
Vegetal Extraction	9,541	.1	7,004	.1	2,537	negl.
Hunting/Fishing	14,935	.1	14,703	.3	232	negl.
Mining	8,761	.1	8,415	.1	346	negl.
Manufacturing	195,599	2.0	17,932	.3	177,667	4.0
Construction	–		–		–	
Utilities	–		–		–	
Retail/Wholesale	322,858	3.2	285,092	5.1	37,766	.9
Finance/Insurance/Real/ Estate	–		–		–	
Personal/Business Services	2,358,759	23.6	134,949	2.4	2,223,810	50.1
Transport/Communication Warehousing	71,986	.7	58,999	1.0	12,987	.3
Social Services	4,725	negl.	3,147	.1	1,578	negl.
Liberal Professions	36,971	.4	25,293	.5	11,678	.3
Public Administration	31,945	.3	31,945	.6	–	
Public Security/National Defense	–		–		–	
Other/Mal-Defined/No Declaration	1,925,118	19.2	1,024,072	18.4	901,046	20.3
Total Economically Active	10,002,868	100.0	5,568,660	100.0	4,434,208	100.0

1920

	Total		Male		Female	
	Number	%	Number	%	Number	%
Agriculture/Silviculture	6,137,751	63.9	5,540,437	68.2	597,314	40.4
Ranching	174,572	1.8	164,967	2.0	9,605	.6
Vegetal Extraction	–		–		–	
Hunting/Fishing	64,557	.7	63,695	.8	862	negl.
Mining	74,650	.8	74,566	.9	84	negl.
Manufacturing	904,143	9.4	474,589	5.8	429,554	29.1
Construction	264,104	2.7	264,104	3.2	–	
Utilities	21,110	.2	21,064	.3	46	negl.
Retail/Wholesale	479,078	5.0	456,835	5.6	22,243	1.5
Finance/Insurance/Real Estate	18,470	.2	17,872	.2	598	negl.
Personal/Business Services	363,879	3.8	70,335	.9	293,544	19.9
Transport/Communication/ Warehousing	253,587	2.6	249,879	3.1	3,708	.3
Social Services	63,525	.7	22,423	.3	41,102	2.8
Liberal Professions	85,957	.9	72,673	.9	13,284	.9
Public Administration	106,992	1.1	106,960	1.3	32	negl.
Public Security/National Defense	97,712	1.0	94,487	1.2	3,225	.2
Other/Mal-Defined/No Declaration	497,525	5.2	434,598	5.3	62,927	4.3
Total Economically Active	9,607,612	100.0	8,129,484	100.0	1,478,128	100.0

Table VI-1 (continued)

1940

	Total		Male		Female	
	Number	%	Number	%	Number	%
Agriculture/Silviculture	9,208,714	52.4	7,949,891	60.2	1,258,823	28.8
Ranching	244,798	1.4	233,422	1.7	11,376	.3
Vegetal Extraction	181,783	1.0	142,735	1.1	39,048	.9
Hunting/Fishing	90,398	.5	89,020	.7	1,378	negl.
Mining	118,379	.7	113,447	.8	4,932	.1
Manufacturing	1,137,356	6.5	846,315	6.4	291,041	6.7
Construction	262,700	1.5	261,056	2.0	1,644	negl.
Utilities	16,750	.1	16,080	.1	670	negl.
Retail/Wholesale	718,632	4.1	671,485	5.1	47,147	1.1
Finance/Insurance/Real Estate	55,305	.3	51,413	.4	3,892	.1
Personal/Business Services	1,450,048	8.2	496,665	3.7	953,383	21.8
Transport/Communication/Warehousing	504,187	2.9	486,475	3.7	17,712	.4
Social Services	202,491	1.2	77,136	.6	125,355	2.9
Liberal Professions	58,382	.3	50,026	.4	8,356	.2
Public Administration	233,416	1.3	211,253	1.6	22,163	.5
Public Security/National Defense	172,212	1.0	170,827	1.3	1,385	negl.
Other/Mal-Defined/No Declaration	2,924,831	16.6	1,345,087	10.2	1,579,744	36.2
Total Economically Active	17,580,382	100.0	13,212,333	100.0	4,368,049	100.0

Table VI-1 (continued)

1950

	Total		Male		Female	
	Number	%	Number	%	Number	%
Agriculture/Siliviculture	9,527,936	55.6	8,801,957	60.2	725,979	29.0
Ranching	358,998	2.1	352,077	2.4	6,921	.3
Vegetal Extraction	251,836	1.5	227,590	1.5	24,246	1.0
Hunting/Fishing	115,475	.7	114,241	.8	1,234	negl.
Mining	115,661	.7	113,153	.8	2,508	.1
Manufacturing	1,608,309	9.4	1,224,621	8.4	383,688	15.3
Construction	584,644	3.4	580,795	4.0	3,849	.2
Utilities	38,252	.2	36,732	.3	1,520	.1
Retail/Wholesale	958,509	5.6	869,448	5.9	89,061	3.5
Finance/Insurance/Real Estate	115,488	.7	102,744	.7	12,744	.5
Personal/Business Services	1,672,802	9.8	746,829	5.1	925,973	36.9
Transport/Communication/ Warehousing	697,089	4.1	668,267	4.6	28,822	1.1
Social Services	434,315	2.5	200,689	1.4	233,626	9.3
Liberal Professions	78,730	.4	64,503	.4	14,227	.6
Public Administration	260,767	1.5	220,636	1.5	40,131	1.6
Public Security/National Defense	251,877	1.5	247,528	1.7	4,349	.2
Other/Mal-Defined/No Declaration	46,674	.3	37,988	.3	8,686	.3
Total Economically Active	17,117,362	100.0	14,609,798	100.0	2,507,564	100.0

1960

	Total		Male		Female	
	Number	%	Number	%	Number	%
Agriculture/Silviculture	11,354,133	49.9	10,192,207	54.6	1,161,926	28.5
Ranching	471,807	2.1	458,974	2.5	12,833	.3
Vegetal Extraction	314,589	1.4	267,184	1.4	47,405	1.1
Hunting/Fishing	136,845	.6	133,977	.7	2,868	.1
Mining	130,925	.6	127,617	.7	3,308	.1
Manufacturing	1,954,187	8.6	1,470,512	7.9	483,675	11.9
Construction	781,247	3.4	774,331	4.1	6,916	.2
Utilities	73,883	.3	70,488	.4	3,395	.1
Retail/Wholesale	1,486,797	6.5	1,315,966	7.0	170,831	4.2
Finance/Insurance/Real Estate	204,392	.9	177,625	1.0	26,767	.6
Personal/Business Services	2,745,958	12.1	1,266,501	6.8	1,479,457	36.3
Transport/Communication/ Warehousing	1,056,227	4.6	1,014,422	5.4	41,805	1.0
Social Services	688,675	3.0	264,620	1.4	424,055	10.4
Liberal Professions	261,934	1.2	212,200	1.1	49,734	1.2
Public Administration	363,669	1.6	290,447	1.6	73,222	1.8
Public Security/National Defense	349,235	1.5	341,907	1.8	7,328	.2
Other/Mal-Defined/No Declaration	375,525	1.7	294,189	1.6	81,336	2.0
Total Economically Active	22,750,028	100.0	18,673,167	100.0	4,076,861	100.0

Table VI-1 (continued)

1970

	Total		Male		Female		Urban		Rural	
Agriculture	Number	%	Number	%	Number	%	Number	%	Number	%
Silviculture	11,799,008	39.9	10,703,851	45.8	1,095,157	17.8	1,421,989	8.6	10,377,019	79.8
Ranching	779,056	2.6	732,524	3.1	46,532	.8	124,894	.8	654,162	5.0
Vegetal Extraction	359,198	1.2	245,971	1.1	113,227	1.8	50,255	.3	308,943	2.4
Hunting Fishing	153,096	.5	150,353	.6	2,743	negl.	67,112	.4	85,984	.7
Mining	175,424	.6	172,276	.7	3,148	.1	98,301	.6	77,123	.6
Manufacturing	3,241,861	11.0	2,633,050	11.2	608,811	9.9	2,886,651	17.4	360,210	2.8
Construction	1,719,714	5.8	1,704,648	7.3	15,066	.2	1,501,726	9.1	217,988	1.7
Utilities	158,428	.5	149,561	.6	8,867	.1	144,763	.9	13,665	.1
Retail Wholesale	2,263,539	7.7	1,893,152	8.1	370,387	6.0	2,080,091	12.6	183.448	1.4
Finance Insurance Real Estate	434,040	1.5	356,329	1.5	77,711	1.3	429,921	2.6	4,119	negl.
Personal Business Services	3,626,494	12.3	1,236,986	5.3	2,389,508	38.8	3,311,595	20.0	314,899	2.4
Transport Communication Warenousing	1,244,395	4.2	1,182,660	5.0	61,735	1.0	1,133,193	6.8	111,202	.8
Social Services	1,470,621	5.0	482,932	2.1	987,689	16.0	1,318,847	8.0	151.774	1.2
Liberal Professions	266,874	.9	204,115	.9	62,759	1.0	259,602	1.5	7,272	.1
Public Administration	633,490	2.1	483,762	2.1	149,728	2.4	602,428	3.6	31,062	.2
Public Security National Defense	518,851	1.8	508,385	2.2	10,466	.2	499,912	3.0	18,939	.1
Other Mal-Defined No Declaration	713,135	2.4	551,222	2.4	161,913	2.6	622,569	3.8	90,566	.7
Total Economically Active	29,557,224	100.0	23,391,777	100.0	6,165,447	100.0	16,548,849	100.0	13,008,375	100.0

Sources: RE 1920D5, pp. VIII-XIII: RE 1940A2, pp. 38-41; RE 1950A1, pp. 34-35; RE 1960A1, pp. 52-53; RE 1970A1, pp. 76-80.

141

Table VI-2. Economically Active and Non-Economically Active Persons in Brazil by Sex, 1872-1970, and by Urban/Rural Residence in 1970

	Total		Male		Female		Urban		Rural	
	Number	%	Number	%	Number	%	Number	%	Number	%
1872										
Economically Active	5,758,364	58.0	3,139,816	61.3	2,618,548	54.5	—	—	—	—
Non-Economically Active	4,172,114	42.0	1,984,053	38.7	2,188,061	45.5	—	—	—	—
Total Population	9,930,478	100.0	5,123,869	100.0	4,806,609	100.0	—	—	—	—
1900										
Economically Active	10,002,868	60.2	5,568,660	66.0	4,434,208	54.1	—	—	—	—
Non-Economically Active	6,624,123	39.8	2,868,413	34.0	3,755,710	45.9	—	—	—	—
Total Population	16,626,991	100.0	8,437,073	100.0	8,189,918	100.0	—	—	—	—
1920										
Economically Active	9,607,612	31.4	8,129,484	52.6	1,478,128	9.7	—	—	—	—
Non-Economically Active	21,027,993	68.6	7,314,334	47.4	13,713,659	90.3	—	—	—	—
Total Population	30,635,605	100.0	15,443,818	100.0	15,191,787	100.0	—	—	—	—
1940										
Economically Active	17,580,382	42.6	13,212,333	64.1	4,368,049	21.2	—	—	—	—
Non-Economically Active	11,457,467	27.8	1,222,278	5.9	10,235,189	49.6	—	—	—	—
Population Under Ten	12,198,466	29.6	6,179,477	30.0	6,018,989	29.2	—	—	—	—
Total Population	41,236,315	100.0	20,614,088	100.0	20,622,227	100.0	—	—	—	—
1950										
Economically Active	17,117,362	32.4	14,609,798	56.5	2,507,564	9.6	—	—	—	—
Non-Economically Active	19,440,628	37.2	3,478,477	13.4	15,962,151	61.3	—	—	—	—
Population Under Ten	15,386,407	30.4	7,796,726	30.1	7,589,681	29.1	—	—	—	—
Total Population	51,944,397	100.0	25,885,001	100.0	26,059,396	100.0	—	—	—	—
1960										
Economically Active	22,750,028	32.4	18,673,167	53.3	4,076,861	11.6	—	—	—	—
Non-Economically Active	26,078,626	37.2	5,519,756	15.7	20,558,870	58.5	—	—	—	—
Other Non-Econ. Active	21,362,716	30.4	10,866,623	31.0	10,496,093	29.9	—	—	—	—
Total Population	70,191,370	100.0	35,059,546	100.0	35,131,824	100.0	—	—	—	—
1970										
Economically Active	29,557,224	31.7	23,391,777	50.5	6,165,447	13.2	16,548,849	31.8	13,008,375	31.7
Non-Economically Active	36,304,895	39.0	9,164,712	19.8	27,140,183	58.0	21,774,407	41.8	14,530,488	35.4
Other Non-Econ. Active	27,276,918	29.3	13,774,854	29.7	13,502,064	28.8	13,761,728	26.4	13,515,190	32.9
Total Population	93,139,037	100.0	46,331,343	100.0	46,807,694	100.0	52,084,984	100.0	41,054,053	100.0

Sources: RE 1920D5, pp. VIII-XI, X-XI, XII-XIII; RE 1940A2, pp. 38-41;
RE 1950A1, pp. 34-35; RE 1960A1, pp. 52-53; RE 1970A1, pp. 76-80.

Table VI-3. Free and Slave Employment in Brazil by Occupation/Industry Group and by Sex, 1972

	Total Population				Slave Population			
	Total	% of Total	Male	Female	Total	% of Total	Male	Female
Lay Religionists	2,225	negl.	2,225	—	—	—	—	—
Regular Religionists	393	negl.	107	286	—	—	—	—
Judges	968	negl.	968	—	—	—	—	—
Lawyers	1,674	negl.	1,674	—	—	—	—	—
Notaries/Scribes	1,493	negl.	1,493	—	—	—	—	—
State-Employed Lawyers	1,204	negl.	1,204	—	—	—	—	—
Justice Officials	1,619	negl.	1,619	—	—	—	—	—
Physicians	1,729	negl.	1,729	—	—	—	—	—
Surgeons	238	negl.	238	—	—	—	—	—
Pharmacists	1,392	negl.	1,392	—	—	—	—	—
Midwives	1,197	negl.	50	1,147	—	—	—	—
Teachers/Professors	3,525	negl.	1,307	2,218	—	—	—	—
Public Employees	10,710	.2	10,710	—	—	—	—	—
Artists	41,203	.7	36,906	4,297	1,858	.2	1,517	341
Military	27,716	.5	27,716	—	—	—	—	—
Merchant Mariners	21,703	.4	21,703	—	1,788	.2	1,788	—
Fishermen	17,742	.3	17,742	—	1,262	.1	1,262	—
Entrepreneurs/Proprietors	31,863	.6	23,140	8,723	—	—	—	—
Manufacturers	19,366	.3	14,496	4,870	—	—	—	—
Business Persons/Bookkeepers	102,133	1.8	93,577	8,556	—	—	—	—
Seamstresses	506,450	8.8	—	506,450	40,766	3.5	—	40,766
Mine/Quarry Workers	4,332	negl.	4,332	—	769	.1	769	—
Metal Workers	19,461	.3	19,461	—	1,075	.1	1,075	—
Wood/Lumber Workers	39,492	.7	39,492	—	5,599	.5	5,599	—
Textile Workers	139,342	2.4	6,313	133,029	13,196	1.1	842	12,354
Construction Workers	20,960	.4	20,960	—	4,013	.3	4,013	—
Leather/Hide Workers	5,627	.1	5,612	15	563	negl.	560	3
Dye Workers	549	negl.	422	127	44	negl.	40	4
Clothing Workers	11,242	.2	11,242	—	1,379	.1	1,379	—
Hat Workers	1,930	negl.	1,711	219	266	negl.	216	50
Shoe Workers	20,001	.3	20,001	—	2,163	.2	2,163	—
Farmers	3,037,466	52.7	2,131,830	905,636	808,401	70.1	503,744	304,657
Ranchers	206,132	3.6	147,443	58,689	—	—	—	—
Daily Wage Workers	409,672	7.1	274,217	135,455	94,488	8.2	49,195	45,293
Domestic Service	1,045,615	18.2	196,784	848,831	175,377	15.2	45,561	129,816
Total Work Force	5,758,364	100.0	3,139,816	2,618,548	1,153,007	100.0	619,723	533,284
Not In The Work Force	4,172,114	42.0	1,984,053	2,188,061	357,799	23.7	185,447	172,352
Total Population	9,930,478	100.0	5,123,869	4,806,609	1,510,806	100.0	805,170	705,636

Source: RE 1872.

Table VI-4. Employment in Brazil by Occupation and by Sex, 1950-70

	1950				1960				1970			
	Total	%	Male	Female	Total	%	Male	Female	Total	%	Male	Female
Total Reporting	18,117,362	100.00			22,750,028	100.00			29,557,224	100.00		
PROFESSIONAL/TECHNICAL PERSONNEL												
Teachers Professors	169,695	.94	29,170	140,525	317,451	1.40	51,654	265,797	726,874	2.50	101,813	625,061
Nurses/Physiotherapists	39,782	.21	12,401	27,381	71,229	.31	20,710	50,519	144,883	.49	29,877	115,006
Accountants/Bookkeepers	46,411	.26	42,330	4,081	91,694	.40	82,052	9,642	117,907	.40	100,668	17,239
Physicians	22,002	.12	21,215	787	34,269	.15	31,920	2,349	44,984	.15	40,468	4,516
Engineers	12,785	.07	12,706	79	29,138	.13	28,873	265	43,905	.15	43,373	532
Laboratory Technicians	8,125	.04	4,868	3,257	27,225	.12	19,250	7,975	38,978	.13	28,568	10,410
Lawyers	15,566	.09	15,220	346	30,066	.13	28,819	1,247	37,719	.13	34,311	3,408
Draftsmen/Cartographers	9,809	.05	9,158	651	19,531	.09	18,394	1,137	36,223	.12	34,290	1,933
Dentists	18,445	.10	17,265	1,180	28,553	.13	26,190	2,363	32,566	.11	28,358	4,208
Clergy	14,590	.08	8,615	5,975	39,664	.17	16,575	23,089	28,457	.10	18,959	9,498
Veterinarians	1,777	negl.	1,167	10	1,949	.01	1,886	63	6,864	.02	6,679	185
MANAGERS/OFFICIALS/PROPRIETORS/MILITARY												
Small Business Owners	380,869	2.10	366,635	14,234	517,746	2.27	494,970	22,776	821,540	2.78	751,110	70,430
Military Personnel(all ranks)	163,425	.90	163,425	0	234,652	1.03	234,020	632	343,705	1.16	343,449	256
Farm Owners	277,418	1.53	269,203	8,215	177,260	.78	170,382	6,878	126,518	.43	122,919	3,599
Factory Owners	62,965	.35	61,880	1,085	64,336	.28	63,145	1,191	97,642	.33	94,293	3,349
Public Administrators	–	–	–	–	33,248	.15	27,783	5,465	80,067	.27	57,013	23,054
Ranch Owners	44,396	.24	42,738	1,658	42,618	.19	41,076	1,542	68,479	.23	66,209	2,270
Bank/Insurance Administrators	–	–	–	–	9,032	.04	8,816	216	46,378	.16	43,678	2,700
Farm/Ranch Administrators	–	–	–	–	12,098	.05	11,992	106	39,078	.13	38,481	597
SERVICE/OFFICE/PRIVATE HOUSEHOLD EMPLOYEES												
Private Household Employees	307,456	1.70	30,629	276,827	947,226	4.16	41,811	905,415	1,697,042	5.74	41,658	1,655,384
Floor Walkers/Sales Clerks	357,961	1.98	309,067	48,894	471,872	2.07	375,172	96,700	781,357	2.64	588,170	193,187
Doorkeepers/Watchmen/Elevator Operators	221,432	1.22	194,022	27,410	373,641	1.64	298,325	75,316	668,824	2.26	524,026	144,798
Door-to-Door Sales Personnel	113,115	.62	108,162	4,953	234,401	1.03	217,703	16,698	321,571	1.09	282,888	38,683
Launderers	123,069	.68	16,374	106,695	225,541	.99	18,240	207,301	254,498	.86	11,337	243,161
Barbers/Hairdressers	55,896	.31	51,302	4,594	97,914	.43	82,090	15,822	116,601	.39	77,468	39,133
Traveling Sales Personnel	43,140	.24	42,781	359	81,445	.36	80,012	1,433	111,607	.38	105,200	6,407
Cooks	373,973	2.06	23,003	350,970	26,596	.12	12,421	14,175	92,722	.31	35,437	57,285
Tellers/Cashiers	24,058	.13	14,345	9,713	44,128	.19	26,575	17,553	89,079	.30	50,697	38,382
Waitpersons	32,126	.18	29,327	2,799	50,887	.22	45,697	5,190	85,136	.29	60,539	24,597
Tax Inspectors/Collectors	–	–	–	–	53,384	.23	28,728	1,444	74,058	.25	70,593	3,465
Police	22,123	.12	22,104	19	24,655	.11	24,527	128	67,475	.23	66,897	578
Typists	18,426	.10	6,485	11,941	43,156	.19	19,678	23,478	60,091	.20	27,200	32,891
Bus Conductors	10,607	.06	9,949	658	22,812	.10	22,255	557	57,231	.19	55,887	1,344
Brokers/Agents	23,162	.13	22,688	474	25,062	.11	24,408	654	56,063	.19	52,581	3,482
Garbage Collectors	14,079	.08	14,071	8	24,183	.11	24,009	174	55,178	.19	54,430	748
Warehouse Personnel	16,512	.09	15,593	919	31,851	.14	29,948	1,903	49,198	.17	46,344	2,854
Gardeners	21,080	.12	20,879	201	26,874	.12	26,337	537	43,897	.15	43,277	620
Commercial Representatives	10,242	.06	10,079	163	9,983	.04	9,636	347	37,800	.13	32,239	5,561
Telephone Operators	10,066	.05	1,517	8,549	17,738	.08	3,385	14,353	34,055	.12	4,850	29,205
Court Reporters/Courtroom Aides	11,976	.06	10,361	1,615	10,501	.05	8,948	1,553	30,247	.10	23,719	6,528
Innkeepers	13,418	.07	8,388	5,030	36,430	.16	23,770	12,660	23,659	.08	13,508	10,151
Telegraphers/Radiotelegraphers	14,813	.08	13,402	1,411	23,466	.10	20,775	2,691	21,039	.07	18,565	2,474

Table VI-4 (continued)

	1950				1960				1970			
	Total	%	Male	Female	Total	%	Male	Female	Total	%	Male	Female
CRAFTS/TRADES/FOREMEN												
Masons	265,876	1.47	265,784	92	400,767	1.76	399,034	1,733	603,187	2.04	601,768	1,419
Carpenters/Joiners	258,001	1.42	256,626	1,375	313,128	1.38	311,307	1,821	410,230	1.39	408,937	1,293
Tailors/Seamstresses	257,804	1.42	81,893	175,911	389,264	1.71	97,053	291,761	405,328	1.37	67,853	337,475
Electricians	46,625	.26	46,316	309	92,795	.41	91,508	1,287	160,985	.54	159,003	1,982
Shoemakers	113,935	.63	104,945	8,990	147,104	.64	137,094	10,010	137,607	.47	117,334	20,273
Painters	60,366	.33	58,888	1,478	91,207	.40	90,290	917	135,725	.46	135,350	375
Potters	72,462	.40	66,521	5,941	109,895	.48	100,878	9,017	98,510	.33	89,550	8,960
Industrial/Construction Foremen	43,081	.24	40,573	2,508	48,039	.21	47,121	918	91,467	.31	87,295	4,172
Bakers	43,181	.24	42,623	558	67,282	.30	65,912	1,370	78,219	.26	77,002	1,217
Pipefitters	22,626	.12	22,603	23	46,476	.20	46,147	329	72,228	.24	72,114	114
Locksmiths	60,986	.34	60,930	56	79,499	.35	79,045	454	68,207	.23	68,028	179
Stonecutters	28,495	.16	28,282	213	31,325	.14	30,795	530	40,602	.14	40,015	587
Typographers	19,727	.11	18,646	1,081	18,900	.08	17,742	1,158	40,410	.14	38,069	2,341
Hatmakers	13,771	.08	2,023	11,748	50,207	.22	2,891	47,316	36,348	.12	655	35,693
Butchers	—	—	—	—	23,839	.10	23,333	506	33,681	.11	33,033	648
OPERATIVES												
Truck Drivers	219,160	1.21	219,086	74	456,079	2.00	454,616	1,463	771,411	2.61	769,385	2,026
Mechanics	165,753	.91	165,160	593	307,470	1.35	304,779	2,691	469,267	1.59	462,097	7,170
Loom Operators	126,794	.70	36,745	90,049	166,439	.73	74,111	92,328	120,323	.41	58,015	62,308
Industrial/Construction Machinery Operators	—	—	—	—	9,388	.04	8,531	857	116,945	.40	107,666	9,279
Packagers/Mailers	—	—	—	—	29,178	.13	16,640	12,538	93,178	.32	55,349	37,895
Lathe Operators	21,686	.12	21,547	139	58,062	.26	57,582	480	80,972	.27	80,468	504
Solderers	14,119	.08	13,628	491	32,717	.14	32,094	623	63,936	.22	62,812	1,124
Carters/Mule Drivers	108,127	.60	107,810	317	102,581	.45	101,974	607	54,595	.18	54,464	131
Fiber Spinners	56,508	.31	12,267	44,241	57,837	.25	18,763	39,074	39,947	.14	14,082	25,865
Spray Painters	—	—	—	—	7,360	.03	7,208	152	32,614	.11	32,133	481
Embroiderers	22,488	.12	338	22,150	38,617	.17	945	37,672	27,422	.09	593	26,829
Charcoal Makers	30,358	.17	29,697	661	29,812	.13	28,690	1,122	24,571	.08	24,083	488
Sheet Metal Workers	15,527	.09	15,284	243	23,431	.10	22,800	631	23,349	.08	23,104	245
Boiler Tenders	21,473	.12	21,226	247	12,312	.05	12,242	70	117	negl.	66	51
NON-RURAL LABORERS												
Hod Carriers	123,517	.68	123,517	0	202,888	.89	201,522	1,366	467,689	1.58	465,512	2,177
Manual Laborers	257,474	1.42	244,720	12,754	212,419	.93	207,610	4,809	380,596	1.29	373,602	6,994
Highway Maintenance Workers	7,862	.04	7,862	0	47,241	.21	47,129	112	33,876	.11	33,837	39
Stevedores	23,696	.13	23,696	0	42,190	.19	42,070	120	26,761	.09	26,734	27
Railroad Maintenance Workers	18,744	.10	18,744	0	42,221	.19	42,103	118	23,709	.08	23,705	4
RURAL LABORERS												
Farm Laborers	9,135,709	50.43	8,421,959	713,750	10,839,839	47.65	9,706,527	1,133,312	11,224,989	37.98	10,168,689	1,056,300
Herders/Ranch Hands	273,020	1.51	268,285	4,735	424,560	1.87	411,776	12,784	739,160	2.50	689,723	49,437
Truck Farm Laborers	61,935	.34	59,838	2,097	226,706	1.00	208,445	18,261	279,720	.95	251,531	28,189
Fishermen	113,182	.62	112,038	1,145	135,268	.59	132,511	2,757	148,422	.50	145,837	2,585
Vegetal Gatherers/Processors	—	—	61,671	662	53,928	.24	15,482	38,446	133,017	.45	26,124	106,893
Woodcutters	62,333	.34	98,728	4,170	73,326	.32	72,278	1,048	102,682	.35	101,271	1,411
Rubber Gatherers	102,898	.57	7,028	1	117,952	.52	112,229	5,723	88,942	.30	85,444	3,498
Tractor Drivers	7,029	.04	42,314	186	35,508	.16	35,371	137	69,910	.24	69,673	237
Sawyers	42,500	.23	34,642	457	44,788	.20	44,479	309	57,259	.19	56,767	492
Gold/Diamond Prospectors/Miners	35,099	.19	9,345	10	32,822	.14	32,004	818	39,320	.13	38,775	545
Miners (other minerals)	9,355	.05			22,128	.10	21,683	445	22,284	.08	22,111	173
All Other Occupations	2,608,089	14.40			2,269,684	9.98			3,676,312	12.43		

Sources: RE 1950A1, pp. 36–45; RE 1960A1, pp. 32–48; RE 1970A1, pp. 50–61.

Table VI-5. Work Forces by Industry Group in Brazil's Most Productive
Political Subdivisions, 1940-70

1940

	Brazil Number	%	São Paulo Number	%	Guanabara Number	%	Rest Of Brazil Number	%
Agriculture/Silviculture/ Ranching	9,453,512	100.0	1,529,055	16.2	18,878	.2	7,905,579	83.6
Vegetal Extraction/Hunting/ Fishing/Mining	390,560	100.0	22,758	5.8	4,582	1.2	363,220	93.0
Manufacturing/Utilities/ Construction	1,416,806	100.0	428,478	30.3	156,497	11.0	831,831	58.7
Retail/Wholesale	718,632	100.0	189,955	26.4	109,470	15.2	419,207	58.4
Finance/Insurance/Real Estate	55,305	100.0	18,315	33.1	11,830	21.4	25,160	45.5
Transportation/Communication/ Warehousing	504,187	100.0	129,524	25.7	64,291	12.8	310,372	61.5
Public Administration	233,416	100.0	70,830	30.3	55,588	23.8	106,998	45.9
National Defense/Public Security	172,212	100.0	24,481	14.2	45,808	26.6	101,923	59.2
Liberal Professions	58,382	100.0	32,345	55.4	19,873	34.0	6,164	10.6
Personal/Business/Social Services	1,652,539	100.0	177,799	10.8	116,057	7.0	1,358,683	82.2
All Other Active & Inactive	14,382,298	100.0	2,563,636	17.8	803,602	5.6	11,015,060	76.6
Total	29,037,849	100.0	5,187,176	17.9	1,406,476	4.8	22,444,197	77.3

1950

	Brazil Number	%	São Paulo Number	%	Guanabara Number	%	Rest Of Brazil Number	%
Agriculture/Silviculture/ Ranching	9,966,965	100.0	1,453,530	14.6	18,100	.2	8,495,335	85.2
Vegetal Extraction/ Hunting/ Fishing/Mining	485,809	100.0	44,501	9.2	6,468	1.3	434,840	89.5
Manufacturing/Utilities/ Construction	2,252,991	100.0	803,590	35.6	251,537	11.2	1,197,864	53.2
Retail/Wholesale	967,237	100.0	250,351	25.9	124,001	12.8	592,885	61.3
Finance/Insurance/Real Estate	116,361	100.0	42,319	36.4	25,805	22.2	48,237	41.4
Personal/Business Services	1,758,800	100.0	426,282	24.2	235,185	13.4	1,097,333	62.4
Transportation/Communication/ Warehousing	698,229	100.0	197,448	28.3	90,059	12.9	410,722	58.8
Liberal Professions	80,791	100.0	26,924	33.3	13,881	17.2	39,986	49.5
Social Services	445,306	100.0	116,024	26.0	72,865	16.4	256,417	57.6
Public Administration	262,917	100.0	57,207	21.7	45,952	17.5	159,758	60.8
National Defense/Public Security	252,093	100.0	35,299	14.0	78,787	31.3	138,007	54.7
Other	48,501	100.0	5,921	12.2	6,446	13.3	36,134	74.5
Total Economically Active	17,336,000	100.0	3,459,396	20.0	969,986	5.6	12,907,518	74.4

1960

	Brazil Number	%	São Paulo Number	%	Guanabara Number	%	Rest Of Brazil Number	%
Agriculture/Silviculture/ Ranching	11,825,940	100.0	1,436,537	12.2	15,081	.1	10,374,322	87.7
Vegetal Extraction/ Hunting/ Fishing/Mining	582,359	100.0	39,195	6.7	5,846	1.0	537,318	92.3
Manufacturing/Utilities/ Construction	2,809,317	100.0	1,053,310	37.5	237,209	8.4	1,518,798	54.1
Retail/Wholesale	1,486,797	100.0	405,714	27.3	157,248	10.6	923,835	62.1
Finance/Insurance/Real Estate/ Personal&Business Services	2,745,958	100.0	137,438	5.0	278,685	10.2	2,329,835	84.8
Transportation/Communication/ Warehousing	1,056,227	100.0	280,923	26.6	109,333	10.4	665,971	63.0
Social Services/Liberal Professions	688,675	100.0	179,051	26.0	91,510	13.3	418,114	60.7
Public Administration & Security/National Defense	712,904	100.0	136,704	19.2	153,910	21.6	422,290	59.2
Other	841,851	100.0	299,669	35.6	127,406	15.1	414,776	49.3
Inactive	26,078,626	100.0	4,805,447	18.4	1,359,893	5.2	19,913,286	76.4
Total	48,828,654	100.0	8,773,988	18.0	2,536,121	5.2	37,518,545	76.8

1970

	Brazil Number	%	São Paulo Number	%	Guanabara Number	%	Rest Of Brazil Number	%
Agriculture/Silviculture/ Ranching/Vegetal Extraction/ Hunting/Fishing	13,090,358	100.0	1,301,830	9.9	14,932	.1	11,773,596	90.0
Manufacturing/Mining/ Construction/Utilities	5,295,427	100.0	2,003,684	37.8	361,653	6.8	2,930,090	55.4
Retail/Wholesale	2,263,539	100.0	627,175	27.7	190,705	8.4	1,445,659	63.9
Personal/Business Services	3,626,494	100.0	1,014,737	28.0	356,660	9.8	2,255,097	62.2
Transportation/Communication/ Warehousing	1,244,395	100.0	351,040	28.2	118,013	9.5	775,342	62.3
Social Services/Liberal Professions	1,470,621	100.0	332,423	22.6	158,170	10.8	980,028	66.6
Public Administration & Security/National Defense	1,152,341	100.0	251,089	21.8	170,576	14.8	730,676	63.4
Other	1,414,049	100.0	487,864	34.5	164,888	11.7	761,297	53.8
Inactive	36,304,895	100.0	6,964,219	19.2	1,867,823	5.1	27,472,853	75.7
Total	65,862,119	100.0	13,334,061	20.2	3,403,330	5.2	49,124,728	74.6

Sources: RE 1940A2, pp. 38-41; SI 1940A, pp. 34 & 36; RE 1950A1, p. 168; RE 1960A1, pp. 100 & 101;
RE 1970A1, pp. 185 & 186.

Chapter VII. Wages, Income Distribution, Housing and Working Conditions

Employment and wages paid in Brazil's mining and manufacturing industries from 1907 to 1970 are shown on Table VII-1. All the pre-1970 data are from the Brazilian censuses; the 1970 data were generated by FIBGE. The 1970 figures on the table are for establishments of five and more employees whose (establishments') value of production was 640 times the largest minimum salary extant in 1970. The number of production workers was reported as of December 31, 1970. The 1960 figures for the number of establishments were for those in existence on January 1, 1960. The number of production workers was the monthly average for 1959 and the annual wages paid were for the year 1959. The 1950 figures for the number of establishments were for those in existence on January 1, 1950. The number of production workers was the 1949 monthly average and the annual wages paid were for the year 1949. The 1940 number of establishments was recorded by the census on September 1, 1940, and the salaries paid were for the year 1939. The 1920 employee remuneration figures included both wages and salaries, not just wages of production workers.

The 1920 census did report the average daily wages of production workers by sex and by age minority for three industry groups. In the textile industry a sample of 108,785 workers was taken and the 41,198 adult males earned a daily average of Cr$ 5.329; the 50,386 adult females Cr$ 3.738. Among the 7,760 minor males the average daily wage was Cr$ 1.973 and among the 9,441 minor females it was Cr$ 1.944. In 1920 majority status was attained at sixteen years of age. In the food industry 37,355 workers were sampled. The 25,990 adult males earned Cr$ 5.111; the 8,267 adult females Cr$ 2.957; the 2,077 minor males Cr$ 2.004; and the 1,021 minor females Cr$ 1.858. The 21,080 workers in the clothing industry produced the following figures: the 10,889 adult males earned Cr$ 6.712 on an average daily basis; the 7,987 adult females Cr$ 3.652; the 1,075 minor males Cr$ 2.174; and the 1,129 minor females Cr$ 1.885.

Table VII-2 presents daily wages of production workers by industry group and sex in Brazil from 1920 to 1970. All data are from Brazilian censuses, which for 1960 and 1970 reported only workers ten years of age and older. The 1920 figures on the table included minors (persons under sixteen years of age), some of whom might have been under ten years of age. The 1920 census reported wages for adults and minors separately. For both male and female minors the highest wage category was Cr$ 4.0 and over. The numbers of minor male workers in this category were added to the adult male Cr$ 4.0-4.9 category to produce the total male category. The pattern of minor male wages suggests that it is unlikely that very many under sixteen years of age earned more than Cr$ 4.9 per day and thus their inclusion in this group does not seriously inflate the total number of males in the Cr$ 4.0-4.9 category nor seriously deflate any higher total male wage categories. In the same manner female minor workers in the Cr$ 4.0 and over category were added to the female adult workers in the Cr$ 4.0-4.9 category to yield the total Cr$ 4.0-4.9 category. The largest female wage category in the 1920 census was Cr$ 8.0 and over. All females in this category were included in the Cr$ 8.0-9.9 category on the table even though a few females may actually have earned more than Cr$ 9.9 daily.

The 1960 and 1970 censuses grouped industries differently in reporting daily wages. In 1960 vegetal extraction, hunting, fishing, and mining formed a separate industry grouping. In 1970 the first three industries were grouped with agriculture, silviculture, and ranching, and mining was grouped with manufacturing, construction, and utilities.

Table VII-3 reports the numbers of hours worked weekly by males and females in major occupations in 1970. The data are from the 1970 census and the occupations are the same as those that appear on Table VI-4.

The numbers of production workers under sixteen years of age by sex for major industry groups in 1920 and 1955 are shown on Table VII-4. The 1920 data are from the 1920 census. Those for 1955 were generated by the Secretaria-Geral do Conselho Nacional de Estatística and published in the Inquéritos econômicos do IBGE. The industrial establishments surveyed for 1955 were in 115 municípios (counties) classified in the 1950 census as most important in industry.

Table VII-5 shows the numbers of employees suffering employment-related illnesses and injuries from 1969 to 1977. All data are from the Instituto Nacional de Previdência

Social (National Institute of Social Welfare). During the eight-year period covered by the table, job-related accidents and illnesses fluctuated but a steady rise was recorded in "in-transit" illnesses and injuries. The sources did not specify what is included in this category but presumably it included transit during work hours while away from a regular job station as well as transit to and from work.

Monthly income for family heads by sex, for family members, and for families by size in 1960 and 1970 is shown on Table VII-6. The data are from the respective censuses. The category "no declaration of income" is not shown on the table. Were it added the family total figures would equal those shown on Table VII-10. The "adoptees" category on Table VII-6 includes agregados and distant relatives who are considered part of the family but does not include household employees who receive an income. Agregados are persons, usually unrelated to the family by blood or marriage, who are living as a part of the family group. In 1970 all husbands were considered heads of families, but in 1960 in a few cases another person was assigned that role.

The federally set monthly minimum wage in each of Brazil's twenty-four regions from 1943 to 1977 is presented on Table VII-7. All wages are given in the monetary scale that prevailed from 1967 on. In that year one new cruzeiro was set to equal 1,000 "old" cruzeiros, but since then the term "new" has been dropped. The data originated in the twenty-three decree laws setting the wages. The first, number 5,473, was promulgated on May 11, 1943, and went into effect in June of that year. The political subdivision names conform to the early-1970s pattern: Rio de Janeiro state had already absorbed Guanabara state, but Mato Grosso had not yet been divided. The country's heavily industrialized regions such as the states of São Paulo, Rio de Janeiro, and Minas Gerais, and the Distrito Federal around Brasília have consistently had the highest minimum wage levels.

Table VII-8 documents annual family expenditures for goods and services for the year 1975. The data were gathered by FIBGE in its Estudo nacional de despesa familiar (National Study of Family Expenditures). The length of the study was usually seven days, with some exceptions, and the results were then expanded to an annual level. The family was the equivalent of the budget unit and included all those persons, related or not, who lived in the same domicile, shared the common food stock, and participated in the formation and expenditure of the budget. The cost of consumption of all goods and services whether they were self-supplied, donated, bartered for, or accepted in lieu of salary, was converted into equivalent monetary value. Payments on long-term

149

mortgage purchases were recorded only for the twelve months immediately preceding the study period.

Table VII-9 compares 1975 and 1946 wage-based family expenditures in Brazil. The 1975 data were taken verbatim from the Rio de Janeiro section of Table VII-8 in this work. The 1946 data appeared in Wythe, Wight, and Midkiff,[1] who reported the results of a survey taken by the Serviço Social da Indústria. The survey covered the families of 3,091 workers in fourteen major establishments in the then Distrito Federal (the city of Rio de Janeiro). The average monthly worker wage was Cr$ 893.30, which, supplemented by an average of Cr$ 279.70 from other sources, yielded an average family income of Cr$ 1173.00.

Table VII-10 reports the size and composition of families by urban/rural residence in 1950, 1960, and 1970. The data are from the respective censuses. For 1950 "other" includes all other related persons plus roomers and employees who were considered as part of the family. The 1960 and 1970 categories "other" include all other related persons plus employees. Roomers were not specified as a group. The inclusion of so many nonrelated persons in the Brazilian family suggests that in the American idiom these data treat with households rather than with families.

The proportion of all families that was headed by females decreased from 1950 to 1960 then rose sharply in the following decade. The average family size declined from 5.13 persons in 1950 to 5.12 in 1960, then fell to 4.85 in 1970. In 1950 in no family size category was the urban proportion as high as 50 percent, but by 1960 more than 50 percent of the families in the four smallest size categories was urban. By 1970 in the five smallest size categories more than 60 percent of the families was urban. From 1950 to 1960 urban single-person families showed the largest proportional gain in Brazil (13.3 percentage points) rising from 42.1 percent of the total in 1950 to 55.4 percent of the 1960 total. Between 1960 and 1970 urban four-person families showed the largest proportional gain, rising from 50.8 to 63.5 percent of the total.

Table VII-11 presents the number and characteristics of the Brazilian urban/rural housing stock from 1940 to 1970 and rents paid in 1960 and 1970. All the data originated with the respective censuses. For 1940 figures were for private domiciles. The exceptions were those for "rooms and bedrooms," which the 1940 census reported only for all domiciles including collective living units. The 1940 census did not specify whether the data were for both occupied and vacant dwellings. The 1950 figures were for private domiciles but no occupied/vacant criterion was noted. For 1970 the rooms and bedrooms figures are slightly understated since the totals were summed from size group data in the census. The last size group is the "11 and over" category, so the number of domiciles in this category was multiplied by 11 bedrooms to establish the number to be added to the rest to obtain the total.

Only the 1940 census classified domiciles by type of construction material. Wood construction, which predominated in rural areas, was twice as common as ceramic, which predominated in urban areas. The 1960 and 1970 censuses classified dwellings on a not-very-useful "permanent-improvised" basis but published no definition of these terms. For 1970 the permanent category was divided into finished and rustic subgroups, the former characterized urban construction and the latter rural construction. The percent of total owner-occupied dwellings increased steadily from 1940 to 1970. The "other" occupance condition, so high a percentage in rural areas, included sharecropped dwellings many of which were paid for in kind. Between 1940 and 1970 the proportion of total dwellings with piped water more than doubled and the proportion with electricity nearly tripled. The proportion of domiciles linked to piped sewage systems had risen to only 13.2 percent by 1970, those with septic tanks to 13.4 percent. By 1970 gas had become as popular as wood for cooking purposes although it has long been accepted that the best cooks in Brazil use wood stoves. The radio and refrigerator proportions both rose sharply between 1960 and 1970. Between 1940 and 1970 the numbers of rooms and bedrooms have remained fairly constant relative to population.

References

1. George Wythe, Royce A. Wight, and Harold M. Midkiff, <u>Brazil, an Expanding Economy</u> (New York: Twentieth Century Fund, 1949).

Table VII-1. Number of Establishments and Production Workers, Workers per Establishment, Annual Wages Paid, and Average Annual Wage per Worker in the Mining Industry and in Manufacturing Industries by Type in Brazil, 1907-70

	1907			1920			
	No. of Estabs.	No. of Prod. Workers	Prod. Workers Per Estab.	No. of Estabs.	No. of Prod. Workers	Prod. Workers Per Estab.	Total Annual Wages and Salaries Paid Cr$1000
MINING AND QUARRYING							
MANUFACTURING	3,258	151,841	46.6	13,336	275,512	20.7	349,467
Metals	208	7,737	37.2	270	8,454	31.3	13,728
Textiles	202	52,584	260.3	1,135	110,549	97.4	110,800
Mechanical	13	284	21.8	116	1,540	13.3	2,285
Transportation Equipment	48	5,340	111.3	232	3,398	14.6	5,354
Food	749	29,123	38.9	2,734	28,590	10.5	45,137
Leather	148	3,276	22.1	723	5,891	8.1	8,489
Soap/Perfumes/Candles	117	2,252	19.2	381	3,587	9.4	5,907
Electrical Equipment	2	45	22.5	3	69	23.0	131
Chemicals	153	4,065	26.6	134	3,001	22.4	4,332
Non-Metallic Minerals	266	6,046	22.7	1,823	20,914	11.5	24,416
Publishing	-	-	-	-	-	-	-
Clothing	337	14,421	42.8	2,076	28,850	13.9	43,276
Lumber/Wood	201	3,780	18.8	1,190	12,997	10.9	21,643
Paper	23	834	36.3	59	3,138	53.2	4,921
Furniture	85	2,843	33.4	545	7,978	14.6	13,418
Beverages	443	5,998	13.5	1,093	9,144	8.4	16,091
Plastics	-	-	-	-	-	-	-
Rubber	2	18	9.0	14	345	24.6	735
Pharmaceuticals	-	-	-	186	1,230	6.6	2,034
Tobacco	104	7,407	71.2	296	14,510	49.0	11,488
Other	157	5,788	36.9	326	11,327	34.7	15,282
TOTAL	3,258	151,841	46.6	13,336	275,512	20.7	349,467

Table VII-1 (continued)

	1940					1950				
	No. of Estabs.	No. of Prod. Workers	Prod. Workers Per Estab.	Total Annual Wages Paid Prod. Wkrs. Cr$1000	Annual Average Wage Cr$	No. of Estabs.	No. of Prod. Workers	Prod. Workers Per Estab.	Total Annual Wages Paid Prod. Wkrs. Cr$1000	Annual Average Wage Cr$
MINING AND QUARRYING	2,267	27,949	12.3	44,015	1,575	1,539	32,708	21.3	288,613	8,824
MANUFACTURING	40,983	669,348	16.3	1,422,988	2,126	82,164	1,144,936	13.9	10,980,285	9,590
Metals	1,460	53,844	36.9	154,046	2,860	2,221	90,203	40.6	1,197,339	13,273
Textiles	2,212	126,477	97.9	405,077	1,871	2,941	313,845	106.7	2,857,726	9,106
Mechanical	327	9,064	27.7	30,932	3,412	762	21,798	28.6	324,548	14,762
Transporation Equipment	248	8,453	34.1	30,519	3,610	539	15,121	28.1	262,861	17,383
Food	14,905	125,736	8.4	222,857	1,772	32,872	211,948	6.4	1,380,740	6,515
Leather	1,297	11,587	8.9	23,481	2,026	2,099	17,309	8.2	154,578	8,930
Soap/Perfumes/Candles	119	4,018	33.8	10,446	2,600	959	8,755	9.2	82,240	9,393
Electrical Equipment	1,780	34,278	19.3	73,097	2,132	341	13,038	38.2	183,512	14,075
Chemicals	4,861	46,466	9.6	96,978	2,087	1,158	41,969	36.2	467,421	11,137
Non-Metallic Minerals	2,207	22,120	10.0	68,876	3,114	12,750	111,269	8.7	913,894	8,213
Publishing	3,203	40,677	12.7	92,404	2,272	2,749	34,491	12.5	507,065	14,701
Clothing	3,545	27,794	7.8	58,915	2,120	5,076	64,140	12.6	640,647	9,988
Lumber & Wood	228	10,642	46.7	22,752	2,138	7,562	56,044	7.4	494,197	8,818
Paper	2,069	23,107	11.2	59,060	2,556	441	22,305	50.6	224,168	10,947
Furniture	1,523	10,610	7.0	25,686	2,421	2,882	31,672	11.0	388,109	12,254
Beverages						4,420	32,762	7.4	269,835	8,236
Plastics						104	2,395	23.0	29,248	12,212
Rubber	65	3,707	57.0	6,954	1,876	119	9,137	76.8	124,395	13,614
Pharmaceuticals						547	12,489	22.8	128,601	10,297
Tobacco	178	11,141	62.6	18,789	1,686	252	14,377	57.1	140,154	9,748
Other	756	9,627	12.7	22,119	2,298	1,370	19,869	14.5	209,007	10,519
TOTAL	43,250	697,297	16.1	1,467,003	2,104	83,703	1,177,644	14.1	11,268,898	9,569

Table VII-1 (continued)

	1960					1970				
	No. of Estabs.	No. of Prod. Workers	Prod. Workers Per Estab.	Total Annual Wages Paid Prod. Wkrs. Cr$1000	Annual Average Wage Cr$	No. of Estabs.	No. of Prod. Workers	Prod. Workers Per Estabs.	Total Annual Wages Paid Prod. Wkrs. Cr$1000	Annual Average Wage Cr%
MINING AND QUARRYING	2,176	35,432	16.3	2,421,326	68,337	1,636	52,702	32.2	263,917	5,007
MANUFACTURING	108,163	1,474,281	13.6	100,196,344	67,963	70,348	2,101,444	29.9	8,973,791	4,184
Metals	4,764	151,801	31.9	13,193,032	86,910	5,085	223,451	43.9	1,103,630	4,939
Textiles	4,267	306,122	71.7	18,910,856	61,776	3,983	313,317	78.7	1,064,991	3,399
Mechanical	1,688	49,000	29.0	4,379,625	89,380	3,499	150,434	43.0	947,148	6,296
Transportation Equipment	2,014	63,229	31.4	5,957,273	94,217	1,885	133,515	70.8	901,815	6,754
Food	33,443	217,621	6.5	11,765,300	54,063	17,162	265,918	15.5	795,165	2,990
Leather	2,350	21,981	9.4	1,301,080	59,191	642	21,529	33.5	67,076	3,115
Soap/Perfumes/Candles	1,070	10,314	9.6	620,065	60,118	531	13,683	25.8	56,259	4,112
Electrical Equipment	972	44,364	45.6	3,881,403	87,490	1,648	97,086	58.9	552,484	5,691
Chemicals	1,777	61,039	34.3	5,337,119	87,438	1,941	81,061	41.8	551,330	6,801
Non-Metallic Minerals	18,127	144,015	7.9	7,775,464	53,991	8,422	171,066	20.3	550,961	3,220
Publishing	3,358	44,860	13.4	3,783,723	84,345	3,350	69,666	20.8	428,589	6,152
Clothing	7,632	85,263	11.2	5,153,485	60,442	4,922	139,209	28.3	377,166	2,709
Lumber & Wood	11,191	74,702	6.7	4,050,624	54,224	5,846	103,107	17.6	263,284	2,554
Paper	766	35,439	46.3	2,622,038	73,987	1,024	56,851	55.5	249,332	4,386
Furniture	8,140	52,974	6.5	3,380,333	63,811	4,255	74,937	17.6	245,735	3,279
Beverages	3,039	31,155	10.3	2,122,733	68,135	1,854	39,533	21.3	161,294	4,080
Plastics	291	7,610	26.2	631,466	82,978	1,026	36,290	35.4	143,636	3,958
Rubber	301	14,741	49.0	1,341,303	90,991	761	27,684	36.4	138,063	4,987
Pharmaceuticals	506	13,539	26.8	1,055,472	77,958	433	20,652	47.7	113,003	5,472
Tobacco	278	18,008	46.8	786,063	60,429	95	12,483	131.4	62,284	4,990
Other	2,189	31,504	14.4	2,147,887	68,178	1,984	49,972	25.9	200,546	4,013
TOTAL	110,339	1,509,713	13.7	102,617,670	67,972	71,984	1,154,146	29.9	9,237,708	4,288

Sources: RE 1920EI, pp. XII-XXII; AN 1956, p. 119; AN 1963, p. 72; AN 1974, p. 208.

Table VII-2. Daily Income in Cruzeiros of All Production Workers in Manufacturing, Construction, and Utility Industry Groups in Brazil by Sex, 1920, and Monthly Income in Cruzeiros of Persons Ten Years of Age and Older in Brazil by Sex and Industry Division, 1920-70

1920

	Cr$0-2.9 Male	Cr$0-2.9 Female	Cr$3.0-3.9 Male	Cr$3.0-3.9 Female	Cr$4.0-4.9 Male	Cr$4.0-4.9 Female	Cr$6.0-7.9 Male	Cr$6.0-7.9 Female	Cr$8.0-9.9 Male	Cr$8.0-9.9 Female
Manufacturing	27,229	40,249	17,741	17,085	43,027	18,684	30,274	6,944	14,315	2,219
Construction	391	51	272	–	549	88	986	–	562	3
Utilities	42	2	67	–	370	–	182	–	195	–
Total	27,662	40,302	18,080	17,085	43,946	18,772	31,442	6,944	15,072	2,222

	Cr$10.0-11.9 Male	Cr$10.0-11.9 Female	Cr$12.0-13.9 Male	Cr$12.0-13.9 Female	Cr$14.0 & Over Male	Cr$14.0 & Over Female	Total Male	Total Female
Manufacturing	5,824	–	2,680	–	1,291	–	142,381	85,323
Construction	209	–	114	–	12	–	3,095	–
Utilities	132	–	16	–	6	–	1,010	2
Total	6,165	–	2,810	–	1,309	–	146,486	85,325

1960

	Cr$0-2100 Male	Cr$0-2100 Female	Cr$2101-3300 Male	Cr$2101-3300 Female	Cr$3301-4500 Male	Cr$3301-4500 Female	Cr$4501-6000 Male	Cr$4501-6000 Female	Cr$6001-10000 Male	Cr$6001-10000 Female
Agriculture/Silviculture/Ranching	2,763,514	282,574	2,016,840	91,833	1,322,568	42,050	1,032,369	25,106	645,038	12,855
Mining/Vegetal Extraction/Hunting/Fishing	79,412	19,100	96,418	6,998	99,874	2,677	97,464	1,296	73,495	878
Manufacturing/Construction/Utilities	137,886	131,257	194,565	65,541	244,836	46,297	577,722	111,966	681,873	86,674
Retail/Wholesale	95,592	25,503	101,931	20,936	114,613	19,681	230,157	38,945	333,794	38,197
Personal/Business Services	139,471	951,992	119,339	222,404	130,925	103,187	265,502	91,671	351,671	51,686
Transportation/Communication/Warehousing	51,149	2,931	61,602	1,819	85,116	2,361	193,675	8,345	346,934	15,417
Social Services/Liberal Professions	13,234	47,381	13,051	28,271	18,694	34,485	43,560	61,542	71,962	114,852
Public Administration & Security/National Defense	49,926	4,138	22,172	3,496	37,079	4,524	82,866	11,167	177,618	27,353
Other	36,448	18,460	34,197	13,818	35,474	12,917	74,608	24,691	135,296	42,141
Economically Inactive	42,211	77,873	77,990	51,942	102,086	39,224	81,902	32,846	91,533	37,254
Total	3,408,843	1,561,209	2,738,105	507,058	2,191,265	307,403	2,679,825	407,575	2,909,214	427,307

	Cr$10001-20000 Male	Cr$10001-20000 Female	Cr$20001-50000 Male	Cr$20001-50000 Female	Cr$50001 & Over Male	Cr$50001 & Over Female	Without Income Male	Without Income Female	Total Male	Total Female
Agriculture/Silviculture/Ranching	226,071	4,416	60,390	1,213	18,189	434	2,466,949	709,038	10,551,928	1,169,519
Mining/Vegetal Extraction/Hunting/Fishing	21,402	369	4,350	81	1,302	17	51,899	22,068	525,616	53,484
Manufacturing/Construction/Utilities	318,711	15,614	92,048	2,751	22,297	328	13,073	24,126	2,283,011	484,554
Retail/Wholesale	260,988	13,439	109,316	2,990	22,354	425	24,215	6,795	1,292,960	166,911
Personal/Business Services	182,385	16,196	36,482	3,551	4,424	470	15,496	11,257	1,245,695	1,455,414
Transportation/Communication/Warehousing	215,866	9,197	38,160	979	4,759	35	4,366	105	1,001,627	41,189
Social Services/Liberal Professions	49,468	87,831	27,891	11,014	5,943	521	17,913	30,676	261,716	416,573
Public Administration & Security/National Defense	150,242	23,318	92,710	4,803	12,576	376	31	29	625,220	79,204
Other	134,413	21,603	98,969	5,671	26,709	520	1,965	375	578,079	140,196
Economically Inactive	84,328	31,098	39,436	10,085	8,621	2,602	4,937,482	20,250,858	5,465,589	20,533,782
Total	1,643,874	223,081	599,752	43,138	127,174	5,728	7,533,389	21,055,327	23,831,441	24,537,826

Table VII-2 (continued)

1970	Cr$0-100		Cr$101-150		Cr$151-250		Cr$251-500		Cr$501-1000	
	Male	Female	Male	Female	Male	Female	Male	Female	Male	Female
Agriculture/Silviculture/Ranching/Vegetal Extraction/Hunting/Fishing	5,558,136	535,058	1,935,402	63,426	1,434,253	32,149	552,075	10,385	125,068	2,433
Manufacturing/Mining/Construction/Utilities	465,166	155,595	591,210	79,654	1,681,672	255,837	1,164,962	95,965	429,464	26,457
Retail/Wholesale	263,764	70,790	211,737	55,667	494,071	136,338	478,483	68,103	255,563	19,791
Personal/Business Services	193,736	1,675,225	135,370	282,811	379,327	263,080	329,739	86,731	125,251	18,931
Transportation/Communication/Warehousing	81,053	3,154	102,138	4,453	323,376	16,537	458,259	27,381	153,519	8,287
Social Services/Liberal Professions	32,496	137,623	48,813	118,722	133,018	276,660	116,317	265,710	61,009	127,061
Public Administration & Security/National Defense	76,176	12,699	64,096	14,458	209,223	35,926	308,923	52,610	191,648	30,249
Other	56,372	37,487	45,353	20,714	140,767	62,856	181,851	69,980	151,318	25,641
Economically Inactive	122,932	294,137	292,050	142,609	218,116	128,013	235,062	120,752	145,782	68,318
Total	6,849,831	2,921,768	3,426,169	782,514	5,013,823	1,207,396	3,825,671	797,617	1,638,622	327,168

	Cr$1001-1500		Cr$1501-2000		Cr$2000 & Over		Without Income		Total	
	Male	Female	Male	Female	Male	Female	Male	Female	Male	Female
Agriculture/Silviculture/Ranching/Vegetal Extraction/Hunting/Fishing	21,704	440	15,248	298	18,275	402	1,969,233	591,777	11,629,394	1,236,368
Manufacturing/Mining/Construction/Utilities	94,284	4,786	55,872	2,242	80,198	1,818	18,199	3,768	4,581,027	626,122
Retail/Wholesale	63,916	3,174	39,002	1,789	40,708	1,362	16,716	7,086	1,863,960	364,100
Personal/Business Services	20,482	2,654	11,119	1,327	11,440	1,179	8,823	5,376	1,215,287	2,337,314
Transportation/Communication/Warehousing	22,834	766	10,670	238	10,110	203	3,477	80	1,165,436	61,099
Social Services/Liberal Professions	27,533	19,980	20,724	7,477	31,003	3,420	7,531	17,892	478,444	974,545
Public Administration & Security/National Defense	64,463	8,095	33,262	2,965	35,894	1,875	-	-	983,685	158,877
Other	56,779	4,908	39,755	2,464	56,665	1,494	177,144	45,940	906,004	271,484
Economically Inactive	46,052	16,504	21,045	8,102	22,428	10,064	8,005,504	26,321,948	9,108,971	27,110,447
Total	418,047	61,307	246,697	26,902	306,721	21,817	10,206,627	26,993,867	31,932,208	33,140,356

Sources: RE 1920E2, pp. 4-5; RE 1960A1, pp. 60-61; RE 1970A1, pp. 95-96.

Table VII-3. Numbers of Hours Worked Weekly in Brazil by Males and Females in Major Occupations, 1970

	Total	%	Total Male	Female	Total	0-15 Hours %	Male	Female	Total	15-39 Hours %	Male	Female
PROFESSIONAL/TECHNICAL PERSONNEL	1,471,152	100.0	210,392	1,260,760	68,419	4.7	9,789	58,630	868,689	59.0	76,486	792,203
Teachers/Professors	143,766	100.0	29,571	114,195	2,178	1.5	477	1,701	25,251	17.6	4,370	20,881
Nurses/Physical Therapists	117,137	100.0	100,030	17,107	904	.8	733	171	11,480	9.8	8,507	2,973
Accountants/Bookkeepers	44,970	100.0	40,465	4,505	540	1.2	431	109	6,588	14.7	5,247	1,341
Physicians	43,729	100.0	43,197	532	291	.7	291	0	3,141	7.2	3,048	93
Engineers	38,621	100.0	28,318	10,303	354	.9	248	106	4,563	11.8	2,609	1,954
Laboratory Technicians	37,671	100.0	34,279	3,392	591	1.6	439	152	6,677	17.7	5,680	997
Lawyers	32,534	100.0	28,338	4,196	759	2.3	539	220	6,745	20.7	5,106	1,639
Dentists	28,450	100.0	18,952	9,498	1,214	4.3	979	235	4,335	15.2	3,059	1,276
Clergy	35,915	100.0	33,997	1,918	291	.8	256	35	4,150	11.6	3,584	566
Draftsmen/Cartographers												
MANAGERS/OFFICIALS/PROPRIETORS/MILITARY	819,925	100.0	749,551	70,374	11,211	1.4	9,437	1,774	54,255	6.6	46,231	8,024
Small Business Operators	343,345	100.0	343,089	256	3,234	1.0	3,226	8	45,529	13.2	45,451	78
Military Personnel(all ranks)	97,578	100.0	94,229	3,349	857	.9	687	170	4,354	4.5	3,924	430
Factory Owners	79,992	100.0	56,959	23,033	841	1.1	503	338	16,346	20.4	8,599	7,747
Public Administrators	46,258	100.0	43,572	2,686	273	.6	243	30	5,740	12.4	5,252	488
Bank/Insurance Administrators												
SERVICE/OFFICE/PRIVATE HOUSEHOLD EMPLOYEES	1,682,457	100.0	41,163	1,641,412	23,819	1.4	777	23,042	170,609	10.1	4,068	166,541
Domestic Employees	767,029	100.0	576,507	190,522	7,793	1.0	5,521	2,272	44,434	5.8	32,112	12,322
Floorwalkers/Sales Clerks	659,654	100.0	515,722	143,932	8,607	1.3	5,116	3,491	82,868	12.6	46,520	36,348
Doorkeepers/Watchmen/Elevator Operators	318,843	100.0	280,323	38,520	9,308	2.9	6,925	2,383	60,252	18.9	48,674	11,578
Door-to-Door Sales Personnel	253,020	100.0	11,119	241,901	16,228	6.4	111	16,117	75,658	29.9	710	74,948
Launderers	115,729	100.0	76,942	38,787	3,265	2.8	1,731	1,534	14,004	12.1	7,309	6,695
Barbers/Hairdressers	110,465	100.0	104,155	6,310	1,094	1.0	848	246	8,172	7.4	6,769	1,403
Traveling Sales Personnel	91,258	100.0	34,663	56,595	1,346	1.5	294	1,052	9,149	10.0	2,207	6,942
Cooks	88,248	100.0	50,373	37,875	629	.7	357	272	11,704	13.3	7,761	3,943
Tellers/Cashiers	83,335	100.0	59,173	24,162	953	1.1	623	330	6,442	7.7	3,925	2,517
Waitpersons	73,682	100.0	70,268	3,414	874	1.2	833	41	10,196	13.8	9,396	800
Tax Inspectors	67,037	100.0	66,463	574	718	1.1	714	4	8,217	12.3	8,112	105
Police	59,517	100.0	26,893	32,624	531	.9	237	294	13,458	22.6	4,708	8,750
Typists	55,002	100.0	53,733	1,269	434	.8	430	4	2,286	4.1	2,202	84
Bus Conductors	55,679	100.0	52,227	3,452	888	1.6	744	144	6,712	12.0	5,829	883
Brokers/Agents	54,856	100.0	54,112	744	805	1.5	798	7	4,384	8.0	4,160	224
Garbage Collectors	48,426	100.0	45,600	2,826	284	.6	263	21	2,782	5.7	2,430	352
Warehouse Personnel	39,082	100.0	38,589	493	647	1.7	623	24	4,439	11.3	4,311	128
Gardeners	37,584	100.0	32,075	5,509	654	1.7	284	370	4,397	11.7	2,611	1,786
Commercial Representatives	38,813	100.0	4,801	29,012	375	1.1	58	317	9,471	28.0	664	8,807
Telephone Operators	30,198	100.0	23,681	6,517	590	1.9	439	151	7,567	25.1	5,384	2,183
Court Reporters/Courtroom Aides	23,625	100.0	13,486	10,139	296	1.3	170	126	1,455	6.2	741	714
Innkeepers	20,919	100.0	18,449	2,470	319	1.5	273	46	4,844	23.2	3,846	998
Telegraphers/Radiotelegraphers												

Table VII-3 (continued)

	40-49 Hours				50 Hours & More			
	Total	%	Male	Female	Total	%	Male	Female
PROFESSIONAL/TECHNICAL/PERSONNEL								
Teachers/Professors	429,987	29.2	89,167	340,820	104,057	7.1	34,950	69,107
Nurses/Physical Therapists	86,739	60.3	18,302	68,437	29,598	20.6	6,422	23,176
Accountants/Bookkeepers	85,785	73.2	73,525	12,260	18,968	16.2	17,265	1,703
Physicians	19,435	43.2	17,406	2,029	18,407	40.9	17,381	1,026
Engineers	30,576	69.9	30,199	377	9,721	22.2	9,659	62
Laboratory Technicians	27,449	71.1	20,303	7,146	6,255	16.2	5,158	1,097
Lawyers	21,889	58.1	20,069	1,820	8,514	22.6	8,091	423
Dentists	17,789	54.7	15,815	1,974	7,241	22.3	6,878	363
Clergy	12,575	54.2	7,689	4,886	10,326	36.3	7,225	3,101
Draftsmen/Cartographers	26,701	74.3	25,548	1,153	4,773	13.3	4,609	164
MANAGERS/OFFICIALS/PROPRIETORS/MILITARY								
Small Business Operators	431,023	52.6	393,040	37,983	323,436	39.4	300,843	22,593
Military Personnel (all ranks)	216,742	63.1	216,593	149	77,840	22.7	77,819	21
Factory Owners	56,804	58.2	54,808	1,996	35,563	36.4	34,810	753
Public Administrators	49,328	61.7	36,623	12,705	13,477	16.8	11,234	2,243
Bank/Insurance Administrators	32,610	70.5	30,666	1,944	7,635	16.5	7,411	224
SERVICE/OFFICE/PRIVATE HOUSEHOLD EMPLOYEES								
Domestic Employees	892,962	53.1	22,832	870,130	595,185	35.4	13,486	581,699
Floorwalkers/Sales Clerks	516,834	67.4	379,385	137,449	197,968	25.8	159,489	38,479
Doorkeepers/Watchmen/Elevator Operators	423,130	64.1	339,057	84,073	145,049	22.0	125,029	20,020
Door-to-Door Sales Personnel	173,290	64.3	155,165	18,125	75,993	23.9	69,559	6,434
Launderers	119,019	47.0	7,837	111,182	42,115	16.7	2,461	39,654
Barbers/Hairdressers	65,697	56.8	43,307	22,390	32,763	28.3	24,595	8,168
Traveling Sales Personnel	73,021	66.1	69,202	3,819	28,178	25.5	27,336	842
Cooks	53,086	58.2	20,760	32,326	27,677	30.3	11,402	16,275
Tellers/Cashiers	61,386	69.6	34,356	27,030	14,529	16.4	7,899	6,630
Waitpersons	49,083	58.9	34,182	14,901	26,857	32.2	20,443	6,414
Tax Inspectors	47,391	64.3	45,186	2,205	15,221	20.7	14,853	368
Police	40,574	60.5	40,189	385	17,528	26.1	17,448	80
Typists	39,795	66.9	18,693	21,102	5,733	9.6	3,255	2,478
Bus Conductors	38,804	61.5	33,088	716	18,478	33.6	18,013	465
Brokers/Agents	35,512	63.8	33,487	2,025	12,567	22.6	12,167	400
Garbage Collectors	38,024	69.3	37,637	387	11,643	21.2	11,517	126
Warehouse Personnel	36,018	74.4	33,935	2,083	9,342	19.3	8,972	370
Gardeners	25,597	65.5	25,322	275	8,399	21.5	8,333	66
Commercial Representatives	23,309	62.1	20,602	2,707	9,224	24.5	8,578	646
Telephone Operators	20,329	60.1	3,112	17,217	3,638	10.8	967	2,671
Court Reporters/Courtroom Aides	17,450	57.8	13,945	3,505	4,591	15.2	3,913	678
Innkeepers	9,634	40.7	5,357	4,277	12,240	51.8	7,218	5,022
Telegraphers/Radiotelegraphers	12,079	57.7	10,856	1,223	3,677	17.6	3,474	203

Table VII-3 (continued)

	Total				0-15 Hours				15-39 Hours			
	Total	%	Male	Female	Total	%	Male	Female	Total	%	Male	Female
CRAFTS/TRADES/FOREMEN												
Masons	587,259	100.0	585,883	1,376	6,492	1.1	6,457	35	26,273	4.5	26,144	129
Carpenters/Joiners	403,211	100.0	401,937	1,274	4,659	1.2	4,644	15	21,036	5.2	20,901	135
Tailors/Seamstresses	402,551	100.0	67,172	335,379	14,416	3.6	1,106	13,310	81,598	20.3	5,711	75,887
Electricians	158,362	100.0	156,423	1,939	1,608	1.0	1,589	19	8,137	5.1	8,043	94
Shoemakers	135,078	100.0	115,035	20,043	1,574	1.2	1,456	118	8,534	6.3	7,602	932
Painters	131,217	100.0	130,855	362	1,324	1.0	1,319	5	8,173	6.2	8,086	87
Potters	97,759	100.0	88,825	8,934	1,066	1.1	941	125	6,193	6.3	5,080	1,113
Industrial/Construction Foremen	90,688	100.0	86,545	4,143	639	.7	603	36	2,361	2.6	2,185	176
Bakers	76,489	100.0	75,288	1,201	1,145	1.5	1,131	14	6,211	8.1	6,093	118
Pipefitters	70,804	100.0	70,690	114	796	1.1	796	0	4,236	6.0	4,236	0
Locksmiths	67,031	100.0	66,856	175	715	1.1	711	4	3,580	5.3	3,554	26
Stonecutters	40,182	100.0	39,599	583	426	1.1	405	21	2,028	5.0	1,931	97
Typographers	39,811	100.0	37,479	2,332	283	.7	275	8	2,057	5.2	1,900	157
Hatmakers	36,321	100.0	651	35,670	1,500	4.2	15	1,485	13,295	36.6	210	13,085
Butchers	32,846	100.0	32,205	641	648	2.0	640	8	3,532	10.8	3,411	121
OPERATIVES												
Truck Drivers	759,378	100.0	757,376	2,002	6,975	.9	6,899	76	35,063	4.6	34,402	661
Mechanics	460,970	100.0	453,941	7,029	3,450	.7	3,400	50	16,944	3.7	16,753	191
Loom Operators	117,810	100.0	56,486	61,324	1,066	.9	482	584	3,647	3.1	1,162	2,485
Industrial/Construction Machinery Operators	114,794	100.0	105,717	9,077	780	.7	731	49	3,006	2.6	2,653	353
Packagers/Mailers	91,454	100.0	54,259	37,195	602	.7	380	222	3,470	3.8	2,096	1,374
Lathe Operators	79,181	100.0	78,685	496	354	.4	354	0	1,705	2.2	1,694	11
Solderers	62,504	100.0	61,405	1,099	516	.8	509	7	1,810	2.9	1,771	39
Carters/Mule Drivers	54,186	100.0	54,055	131	944	1.7	932	12	5,711	10.5	5,691	20
Thread Spinners	38,930	100.0	13,655	25,275	312	.8	81	231	1,347	3.5	290	1,057
Spray Painters	31,862	100.0	31,391	471	223	.7	219	4	1,080	3.4	1,069	11
Embroiderers	27,286	100.0	589	26,697	1,697	6.2	8	1,689	8,506	31.2	34	8,472
Sheet Metal Workers	22,950	100.0	22,705	245	270	1.2	254	16	1,355	5.9	1,315	40
Boiler Tenders	9,350	100.0	9,287	63	64	.7	60	4	230	2.5	226	4
NON-RURAL LABORERS												
Hod Carriers	448,105	100.0	445,967	2,138	4,498	1.0	4,472	26	19,771	4.4	19,596	175
Manual Laborers	372,284	100.0	365,412	6,872	4,643	1.2	4,495	148	25,184	6.8	24,578	606
Highway Maintenance Workers	33,717	100.0	33,678	39	290	.9	290	0	1,305	3.9	1,297	8
Stevedores	26,525	100.0	26,502	23	402	1.5	402	0	2,538	9.6	2,534	4
Railroad Maintenance Workers	23,626	100.0	23,622	4	214	.9	214	0	806	3.4	806	0
RURAL LABORERS												
Farm Laborers	4,322	100.0	3,881	441	60	1.4	37	23	370	8.6	241	129
Herders	3,713	100.0	3,684	29	13	.4	13	0	268	7.2	260	8
Fishermen	147,760	100.0	145,200	2,560	5,133	3.5	4,987	146	29,393	19.9	28,523	870
Tractor Drivers	20,888	100.0	20,766	122	190	.9	185	5	748	3.6	745	3
Gold/Diamond Miners/Prospectors	39,174	100.0	38,629	545	415	1.1	387	28	2,949	7.5	2,828	121
Miners (other minerals)	22,052	100.0	21,883	169	115	.5	111	4	3,608	16.4	3,573	35

159

Table VII-3 (continued)

	40-49 Hours				50 Hours & More			
	Total	%	Male	Female	Total	%	Male	Female
CRAFTS/TRADES/FOREMEN								
Masons	399,073	68.0	398,221	852	155,421	26.4	155,061	360
Carpenters/Joiners	273,459	67.8	272,604	855	104,057	25.8	103,788	269
Tailors/Seamstresses	233,309	57.9	42,286	191,023	73,228	18.2	18,069	55,159
Electricians	111,306	70.3	109,754	1,552	37,311	23.6	37,037	274
Shoemakers	97,065	71.9	80,401	16,664	27,905	20.6	25,576	2,329
Painters	90,882	69.3	90,662	220	30,838	23.5	30,788	50
Potters	61,890	63.3	56,277	5,613	28,610	29.3	26,527	2,083
Industrial/Construction Foremen	64,813	71.5	61,482	3,331	22,875	25.2	22,275	600
Bakers	46,077	60.2	45,322	755	23,056	30.2	22,742	314
Pipefitters	48,512	60.5	48,420	92	17,260	24.4	17,238	22
Locksmiths	45,923	68.5	45,805	118	16,813	25.1	16,786	27
Stonecutters	26,243	65.3	25,867	376	11,485	28.6	11,396	89
Typographers	29,940	75.2	28,081	1,859	7,531	18.9	7,223	308
Hatmakers	17,751	48.8	364	17,387	3,775	10.4	62	3,713
Butchers	19,000	57.8	18,592	408	9,666	29.4	9,562	104
OPERATIVES								
Truck Drivers	417,338	55.0	416,369	969	300,002	39.5	299,706	296
Mechanics	324,633	70.4	318,686	5,947	115,943	25.2	115,102	841
Loom Operators	94,266	71.0	44,506	49,760	18,831	16.0	10,336	8,495
Industrial/Construction Machinery Operators	81,478	71.0	73,941	7,537	29,530	25.7	28,392	1,138
Packagers/Mailers	69,273	75.7	39,632	29,641	18,109	19.8	12,151	5,958
Lathe Operators	60,630	76.6	60,246	384	16,492	20.8	16,391	101
Solderers	45,476	72.8	44,535	941	14,702	23.5	14,590	112
Carters/Mule Drivers	33,571	62.0	33,486	85	13,960	25.8	13,946	14
Thread Spinners	31,973	82.1	11,168	20,805	5,298	13.6	2,116	3,182
Spray Painters	23,577	74.0	23,157	420	6,982	21.9	6,946	36
Embroiderers	13,724	50.3	422	13,302	3,359	12.3	125	3,234
Sheet Metal Workers	16,133	70.3	16,013	120	5,192	22.6	5,123	69
Boiler Tenders	6,278	67.1	6,239	39	2,778	29.7	2,762	16
NON-RURAL LABORERS								
Hod Carriers	305,744	68.2	304,186	1,558	118,092	26.4	117,713	379
Manual Laborers	244,856	65.8	239,980	4,876	97,601	26.2	96,359	1,242
Highway Maintenance Workers	24,291	72.0	24,268	23	7,831	23.2	7,823	8
Stevedores	16,942	63.9	16,930	12	6,643	25.0	6,636	7
Railroad Maintenance Workers	17,102	72.4	17,098	4	5,504	23.3	5,504	0
RURAL LABORERS								
Farm Laborers	2,960	68.5	2,746	214	932	21.5	857	75
Herders	2,682	72.2	2,665	17	750	20.2	746	4
Fishermen	79,098	53.5	77,804	1,294	34,136	23.1	33,886	250
Tractor Drivers	12,671	60.7	12,576	95	7,279	34.8	7,260	19
Gold/Diamond Miners/Prospectors	25,883	66.1	25,603	280	9,927	25.3	9,811	116
Miners (other minerals)	13,064	59.2	12,963	101	5,265	23.9	5,236	29

Source: RE 1970A1, pp. 62-73

Table VII-4. Numbers of Minor Production Workers by Industry Group and
Sex, 1920 and 1955

	No. of Estabs. Rptg.	Prod. Workers Total	Minors Total	% of Prod. Workers	Males	Females
			1920			
Textiles		108,804	17,201	15.8	7,762	9,439
Metals		12,031	1,887	15.7	1,706	181
Chemicals		12,432	1,883	15.1	780	1,103
Ceramics		12,281	1,693	13.8	1,515	178
Transportation Equipment		3,237	400	12.4	351	49
Clothing		21,180	2,204	10.4	1,075	1,129
Furniture		6,631	686	10.3	632	54
Food		37,356	3,098	8.3	2,077	1,021
Leather		3,806	207	5.4	163	44
Publishing		2,571	129	5.0	129	0
Lumber & Wood		9,614	415	4.3	395	20
Utilities		1,012	15	1.5	15	0
Other		856	235	27.5	181	54
Total		231,811	30,053	13.0	16,781	13,272
			1955			
Clothing	547	41,131	7,879	19.2	3,440	4,439
Textiles	585	226,596	41,985	18.5	12,590	29,395
Publishing	276	25,143	3,548	14.1	2,194	1,354
Non-Metallic Minerals	704	57,034	7,854	13.8	5,180	2,674
Furniture	369	19,339	2,346	12.1	2,022	324
Chemicals/Pharmaceuticals	197	43,599	5,090	11.7	1,348	3,742
Food	960	26,130	6,699	10.8	2,878	3,821
Lumber & Wood	590	14,847	1,477	9.9	1,236	241
Paper	96	14,206	1,398	9.8	523	875
Leather	225	10,418	925	8.9	633	292
Mechanical	100	15,732	1,202	7.6	1,187	15
Electrical Equipment	32	12,120	870	7.2	500	370
Metals	153	64,081	4,273	6.7	3,253	1,020
Tobacco	19	7,128	241	3.4	110	131
Beverages	113	15,404	450	2.9	224	226
Rubber	4	3,933	50	1.3	49	1
Transportation Equipment	9	7,993	27	.3	27	0
Other	123	14,340	2,686	18.7	1,268	1,418
Total	5,102	655,174	89,000	13.6	38,662	50,338

Sources: RE 1920E2, p. VII; AN 1956, p. 132

Table VII-5. Numbers of Employees Suffering Employment Related
Injuries or Illnesses, 1969-77

Date	Total	Injured On Job	Taken Ill On Job	Injured Or Taken Ill In Transit
1969	1,059,296	1,050,086	606	8,604
1970	1,220,111	1,199,672	5,937	14,502
1972	1,504,723	1,479,318	2,389	23,016
1974	1,796,761	1,756,649	1,839	38,273
1976	1,743,825	1,692,833	2,598	48,394
1977	1,614,750	1,562,957	3,013	48,780

Sources: AN 1970, p. 620; AN 1971, p. 601; AN 1973, p. 705;
AN 1975, p. 727; AN 1977, p. 669; AN 1978, p. 685.

Table VII-6. Monthly Income for Heads of Families by Sex and for Family Members in Brazil, 1960-70, and by Family Size in 1970

1960

Monthly Income in Cruzeiros	0-2100	2101-3300	3301-4500	4501-6000	6001-10000	10001-20000	20001-50000	50001 & Over	Without Income	Total
HEADS OF FAMILIES										
Male	2,055,266	1,916,386	1,630,951	1,941,148	2,182,253	1,333,982	523,164	117,535	181,413	11,882,098
%	17.3	16.1	13.7	16.4	18.4	11.2	4.4	1.0	1.5	100.0
Female	342,808	138,562	84,956	83,104	78,347	49,194	15,665	2,804	630,947	1,426,387
%	24.0	9.7	6.0	5.8	5.5	3.5	1.1	.2	44.2	100.0
FAMILY MEMBERS										
Husbands	372	377	563	610	844	430	280	50	105	3,631
Wives	1,833,498	1,734,921	1,490,577	1,783,925	2,016,978	1,248,156	490,911	109,646	132,005	10,840,617
Children, Natural/Step/Grand	6,776,581	6,180,564	5,285,572	6,103,003	6,555,172	3,670,238	1,285,062	288,383	1,873,729	38,018,304
Parents/In-Laws	120,860	116,072	108,170	151,100	197,245	141,220	58,372	12,262	23,095	928,396
Other Relatives	465,779	418,405	383,850	491,165	616,975	405,368	145,800	29,462	241,818	3,198,622
Adoptees	78,966	67,194	62,147	73,156	97,093	83,412	48,824	14,411	36,647	561,850
Retirees	—	—	—	—	—	—	—	—	—	—

1970

Monthly Income in Cruzeiros	0-100	101-150	151-250	251-500	501-1000	1001-1500	1501-2000	2001 & Over	Without Income	Total
HEADS OF FAMILIES										
Male	4,102,359	2,445,813	3,526,019	3,058,615	1,406,581	376,774	226,674	289,474	404,938	15,837,247
%	25.9	15.4	22.3	19.3	8.9	2.4	1.4	1.8	2.6	100.0
Female	702,026	193,486	221,830	174,129	84,964	21,409	10,906	9,272	963,211	2,381,233
%	29.5	8.1	9.3	7.3	3.6	.9	.5	.4	40.4	100.0
FAMILY MEMBERS										
Husbands	—	—	—	—	—	—	—	—	—	—
Wives	3,717,677	2,235,718	3,262,142	2,873,091	1,328,864	355,511	213,444	273,498	324,193	14,584,138
Children, Natural/Grand/Step	13,320,851	7,746,140	10,962,677	8,986,371	3,508,742	848,193	500,706	631,455	2,551,743	49,056,878
Parents/In-Laws	192,538	130,822	211,217	210,166	111,865	31,819	19,246	23,949	30,389	962,011
Other Relatives	853,436	492,077	689,401	649,859	296,870	73,392	39,405	42,983	425,666	3,563,089
Adoptees	140,177	84,872	130,084	156,004	88,870	28,463	18,702	23,133	50,909	721,214
Retirees	93,096	72,941	127,724	128,991	60,159	14,464	9,696	11,489	35,407	553,967
SIZE OF FAMILIES (Including Heads)										
1	299,969	116,794	134,186	91,968	42,149	11,553	6,882	7,278	175,898	886,677
%	33.9	13.2	15.1	10.4	4.7	1.2	.8	.8	19.9	100.0
2	739,566	355,043	457,852	378,818	187,660	49,664	27,013	27,212	380,821	2,603,649
%	28.4	13.6	17.7	14.6	7.2	1.9	1.0	1.0	14.6	100.0
3	785,596	408,933	589,437	524,690	260,041	66,711	36,782	40,269	271,743	2,984,202
%	26.3	13.8	19.7	17.6	8.7	2.2	1.3	1.3	9.1	100.0
4	698,502	390,425	599,607	579,964	312,321	85,487	48,388	53,487	188,268	2,956,449
%	23.6	13.2	20.3	19.6	10.6	2.9	1.6	1.8	6.4	100.0
5	613,194	353,487	537,217	494,628	250,296	72,266	44,998	57,843	130,237	2,554,166
%	24.0	13.8	21.0	19.4	9.8	2.8	1.8	2.3	5.1	100.0
6-10	1,500,947	908,362	1,279,923	1,034,199	397,612	104,555	68,692	106,448	208,190	5,608,928
%	26.8	16.2	22.8	18.4	7.1	1.9	1.2	1.9	3.7	100.0
11-14	159,112	101,201	142,105	120,634	38,302	7,315	4,411	5,679	12,403	591,162
%	26.9	17.1	24.0	20.4	6.5	1.2	.8	1.0	2.1	100.0
15 & Over	7,499	5,054	7,522	7,843	3,164	632	414	530	589	33,247
%	22.6	15.2	22.6	23.6	9.5	1.9	1.2	1.6	1.8	100.0

Sources: RE 1960A1, pp. 114-117; RE1970A1, pp. 214-218

Table VII-7. Monthly Minimum Wage in Cruzeiros for Twenty-Five Regions in Brazil, 1943-77

Date Wage Became: REGION	Effective: POLITICAL SUBDIVISION	June 1943	Dec. 1943	Jan. 1952	July 1954	Aug. 1956	Jan. 1959	Oct. 1960	Oct. 1961	Jan. 1963	Feb. 1964	Mar. 1965	Mar. 1966	Mar. 1967	Mar. 1968	May 1969	May 1970	May 1971	May 1972	May 1973	May 1974	May 1975	May 1976	May 1977
São Paulo	São Paulo	.27	.36	1.19	2.30	3.70	5.90	9.44	13.21	21.00	42.00	66.00	84.00	105.00	129.60	156.00	187.20	225.60	268.80	312.00	376.80	532.80	768.00	1106.40
Rio de Janeiro	Rio de Janeiro	.30	.38	1.20	2.40	3.80	6.00	9.60	13.44	21.00	42.00	66.00	84.00	105.00	129.60	156.00	187.20	225.60	268.80	312.00	376.80	532.80	768.00	1106.40
Belo Horizonte	Minas Gerais	.21	.27	.90	2.20	3.30	5.30	8.48	11.87	21.00	42.00	64.32	81.00	101.25	124.80	148.80	177.60	216.00	268.00	312.00	376.80	532.80	768.00	1106.40
Brasília	Distrito Federal									21.00	42.00	63.60	81.00	101.25	124.80	148.80	177.60	216.00	268.00	312.00	376.80	532.80	768.00	1106.40
Pôrto Alegre	Rio Grande do Sul	.25	.32	.80	1.80	3.10	5.00	8.00	11.20	18.30	36.60	60.00	76.50	95.63	117.60	141.60	170.40	208.80	249.60	288.00	350.40	494.40	712.80	1027.20
Curitiba	Paraná	.22	.29	.65	1.50	2.70	4.50	7.20	10.08	17.80	35.60	60.00	76.50	95.63	117.60	141.60	170.40	208.80	249.60	288.00	350.40	494.40	712.80	1027.20
Florianópolis	Santa Catarina	.21	.27	.65	1.05	2.40	4.50	7.20	10.08	17.80	35.60	60.00	76.50	95.63	117.60	141.60	170.40	208.80	249.60	288.00	350.40	494.40	712.80	1027.20
Vitória	Espírito Santo	.20	.26	.80	1.80	2.80	4.50	7.20	10.08	17.20	32.40	51.60	66.00	82.50	100.80	124.80	156.00	187.20	225.60	261.60	321.60	453.60	655.20	945.60
Recife	Pernambuco	.18	.24	.65	1.60	2.70	4.50	7.20	10.08	16.50	33.00	51.60	66.00	82.50	100.80	120.00	144.00	172.80	206.40	240.00	295.20	417.60	602.40	868.80
Salvador	Bahia	.18	.24	.70	1.55	2.30	3.80	6.24	8.51	16.50	33.00	51.60	66.00	82.50	100.80	120.00	144.00	172.80	206.40	240.00	295.20	417.60	602.40	868.80
Cuiabá	Mato Grosso	.18	.24	.57	1.20	2.40	3.90	6.08	8.73	16.60	33.00	51.84	66.00	82.50	100.80	120.00	144.00	172.80	206.40	240.00	295.20	417.60	602.40	868.80
Goiânia	Goiás	.18	.24	.69	1.30	2.40	4.40	7.04	9.85	18.00	34.00	51.84	66.00	82.50	100.80	120.00	144.00	172.80	206.40	240.00	295.20	417.60	602.40	868.80
Pôrto Velho	Rondônia	-	.29	.76	1.26	2.90	4.80	7.68	10.75	14.50	34.00	48.00	61.00	76.25	93.60	112.80	134.40	172.80	206.40	240.00	295.20	417.60	602.40	868.80
Rio Branco	Acre	.21	.27	.89	1.42	2.90	4.40	7.04	9.85	15.10	30.90	48.00	61.00	76.25	93.60	112.80	134.40	172.80	206.40	240.00	295.20	417.60	602.40	868.80
Manaus	Amazonas	.20	.26	.76	1.26	2.90	4.00	6.40	8.96	16.90	34.00	48.00	61.00	76.25	93.60	112.80	134.40	172.80	206.40	240.00	295.20	417.60	602.40	868.80
Boa Vista	Roraima	-	.21	.59	.95	2.50	4.80	7.68	10.75	15.70	34.00	48.00	61.00	78.25	93.60	112.80	134.40	172.80	206.40	240.00	295.20	417.60	602.40	868.80
Belém	Pará	.18	.24	.64	.99	2.80	4.00	6.40	8.96	16.50	31.00	48.00	61.00	76.25	93.60	112.80	134.40	172.80	206.40	240.00	295.20	417.60	602.40	868.80
Macapá	Amapá	-	.19	.46	.75	2.30	3.70	5.92	8.28	13.40	31.00	48.00	61.00	76.25	93.60	112.80	134.40	172.80	206.40	240.00	295.20	417.60	602.40	868.80
Fortaleza	Ceará	.18	.24	.69	1.12	2.25	3.40	5.44	7.61	14.70	25.20	39.60	51.00	63.75	79.20	98.40	124.80	151.20	182.40	213.60	266.40	376.80	544.80	787.20
São Luís	Maranhão	.15	.20	.66	1.20	2.00	2.50	4.00	5.60	12.00	25.20	39.60	51.00	73.75	79.20	98.40	124.80	151.20	182.40	213.60	266.40	376.80	544.80	787.20
Teresina	Piauí	.15	.20	.54	.90	1.50	3.60	4.00	8.06	9.00	20.00	36.00	48.00	60.00	76.80	98.40	124.80	151.20	182.40	213.60	266.40	376.80	544.80	787.20
Natal	Rio Grande do Norte	.16	.21	.50	.84	1.80	3.60	5.76	8.06	13.50	25.20	39.60	51.00	63.75	79.20	98.40	124.80	151.20	182.40	213.60	266.40	376.80	544.80	787.20
João Pessoa	Paraíba	.16	.21	.55	1.20	2.20	3.60	5.76	8.06	13.90	25.20	39.60	51.00	63.75	79.20	98.40	124.80	151.20	182.40	213.60	266.40	376.80	544.80	787.20
Maceió	Alagoas	.15	.21	.59	1.00	2.20	3.60	5.76	8.06	14.20	26.20	39.60	51.00	63.75	79.20	98.40	124.80	151.20	182.40	213.60	266.40	376.80	544.80	787.20
Aracaju	Sergipe	.15	.21	.59	1.08	2.20	3.60	5.76	8.06	13.10	25.10	39.60	51.00	63.75	79.20	98.40	124.80	151.20	182.40	213.60	266.40	376.80	544.80	787.20

Sources: AN 1971, p. 538; AN 1977, p. 657

Table VII-8. Annual Family Expenditures in Five Regions of Brazil by Activity of Family Head, 1975

RIO de JANEIRO

Activities of Family Head / Amount & % Expended	ALL ACTIVITIES		AGRICULTURAL ACTIVITIES						NON AGRICULTURAL ACTIVITIES			
			Employer		Self-Employed		Employee		Employer/Professional		Business-person	
EXPENDITURE CATEGORY	Cr$	%	Cr$	%	Cr$	%	Cr$	%	Cr$	%	Cr$	%
Housing	10,543	26.3	8,769	19.4	2,676	18.1	1,669	18.6	28,694	23.8	12,199	28.4
Food	8,528	21.3	9,480	21.0	6,937	47.0	5,311	59.2	12,430	10.3	10,254	23.9
Clothing	2,192	5.5	2,016	4.5	1,006	6.8	534	5.9	7,160	5.9	1,679	3.9
Transportation	2,112	5.3	3,816	8.5	499	3.4	224	2.5	7,073	5.8	2,519	5.9
Health & Hygiene	2,000	5.0	2,029	4.5	665	4.5	386	4.3	5,312	4.4	1,993	4.6
Education	855	2.1	961	2.1	155	1.0	71	.8	2,632	2.2	1,276	3.0
Tobacco	615	1.5	472	1.0	354	2.4	206	2.3	891	.7	592	1.4
Recreation	587	1.4	423	.9	114	.8	35	.4	1,692	1.4	529	1.2
Other Consumption	1,199	3.0	1,378	3.1	305	2.1	121	1.3	4,812	4.0	1,491	3.5
Taxes/Pensions/Contributions	2,846	7.1	1,501	3.3	308	2.1	129	1.4	10,212	8.5	2,503	5.8
Upkeep/Property/Investments	6,760	16.9	12,845	28.5	1,555	10.5	257	2.9	32,231	26.7	5,961	13.9
Savings	1,838	4.6	1,441	3.2	188	1.3	32	.4	7,584	6.3	1,928	4.5
Total	40,075	100.0	45,131	100.0	14,762	100.0	8,975	100.0	120,723	100.0	42,924	100.0
No. of Families Surveyed	2,169,000		23,000		41,000		71,000		87,000		57,000	
Average Family Size	4		5		6		6		4		5	

SÃO PAULO

EXPENDITURE CATEGORY	Cr$	%	Cr$	%	Cr$	%	Cr$	%	Cr$	%	Cr$	%
Housing	10,387	24.4	9,230	16.9	4,028	17.4	2,660	21.2	29,179	23.7	15,283	21.3
Food	8,372	19.6	10,701	19.6	8,699	37.5	6,425	51.2	12,830	10.4	11,163	15.6
Clothing	2,234	5.2	3,056	5.6	1,310	5.6	919	7.3	4,992	4.0	2,613	3.6
Transportation	2,197	5.2	3,142	5.8	1,022	4.4	230	1.8	6,629	5.4	3,648	5.1
Health & Hygiene	1,864	4.4	2,729	5.0	1,095	4.7	559	4.5	4,498	3.7	2,985	4.2
Education	717	1.7	1,006	1.8	208	.9	75	.6	2,266	1.8	1,089	1.5
Tobacco	597	1.4	536	1.0	256	1.1	308	2.5	832	.7	742	1.0
Recreation	466	1.1	362	.7	137	.6	68	.5	1,438	1.2	875	1.2
Other Consumption	1,179	2.8	1,718	3.2	737	3.2	211	1.7	3,449	2.8	1,993	2.8
Taxes/Pensions/Contributions	2,454	5.8	2,144	3.9	383	1.7	159	1.3	6,466	5.3	2,828	3.9
Upkeep/Property/Investments	10,190	23.9	19,204	35.3	4,973	21.4	895	7.1	43,596	35.4	24,124	33.6
Savings	1,923	4.5	650	1.2	342	1.5	43	.3	6,926	5.6	4,441	6.2
Total	42,580	100.0	54,478	100.0	23,190	100.0	12,552	100.0	123,101	100.0	71,784	100.0
No. of Families Surveyed	4,168,000		102,000		174,000		400,000		204,000		159,000	
Average Family Size	5		5		6		5		4		5	

PARANÁ/SANTA CATARINA/RIO GRANDE do SUL

EXPENDITURE CATEGORY	Cr$	%	Cr$	%	Cr$	%	Cr$	%	Cr$	%	Cr$	%
Housing	5,761	19.8	5,607	13.2	3,263	16.1	1,940	19.6	19,842	18.3	9,818	22.1
Food	7,711	26.6	9,408	22.1	8,089	40.0	5,623	56.8	12,238	11.3	9,168	20.6
Clothing	1,844	6.4	2,188	5.1	1,412	7.0	654	6.6	5,302	4.9	2,723	6.1
Transportation	1,288	4.4	2,028	4.8	689	3.4	141	1.4	5,565	5.1	2,514	5.7
Health & Hygiene	1,452	5.0	2,216	5.2	1,257	6.2	557	5.6	4,169	3.8	1,826	4.1
Education	400	1.4	344	.8	177	.9	64	.6	1,798	1.7	929	2.1
Tobacco	423	1.5	364	.9	218	1.1	223	2.3	903	.8	653	1.5
Recreation	301	1.0	244	.6	101	.5	49	.5	1,585	1.5	504	1.1
Other Consumption	1,000	3.5	1,726	4.1	624	3.1	193	1.9	4,130	3.8	1,127	2.5
Taxes/Pensions/Contributions	1,262	4.3	1,526	3.6	270	1.3	90	.9	6,944	6.4	1,878	4.2
Upkeep/Property/Investments	6,693	23.0	16,019	37.7	3,859	19.0	356	3.6	41,241	38.0	11,494	25.9
Savings	904	3.1	827	1.9	288	1.4	15	.2	4,795	4.4	1,799	4.1
Total	29,039	100.0	42,497	100.0	20,247	100.0	9,905	100.0	108,512	100.0	44,433	100.0
No. of Families Surveyed	3,548,000		286,000		930,000		329,000		117,000		117,000	
Average Family Size	5		5		6		5		5		5	

Table VII-8 (continued)

NON AGRICULTURAL ACTIVITIES

Activities of Family Head Amount & % Expended Region of Brazil	Self Employed-Established Cr$	%	Self Employed-Beginning Cr$	%	Upper Level Employee Cr$	%	Middle Level Employee Cr$	%	Skilled Laborer Cr$	%	Unskilled Laborer Cr$	%
EXPENDITURE CATEGORY												
RIO de JANEIRO												
Housing	7,906	25.5	6,686	26.8	46,330	27.4	19,179	28.3	9,096	26.6	5,166	24.6
Food	8,658	27.9	8,081	32.4	15,583	9.2	10,837	16.0	8,535	25.0	7,689	36.6
Clothing	1,835	5.9	1,357	5.5	6,551	3.9	4,319	6.4	2,140	6.3	1,337	6.4
Transportation	1,660	5.3	1,853	7.4	7,334	4.3	3,514	5.2	2,304	6.7	1,176	5.6
Health & Hygiene	1,722	5.5	1,278	5.1	7,088	4.2	3,289	4.9	1,876	5.5	991	4.7
Education	737	2.4	477	1.9	4,254	2.5	1,966	2.9	658	1.9	344	1.6
Tobacco	797	2.6	617	2.5	727	.4	719	1.1	703	2.0	583	2.8
Recreation	649	2.1	242	1.0	2,623	1.5	1,177	1.7	484	1.4	237	1.1
Other Consumption	462	1.5	523	2.1	5,764	3.4	2,270	3.4	876	2.6	458	2.2
Taxes/Pensions/Contributions	2,191	7.0	1,030	4.1	17,578	10.4	6,953	10.3	2,176	6.4	1,285	6.1
Upkeep/Property/Investments	3,106	10.0	1,930	7.8	45,421	26.9	8,769	12.9	3,575	10.5	1,136	5.5
Savings	1,321	4.3	852	3.4	9,897	5.9	4,701	6.9	1,730	5.1	595	2.8
Total	31,044	100.0	24,926	100.0	169,150	100.0	67,693	100.0	34,153	100.0	20,997	100.0
No. of Families Surveyed	49,000		169,000		78,000		139,000		254,000		685,000	
Average Family Size	4		5		4		3		4		5	
SÃO PAULO												
Housing	9,611	26.1	10,145	26.5	35,173	21.0	19,720	25.0	10,526	24.2	6,836	26.8
Food	9,189	24.9	8,333	21.8	11,555	6.9	9,795	12.4	9,024	20.8	7,499	29.3
Clothing	2,283	6.2	2,291	6.0	6,558	3.8	4,285	5.4	2,696	6.2	1,678	6.6
Transportation	1,969	5.3	2,487	6.5	8,295	5.0	5,080	6.4	2,733	6.3	1,225	4.8
Health & Hygiene	1,879	5.1	1,737	4.5	6,449	3.9	3,403	4.3	2,099	4.8	1,176	4.6
Education	687	1.9	638	1.7	3,431	2.1	2,084	2.7	814	1.9	348	1.4
Tobacco	730	2.0	622	1.6	670	.4	718	.9	760	1.7	598	2.3
Recreation	403	1.1	388	1.0	2,285	1.4	1,191	1.5	526	1.2	229	.9
Other Consumption	677	1.8	1,131	3.0	6,551	3.9	2,515	3.2	1,199	2.8	627	2.4
Taxes/Pensions/Contributions	1,705	4.6	2,192	5.8	19,343	11.6	5,800	7.3	2,896	6.7	1,555	6.1
Upkeep/Property/Investments	6,043	16.4	7,084	18.5	53,541	32.0	19,311	24.4	7,998	18.4	2,905	11.4
Savings	1,673	4.6	1,194	3.1	13,350	8.0	5,161	6.5	2,160	5.0	873	3.4
Total	36,849	100.0	38,242	100.0	167,201	100.0	79,063	100.0	43,431	100.0	25,549	100.0
No. of Families Surveyed	121,000		261,000		82,000		235,000		405,000		1,337,000	
Average Family Size	5		4		3		3		4		5	
PARANÁ/SANTA CATARINA/RIO GRANDE do SUL												
Housing	7,109	20.0	5,701	23.3	27,189	22.6	12,928	22.5	8,326	23.3	4,472	23.3
Food	9,292	26.2	7,232	29.5	11,606	9.6	8,547	14.8	7,730	21.7	6,933	36.0
Clothing	2,429	6.9	1,810	7.4	6,438	5.3	3,741	6.5	2,436	6.8	1,449	7.5
Transportation	1,530	4.3	1,411	5.8	8,320	6.9	3,591	6.2	2,036	5.7	655	3.4
Health & Hygiene	1,600	4.5	1,461	6.0	4,167	3.5	2,499	4.3	1,698	4.8	944	4.9
Education	550	1.6	355	1.4	3,096	2.6	1,357	2.4	553	1.6	244	1.3
Tobacco	616	1.7	514	2.1	951	.8	852	1.5	647	1.8	476	2.5
Recreation	327	.9	233	1.0	2,238	1.9	1,111	1.9	427	1.2	171	.9
Other Consumption	1,032	2.9	827	3.4	4,977	4.1	2,210	3.8	1,331	3.7	561	2.9
Taxes/ Pensions/Contributions	1,281	3.6	921	3.8	11,790	9.8	4,391	7.6	2,074	5.8	975	5.1
Upkeep/Property/Investments	8,390	23.6	3,334	13.6	32,166	26.7	12,380	21.5	6,653	18.7	1,931	10.0
Savings	1,354	3.8	668	2.7	7,508	6.2	4,001	7.0	1,745	4.9	416	2.2
Total	35,510	100.0	24,467	100.0	120,446	100.0	57,608	100.0	35,656	100.0	19,227	100.0
No. of Families Surveyed	96,000		195,000		34,000		116,000		179,000		714,000	
Average Family Size	5		5		4		4		4		5	

Table VII-8 (continued)

MINAS GERAIS/ESPÍRITO SANTO

Activities of Family Head	ALL ACTIVITIES		AGRICULTURAL ACTIVITIES						NON AGRICULTURAL ACTIVITIES			
			Employer		Self-Employed		Employee		Employer/Professional		Business-person	
Amount & % Expended	Cr$	%	Cr$	%	Cr$	%	Cr$	%	Cr$	%	Cr$	%
EXPENDITURE CATEGORY												
Housing	4,650	19.7	5,743	12.7	2,082	13.0	1,082	14.4	22,435	16.5	7,666	22.5
Food	6,619	28.0	9,618	21.3	7,103	44.3	4,691	62.6	12,150	8.9	8,437	24.8
Clothing	1,610	6.8	2,582	5.7	1,301	8.1	573	7.6	5,774	4.2	2,439	7.2
Transportation	963	4.1	3,274	7.2	546	3.4	97	1.3	4,998	3.7	1,475	4.3
Health & Hygiene	1,262	5.3	2,600	5.7	1,052	6.6	354	4.7	4,639	3.4	2,032	6.0
Education	426	1.8	571	1.3	196	1.2	44	.6	2,401	1.7	742	2.2
Tobacco	319	1.3	350	.8	148	.9	136	1.8	664	.5	489	1.4
Recreation	275	1.2	285	.6	92	.6	28	.4	1,816	1.3	480	1.4
Other Consumption	889	3.8	2,214	4.9	582	3.6	156	2.1	4,786	3.5	1,411	4.2
Taxes/Pensions/Contributions	1,034	4.3	2,926	6.5	211	1.3	44	.6	7,738	5.7	1,426	4.2
Upkeep/Property/Investments	5,027	21.2	13,836	30.6	2,558	15.9	278	3.7	64,827	47.6	6,554	19.2
Savings	587	2.5	1,222	2.7	173	1.1	14	.2	4,053	3.0	889	2.6
Total	23,661	100.0	45,231	100.0	16,044	100.0	7,497	100.0	136,281	100.0	34,040	100.0
No. of Families Surveyed	2,592,000		150,000		439,000		480,000		62,000		96,000	
Average Family Size	5		5		6		5		5		5	

MARANHÃO/PIAUÍ/CEARÁ/RIO GRANDE do NORTE/PARAÍBA/PERNAMBUCO/ALAGOAS/SERGIPE/BAHIA

Activities of Family Head	ALL ACTIVITIES		AGRICULTURAL ACTIVITIES						NON AGRICULTURAL ACTIVITIES			
			Employer		Self-Employed		Employee		Employer/Professional		Business-person	
	Cr$	%	Cr$	%	Cr$	%	Cr$	%	Cr$	%	Cr$	%
Housing	2,637	19.9	2,324	14.6	989	13.6	798	14.5	14,570	21.5	3,408	9.7
Food	5,145	38.9	6,180	38.9	4,400	60.3	3,619	65.8	11,850	17.5	6,725	38.8
Clothing	971	7.3	1,103	7.0	622	8.5	398	7.2	4,113	6.1	1,403	8.1
Transportation	485	3.7	594	3.7	119	1.6	49	.9	3,884	5.7	695	4.0
Health & Hygiene	638	4.8	922	5.8	328	4.5	203	3.7	2,876	4.2	831	4.8
Education	213	1.6	144	.9	46	.6	19	.4	1,638	2.4	243	1.4
Tobacco	208	1.6	172	1.1	110	1.5	121	2.2	702	1.0	281	1.6
Recreation	146	1.1	111	.7	34	.5	30	.6	1,185	1.8	171	1.0
Other Consumption	320	2.4	614	3.9	150	2.1	74	1.3	1,850	2.7	356	2.1
Taxes/Pensions/Contributions	553	4.2	632	4.0	93	1.3	57	1.0	5,052	7.4	527	3.0
Upkeep/Property/Investments	1,628	12.3	2,909	18.3	382	5.2	128	2.3	16,840	24.8	2,485	14.3
Savings	286	2.2	179	1.1	23	.3	5	.1	3,309	4.9	199	1.2
Total	13,230	100.0	15,884	100.0	7,296	100.0	5,501	100.0	67,869	100.0	17,324	100.0
No. of Families Surveyed	5,791,000		487,000		1,239,000		1,112,000		84,000		343,000	
Average Family Size	5		6		6		5		6		6	

Table VII-8 (continued)

NON AGRICULTURAL ACTIVITIES

Region: MINAS GERAIS/ESPÍRITO SANTO

Activities of Family Head / Amount & % Expended / EXPENDITURE CATEGORY	Self Employed- Established Cr$	%	Self Employed- Beginning Cr$	%	Upper Level Employee Cr$	%	Middle Level Employee Cr$	%	Skilled Laborer Cr$	%	Unskilled Laborer Cr$	%
Housing	6,007	19.4	4,057	22.8	30,996	21.6	13,429	24.9	8,341	24.3	3,778	23.2
Food	7,956	25.7	5,924	33.2	14,278	10.0	9,813	18.2	7,561	22.0	6,050	37.2
Clothing	1,959	6.3	1,347	7.5	8,404	5.9	4,128	7.6	2,464	7.2	1,324	8.1
Transportation	1,597	5.2	938	5.3	5,769	4.0	2,742	5.1	1,514	4.4	543	3.3
Health & Hygiene	1,684	5.5	1,102	6.2	5,294	3.7	3,034	5.6	1,697	4.9	890	5.5
Education	668	2.2	346	1.9	3,309	2.3	1,601	3.0	808	2.3	299	1.8
Tobacco	635	2.0	340	1.9	1,061	.7	691	1.3	541	1.6	371	2.3
Recreation	456	1.5	277	1.6	2,478	1.7	1,154	2.1	535	1.6	148	.9
Other Consumption	768	2.5	563	3.2	8,910	6.2	2,216	4.1	1,388	4.0	510	3.1
Taxes/Pensions/Contributions	1,205	3.9	444	2.5	11,851	8.3	3,273	6.1	1,866	5.4	774	4.8
Upkeep/Property/Investments	6,674	21.6	2,045	11.5	42,968	30.0	9,253	17.1	6,616	19.2	1,341	8.2
Savings	1,301	4.2	424	2.4	8,056	5.6	2,657	4.9	1,070	3.1	264	1.6
Total	30,910	100.0	17,807	100.0	143,374	100.0	53,991	100.0	34,401	100.0	16,292	100.0
No. of Families Surveyed	43,000		180,000		19,000		68,000		123,000		526,000	
Average Family Size	5		5		4		4		5		5	

Region: MARANHÃO/PIAUÍ/CEARÁ/RIO GRANDE do NORTE/PARAÍBA/PERNAMBUCO/ALAGOAS/SERGIPE/BAHIA

EXPENDITURE CATEGORY	Self Employed- Established Cr$	%	Self Employed- Beginning Cr$	%	Upper Level Employee Cr$	%	Middle Level Employee Cr$	%	Skilled Laborer Cr$	%	Unskilled Laborer Cr$	%
Housing	2,800	19.5	2,260	20.9	29,573	21.5	13,442	25.8	5,499	24.0	2,646	22.2
Food	6,193	43.0	4,892	45.3	13,726	10.0	9,420	18.1	7,201	31.4	5,351	44.8
Clothing	1,248	8.7	879	8.2	6,750	4.8	3,518	6.7	1,865	8.1	927	7.8
Transportation	440	3.1	375	3.5	8,503	6.2	2,751	5.3	1,089	4.7	403	3.4
Health & Hygiene	693	4.8	557	5.2	5,639	4.1	2,570	4.9	1,190	5.1	596	5.0
Education	191	1.3	166	1.5	3,244	2.4	1,644	3.2	519	2.2	191	1.6
Tobacco	252	1.8	235	2.1	884	.6	489	.9	405	1.8	290	2.4
Recreation	158	1.1	118	1.1	2,107	1.5	880	1.7	354	1.5	116	1.0
Other Consumption	305	2.1	250	2.3	4,169	3.0	1,664	3.2	574	2.5	235	2.0
Taxes/Pensions/Contributions	438	3.0	248	2.3	11,944	8.7	3,870	7.4	1,323	5.8	560	4.7
Upkeep/Property/Investments	1,481	10.3	725	6.7	43,355	31.4	8,695	16.7	2,184	9.5	444	3.7
Savings	189	1.3	97	.9	7,965	5.8	3,189	6.1	789	3.4	169	1.4
Total	14,388	100.0	10,802	100.0	137,859	100.0	52,132	100.0	22,992	100.0	11,928	100.0
No. of Families Surveyed	147,000		457,000		37,000		96,000		200,000		848,000	
Average Family Size	6		5		4		5		5		6	

Source: AN 1978, pp. 710-734

Table VII-9. Monthly Expenditures by Factory Workers in the Distrito Federal in 1946 and Annual Family Expenditures for Skilled and Unskilled Workers in Rio de Janeiro State in 1975

	1946		1975			
	Monthly Expenditures		Annual Expenditures			
	Factory Workers		Skilled Laborer		Unskilled Laborer	
EXPENDITURE CATEGORY	Cr$	%	Cr$	%	Cr$	%
Housing	125.10	10.7	9,096	26.6	5,166	24.6
Food	601.00	51.2	8,535	25.0	7,689	36.6
Clothing	122.60	10.5	2,304	6.7	1,337	6.4
Transportation	37.60	3.2	2,140	6.3	1,176	5.6
Health & Hygiene	75.50	6.4	1,876	5.5	991	4.7
Education	17.70	1.5	658	1.9	344	1.6
Tobacco	-	-	703	2.0	583	2.8
Recreation	37.80	3.2	484	1.4	237	1.1
Other Consumption	45.90	3.9	876	2.6	458	2.2
Taxes/Pensions/Contributions	47.60	4.1	2,176	6.4	1,285	6.1
Upkeep/Property/Investments	-	-	3,575	10.5	1,136	5.5
Savings	62.20	5.3	1,730	5.1	595	2.8
Total	1,173.00	100.0	34,153	100.0	20,997	100.0
No. of Families Surveyed	3,091		254,000		685,000	
Average Family Size	-		4		5	

Sources: Wythe, Wright, Midkiff, p. 246; AN 1978, p. 710.

Table VII-10. Size and Composition of Families by Urban/Rural Domicile in Brazil, 1950-70

Brazil Total:	1950		1960		1970	
	Number	%	Number	%	Number	%
Heads of Families						
Male	8,827,218	87.9	12,082,817	89.3	16,137,061	87.0
Female	1,218,981	12.1	1,449,325	10.7	2,417,364	13.0
Total	10,046,199	100.0	13,532,142	100.0	18,554,425	100.0
Family Members						
Husbands	7,025	negl.	3,698	negl.	-	-
Wives	7,902,888	19.0	11,017,779	19.8	14,843,469	20.8
Children/natural grand/step	27,932,372	67.3	38,567,106	69.2	49,841,672	69.8
Parents/In-laws	712,390	1.7	943,214	1.7	977,383	1.4
Agregados	970,701	2.3	568,608	1.0	731,780	1.0
Other	4,004,434	9.7	4,604,738	8.3	5,013,183	7.0
Total	41,529,810	100.0	55,705,143	100.0	71,407,487	100.0
Average Family Size		5.12		5.12		4.85

Urban/Rural:

Size of Families	1950				1960			
	Numbers of Families				Numbers of Families			
	Total	% of Total	Urban	% Urban	Total	% of Total	Urban	% Urban
1	503,044	5.0	211,586	42.1	646,380	4.8	357,852	55.4
2	1,198,411	11.9	476,906	39.8	1,592,112	11.8	813,138	51.1
3	1,500,893	14.9	593,349	39.5	2,031,388	15.0	1,037,163	51.1
4	1,525,456	15.2	607,889	39.8	2,205,777	16.3	1,120,659	50.8
5	1,371,779	13.7	525,839	38.3	1,841,190	13.6	916,300	49.8
6	1,147,664	11.4	415,764	36.2	1,534,415	11.3	709,861	46.3
7	902,910	9.0	306,475	33.9	1,177,475	8.7	502,370	42.7
8	700,343	7.0	221,221	31.6	883,755	6.5	348,788	39.5
9	461,382	4.6	141,786	30.7	611,066	4.5	226,790	37.1
10	310,824	3.1	91,962	29.6	482,857	3.6	158,298	32.8
11-14	388,520	3.9	121,124	31.2	481,329	3.6	165,684	34.4
15 and over	34,973	.3	16,467	47.1	44,398	.3	17,730	39.9
Total	10,046,199	100.0	3,730,368	37.1	13,532,142	100.0	6,374,633	47.1

Size of Families	1970			
	Numbers of Families			
	Total	% of Total	Urban	% Urban
1	916,757	4.9	560,651	61.2
2	2,664,604	14.4	1,652,103	62.0
3	3,039,907	16.4	1,890,291	62.2
4	3,006,456	16.2	1,909,013	63.5
5	2,595,114	14.0	1,589,021	61.2
6	1,950,352	10.5	1,133,374	58.1
7	1,455,633	7.8	788,635	54.2
8	1,055,480	5.7	536,565	50.8
9	723,948	3.9	347,796	48.0
10	512,657	2.8	229,509	44.8
11-14	599,783	3.2	253,543	42.3
15 and over	33,735	.2	13,812	40.9
Total	18,554,426	100.0	10,904,313	58.8

Sources: RE 1950A1, pp. 280-281; RE 1960A1, pp. 112 & 114-115; RE 1970A1, pp. 206 & 214-218.

Table VII-11. Physical Structure, Condition of Occupance, Numbers of Rooms, Bedrooms, Utility Hook-ups, Appliances, and Automobiles for Urban/Rural Dwellings in Brazil, 1940-70, and Rents Paid in 1960 and 1970

	1940				Number Rural as % of Col. 1	1950				Number Rural as % of Col. 1
	Total Number	% of Total	Number Rural	% of Rural	This Line	Total Number	% of Total	Number Rural	% of Rural	This Line
Physical Structure										
Ceramic	2,579,659	32.7	1,022,045	19.0	39.6	-	-	-	-	-
Wood	5,192,297	65.7	4,276,637	79.4	82.4	-	-	-	-	-
Other (No Decl.)	125,813	1.6	89,448	1.6	71.1	-	-	-	-	-
Units Censused	7,897,769	100.0	5,388,130	100.0	68.2	10,046,199	100.0	6,315,831	100.0	62.9
Occupance Condition										
Owner Occupied	3,450,109	43.7	2,445,678	45.4	70.9	5,236,178	52.1	3,511,521	55.6	67.1
Renter Occupied	1,647,961	20.9	419,592	7.8	25.5	2,323,573	23.1	569,767	9.0	24.5
Other (No Decl.)	2,799,699	35.4	2,522,860	46.8	90.1	2,486,448	24.8	2,234,543	35.4	89.9
Units Censused	7,897,769	100.0	5,388,130	100.0	68.2	10,046,199	100.0	6,315,831	100.0	62.9
Utilities										
Piped Water	1,025,562	13.0	67,269	1.2	6.6	1,563,272	15.6	88,585	1.4	5.7
Well/Spring	-	-	-	-	-	-	-	-	-	-
Electricity	1,317,967	16.7	131,953	2.4	10.0	2,466,898	24.6	229,188	3.6	9.3
Piped Sewage	-	-	-	-	-	863,444	8.6	14,295	.2	1.7
Septic Tank	-	-	-	-	-	451,811	4.5	40,132	.6	8.9
Units Censused	7,897,679	100.0	5,388,130	100.0	68.2	10,046,199	100.0	6,315,831	100.0	62.9
		Persons Per Room					Persons Per Room			
Rooms/Bedrooms										
Rooms	35,863,941	1.16	22,682,873	1.26	-	45,845,526	1.13	27,123,703	1.22	-
Bedrooms	16,104,367	2.58	10,684,011	2.67	-	20,600,282	2.50	12,754,732	2.60	-
Persons Censused	41,566,410	-	28,517,419	-	-	51,584,665	-	33,262,177	-	-

	1960				Number Rural as % of Col. 1	1970				Number Rural as % of Col. 1
	Total Number	% of Total	Number Rural	% of Rural	This Line	Total Number	% of Total	Number Rural	% of Rural	This Line
Physical Structure										
Permanent	13,497,823	99.2	7,147,697	99.9	53.0	17,628,629	99.9	7,352,359	99.9	41.7
Finished	-	-	-	-	-	13,007,920	73.7	4,228,365	57.5	32.6
Rustic	-	-	-	-	-	4,620,779	26.2	3,123,994	42.4	67.6
Improvised	6,802	.1	1,656	negl	24.3	14,688	.1	7,629	.1	51.9
Units Censused	13,504,624	100.0	7,149,353	100.0	52.9	17,643,387	100.0	7,359,988	100.0	41.7
Occupance Condition										
Owner Occupied	7,703,245	57.1	4,491,201	62.8	58.3	10,631,603	60.3	4,473,859	60.8	42.1
Renter Occupied	3,006,609	22.3	296,744	4.2	9.9	3,356,051	19.0	209,652	2.9	6.2
Other	2,787,969	20.6	2,359,752	33.0	84.6	3,641,045	20.7	2,668,848	36.3	73.3
Units Censused	13,497,823	100.0	7,147,697	100.0	53.0	17,628,699	100.0	7,352,359	100.0	41.7
Utilities										
Piped Water	2,845,620	21.1	88,030	1.2	3.1	5,784,268	32.8	191,662	2.6	3.3
Well/Spring	4,467,018	33.1	2,708,822	37.9	60.6	4,332,655	24.6	1,907,210	25.9	44.0
Electricity	5,201,521	38.5	5,974,464	8.4	11.5	8,383,994	47.6	615,273	8.4	7.3
Piped Sewage	1,772,806	13.1	20,732	.3	1.2	2,318,402	13.2	27,829	.4	1.2
Septic Tank	1,439,459	10.7	190,976	2.7	13.3	2,366,075	13.4	117,308	1.6	5.0
Units Censused	13,497,823	100.0	7,147,697	100.0	53.0	17,628,699	100.0	7,352,359	100.0	41.7
Appliances/Autos										
Wood Stove	8,290,532	61.4	5,728,188	80.1	69.1	7,947,125	45.1	5,802,394	81.2	73.0
Gas Stove	2,464,528	20.5	147,283	2.1	6.0	7,528,287	42.7	403,391	5.6	5.4
Radio	4,776,300	35.4	864,062	12.1	18.1	10,386,763	58.9	2,947,282	41.2	28.4
Refrigerator	1,570,924	11.6	91,625	1.3	5.8	4,594,920	26.1	232,239	3.2	5.1
Television	621,919	4.6	20,367	.3	3.3	4,250,404	24.1	116,092	1.6	2.7
Automobile	-	-	-	-	-	1,594,465	9.0	187,437	2.6	11.8
Units Censused	13,497,823	100.0	7,147,697	100.0	53.0	17,628,699	100.0	7,147,697	100.0	40.5
		Persons Per Room					Persons Per Room			
Rooms/Bedrooms										
Rooms	62,598,389	1.10	31,882,215	1.21	-	83,152,217	1.08	33,194,481	1.19	-
Bedrooms	27,986,958	2.47	15,097,231	2.55	-	36,227,685	2.48	15,440,124	2.56	-
Persons Censused	69,222,849	-	38,628,462	-	-	90,020,290	-	39,580,023	-	-

Rents Paid Cr$ 1960	Number of Dwellings	% of Total	Rents Paid Cr$ 1970	Number of Dwellings	% of Total
1-500	862,400	28.9	1-15	348,059	10.4
501-1000	605,199	20.3	16-30	528,177	15.8
1001-2000	568,067	19.0	31-60	745,489	22.3
2001-4000	523,248	17.5	61-120	708,406	21.2
4001-6000	239,580	8.0	121-240	571,743	17.2
6001-10000	135,648	4.5	241-480	346,576	10.4
10001-20000	47,728	1.6	481-960	75,870	2.3
20001 & over	5,142	.2	961 & over	13,281	.4
Brazil Total	2,987,012	100.0	Brazil Total	3,337,601	100.0

Sources RE 1940A2, pp. 161-162; RE 1950A1, pp. 293-299; RE 1960A1, pp. 124-129; RE 1970A1, pp. 240-257.

Chapter VIII. Labor Organizations, Unemployment and Cooperatives

Table VIII-1 presents the numbers of unions and union membership in Brazil from 1941 to 1977. The data for 1960 and earlier originated with the Serviço de Estatística da Previdência (Welfare) e Trabalho (Labor). The 1970 data originated with the Centro de Documentação e Informática da Ministério de Trabalho e Previdência Social, and those for 1977 with the same Centro of the Ministério de Trabalho. Syndicates (<u>sindicatos</u>) are equivalent to local unions. Federations are state and regional groupings of locals, or locals grouped by related industries or on an industry-wide basis. According to the <u>Anuário estatístico do Brasil, 1937</u>, p. 551 (no data origin given), from 1931 through 1936, 694 new employee syndicates were officially recognized and official recognition was given to 538 new employer syndicates, to 77 new liberal profession syndicates, and to 13 new syndicates of workers on their own accounts.

The numbers and financial values of labor disputes handled by Brazilian labor courts from 1941 to 1977 are shown on Table Table VIII-2. All data originated with the Secretaria do Tribunal Superior do Trabalho (Superior Labor Court). The cases reported on the table are those heard by Juntas de Conciliação e Julgamento. These are first-level courts composed, according to the <u>Pequeno diccionário brasileiro da língua portuguêsa</u>,[1] of a judge-president and two lawyers, one representing the employee(s) and the other the employer(s).

Table VIII-3 presents membership in and benefits paid by Brazil's social security system from 1925 to 1977. Stimulated by 1919 enabling legislation Brazil's first social security program was set up four years later. In 1923, according to Alim Pedro,[2] the Railroad Workers Retirement and Pensions Fund (Caixas de Aposentadoria e Pensões dos Ferroviários) was created to offer protection against job-related accidents. Payments, however, were the responsibility of the employers who could choose to enroll their companies with private insurers. Wythe, Wight, and Midkiff[3] report that by 1925 twenty-seven separate social security funds were in operation in Brazil. Most of them were local or regional in scope including only employees of a company or group of companies. In 1933, however, the first nationwide program based on job activity rather than on company or locale was established. Enrollment was obligatory in this program entitled the Retirement and Pensions Institute for Maritime Workers (Instituto de Aposentadoria e Pensões dos Marítimos-IAPM). Since 1925 the number of smaller funds (Caixas) had been growing. Their numbers reached a peak of 183 in 1936 and then began a long, steady decline as they were merged with the increasing numbers of Institutes. By 1951 only 35 Caixas and Institutos were in operation. In the late 1960s most of the existing programs were brought under the umbrella of the National Institute for Social Welfare (Instituto Nacional de Previdência Social-INPS). Rural workers were mandatorily enrolled in the social security system by law number 4,214, March 2, 1963, which set up the Fundo de Assistência e Previdência do Trabalhador Rural. Coimbra[4] notes that 1 percent of the value of the agricultural harvest was to be paid into the fund by the producer.

All data on Table VIII-3 from 1925 through 1950 were generated by the Departamento Nacional de Previdência Social. The 1960 data were originated by various Institutos de Aposentadorias e Pensões, and by the Serviço Social aos Servidores Economiários (Administrators). All post-1960 data originated with the Instituto Nacional de Previdência Social (INPS).

The figures on Table VIII-3 for the years 1925 through 1950 cover all Caixas (Funds) and Institutos (Institutes) except those for federal employees. Pedro,[2] in a publication dated 1950, reported that 2,820,000 Brazilians with 5,180,000 beneficiaries were provided mandatory coverage by the country's 30 Caixas and Institutos. He gave no date for these figures. He reported the five largest Institutes and the numbers enrolled (excluding beneficiaries) in each to be as follows: Industrial Workers, 1,464,000; Retail/Wholesale Workers, 596,000; Teamsters, 244,000; Maritime Workers, 68,000; and Bank Employees, 54,000. The two largest Caixas were those for Railroad Workers with 205,000 enrollees, and for Public Utilities with an enrollment of 176,000.

The 1960 figures on Table VIII-3 are for eight Institutes including Bank Employees, Retail/Wholesale Workers, Teamsters, Railroad/Public Service Workers, Industrial Workers, Maritime Workers, Federal Employees, and Administrators. The 1960 retirement total included payments to employees in quasi-government authorities (autarquias). Figures for 1969 and 1974 were separated into those for INPS, the umbrella institute, and those for three other public employee institutes: federal, state, and municipal.

The 1976 data for the Rural Workers Fund were reported separately from the INPS by the sources. The numbers of retirees and pensioners shown on Table VIII-3 do not represent individuals but instead are the numbers of benefits paid which in some cases results in double-counting individuals who received both retirement and pension benefits. Sources for the INPS data did not include three public employee Institutes or the Rural Workers Fund. Again, the numbers of retirees and pensioners did not represent individuals but benefits paid and the caveat noted above pertains here as well.

Table VIII-4 reports the numbers of unemployed by sex in Brazil in 1960 and 1970. The data are from the respective censuses and therefore represent individuals who themselves said they were unemployed when the census was taken. The censuses did not publish a lower age limit for classifying a person as unemployed. The industry groups listed on the table are those in which the person worked the week before the census was taken, so unemployment is probably under-stated.

The numbers of cooperatives and cooperative memberships in Brazil from 1902 to 1976 are shown on Table VIII-5. The data for 1960 and earlier were generated by the Serviço de Economia Rural do Ministério da Agricultura. The 1964 and 1970 data were generated by the Instituto Nacional de Colonizição e Reforma Agrária (INCRA), Divisão de Cooperativismo, and the 1976 data by INCRA. All cooperatives reported on the table were registered with or authorized by the appropriate federal agency. The number of unregistered/unauthorized cooperatives may for any given year exceed the number given government sanction. The counts of these cooperatives, however, were intermittent, making longitudinal comparisons difficult. In 1936, for example, there were 462 unregistered cooperatives and only 189 registered organizations.

Brazil's first cooperative was founded in 1902. From that date through 1941 a total of 1,380 cooperatives was founded and registered, but also in this period 61 registered cooperatives ceased to exist so that by the end of 1941 Brazil had 1,319 registered cooperatives. The late 1930s and the decade of the 1940s saw a boom in the cooperative movement in Brazil, which subsequently slowed and then declined. Rio Grande do Sul state with its German, Italian, and Polish ethnic farmers had more than 35 percent of Brazil's registered cooperatives in 1936. By 1951, however,

São Paulo state with its Japanese ethnic farmers had become the leading state in the number of registered cooperatives. By 1960 São Paulo state's total registered cooperative membership had reached 432,592, or 23.2 percent of the Brazilian total. Rio Grande do Sul State had 19.3 percent of the country's total registered cooperative membership in 1976 (432,592). The total of "other" cooperatives in 1976 is large in part because it reflects the growing numbers of school cooperatives.

References

1. _Pequeno diccionário da língua portuguêsa_, 10th ed., ed Aurelio Buarque de Hollanda Ferreira (Rio de Janeiro: Editôra Civilizaçao Brasileira, S.A., 1961).

2. Pedro Alim, _O seguro social, a industria brasileria, o instituto dos industriários_, Relatório estudo do Engenheiro Alim Pedro, Presidente do I.A.P.I. no período de 26-4-46 a 29-1-51, 1950.

3. George Wythe, Royce A. Wight, and Harold M. Midkiff, _Brazil: An Expanding Economy_ (New York: Twentieth Century Fund, 1949).

4. _O trabalhador rural e a previdência social, lei e regulamento_, comentários por J. R. Feijó Coimbra, ed. José Konfino (Rio de Janeiro, 1968). No publisher given.

Table VIII-1. Unions and Union Membership in Brazil, 1941-77

	1941	1950	1960	1970	1977
Number of Unions	732	1,985	2,892	3,523	3,665
Confederations	–	4	9	13	–
Employee	–	2	5	8	–
Employer	–	2	3	4	–
Liberal Professions	–	–	1	1	–
Federations	–	90	154	217	232
Employee	–	48	91	88	137
Employer	–	39	59	123	86
Liberal Professions	–	3	4	6	9
Syndicate	732	1,891	2,729	3,293	3,433
Employee	395	1,075	1,608	1,991	1,975
Employer	300	729	1,005	1,190	1,317
Liberal Professions	37	87	116	112	141
Syndicate Membership					
Employee Syndicate	–	–	1,217,655	2,132,086	3,509,915
Industry	–	–	692,184	1,239,363	2,079,607
Commerce	–	–	203,469	364,590	672,991
Land Transport	–	–	122,466	180,295	287,117
Banks	–	–	67,670	142,010	191,247
Water/Air Transport	–	–	89,135	93,042	100,591
Communication/Publication	–	–	25,476	58,937	91,275
Education/Culture	–	–	17,255	53,849	87,087
Employer Syndicates	–	–	132,188	235,118	359,205
Commerce	–	–	61,323	122,048	190,705
Land Transport	–	–	40,656	63,937	106,832
Industry	–	–	22,038	32,211	40,914
Communication/Publication	–	–	1,536	7,970	11,473
Education/Culture	–	–	1,817	4,484	5,101
Banks	–	–	1,830	3,409	3,304
Water/Air Transport	–	–	2,988	1,059	876
Liberal Professions	–	–	40,491	72,969	125,241
Accountants	–	–	15,207	33,168	49,356
Physicians	–	–	9,631	9,588	20,073
Engineers	–	–	3,617	7,647	14,274
Dentists	–	–	3,714	6,250	15,898
Lawyers	–	–	705	5,498	6,795
Economists	–	–	3,270	4,491	6,904
Chemists	–	–	1,034	1,561	1,829
Composers/Artists/ Musicians	–	–	–	1,379	575
Pharmacists	–	–	1,049	1,170	2,619
Social Workers	–	–	541	1,164	1,581
Other	–	–	–	–	5,337

Sources: AN 1952, p. 422; AN 1961, p. 348; AN 1962, pp. 272-273;
AN 1972, pp. 539 & 559-560; AN 1978, pp. 697-698

Table VIII-2. Number and Financial Value of Disputes Handled by
         Brazilian Labor Courts, 1941-77

	1941	1950	1960	1970	1977
Cases Resolved	8,089	66,065	124,347	430,795	452,248
By Conciliation	2,883	22,630	38,786	141,839	221,999
Cr$ Amount(000's)	1,557	40,822	684,681	95,072	1,220,797
By Decision	4,830	38,808	73,962	192,836	201,063
Cr$ Amount(000's)	3,793	133,608	1,820,531	193,397	1,638,760
Other Judgements Rendered	376	4,627	11,599	96,120	29,186

Sources: AN 1952, p. 420; AN 1961, p. 347; AN 1971, p. 544; AN 1978, p. 302.

Table VIII-3. Membership In and Benefits Paid by the Brazilian Social
Security System, 1925-77

	1925	1930	1935	1940	1950	1960
	All Social Security Units					
Membership						
Active	41,192	142,464	495,363	1,912,972	3,030,708	4,359,196
Retirees	0	8,009	13,759	34,837	181,267	518,024
Pensioners	0	7,013	16,102	63,138	202,838	697,852
Payments(Cr$000's)	9,647	40,658	79,535	280,864	4,056,484	42,577,726
To Retirees	5,218	26,985	44,027	94,913	1,179,082	26,378,132
Time in Service	-	-	-	-	-	-
Old Age	-	-	-	-	-	-
Disability	-	-	-	-	-	-
To Pensioners	480	3,790	12,697	39,995	456,277	8,726,339
For Medical/Natal/Funeral	2,412	5,624	10,010	34,939	271,874	⎤ 7,473,255
For Other Social Needs	1,537	4,259	12,801	111,017	2,149,251	⎦

	1969		1974		1976	1977
	INPS*	Public Employee Units	INPS*	Public Employee Units	Rural Workers	INPS*
Membership						
Active	8,776,455	1,333,746	14,065,817	1,747,192	-	18,595,367
Retirees	725,272	2,977	1,179,165	2,891	1,373,463	1,606,589
Pensioners	-	97,622	825,337	121,974	227,098	1,028,611
Payments(Cr$000's)	3,975,648	143,442	18,634,602	1,966,595	6,578,129	75,023,758
To Retirees	1,683,668	16,456	8,829,823	9,433	4,941,914	33,810,818
Time in Service	8,984,480	-	5,404,210	-	-	20,211,057
Old Age	208,363	-	914,726	-	4,511,023	3,427,324
Disability	576,825	-	2,510,887	-	430,891	10,171,937
To Pensioners	510,382	102,360	2,879,590	399,513	807,680	9,952,767
For Medical/Natal/Funeral	755,060	12,454	3,479,934	4,804	76,922	10,098,126
For Other Social Needs	1,026,538	12,172	3,445,255	1,552,845	751,613	21,162,047

Sources: AN 1952, p. 393; AN 1961, p. 337; AN 1970, pp. 616-619; AN 1971, pp. 606-608;
AN 1975, pp. 723-727; AN, 1977, pp. 670-672; AN 1978, pp. 680-684 & 689-690

* Instituto Nacional de Previdência Social (National Institute for Social Welfare)

Table VIII-4. Unemployment in Brazil by Sex and by Industry Group in Which Person Last Worked, 1960-70

1960	Total			Male			Female		
	Workers Reporting	Unemployed Number	%	Workers Reporting	Unemployed Number	%	Workers Reporting	Unemployed Number	%
Agriculture/Silviculture/Ranching	11,825,371	31,579	.3	10,650,640	28,886	.3	1,174,731	2,693	.2
Vegetal Extraction/Hunting/Fishing/Mining	582,247	2,547	.4	528,678	2,490	.5	53,569	57	.1
Manufacturing/Utilities/Construction	2,808,617	27,030	1.0	2,314,725	22,913	.9	493,892	4,117	.8
Retail/Wholesale	1,486,292	8,984	.6	1,315,495	7,690	.6	170,797	1,294	.8
Finance/Insurance/Real Estate/Personal & Business Services	2,745,131	18,073	.7	1,266,098	9,126	.7	1,479,033	8,947	.6
Transportation/Communication/Warehousing	1,055,951	7,588	.7	1,014,165	7,371	.7	41,786	217	.5
Social Services/Liberal Professions	688,379	1,951	.3	264,485	798	.3	423,894	1,153	.3
Public Administration & Security/National Defense	712,609	1,146	.2	632,106	1,027	.2	80,503	119	.1
Other	810,481	77,394	9.5	659,746	70,989	1.1	150,735	6,405	4.2
Total	22,715,078	176,292	.8	18,646,138	151,290	.8	4,068,940	25,002	.6

1970	Total			Male			Female		
	Workers Reporting	Unemployed Number	%	Workers Reporting	Unemployed Number	%	Workers Reporting	Unemployed Number	%
Agriculture/Silviculture/Ranching/Vegetal Extraction/Hunting/Fishing	13,090,260	24,110	.2	11,832,616	23,146	.2	1,257,644	964	negl.
Manufacturing/Utilities/Mining/Construction	5,295,378	104,839	2.0	4,659,490	96,008	2.0	635,888	8,831	1.4
Retail/Wholesale	2,263,520	24,375	1.1	1,893,142	20,481	1.1	370,378	3,894	1.1
Finance/Insurance/Real Estate/Personal & Business Services	3,626,483	36,656	1.0	1,236,983	18,170	1.5	2,389,500	18,486	.8
Transportation/Communication/Warehousing	1,244,395	17,693	1.4	1,182,660	17,241	1.5	61,735	452	.7
Social Services/Liberal Professions	1,470,613	5,162	.4	482,932	2,125	.4	987,681	3,037	.3
Public Administration & Security/National Defense	1,152,328	2,467	.2	992,138	2,258	.2	160,190	209	.1
Other	1,192,366	160,775	13.5	935,448	140,155	15.0	256,918	20,620	8.0
Total	29,335,343	376,077	12.8	23,215,409	319,584	13.8	6,119,934	56,493	.1

Sources: RE 1960A1, p. 51; RE 1970A1, pp. 74-75

Table VIII-5. Cooperatives and Cooperative Membership in Brazil, 1902-76

	1902	1911	1921	1931	1936	1941	1951	1960	1964	1970	1976
Number of Cooperatives	1	5	30	202	189	1,319	3,113	4,627	5,893	3.305	2,317
Consumer	-	-	-	-	21	-	1,488	2,228	2,880	788	363
Credit	-	-	-	-	69	-	363	502	532	-	-
Producer	-	-	-	-	70	-	1,147	1,739	2,211	1,728	343
Other	-	-	-	-	29	-	115	158	270	799	1,611
Membership	-	-	-	-	-	-	-	1,859,079	2,899.372	-	-
Consumer	-	-	-	-	-	-	-	918,875	1,278,979	-	-
Credit	-	-	-	-	-	-	-	503,900	620,920	-	-
Producer	-	-	-	-	-	-	-	406,486	819,904	-	-
Other	-	-	-	-	-	-	-	29,818	179,569	-	-

Sources: AN 1941/45, pp. 374-375; AN 1952, p. 415; AN 1961, pp. 345-346; AN 1966, p. 380; AN 1972, p. 670; AN 1978, p. 358.

181

Chapter IX. Agriculture, Domesticated Animals and Products, and Wild Gathered Vegetal, Animal and Aquatic Products

The numbers of Brazilian agricultural establishments and the areas in annual and perennial crops by agricultural establishment size groupings from 1920 to 1970 are presented on Table IX-1. The 1920 and 1950 data were from the respective censuses, but the origin of the 1931 data was not given. The 1940 data were from the Comissão Censitária Nacional's Sinopse do censo agrícola, published in 1948, and the 1960 and 1970 data originated with FIBGE. For 1920 the establishments of less than ten hectares are included in the 10-99-hectare category.

Table IX-2 shows land use in detail for all agricultural establishments from 1920 to 1970. The data origins are the same as those for Table IX-1.

The value of land, improvements and machinery on Brazilian agricultural establishments by the most important political subdivisions is shown for 1920 to 1970 on Table IX-3. Data origins are the same as those for Table IX-1.

Table IX-4 reports farm machinery in Brazil and the most important political subdivisions having it from 1920 to 1970. The 1920 to 1940 data originated with the respective censuses; the 1970 data with FIBGE.

Table IX-5 presents the status of operators of Brazilian rural establishments from 1920 to 1975. The data origins are the same as those for Table IX-4. The owners category includes institutions, receivers, and other nonindividual, nonfarm entities.

Table IX-6 shows employment status of farm personnel in Brazil from 1920 to 1970. Origins of data for 1920 to 1950 were the respective censuses. IBGE's Serviço Nacional de Recenseamento originated the 1960 data, and FIBGE was the origin of the 1970 data.

Table IX-7 reports the harvest value, numbers of hectares cultivated, and quantity produced of Brazil's fifty-two highest-value crops from 1920 to 1975. The 1920 data originated with the 1920 census, but no origin was given for the 1931 data. Data for 1940 through 1960 were originated by the Serviço de Estatística da Produção, the 1970 data by FIBGE, and the 1975 data by FIBGE and the Instituto Brasileiro do Café. All values on Table IX-7 are in Cr$ 1000 and all areas are in hectares. Quantities are in metric tons and yields in kilograms per hectare except for eighteen crops. The quantities of bananas are in stems (cachos) and the yields are in stems per hectare. Quantities are in 1,000 fruits and the yields are in fruits per hectare for these seventeen crops: oranges, coconuts, mangoes, pineapples, garlic, watermelons, tangerines, cashews, avocados, lemons, peaches, pears, quinces, figs, persimmons, apples, and cantaloupes.

The harvest of cotton included that for both herbaceous (shrub) and arboreal (tree) plants. Sources specified that the areas for the following tree and fiber crops included only those with producing plants and not those with new plantings: avocados, sisal, olives, cacao, coffee, persimmons, chestnuts, tea, coconuts, figs, oranges, lemons, apples, mangoes, quinces, walnuts, pears, peaches, black pepper, tangerines, tung nuts, grapes, and bananas. The 1920 agricultural census recorded coffee production by both metric tons and sacks of 60 kilograms. The total coffee production for tons and sacks was the same leading to the conclusion that the 1920 data reported processed (beneficiado) coffee since this is usually the form in which coffee is sacked in Brazil. For coffee, the 1940 through 1960 data reported processed coffee. In 1960 the coffee quantity was for coffee cherries (café em coco), which are shells carrying two beans each. This may account for the widely differing yields between 1955 and 1960.

Corn is often interplanted with beans and mandioca. In 1920 the areas of these latter two crops were included with that of corn and thus were not added to the bean or mandioca areas. Cotton for all years was reported in three ways. Bolls with seeds were the primary harvest, and cotton fibers and cotton seeds were reported separately from these. Fiber and seed production equaled the production of bolls with seeds. Tobacco in all years was reported in leaf form. Cashews were first reported as an agricultural crop in 1955. Prior to that time nearly all were wild-gathered. For 1975 the source grouped data on nuts in a way that prevented distinguishing the chestnut and walnut categories.

Table IX-8 shows the political subdivisions that have been the leading producers by quantity of Brazil's fifty-two leading agricultural and silvicultural crops from 1920 to 1975. The 1920 data were from the census of that year, but no origin was given for the 1931 data. The 1940, 1950, and 1960 data originated with the Serviço de Estatística da Produção, the 1970 data with the Equipe Técnico de Estatística Agropecuária, and the 1977 data with FIBGE.

Table IX-9 reports the quantum and producer prices of agricultural production from 1939 to 1975. The data for the 1948 base year were originated by the Laboratório de Estatística of the Conselho Nacional de Estatística, and for the first 1955 base year by the Laboratório de Estatística, IBGE. The data for the second 1955 base year were generated by the Instituto Brasileiro de Estatística, and those for the 1966 base year by the Fundação Getúlio Vargas, Instituto Brasileiro de Economia. The quantum data for the 1948 base year and for the first and second 1955 base years were calculated using the Paasche model. The producer prices for these same three base years were derived by the use of the Laspeyres model. The models used to calculate the quantum and producer price indices for the 1966 base year were not specified by the sources. The annual price indices for the 1966 base year were given by the sources on a monthly basis for each year. The price index for each year on Table IX-9 represents the average index for the twelve months of that year.

The indices for the base year 1948 were built on the following nineteen crops: pineapples, alfalfa, cotton in bolls, rice, bananas, white potatoes, cacao, coffee, sugar cane, cotton seeds, coconuts, black beans, tobacco, oranges, castor beans (mamona), mandioca, corn, wheat, and grapes. Indices for the two 1955 base years were calculated from harvests of forty-six crops. These included all the fifty-two crops listed on Table IX-7 in this work except cotton fiber, cotton seed, tea, cashews, flaxseed, and olives.

Table IX-10 shows the numbers of domesticated animals in Brazil by most productive political subdivisions from 1912 to 1976. Data origins for the 1912 figures were the Relatório of the Diretoria Geral da Estatística for the years 1915 and 1916/1917, and the Resumos of various "Estatísticas econômico-financeiras" of the same Diretoria. The data for 1920 through 1950 were from the census of 1950. The data for 1960 originated with the Serviço de Estatística da Produção, and those for 1970 and 1976 with the Equipe Técnica de Estatística Agropecuária. The figures recorded all animals on rural establishments, including work and saddle animals, and all animals censused outside rural establishments. The 1912 figures did not include Acre and the Distrito Federal (later, Guanabara state). The fowl category included ducks, geese, and turkeys, but in nearly every year reported more than 95 percent of the category was made up of chickens.

Table IX-11 reports the quantities and values of animal-created products in Brazil by major producing political subdivisions from 1919 to 1976. The 1919, 1939, and 1949 data were from the 1920, 1940, and 1950 censuses, respectively. The 1960 data originated with the Serviço de Estatística da Produção, those for 1970 with the Equipe Técnica de Estatística Agropecuária, and those for 1976 with FIBGE. Milk for 1920 included cream, but sources for subsequent years did not specify whether cream was included in milk production.

Table IX-12 shows the value and quantity of wood and vegetal extracts in Brazil from 1920 to 1975. The 1920 data were from the census of that year, but no origin was given for the 1935 data. Data for 1940 to 1960 were originated by the Serviço de Estatística da Produção, those for 1970 by the Equipe Técnica de Estatística Agropecuária, and those for 1975 by FIBGE. All values are in Cr$ 1,000. The quantities of wood are in cubic meters, but all other quantities are in metric tons.

All the Brazilian common names in the following paragraphs on plant and animal species are taken from the *Pequeno diccionario brasileiro da língua portuguêsa*.[1] Most of the scientific names are taken from the eight major plant and animal references noted at the end of this chapter. Four plant genuses, however, Hancornia, Bactris, Licania and Spondias do not appear in these works so these names come from the *Pequeno diccionário*. Babaçu oil nuts grow on the palm Orbignya martiana. Erva mate is a tea made by drying and grinding the leaves of the tree whose scientific name is Ilex paraguariensis. Brazil nuts (castanhas do Pará) are gathered from the tree Bertholletia excelsa. Palm hearts are the soft interiors of new palm stems and are usually taken from the tree Euterpe edulis.[2] The pine nut is the fruit of the araucaria pine tree, Araucaria angustofolia.[3] Cashew nuts are gathered from the tree Anacardium occidentale. The umbu is the edible, plum-sized fruit of a tree in the family Anacardiaceae, either Spondias tuberosa or Spondias purpurea. The genus name Spondias comes from the *Pequeno diccionario*; it does not appear in the major plant reference books. The cashew tree, however, is referred to in the *Pequeno diccionário* as Spondias lutea, and in Milne[4] as Anacardium occidentale. It is possible that the umbu is now also classified as genus Anacardium rather than Spondias.

Licuri is the common name of two palm species, Cocos coronata and Cocos schizophylla whose nuts produce oil and whose leaves yield a wax. Acaí is the potable juice-producing fruit of the Amazon palms Euterpe edulis and E. oleracea. Oiticica oil is pressed from the nuts of the tree Licania rigida. Tucum oil comes from the nuts of the palm Bactris setosa. Mangaba is the fruit of the tree Hancornia speciosa, which tree also produces a latex sap. The pequi is the walnut-sized fruit of a tree common in the campos cerrados of the interior. In Goiás it is cooked with rice and the mealy, orange-colored rind is stripped gingerly in the mouth to avoid the short spikes that lie just under the rind. Guaraná seeds are produced by the shrub Paullinia cupana. Amazon Indians have long mixed dried, powdered guaraná seeds with water to produce a drink that is reputed to provide quick energy. A carbonated, commercially made version is known as Brazil's "national" soft drink. The flavor is now artificially produced.

Nearly all of the rubber gathered in Brazil is from the tree whose scientific name is Hevea brasiliensis. Rubber is gathered from many other trees as well, including the caucho, Castilloa ulei, and the maniçoba plant, Manihot glaziovii, of the dry Northeast. Carnaúba wax is scraped from the leaves of the palm Copernicia cerifera. Piaçava fibers are used in brooms and come from two palms, Attalea funifera and Leopoldina passaba. Malva and guaxima fibers are taken from various plants, chief among which is the Urena lobata, a plant reputed to have medicinal properties as well. Vegetal hairs (painas) are silky fibers, similar to cotton and used industrially, from various plants of the families Bombacaceae, Asclepiadaceae, and Tifaceae. Caroá is a jute/linen-like fiber from the plant Neoglaziovia variegata. Agave, Agave americana, is an introduction from Mexico to the dry Northeast that provides fibers for cordage. Jute, Corchorus capsularis, produces a fiber for coarse textiles.

Sorva is a resin from a tree of the family Apocynaceae. Maçaranduba and balata are gums from a tree of the family Sapotaceae. Jaborandi is a medicinal product derived from a plant of the family Piperaceae. Ipecac is an emetic from the plant Cephaelis ipecacuanha. Timbó is a poison, often used to paralyze fish, which comes from a variety of plants, chief among which is Clitoria canjanifolia. Quebracho is a tannin made from the bark of various species of quebracho trees, the most important of which is Schinopsis quebracho-colorado. Barbatimão tannin comes from a tree of the campos cerrados, Stryphnodendrum barbatiman, and angico is a tannin from the bark of the angico tree, family Mimosaceae.

187

Table IX-13 presents those Brazilian political subdivisions with the largest shares of wood and vegetal extract production for the years 1920 to 1975. Data origins were the same as those for Table IX-12 except for the addition of the Escritório de Estatística do Ministério da Agricultura for the 1970 data. All subdivision percentages are based on values in Cr$ except those for 1920, which are based on quantities in metric tons.

Table IX-14 reports the harvest of wild animal hides and skins in Brazil by major producing subdivisions from 1960 to 1969. The data from 1960 to 1966 were originated by the Serviço de Estatística da Produção, and those for 1967 to 1969 by the Equipe Técnica Estatística Agropecuária. Detailed data on the harvest of wild animal hides and skins were published in the Anuários estatísticos during the decade of the 1960s, but before and after this period the only official clues to the harvest lay in export data from the Anuários estatísticos. For example, snake, crocodilian, and lizard skins were exported in the following amounts in 1944: 34 metric tons worth Cr$ 12,079; in 1945, 52 metric tons worth Cr$ 18,987; and in 1946, 93 metric tons worth Cr$ 43,159. In 1948 the hide exports were categorized by type: wild pigs, 404 metric tons worth Cr$ 20,400,000; big cats, 22 metric tons worth Cr$ 8,584,000; and snake/crocodilian/lizard skins, 204 metric tons worth Cr$ 29,105,000. In 1949 the figures were: wild pigs, 385 metric tons worth Cr$ 16,015,000; big cats, 24 metric tons worth Cr$ 6,812,000; and snake/crocodilian/lizard hides, 229 metric tons worth Cr$ 33,949,000. In 1950 the export figures were: wild pigs, 449 metric tons worth Cr$ 18,275,000; big cats, 21 metric tons worth Cr$ 6,130,000; and snake/crocodilian/lizard skins, 397 metric tons worth Cr$ 52,556,000. By 1971 the export of big cat hides had fallen to 17 metric tons worth Cr$ 8,900,000. None was exported in 1972, but in 1973, the last year reported, one metric ton of big cat hides worth Cr$ 528,000 was exported.

The classification "big cats" used on Table IX-14 is made up mostly of animals the Brazilians call onças (jaguars in the United States). As an example of the makeup of the category, about one-half of the 1960 harvest was comprised of the pintada (spotted) cat, the Panthera onca.[5] This is the largest and most aggressive of the big Brazilian cats. Some are solid black (oncas-pretas) but are classed by the data sources with the pintadas. The other half of the harvest in 1960 was made up of slightly smaller cats including the maracajá, Felis pardalis brasiliensis, and the jaguatirica, Leopardus pardalis chibiquazu.[6]

Lizard skins were mostly from the large animal called by
Brazilians the tejuaçu, a member of the family <u>Teiidae</u>.
Crocodilian hides were from the reptile commonly called
jacaré in Brazil. They are all of the genus <u>Caiman</u> and
include the jacaré-açu, <u>Caiman niger</u>;[7] the jacaré-caroa,
<u>Caiman trigonatus</u>; and the jacaré-de-óculos, <u>Caiman sclerops</u>.
Most of the wild pig hides were from the animal called
caititu in Brazil, the <u>Tayassu tajacu</u>, but some came from the
quexada, the <u>Tayassu pecari</u>. Otter skins were from the
semi-aquatic carnivore called ariranha by Brazilians, the
<u>Pteronura brasiliensis</u>. Deer skins were from a wide variety
of animals. Some of the more common are the deer called by
Brazilians the veado-campeiro, which include <u>Dorcelaphus
bezoarticus</u> and <u>Ozotoceros bezoarticus</u>. Spelling of the
former scientific names is taken directly from the <u>Pequeno
diccionário</u> because it does not appear in Walker, Grzimek,[8]
or Whitehead.[9] Spelling of the latter scientific name is
from Whitehead and differs from the <u>Pequeno diccionário</u>.
Other Brazilian deer include the heavy-antlered swamp deer
called veado-galheiro, <u>Blastocerus dichotomus</u>; the gray deer
called veado-pardo, <u>Mazama americana</u>; the black deer called
veado-negro, <u>Mazama rondoni</u>; and the red deer called
veado-roxo, <u>Mazama simplicornis</u>. Capivara (also spelled
capibara) skins are from the large rodent <u>Hydrochoerus
hydrochaeris</u>.

The characteristics of the Brazilian fishing fleet and
the numbers of fishermen by important political subdivisions
from 1958 to 1968 are shown on Table IX-15. The 1958 data
were from Heare.[10] Data for 1960 were generated by the
Serviço de Estatística da Produção and those for 1970 by the
Equipe Técnica de Estatística Agropecuária.

Table IX-16 reports the aquatic food harvest for Brazil
and its most productive political subdivisions from 1938 to
1975. The 1938-44 data for Guanabara state (then the
Distrito Federal) were originated by the Divisão de Caça e
Pesca. The national and subdivision data from 1946 on were
originated by the Serviço de Estatística da Produção, the
Equipe Técnica de Estatística Agropecuaria, the Superintendência do Desenvolvimento da Pesca, and the Ministério da
Agricultura, Superintendência do Desenvolvimento da Pesca,
Secretaria de Planajamento e Orçamento. The fishing harvest
excluded shrimp and allied catches by foreign fleets as well
as fish harvested for subsistence and sport. For 1964
through 1966 figures for Rio Grande do Sul state did not
include those for the <u>município</u> of Rio Grande do Sul. For
1966, figures for Amazonas state did not include those for
the <u>município</u> of Manaus. In the 1940s Guanabara state (then
the Distrito Federal) counted as local production some fish
from other states. Most of these cargoes were in trawlers

coming from Bahia, Rio Grande do Sul, and São Paulo states.

References

1. Pequeno diccionário (see reference 7, Chapter III).

2. Simon and Schuster's Guide to Trees (New York: Simon and Schuster, 1977).

3. H.C.D. de Wit, Plants of the World, The Higher Plants I and II, trans. A.J. Pomerans (New York: E.P. Dutton, 1966).

4. Lorus and Margery Milne, Living Plants of the World (New York: Random House, 1975).

5. Ernest P. Walker, Mammals of the World, vol. II (Baltimore: The Johns Hopkins Press, 1964).

6. C.A.W. Guggisberg, Wild Cats of the World (London: David and Charles, 1975).

7. R.L. Ditmars, Reptiles of the World, rev. ed. (New York: Macmillan, 1953).

8. Bernhard Grzimek, Grzimek's Animal Life Encyclopedia (New York: Van Nostrand Reinhold, 1968), 13 vols.

9. G. Kenneth Whitehead, Deer of the World (London: Constable, 1972).

10. Gertrude Heare, Brazil: Information for United States Businessmen (Washington, D.C.: United States Department of Commerce, Bureau of International Programs, 1961).

Table IX-1. Number of Brazilian Agricultural Establishments, Their Total Areas and Areas in Annual and Perennial Crops by Size Groupings in Hectares, 1920-70

Hectares	Less Than 10		10-99		100-999		1,000-9,999		10,000 & Over		No Declaration		Total	
	Number	%	Number	%	Number	%	Number	%	Number	%	Number	%	Number	%
1920														
Number of Establishments	--	--	463,879	71.5	157,959	24.4	24,647	3.8	1,668	.3	--	--	648,153	100.0
Total Area of Establishments	--	--	15,708,314	9.0	48,415,737	27.6	65,487,928	37.4	45,492,696	26.0	--	--	175,104,675	100.0
Area in Annual & Perennial Crops	--	--	--	--	--	--	--	--	--	--	--	--	6,642,057	100.0
1931														
Number of Establishments	--	--	--	--	--	--	--	--	--	--	--	--	--	--
Total Area of Establishments	--	--	--	--	--	--	--	--	--	--	--	--	--	--
Area in Annual & Perennial Crops	--	--	--	--	--	--	--	--	--	--	--	--	10,008,250	100.0
1940														
Number of Establishments	654,557	34.3	975,438	51.2	243,818	12.8	26,539	1.4	1,273	.1	2,964	.2	1,904,589	100.0
Total Area of Establishments	2,893,439	1.5	33,112,160	16.7	66,184,999	33.5	62,024,817	31.4	33,504,832	16.9	--	--	197,720,247	100.0
Area in Annual & Perennial Crops	1,638,141	8.7	8,081,252	42.9	6,463,959	34.3	2,289,756	12.2	362,322	1.9	--	--	18,835,430	100.0
1950														
Number of Establishments	710,934	34.4	1,052,557	51.0	268,159	13.0	31,017	1.5	1,611	.1	364	negl.	2,064,642	100.0
Total Area of Establishments	3,025,372	1.3	35,562,747	15.3	75,520,717	32.5	73,093,482	31.5	45,008,788	19.4	--	--	232,211,106	100.0
Area in Annual & Perennial Crops	1,703,783	8.9	8,667,028	45.4	6,349,039	33.3	2,063,556	10.8	311,651	1.6	--	--	19,095,057	100.0
1960														
Number of Establishments	1,495,020	44.8	1,491,415	44.7	314,831	9.5	30,883	.9	1,597	negl.	4,023	.1	3,337,769	100.0
Total Area of Establishments	5,952,381	2.4	47,566,290	19.0	86,029,455	34.4	71,420,904	28.6	38,893,112	15.6	--	--	249,862,142	100.0
Area in Annual & Perennial Crops	3,958,826	13.8	13,213,628	46.0	8,859,018	30.9	2,438,974	8.5	241,763	.8	--	--	28,712,209	100.0
1970														
Number of Establishments	2,524,982	51.2	1,935,130	39.2	415,224	8.5	35,772	.7	1,391	negl.	19,703	.4	4,932,202	100.0
Total Area of Establishments	9,110,960	3.1	60,162,785	20.5	108,909,743	37.2	80,398,983	27.4	34,429,697	11.8	--	--	293,012,168	100.0
Area in Annual & Perennial Crops	5,976,354	17.5	15,752,884	46.2	9,569,163	28.1	2,558,664	7.5	224,378	.7	--	--	34,081,443	100.0

Sources: RE 1920 C2, pp. IX and 3; AN 1936, p. 96; AN 1949, p. 85; AN 1956, p. 492; AN 1973, pp. 159-160.

191

Table IX-2. Number of Agricultural Establishments, Hectares in Rural Land Uses and Hectares of Land Not in Establishments in Brazil, 1920-70

	1920 Number	1920 % of Brazil Area	1931 Number	1931 %	1940 Number	1940 %	1950 Number	1950 %	1960 Number	1960 %	1970 Number	1970 %
Number of Establishments	648,153	-	-	-	1,904,589	-	2,064,642	-	3,337,769	-	4,924,019	-
Total Area of Establishments	175,104,675	20.6	-	-	197,720,247	23.2	232,211,106	27.2	249,862,142	29.4	294,145,466	34.6
Annual Crops	4,072,244	.5	6,038,130	.7	} 18,835,430	2.2	14,692,631	1.7	20,914,721	2.5	25,999,728	3.1
Perennial Crops	2,569,813	.3	3,970,120	.5	}	.5	4,402,426	.5	7,797,488	.9	7,984,068	.9
Pasture	-	-	-	-	88,141,733	10.3	107,633,043	12.6	122,335,386	14.4	154,138,529	18.1
Forest	48,916,653	5.7	-	-	49,085,464	5.8	55,999,081	6.6	57,945,105	6.8	57,881,182	6.8
Uncultivated Land	-	-	-	-	29,296,493	3.4	34,310,721	4.0	28,174,779	3.3	33,410,460	3.9
Unusable Land	-	-	-	-	12,361,127	1.5	15,173,204	1.8	12,694,663	1.5	14,731,499	1.8
Use Unkown	119,545,965	14.1	-	-	-	-	-	-	-	-	-	-
Land Outside of Establishments	676,014,225	79.4	-	-	653,883,453	76.8	620,432,994	72.8	601,334,358	70.6	557,051,034	65.4
Total Land Area of Brazil	851,118,900	100.0	851,118,900	100.0	851,603,700	100.0	852,644,100	100.0	851,196,500	100.0	851,196,500	100.0

Sources: RE 1920 C2, pp. IX, XIV and 3; AN 1949, pp. 6 and 8; AN 1956, pp. 5,96 and 492-3; AN 1967, p. 90; AN 1975, p. 140.

Table IX-3. Value of Land, Improvements and Machinery on Brazilian Agricultural Establishments, and the Political Subdivisions with the Highest Values of Land and Improvements, 1920-70

	1920		1940		1950		1960		1970	
	Cr$1000	%	Cr$1000	%	Cr$1000	%	Cr$1000	%	Cr$1000	%
BRAZIL										
Land	8,325,276	78.8	19,897,156	76.2	121,220,928	82.6	1,370,852,877	81.7	881,569	31.4
Improvements	1,918,187	18.1	5,316,139	20.4	22,374,496	15.2	255,304,091	15.2	1,293,302	46.0
Machinery	324,546	3.1	880,743	3.4	3,218,197	2.2	51,567,095	3.1	636,237	22.6
Total	10,568,009	100.0	26,094,038	100.0	146,813,621	100.0	1,677,724,063	100.0	2,811,108	100.0

HIGHEST POLITICAL SUBDIVISIONS

Land	1920			1940			1950			1960			1970		
		Cr$1000	%		Cr$1000	%		Cr$1000	%		Cr$1000	%		Cr$1000	%
	SP	2,237,008	26.9	RS	4,574,023	23.0	SP	29,774,230	24.6	SP	293,201,449	21.4	SP	174,105	19.7
	RS	1,717,040	20.6	MG	4,106,804	20.6	RS	20,701,327	17.1	MG	206,864,456	15.1	RS	171,474	19.5
	MG	1,630,509	19.6	SP	3,963,744	19.9	MG	20,148,363	16.6	RS	201,703,843	14.7	PR	143,958	16.3
	BA	405,020	4.9	BA	831,785	4.2	PR	10,922,129	9.0	PR	166,515,766	12.1	MG	140,757	16.0
	RJ	322,454	3.9	RJ	811,760	4.1	BA	7,682,960	6.3	BA	95,288,048	7.0	GO	62,465	7.1
	PE	305,479	3.7	PR	750,732	3.8	SC	4,447,397	3.7	GO	84,101,120	6.1	MT	56,106	6.4
	PR	244,358	2.9	PE	678,630	3.4	RJ	3,993,799	3.3	MT	52,724,617	3.8	SC	42,454	4.8

Improvements	1920			1940			1950			1960			1970		
	SP	531,423	27.7	SP	1,166,273	21.9	SP	5,021,967	22.4	SP	60,305,427	23.6	SP	215,873	16.7
	MG	284,216	14.8	RS	1,052,075	19.8	RS	4,167,092	18.6	RS	44,949,265	17.6	RS	165,458	12.8
	RS	247,437	12.9	MG	789,455	14.8	MG	2,765,036	12.4	PR	32,203,111	12.6	MG	160,760	12.5
	BA	144,675	7.5	BA	361,025	6.8	PR	1,582,019	7.1	MG	24,577,966	9.6	PR	130,961	10.1
	RJ	107,107	5.6	PE	217,633	4.1	BA	1,570,289	7.0	BA	16,664,891	6.5	BA	106,368	8.2
	ES	81,790	4.3	CE	199,638	3.7	SC	1,095,846	4.9	SC	13,767,119	5.4	GO	73,967	5.7
	PE	73,278	3.8	RJ	195,570	3.7	RJ	913,674	4.1	GO	9,799,395	3.8	SC	71,429	5.5

Sources: RE 1920C3, p. 4; AN 1949, p. 90; AN 1956, p. 99, RE1960C1, pp. 2 and 18; AN 1975, p. 153.

Table IX-4. Number of Tractors, Plows and Combines in Brazil and in the Political Subdivisions with the Largest Shares of the National Total, 1920-70

TRACTORS

	1920 Number	%		1940 Number	%		1950 Number	%		1960 Number	%		1970 Number	%
BRAZIL Political Subdivisions	1,706	100.0		3,380	100.0		8,372	100.0		61,345	100.0		157,346	100.0
RS / SP / SP / SP / SP	817	47.8	SP	1,410	41.7	SP	3,819	45.6	SP	27,176	44.3	SP	65,801	41.8
SP / RS / RS / RS / RS	401	23.5	RS	1,104	32.7	RS	2,245	26.8	RS	15,169	24.7	RS	38,358	24.4
MG / MG / MG / PR / PR	153	9.0	MG	253	7.5	MG	763	9.1	PR	5,181	8.4	PR	17,258	11.0
PR / RJ / RJ / MG / MG	95	5.6	RJ	140	4.1	RJ	457	5.5	MG	4,772	7.8	MG	9,332	5.9
SC / SC / PR / RJ / GO	94	5.5	SC	71	2.1	PR	280	3.3	RJ	1,538	2.5	GO	5,294	3.4
RJ / PR / PE / GO / SC	58	3.4	PR	65	1.9	PE	142	1.7	GO	1,349	2.2	SC	5,068	3.2
PE / BA / GO / SC / MT	36	2.1	BA	43	1.3	GO	89	1.1	SC	1,106	1.8	MT	4,044	2.6

PLOWS

	1920 Number	%		1940 Number	%		1950 Number	%		1960 Number	%		1970 Number	%
BRAZIL Political Subdivisions	141,196	100.0		500,853	100.0		714,259	100.0		1,031,930	100.0		1,878,925	100.0
RS	73,403	51.4	RS	222,657	44.5	RS	312,001	43.7	RS	440,467	42.7	RS	641,976	34.2
SP	27,922	19.7	SP	168,073	33.5	SP	224,947	31.5	SP	286,580	27.8	SP	401,645	21.4
MG	17,513	12.6	MG	49,373	9.8	MG	73,968	10.4	MG	93,040	9.0	PR	302,098	16.1
PR	7,000	4.9	SC	21,481	4.2	SC	41,029	5.7	PR	82,324	8.0	SC	160,794	8.6
SC	6,126	4.2	PR	20,498	4.0	PR	30,405	4.3	SC	81,259	7.9	MG	154,880	8.2
RJ	4,234	3.0	RJ	8,248	1.6	RJ	12,020	1.6	RJ	12,314	1.2	BA	40,177	2.1
PE	2,368	1.6	PE	3,213	.6	BA	4,647	.6	GO	6,388	.6	MT	32,513	1.7

COMBINES

	1920 Number	%	1940 Number	%	1950 Number	%	1960 Number	%		1970 Number	%
BRAZIL Political Subdivisions	–	–	–	–	–	–	–	–		98,184	100.0
	–	–	–	–	–	–	–	–	SP	24,241	24.7
	–	–	–	–	–	–	–	–	PR	19,719	20.1
	–	–	–	–	–	–	–	–	RS	18,619	19.0
	–	–	–	–	–	–	–	–	SC	16,161	16.5
	–	–	–	–	–	–	–	–	MG	10,661	10.9
	–	–	–	–	–	–	–	–	RJ	1,701	1.7

Sources: RE 1920 Ce, pp. 6-7; AN 1949, p. 97; AN 1963, p. 58; AN 1973 p. 164; AN 1975, p. 151

Table IX-5. Status of Operators of Rural Establishments, 1920-75

Status	1920 No. of Estabs	% of Brazil Total	Area In Hectares	%	1940 No. of Estabs	% of Brazil Total	Area In Hectares	%	1950 No. of Estabs	% of Brazil Total	Area In Hectares	%
Owner	577,210	89.1	126,787,281	72.4	1,376,602	72.3	127,276,879	64.4	1,553,349	75.2	154,480,678	66.5
Renter	23,371	3.6	8,575,917	4.9	221,505	11.6	19,117,981	9.6	186,949	9.1	12,946,538	5.6
Squatter	-	-	-	-	109,016	5.7	5,278,125	2.7	208,657	10.1	9,947,607	4.3
Administrator	47,572	7.3	39,741,477	22.7	178,376	9.4	44,832,481	22.7	115,512	5.6	54,837,701	23.6
No Declaration	-	-	-	-	10,090	1.0	1,214,781	.6	175	negl.	1,418	negl.
Total	648,153	100.0	175,104,675	100.0	1,904,589	100.0	197,720,247	100.0	2,064,642	100.0	232,211,106	100.0

Status	1960 No. of Estabs	% of Brazil Total	Area In Hectares	%	1970 No. of Estabs	% of Brazil Total	Area In Hectares	%	1975 No. of Estabs	% of Brazil Total	Area In Hectares	%
Owner	2,234,960	66.9	161,102,822	64.5	3,094,861	62.8	254,425,898	86.5	3,085,299	61.6	281,430,040	87.2
Renter	579,969	17.4	18,109,824	7.3	1,017,791	20.7	18,522,300	6.3	914,179	18.3	15,005,583	4.7
Squatter	356,502	10.7	9,087,028	3.6	811,367	16.5	21,197,268	7.2	987,386	19.7	25,870,543	8.0
Administrator	166,236	5.0	61,548,812	24.6	-	-	-	-	-	-	-	-
No Declaration	102	negl.	13,656	negl.	-	-	-	-	19,805	.4	314,833	.1
Total	3,337,769	100.0	249,862,142	100.0	4,924,019	100.0	294,145,466	100.0	5,006,669	100.0	322,620,999	100.0

Sources: AN 1956, pp. 98 & 493; AN 1977, p. 304.

Table IX-6. Employment Status of Personnel on Brazilian Agricultural Establishments, 1920-70

Status	1920 No of Persons	1920 % of Brazil Total	1940 No of Persons	1940 % of Brazil Total	1950 No of Persons	1950 % of Brazil Total	1960 No of Persons	1960 % of Brazil Total	1970 No of Persons	1970 % of Brazil Total
Owners/Unpaid Family Members	–	–	–	–	6,022,033	54.8	9,848,727	63.0	14,106,190	80.2
Permanent Employees	–	–	–	–	1,420,867	12.9	1,429,350	9.1	1,155,292	6.6
Temporary Employees	–	–	–	–	2,308,377	21.0	2,983,324	19.1	1,488,416	4.7
Renters/Sharecroppers	–	–	–	–	1,245,557	11.3	1,372,584	8.8	832,191	8.5
	6,312,323	100.0	10,105,411	100.0	10,996,834	100.0	15,633,985	100.0	17,582,089	100.0

Sources: RE 1920C3, p. XII; RE 1940A3, p. 20; AN 1956, pp. 101-103; AN 1967, pp. 94-96; AN 1975, pp. 144-145.

Table IX-7. Value of Harvest, Number of Hectares Cultivated, Quantity
Produced, and Yield per Hectare for Each of Brazil's
Fifty-two Highest Value Agricultural and Silvicultural
Crops, 1920-75

	1920	1931	1940	1945	1950	1955	1960	1970	1975
RICE									
Value	415,748	-	684,699	2,441,353	5,399,028	17,180,419	51,965,924	2,254,806	-
Area	532,384	719,350	871,717	1,498,117	1,964,158	2,511,689	2,965,684	4,979,165	5,306,270
Production	831,495	1,078,458	1,319,973	2,146,965	3,217,690	3,737,471	4,794,810	7,553,083	7,781,538
Yield	1,562	1,499	1,514	1,433	1,180	1,488	1,617	1,571	1,466
CORN (MAIZE)									
Value	999,940	-	1,186,933	3,380,417	5,581,366	16,045,324	49,074,757	2,198,940	-
Area	2,451,382	3,170,000	3,903,940	4,092,054	4,681,827	5,623,134	6,681,165	9,858,108	10,672,450
Production	4,999,698	4,749,995	4,875,533	4,846,557	6,023,549	6,689,930	8,671,952	14,216,009	16,334,516
Yield	2,040	1,498	1,249	1,184	1,287	1,190	1,298	1,442	1,504
SUGAR CANE									
Value	349,650	-	651,315	1,682,100	3,253,471	7,794,540	29,584,005	1,578,945	-
Area	414,578	348,450	564,164	656,921	828,182	1,072,902	1,339,933	1,725,121	1,969,227
Production	13,985,999	16,249,830	22,252,220	25,178,584	32,670,814	40,946,305	56,926,882	79,752,936	91,524,559
Yield	33,736	46,635	39,443	38,238	39,459	38,164	42,485	46,230	46,477
COFFEE									
Value	1,025,034	-	1,377,833	3,717,173	15,884,691	41,557,570	77,462,446	1,477,219	-
Area	2,215,658	3,651,880	2,519,111	2,381,561	2,663,117	3,265,541	4,419,537	2,402,993	2,216,921
Production	788,488	1,301,670	1,002,062	834,916	1,071,437	1,369,759	4,169,586	1,509,520	2,544,598
Yield	356	356	398	351	402	419	943	638	1,148
BLACK BEANS									
Value	253,774	-	445,214	1,177,968	2,248,591	8,477,344	39,948,444	1,412,026	-
Area	672,912	522,210	978,508	1,432,190	1,807,956	2,228,539	2,560,281	3,484,778	4,145,916
Production	725,069	687,112	767,314	1,002,446	1,248,138	1,474,985	1,730,795	2,211,449	2,282,466
Yield	1,078	1,316	784	700	690	662	676	635	550
MANDIOCA									
Value	86,957	-	514,168	1,688,982	3,138,657	6,744,611	23,699,681	1,397,138	-
Area	215,234	227,100	584,094	897,988	957,493	1,149,123	1,342,403	2,024,557	2,041,416
Production	2,898,570	5,209,500	7,331,862	11,414,680	12,532,482	14,863,193	17,613,213	29,464,275	26,117,614
Yield	13,467	22,939	12,553	12,711	13,089	12,934	13,121	14,553	12,793
COTTON (BOLLS WITH SEEDS)									
Value	664,676	-	1,757,150	2,315,910	6,925,425	13,670,015	42,775,472	1,343,567	-
Area	378,599	738,495	2,412,484	2,721,584	2,689,185	2,617,086	2,930,361	4,298,573	3,876,389
Production	332,338	375,408	1,562,307	1,124,015	1,167,091	1,241,301	1,609,275	1,954,993	1,748,144
Yield	878	508	647	413	434	474	549	455	451
COTTON FIBER									
Value	-	-	1,474,854	2,039,948	6,273,524	12,034,430	-	-	-
Area	-	738,495	2,412,484	2,721,584	2,689,185	2,617,086	-	-	-
Production	-	112,789	468,695	378,495	393,000	428,474	-	-	-
Yield	-	*	153	194	139	116	164	-	-	-
COTTON SEED									
Value	-	-	282,296	275,962	651,901	1,635,585	-	-	-
Area	-	738,495	2,412,484	2,721,584	2,689,185	2,617,086	-	-	-
Production	-	262,619	1,093,612	745,520	774,091	812,827	-	-	-
Yield	-	356	453	274	288	310	-	-	-
WHEAT									
Value	43,590	-	69,813	241,775	1,304,141	7,076,984	1,721,474	882,286	
Area	136,069	141,610	201,091	315,548	652,453	1,196,063	1,141,015	1,895,249	2,931,508
Production	87,181	141,580	101,739	233,298	532,351	1,101,315	713,124	1,844,263	1,788,180
Yield	641	1,999	506	739	816	921	621	973	610
BANANAS									
Value	-	-	117,397	414,328	1,012,735	2,938,157	10,914,118	755,910	-
Area	-	46,020	80,414	84,205	110,126	155,567	184,530	277,744	313,650
Production	-	70,000	75,175	107,311	162,874	204,275	256,339	492,900	363,684
Yield	-	1,521	935	1,274	1,479	1,403	1,289	1,775	1,159

197

Table IX-7 (continued)

	1920	1931	1940	1945	1950	1955	1960	1970	1975
ORANGES									
Value	-	-	223,961	296,397	625,516	1,916,400	6,013,319	451,229	-
Area	-	-	124,589	73,183	77,018	77,738	112,241	202,037	403,192
Production	-	-	6,399,333	5,037,305	6,015,129	6,501,670	8,359,854	15,497,198	31,565,854
Yield	-	-	51,364	68,832	78,100	83,636	74,481	76,705	78,289
SOYBEANS									
Value	-	-	-	-	-	260,589	2,060,348	430,028	-
Area	-	-	-	-	-	73,971	171,440	1,318,809	5,824,492
Production	-	-	-	-	-	106,884	205,744	1,508,540	9,893,008
Yield	-	-	-	-	-	1,445	1,200	1,144	1,698
WHITE POTATOES									
Value	43,796	-	205,068	632,048	1,301,501	3,328,483	9,740,247	412,493	-
Area	19,902	24,000	66,420	115,855	147,739	178,614	198,772	214,155	191,216
Production	145,985	160,797	433,746	595,670	707,159	898,184	1,112,640	1,583,465	1,654,767
Yield	7,345	6,700	6,530	5,141	4,787	5,029	5,598	7,394	8,653
CACAO									
Value	80,259	-	141,048	221,341	1,029,926	3,282,733	8,001,292	376,000	-
Area	197,129	153,670	229,884	267,920	275,970	368,297	470,806	443,916	451,145
Production	66,883	76,738	128,016	119,656	152,902	157,921	163,223	197,061	281,887
Yield	339	499	557	447	554	427	347	444	624
PEANUTS									
Value	-	-	-	33,731	259,753	648,738	6,463,145	366,758	-
Area	-	-	-	40,617	127,428	166,306	219,025	669,688	345,095
Production	-	-	-	28,584	118,192	185,856	408,410	928,073	441,987
Yield	-	-	-	704	928	1,118	1,403	1,386	1,280
TOBACCO									
Value	110,471	-	178,538	515,219	699,151	1,742,638	6,849,868	289,525	-
Area	106,145	86,680	96,419	143,565	141,931	196,084	213,203	245,207	253,736
Production	73,647	97,550	94,768	113,449	107,950	148,205	161,426	244,000	285,934
Yield	694	1,125	983	790	761	756	757	995	1,126
TOMATOES									
Value	-	-	-	89,942	227,109	873,767	3,590,196	269,985	-
Area	-	-	-	6,591	13,521	24,060	28,887	44,980	46,935
Production	-	-	-	58,903	135,645	237,123	397,112	764,119	1,049,724
Yield	-	-	-	8,937	10,032	9,855	13,747	16,987	22,365
GRAPES									
Value	-	-	69,241	156,413	321,906	1,289,384	3,292,504	183,509	-
Area	-	45,500	32,492	32,002	37,035	48,447	61,315	66,197	57,709
Production	-	222,000	214,297	209,028	229,646	297,854	427,125	598,016	580,586
Yield	-	4,879	6,595	6,532	6,201	6,148	6,966	9,034	10,060
COCOANUTS									
Value	30,855	-	31,041	95,024	266,220	677,611	3,204,167	173,990	-
Area	30,194	15,950	44,426	37,148	52,105	61,504	73,583	117,193	157,282
Production	154,275	130,636	133,900	137,712	229,261	298,697	436,430	656,750	482,390
Yield	5,109	8,190	3,014	3,707	4,400	4,857	5,931	5,604	3,067
SWEET POTATOES									
Value	-	-	-	278,751	451,854	1,170,607	3,642,555	172,847	-
Area	-	-	-	107,916	102,265	113,462	133,277	180,789	153,413
Production	-	-	-	967,921	833,376	1,042,321	1,283,087	2,133,983	1,599,906
Yield	-	-	-	8,969	8,149	9,187	9,627	11,804	10,428
CASTOR BEANS (MAMONA)									
Value	12,887	-	80,161	132,818	350,229	454,206	2,347,731	130,452	-
Area	33,185	-	140,749	200,073	233,158	206,026	254,595	380,986	398,709
Production	42,958	-	148,141	160,436	183,996	163,996	224,695	348,546	353,904
Yield	1,295	-	1,053	802	789	796	882	915	887

Table IX-7 (continued)

	1920	1931	1940	1945	1950	1955	1960	1970	1975
					ONIONS				
Value	-	-	-	149,441	300,496	779,702	2,976,795	99,724	-
Area	-	-	-	21,895	23,759	31,996	41,228	51,719	52,258
Production	-	-	-	78,096	125,772	155,186	210,265	284,603	346,484
Yield	-	-	-	3,567	5,294	4,850	5,100	5,503	6,630
					PINEAPPLES				
Value	-	-	25,094	52,607	145,293	346,828	1,191,172	92,975	-
Area	-	8,800	9,282	11,422	14,604	16,980	24,716	32,189	28,200
Production	-	80,000	85,368	74,906	97,592	125,620	177,950	282,602	351,384
Yield	-	9,090	9,197	6,558	6,477	7,398	7,200	8,779	12,460
					SISAL (AGAVE)				
Value	-	-	-	-	305,872	387,916	3,170,393	72,187	-
Area	-	-	-	-	-	93,000	141,159	287,486	326,982
Production	-	-	-	-	52,477	89,798	164,076	263,299	314,314
Yield	-	-	-	-	-	966	1,162	916	961
					TANGERINES				
Value	-	-	-	-	-	265,481	788,739	71,710	-
Area	-	-	-	-	-	12,003	15,874	26,312	33,351
Production	-	-	-	-	-	1,179,683	1,494,977	2,444,854	2,969,643
Yield	-	-	-	-	-	98,282	94,178	92,918	89,042
					MANGOES				
Value	-	-	-	-	-	445,433	1,518,303	71,531	-
Area	-	-	-	-	-	35,121	37,568	44,665	42,080
Production	-	-	-	-	-	1,706,757	1,823,799	2,148,507	2,141,946
Yield	-	-	-	-	-	48,597	48,547	48,103	50,901
					CASHEWS				
Value	-	-	-	-	-	-	657,540	70,090	-
Area	-	-	-	-	-	-	49,423	81,220	110,052
Production	-	-	-	-	-	-	2,147,857	4,057,622	4,661,289
Yield	-	-	-	-	-	-	43,459	49,958	42,355
					WATERMELON (MELANCIA)				
Value	-	-	-	-	-	216,755	1,161,754	49,832	-
Area	-	-	-	-	-	74,629	114,961	103,429	82,719
Production	-	-	-	-	-	54,977	86,740	82,449	91,118
Yield	-	-	-	-	-	737	755	797	1,101
					BLACK PEPPER				
Value	-	-	-	-	-	151,188	703,206	44,683	-
Area	-	-	-	-	-	1,054	2,392	5,473	9,909
Production	-	-	-	-	-	1,232	4,069	14,267	27,876
Yield	-	-	-	-	-	1,169	1,701	2,607	2,898
					BROAD BEANS (FAVA)				
Value	-	-	-	38,764	66,920	191,978	813,681	41,859	-
Area	-	-	-	59,208	78,459	96,927	109,831	169,265	198,787
Production	-	-	-	34,520	35,593	38,036	54,169	73,434	74,950
Yield	-	-	-	583	454	392	493	434	377
					GARLIC				
Value	-	-	-	69,417	115,429	318,280	1,057,550	41,488	-
Area	-	-	-	5,561	7,499	10,141	11,435	14,121	5,484
Production	-	-	-	12,703	15,785	21,853	27,276	36,377	14,174
Yield	-	-	-	2,284	2,105	2,155	2,385	2,576	2,584
					LEMONS				
Value	-	-	-	-	-	109,939	422,305	35,861	-
Area	-	-	-	-	-	5,112	7,817	11,414	19,868
Production	-	-	-	-	-	461,825	793,994	1,355,833	2,075,212
Yield	-	-	-	-	-	90,341	101,573	118,787	104,450
					ALFALFA				
Value	-	-	28,854	78,017	173,637	358,044	1,044,687	34,516	-
Area	-	12,630	20,325	26,564	25,830	27,170	30,679	23,669	17,073
Production	-	113,831	111,137	148,406	184,845	205,851	227,127	176,178	92,978
Yield	-	9,013	5,468	5,597	7,156	7,576	7,403	7,443	5,445

Table IX-7 (continued)

	1920	1931	1940	1945	1950	1955	1960	1970	1975
AVOCADOS									
Value	-	-	-	-	-	183,206	590,039	34,483	-
Area	-	-	-	-	-	5,999	7,635	15,784	18,870
Production	-	-	-	-	-	260,641	321,245	612,693	583,349
Yield	-	-	-	-	-	43,447	42,075	38,817	30,914
JUTE									
Value	-	-	-	29,597	61,223	158,777	1,083,965	29,601	-
Area	-	-	-	-	-	2,471	28,007	33,304	27,648
Production	-	-	-	6,598	14,054	24,466	38,891	38,172	30,738
Yield	-	-	-	-	-	1,139	1,389	1,146	1,111
PEACHES									
Value	-	-	-	-	-	113,804	320,792	29,234	-
Area	-	-	-	-	-	7,329	8,118	12,747	22,106
Production	-	-	-	-	-	442,486	516,506	1,197,363	1,442,042
Yield	-	-	-	-	-	60,375	63,625	93,933	65,233
TEA									
Value	-	-	-	6,352	12,275	36,297	3,170,393	16,801	-
Area	-	-	-	1,510	2,087	5,347	4,136	4,452	5,315
Production	-	-	-	409	835	729	2,716	5,848	7,618
Yield	-	-	-	271	406	136	657	1,314	1,445
FIGS									
Value	-	-	-	-	-	74,929	172,514	10,681	-
Area	-	-	-	-	-	1,977	2,612	3,044	5,588
Production	-	-	-	-	-	248,962	304,625	441,980	864,531
Yield	-	-	-	-	-	125,929	155,625	145,197	154,712
BARLEY									
Value	-	-	5,537	10,280	27,653	149,568	321,908	10,403	-
Area	-	9,300	12,727	13,757	12,758	3,051	36,731	25,044	23,732
Production	-	9,274	12,761	14,892	15,233	34,576	28,722	26,735	25,463
Yield	-	997	1,003	1,083	1,194	1,147	782	1,068	1,072
PEARS									
Value	-	-	-	-	-	67,847	179,905	10,293	-
Area	-	-	-	-	-	2,827	8,118	4,703	5,079
Production	-	-	-	-	-	242,874	279,628	404,504	273,227
Yield	-	-	-	-	-	85,912	63,625	85,010	53,795
FLAXSEED									
Value	-	-	-	-	-	-	558,988	9,528	-
Area	-	-	-	-	-	-	42,669	32,006	7,804
Production	-	-	-	-	-	-	30,172	22,370	5,099
Yield	-	-	-	-	-	-	707	699	653
OATS									
Value	-	-	3,067	9,271	17,258	62,188	193,122	9,466	-
Area	-	11,740	8,263	12,677	14,857	20,203	27,597	30,705	44,793
Production	-	11,936	6,942	11,185	10,028	16,159	18,610	26,754	41,593
Yield	-	1,017	840	882	675	800	674	871	928
APPLES									
Value	-	-	-	-	-	58,917	161,225	7,895	-
Area	-	-	-	-	-	1,746	2,080	2,880	5,123
Production	-	-	-	-	-	88,148	95,136	154,249	170,958
Yield	-	-	-	-	-	50,485	45,738	53,559	33,370
RYE									
Value	-	-	7,428	11,468	29,056	83,032	223,966	7,629	-
Area	-	17,765	12,888	13,800	24,270	26,553	25,962	22,929	20,857
Production	-	17,755	12,754	10,160	17,864	20,324	19,259	18,972	19,430
Yield	-	999	990	736	736	768	742	837	931
PERSIMMONS									
Value	-	-	-	-	-	32,246	144,232	5,748	-
Area	-	-	-	-	-	1,310	2,242	3,444	3,551
Production	-	-	-	-	-	90,837	144,489	216,586	221,140
Yield	-	-	-	-	-	69,341	64,446	62,888	62,275

Table IX-7 (continued)

	1920	1931	1940	1945	1950	1955	1960	1970	1975
CANTALOUPES									
Value	-	-	-	-	-	14,854	68,338	4,896	-
Area	-	-	-	-	-	4,087	5,569	4,777	4,109
Production	-	-	-	-	-	3,164	4,259	6,527	10,651
Yield	-	-	-	-	-	774	765	1,366	2,592
QUINCES									
Value	-	-	-	-	-	64,470	120,256	4,836	-
Area	-	-	-	-	-	4,212	6,379	8,343	4,155
Production	-	-	-	-	-	122,034	131,007	103,718	112,482
Yield	-	-	-	-	-	28,973	20,537	12,432	27,071
TUNG NUTS									
Value	-	-	-	7,508	7,863	14,084	41,045	2,606	-
Area	-	-	-	4,456	8,283	4,800	5,132	4,834	3,775
Production	-	-	-	3,598	6,542	5,723	8,313	14,725	9,904
Yield	-	-	-	807	790	1,192	1,620	3,046	2,623
OLIVES									
Value	-	-	-	-	-	3,697	16,947	1,395	-
Area	-	-	-	-	-	230	379	893	559
Production	-	-	-	-	-	213	388	1,086	1,059
Yield	-	-	-	-	-	927	1,024	1,216	1,894
CHESTNUTS									
Value	-	-	-	-	-	1,163	4,922	1,395	-
Area	-	-	-	-	-	43	73	893	-
Production	-	-	-	-	-	78	176	1,086	-
Yield	-	-	-	-	-	1,835	2,411	1,216	-
WALNUTS									
Value	-	-	-	-	-	4,736	17,072	1,261	-
Area	-	-	-	-	-	519	483	527	-
Production	-	-	-	-	-	282	294	431	-
Yield	-	-	-	-	-	543	609	903	-

Sources: RE 1920C, p. XIX; AN 1936, pp. 96, 102 & 110; AN 1956, pp. 494-505; AN 1963, pp. 59-60;
AN 1971, pp. 145-146; AN 1977, p. 340.

Table IX-8. Political Subdivisions Producing the Largest Shares by
Quantity of Output of Each of Brazil's Major Agricultural
and Silvicultural Crops, 1920-75

	1920 PS	%	1931 PS	%	1940 PS	%	1950 PS	%	1960 PS	%	1970 PS	%	1975 PS	%
Rice	SP	41.9	SP	61.6	MG	28.2	SP	30.9	SP	23.2	GO	20.4	RS	13.9
	MG	20.8	RS	18.2	RS	23.4	MG	21.5	MG	20.4	MG	15.4	MT	12.9
	RS	13.5	MG	17.5	SP	15.7	RS	18.1	RS	16.6	RS	13.9	MA	11.7
Corn	MG	25.4	MG	25.3	MG	31.6	MG	23.6	MG	21.5	PR	25.0	PR	23.3
	SP	23.8	SP	23.4	RS	19.4	SP	21.0	RS	20.1	SP	18.8	RS	14.5
	RS	23.0	RS	22.1	PR	12.8	RS	17.6	SP	18.2	RS	16.8	MG	14.2
Sugar Cane	MG	20.1	PE	22.5	PE	17.7	SP	21.2	SP	39.4	SP	38.1	SP	40.0
	RJ	18.5	BA	14.4	MG	16.3	PE	16.6	PE	15.3	PE	13.6	PE	14.0
	PE	16.9	MG	13.9	RJ	14.8	MG	14.0	RJ	9.3	MG	10.8	AL	11.5
Coffee	SP	42.4	SP	59.5	SP	61.3	SP	43.8	SP	49.9	SP	39.0	PR	48.2
	MG	32.0	MG	19.6	MG	19.3	MG	21.0	PR	28.5	MG	26.0	SP	34.9
	RJ	10.3	ES	7.7	ES	6.9	PR	18.9	MG	10.9	ES	15.1	MG	9.4
Black Beans	SP	29.4	SP	29.3	MG	30.4	MG	22.9	MG	22.7	PR	33.0	SP	26.6
	MG	21.2	RS	23.2	RS	15.8	PR	19.1	PR	18.6	MG	13.0	MG	12.5
	RS	16.7	MG	20.2	SP	10.9	SP	14.2	SP	12.7	RS	11.1	BA	8.5
Mandioca	BA	17.2	RS	26.5	BA	17.5	BA	17.4	RS	17.2	BA	13.6	RS	12.1
	RS	13.9	PE	12.8	MG	12.1	RS	11.2	BA	11.8	RS	12.2	MG	8.6
	PA	9.8	SP	8.7	PE	9.3	SC	10.7	PE	10.0	SC	10.2	BA	5.8
Cotton	SP	31.3	PB	20.4	SP	66.6	SP	52.3	SP	36.7	SP	36.2	SP	27.9
	PE	18.7	PE	13.3	PB	8.6	CE	15.4	PB	14.2	PR	27.9	PR	21.6
	PB	10.6	RN	12.7	RN	6.5	RN	7.3	CE	12.0	CE	8.8	CE	12.3
Wheat	RS	96.1	RS	78.9	RS	72.5	RS	70.6	RS	75.3	RS	78.6	RS	69.0
	PR	1.8	PR	18.3	SC	15.8	SC	20.2	SC	14.6	PR	15.3	PR	24.8
	SC	1.7	SC	2.8	PR	10.8	PR	8.8	PR	9.4	SC	5.0	SP	3.9
Bananas	-	-	SP	36.6	RJ	23.1	SP	18.0	SP	17.4	CE	19.7	CE	18.1
	-	-	RJ	20.7	SP	18.0	MG	15.7	CE	13.5	SP	13.0	BA	11.5
	-	-	MG	10.7	MG	16.1	RJ	2.7	RJ	13.2	MG	11.9	RJ	9.1
Oranges	-	-	SP	45.9	SP	33.0	RJ	26.9	SP	24.0	SP	44.6	SP	67.1
	-	-	RJ	30.0	RJ	30.9	MG	16.2	RJ	20.3	MG	11.0	RJ	8.5
	-	-	RS	6.5	MG	13.9	SP	16.1	MG	11.7	RJ	10.8	RS	5.1
Soybeans	-	-	-	-	-	-	-	-	RS	92.4	RS	64.8	RS	47.4
	-	-	-	-	-	-	-	-	PR	2.6	PR	24.4	PR	36.6
	-	-	-	-	-	-	-	-	SP	2.0	SP	6.0	SP	6.8
White Potatoes	RS	43.0	SP	40.0	RS	42.7	SP	34.2	SP	40.6	PR	25.9	PR	25.8
	SP	27.9	RS	35.7	PR	27.3	RS	32.7	RS	24.1	RS	23.4	RS	23.9
	PR	9.6	PR	11.9	SP	10.9	PR	15.5	PR	14.9	SP	22.6	SP	18.9
Cacao	BA	88.8	BA	97.0	BA	96.1	BA	96.6	BA	96.9	BA	95.7	BA	96.4
	PA	6.3	PA	2.1	PA	1.8	ES	2.2	ES	2.2	ES	3.2	ES	2.7
	AM	2.9	AM	.5	AM	1.0	PA	.7	PA	.5	PA	.7	PA	.6
Peanuts	-	-	-	-	-	-	SP	82.6	SP	95.3	SP	76.1	SP	59.4
	-	-	-	-	-	-	RS	5.6	RS	1.3	PR	16.6	PR	24.9
	-	-	-	-	-	-	MG	4.6	MG	1.1	MT	3.9	MT	8.8
Tobacco	BA	39.0	BA	35.8	BA	33.6	RS	31.2	BA	27.8	RS	40.8	RS	34.2
	RS	19.7	RS	26.6	RS	32.7	BA	25.5	RS	22.1	SC	20.6	SC	27.5
	MG	15.6	MG	15.7	MG	11.7	MG	15.6	MG	16.6	BA	13.0	BA	11.9
Tomatoes	-	-	-	-	-	-	PE	40.4	SP	60.7	SP	48.6	SP	49.6
	-	-	-	-	-	-	SP	36.2	RJ	18.0	RJ	18.1	PE	9.5
	-	-	-	-	-	-	MG	13.1	MG	6.6	PE	13.0	RJ	7.1
Grapes	-	-	RS	90.1	RS	84.3	RS	69.2	SP	40.1	RS	68.8	RS	62.0
	-	-	SP	5.0	SC	5.3	SP	11.7	RS	40.0	SP	16.2	SP	23.1
	-	-	SC	2.0	MG	4.2	SC	9.5	SC	7.6	SC	8.8	SC	10.1
Cocoanuts	BA	35.4	BA	28.9	SE	21.7	BA	2.61	BA	24.5	BA	27.9	BA	20.2
	PE	18.4	AL	24.9	AL	20.1	AL	16.4	AL	19.9	AL	15.7	SE	14.6
	AL	14.4	SE	9.6	BA	19.0	SE	14.9	CE	13.5	SE	14.1	AL	14.3

Table IX-8 (continued)

	1920 PS	%	1931 PS	%	1940 PS	%	1950 PS	%	1960 PS	%	1970 PS	%	1975 PS	%
Sweet Potatoes	-	-	-	-	-	-	RS	21.9	RS	25.8	SC	29.9	RS	24.0
	-	-	-	-	-	-	SC	21.1	PR	10.4	RS	18.0	SC	22.6
	-	-	-	-	-	-	MG	9.8	SC	9.3	PR	16.7	PR	18.2
Castor Beans	-	-	-	-	BA	25.3	BA	29.4	BA	40.0	BA	45.2	BA	36.3
	-	-	-	-	PE	17.6	CE	20.5	SP	18.7	SP	16.9	PR	27.3
	-	-	-	-	CE	16.9	SP	19.2	PE	18.3	PR	16.5	SP	10.6
Onions	-	-	-	-	-	-	RS	52.9	RS	41.5	RS	45.4	RS	39.2
	-	-	-	-	-	-	SP	21.2	SP	24.1	SP	17.4	SP	28.6
	-	-	-	-	-	-	MG	9.1	PE	7.7	PE	10.7	SC	11.0
Pineapple	-	-	PE	31.3	PE	27.9	SP	22.6	SP	22.4	PB	24.3	MG	18.8
	-	-	SP	22.5	MG	17.4	PB	20.2	MG	17.7	SP	11.8	BA	12.8
	-	-	RJ	19.2	RJ	15.8	PE	16.3	PB	17.2	MG	8.7	ES	11.8
Sisal	-	-	-	-	-	-	-	-	BA	46.0	BA	34.1	BA	60.0
	-	-	-	-	-	-	-	-	PB	33.0	RN	30.3	PB	26.6
	-	-	-	-	-	-	-	-	PE	10.5	PB	29.5	RN	11.5
Tangerines	-	-	-	-	-	-	-	-	-	-	-	-	SP	44.0
	-	-	-	-	-	-	-	-	-	-	-	-	RS	16.7
	-	-	-	-	-	-	-	-	-	-	-	-	RJ	9.3
Mangoes	-	-	-	-	-	-	-	-	-	-	-	-	CE	16.9
	-	-	-	-	-	-	-	-	-	-	-	-	MG	16.2
	-	-	-	-	-	-	-	-	-	-	-	-	PB	12.5
Cashews	-	-	-	-	-	-	-	-	-	-	-	-	CE	58.4
	-	-	-	-	-	-	-	-	-	-	-	-	RN	13.8
	-	-	-	-	-	-	-	-	-	-	-	-	PE	10.9
Watermelons	-	-	-	-	-	-	-	-	-	-	-	-	BA	21.5
	-	-	-	-	-	-	-	-	-	-	-	-	RS	14.3
	-	-	-	-	-	-	-	-	-	-	-	-	MA	10.1
Black Pepper	-	-	-	-	-	-	-	-	-	-	-	-	PA	93.8
	-	-	-	-	-	-	-	-	-	-	-	-	BA	2.7
	-	-	-	-	-	-	-	-	-	-	-	-	PB	1.4
Broad Beans	-	-	-	-	-	-	PB	28.7	-	-	-	-	PE	29.8
	-	-	-	-	-	-	PE	20.9	-	-	-	-	PB	17.1
	-	-	-	-	-	-	MG	14.2	-	-	-	-	MG	14.5
Garlic	-	-	-	-	-	-	MG	42.5	-	-	MG	32.5	MG	35.2
	-	-	-	-	-	-	RS	18.0	-	-	RS	19.2	RS	20.5
	-	-	-	-	-	-	SP	14.0	-	-	PR	19.1	PR	16.2
Lemons	-	-	-	-	-	-	-	-	-	-	-	-	SP	60.2
	-	-	-	-	-	-	-	-	-	-	-	-	RJ	8.2
	-	-	-	-	-	-	-	-	-	-	-	-	RS	5.2
Alfalfa	-	-	RS	89.9	RS	82.2	RS	72.1	-	-	-	-	RS	70.4
	-	-	SP	5.6	SC	10.8	SP	11.3	-	-	-	-	PR	21.8
	-	-	SC	2.4	SP	6.3	SC	10.6	-	-	-	-	SC	5.7
Avocado	-	-	-	-	-	-	-	-	-	-	-	-	SP	33.8
	-	-	-	-	-	-	-	-	-	-	-	-	MG	17.8
	-	-	-	-	-	-	-	-	-	-	-	-	CE	8.7
Jute	-	-	-	-	-	-	-	-	-	-	-	-	AM	78.1
	-	-	-	-	-	-	-	-	-	-	-	-	PA	21.9
	-	-	-	-	-	-	-	-	-	-	-	-	-	-
Peaches	-	-	-	-	-	-	-	·	-	-	-	-	RS	81.3
	-	-	-	-	-	-	-	-	-	-	-	-	SP	6.7
	-	-	-	-	-	-	-	-	-	-	-	-	SC	4.4
Tea	-	-	-	-	-	-	SP	89.9	-	-	-	-	SP	99.9
	-	-	-	-	-	-	MG	10.1	-	-	-	-	MG	.1
	-	-	-	-	-	-	-	-	-	-	-	-	-	-

Table IX-8 (continued)

	1920 PS	%	1931 PS	%	1940 PS	%	1950 PS	%	1960 PS	%	1970 PS	%	1975 PS	%
Figs	-	-	-	-	-	-	-	-	-	-	-	-	RS	73.9
	-	-	-	-	-	-	-	-	-	-	-	-	SP	17.0
	-	-	-	-	-	-	-	-	-	-	-	-	MG	5.8
Barley	-	-	RS	89.0	RS	87.9	-	-	-	-	RS	90.1	RS	45.2
	-	-	PR	10.1	PR	6.1	-	-	-	-	SC	7.4	PR	40.7
	-	-	SC	.9	SC	6.0	-	-	-	-	PR	2.5	SC	14.0
Pears	-	-	-	-	-	-	-	-	-	-	-	-	RS	33.6
	-	-	-	-	-	-	-	-	-	-	-	-	SP	6.7
	-	-	-	-	-	-	-	-	-	-	-	-	SC	4.4
Flaxseed	-	-	-	-	-	-	-	-	-	-	-	-	RS	87.7
	-	-	-	-	-	-	-	-	-	-	-	-	SC	12.3
	-	-	-	-	-	-	-	-	-	-	-	-	-	-
Oats	-	-	RS	87.3	RS	91.5	RS	85.3	-	-	RS	85.5	RS	58.1
	-	-	PR	6.9	PR	4.6	SC	11.0	-	-	PR	10.2	PR	34.0
	-	-	SC	5.8	SC	3.9	PR	3.7	-	-	SC	4.3	SC	7.9
Apples	-	-	-	-	-	-	-	-	-	-	-	-	SP	38.4
	-	-	-	-	-	-	-	-	-	-	-	-	SC	32.1
	-	-	-	-	-	-	-	-	-	-	-	-	RS	23.4
Rye	-	-	PR	45.9	PR	72.4	PR	84.4	-	-	PR	61.7	PR	41.7
	-	-	RS	39.5	SC	22.5	SC	14.4	-	-	SC	23.4	RS	36.4
	-	-	SC	14.6	RS	5.1	RS	.6	-	-	RS	14.9	SC	21.9
Persimmons	-	-	-	-	-	-	-	-	-	-	-	-	SP	48.9
	-	-	-	-	-	-	-	-	-	-	-	-	RS	28.5
	-	-	-	-	-	-	-	-	-	-	-	-	PR	8.1
Cantaloupes	-	-	-	-	-	-	-	-	-	-	-	-	RS	28.8
	-	-	-	-	-	-	-	-	-	-	-	-	SP	27.1
	-	-	-	-	-	-	-	-	-	-	-	-	PE	19.9
Quinces	-	-	-	-	-	-	-	-	-	-	-	-	MG	60.2
	-	-	-	-	-	-	-	-	-	-	-	-	RS	35.3
	-	-	-	-	-	-	-	-	-	-	-	-	SC	2.3
Tung Nuts	-	-	-	-	-	-	PR	56.0	-	-	-	-	RS	95.3
	-	-	-	-	-	-	RS	34.0	-	-	-	-	PR	4.7
	-	-	-	-	-	-	SP	8.6	-	-	-	-	-	-
Olives	-	-	-	-	-	-	-	-	-	-	-	-	RS	99.7
	-	-	-	-	-	-	-	-	-	-	-	-	MG	.3
	-	-	-	-	-	-	-	-	-	-	-	-	-	-
Chestnuts/Walnuts	-	-	-	-	-	-	-	-	-	-	-	-	RS	77.1
	-	-	-	-	-	-	-	-	-	-	-	-	SP	9.6
	-	-	-	-	-	-	-	-	-	-	-	-	PR	9.0

Sources: RE 1920 C2, pp. 4-7; AN 1936, pp, 104-110; AN 1941-45, pp. 59-97; AN 1951, pp. 80-113; AN 1963, pp. 61-67; AN 1971, pp. 148-156; AN 1977, pp. 341-354.

Table IX-9. Indices of Quantum and Producer Prices of Brazilian Agricultural Products, 1939-75

	Quantum	Producer Prices	Quantum	Producer Prices	Quantum	Producer Prices	Quantum	Producer Prices
	Base Year= 1948		Base Year= 1955		Base Year= 1955		Base Year= 1966	
1939	86.7	28.6						
1940	83.2	28.3						
1941	88.1	29.8						
1942	82.7	33.5						
1943	92.3	40.5						
1944	92.5	56.1						
1945	87.6	66.5						
1946	96.8	79.0						
1947	96.5	88.9						
1948	100.0	100.0						
1949	106.0	110.2						
1950	110.3	136.4						
1951	108.0	153.1						
1952	115.5	172.9						
1953	115.4	215.8	85.4	71.9				
1954	119.9	260.7	89.4	86.4				
1955	135.4	301.7	100.0	100.0				
1956			90.9	118.2				
1957			105.1	130.3				
1958			109.2	139.1				
1959			142.2	163.0				
1960			147.2	213.9				
1961			155.9	274.2	162.5	313.5		
1962			159.3	500.0	148.6	537.5		
1963					143.2	926.8		
1964					119.1	1824.0		
1965					184.5	2184.2		
1966					145.9	3268.9		
1967					164.5	4037.1		
1968					154.5	5295.1		
1969					164.0	6651.0		
1970					158.7	8110.7		
1971							–	321.8
1972							–	386.7
1973							–	543.8
1974							–	733.6
1975							–	1004.9

Sources: AN 1956, p. 104; AN 1963, p. 58; AN 1971, p. 144; AN 1975, p. 439.

Table IX-10. Number of Domesticated Animals in Brazil and Percentage of the Total in the Most Productive Political Subdivisions, 1912-76

	1912	1920	1940	1950	1960	1970	1976
CATTLE							
Brazil: No.(000's)	30,705	34,271	34,458	47,069	73,962	97,864	107,349
and %	100.0	100.0	100.0	100.0	100.0	100.0	100.0
Political Subdivision: %	RS 23.6	RS 24.8	MG 22.6	MG 22.3	MG 21.9	MG 21.3	MG 19.6
	MG 22.3	MG 21.4	RS 21.7	RS 19.6	RS 14.1	RS 12.8	GO 12.9
	BA 8.7	GO 8.8	SP 9.2	SP 12.6	SP 13.0	SP 11.7	RS 12.0
	MT 8.3	MT 8.3	GO 8.6	BA 8.6	MT 8.6	MT 10.4	MT 11.8
	GO 6.1	BA 7.9	BA 8.0	GO 7.5	GO 8.6	GO 10.1	SP 11.1
SWINE							
Brazil: No.(000's)	18,401	16,169	16,850	23,034	47,944	66,374	38,742
and %	100.0	100.0	100.0	100.0	100.0	100.0	100.0
Political Subdivision: %	MG 36.5	MG 30.1	RS 18.8	RS 18.2	MG 18.4	MG 15.3	PR 15.8
	BA 13.1	RS 20.8	SP 15.9	MG 16.1	RS 11.8	PR 13.1	RS 14.7
	RS 12.0	SP 18.1	MG 15.2	SP 11.6	PR 10.6	RS 11.4	MG 11.0
	SP 10.5	BA 4.8	PR 8.9	PR 8.9	SP 10.3	GO 8.3	SC 9.4
	RJ 4.0	PR 4.8	SC 6.7	MA 7.7	SC 9.0	SP 8.2	MA 9.0
SHEEP							
Brazil: No.(000's)	10,550	7,933	9,287	13,073	18,162	24,727	18,002
and %	100.0	100.0	100.0	100.0	100.0	100.0	100.0
Political Subdivision: %	RS 35.5	RS 56.5	RS 55.9	RS 55.5	RS 55.5	RS 54.6	RS 63.3
	BA 21.1	BA 12.0	BA 13.8	BA 13.3	BA 11.9	BA 11.3	BA 12.0
	CE 12.4	PE 5.3	CE 7.4	CE 8.5	CE 6.1	CE 6.0	CE 6.3
	PI 4.9	CE 5.0	PI 4.6	PB 4.1	PI 5.2	PB 4.9	PI 4.7
	PB 4.6	MG 3.9	PB 3.9	PI 3.9	PE 3.8	PI 4.9	PE 2.9
GOATS							
Brazil: No.(000's)	10,049	5,087	6,523	6,963	11,195	14,609	7,485
and %	100.0	100.0	100.0	100.0	100.0	100.0	100.0
Political Subdivision: %	PE 29.9	PE 27.9	BA 30.3	BA 29.3	BA 23.9	BA 21.8	BA 34.6
	CE 16.8	PB 16.8	PE 16.5	PE 16.1	PE 13.4	PI 12.6	PI 19.1
	PB 14.9	BA 10.7	CE 15.6	CE 15.1	CE 12.6	PE 10.8	PE 15.1
	BA 8.4	CE 10.4	PI 13.0	PI 11.3	PI 11.1	CE 10.5	CE 9.6
	PI 6.3	PI 5.9	PB 6.6	PB 7.3	PB 5.9	PB 8.2	PB 5.8
HORSES							
Brazil: No.(000's)	7,290	5,254	4,684	5,258	8,273	9,114	5,157
and %	100.0	100.0	100.0	100.0	100.0	100.0	100.0
Political Subdivision: %	MG 23.9	RS 27.7	RS 20.6	RS 20.6	MG 17.6	MG 14.8	MG 16.1
	RS 19.5	MG 22.5	MG 17.1	MG 17.6	RS 14.7	RS 14.6	RS 12.0
	BA 11.3	SP 9.6	SP 10.1	SP 10.8	SP 11.0	BA 11.1	GO 12.0
	SP 7.0	BA 7.5	GO 8.1	BA 8.4	BA 8.5	GO 9.0	SP 10.2
	GO 4.3	GO 5.1	BA 7.9	GO 6.9	GO 7.8	SP 8.2	BA 9.6
MULES/ASSES							
Brazil: No.(000's)	3,208	1,865	2,135	2,503	6,161	7,745	2,095
and %	100.0	100.0	100.0	100.0	100.0	100.0	100.0
Political Subdivision: %	MG 24.3	MG 20.6	BA 17.3	BA 18.5	BA 21.3	MG 24.3	MG 33.9
	BA 17.8	SP 17.5	SP 17.2	SP 16.1	SP 11.3	BA 11.0	CE 18.3
	SP 13.0	BA 13.4	CE 12.8	CE 12.3	CE 8.8	SP 9.2	BA 14.6
	CE 8.8	RS 11.5	MG 11.3	MG 11.3	PI 8.5	CE 8.5	PI 14.4
	RS 6.3	CE 6.3	PI 8.0	PI 7.3	PE 6.6	PI 6.4	SP 13.3
FOWL							
Brazil: No.(000's)	—	52,940	62,912	77,830	184,133	302,668	344,827
and %	—	100.0	100.0	100.0	100.0	100.0	100.0
Political Subdivision: %	—	MG 19.6	MG 18.5	MG 16.9	SP 20.4	SP 21.1	SP 24.4
	—	SP 17.0	SP 17.2	SP 16.3	MG 19.0	MG 16.3	MG 11.6
	—	RS 16.7	RS 12.7	RS 13.6	PR 9.4	PR 9.7	RS 10.4
	—	BA 6.8	BA 6.7	BA 6.2	RS 8.3	RS 8.4	PR 9.8
	—	SC 4.8	SC 4.8	SC 6.0	GO 5.5	GO 6.1	SC 9.3

Sources: AN 1939-40, pp. 1315-1318; RE 1950A2, pp. 128-129; AN 1961, pp. 81-83 & 86-87; AN 1971, pp. 160-167; AN 1978, pp. 387-392

Table IX-11. Animal-Created Products by Value and Quantity, and Share of
Total Brazilian Quantity by Most Productive Political
Subdivisions, 1920-76

	1919		1939		1949		1960		1970		1976	

MILK

	1919		1939		1949		1960		1970		1976	
Total Value Cr$1000	–		–		–		50,843,570		2,502,018		20,071,647	
Total Quantity	221,911		1,829,755		2,750,892		4,899,816		7,132,049		8,256,942	
% of Quantity	–	–	MG	36.9	MG	31.8	MG	33.1	MG	34.3	MG	29.4
	–		RS	14.9	SP	18.7	SP	24.6	SP	19.0	SP	16.8
	–		SP	13.1	RS	16.3	RS	7.8	RS	9.3	RS	9.7
	–		SC	5.6	SC	5.8	GO	6.7	PR	6.6	PR	7.0
	–		RJ	5.1	BA	4.7	GB	6.7	GO	5.6	GO	6.8

WOOL

	1919		1939		1949		1960		1970		1976	
Total Value Cr$1000	952,670		–		720,957		3,044,730		112,303		509,368	
Total Quantity	3,604		4,464		19,659		22,686		31,713		30,591	
% of Quantity	RS	96.3	RS	95.1	RS	98.1	RS	97.4	RS	96.6	RS	98.6
	MG	1.6	SC	1.6	SC	.7	SC	.9	PR	1.8	SC	.6

EGGS

	1919		1939		1949		1960		1970		1976	
Total Value Cr$1000	–		–		–		21,777,647		1,162,613		5,068,014	
Total Quantity	–		116,436		187,875		520,344		840,986		920,504	
% of Quantity	–	–	RS	21.5	SP	23.3	SP	30.9	SP	32.5	SP	40.3
	–	–	MG	18.8	MG	17.7	MG	16.0	MG	14.7	MG	19.6
	–	–	SP	16.0	RS	13.6	PR	8.8	PR	9.1	PR	8.1
	–	–	SC	5.4	BA	5.5	RS	8.0	RS	8.1	RS	8.1

HONEY

	1919		1939		1949		1960		1970		1976	
Total Value Cr$1000	–		–		33,241		261,413		17,659		111,784	
Total Quantity	–		–		6,156		7,539		6,315		5,902	
% of Quantity	–	–	–	–	RS	41.3	SC	23.1	RS	35.1	SC	36.4
	–	–	–	–	SC	21.7	RS	21.7	SC	19.6	RS	27.7
	–	–	–	–	PR	16.5	PR	20.9	PR	10.9	BA	7.3
	–	–	–	–	SP	5.7	SP	15.4	SP	7.2	PR	7.0

BEESWAX

	1919		1939		1949		1960		1970		1976	
Total Value Cr$1000	–		–		14,019		97,641		4,201		14,775	
Total Quantity	219		–		927		1,161		1,193		624	
% of Quantity	RS	45.5	–	–	RS	29.0	PR	24.5	RS	29.7	RS	33.8
	PR	10.6	–	–	SC	20.0	SC	23.0	SC	16.6	SC	22.1
	SC	10.0	–	–	PR	19.5	RS	17.7	PR	13.2	BA	10.1

SILK

	1919		1939		1949		1960		1970		1976	
Total Value Cr$1000	–		–		19,164		217,497		16,386		216,709	
Total Quantity	–		–		764		1,143		2,463		9,132	
% of Quantity	–	–	–	–	SP	98.7	SP	99.2	SP	99.2	SP	78.2
	–	–	–	–	ES	1.0	RS	.3	PR	.6	PR	13.1
	–	–	–	–	MG	.3	ES	.2	RS	.1	MT	8.2

Milk quantity is in 1,000 liters, egg quantity in 1,000 dozen. All others are in metric tons.
Sources: RE 1920 C2, pp. 13-15; RE 1950 A2, p. 130; AN 1952, pp. 130-132; AN 1963, pp. 69-71; AN 1971, pp. 165,168-170; AN 1978, pp. 390-393.

Table IX-12. Value and Quantity of Wood and Major Vegetal Extracts in Brazil, 1920-75

	1920 Quantity	1920 Value	1935 Quantity	1935 Value	1940 Quantity	1940 Value	1950 Quantity	1950 Value	1960 Quantity	1960 Value	1970 Quantity	1970 Value	1975 Quantity	1975 Value
WOODS	--	--	164,815,944	--	--	--	--	--	102,840,625	15,358,284	134,804,000	642,498,000	31,527,908	--
FIREWOOD	--	38,012	--	--	--	--	--	--	971,150	2,085,987	1,589,556	152,718	122,069,682	--
CHARCOAL	--	--	88,000	--	--	--	--	--	--	--	--	--	2,396,236	--
FOODS/OILS														
Babaçu Oil Nuts	--	--	29,081	12,358	68,162	54,128	74,795	231,289	100,708	2,856,457	180,897	110,727	212,723	487,100
Erva Mate Tea	118,641	--	83,545	42,885	83,815	42,908	60,321	92,182	110,676	1,223,173	113,460	39,901	94,636	201,427
Brazil Nuts	--	--	51,097	71,842	40,527	35,985	22,636	98,779	39,382	1,680,275	104,487	54,642	51,719	100,972
Palm Hearts	--	--	--	--	--	--	--	--	--	--	--	--	200,154	91,352
Pine Nuts	--	--	--	--	--	--	--	--	--	--	--	--	21,616	41,165
Cashew Nuts	--	--	--	--	--	--	--	--	5,506	34,701	20,309	9,347	20,490	26,948
Umbu Fruit	--	--	--	--	--	--	--	--	--	--	--	--	29,815	21,998
Licurí Oil Nuts	--	--	--	--	2,720	3,795	3,056	8,605	7,818	204,710	46,422	11,268	7,337	17,720
Açaí Fruit	--	--	--	--	--	--	--	--	--	--	--	--	17,474	16,694
Oiticica Oil Nuts	--	--	9,001	--	29,785	38,881	33,529	36,727	37,934	284,505	20,064	4,082	24,079	16,399
Tucum Oil Nuts	--	--	2,000	--	--	--	--	--	5,152	70,547	7,263	2,933	9,542	15,642
Mangaba Fruit	--	--	--	--	--	--	--	--	--	--	--	--	1,028	2,004
Pequi Fruit	--	--	--	--	--	--	--	--	--	--	--	--	841	1,247
Guaraná Seeds	19,987	2,263	140	--	172	1,675	198	4,410	178	9,762	188	469	--	--
RUBBERS	--	--	16,543	4,780	18,284	88,927	27,829	358,772	30,895	2,590,901	52,190	132,501	14,311	106,253
WAXES														
Carnaúba	--	--	7,785	35,028	9,892	159,187	10,625	285,837	10,980	1,930,445	20,378	34,711	18,103	203,629
Licurí	--	--	--	--	1,200	12,000	1,560	31,794	212	13,480	148	133	109	612
FIBERS														
Piaçava	--	--	5,600	--	5,621	6,089	5,494	20,461	15,621	393,656	21,654	19,833	48,705	174,234
Malva/Guaxima	--	--	--	--	--	--	5,902	29,151	11,585	286,619	14,972	5,866	7,492	23,225
Vegetal Hairs	--	--	--	--	--	--	--	--	--	--	--	--	2,000	1,413
Caroá	--	--	2,960	--	5,426	8,252	4,630	14,656	3,267	41,052	1,463	601	585	1,105
Agave	--	--	802	--	--	--	52,477	305,872	--	--	--	--	--	--
Jute	--	--	33	--	--	--	14,054	61,223	--	--	--	--	--	--
RESINS/GUMS														
Sôrva	--	--	--	--	--	--	--	--	1,361	34,913	4,692	5,757	3,294	9,878
Maçaranduba	--	--	--	--	--	--	--	--	763	28,082	595	776	496	1,902
Balata	1,905	--	--	--	--	--	--	--	1,217	269,326	474	1,077	283	1,510
MEDICINALS/TOXINS														
Jaborandi	371	--	--	--	--	--	--	--	--	--	--	--	2,367	6,603
Ipecac	71	--	--	--	--	--	--	--	83	108,831	53	902	31	608
Timbó	--	--	743	2,588	--	--	4	9	183	1,999	138	112	6	8
TANNINS														
Quebracho	520	--	--	--	--	--	--	--	--	--	--	--	21,865	4,373
Barbatimão	--	--	--	--	--	--	--	--	--	--	--	--	5,696	4,035
Angico	--	--	--	--	--	--	--	--	30,506	58,556	6,371	964	5,280	3,651

All quantities are in metric tons

Sources: RE 1920C3, pp. 12-13; AN 1936, pp. 87-88; AN 1937, p. 198; AN 1941-45, pp. 54-58; AN 1951, pp. 72-74; AN 1963, pp. 43-48; AN 1971, p. 129; AN 1972, pp. 131-132; AN 1978, pp. 381-382.

Table IX-13. Political Subdivisions with Largest Shares of Brazil's
Production of Wood and Major Vegetal Extracts, 1920-75

	1920		1935		1940		1950		1960		1970		1975	
	PS	%	PS	%	PS	%	PS	%	PS	%	PS	%	PS	%
WOODS	MG	18.1	AM	43.8	-	-	-	-	-	-	-	-	PA	27.4
	SP	16.4	MT	4.8	-	-	-	-	-	-	-	-	SC	19.5
	RS	16.1	SP	2.1	-	-	-	-	-	-	-	-	BA	7.9
FIREWOOD	-	-	-	-	-	-	-	-	MG	26.5	MG	18.5	MG	18.9
	-	-	-	-	-	-	-	-	SC	11.2	PR	12.2	BA	14.2
	-	-	-	-	-	-	-	-	RS	10.4	RS	12.2	SC	9.8
CHARCOAL	-	-	MG	100.0	-	-	-	-	MG	52.7	MG	70.8	MG	74.2
	-	-	-	-	-	-	-	-	SP	15.6	SP	6.6	ES	4.9
	-	-	-	-	-	-	-	-	PE	5.7	PE	3.5	BA	4.8
FOODS/OILS														
Babaçu Oil Nuts	-	-	MA	71.9	MA	68.4	MA	75.5	MA	83.3	MA	82.7	MA	74.6
	-	-	PI	27.6	PI	29.3	PI	20.4	PI	9.6	GO	8.3	GO	14.4
	-	-	GO	.3	GO	1.0	GO	2.8	GO	5.0	PI	7.1	PI	9.0
Erva Mate Tea	PR	74.5	PR	51.3	PR	37.2	RS	41.9	SC	30.8	RS	51.9	RS	34.0
	SC	11.8	RS	19.6	RS	29.8	PR	24.6	PR	28.0	PA	29.6	SC	33.6
	RS	10.0	SC	17.4	MT	24.4	MT	18.2	RS	26.4	SC	18.4	PR	31.3
Brazil Nuts	-	-	AM	43.5	PA	44.3	PA	35.8	PA	39.7	AM	53.9	PA	52.3
	-	-	PA	43.1	AM	40.4	AM	47.3	AM	34.9	PA	24.5	RO	21.1
	-	-	MT	1.2	AC	13.7	AP	6.5	AC	13.1	AC	14.9	AM	12.1
Palm Hearts	-	-	-	-	-	-	-	-	-	-	-	-	PA	81.9
	-	-	-	-	-	-	-	-	-	-	-	-	PR	6.5
	-	-	-	-	-	-	-	-	-	-	-	-	SP	5.2
Pine Nuts	-	-	-	-	-	-	-	-	-	-	-	-	SC	66.9
	-	-	-	-	-	-	-	-	-	-	-	-	PR	24.8
	-	-	-	-	-	-	-	-	-	-	-	-	MG	6.5
Cashew Nuts	-	-	-	-	-	-	-	-	CE	46.7	CE	61.2	CE	45.1
	-	-	-	-	-	-	-	-	PE	20.6	RN	13.7	RN	20.8
	-	-	-	-	-	-	-	-	BA	10.9	PE	11.8	PE	11.8
Umbu Fruit	-	-	-	-	-	-	-	-	-	ᵗ	-	-	BA	97.0
	-	-	-	-	-	-	-	-	-	-	-	-	PE	2.7
	-	-	-	-	-	-	-	-	-	-	-	-	PB	.2
Licuri Oil Nuts	-	-	-	-	-	-	-	-	BA	100.0	BA	93.8	BA	100.0
	-	-	-	-	-	-	-	-	-	-	AC	6.2	-	-
Acaí Fruit	-	-	-	-	-	-	-	-	-	-	-	-	PA	81.7
	-	-	-	-	-	-	-	-	-	-	-	-	MA	17.7
	-	-	-	-	-	-	-	-	-	-	-	-	AP	.4
Oiticica Oil Nuts	-	-	CE	88.9	CE	75.7	CE	42.1	CE	66.1	CE	50.9	CE	69.9
	-	-	PB	11.1	RN	15.2	PB	38.2	PB	22.1	PB	31.5	PB	16.5
	-	-	-	-	PB	7.9	RN	7.1	RN	10.9	RN	16.4	RN	13.4
Tucum Oil Nuts	-	-	-	-	-	-	-	-	PI	50.6	PI	82.1	PI	83.9
	-	-	-	-	-	-	-	-	MA	49.0	MA	17.5	MA	16.1
	-	-	-	-	-	-	-	-	BA	.3	ES	.3	-	-
Mangaba Fruit	-	-	-	-	-	-	-	-	-	-	-	-	PB	96.1
	-	-	-	-	-	-	-	-	-	-	-	-	BA	1.9
	-	-	-	-	-	-	-	-	-	-	-	-	SE	1.5
Pequi Fruit	-	-	-	-	-	-	-	-	-	-	-	-	CE	84.7
	-	-	-	-	-	-	-	-	-	-	-	-	BA	10.9
	-	-	-	-	-	-	-	-	-	-	-	-	MT	2.3
Guaraná Seeds	AM	100.0	AM	100.0	AM	100.0	AM	100.0	AM	100.0	AM	100.0	-	-
RUBBERS	AM	39.4	AM	37.4	AM	47.7	AM	28.4	AC	35.8	AM	59.9	AC	45.8
	AC	27.8	PA	28.4	AC	26.3	AC	24.1	RO	25.8	AC	20.0	AM	25.9
	PA	26.3	MT	6.7	PA	17.2	PA	18.3	AM	18.8	RO	11.0	RO	19.2
WAXES														
Carnaúba	-	-	PI	42.6	CE	43.5	CE	41.9	CE	38.9	CE	38.9	CE	50.0
	-	-	CE	36.1	PI	38.6	PI	38.2	PI	28.8	PI	24.1	RN	24.0
	-	-	RN	11.8	MA	7.3	RN	9.7	RN	15.3	MA	19.1	PI	20.9

Table IX-13 (continued)

	1920		1935		1940		1950		1960		1970		1975	
	PS	%	PS	%	PS	%	PS	%	PS	%	PS	%	PS	%
FIBERS														
Piaçava	-	-	BA	84.8	BA	81.3	BA	92.2	BA	92.6	BA	95.1	BA	98.1
	-	-	AM	15.2	AM	18.7	AM	7.7	AM	7.4	AM	4.9	AM	1.9
Malva/Guaxima	-	-	-	-	-	-	-	-	PA	87.9	PA	85.2	PA	99.9
	-	-	-	-	-	-	-	-	MA	10.4	AC	7.5	BA	.1
	-	-	-	-	-	-	-	-	MG	1.5	MA	7.2	-	-
Vegetal Hairs	-	-	-	-	-	-	-	-	-	-	-	-	SC	61.1
	-	-	-	-	-	-	-	-	-	-	-	-	RS	20.2
	-	-	-	-	-	-	-	-	-	-	-	-	PR	15.9
Caroá	-	-	PE	62.4	PE	74.3	PE	61.4	PE	74.1	PE	64.6	PE	57.0
	-	-	PB	16.2	PB	13.3	BA	26.3	BA	19.7	BA	22.8	BA	31.3
	-	-	BA	13.2	BA	11.0	PB	9.1	PB	3.3	PI	4.0	PB	8.8
Agave	-	-	PB	100.0	-	-	PB	90.6	-	-	-	-	-	-
	-	-	-	-	-	-	RN	4.8	-	-	-	-	-	-
	-	-	-	-	-	-	BA	3.4	-	-	-	-	-	-
Jute	-	-	-	-	-	-	AM	49.5	-	-	-	-	-	-
	-	-	-	-	-	-	PA	49.0	-	-	-	-	-	-
RESINS/GUMS														
Sôrva	-	-	-	-	-	-	-	-	-	-	-	-	AM	84.5
	-	-	-	-	-	-	-	-	-	-	-	-	RO	12.3
	-	-	-	-	-	-	-	-	-	-	-	-	RN	2.2
Maçaranduba	-	-	-	-	-	-	-	-	-	-	-	-	PA	97.6
	-	-	-	-	-	-	-	-	-	-	-	-	AM	1.6
	-	-	-	-	-	-	-	-	-	-	-	-	AP	.8
Balata	-	-	-	-	-	-	-	-	-	-	-	-	PA	97.5
	-	-	-	-	-	-	-	-	-	-	-	-	AP	1.8
	-	-	-	-	-	-	-	-	-	-	-	-	RO	.4
MEDICINALS/TOXINS														
Jaborandi	-	-	MA	43.9	-	-	-	-	-	-	-	-	MA	94.4
	-	-	PI	56.1	-	-	-	-	-	-	-	-	PI	4.7
	-	-	-	-	-	-	-	-	-	-	-	-	PB	.6
Ipecac	-	-	MT	56.4	-	-	-	-	MT	92.0	MT	46.9	RO	76.0
	-	-	BA	25.0	-	-	-	-	RO	3.6	RO	41.4	MT	17.3
	-	-	PB	17.6	-	-	-	-	ES	2.4	MG	5.4	BA	4.1
Timbó	-	-	AM	100.0	PA	92.9	PA	100.0	PA	83.0	MA	81.2	-	-
	-	-	-	-	AM	7.1	-	-	AM	9.9	PA	14.3	-	-
	-	-	-	-	-	-	-	-	AP	7.0	AP	4.5	-	-
TANNINS														
Quebracho	-	-	MT	100.0	-	-	-	-	-	-	-	-	MT	100.0
Barbatimão	-	-	-	-	-	-	-	-	-	-	-	-	MG	77.3
	-	-	-	-	-	-	-	-	-	-	-	-	SP	16.5
	-	-	-	-	-	-	-	-	-	-	-	-	GO	5.0
Angico	-	-	MG	100.0	-	-	-	-	MT	53.2	BA	55.9	BA	30.4
	-	-	-	-	-	-	-	-	BA	14.3	PE	10.6	MT	20.9
	-	-	-	-	-	-	-	-	PE	13.3	MG	5.7	MG	12.3

Sources: RE 1920C2, pp. 7 & 12; AN 1936, pp. 83-86; AN 1941-45, pp. 56-58; AN 1951, pp. 72-74; AN 1963, pp. 46-48; AN 1971, pp. 130-133; AN 1972, pp. 131-132; AN 1978, pp. 381-385.

Table IX-14. Number and Value of Wild Animal Hides and Skins Taken in Brazil, and the Political Subdivisions Producing the Largest Shares of the Total Number Taken, 1960-69

	1960	1961	1962	1963	1964	1965	1966	1967	1968	1969
BIG CATS										
Value Cr$1000	222,735	281,022	502,259	1,518,968	2,412,104	3,956,111	3,711,565	4,339,172	6,593,222	8,753,020
Number	116,886	121,294	119,410	124,254	131,998	168,459	151,160	113,680	139,094	129,038
Major Prod.	BA CE MA PE GO	BA CE PE MA GO	CE BA PE MA GO	BA CE MA GO AC	CE BA MA PA PI	CE BA AC MA PI	CE BA MA PI GO	CE BA MA PI GO	CE BA PA MA PI	BA CE PA MA PI
Subdvs. by %	18.1 17.7 12.4 12.1 11.3	19.8 19.4 14.7 11.4 7.3	18.3 15.6 15.2 12.7 8.1	19.4 18.8 12.6 7.6 6.3	19.8 18.6 11.4 11.1 9.4	27.9 16.1 9.3 8.2 6.7	28.0 19.7 8.9 6.5 5.6	28.6 23.0 10.5 9.1 8.1	22.2 19.1 10.1 8.4 7.8	18.9 18.7 18.0 8.6 8.4
LIZARDS										
Value Cr$1000	49,287	54,119	72,781	153,470	674,504	809,328	875,925	1,388,291	2,505,975	2,423,442
Number	803,364	860,383	1,003,626	948,942	1,182,886	1,275,239	1,302,608	1,284,359	1,380,964	1,369,560
Major Prod.	CE BA PI	CE PI BA	CE BA PI	CE BA PI	CE PI BA	CE BA PI	CE BA PI	CE BA PI	CE BA PI	CE BA PI
Subdvs. by %	49.6 18.5 14.8	48.2 15.7 14.3	50.6 14.9 11.1	47.1 15.8 15.4	40.2 15.8 15.2	43.6 14.2 12.3	42.7 14.0 12.1	40.1 20.8 13.6	36.8 22.1 13.5	37.2 22.7 13.2
CROCODILIANS										
Value Cr$1000	46,786	81,964	156,101	237,737	582,817	996,872	1,324,876	4,654,571	2,509,827	2,307,015
Number	94,419	137,239	162,426	163,008	528,512	565,961	444,794	757,902	472,214	341,412
Major Prod.	AM PA GO	AM GO PA	AM PA GO	AM PA GO	MT AM GO	MT AM PA	MT AM PA	MT AM MA	MT AM MA	MT AM PA
Subdvs. by %	35.0 29.0 22.0	33.0 23.7 21.0	27.9 17.8 14.4	29.9 25.8 23.4	70.1 9.8 9.5	75.8 8.9 6.9	54.0 27.5 9.4	53.3 20.4 9.4	44.7 18.7 11.2	37.6 24.4 14.8
WILD PIGS										
Value Cr$1000	35,025	56,468	104,850	286,319	492,055	639,546	1,020,399	1,306,033	1,663,418	2,630,473
Number	344,771	403,331	468,092	510,382	535,611	574,637	670,007	687,825	629,153	776,864
Major Prod.	GO MA AC	AC GO MA	AC AM MA	AM AC MA	AM GO AC	AM AC GO	AM AC GO	AM AC GO	AM AC GO	AC AM PA
Subdvs. by %	20.2 19.2 18.0	22.1 17.2 15.5	20.8 17.1 15.0	11.6 10.3 10.2	25.1 15.6 13.6	27.8 15.7 14.5	32.2 19.8 12.4	27.8 24.4 13.3	22.1 20.9 13.6	42.9 16.8 11.9
OTTERS										
Value Cr$1000	22,504	18,885	42,960	150,632	160,699	224,738	211,530	249,551	304,188	358,911
Number	4,929	3,971	4,979	6,228	5,496	6,099	4,367	4,594	4,674	5,305
Major Prod.	MG GO PA	MT PA GO	MT GO PA	MG MT PA	MT MG PA	MT AM MG	MT GO MG	GO MT PA	PA AM MT	AM PA MT
Subdvs. by %	30.7 17.0 14.5	25.4 15.4 12.6	35.4 14.8 11.5	18.6 23.0 12.4	22.0 18.3 15.9	27.1 19.4 13.6	32.7 18.1 13.1	17.4 16.9 13.1	17.7 17.3 15.8	23.1 18.1 13.5
DEER										
Value Cr$1000	22,072	34,560	63,938	211,705	190,184	263,759	421,807	551,661	730,437	902,892
Number	235,014	271,323	297,606	329,040	322,092	349,831	336,324	356,953	320,854	296,082
Major Prod.	MA AC GO	AC MA GO	MA PA AM	AC AM MA	MA PA AC	AM MA AC	AC MA PA	AM AC MA	AC MA MA	AC MA AM
Subdvs. by %	28.4 20.0 11.7	27.8 23.2 10.7	20.9 12.8 12.7	18.0 16.0 15.9	18.5 15.9 15.6	18.3 17.5 15.7	22.0 17.5 12.9	24.0 21.5 15.9	19.8 16.3 15.6	30.0 16.3 11.1
CAPIVARA										
Value Cr$1000	14,984	25,669	80,039	109,486	159,324	206,837	221,513	206,379	186,134	152,621
Number	126,993	184,651	311,760	243,331	159,998	169,442	126,221	102,114	75,720	46,466
Major Prod.	MT AM PA	MT AM PA	AM MT MG	MT AM MG	MT AM PA	MT MA PA	MT AM PA	MT AM PA	MT AM PA	MT PA AM
Subdvs. by %	72.7 12.7 6.0	68.6 18.4 4.9	47.4 42.6 5.6	50.5 33.4 4.0	71.8 11.2 7.8	72.5 11.8 7.8	64.9 17.2 8.7	60.4 19.8 11.4	70.1 10.4 9.2	47.3 25.2 13.0

Sources: AN 1963, pp. 49-51; AN 1965, pp. 81-83; AN 1967, pp. 77-78; AN 1970, pp. 103-104.

Table IX-15. Number of Professional Fishermen and Characteristics of the Fishing Fleet in Brazil, 1958-68

	1958	1960		1968	
Number of Professional Fishermen	223,800	239,761		311,824	
Number of Boats	111,481	121,271		54,695	
Cargo Capacity of Boats (metric tons)	92,000	99,458		69,613	
Value of Boats (Cr$1000)	–	1,712,711		–	
Number of Motorships	–	3,176		4,593	
Enclosed Deck	–	2,518		–	
Open Deck	–	658		–	
Number of Sailboats	–	22,968		20,982	
Enclosed Deck	–	1,270		–	
Open Deck	–	21,698		–	
Number of Rowed Boats	–	95,127		29,120	
Enclosed Deck	–	843		–	
Open Deck	–	94,284		–	
Most Important Political Subdivisions					
Number of Fishermen	–	MA	32,321	MA	64,925
	–	AM	31,508	CE	29,813
	–	CE	25,258	BA	28,068
	–	PA	22,514	PA	27,451
	–	BA	21,227	SP	26,595
	–	AM	23,458	MA	9,478
	–	MA	16,116	SC	6,891
	–	PA	12,629	PA	6,506
	–	BA	8,691	RJ	5,601
	–	SC	8,085	RS	5,308
Number of Boats	–	GB	594,532	–	
	–	SP	198,070	–	
	–	CE	112,683	–	
Value of Boats	–	MA	106,373	–	
	–	RN	91,209	–	

Sources: Heare, p. 91; AN 1962, pp. 50-51; AN 1971, pp. 135-137.

212

Table IX-16. Quantity and Value of Commercial Harvests of Salt and Fresh Water Animal Life by the Most Productive Political Subdivisions, 1938-79

	1938	1939	1940	1941	1942	1943	1944	1946	1947	1948	1949
Total (metric tons)	—	—	—	—	—	—	—	122,410	139,732	144,767	152,606
Largest Producer (metric tons)	GB 16,031	GB 18,530	GB 18,488	GB 19,185	GB 17,195	GB 17,958	GB 22,469	RJ 30,438	RJ 26,555	RJ 26,401	MA 31,590
								RS 17,972	GB 21,291	MA 24,870	RJ 23,563
								SP 15,429	MA 18,242	RS 22,055	RS 19,777
								GB 13,546	RS 17,377	SP 18,085	SP 16,397
								MA 10,053	SP 16,703	GB 13,206	GB 10,798
Total (Cr$ 000)	—	—	—	—	—	—	—	385,935	421,023	453,038	522,499
Largest Producers (Cr$ 000)	GB 26,386	GB 27,759	GB 27,998	GB 28,527	GB 29,844	GB 25,140	GB 33,799	GB 72,530	RJ 82,671	RJ 96,166	RJ 99,799
								RJ 62,019	SP 66,073	MA 63,996	MA 93,032
								SP 38,471	MA 46,427	SP 50,580	SP 47,715
								RS 31,834	SP 43,941	GB 48,409	GB 47,455
								MA 24,646	RS 30,277	RS 32,280	RS 35,304
Fish (metric tons)	—	—	—	—	—	—	—	—	—	—	—
Fish (Cr$ 000)	—	—	—	—	—	—	—	—	—	—	—
Crustaceans (metric tons)	—	—	—	—	—	—	—	—	—	—	—
Crustaceans (Cr$ 000)	—	—	—	—	—	—	—	—	—	—	—
Aquatic Mammals (m. tons)	—	—	—	—	—	—	—	—	—	—	—
Aquatic Mammals (Cr$ 000)	—	—	—	—	—	—	—	—	—	—	—
Molluscs (metric tons)	—	—	—	—	—	—	—	—	—	—	—
Molluscs (Cr$ 000)	—	—	—	—	—	—	—	—	—	—	—
Turtles (metric tons)	—	—	—	—	—	—	—	—	—	—	—
Turtles (Cr$ 000)	—	—	—	—	—	—	—	—	—	—	—

	1950	1951	1952	1953	1954	1955	1956	1957	1958	1959
Total (metric tons)	153,107	158,297	174,630	160,677	172,033	190,287	208,285	216,239	214,899	253,100
Largest Producers (metric tons)	MA 34,285	MA 30,089	RS 31,570	MA 30,917	RS 27,277	RJ 28,303	SP 29,889	SP 35,161	SP 38,887	RS 45,781
	RJ 28,137	RJ 27,432	MA 29,027	RS 24,552	MA 24,080	RS 27,702	MA 28,363	MA 33,352	MA 31,560	SP 37,512
	RS 21,770	RS 21,951	RJ 26,648	GB 18,911	RJ 22,755	MA 25,595	RS 27,123	RS 27,407	RS 29,007	MA 31,128
	SP 12,611	GB 16,399	GB 21,017	SP 16,370	GB 19,561	GB 23,721	GB 24,790	GB 24,765	GB 21,308	RJ 23,505
	SC 10,056	SP 14,135	SP 15,974	SC 14,707	SP 19,418	SP 15,646	RJ 23,674	RJ 17,764	RJ 18,043	RJ 22,365
Total (Cr$ 000)	570,887	—	826,260	982,454	1,251,404	1,530,701	2,159,400	2,517,564	3,222,327	4,652,117
Largest Producers (Cr$ 000)	MA 106,144	—	GB 120,912	MA 133,556	MA 156,977	GB 190,151	SP 255,608	SP 373,321	MA 464,610	SP 712,549
	RJ 88,100	—	SP 112,431	RJ 131,634	RJ 155,291	MA 186,159	RJ 249,421	MA 356,113	SP 456,231	MA 541,066
	SP 66,612	—	MA 98,702	GB 129,012	SP 144,292	RJ 184,301	MA 244,467	GB 273,594	GB 374,446	GB 517,665
	GB 48,645	—	RJ 92,292	SP 120,880	GB 137,858	SC 179,368	GB 238,897	SC 190,440	BA 271,917	RJ 393,133
	RS 45,171	—	RS 67,586	SC 71,967	SC 123,261	RS 115,098	SC 188,615	CE 180,509	RS 241,662	BA 371,706
Fish (metric tons)	—	—	—	—	—	—	—	157,352	158,366	211,116
Fish (Cr$ 000)	—	—	—	—	—	—	—	1,809,791	2,416,235	3,754,862
Crustaceans (metric tons)	—	—	—	—	—	—	—	23,796	23,347	25,741
Crustaceans (Cr$ 000)	—	—	—	—	—	—	—	342,078	481,032	785,669
Aquatic Mammals (m. tons)	—	—	—	—	—	—	—	4,012	2,966	9,600
Aquatic Mammals (Cr$ 000)	—	—	—	—	—	—	—	48,739	8,188	23,362
Molluscs (metric tons)	—	—	—	—	—	—	—	2,635	2,171	1,921
Molluscs (Cr$ 000)	—	—	—	—	—	—	—	3,486	7,584	18,832
Turtles (metric tons)	—	—	—	—	—	—	—	486	608	516
Turtles (Cr$ 000)	—	—	—	—	—	—	—	5,138	12,134	12,981

Table IX-16 (continued)

1960–1969

	1960	1961	1962	1963	1964	1965	1966	1967	1968	1969
Total (metric tons)	281,512	330,140	414,640	421,356	333,085	376,912	435,787	429,422	500,387	501,197
Largest Producers (metric tons)	SP 47,138; RS 43,049; RJ 32,464; MA 31,022; GB 20,797	RJ 50,074; SP 42,526; RS 42,006; SC 36,673; MA 35,634	MA 85,618; RS 83,392; SC 55,731; SP 38,471; RJ 36,046	RS 106,353; SC 74,976; MA 42,637; SP 41,838; RJ 28,032	SC 54,935; MA 39,643; SP 38,660; RS 35,627; PA 30,180	SC 58,483; RS 50,221; MA 47,660; SP 45,792; PA 34,347	RS 101,707; SC 54,501; SP 52,261; MA 48,625; GB 34,920	SP 59,949; MA 53,451; SC 50,286; RS 33,958	SP 81,251; GB 61,035; MA 56,080; RS 51,117; SC 46,173	RS 75,145; SP 60,294; SC 56,830; RJ 50,856; MA 48,537
Total (Cr$ 000)	8,100,251	12,031,768	23,240,379	39,842,150	59,374,577	108,085,217	160,914,501	213,246,398	302,829,509	421,475
Largest Producers (Cr$ 000)	SP 2,232,889; RS 829,909; SC 763,659; MA 632,987; RJ 521,272	SP 3,029,336; RS 1,079,205; SC 1,020,645; MA 958,626; GB 870,678	MA 4,289,313; SP 3,663,424; RS 2,608,314; SC 2,484,803; CE 1,461,138	SC 6,490,339; SP 5,150,268; RS 4,886,030; MA 4,279,299; CE 2,616,096	SP 8,804,535; MA 7,557,084; SC 7,151,715; GB 5,345,125; CE 5,270,688	SP 15,293,890; MA 13,860,978; SC 13,358,486; RS 9,813,065; CE 7,848,652	SP 29,627,191; MA 20,168,512; SC 17,100,287; RS 17,075,071; GB 10,394,187	SP 41,285,729; MA 26,570,167; GB 21,632,045; SC 18,100,287; RS 13,565,025	SP 62,638,081; GB 34,900,132; MA 32,582,018; RS 24,653,542; SC 24,143,348	SP 71,859; GB 47,153; MA 44,214; RJ 36,925; SC 34,935
Fish (metric tons)	217,550	233,903	329,508	364,581	283,927	318,009	368,367	361,688	414,529	418,541
Fish (Cr$ 000)	6,552,269	9,375,994	18,436,310	33,270,298	47,266,239	85,354,670	120,377,238	162,768,467	219,574,915	297,970
Crustaceans (m. tons)	30,639	38,265	48,711	44,518	43,316	51,390	57,587	55,564	70,814	70,400
Crustaceans (Cr$ 000)	1,292,763	1,921,208	3,488,135	5,532,337	10,763,057	20,269,714	37,734,079	47,095,624	76,321,365	116,686
Aquatic Mammals (m. tons)	24,662	48,472	22,922	7,276	2,235	3,538	6,852	6,844	8,461	7,607
Aquatic Mammals (Cr$ 000)	71,592	333,532	533,251	445,564	717,345	1,078,555	1,350,209	1,393,220	2,064,546	2,954
Molluscs (metric tons)	2,051	2,403	2,545	1,798	2,630		2,155	4,698	4,775	3,018
Molluscs (Cr$ 000)	23,834	35,657	66,230	144,448	275,018	661,566	862,010	1,352,762	2,555,419	2,036
Turtles (metric tons)	507	558	695	498	354	590	419	280	237	250
Turtles (Cr$ 000)	16,662	28,800	41,960	82,436	117,254	269,612	266,340	203,905	234,366	293

1970–1979

	1970	1971	1972	1973	1974	1975	1976	1977	1978	1979
Total (metric tons)	526,292	591,543	604,673	698,802	731,383	759,792	658,847	752,607	806,328	858,183
Largest Producers (metric tons)	RS 117,771; SP 69,021; SC 60,707; MA 52,526; GB 39,859	RS 124,033; SC 73,088; SP 65,604; GB 61,643; RJ 49,624	RS 109,421; SC 88,849; GB 76,788; SP 65,574; RS 51,372	RJ 158,652; SC 135,799; RS 126,295; SP 52,489; MA 49,961	RJ 162,525; SC 112,525; RS 104,406; SP 72,643; MA 47,464	RJ 144,596; RS 122,013; SC 107,264; SP 74,970; PA 65,964	RS 143,358; RJ 106,404; SP 80,463; SC 64,787; PA 63,744	RS 138,117; RJ 127,197; MA 95,685; SC 86,868; SP 83,413	RJ 164,081; SC 144,698; MA 92,136; PA 91,455	SC 227,605; RJ 178,361; SP 91,687; RS 87,216; PA 69,503
Total (Cr$ 000)	498,611	856,606	1,120,931	1,751,089	2,144,625	2,184,065	3,271,433	4,420,822	6,404,396	15,354,201
Largest Producers (Cr$ 000)	SP 96,084; GB 54,902; MA 50,717; SC 48,818; RS 45,029	CE 156,426; SP 109,935; SC 87,788; GB 71,896; SC 69,292	CE 196,668; SP 164,186; GB 105,472; SC 99,940; RS 88,734	RJ 434,238; CE 314,303; SP 164,127; SC 156,406; RS 129,615	RJ 499,737; SP 306,095; CE 207,382; SC 189,538; SC 160,956	SP 310,894; RS 236,738; SC 214,426; RN 214,243; PA 200,996	SP 459,308; RS 420,954; CE 324,961; PE 318,104; MA 278,958	SP 580,595; RS 515,252; SC 513,371; PA 451,820; PA 439,330	SP 946,190; PA 829,300; RS 673,699; RJ 666,825; SC 628,501	SP 2,521,983; CE 2,062,028; RJ 1,670,936; RS 1,586,066; RS 1,460,867
Fish (metric tons)	449,322	499,281	509,504	600,417	650,654	680,014	585,123	663,258	703,050	660,207
Fish (Cr$ 000)	349,878	468,257	587,896	984,596	1,358,730	1,501,836	2,269,017	3,030,331	4,437,824	9,431,409
Crustaceans (m. tons)	64,044	76,693	87,263	83,547	71,174	69,022	63,790	79,470	84,241	104,509
Crustaceans (Cr$ 000)	140,973	376,423	525,605	752,595	766,475	661,259	982,670	1,339,595	1,893,245	5,064,563
Aquatic Mammals (m. tons)	3,269	9,813	3,069	7,375	5,388	6,631	5,816	4,120	3,700	3,064
Aquatic Mammals (Cr$000)	3,545	4,420	2,291	4,122	5,288	6,498	4,045	11,380	9,920	2,873
Molluscs (metric tons)	2,861	4,466	4,619	7,369	4,056	3,884	4,036	5,708	12,884	
Molluscs (Cr$ 000)		4,057	4,592	9,328	13,813	13,377	15,101	38,956	48,678	77,951
Turtles (metric tons)	473	280	200	94	36	68	82	51	46	40
Turtles (Cr$ 000)	638	439	501	448	130	334	600	560	913	1,170

Sources: AN 1941–45, p. 59; AN 1952, p. 89; AN 1954, p. 75; AN 1956, p. 95; AN 1957, p. 69; AN 1960, pp. 46–49; AN 1961, pp. 69–72; AN 1962, p. 52; AN 1963, pp. 52–53; AN 1966, pp. 95–98; AN 1970, pp. 109–112; AN 1973, pp. 155–158; AN 1975, pp. 125–129;

Chapter X. Mining and Energy

Table X-1 presents the values and quantities of ores, minerals, and building materials extracted in Brazil from 1920 to 1977. The Serviço de Estatística da Produção generated the data for 1920 to 1960. The 1968 data originated with IBGE and the Escritório de Estatística do Ministério da Agricultura. Data for 1970 and 1977 were originated by the Departamento Nacional da Produção Mineral.

For all years (except where noted) the values and quantities of the following ores were reported after they had been beneficiated or concentrated: columbite/tantalite, tin, tungsten (except 1968), zirconium, gold, and silver. For 1970 and 1977 the flourite figures were for the concentrates. The 1930 sea salt figures were estimted by the Serviço de Estatística da Produção on the basis of 1925-29 production. For 1938, quartz and diamond figures were for exports. The same is true for the quartz figures for 1940 and the manganese figures for 1940 and 1950. Iron ore production in 1940 was the sum of internal consumption and exports.

Table X-2 shows the major political subdivisions of Brazil producing coal, ores, minerals and building materials from 1940 to 1977. The data origins are the same as those for Table X-1.

Indices for quantum and producer prices of Brazilian minerals from 1950 to 1968 appear on Table X-3. The data origin for the base year 1953 and for the first 1955 base year was the Laboratório de Estatística of IBGE, and for the second 1955 base year, IBGE. The quantum index is based on the Laspeyres model; the producer price index on the Paasche model. The calculations of these indices included quantities and prices for twenty-five products. Eleven were metallic minerals: aluminum, beryl, columbite/tantalite, chrome, tin, iron, manganese, nickel, titanium, tungsten, and zirconium. Fourteen were nonmetallic minerals: asbestos, barite, dolomite, phosphorite, gypsum, graphite, mica, quartz, sea salt, talc, marble, coal, natural gas, and crude petroleum.

215

For the period 1961-64 the price of iron ore was set at its export price.

Table X-4 reports Brazilian natural gas and petroleum output by political subdivisions from 1940 to 1970. Data for 1940 to 1950 originated with the Conselho Nacional de Petróleo, and those for 1955 with the Serviço Nacional da Produção and Petróleo Brasileiro, S.A. (Petrobrás). Petrobrás also originated data for the remaining years on the table, but some data for 1977 also came from the Conselho Nacional de Petróleo. The 1970 figures for petroleum production included 151,720 cubic meters (954,000 barrels) of liquid natural gas.

Wyeth[1] notes that between 1918 and 1930 the Geological and Mineralogical Service of the Ministry of Agriculture drilled more than seventy wells but no oil or gas production resulted so interest waned in the 1930s. In 1939 the Department of Mineral Production brought in the first well in the Lobato-Joanes field near Salvador, Bahia. It yielded only a few liters per day. Between 1939 and 1946 on the margins of the Bahia de Todos os Santos (Bay of All Saints) in the state of Bahia, four new fields were discovered: Candeias, Aratu, Itaparica, and Dom João. In 1938 the National Petroleum Council, a government monopoly, was established to pursue exploration and development, but lack of refinery capacity proved to be a bottleneck in the flow of petroleum products to market. During World War II the Council set up refineries in Bahia state, at Aratu and Candeias, with a combined daily capacity of 150 barrels of crude. During the 1940s three privately owned refineries, one at Rio Grande do Sul in Rio Grande do Sul state, operated on crude imported from Venezuela. In 1947 the Council completed a pilot plant to produce oil shale from the coal/shale beds in south Brazil (Wyeth does not give a location for this project).

Table X-5 reports Brazil's petroleum and coal energy balance from 1902 to 1976. Data origins included the Serviço de Estatística da Produção, the Serviço Estatística Econômica e Financeira, the Centro de Informaçoes Econômicos Fiscais, the Conselho Nacional de Petróleo, the Instituto Nacional de Siderurgia, the Departamento Nacional de Produção Mineral, Petróleo Brasileiro, S.A. (Petrobrás), and the Banco do Brasil's Carteira de Comércio Exterior.

All petroleum figures are given in 42-gallon barrels. Where data origins gave the quantities in metric tons the conversion used was 7.454 barrels per metric ton which is the American Petroleum Institute's standard for crude at 36 degrees. Gasoline imports for all years included aviation

216

gasoline as well as other types of gasoline. For 1902 the kerosene figures included some gasoline. The 1970 "other" category of petroleum imports included some petroleum coke (3,922 metric tons) and some lubricating oils mixed with vegetable oils.

Coke was included in coal imports in 1960 (30,246 metric tons), 1970, and 1976 on Table X-5. Prior to 1902 some easily mined coal in Santa Catarina and Rio Grande do Sul states was probably used locally, but according to Wyeth[1] the only commercial coal mine was at São Jerônimo, Rio Grande do Sul, which produced 15,000 metric tons in 1913. A 1931 law requiring importers to mix Brazilian coal with all imports provided a stimulus to national production.

Table X-6 shows Brazil's potential and actual electrical energy production by major political subdivisions from 1889 to 1975. Data origins included the Divisão de Águas do Departamento Nacional da Produção Mineral, the Conselho Nacional de Águas e Energia Elétrica, the Serviço de Estatística do Departamento Nacional de Águas e Energia Elétrica, and the Departamento Nacional de Águas e Energia Elétrica. The rise of Goiás state to fourth place in installed potential by 1970 reflected the development of electrical power sources, mostly hydraulic, that accompanied the creation of Brasília and surrounding regional infrastructure in the 1960s.

Table X-7 reports the consumption of electrical energy by major users in Brazil from 1952 to 1976. Data origins for 1952 and 1960 were the Conselho Nacional de Águas e Energia Elétrica, for 1970 the Serviço de Estatística do Departamento Nacional de Águas e Energia Elétrica, and for 1976 the Departamento Nacional de Águas e Energia Elétrica. Although electrical energy production (see Table X-6) in 1952 matched consumption on Table X-7, production for 1960 and 1970 on Table X-6 exceeded consumption reported on Table X-7. The sources offered no explanations for these discrepancies. In 1952, however, the power losses through transmission and transformers amounted to about 15 percent of total production. This percentage approximates the differences between production on Table X-6 and consumption on Table X-7 for 1960 and 1970.

Table X-8 presents the indices of the quantum of Brazilian electrical energy output from 1944 to 1971. The data origin for the 1948 base year was the Fundação Getúlio Vargas and for the base years 1953 and 1962 the Instituto Brasileiro de Economia. The 1968 base year data originated with FIBGE which calculated the indices from data supplied by the Departamento Nacional de Águas e Energia Elétrica and the

Ministério das Minas e Energia. The source (AN 1956) noted
that the 1948 base year data are provisional. The indices
for the 1968 base year included electricity produced by every
possible entity in Brazil including all levels of government,
government concessionaires, private and mixed (private/
public) companies, and private producers of electricity for
their own use. The latter included factories, mills, mines,
and railroads. No such specifications were given for indices
for other base years.

Table X-9 shows Brazilian consumption of primary energy
by sources of energy in petroleum-equivalents from 1967 to
1977. The data originated with the Ministério das Minas e
Energia. During the period the hydroelectric proportion of
the total rose by 9.6 percentage points (from 16.5 percent of
the total in 1967 to 26.1 percent in 1977). The proportion
produced by petroleum rose by 7.9 percentage points and the
proportion generated by wood fell by 17.2 percentage points.
The category "cane refuse" refers to bagasse, the stalks
after the juice has been pressed from them.

Table X-10 reports Brazil's production of gasohol
(alcohol mixed with gasoline) from 1931 to 1978. The origin
of the data from 1931 to 1966 was the Instituto de Açúcar e
do Álcool. The data for 1967 to 1978 originated with Yang
and Trindade.[2] In the years 1938 through 1944 (excepting
1940) kerosene and other nonalcohol substances were added to
gasohol. The amounts introduced were negligible, never
equaling 0.1 percent of the total volume, although in 1942
these additives totaled 264,000 liters and in 1944 127,000
liters. The 1978 percent of alcohol in the total mix was
estimated by Yang and Trindade.

Not all political subdivisions used gasohol proportionate to gasoline consumption or mixed the same percentages
of alcohol with gasoline. In 1955 São Paulo state produced
46.4 percent of the Brazilian gasohol total, Guanabara 34.8
percent, and Pernambuco 15 percent of the total. The product
was not shipped far so production by state is nearly
tantamount to consumption by state. In 1965 São Paulo
state's production of gasohol reached 61.7 percent of
Brazil's total, Pernambuco's rose to 19.3 percent and
Guanabara's fell to 10.1 percent. The proportion of alcohol
mixed with gasoline has consistently been higher in São Paulo
state, Brazil's largest gasoline consumer and sugar cane
producer, than in the nation as a whole.

Brazil's early interest in mixing alcohol (anhydrous
ethanol, EtOH, derived from sugar cane) with gasoline was
triggered less by a shortage of gasoline than by a surplus of
sugar produced from cane. From 1930 to 1931 the value of

Brazil's sugar exports fell by 82 percent, resulting in huge domestic stockpiles of the commodity. At the time Brazil was importing all its petroleum needs and paying for them with ever smaller currency reserves. Faced with these conditions, in 1931 Brazil legislated the use of alcohol as a motor fuel additive. All importers of gasoline were required to purchase and mix alcohol with gasoline so from that year hence all gasoline sold in Brazil has been gasohol. In 1931 the mix was set at 95:5, gasoline to alcohol, but has fluctuated sharply from year to year since then.

During Brazil's economic boom of the late 1960s and early 1970s alcohol production did not keep pace with the huge petroleum imports so the percentage of alcohol mixed with gasoline fell to very low levels. In 1975 the National Alcohol Commission was empowered to stimulate construction of alcohol distilleries and the production of sugar cane as a feedstock for these distilleries. The production of alcohol (anhydrous ethanol) was 277,353 cubic meters in 1976. By 1977 it had risen to 1,087,924 cubic meters, by 1978 to 1,943,455 cubic meters and by 1979 to 2,832,036 cubic meters. Brazil's short term goal was to increase the annual production of anhydrous ethanol to 5,000,000 cubic meters by 1982. Thus from 1977, when this program began using new sugar cane plantings, to 1982 total annual ethanol production will have had to rise by more than 3,900,000 cubic meters to meet this goal. Ludwig[3] calculated that such production would require 979,000 hectares (2.4 million acres) of new cane plantings.

References

1. George Wyeth, Royce A. Wight, and Harold M. Midkiff, Brazil: An Expanding Economy (New York: Twentieth Century Fund, 1949).

2. V. Yang and S.C. Trindade, "Brazil's New Gasohol Program," Chemical Engineering Progress, April 1979, pp. 11-19.

3. Armin K. Ludwig, "Brazil's New Gasohol Program: Its Sugar Cane Production and Land Requirements," in New Issues in Latin America, ed. Barry Lentnek, Proceedings of the Conference of Latin Americanist Geographers, Buffalo, New York, October 15-18, 1981.

Table X-1. Value and Quantity of Ores, Minerals, and Building Materials Extracted in Brazil, 1920-77

	1920 Value Cr$1000	1920 Quantity	1930 Value Cr$1000	1930 Quantity	1940 Value Cr$1000	1940 Quantity	1950 Value Cr$1000	1950 Quantity	1960 Value Cr$1000	1960 Quantity	1968 Value Cr$1000	1968 Quantity	1970 Quantity	1977 Quantity
Coal	12,458	306,930	15,021	385,148	72,473	1,336,301	371,754	1,958,649	2,765,024	2,330,088	356,367	4,827,590	36,381,230	10,045,302
Iron Ore	-	-	-	-	11,872	593,581	64,382	1,987,425	1,458,123	9,345,117	-	25,123,313	-	100,817,295
Sea Salt	2,871	287,061	3,915	333,777	18,105	466,122	794,181	103,879	1,125,067	922,914	-	1,248,058	-	2,481,331
Tin	-	-	-	-	-	305	4,769	305	842,774	2,635	15,302	2,870	5,421	9,525
Manganese	39,829	453,737	14,486	192,122	31,237	313,391	31,237	313,391	538,048	999,163	69,404	2,096,595	2,731,582	2,736,458
Quartz Crystals	-	-	-	-	27,863	1,103	24,225	1,103	343,462	1,177	4,034	1,182	4,075	45,530
Tungsten	-	-	-	-	-	-	11,162	482	206,890	1,412	3,050	151,583	995	2,026
Lead	-	-	-	-	-	-	-	-	205,509	140,903	7,438	320,553	354,046	266,377
Marble	-	-	-	-	2,282	14,373	14,652	23,817	93,699	49,533	2,136	40,993	41,273	145,257
Beryl	-	-	-	-	721	1,472	7,625	2,201	82,099	1,696	577	744	14,908	-
Phosphorite	-	-	-	-	-	-	-	-	69,708	226,146	-	353,091	608,404	1,662,721
Dolomite	-	-	-	-	-	-	-	-	54,926	676,447	3,228	66,447	-	1,512,997
Asbestos	-	-	-	-	85	142	844	623	41,859	98,366	1,289	345,442	330,086	190,178
Mica	-	-	-	-	21,970	1,151	31,753	1,813	40,652	2,014	187	483	-	621
Talc	-	-	-	-	133	1,334	4,386	12,631	39,076	19,918	2,551	79,490	79,496	370
Copper	-	-	-	-	-	-	-	-	36,525	70,241	1,992	162,482	111,200	-
Columbite/Tantalite	-	-	-	-	-	-	-	-	34,016	213	725	130	250	137
Bauxite	-	-	-	-	483	6,019	2,220	18,570	35,232	120,763	1,345	313,748	509,803	1,352,065
Apatite	-	-	-	-	-	-	-	-	28,464	203,184	4,199	582,703	216,402	543,046
Gypsum	-	-	-	-	-	-	-	-	27,430	103,101	2,773	216,798	173,749	481,154
Barite	-	-	-	-	-	-	-	-	21,839	39,758	2,326	99,980	-	53,603
Graphite	-	-	-	-	-	-	2,329	471	18,200	1,300	2,092	22,000	33,503	39,575
Magnesite	-	-	-	-	-	-	-	-	17,892	63,315	7,554	137,820	73,455	683,147
Chrome	-	-	-	-	-	-	1,102	3,227	10,037	5,666	677	17,032	4,024	13,268
Zircon	-	-	-	-	-	-	1,980	3,016	8,729	5,768	17	328	-	4,649
Titanium	-	-	-	-	-	-	-	-	6,084	216	1	1	-	-
Nickel	-	-	-	-	-	-	-	-	3,400	5,005	230	67,744	202,078	339,275
Gold (kilograms)	17,484	4,160	25,472	4,189	111,634	4,660	154,326	4,082	-	-	-	-	5,830	5,355
Mineral Water(000 ltrs)	-	-	-	-	-	-	-	-	-	-	-	-	-	396,099
Arsenic	-	-	308	202	21,376	20,749	64,455	37,806	-	-	-	-	-	-
Silver (kilograms)	-	-	582	70	2,720	1,088	5,750	1,067	-	-	-	-	11,108	11,583
Diamonds (grams)	-	-	-	-	169	768	439	665	-	-	-	-	12,864	12,864
Limestone	-	-	-	-	81,403	50,866	461	627	-	-	-	-	16,524,765	39,303,119
Kaolin	-	-	-	-	-	-	-	-	-	-	-	-	400,037	939,666
Flourite	-	-	-	-	-	-	-	-	-	-	-	-	36,568	115,960
Bentonite	-	-	-	-	-	-	-	-	-	-	-	-	28,062	108,359
Feldspar	-	-	-	-	-	-	-	-	-	-	-	-	43,088	99,767
Diatomite	-	-	-	-	-	-	-	-	-	-	-	-	3,160	11,204

All quantities are in metric tons except where specified
Sources: AN 1939-40, pp. 1310,11; AN 1956, pp. 482-487; AN 1963, pp. 125-128; AN 1972, pp. 173-175; AN 1978, pp. 418-423.

Table X-2. Brazilian Political Subdivisions with the Largest Percentages by Quantity of the National Output of Coal, Ores, Minerals, and Building Materials, 1940–77

Coal, Ore, Mineral	1940 (PS[a] %)	1950 (PS %)	1960 (PS %)	1968 (PS %)	1977 (PS %)
COAL	RS 79.7 / SC 19.9 / PR .2	SC 51.3 / RS 43.6 / PR 5.1	SC 69.8 / RS 27.6 / PR 2.6	SC 72.3 / RS 20.6 / PR 7.1	SC 83.9 / RS 13.2 / PR 2.9
IRON ORE	MG 99.7 / PR .3	MG 99.2 / PR .8	MG 98.9 / PR .8	MG 99.7 / PR .2	MG 99.9
SEA SALT	RN 63.7 / RJ 17.4 / CE 7.5	RN 73.8 / CE 11.8 / RJ 6.5	RN 63.3 / CE 16.1 / RJ 11.9	RN 62.2 / RJ 16.1 / CE 13.7	RN 75.1 / RJ 19.6 / MA 2.3
TIN	—	RJ 96.7	RJ 83.0 / GO 11.8	RO 62.8 / GO 9.9 / MG 9.2	RO 62.8 / GO 9.9 / PA 9.2 / AP 2.1
MANGANESE	MG 97.3 / BA 2.4 / PR .3	MG 94.6 / BA 5.4	AP 76.1 / MG 15.8 / MT 6.5	AP 77.4 / MG 18.4 / MT 4.0	AP 59.7 / MG 28.1 / MT 8.6
QUARTZ	—	—	GO 52.0 / BA 26.4 / MG 21.5	GO 47.0 / MT 46.2 / BA 5.8	MG 91.5 / SP 6.9 / RJ .9
TUNGSTEN	—	—	RN 99.9	RN 100.0	RN 100.0
LEAD	—	—	BA 50.1 / PR 44.8	BA 71.8 / PR 28.2	BA 81.5 / PA 18.5
MARBLE	MG 50.3 / RJ 28.3 / SC 11.1	MG 65.6 / RJ 24.9 / SC 2.9	RJ 34.3 / MG 32.6 / RN 11.9	MG 61.0 / BA 14.1 / RJ 11.3	ES 61.8 / MG 21.8 / RN 5.1
BERYL	—	—	BA 84.2 / MG 8.9	BA 97.8	—
DOLOMITE	—	—	SP 48.4 / MG 29.6 / RJ 21.1	MG 66.8 / RJ 20.1 / SP 10.0	MG 41.1 / SP 40.2 / PR 11.9
PHOSPHORITE	—	—	PE 98.4 / SP 1.6	PE 68.0 / SP 32.0	—
ASBESTOS	—	—	BA 88.3 / AL 10.9	AL 80.0 / GO 19.5	GO 99.5 / AL .4
MICA	MG 92.8 / RJ 5.1 / PB 1.3	MG 53.8 / BA 42.7 / PB 5.5	MG 94.2 / GO 3.0 / RN 2.6	MG 58.4 / GO 41.4 / PB .2	—
TALC	MG 56.4 / PR 23.8 / BA 19.8	—	PR 45.7 / MG 30.1 / BA 12.5	PR 63.4 / MG 24.5 / BA 9.7	PR 80.5 / BA 11.2 / MG 5.7
COPPER	—	—	RS 100.0	RS 98.4 / BA 1.6	SP 100.0
COLUMBITE/TANTALITE	—	—	MG 78.9 / BA 9.9 / AP 7.0	MG 80.8 / BA 14.6 / AP 3.1	—
BAUXITE	MG 97.3 / SP 2.7	—	—	—	MG 94.5 / SP 5.5
APATITE	—	—	SP 96.5 / MG 3.3	SP 81.1 / MG 18.9	—
GYPSUM	—	—	RN 55.0 / CE 34.2 / RJ 5.8	PE 79.8 / CE 14.2 / PI 3.2	PE 93.5 / CE 3.8 / RN 2.7

Coal, Ore, Mineral	1940 (PS %)	1950 (PS %)	1960 (PS %)	1968 (PS %)	1977 (PS %)
BARITE	—	—	BA 99.4 / MG .6	BA 100.0	BA 99.9 / PR .1
GRAPHITE	—	MG 100.0	MG 100.0	MG 99.0 / GO .8	MG 100.0
MAGNESITE	—	—	BA 77.7 / CE 22.3	BA 96.1 / CE 3.9	BA 96.3 / CE 3.3
CHROME	—	—	BA 67.2 / MG 26.1 / GO 6.7	BA 79.3 / MG 11.3 / GO 9.4	BA 99.9 / MG .1
ZIRCONIUM	—	—	MG 90.1 / SP 7.6 / ES 2.3	—	RJ 93.1 / MG 6.9
TITANIUM	—	—	CE 46.3 / GO 37.5 / MG 15.3	MG 100.0	—
NICKEL	—	—	MG 100.0	MG 99.5 / GO .5	MG 99.9
GOLD	MG 95.2 / PR 4.8	MG 99.9	—	—	MG 70.0 / PA 27.6 / AM 2.1
DIAMONDS	—	—	—	—	SP 46.0 / MG 11.2 / RS 9.6
MINERAL WATER	—	—	—	—	—
ARSENIC	MG 100.0	MG 100.0	—	—	—
SILVER	MG 96.2 / PR 3.8	MG 100.0	—	—	—
LIMESTONE	—	—	—	—	MG 36.3 / SP 25.8 / RJ 6.3
KAOLIN	—	—	—	—	SP 39.2 / MG 35.4 / AP 16.2
FLOURITE	—	—	—	—	SC 99.8 / RJ .2
BENTONITE	—	—	—	—	PB 100.0
FELDSPAR	—	—	—	—	MG 40.0 / SP 36.8 / RJ 21.6
DIATOMITE	—	—	—	—	BA 41.0 / RN 24.5 / SC 17.7

Sources: AN 1941–45, pp. 51–52; AN 1951, pp. 68–69; AN 1963, pp. 125–128; AN 1972, pp. 173–175; AN 1978, pp. 419–420.

[a]PS = political subdivision

Brazil: A Handbook of Historical Statistics

Table X-3. Indices of Quantum of Producer Prices of Brazilian Mineral
Products, 1950-68

	Quantum	Producer Prices	Quantum	Producer Prices	Quantum	Producer Prices
	Base Year = 1953		Base Year = 1955		Base Year = 1955	
1950	76.3	80.5				
1951	97.1	84.6				
1952	96.2	90.0				
1953	100.0	100.0	94.0	88.3		
1954	102.8	113.9	92.0	106.0		
1955	110.0	150.0	100.0	100.0		
1956	123.3	180.9	117.7	122.4		
1957	141.9	233.1	159.3	149.1		
1958	192.4	255.3	232.5	154.8		
1959			295.9	238.0		
1960			351.7	369.0	343.6	268.2
1961					343.2	496.3
1962					346.2	677.6
1963					373.1	1185.9
1964					442.2	2301.0
1965					515.1	3039.2
1966					614.7	3548.4
1967					674.4	4095.4
1968					743.8	4329.1

Sources: AN 1960, p. 37; AN 1965, p. 127; AN 1971, p. 171.

Table X-4. Petroleum and Natural Gas Production in Brazil and in Its
Political Subdivisions with Largest Shares of National Total, 1940-77

	1940	1945	1950	1955	1960	1965	1970	1977
Petroleum (42 gallon barrels)	2,088	79,327	338,704	2,021,899	29,613,000	34,341,811	60,926,345	60,735,189
Major Producing Subdivisions	BA 100.0	BA 100.0	BA 100.0	BA 100.0	BA 100.0	BA 99.4	BA 81.4	BA 57.1
	—	—	—	—	—	AL .4	SE 17.9	CP[a] 23.1
	—	—	—	—	—	SE .2	AL .4	SE 16.4
	—	—	—	—	—	—	CP[a] .3	AL 1.8
	—	—	—	—	—	—	—	ES 1.6
Natural Gas (1000 cubic meters)	—	—	—	61,822	534,881	684,037	1,263,605	1,807,604
Major Producing Subdivisions	—	—	—	BA 100.0	BA 100.0	BA 100.0	BA 97.3	BA 60.1
	—	—	—	—	—	—	SE 2.3	CP[a] 33.1
	—	—	—	—	—	—	CP[a] .3	SE 3.9
	—	—	—	—	—	—	AL .1	AL 2.3
	—	—	—	—	—	—	—	ES .6

[a]CP = Continental Platform

Sources: AN 1951, p. 70; AN 1956, p. 87; AN 1957, p. 66; AN 1962, p. 46; AN 1968, p. 178; AN 1972, p. 176; AN 1978, p. 502.

223

Table X-5. Brazil's Petroleum and Coal Energy Balance, 1902–76

	1902 Metric Tons	1902 % of Total Consump.	1910 Metric Tons	1910 % of Total Consump.	1920 Metric Tons	1920 % of Total Consump.	1930 Metric Tons	1930 % of Total Consump.	1940 Metric Tons	1940 % of Total Consump.
Petroleum & Petroleum Derivatives										
Import Total	67,775	100.0	113,067	100.0	338,627	100.0	768,978	100.0	1,257,888	100.0
Crude Oil	-	-	-	-	-	-	-	-	49,266	3.9
Diesel & Fuel Oil	-	-	3,369	3.0	228,651	67.5	374,457	48.7	694,092	55.2
Gasoline	-	-	10,168	9.0	36,384	10.7	279,495	36.3	368,398	29.3
Lubricants	5,515	8.1	-	-	15,092	4.5	24,561	3.2	44,485	3.5
Kerosene	62,240	91.9	99,530	88.0	58,500	17.3	90,465	11.8	101,647	8.1
Other	-	-	-	-	-	-	-	-	-	-
Export Total	-	-	-	-	-	-	-	-	-	-
Net Import Total(Imp. minus Exp.)	67,755	100.0	113,067	100.0	338,627	100.0	768,978	100.0	1,257,888	100.0
Domestic Production of Crude	-	-	-	-	-	-	-	-	273	negl.
Total Brazilian Consumption	67,555	100.0	113,067	100.0	338,627	100.0	768,978	100.0	1,258,161	100.0
Coal										
Import Total	943,564	100.0	1,581,719	100.0	1,120,575	78.5	1,745,826	81.9	1,149,544	46.4
Export Total	-	-	-	-	-	-	-	-	6,900	(-) .3
Net Import Total(Imp. minus Exp.)	943,564	100.0	1,581,719	100.0	1,120,575	78.5	1,745,826	81.9	1,142,644	46.1
Domestic Production of Coal	-	-	-	-	306,930	21.5	385,148	18.1	1,336,301	53.9
Total Brazilian Consumption	943,564	100.0	1,581,719	100.0	1,427,505	100.0	2,130,974	100.0	2,478,945	100.0

	1950 Metric Tons	1950 % of Total Consump.	1960 Metric Tons	1960 % of Total Consump.	1970 Metric Tons	1970 % of Total Consump.	1976 Metric Tons	1976 % of Total Consump.
Petroleum & Petroleum Derivatives								
Import Total	4,289,709	99.0	10,042,894	75.1	17,879,664	72.0	42,433,669	88.7
Crude Oil	11,004	.3	5,683,919	42.5	15,796,648	63.6	40,094,943	83.8
Diesel & Fuel Oil	2,308,688	53.3	2,981,485	22.3	-	-	682,794	1.4
Gasoline	1,618,008	37.3	890,985	6.7	74,428	.3	69,358	.2
Lubricants	115,526	2.7	212,242	1.6	420,260	1.7	287,751	.6
Kerosene	236,483	5.4	98,196	.7	7,668	negl.	-	-
Other	-	-	176,067	1.3	1,580,660	6.4	1,298,823	2.7
Export Total	-	-	647,368	(-)4.8	1,026,080	(-)4.1	2,823,653	(-)5.9
Net Import Total(Imp. minus Exp.)	4,289,709	99.0	9,395,526	70.3	16,853,584	67.9	39,610,016	82.8
Domestic Production of Crude	44,268	1.0	3,973,473	29.7	7,961,597	32.1	8,224,467	17.2
Total Brazilian Consumption	4,333,977	100.0	13,368,999	100.0	24,815,181	100.0	47,834,483	100.0
Coal								
Import Total	1,082,722	35.6	1,046,878	31.0	2,100,916	28.9	3,231,574	29.1
Export Total	-	-	-	-	-	-	58	negl.
Net Import Total(Imp. minus Exp.)	1,082,722	35.6	1,046,878	31.0	2,100,916	28.9	3,231,516	29.1
Domestic Production of Coal	1,958,649	64.4	2,330,088	69.0	5,171,673	71.1	7,876,081	70.9
Total Brazilian Consumption	3,041,371	100.0	3,376,966	100.0	7,272,589	100.0	11,107,597	100.0

Sources: AN 1937, pp. 840 & 191; AN 1939-40, p. 1310; AN 1941-45, pp. 262 & 265; AN 1951, p. 261; AN 1956, p. 531; AN 1963, pp. 125-128, 170 & 175; AN 1971, pp. 308, 318-319; AN 1978, pp. 420, 502, 542 & 559.

Table X-6. Electrical Power, Installed Potential in Kilowatts and Amount
Generated in Kilowatt Hours, in Brazil and Its Most
Productive Political Subdivisions, 1889-1975

Installed Potential in Kilowatts

	1889	1900	1910	1920	1930	1940	1950	1960	1970
Brazil	4,618	12,085	159,860	357,203	747,101	1,243,877	1,882,500	4,800,082	11,233,400
Major Subdivisions	—	—	—	—	SP 42.5	SP 45.4	SP 45.0	SP 37.0	SP 32.1
(% of Brazil Total)	—	—	—	—	RJ 22.9	RJ 21.2	RJ 22.5	RJ 17.2	MG 21.1
	—	—	—	—	MG 11.7	MG 11.6	MG 11.2	MG 15.5	RJ 11.0
	—	—	—	—	RS 5.2	RS 5.3	RS 5.1	BA 4.9	GO 8.5
	—	—	—	—	PE 4.0	PE 3.9	PE 3.0	RS 4.5	BA 6.4
	—	—	—	—	BA 2.9	BA 2.0	DF 2.2	PR 2.7	RS 5.6
	—	—	—	—	DF 2.0	PR 1.4	PR 2.1	SC 1.9	PR 3.8

Source:

	1889	1900	1910	1920	1930	1940	1950	1960	1970
Hydraulic	1,475	5,500	137,864	279,378	618,476	1,009,346	1,535,670	—	8,828,400
Thermic	3,143	6,585	21,996	77,825	128,625	234,531	346,830	—	2,405,000

Production in 1000 Kilowatt Hours

	1952	1960	1970	1975
Brazil	10,028,520	22,864,928	45,459,803	77,273,462
Major Subdivisions		SP 39.3	SP 31.0	SP 35.2
(% of Brazil Total)		RJ 21.7	MG 23.6	MG 31.8
		MG 13.5	RJ 14.0	BA 11.1
		BA 4.3	BA 8.5	RJ 6.6
		RS 3.7	MT 7.5	RS 3.4
		PR 2.7	RS 4.6	SC 3.2
		SC 1.4	PR 2.8	PR 3.1

Source:

	1952	1960	1970	1975
Hydraulic	9,183,971	18,384,240	39,863,000	71,292,028
Combustible Liquid or Gas	526,228	3,825,576	3,894,206	⎤ 5,981,434
Combustible Solid	318,321	655,112	1,702,597	⎦

Sources: AN 1951, pp. 158-160; AN 1954, p. 161; AN 1956, p. 159; AN 1961, pp. 160-161;
AN 1963, p. 159; AN 1971, pp. 289-190; AN 1978, p. 498.

Table X-7. Consumption of Electrical Energy by Major Users in Brazil, 1952-76

Consumer	1952 1000 KWH	1952 %	1960 1000 KWH	1960 %	1970 1000 KWH	1970 %	1976 1000 KWH	1976 %
Industry	⌐4,141,377	41.3	9,173,876	46.8	19,345,230	51.3	43,479,401	56.4
Ore Smelting			1,320,240	6.7	–	–	–	–
Electro-chemical & Metallurgy			947,834	4.9	–	–	–	–
Other	⌐		6,905,802	35.2	–	–	–	–
Commercial			2,621,427	13.3	5,193,760	13.8	9,859,233	12.8
Residential	⌐3,596,532	35.9	3,869,730	19.7	8,405,802	22.3	1,474,786	19.1
Public Illumination	⌐		1,456,387	7.4	3,375,934	9.0	–	–
Raising Water in Hydro-electric Reservoirs	–	–	–	–	–	–	–	–
Electric Traction	775,409	7.7	1,294,236	6.6	–	–	–	–
Other	–	–	925,087	4.7	–	–	–	–
Losses in Transmission/Transformers	1,515,202	15.1	299,027	1.5	1,351,969	3.6	9,055,514	11.7
Total	10,028,520	100.0	19,639,770	100.0	37,672,695	100.0	77,141,934	100.0

Sources: AN 1954, p. 161; AN 1963, p. 259; AN 1971, p. 504; AN 1978, p. 500.

Table X-8. Indices of the Quantum of Brazilian
Electrical Energy Output, 1944-71

Year	Base Year 1948	Base Year 1953	Base Year 1962	Base Year 1968
1944	69			
1945	76			
1946	83			
1947	90			
1948	100			
1949	108	99		
1950	117	104		
1951	126	110		
1952	136	104		
1953	138	100		
1954	154	113		
1955	168	129		
1956		146		
1957		165		
1958		183		
1959		196		
1960		214		
1961		228		
1962		254	100.0	71.13
1963		261	102.6	72.99
1964		287	110.0	76.20
1965				78.91
1966				85.52
1967				89.67
1968				100.00
1969				109.08
1970				119.06
1971				113.54

Sources: AN 1956, p. 163; AN 1965, p. 127; AN 1973, p. 284.

Brazil: A Handbook of Historical Statistics

Table X-9. Brazilian Consumption of Primary Energy by Sources of Energy in Petroleum-Equivalent Units, 1967-77

	1967 Tons (000)	%	1968 Tons (000)	%	1969 Tons (000)	%	1970 Tons (000)	%	1971 Tons (000)	%
Petroleum	17,371	33.8	20,279	37.9	21,993	38.7	23,311	38.1	26,186	39.9
Natural Gas	105	.2	93	.2	96	.2	104	.2	140	.2
Alcohol	367	.7	160	.3	27	negl.	155	.2	213	.3
Hydraulic	8,465	16.5	8,860	16.6	9,481	16.7	11,560	18.9	12,549	19.1
Coal	2,048	4.0	2,317	4.3	2,342	4.0	2,391	3.9	2,431	3.9
Wood	19,291	37.4	18,048	33.8	18,999	33.4	18,809	30.8	18,862	28.8
Cane Refuse	2,825	5.5	2,564	4.8	2,762	4.9	3,356	5.5	3,559	5.4
Charcoal	1,003	1.9	1,094	2.1	1,191	2.1	1,484	2.4	1,655	2.5
Total	51,475	100.0	53,415	100.0	56,891	100.0	61,170	100.0	65,595	100.0

	1972 Tons (000)	%	1973 Tons (000)	%	1974 Tons (000)	%	1975 Tons (000)	%	1976 Tons (000)	%	1977 Tons (000)	%
Petroleum	28,740	41.0	34,240	43.9	36,947	43.8	39,300	43.5	42,894	43.3	43,063	41.7
Natural Gas	166	.2	178	.2	339	.4	369	.4	367	.4	505	.5
Alcohol	328	.4	260	.3	160	.2	136	.1	144	.1	537	.5
Hydraulic	14,918	21.3	17,055	21.9	19,011	22.5	21,412	23.7	23,626	23.8	26,953	26.1
Coal	2,491	3.6	2,493	3.2	2,469	2.9	2,850	3.2	3,435	3.5	4,106	4.0
Wood	17,661	25.2	17,429	22.4	18,541	22.0	19,328	21.4	21,294	21.5	20,885	20.2
Cane Refuse	3,990	5.7	4,459	5.7	4,361	5.2	4,032	4.5	4,156	4.2	4,714	4.6
Charcoal	1,822	2.6	1,897	2.4	2,536	3.0	2,897	3.2	3,154	3.2	2,489	2.4
Total	70,116	100.0	78,011	100.0	84,364	100.0	90,324	100.0	99,080	100.0	103,252	100.0

Source: AN 1978, p. 496.

Table X-10. Brazilian Gasohol Production, 1931-78

Year	Gasohol Produced 1000 liters	Alcohol Content 1000 liters	%	Sao Paulo State Alcohol Content (%)
1931	—	—	5.0	
1938	213,478	32,690	15.3	
1939	312,684	49,066	15.7	
1940	299,217	44,835	15.0	
1941	462,509	102,789	22.2	
1942	290,575	104,691	36.0	
1943	144,472	87,943	60.9	
1944	141,736	82,831	58.4	
1945	111,242	36,134	32.5	
1946	117,813	28,222	24.0	
1947	558,780	76,068	13.6	
1948	633,580	92,904	14.7	
1949	466,752	70,725	15.2	
1950	111,449	10,853	9.7	
1951	81,183	15,187	18.7	
1952	402,175	51,835	12.9	
1953	848,429	105,165	12.4	
1954	1,007,838	132,400	13.1	
1955	1,105,050	207,666	18.8	
1956	619,658	95,729	15.4	
1957	853,892	159,141	18.6	
1958	1,400,622	277,319	19.8	—
1959	1,213,557	248,301	20.5	—
1960	1,361,221	233,285	17.1	—
1961	1,005,283	130,607	13.0	—
1962	874,018	139,946	16.0	—
1963	609,791	62,704	10.3	—
1964	662,015	82,442	12.5	—
1965	1,306,965	224,217	17.2	—
1966	1,985,570	338,125	17.0	—
1967	—	—	6.2	13.5
1968	—	—	2.3	5.1
1969	—	—	.3	.4
1970	—	—	1.9	4.6
1971	—	—	2.5	5.8
1972	—	—	3.5	8.6
1973	—	—	2.5	7.0
1974	—	—	1.4	3.1
1975	—	—	1.1	2.4
1976	—	—	1.2	2.6
1977	—	—	4.6	8.2
1978	—	—	12.0	20.0

Sources: AN 1956, p. 146; AN 1959, p. 130; AN 1961, p. 118; AN 1962, p. 88;
AN 1965, p. 147; AN 1967, p. 194; Yang and Trindade, p. 12.

Chapter XI. Infrastructure

Table XI-1 reports the characteristics of the Brazilian railroad system from 1854 to 1977. The source for the 1854 to 1900 data (AN 1908/1912) gave no origin for them, nor did the sources for the 1920 and 1930 data (RS 1924 and BT 1930, respectively). The 1916 data originated with the Relatórios (Reports) of the Inspetoria Federal das Estradas (sic) da Ministério da Viação e Obras Públicas (confirmed by the railroad companies themselves). Data for all the remaining years were originated by either the Departamento Nacional de Estradas de Ferro, the Rêde Ferroviária Federal, S.A., or the Secretaria Geral de Conselho Nacional de Estatística.

The term "trackage" on Table XI-1 refers to actual trackage carrying traffic and not just to rights-of-way. Federally owned trackage was not all federally administered. The ownership/administration relationship has been a complex one in Brazil and is dealt with in detail in the text for Table XI-2. The area of Brazil used to establish the kilometers of track per 1,000 square kilometers was that given for 1960, 8,511,965 square kilometers. Prior to 1970 animals transported by rail were reported in thousands of head by the sources but for 1970 and 1977 they were reported in thousands of metric tons. Passenger/kilometers reported on Table XI-1 were developed by multiplying each passenger by the length of trip taken. Thus, one passenger making a 100-kilometer trip produced 100 passenger/kilometers and 100 passengers each making a one-kilometer trip also produced 100 passenger/kilometers. For baggage and freight the number of tons likewise was multiplied by the number of kilometers they were carried. Thus, ten tons of freight hauled a distance of 10 kilometers produced 100 freight ton/kilometers. Prior to 1970 sources used numbers of animals as the multiplier in the animal/kilometer category, but for 1970 and 1977 the metric tonnage of animals was used. The number of personnel employed in 1940 was actually for the year 1939. In the receipts and expenditures category for 1916, figures for one railroad, the Estrada de Ferro Noroeste, were not included.

Table XI-2 characterizes the twenty largest railroad systems in Brazil in 1945, 1955, and 1962, and those of the twenty that could be identified by name in 1912. No origin was given for the 1912 data, nor did Abreu,[1] reporting the 1945 trackage by administration, give the origin for his data. All other data originated with the Departamento Nacional de Estradas de Ferro. In 1955 headquarters locations were given by the initials of the political subdivisions. Between 1945 and 1955 the Estradas de Ferro Dourado was absorbed by the Companhia Paulista de Estradas de Ferro. For 1962 the total of 1.60-meter-gauge lines (3,167 kilometers) included 194 kilometers of 1.44-meter-gauge line (4 feet, 8 1/2 inches) of the American-built Amapá Railroad in the Territory of Amapá.

Abreu reports that of the total of 31,967 kilometers of railroad lines in 1929 the government owned 19,079 kilometers but administered only 9,267. The remainder was operated by the states and private companies under a variety of agreements. The states in 1929 owned only 2,239 kilometers of lines but administered 6,270 kilometers, and private companies owned 10,649 kilometers but administered 16,430 kilometers of railroad line. By 1937, of the nation's total trackage of 34,095 kilometers, the federal government owned 21,207 and administered 12,808, the states owned 3,158 kilometers and administered 10,410, and private companies owned 9,730 and administered 10,877 kilometers of railroad line. By 1945 the federal government owned 23,872 kilometers and administered 14,363, the states owned 3,286 and administered 10,990, and private companies owned 8,122 kilometers and administered 9,927. In 1953 the ownership/administration of Brazil's 36,977 kilometers of railroad trackage was as follows: federal government 29,192/25,377; the states 5,550/9,365; and private companies 2,235/2,235.

Maps XI-1, 2 and 3 show the routes, kilometrage, and important stops on eight of the twenty largest Brazilian railroad systems as of 1955. The maps were taken directly from Ferrovias do Brasil, a 1958 IBGE publication. Except for the Companhia Paulista de Estradas de Ferro, which is the dominant system in São Paulo, Brazil's most productive state, all the systems shown on the maps administered more than 2,000 kilometers of trackage.

The Brazilian highway system is characterized on Table XI-3. No origin was given by the source for the 1930 data and Wilkins[2] gave no source for his part of the 1952 data. The 1939 data originated with the Sistema Regional e Secção de Sistematização da Secretaria Geral do IBGE. The Departamento Nacional de Estradas de Rodagem originated the data for 1960, 1970, and 1977, and this Departamento plus the Departamento de Estradas de Rodagem do Distrito Federal originated parts of the data for 1952.

None of the sources defined explicitly what constituted a highway in Brazil. Their use of the terms estradas de rodagem (vehicular roads) and rêde rodoviária (highway network) and their inclusion of the category "unimproved roads" suggested that all routes passable by wheeled motor vehicles were considered highways. No source explicitly indicated that urban streets were excluded from the route kilometrage reported. Judging by some of the more detailed data, however, the author has concluded that such streets were not included. For example, the 1939 data for the municípios (counties) of most of the state capital cities in the north and northeast reported no paved route kilometrage. The states likewise had no paved road kilometrage. At least some streets in these cities were probably paved and thus some kilometrage of paved roads would have been reported for the municípios, and therefore for the states, if urban streets had been included in the accounting.

The 1939 total highway system figures for Paraná and Santa Catarina states were for the year 1937 because the states' questionnaires for 1939 had not been returned to the federal highway department. For 1952 the percentage of the paved road network by political subdivision excluded 676 kilometers which according to Wilkin's[2] data were not distributed by political subdivision. For 1960 the município (county) highway data were for the year 1959, and the Goiás state percentage of the total system included the route kilometrage in the new Distrito Federal around Brasília. The 1976 state highway data were preliminary. The area of Brazil used to calculate densities was that given for 1960, 8,511,965 square kilometers. Stretches of federal highways surfaced with paralelepípidos (paving blocks or cobblestones) were included in the category of paved highways by the sources.

Map XI-4 shows the pattern and status of the Brazilian federal highway network at the end of 1960. Most of the basic information and route numbers were taken from the map in Heare,[3] which provided no source for its data. These data were modified by reference to maps by the highway departments of São Paulo state, 1958; Bahia, 1961; Minas Gerais, 1961; and Rio de Janeiro state, no date. The route numbering system (the BR prefixes are not shown on Map XI-4) was that in use in 1960. It was subsequently changed. Those federal routes projected as part of the Five Year Development Plan, 1961-1965, are not shown on the map.

Brazil: A Handbook of Historical Statistics

Table XI-4 documents the numbers of motor vehicles in Brazil from 1925 to 1976. No data origins were provided by the sources for the 1925 and 1929 data. The 1942 and 1944 data originated with the Sistema Regional e Serviço de Inquéritos da Secretaria Geral do IBGE. IBGE and the Departamento de Geografia e Estatística da Prefeitura do Distrito Federal originated the 1946 data. The 1950 data were generated by the Secretaria-Geral do Conselho Nacional de Estatística. Those for 1960 came from the Departamentos Estaduais de Estatística, and the Serviço de Emplacamento and the Departamento de Geografia e Estatística of the Estado de Guanabara.

Table XI-4 reports only licensed, self-propelled, over-the-road vehicles. For 1960, however, the source listed 77,328 "other cargo vehicles" some of which may not have been over-the-road types. These are included in the cargo vehicle category on the table. For 1970 the total number of vehicles reported by the source included 46,924 that were licensed but which could not move under their own power. These are not included in the 1970 total on the table. The 1970 total also excluded 16,857 vehicles reported by the source in the "other" category. Some of these may have been for over-the-road passenger or cargo use.

Table XI-5 notes the characteristics of Brazil's commercial air traffic from 1927 to 1977. Data for 1927 to called São José do Rio Prêto in São Paulo state. Also in 1934 the Brazilian government contracted with Panair do Estatística. Data for the years 1938 to 1960 were generated by the Diretoria de Aeronáutica Civil, and those for 1970 and 1977 originated with the Departamento de Aviação-Civil.

Sources for the 1927 to 1938 data used the term _vôos_ which is translated as "flights." Sources for the 1945 to 1960 data used the term _viagens_ which is translated "trips." Apparently there is no distinction between these terms because two different sources for the 1938 data reported the same number of movements (8,052) but one referred to them as "flights" and the other as "trips." Sources for the 1960 to 1977 period specified that all data included both domestic and international movements. Sources for the 1927 to 1951 data did not so specify, but supporting detailed data indicated that both domestic and international movements were reported for these years.

According to _Civil Aviation in Brazil_,[4] commercial air service began in the country in June 1927, with the establishment of a regional airline serving the state of Rio Grande do Sul. The company's formal name was Emprêsa de Viação Aérea Rio Grandense, but it became known by its acronym VARIG and is at this writing the largest airline in Brazil and one of the largest in the world. In November 1927 a company (apparently French) called Compagnie Générale d'Entreprises Aéronautiques-Lignes Latécoère had inaugurated service between Toulouse, France, and Buenos Aires. Presumably, though not specified by Civil Aviation in Brazil, the line made stops in Brazil thus linking the nation with both France and Argentina. In 1928 a Brazilian airline, "Sindicato Condor Limitada," started service on a 720-mile route between the cities of Rio de Janeiro and Pôrto Alegre, Rio Grande do Sul. In 1930 it extended its route 1,456 miles north from Rio de Janeiro to Natal in Rio Grande do Norte state. Seaplanes were used on these lines. Also in 1930 this company initiated commercial service on a 270 mile line between Corumbá and Cuiabá both in Mato Grosso state. In the same year the Brazilian company Nyrba do Brasil, S.A., began seaplane service from Belém, Pará, to Brazilian cities along the east coast and thence to Buenos Aires, Argentina. In Belém this line linked with the New York, Rio de Janeiro, and Buenos Aires Airline whose route from Miami island-hopped the Caribbean to Venezuela and the Guianas to reach Belém. Nyrba later became Panair do Brasil, S.A. In 1934 the Viação Aérea São Paulo (VASP), a major airline in Brazil at this writing, had begun service on two routes, one covering the 298 miles between the city of São Paulo and Uberaba, Minas Gerais, and the other the 260 miles from São Paulo city to Rio Prêto, now called São José do Rio Prêtal in São Paulo state. Also in 1934 the Brazilian government contracted with Panair do Brasil for once-a-week seaplane service over the 930-mile Amazon River route between Belém, Pará, and Manaus, Amazonas.

Table XI-6 shows the values of goods traded among Brazil's political subdivisions via noncoastwise routes in 1939, 1960, and 1970. The 1939 data originated with the Sistema Regional of the Serviço de Estatística Econômica e Financeira and the Secçao de Sistematização de Secretaria Geral do IBGE. The 1960 data were generated by the Orgãos Regionais do sistema estatística nacional and the Secretaria Geral do Conselho Nacional de Estatística. IBGE was the originator of the 1970 data. The sources did not specify the modes of transportation involved but presumably they included all land, air, and internal waterway movements.

The 1939 and 1960 data were for the years 1939 and 1960, but the 1970 data were not all for the year 1970. Data for Piauí, Rio de Janeiro, Santa Catarina, Rio Grande do Sul, and Goiás were for the year 1967. Data for Roraíma, Ceará, Alagoas, and São Paulo were for 1968, and those for Paraíba, Pernambuco, Minas Gerais, and Paraná were for 1969. For 1960 exports from Paraíba, Alagoas, Minas Gerais, São Paulo, Goiás, Paraná, and Mato Grosso were estimated by the data

originator. Minas Gerais exports were in the Brazil total
for 1970 but the source notes that only those to Espírito
Santo were discriminated by political subdivision. The
remainder is presumably the Cr$ 77,484,000 in the
"unspecified" category.

Only the industrial states of São Paulo and Guanabara
had positive trade balances in all years shown. The
construction of Brasilia gave the Distrito Federal a large
trade deficit in 1960 which was not compensated by any
exports whatsoever.

Table XI-7 reports the numbers and tonnages of ships
registered by Brazilian companies from 1908 to 1977. Data
for the 1908 to 1930 period originated with the Departamento
Nacional de Estatística's publication Estatísticos dos meios
de transporte no Brasil, the Relatório for 1916/17 of the
Directoria Geral de Estatística, the Anuário estatístico do
Brasil, ano IV and ano V, and the Departamento Nacional de
Pôrtos e Navegação. Data for 1941 were originated by the
Comissão de Marinha Mercante and the Serviço de
Sistematização da Secretaria Geral do Conselho Nacional de
Estatística, and those for 1960 by the Comissão alone. Data
for 1970 and 1977 were generated by the Superintêndencia
Nacional de Marinha Mercante.

Ship tonnage for the period 1908 to 1930 was in crude
tonnage (tonelagem bruta). This measure according to AN
1952, page 228, included the weight of all enclosed parts of
the ship. It would appear to refer to total displacement.
Tonnage for 1941 to 1977 was in cargo tonnage. A cargo ton
contained 1,016 kilograms, the weight of one cubic meter of
sea water (AN 1952, p. 228). The 1941 and 1960 data sources
did not specify what tonnage definition was used. The 1970
and 1977 sources reported cargo tonnage as TPB (toneladas de
porte brutas), or tons of crude capacity, but did not define
this term.

Data for 1908 to 1930 included all Brazilian-registered
ships regardless of weight. Data for 1941 and 1950 included
only those ships of 100 and more crude tons owned by private
companies transporting 10,000 and more crude tons of cargo.
The data for 1960 were restricted to ships of 100 and more
crude tons but no restriction was noted on the amount of
tonnage that a private company had to carry to have its ships
included in the data. The 1970 and 1977 data were also
restricted. For these years among dry cargo carriers only
those private companies carrying 10,000 tons (TPB) of cargo
were included. Among tanker-operating carriers only those
private companies carrying 1,000 tons (TPB) of cargo were
included. All government carriers were included.

Table XI-8 shows the numbers and registered tonnage of ships calling at Brazilian ports from 1840/41 to 1977. Data origins for 1840/41 to 1930 were the Resumos of various Estatísticas Econômico-Financeiras of the Diretoria Geral de Estatística, and the Quadros estatísticos, numeros 1 and 2, of the Serviço Estatístico Econômica e Financeira. For the period 1938-60 data were generated by the Serviço de Estatística Econômica e Financeira. Data for 1970 were originated by the Departamento Nacional de Pôrtos e Vias Navegáveis, and those for 1977 by the Emprêsa de Pôrtos do Brasil.

None of the sources specified the measure of tonnage, so it is assumed to be metric. Coastwise shipping was included by all the data sources for Table XI-8. Data for 1840/41 to 1930 were for embarkations (embarcações) as were data for 1970 and 1977. Data for the period 1938-55 were for ships entering port (entradas). The differences between embarcações and entradas tended to be small enough to make the table longitudinally useful. In 1938, the only year for which both were available in these sources, embarcações numbered 33,299 of 46,506,000 tons and entradas numbered 34,838 of 51,259,000 tons. The data for 1938 to 1977 recorded movements at all major Brazilian ports which included the fresh-water ports along the Amazon River and along the upper Paraguay River in Mato Grosso state.

Table XI-9 shows the values of tonnages of major commodities moved by coastwise shipping among Brazil's principal political subdivisions from 1921 to 1977. The 1921 to 1930 data originated in the reports by the Serviço de Estatística Econômica e Financeira entitled Comércio de Cabotagem do Brasil, no. 4-C.C.F. and no. 8. The 1938 to 1960 data were generated by the Serviço de Estatística Econômica e Financeira. The Centro de Informações Econômico Fiscais originated the 1970 data and the Superintendência da Marinha Mercante the 1977 data. For the numbers and tonnages of ships engaged in Brazilian coastwise traffic see Table IX-7.

Writing in 1954, Labouriau[5] called coastwise shipping "the only truly national transportation in Brazil." Until 1950 coastwise shipping carried more than 90 percent of all domestic Brazilian trade by tonnage and more than 80 percent of all this trade by value. By 1960, although the actual tonnage and value of coastwise commerce had increased, the development of the highway system and the concomitant reduction of government subsidies to shipping had brought the coastwise percentage down sharply. Between 1946 and 1977 the dominant cargoes carried along coastwise routes shifted from food and manufactured products to petroleum and mineral raw materials. Labouriau noted that in the early 1950s nearly the entire wheat and rice crops of Rio Grande do Sul, Brazil's major cereal-producing state, moved along coastwise routes. He also reported that the entire output of salt from Rio Grande do Norte, representing 80 percent of Brazil's production, moved via coasting steamers.

Table XI-10 reports the characteristics and facilities of Brazil's major maritime ports from 1938 to 1977. The data for 1938 originated with the Departamento Nacional de Pôrtos e Navegação, those for 1960 with the Departamento Nacional de Pôrtos, Rios e Canais, and those for 1978 with the Emprêsa de Pôrtos do Brasil. The 1960 data for Natal, Rio Grande do Norte were for the year 1959. For 1960 the category "depth of water at quays" on the table was reported by the source as the depth of water at anchorage. The 1978 source reported the depth of water at the quays for the port of Rio Grande, Rio Grande do Sul, to be 55/10 meters. This was probably meant to read 5.5/10 and is so reported on the table. The only 1978 data reported by the source for Brazil's two specialized iron ore ports in Espírito Santo state were the sizes of the dock storage areas. Tuberão had 133,000 square meters of such space, all out in the open, and Ponta de Umbu had 258,800 square meters, all uncovered.

Table XI-11 reports the structure, personnel, traffic, and finances of the Brazilian postal and telegraph system from 1840 to 1977. The 1840 to 1930 data originated with the Anuário estatístico do Brasil, ano I, vol. II, and ano V; the Relatório of the Diretoria Geral dos Correios, 1907 to 1930; the Relatório of the Departamento dos Correios e Telégrafos, 1931 to 1939; the Carteira Estatística de Minas Gerais, 1929; and the Quadros estatísticos, número 1 and número 2 of the Serviço de Estatística Econômica e Financeira. The Departamento dos Correios e Telégrafos originated the data for 1939 and 1950, and the Secção da Diretoria de Correios do Departamento dos Correios e Telégrafos originated the 1960 data. The 1968, 1970, and 1977 data were generated by the Emprêsa Brasileira de Correios e Telégrafos.

The category "agencies" on Table XI-11 includes both railroad and horse-drawn post offices. Many postal-telegraph agencies also offered regular mail service. The postal-radiotelegraph agencies functioned principally to contact ships at sea. The category "correspondence" included letters, post cards, samples, money orders, newspapers, books, and other printed material. Sources for the 1840 to 1939 postal data did not indicate whether international mail was also included in their counts. International mail was included in all later data. Postal traffic data for 1880 are for the period 1879-80. The source did not specify whether this period represented two calendar years or overlapping parts of fiscal years. In the 1950 "types of correspondence handled" category only those items posted/received were reported. Those items distributed/forwarded or in transit were not reported. In the 1970 "types of correspondence handled" category only items posted/received or distributed/ forwarded were reported. Those items in transit were not reported. Telegraph data for 1870 were for the period 1869-70 and those for 1880 were for the period 1879-80. The exact lengths of these periods were not specified by the sources. The category "postal expenditures" also included those for the telegraph system in the years 1939 to 1977. Prior to 1939 only postal expenditures were included in this category.

Table XI-12 characterizes the telephone system in Brazil from 1907 to 1976. No data origin was given by the 1907 source. The 1937 and 1938 data originated with the Sistema Regional e Secção de Sistematização da Secretaria Geral do IBGE. The 1944 data were generated by IBGE and those for 1950 by the Secretaria Geral do Conselho Nacional de Estatística. The data for 1959 were developed by the Orgãos Regionais de Estatística e Diretoria de Levantamentos Estatísticos of IBGE. The 1969 data originated with the Instituto Brasileiro de Estatística, and those for 1976 with FIBGE.

The 1938 data were for **municípios** (counties) of the capitals of Brazil's political subdivisions. These data totals may nearly have been tantamount to the national totals, for as late as 1961 these **municípios** contained 81.1 percent of all the country's telephones and 76.8 percent of its phone subscribers. In the totals for 1944 the data for Rio Grande do Norte were for 1943 and those for the state of Pará were for the city of Belém. In the 1950 totals the data for Ceará, São Paulo and Guanabara were for 1949, and employee totals excluded persons working for the national telephone company in the states of Minas Gerais, Espírito Santo and Rio de Janeiro. Sources for the 1976 and 1979 data specified that the numbers of telephones were those of the "urban service system" as opposed to the "interurban service system." This would appear to include most of the telephones in Brazil since the equipment listed as belonging to the interurban system included no telephones per se but only larger scale transmission and switching machinery.

The development of Brazil's radio and television systems is shown on Table XI-13. The sources for the 1923 to 1935 data provided no origins for them. The 1940 to 1950 data were originated by the Serviço de Estatística da Educação e

Saúde. Data for the 1961-74 period were generated by the Serviço de Estatística de Educação e Cultura. All the data referred to radio and television stations serving the public. They excluded amateur operators (hams) and some private organizations that amplified sound through loud speakers. According to Brazil, 1966[6] all Brazilian radio and television operations were in the private (non-government) sector. Nevertheless, in 1944, of the 106 radio stations, 9 were listed as official, presumably meaning government or school-system operated. No sources for years previous to or subsequent to 1944 distinguished private from government operated stations.

The data for radio stations in 1974 on Table XI-13 included retransmission stations in Rio de Janeiro and Guanabara states, and an experimental station in Paraná state. The data for television stations in 1974 included an experimental station in the territory of Roraíma in the Amazon region, and retransmission stations in Rio de Janeiro and São Paulo states. Power in 1944 was in potential wattage and in 1950 was in maximum potential wattage. The weekly radio and television hours broadcast in 1974 were for the first week in December. For all other years sources did not specify how the weekly hours broadcast data were developed. Seven of the 803 radio stations listed by sources for 1961 did not function in that year.

Brazil's first radio station began operating in the city of Rio de Janeiro in 1923. The station, Rádio Sociedade Rio de Janeiro, had as its call letters PRA2 and operated at a frequency of 780 kilocycles and 385 meters. The following year the Rádio Club do Brasil (PRA3) began operating in the city of Rio de Janeiro, the Rádio Sociedade da Bahia (PRA4) in Salvador, and the Rádio Club Paranaense (PRB2) in Curitiba, Paraná. The first station in the city of São Paulo, the Rádio Club de São Paulo, began operating as PRA5 in 1925.

Table XI-14 shows the numbers, copies printed, and languages of newspapers in Brazil from 1933 to 1974. No origin was given for the 1933 data, but the Serviço de Estatística da Educação e Saúde originated the data for all the other years. None of the sources prior to 1954 attempted to define the term "newspaper." Each source used the term jornal, which translates as "newspaper," and did distinguish it to some extent by reporting parallel data for bulletins, magazines, and books. Nevertheless, the category jornal may have included school newspapers and the house organs of companies, political groups, churches, and government agencies. For those years in which sources reported "daily newspapers" the total numbers of newspapers probably more closely approximated the actual numbers of commercial newspapers carrying general news items. The source for the 1954 data specifically referred to daily newspapers whose chief subject was news (notícias). The 1963 and 1977 data sources referred to newspapers of general information (jornais de informações geral) and specifically excluded advertising, school, and other parochial publications from the category. Sources did not report circulation as such. Instead, they reported numbers of copies printed for each printing or for the year.

References

1. Ruben E. de Freitas Abreu, "The Panorama of Brazilian Railway Transportation," pp. 3-104 in Brazilian Technical Studies, prepared for the Joint Brazil-United States Economic Development Commission (Washington, D.C.: Institute of Inter-American Affairs, Foreign Operations Administration, 1954). This work accompanies The Development of Brazil, a report by the Joint Brazil-United States Economic Development Commission (Washington, D.C.: United States Government Printing Office, 1954).

2. Galyn G. Wilkins, "Comments on the Brazilian Highway Problem," pp. 265-70 in Brazilian Technical Studies (see reference 1 above).

3. Gertrude E. Heare, Brazil: Information for United States Businessmen (Washington, D.C.: United States Department of Commerce, Bureau of International Programs, 1961, p. 80).

4. Civil Aviation in Brazil: Its Beginnings, Growth, Present State (São Paulo: "Graphicars," Romiti & Lazara, 1938). No author is given for this work. No date is given, but the first line of the work notes that "it has been eleven years since commercial air transit began in Brazil." The first air transit began in Brazil in June 1927. The wording of this work indicates that it had been translated into English from a Brazilian source, which remains unknown.

5. Ivan Gouvea Labouriau, Robert H. Tarr, and Howard P. Du Temple, "Brazil's Coastwise Shipping: A Report to the Subcommission on Shipping," pp. 187-208 in Brazilian Technical Studies (see reference 1 above).

6. Brazil, 1966: Resources and Possibilities (Brasília: Administration Department, Ministry of External Relations, 1966).

Table XI-1. The Brazilian Railroad Network: Length of Trackage by Major Political Subdivisions; Density, Ownership, and Gauge of Network; Rolling Stock; Traffic Volumes; Personnel; and Finances, 1854–1977

	1912	1916	1920	1930	1940	1950	1960	1970	1977
Total Trackage in Use(kms)(a)	23,491	27,015	28,553	32,478	34,252	36,681	38,287	32,102	29,855
Percent by Political Subdivisions									
Minas Gerais	-	-	23.2	24.1	23.9	23.6	22.4	20.8	20.6
São Paulo	-	-	23.3	21.7	21.7	20.7	20.0	18.3	19.2
Rio Grande do Sul	-	-	9.5	9.5	10.2	10.2	10.1	11.4	11.8
Paraná	-	-	3.9	4.1	4.6	4.8	5.1	6.0	7.3
Rio de Janeiro	-	-	9.2	8.4	7.9	7.2	7.3	5.0	5.3
Bahia	-	-	6.2	6.4	6.3	7.1	6.8	6.1	5.3
Density									
Kms of Track per 1000 Sq. Kms.(b)	2.5	3.2	3.4	3.8	4.0	4.3	4.5	3.8	3.5
Kms of Track per 100,000 Persons(c)	92.6	96.5	93.1	86.3	83.1	70.1	54.5	34.5	26.2
Federally-Owned Trackage (Kms)	12,199	-	-	-	22,573	28,424	29,940	25,101	23,649
Trackage by Gauge (Kms)									
Narrow (<1.00 meter)	-	-	-	-	1,212	1,062	811	231	202
Standard (1.00 meter)	-	-	-	-	30,956	33,254	34,017	28,319	26,062
Wide (1.44–1.60 meters)	-	-	-	-	2,084	2,365	3,459	3,552	3,591
Electrified Trackage (Kms)	-	-	-	-	-	-	2,514	2,610	2,285
Rolling Stock									
Locomotives	-	-	-	2,898	3,619	3,950	4,454	2,351	1,961
Diesel	-	-	-	-	-	-	829	1,508	1,783
Electric	-	-	-	-	-	-	231	246	152
Steam	-	-	-	-	-	-	3,394	597	26
Freight Cars	-	-	-	36,532	50,632	61,066	68,500	59,382	68,787
Passenger Cars	-	-	-	3,601	3,972	5,096	5,419	4,611	2,852
Traffic									
Passengers (000's)	-	54,472	75,516	148,271	193,739	342,709	420,583	332,410	344,224
Animals (see text)	-	2,258	2,768	2,680	4,103	4,596	4,339	568	290
Baggage (000 metric tons)	-	343	551	684	1,110	1,294	706	135	40
Freight (000 metric tons)	-	13,015	16,555	18,949	35,066	38,040	43,727	49,666	131,544
Passenger/Kms (000's)	-	1,412,661	2,194,379	4,396,539	6,428,278	10,466,976	15,394,764	12,350	11,699
Animal/Kms (see text)	-	428,155	475,619	506,600	1,177,572	1,560,183	1,605,524	265	145
Baggage/Kms (000 metric tons)	-	30,569	68,495	133,272	175,712	216,289	131,247	28,797	11,000
Freight/Kms (000 metric tons)	-	1,691,274	2,230,822	3,556,833	6,074,578	8,066,303	12,078,817	17,260,000	60,505,000
Personnel Employed	-	-	-	-	154,956	196,875	203,955	169,714	128,188
Finances (Cr$ 000)									
Receipts	-	201,442	334,902	658,850	1,291,718	4,170,690	23,347,587	961,322	11,320,000
Expenditures	-	169,043	305,614	635,478	1,261,713	5,467,082	44,832,736	1,725,977	18,640,000

	1854	1860	1870	1880	1890	1900
(a)Total Trackage in Use(kms)	14	223	744	3,398	9,973	15,316
(b)Kms of Track per 1000 Sq. Kms.	negl.	negl.	.1	.4	1.2	1.8
(c).Kms of Track per 100,000 Persons	.2	2.6	7.7	28.6	69.6	87.8

Sources: AN 1908-1912, pp. 31–51; RS 1924, pp. 80–82; BT 1930, pp. 167–173; AN 1939-40, pp. 1336–1338; AN 1946, pp. 177–183; AN 1952, pp. 208–212; AN 1956, pp. 510–511; AN 1962, pp. 107–108; AN 1971, pp. 381–383; AN 1978, pp. 585–590.

Table XI-2. Brazil's Federal, State, and Private Railroad Networks and Twenty Largest Railroad Systems, 1912–62; Their Extents, Gauges, Locations, Administrations, and Electrified Lines

Railroad System	1912 Adm.[1]	1912 Length of Lines (kms) Total	1945 Length of Lines (kms) Total	1955 Adm.	1955 Hdqtrs. Location	1955 Total	1955 Gauges in Meters 1.60	1955 Gauges in Meters 1.00	1955 Gauges in Meters <1.00	1962 Adm.	1962 Total	1962 Gauges in Meters 1.60	1962 Gauges in Meters 1.00	1962 Gauges in Meters <1.00	1962 Electrified
Rêde Mineira de Viação	O	-	3,985	F	MG	3,989	-	3,260	729	F	3,507	-	2,857	650	512
Via Férrea de Rio Grande do Sul	O	2,170	3,575	S	RS	3,701	-	3,701	-	F	3,612	-	3,612	-	-
Estrada de Ferro Central do Brasil	F	2,033	3,355	F	GB	3,737	1,494	2,243	-	F	3,474	1,516	1,958	-	378
Estrada de Ferro Leopoldina	P	2,659	3,082	F	GB	3,057	-	3,057	-	F	3,056	-	3,056	-	-
Rêde Viação Paraná-Santa Catarina	P	-	2,458	S	PR	2,666	-	2,666	-	O	2,723	-	2,723	-	52
Estrada de Ferro Sorocabana	P	1,311	2,215	F	SP	2,074	-	2,074	-	F	2,051	-	2,051	-	573
Viação Férrea Federal Leste Brasileiro	P	1,406	2,209	P	BA	2,545	-	2,545	-	O	2,545	-	2,545	-	194
Companhia Mogiana de Estradas de Ferro	P	1,596	1,959	F	SP	1,959	-	1,874	85	O	1,844	-	1,844	-	-
Rêde de Viação Cearense	-	-	1,932	F	CE	1,596	-	1,596	-	F	1,452	-	1,452	-	-
Rêde Ferroviária do Nordeste	P	1,609	1,657	F	PE	1,863	-	1,863	-	F	2,965	-	2,965	-	-
Estrada de Ferro Noroeste do Brasil	P	935	1,539	F	SP	1,762	-	1,762	-	F	1,658	-	1,658	-	-
Companhia Paulista de Estradas de Ferro	P	-	1,536	P	SP	2,156	991	1,103	62	O	2,121	887	1,234	-	493
Estrada de Ferro São Luís-Teresina	-	528	645	P	MA	471	-	471	-	O	452	-	452	-	-
Estrada de Ferro Vitória-Minas	P	-	597	P	ES	569	-	569	-	F	569	-	569	-	-
Estrada de Ferro Bahia-Minas	-	-	582	F	MG	582	-	582	-	O	582	-	582	-	-
Estrada de Ferro Goiás	P	226	392	S	MG	478	-	478	-	F	481	-	481	-	-
Estrada de Ferro Araraquara	P	245	379	P	SP	482	-	482	-	O	482	431	51	-	-
Estrada de Ferro Madeira-Mamoré	P	364	366	P	RO	366	-	366	-	F	366	-	366	-	-
Estrada de Ferro Nazaré	-	-	325	S	BA	324	-	324	-	O	324	-	324	-	-
Estrada de Ferro Dourado	P	225	317	-	-	-	-	-	-	-	-	-	-	-	-
Others (1912)	P	8,184	-	-	-	-	-	-	-	-	-	-	-	-	-
Others (26 in 1945)	-	-	2,175	-	-	-	-	-	-	-	-	-	-	-	-
Others (22 in 1955)	-	-	-	-	-	2,720	139	2,305	186	-	-	-	-	-	-
Others (20 in 1962)	-	-	-	-	-	-	-	-	-	-	2,308	333	1,891	84	183
Total	-	23,491	35,280	-	-	37,092	2,624	33,406	1,062	-	36,572	3,167	32,671	734	2,385
All Federally-Administered Networks	-	3,531	14,363	-	-	25,075	1,633	22,606	836	-	28,474	-	-	-	-
All State-Administered Networks	-	690	10,990	-	-	7,219	-	7,164	55	-	3,289	-	-	-	-
All Privately-Administered Networks	-	19,270	9,927	-	-	4,798	991	3,636	171	-	4,809	-	-	-	-

Sources: AN 1908–1912, pp. 32–34; Abreu, 1954, p. 98; Ferrovias do Brasil, 1956, pp. 7 and 11.

[1] Adm. = administrative entity.
    F = federal government
    S = state government
    P = private company
    O = private or state (not distinguished by source)

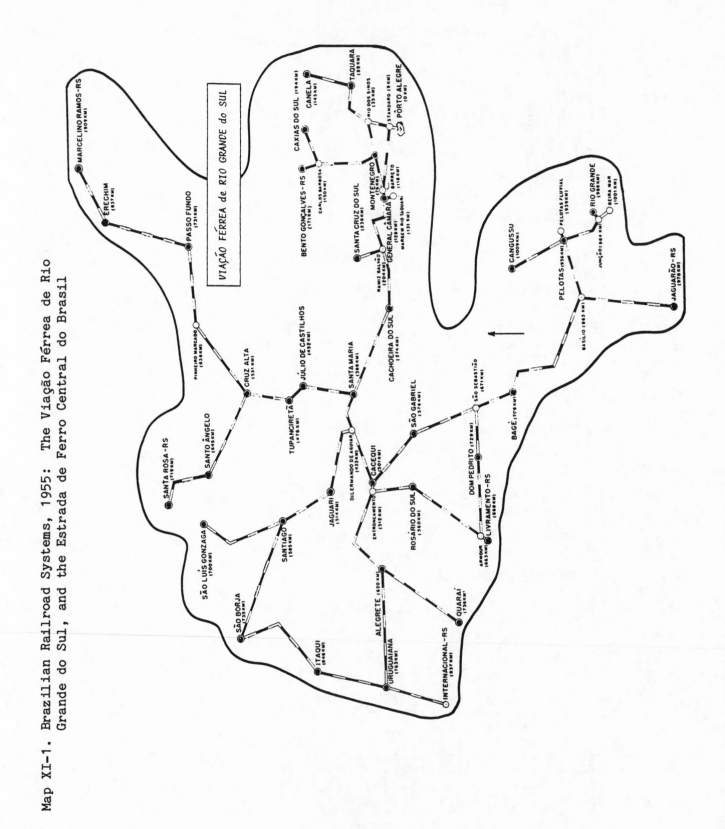

Map XI-1. Brazilian Railroad Systems, 1955: The Viação Férrea de Rio Grande do Sul, and the Estrada de Ferro Central do Brasil

Map XI-1 (continued)

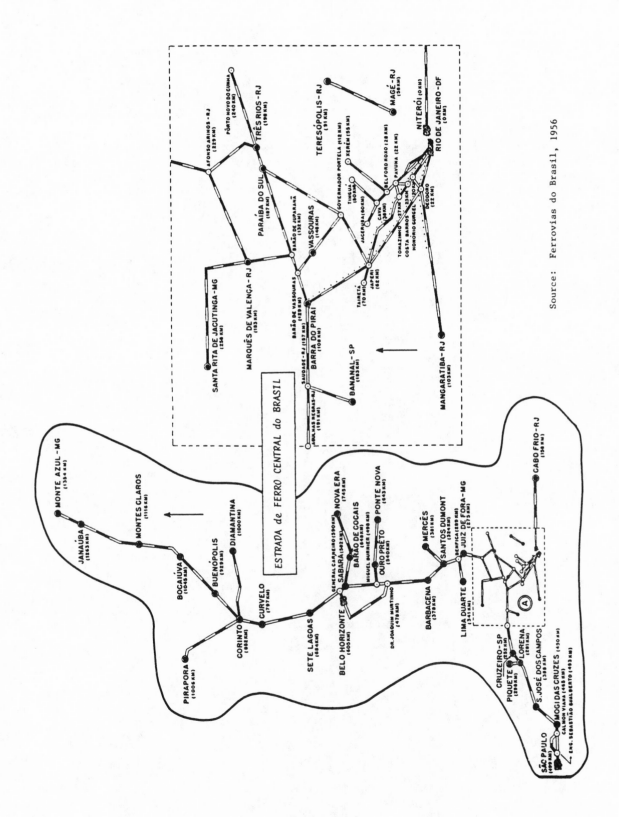

Source: Ferrovias do Brasil, 1956

Map XI-2. Brazilian Railroad Systems, 1955: The Estrada de Ferro Sorocabana, the Companhia Paulista de Estradas de Ferro, and the Rêde Mineira de Viação

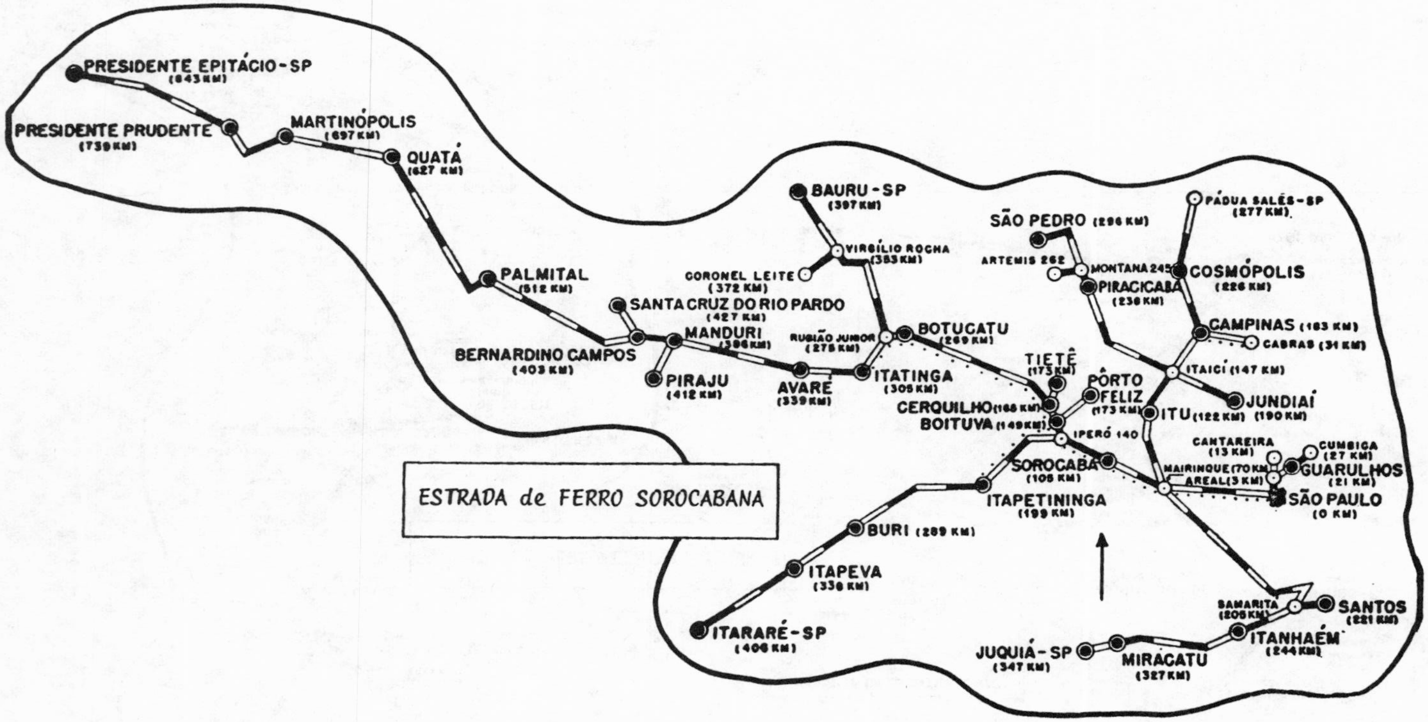

ESTRADA de FERRO SOROCABANA

PÁDUA SALES-SP (277 KM)
COSMÓPOLIS (226 KM)
CAMPINAS (163 KM)
CABRAS (34 KM)
CUMBICA (27 KM)
GUARULHOS (21 KM)
SÃO PAULO (0 KM)
SANTOS (221 KM)
ITANHAÉM (244 KM)
SAMARITA (204 KM)
ITAICI (147 KM)
JUNDIAÍ (190 KM)
CANTAREIRA (13 KM)
MAIRINQUE(TOKA)
AREAL(3 KM)
MONTANA 245
PIRACICABA (236 KM)
SÃO PEDRO (296 KM)
ARTEMIS 262
PÔRTO FÉLIZ (173 KM)
ITU (122 KM)
IPERÓ 140
MIRAGATU (327 KM)
TIETÊ (173 KM)
SOROCABA (106 KM)
ITAPETININGA (159 KM)
JUQUIÁ-SP (347 KM)
CERQUILHO(188 KM)
BOITUVA (140 KM)
BOTUCATU (269 KM)
ITATINGA (305 KM)
BURI (209 KM)
VIRGÍLIO ROCHA (355 KM)
RUBIÃO JUNIOR (278 KM)
AVARÉ (339 KM)
ITAPEVA (330 KM)
BAURU-SP (397 KM)
CORONEL LEITE (372 KM)
SANTA CRUZ DO RIO PARDO (427 KM)
MANDURI (396 KM)
PIRAJU (412 KM)
ITARARÉ-SP (405 KM)
PALMITAL (512 KM)
BERNARDINO CAMPOS (403 KM)
QUATÁ (527 KM)
MARTINÓPOLIS (697 KM)
PRESIDENTE EPITÁCIO-SP (843 KM)
PRESIDENTE PRUDENTE (739 KM)

246

Map XI-2 (continued)

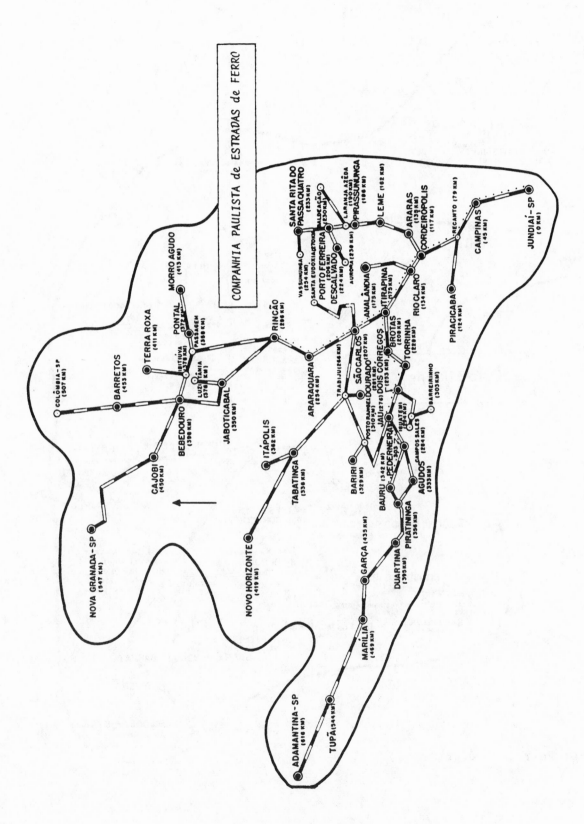

COMPANHIA PAULISTA de ESTRADAS de FERRO

247

Map XI-2 (continued)

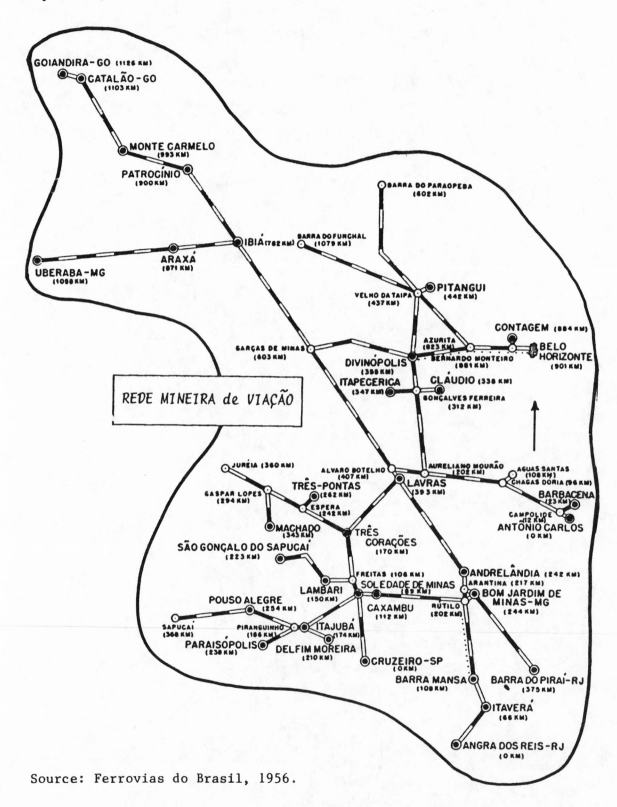

Source: Ferrovias do Brasil, 1956.

Map XI-3. Brazilian Railroad Systems: The Viação Férrea Federal Leste
Brasileiro, the Rêde Viação Paraná-Santa Catarina and the
Estrada de Ferrro Leopoldina

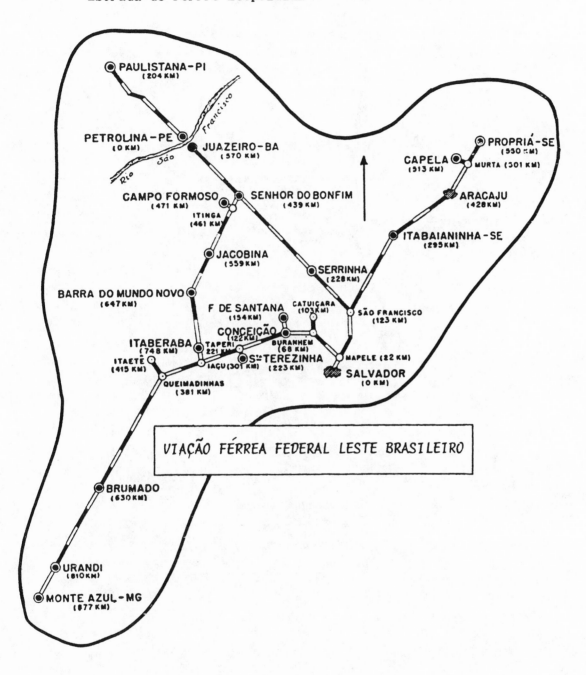

Map XI-3 (continued)

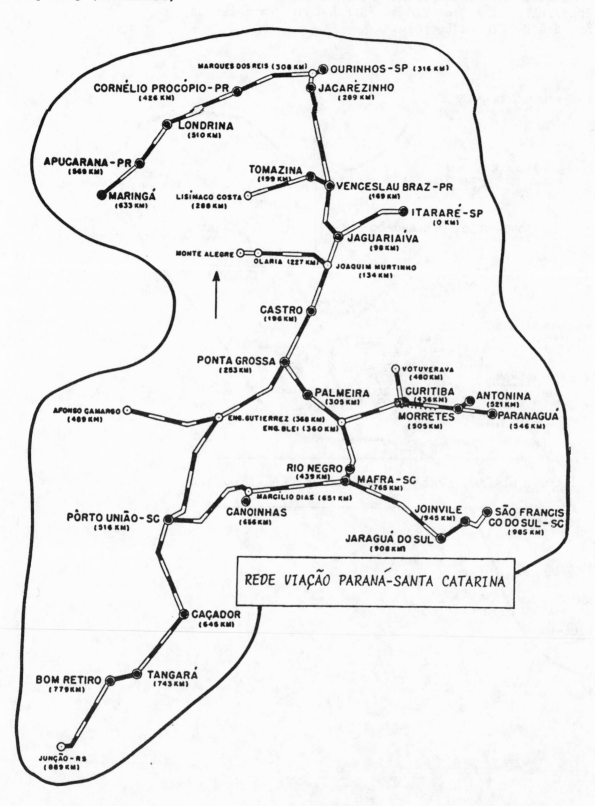

REDE VIAÇÃO PARANÁ-SANTA CATARINA

Map XI-3 (continued)

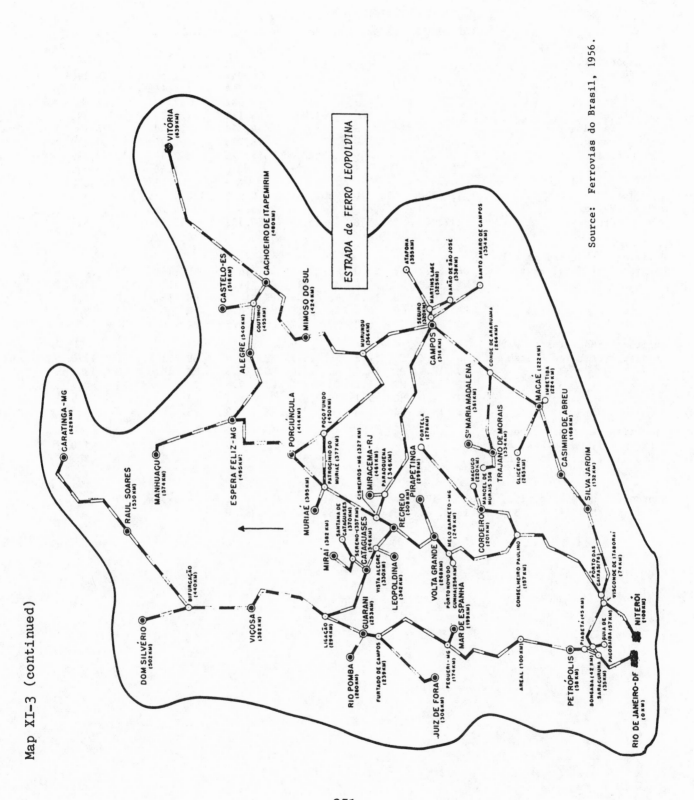

ESTRADA de FERRO LEOPOLDINA

Source: Ferrovias do Brasil, 1956.

Table XI-3. The Brazilian Highway System: Length by Construction and
Maintenance Responsibility, Surface Types, and Major
Political Subdivisions; and Density of the Nation's Network,
1930-76

	1930	1939	1952	1960	1970	1976
Total Highway System						
by Responsibility (kms)						
Federal	-	-	12,315	34,051	51,540	70,198
Paved	-	-	-	9,019	24,146	41,762
Unpaved	-	-	-	25,032	27,394	28,436
State	-	-	51,032	83,116	125,334	121,396
Paved	-	-	-	4,338	23,428	26,106
Unpaved	-	-	-	78,778	101,906	95,290
Municipal	-	-	238,800	359,771	862,905	1,257,099
Paved	-	-	-	-	1,689	3,249
Unpaved	-	-	-	-	861,216	1,253,850
Total	113,250	258,390	302,147	476,938	1,039,779	1,448,693
Paved	910	2,842	-	13,357	49,263	71,117
Unpaved	112,240	255,548	-	463,581	990,516	1,377,576

Political Subdivisions With												
Largest % of Total System	SP	24.8	SP	20.0	SP	29.6	SP	16.6	SP	14.9	SP	14.8
	MG	11.0	MG	16.4	MG	11.7	RS	11.7	MG	14.8	MG	14.4
	RS	10.2	RS	14.2	RS	8.9	PR	10.2	RS	13.1	RS	11.3
	PR	7.5	GO	6.5	PR	8.6	MG	10.1	PR	9.8	PR	8.9
	SC	6.2	SC	6.0	SC	8.2	GO	7.5	BA	6.9	GO	7.0

Political Subdivisions With												
Largest % of Paved System	GB	29.8	SC	52.2	SP	36.1	SP	33.0	SP	31.1	SP	19.0
	RJ	19.9	RS	14.4	MG	11.0	MG	14.3	MG	16.0	MG	13.4
	SP	12.9	MT	11.2	GB	9.7	RJ	9.6	PR	6.8	RS	8.7
	PR	11.0	MG	7.1	RS	9.6	PE	5.5	RJ	6.6	PR	7.5
	PE	11.0	RJ	5.4	PE	2.7	RS	5.2	RS	6.4	BA	6.3

Densities of Total System						
Kms per 1,000 Sq.Kms. of Area	13	30	35	56	122	170
Kms per 100,000 Inhabitants	301	632	543	679	1,116	1,304

Sources: AN 1936, p. 152; AN 1939-1940, pp. 273-275; AN 1953, p. 206; Wilkins, 1954, p. 267;
AN 1961, p. 153; AN 1971, p. 398; AN 1978, pp. 591-592.

Table XI-4. Motor Vehicles Registered in Brazil by Major Political Subdivisions, 1925-76

	1925	1929	1942	1944	1946	1950	1960	1970	1976
Total Motor Vehicles	73,537	166,926	190,669	145,328	219,385	409,486	1,035,887	3,062,778	7,313,498
Passenger Vehicles	–	109,810	117,165	72,263	129,216	237,484	647,575	2,464,285	6,008,488
Automobiles	–	105,125	103,987	57,401	114,388	200,141	502,546	–	5,116,290
Other	–	4,685	13,178	14,862	14,828	37,343	145,029	–	892,198
Cargo Vehicles	–	57,116	73,504	73,065	90,169	172,002	388,312	598,493	1,305,010
Political Subdivisions	SP 50.8	SP 47.8	SP 38.9	SP 36.7	SP 37.8	SP 34.7	SP 36.7	SP 36.6	SP 39.0
With Largest Numbers	GB 12.8	RS 11.4	GB 16.8	GB 15.8	GB 18.7	GB 16.2	GB 11.2	GB 11.3	RJ 12.8
of Motor Vehicles	MG 10.5	GB 10.1	MG 10.3	MG 10.6	MG 9.9	RS 12.6	MG 10.8	RS 10.9	RS 9.1
(% of Total Vehicles)	RS 8.6	MG 9.8	RS 8.6	RS 8.5	RS 8.3	MG 10.6	RS 10.7	MG 9.8	MG 8.8
	PE 3.6	RJ 4.9	RJ 5.5	RJ 5.9	RJ 5.4	PR 5.3	PR 7.1	PR 7.4	PR 8.4

Sources: AN 1936, pp. 147 & 148-149; AN 1946, p. 192; AN 1947, p. 192; AN 1951, p. 174; AN 1963, p. 215; AN 1972, p. 401; AN 1978, pp. 594 & 596.

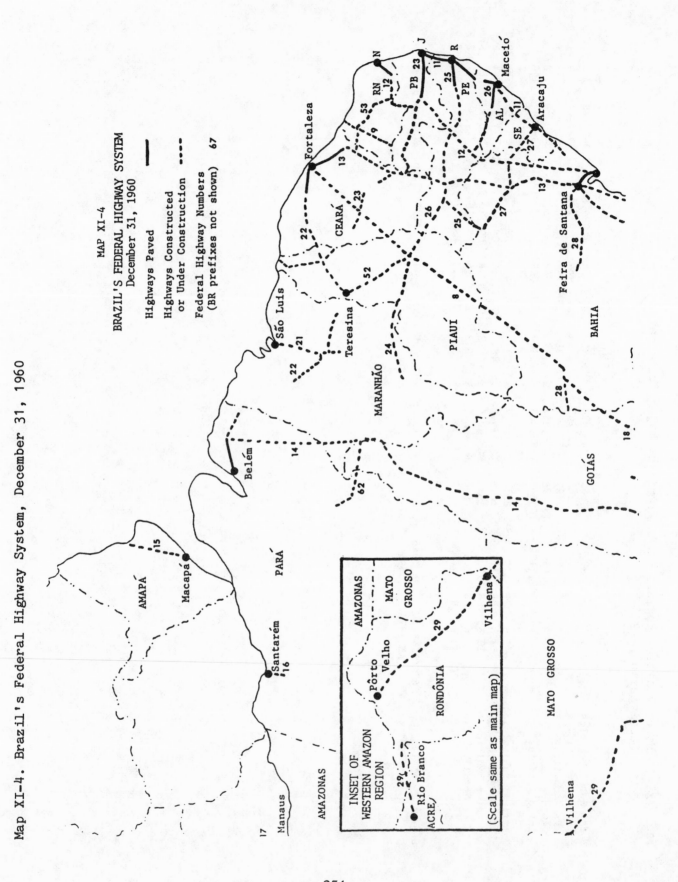

Map XI-4. Brazil's Federal Highway System, December 31, 1960

MAP XI-4

BRAZIL'S FEDERAL HIGHWAY SYSTEM
December 31, 1960

Highways Paved

Highways Constructed
or Under Construction

Federal Highway Numbers   67
(BR prefixes not shown)

Map XI-4 (continued)

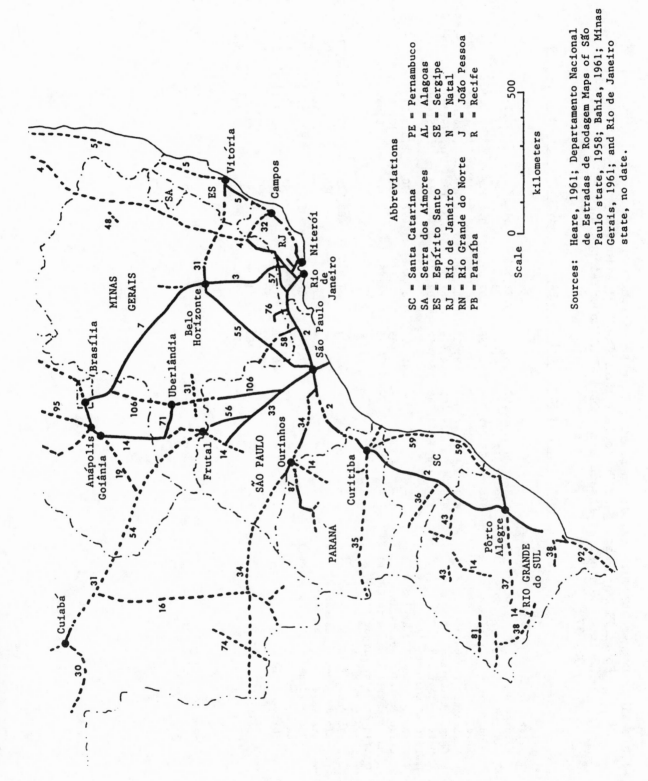

Table XI-5. Commercial Air Traffic in Brazil; Flights, Kilometers and Hours Flown; Passenger, Cargo, and Mail Traffic; Kilometer Indices; Numbers of Passengers Embarked at Major Airports, 1927-77

	1927	1928	1930	1938	1945	1951	1960	1970	1977
Brazil									
Flights									
Numbers	158	1,178	1,767	8,052	22,553	110,538	139,794	-	179,453
Kilometers (000's)	120	912	1,708	9,620	23,466	96,068	145,832	-	258,000
Hours	844	6,615	12,013	32,558	97,001	374,952	462,042	-	-
Traffic									
Passengers (numbers)	643	2,504	4,667	63,423	289,580	2,241,400	4,124,047	-	9,207,000
Cargo (kilograms)	210	1,911	9,609	354,975	4,781,550	51,037,103	101,079,339	-	-
Mail (kilograms)	257	9,688	31,946	185,642	562,775	1,444,473	3,935,479	-	-
Traffic/Kilometers									
Passenger Kms (000's)	-	-	-	41,504	258,466	1,492,370	3,529,373	-	-
Cargo (metric ton/kms in 000's)	-	-	-	439	6,729	48,692	112,447	-	612,158
Mail (metric ton/kms in 000's)	-	-	-	478	867	2,993	9,659	-	18,188
Traffic at Major Airports									
Passengers Embarked									
São Paulo (Congonhas)	-	-	-	10,077	57,974	463,879	770,894	740,574	2,241,102
Rio de Janeiro (Galeão)	-	-	-	-	-	62,085	132,577	516,089	1,962,479
Brasília	-	-	-	-	-	-	172,546	130,824	683,843
Rio de Janeiro (Santos Dumont)	-	-	-	17,018	86,186	439,201	737,671	544,782	677,126
Belo Horizonte	-	-	-	2,465	10,406	129,081	213,032	117,176	472,267
Pôrto Alegre	-	-	-	6,193	18,621	106,283	192,331	120,789	377,078
Salvador	-	-	-	2,252	9,139	49,961	131,311	110,300	375,071
Recife	-	-	-	2,281	11,506	51,595	129,425	123,402	307,150
Curitiba	-	-	-	416	3,743	82,845	156,767	53,344	247,728

Sources: AN 1939-40; p. 1341; AN 1953, p. 223; AN 1963, pp. 222-223; AN 1971, pp. 427-428; AN 1978, pp. 606-608.

Table XI-6. Trading among Brazil's Political Subdivisions via Internal
(Non-Coastwise) Transportation by Value of Merchandise
Exchanged, 1939, 1960, and 1970

	Exported From:			Imported By:		
	1939	1960	1970	1939	1960	1970
	000 Cr$	000 Cr$	000 Cr$	000 Cr$	000 Cr$	000 Cr$
Political Subdivisions						
São Paulo	1,519,058	195,543,000	10,988,980	812,653	113,660,000	6,528,631
Guanabara	–	127,526,000	5,362,227	1,466,045	99,619,000	4,556,675
Minas Gerais	1,485,750	77,166,000	3,406,695	456,810	63,739,000	2,560,982
Paraná	193,401	36,383,000	2,596,110	228,287	47,638,000	1,717,779
Pernanbuco	138,261	26,953,000	1,034,785	59,026	18,901,000	1,167,931
Rio Grande do Sul	41,550	44,354,000	833,435	92,194	42,751,000	1,885,222
Santa Catarina	81,050	18,508,000	604,408	69,570	21,775,000	834,841
Bahia	17,918	4,861,000	518,066	46,404	15,190,000	1,207,025
Rio de Janeiro	–	47,136,000	490,735	263,449	48,426,000	2,721,756
Espírito Santo	51,301	5,060,000	366,587	45,155	6,423,000	444,094
Mato Grosso	62,474	2,877,000	261,528	110,045	3,950,000	379,238
Goiás	96,432	9,404,000	210,849	65,427	13,774,000	696,474
Paraíba	28,027	8,484,000	205,149	100,141	10,661,000	372,093
Rio Grande do Norte	5,361	2,428,000	164,877	34,236	5,192,000	262,071
Pará	–	1,067,000	155,807	3,858	2,630,000	313,802
Ceará	24,033	4,062,000	150,868	24,290	11,281,000	676,368
Maranhão	23,609	2,526,000	148,705	3,137	3,842,000	234,540
Alagoas	162,442	4,805,000	122,858	31,476	5,592,000	288,092
Sergipe	11,823	2,557,000	122,694	11,563	3,513,000	271,538
Rondônia	–	39,000	54,849	–	181,000	34,639
Piauí	11,275	1,368,000	41,934	28,541	3,186,000	185,092
Amazonas	4,315	115,000	38,021	3,301	762,000	57,253
Acre	12,000	5,000	1,854	616	123,000	12,432
Roraíma	–	13,000	29	–	46,000	4,891
Amapá	–	47,000	19	–	174,000	11,886
Distrito Federal	–	–	–	–	3,067,000	454,812
Fernando de Noronha	–	–	–	–	1,000	9
Unspecified	–	–	–	12,856	77,184,000	1,903
Total	3,970,080	623,287,000	27,882,069	3,970,080	623,287,000	27,822,069

Sources: AN 1939-40, pp. 449-450; AN 1963, p. 194; AN 1972, pp. 345 & 349.

Table XI-7. The Brazilian Overseas, Coastwise, and Interior Merchant Fleet: Number, Type, and Ownership of Ships, and Ship Tonnage, 1908-77

	1908	1910	1920	1930	1941	1950	1960	1970	1977
Number of Ships	141	196	239	196	160	406	516	346	875
Dry Cargo	—	—	—	—	—	—	468	298	724
Official	—	—	—	—	—	—	155	100	212
Private	—	—	—	—	—	—	313	198	512
Tanker	—	—	—	—	—	—	48	48	151
Official	—	—	—	—	—	—	38	34	51
Private	—	—	—	—	—	—	10	14	100
Overseas	—	—	—	—	—	—	89	91	148
Coastwise	—	—	—	—	—	—	293	119	110
Interior	—	—	—	—	—	—	134	136	617
Ship Tonnage	128,000	184,000	285,000	400,000	512,525	568,789	1,299,633	2,338,727	5,612,719
Dry Cargo	—	—	—	—	—	—	827,530	1,470,460	2,637,850
Official	—	—	—	—	—	—	471,539	843,221	1,281,126
Private	—	—	—	—	—	—	355,991	627,239	1,356,724
Tanker	—	—	—	—	—	—	472,103	868,267	2,974,869
Official	—	—	—	—	—	—	462,005	854,806	2,915,094
Private	—	—	—	—	—	—	10,098	13,461	59,775
Overseas	—	—	—	—	—	—	704,620	1,816,581	4,680,015
Coastwise	—	—	—	—	—	—	557,353	471,471	672,384
Interior	—	—	—	—	—	—	37,660	50,675	260,320

Sources: AN 1939-40, pp. 1338-1339; AN 1941-45, p. 181; AN 1961, p. 161; AN 1971, p. 424; AN 1978, p. 602.

Table XI-8. Numbers and Registered Tonnage of Ships Calling at Brazilian Ports, 1840/41-1977

	1840-1841		1870-1871		1880-1881		1902	
	Number	Tonnage (000)	Number	Tonnage (000)	Number	Tonnage (000)	Number	Tonnage (000)
Brazil Total	5,825	795	9,944	2,883	7,981	3,902	15,659	11,334

	1910		1915		1921		1930	
	Number	Tonnage (000)	Number	Tonnage (000)	Number	Tonnage (000)	Number	Tonnage (000)
Brazil Total	22,343	21,405	22,599	19,495	22,728	18,286	32,389	47,767

		1938		1948		1955		1960	
		Number	Tonnage (000)	Number	Tonnage (000)	Number	Tonnage (000)	Number	Tonnage (000)
Brazil Total		35,882	51,258	35,267	44,432	35,008	50,677	31,081	59,294
Major Ports									
Santos	SP	3,639	11,608	4,402	5,349	9,456	13,258	4,424	14,729
Rio de Janeiro	GB	4,411	12,361	4,997	11,505	4,610	12,865	4,173	13,681
Salvador	BA	1,507	4,141	1,319	3,192	1,162	3,333	1,444	4,866
Recife	PE	1,825	4,001	1,854	3,586	1,534	4,024	1,502	3,666
Vitória	ES	1,618	1,862	868	1,315	895	2,059	1,004	3,328
Rio Grande	RS	903	2,225	921	1,743	1,163	2,321	961	2,435
Paranaguá	PR	877	1,008	964	1,133	786	1,653	892	2,250
Pôrto Alegre	RS	983	992	1,379	1,230	1,748	1,481	1,544	1,512
Belém	PA	796	1,221	774	1,416	901	1,461	825	1,343
Fortaleza	CE	629	1,198	884	1,541	815	1,154	733	1,228
Angra dos Reis	RJ	304	546	194	297	229	260	420	1,173

		1970		1977	
		Number	Tonnage (000)	Number	Tonnage (000)
Brazil Total		40,966	–	47,745	–
Major Ports					
Santos	SP	3,280	–	3,528	–
Rio de Janeiro	GB	2,709	–	2,968	–
Salvador	BA	864	–	1,724	–
Recife	PE	1,138	–	1,101	–
Vitória	ES	636	–	1,535	–
Rio Grande	RS	1,476	–	4,880	–
Paranaguá	PR	862	–	1,238	–
Pôrto Alegre	RS	18,293	–	11,233	–
Belém	PA	2,030	–	4,185	–
Fortaleza	CE	672	–	754	–
Angra dos Reis	RJ	151	–	219	–

Sources: AN 1939-40, pp. 1339-1340; AN 1956, p. 179; AN 1963, pp. 220-221; AN 1971, p. 425; AN 1978, p. 604

Table XI-9. Brazilian Coastwise Shipping: Major Commodities Moved by
Tonnage and Value, and Major Exporting and Importing
Political Subdivisions, 1921-77

	1921	1925	1930	1938		1945	
Tonnage							
Total (000 metric tons)	1,804	1,760	1,560		1,607		3,332
Major Commodities	-	-	-		-	Coal	510
	-	-	-		-	Sugar	415
	-	-	-		-	Salt	329
	-	-	-		-	Lumber	204
	-	-	-		-	Rice	135
	-	-	-		-	Gasoline	102
Major Exporting Political	-	-	-	RS	21.7	SC	22.8
Subdivisions (% of total tonnage)	-	-	-	GB	14.3	GB	13.7
	-	-	-	RN	11.6	RS	12.8
	-	-	-	SC	10.5	PE	10.2
	-	-	-	PE	10.2	RN	9.2
	-	-	-	SP	7.2	SP	7.7
Major Importing Political	-	-	-	GB	34.2	GB	36.8
Subdivisions (% of total tonnage)	-	-	-	SP	19.7	SP	21.4
	-	-	-	RS	11.2	RS	11.7
	-	-	-	BA	6.6	PE	5.3
	-	-	-	CE	5.3	BA	4.4
	-	-	-	PE	5.2	SC	2.6
% Internal Trade Via Coastwise Routes	92.7	91.7	93.2		93.9		90.8
Value							
Total (Cr$000)	1,156,423	2,979,084	2,058,446		4,100,427		12,472,025
Major Commodities	-	-	-		-	Cott Tex	1,572,331
	-	-	-		-	Sugar	850,093
	-	-	-		-	Dri Beef	416,442
	-	-	-		-	Machy	413,837
	-	-	-		-	Hides	325,137
	-	-	-		-	Pharms	304,985
Major Exporting Political	-	-	-	GB	30.0	GB	27.4
Subdivisions (% of total value)	-	-	-	RS	17.6	SP	18.9
	-	-	-	SP	17.0	RS	14.5
	-	-	-	PE	10.6	PE	10.5
	-	-	-	SC	4.0	SC	5.8
	-	-	-	BA	3.1	PA	3.8
Major Importing Political	-	-	-	RJ	20.3	GB	22.6
Subdivisions (% of value)	-	-	-	RS	16.0	SP	13.9
	-	-	-	SP	12.3	RS	13.1
	-	-	-	BA	11.0	PE	12.2
	-	-	-	PE	9.1	BA	8.4
	-	-	-	CE	5.4	CE	4.4
% Internal Trade Via Coastwise Routes	87.2	86.8	86.4		87.8		89.2

Abbrevations Used: Crude = Crude Oil   Diesel = Diesel Oil   Coff Bns = Coffee Beans   Cott Tex = Cotton Tex
Dri Beef = Dried Beef   Machy = Machinery   Pharms = Pharmaceutical   Raw Cott = Raw Cott
Chems = Chemicals   Babaçu = Babaçu Nuts   Fe Ore = Iron Ore   Wood Prd = Wood Products

Sources: AN 1939-1940, p. 1357; AN 1947, pp. 311-312; AN 1951, p. 293; Labouriau, 1954, p. 192-194;
AN 1956, pp. 281-282; AN 1963, pp. 189-193; AN 1972, pp. 334-341; AN 1978, pp. 575-579.

Table XI- 9   (continued)

1950		1960		1970		1977	
	4,190		7,650		5,925		17,653
Salt	559	Crude	1,656	Crude	1,503	Diesel	5,088
Coal	521	Salt	688	Salt	1,226	Crude	4,443
Sugar	478	Gasoline	657	Diesel	871	Gasoline	1,574
Lumber	406	Coal	652	Coal	744	Fe Ore	1,244
Rice	155	Sugar	502	Gasoline	651	Salt	1,151
Wd Prd	138	Diesel	312	Coff Bns	103	Coal	1,020
SC	20.5	BA	32.7	SE	25.1	BA	21.0
RS	14.4	SC	12.3	RN	19.4	RJ	19.4
RN	12.6	SP	10.8	BA	14.4	SE	14.5
GB	11.2	RN	8.7	SC	12.8	SP	14.1
PE	10.8	RS	7.7	GB	11.5	RN	6.8
SP	6.1	PE	7.6	RS	3.6	SC	5.8
GB	36.6	SP	33.7	SP	29.9	SP	30.9
SP	19.3	GB	23.9	GB	28.1	RJ	17.8
RS	10.0	RJ	6.9	PE	7.1	ES	9.2
PE	6.7	RS	6.2	PR	5.4	BA	9.1
BA	5.0	PE	4.7	SC	4.8	PE	8.5
CE	3.3	PA	4.5	PA	4.0	PA	6.0
	93.4		27.5		16.8		−
	20,882,000		107,689,284		1,389,872		1,838,142
Cott Tex	2,012,000	Sugar	6,923,277	Gasoline	242,983	Salt	258,810
Sugar	1,548,000	Rice	6,391,005	Diesel	164,336	Diesel	254,660
Raw Cott	1,191,000	Gasoline	5,710,421	Coal	69,429	Crude	151,861
Chems	879,000	Rubber	4,902,349	Coff Bns	69,366	Wheat	132,550
Steel	776,000	Cotton	4,023,473	Sugar	46,057	Coal	131,337
Dri Beef	730,000	Babaçu	3,168,191	Rice	44,743	Fe Ore	113,766
GB	22.7	SP	16.9	GB	23.7	RJ	18.9
RS	17.1	GB	16.6	BA	11.7	RN	14.1
SP	16.3	RS	15.2	SP	11.4	SP	12.7
PE	10.8	BA	7.9	PA	10.2	BA	11.6
SC	4.7	PE	6.8	RS	7.4	RS	11.5
PA	4.0	PA	6.6	PR	5.7	SC	7.5
GB	22.4	GB	21.1	AM	21.3	SP	23.0
SP	16.1	SP	17.6	SP	14.6	RJ	14.2
PE	13.1	PE	12.1	PA	10.8	AM	13.9
RS	10.3	PA	11.5	GB	10.4	PE	8.0
BA	9.4	BA	6.1	PE	10.0	BA	7.8
PA	4.6	RS	6.0	PR	6.2	PA	7.7
	91.0		14.7		4.7		−

Table XI-10. Characteristics and Facilities of Brazil's Major Maritime Ports, 1938-78

1938 Port	Pol. Subdv.	Init. Dev. Date	Quay Length (meters)	Std. Cranes	Bridge Cranes	Warehouses No.	Warehouses Sq. Meters	Railroad Trackage (meters)
Pôrto Alegre	RS	1921	2,614	29	15	15	26,168	7,365
Rio de Janeiro	RJ	1910	4,677	112	152	25	104,000	34,195
Santos	SP	1892	5,021	143	123	59	281,612	85,600
Recife	PE	1918	3,271	56	52	16	41,343	20,171
Rio Grande	RS	1915	2,355	39	60	18	33,400	14,220
Salvador	BA	1913	1,480	22	18	10	19,600	7,865
Belém	PA	1909	1,860	21	44	15	35,600	6,000
Paranaguá	PR	1935	500	4	–	3	6,000	4,350
Vitória	ES	1940	–	–	–	–	–	–
Fortaleza	CE	–	–	–	–	–	–	–
Manaus	AM	1903	1,314	12	–	19	19,031	–
Itajaí	SC	–	–	–	–	–	–	–
Maceió	AL	1942	–	–	–	–	–	–
Cabedelo	PB	1935	400	5	5	3	400	2,538
São Francisco do Sul	SC	–	–	–	–	–	–	–
Pelotas	RS	1940	–	–	–	–	–	–
Niterói	RJ	1930	1,470	2	4	2	3,440	2,200
São Sebastião	SP	–	–	–	–	–	–	–
Antonina	PR	–	–	–	–	–	–	–
Natal	RN	1932	200	4	–	2	3,553	1,196
Angra dos Reis	RJ	1934	500	4	2	2	6,078	3,022
Imbituba	SC	–	–	–	–	–	–	–
Laguna	SC	1943	–	–	–	–	–	–
Ilheus	BA	1925	454	–	–	4	5,555	597
Aracaju	SE	–	–	–	–	–	–	–
Itaqui	MA	–	–	–	–	–	–	–
Henrique Laje	SC	–	–	–	–	–	–	–
Santarém	PA	–	–	–	–	–	–	–

Table XI-10 (continued)

Infrastructure

1960 Port	Pol. Subdv.	Init. Dev. Date	Quay Length (meters)	Water Depth At Quays (meters)	Std. Cranes	Bridge Cranes	Warehouses No.	Warehouses Sq. Meters	Railroad Trackage (meters)
Pôrto Alegre	RS	1921	6,622	8.0	46	-	21	46,213	8,459
Rio de Janeiro	RJ	1910	6,909	24.0	217	194	35	164,300	94,700
Santos	SP	1892	7,787	8.4	209	148	60	308,693	125,464
Recife	PE	1918	2,950	8.5	53	47	20	48,151	14,758
Rio Grande	RS	1915	2,408	9.0	39	16	24	56,860	17,260
Salvador	BA	1913	1,480	10.0	34	18	10	19,600	7,010
Belém	PA	1909	1,935	6.0	24	52	15	35,600	6,000
Paranaguá	PR	1935	1,590	11.0	22	3	15	31,416	14,496
Vitória	ES	1940	1,460	8.4	21	8	5	8,721	5,472
Fortaleza	CE	-	-	-	-	-	-	-	-
Manaus	AM	1903	1,689	7.5	17	-	18	19,530	-
Itajaí	SC	-	-	-	-	-	-	-	-
Maceió	AL	1942	420	7.3	5	-	3	8,778	4,280
Cabedelo	PB	1935	600	9.0	10	4	4	6,450	3,086
São Francisco do Sul	SC	-	450	7.7	3	-	2	8,000	1,810
Pelotas	RS	1940	434	5.5	5	-	4	7,387	-
Niterói	RJ	1930	436	24.0	4	4	2	3,425	2,570
São Sebastião	SP	-	400	8.3	2	-	1	600	-
Antonina	PR	-	-	-	-	-	-	-	-
Natal	RN	1932	400	5.8	10	-	3	4,822	2,664
Angra dos Reis	RJ	1934	300	10.0	5	2	2	2,956	1,295
Imbituba	SC	-	-	-	-	-	-	-	-
Laguna	SC	1943	300	4.5	4	-	3	1,992	5,000
Ilheus	BA	1925	478	5.0	1	-	6	8,100	703
Aracaju	SE	-	-	-	-	-	-	-	-
Itaqui	MA	-	-	-	-	-	-	-	-
Henrique Laje	SC	-	140	10.0	12	-	24	8,982	7,670
Santarém	PA	-	-	-	-	-	-	-	-

Table XI-10 (continued)

1978 Port	Pol. Subdv.	Init. Dev. Date	Quay Length (meters)	Water Depth At Quays (meters)	Std. Cranes	Bulk Loaders	Warehouses Sq. Meters
Pôrto Alegre	RS	1921	8,014	2.5/6	35	48	54,450
Rio de Janeiro	RJ	1910	7,391	7/11	103	314	117,223
Santos	SP	1892	7,277	5/11	123	436	397,850
Recife	PE	1918	3,060	8/10	36	59	32,651
Rio Grande	RS	1915	2,612	5.5/10	28	64	53,951
Salvador	BA	1913	2,016	8/10	34	36	20,602
Belém	PA	1909	1,852	7	26	46	30,800
Paranaguá	PR	1935	1,736	8	20	-	190,125
Vitória	ES	1940	1,495	8/13	20	39	14,893
Fortaleza	CE	-	1,116	6/10	4	25	55,754
Manaus	AM	1903	1,103	-	-	50	14,646
Itajaí	SC	-	703	4/6.3	4	28	13,856
Maceió	AL	1942	670	4/10	5	3	26,828
Cabedelo	PB	1935	602	7/10	5	28	17,241
São Francisco do Sul	SC	-	600	6.5/8	2	10	7,400
Pelotas	RS	1940	500	6.5	-	15	6,290
Niterói	RJ	1930	436	7	-	3	18,300
São Sebastião	SP	-	420	2/8.2	-	15	11,700
Antonina	PR	-	417	6/7	-	52	7,550
Natal	RN	1932	400	6	-	8	14,248
Angra dos Reis	RJ	1934	350	10	6	15	5,364
Imbituba	SC	-	308	8/10	2	5	3,300
Laguna	SC	1943	300	5	-	-	-
Ilheus	BA	1925	66	4	5	15	8,940
Aracaju	SE	-	56	8	-	1	2,358
Itaqui	MA	-	-	-	8	7	4,481
Henrique Laje	SC	-	-	-	-	-	-
Santarém	PA	-	-	-	2	5	4,800

Sources: Ports, Rivers & Navigation of Brazil, 1939, p. 26; AN 1961, pp. 158-159;
AN 1979, pp. 574-575.

Table XI-11. The Brazilian Postal and Telegraph System: Structure, Personnel, Traffic, and Finances, 1840-1977

	1840	1850	1860	1870	1880	1890	1900	1910
Number of Agencies	-	-	-	-	-	-	2,648	3,415
Postal Only	-	-	-	-	-	-	-	-
Postal-Telegraph	-	-	-	-	-	-	-	-
Postal-Radiotelegraph	-	-	-	-	-	-	-	-
Persons Employed	-	-	-	-	-	-	5,198	7,386
In Agencies	-	-	-	-	-	-	3,039	4,191
On Postal Lines	-	-	-	-	-	-	2,159	3,195
Postal Routes								
Number	-	-	-	-	-	-	1,245	1,743
Kilometers	-	-	-	-	-	-	85,997	141,737
Telegraph Network								
Kilometers of Routes	-	-	-	-	-	11,896	21,066	31,332
Kilometers of Lines	-	-	-	-	-	20,299	41,678	57,140
Postal Traffic (1000 Units)								
Total Correspondence Handled	872	1,815	5,731	9,723	19,452	50,441	278,480	543,669
Telegraph Traffic (1000 Telegrams)	-	-	-	46	254	751	1,354	2,789
National	-	-	-	-	-	-	-	-
International	-	-	-	-	-	-	-	-
Radio Service	-	-	-	-	-	-	-	-
Postal Finances (Cr$ 000)								
Receipts	-	-	-	-	-	2,551	6,608	8,891
Expenditures	-	-	-	-	-	3,847	8,986	18,819

	1920	1930	1939	1950	1960	1968	1970	1977
Number of Agencies	3,913	4,756	4,688	5,105	5,617	5,605	3,709	6,677
Postal Only	-	-	3,178	3,008	3,140	1,395	774	3,997
Postal-Telegraph	-	-	1,442	1,941	2,326	4,057	2,776	2,488
Postal-Radiotelegraph	-	-	68	156	151	153	159	192
Persons Employed	8,656	10,378	10,284	42,560	53,431	71,376	63,312	84,710
In Agencies	5,041	6,908	6,852	-	51,244	-	-	-
On Postal Lines	3,615	3,470	3,432	-	2,187	-	-	-
Postal Routes								
Number	2,408	2,927	2,686	3,380	3,987	4,180	-	-
Kilometers	151,023	173,763	139,351	-	-	-	-	-
Telegraph Network								
Kilometers of Routes	44,447	58,948	61,223	71,783	82,717	78,003	87,310	-
Kilometers of Lines	79,930	114,475	124,867	150,620	170,083	159,671	-	-
Postal Traffic (1000 Units)								
Total Correspondence Handled	642,376	1,909,312	3,141,107	-	11,842,460	7,933,257	-	-
Types of Handling								
Posted/Received	-	-	1,308,352	2,003,358	4,156,975	4,159,619	780,949	2,117,000
Distributed/Forwarded	-	-	1,227,106	-	4,394,245	2,764,896	752,427	-
In Transit	-	-	605,649	-	3,291,240	1,008,742	-	-
Types of Correspondence Handled								
Letters	-	-	1,405,188	1,175,328	-	-	942,525	-
Printed Matter	-	-	1,636,053	743,310	-	-	-	-
Parcels Handled	-	-	16,934	-	123,603	39,736	-	-
Telegraph Traffic (1000 Telegrams)	6,556	5,537	10,676	28,264	26,388	20,522	19,064	17,553
National	-	-	10,610	27,871	26,094	20,394	18,927	17,395
International	-	-	66	393	277	117	129	158
Radio Service	-	-	-	-	17	11	8	-
Postal Finances (Cr$ 000)								
Receipts	14,927	46,188	109,471	-	2,549,427	86,022	140,595	4,064,300
Expenditures	29,408	71,576	185,054	-	9,325,366	289,891	391,855	3,751,638

Sources: AN 1939-40, pp. 328-335, 345 & 1342-1346; AN 1952, pp. 243-247; AN 1963, pp. 224-226; AN 1970, pp. 423-425; AN 1972, pp. 427-431; AN 1978, pp. 611-612.

Table XI-12. The Brazilian Telephone System: Numbers of Telephones in
Operation and Numbers of Subscribers and Employees, 1907-76

	1907	1937	1938	1944	1950	1959	1969	1976
Number of Telephones	15,203	170,663	187,230	373,499	521,222	1,007,163	1,789,001	4,025,408
Number of Subscribers	-	134,624	140,078	309,489	405,441	743,333	-	-
Number of Employees	-	6,304	6,508	13,993	14,052	21,950	51,024	90,254

Sources: AN 1908-1912, p. 94; AN 1936, p. 187; AN 1939-1940, pp. 350-351; AN 1947, p. 231; AN 1952, p. 248; AN 1963, p. 227; AN 1972, pp. 435-437; AN 1978, pp. 613-615.

Table XI-13. The Brazilian Radio and Television System: Numbers of Stations by Wavelengths and Power, Numbers of Employees and Hours Broadcast, and Numbers and Types of Stations by Political Subdivisions, 1923-74

Radio Stations — Number Operating

1923	1925	1930	1935	1940
2	7	16	52	75

1944	1950	1961	1968	1974
106	300	803	990	977

Radio Stations — detail

	1944	1950	1961	1968	1974
Number Operating	106	300	803	990	977
Wavelengths					
AM	–	–	637	788	802
FM	–	–	26	47	33
Tropical	–	–	68	76	112
Short	–	–	72	79	30
Power in Watts					
100	–	133	–	–	–
101–500	59	66	–	–	–
501–1000	9	38	–	–	–
1001–5000	24	30	–	–	–
5001–10000	9	19	–	–	–
10001–20000	1	6	–	–	–
20001–50000	6	6	–	–	–
50001–100000	1	1	–	–	–
Unknown	1	1	–	–	–
Total Daytime Wattage by Wavelength	792,350	–	–	2,720,510	2,693,510
AM	–	–	–	1,749,210	1,973,000
FM	–	–	–	27,600	105,310
Tropical	–	–	–	118,350	432,200
Short	–	–	–	825,530	183,000
Weekly Hours Broadcast	–	20,586	67,829	114,676	99,164
Number of Personnel	–	9,625	16,931	17,012	17,231
Male	–	7,925	14,456	–	–
Female	–	1,700	2,475	–	–

Television Stations

	1961	1968	1974
Number Operating	23	40	75
Total Daytime VHF Power in Watts	–	772,500	756,460
Weekly Hours Telecast	1,205	2,865	5,120
Number of Personnel	3,245	4,630	9,529
Male	2,869	–	–
Female	376	–	–

Numbers of Stations By Major Pol. Subdivs. and Cities

	Radio Stations 1935	1944	1950	1968	1974	Television Stations 1968	1974
Total	52	106	300	990	977	40	75
São Paulo	24	41	97	263	240	7	9
São Paulo	10	–	–	49	–	5	–
Rio Grande do Sul	3	6	40	124	125	2	9
Pôrto Alegre	2	–	–	2	–	2	2
Paraná	1	6	19	94	103	4	8
Curitiba	–	–	–	20	–	3	–
Minas Gerais	3	18	55	114	125	6	7
Belo Horizonte	1	–	–	15	–	4	–
Distrito Federal	–	–	–	8	13	3	4
Brasília	–	–	–	–	–	–	–
Guanabara	12	13	14	47	–	5	–
Rio de Janeiro	12	13	14	47	63	5	4
Niterói	3	4	13	37	–	–	–
Pernambuco	1	–	–	6	29	3	4
Recife	1	1	2	29	29	3	–
Amazonas	–	–	–	16	12	–	4
Manaus	–	–	2	11	12	3	–
Mato Grosso	–	–	–	6	–	–	–
Cuiabá	–	3	4	17	19	1	3
Ceará	1	–	–	4	–	–	–
Fortaleza	1	2	2	25	24	2	3
Goiás	–	–	–	11	–	1	–
Goiânia	–	1	5	34	33	2	2
Pará	1	–	–	15	–	2	–
Belém	1	1	2	12	13	2	2
Maranhão	–	–	–	7	–	2	–
São Luís	–	1	2	10	10	1	2
Rondônia	–	–	–	9	–	–	–
Pôrto Velho	–	–	–	3	3	1	–
Bahia	–	2	7	33	32	1	2
Salvador	3	–	–	13	–	1	–
Santa Catarina	3	2	23	61	63	–	2
Florianópolis	–	–	–	7	–	–	–
Paraíba	–	1	3	12	11	1	1
João Pessoa	–	–	–	4	–	1	–
Espírito Santo	–	1	2	11	10	1	1
Vitória	–	–	–	6	–	1	–
Rio Grande do Norte	–	2	2	13	12	1	–
Natal	–	–	–	6	–	–	–
Sergipe	–	1	1	7	7	–	–
Aracaju	–	–	–	6	–	–	–
Piauí	–	1	2	6	9	–	–
Teresina	–	–	–	6	9	–	–
Amapá	–	1	–	4	4	–	–
Macapá	–	–	–	4	–	–	–
Roraima	–	–	–	1	1	–	–
Boa Vista	–	–	–	–	–	–	–
Acre	–	1	1	3	7	–	–
Rio Branco	–	–	–	3	–	–	–
Alagoas	–	1	1	9	9	–	–
Maceió	–	–	–	6	–	–	–

Sources: AN 1936, p. 377; AN 1941-45, p. 451; AN 1952, pp. 482-483; AN 1963, p. 396; AN 1970, pp. 701-704; AN 1978, pp. 626-634.

Table XI-14. Newspapers Published in Brazil by Major Political Subdivisions and Major Cities: Numbers, Copies Printed, and Language of Text, 1933-74

Numbers and Copies Printed	1933 Number Total	1933 Daily	1944 Number Total	1944 Daily	1954 Number Total	1954 Daily	1954 Copies Printed Per Printing	1963 Number Total	1963 Daily	1963 Copies Total	1963 Copies Daily	1974 Number Total	1974 Daily	1974 Copies Total	1974 Copies Daily
Brazil Total	916	100	772	192	1,281	261	2,928,552	1,047	246	5,519,135	3,301,080	1,151	284	1,300,628	1,175,776
São Paulo	248	27	221	42	–	69	–	340	69	1,641,312	697,472	387	97	584,690	522,972
São Paulo	–	–	–	–	–	–	–	39	19	803,032	428,782	49	22	435,180	405,325
Guanabara	39	13	38	29	–	26	–	36	20	1,618,170	1,504,710	–	–	–	–
Rio de Janeiro	39	13	38	29	–	26	–	36	20	1,618,170	1,504,710	25	16	289,192	283,160
Rio de Janeiro	49	5	56	11	–	16	–	88	16	282,450	48,500	99	26	310,731	294,872
Niterói	–	–	–	–	–	–	–	10	5	41,500	22,000	–	–	–	–
Rio Grande do Sul	71	14	62	20	–	23	–	81	18	427,908	258,148	99	17	104,749	89,050
Pôrto Alegre	–	–	–	–	–	–	–	8	8	215,148	215,148	13	8	82,686	81,519
Minas Gerais	191	7	157	15	–	23	–	153	23	446,345	192,100	203	20	69,106	55,040
Belo Horizonte	–	–	–	–	–	–	–	12	8	181,500	130,500	9	6	43,062	42,719
Paraná	19	6	13	6	–	14	–	75	22	293,902	127,152	82	20	53,455	48,182
Curitiba	–	–	–	–	–	–	–	15	10	121,500	85,500	13	9	34,441	33,567
Bahia	62	2	62	9	–	8	–	45	4	100,090	27,300	47	8	28,769	26,644
Salvador	–	–	–	–	–	–	–	5	2	40,000	24,000	7	5	25,861	25,246
Distrito Federal	–	–	–	–	–	–	–	2	2	9,000	9,000	12	9	25,055	24,236
Brasília	–	–	–	–	–	–	–	2	2	9,000	9,000	12	9	25,055	24,236
Pernambuco	96	7	26	6	–	7	–	21	4	130,288	106,088	16	5	21,366	20,555
Recife	–	–	–	–	–	–	–	5	4	111,088	106,088	7	5	–	–
Santa Catarina	19	3	31	6	–	6	–	43	8	98,170	28,000	40	10	16,629	14,628
Florianópolis	–	–	–	–	–	–	–	4	3	24,300	12,800	4	3	6,250	6,238
Amazonas	9	1	7	5	–	7	–	7	6	30,200	29,700	6	6	12,491	12,491
Manaus	–	–	–	–	–	–	–	7	6	30,200	29,700	6	6	12,491	12,491
Pará	14	5	11	5	–	9	–	11	5	142,180	105,000	7	4	14,403	14,109
Belém	–	–	–	–	–	–	–	9	5	141,000	105,000	5	4	14,296	14,109

Languages	1954 Number Daily	1968 Number Total	1968 Number Daily	1968 Copies Annual in 000's Total	1968 Copies Daily	1974 Number Total	1974 Number Daily	1974 Copies Annual in 000's Total	1974 Copies Daily
All Languages	261	957	219	1,087,265	1,103,947	1,151	284	1,300,628	1,175,776
Portuguese	255	935	214	1,065,015	995,211	1,140	283	1,296,501	1,172,991
Foreign	2	6	2	4,670	3,297	9	1	4,078	2,785
German	1	2	1	4,147	3,107	3	–	788	–
Japanese	1	1	1	10	–	1	–	32	–
English	1	1	1	190	190	1	1	2,785	2,785
Spanish	–	–	–	–	–	1	–	182	–
Italian	–	1	–	204	–	1	–	291	–
Other	1	1	–	119	–	2	–	–	–
Portuguese/Foreign	4	16	3	17,580	15,439	2	–	49	–
Portuguese/German	1	6	–	1,065	–	1	–	13	–
Portuguese/Japanese	–	4	3	15,414	15,439	–	–	–	–
Portuguese/English	–	–	–	102	–	–	–	–	–
Portuguese/Spanish	1	1	–	–	–	–	–	–	–
Portuguese/Italian	2	–	–	–	–	1	–	–	–
Portuguese/Other	1	5	–	969	–	–	–	36	–

Sources: AN 1936, p. 376; AN 1941-1945, pp. 449-450; AN 1952, pp. 480-481; AN 1956, pp. 378-379; AN 1965, p. 457; AN 1970, pp. 706-708; AN 1976, pp. 709-711.

Chapter XII. Manufacturing,
Industry and
Trade Construction

Table XII-1 reports the value of output by Brazilian manufacturing industry groups from 1907 to 1974. The data for 1907, 1920, 1939, 1949, and 1959 originated with the Serviço Nacional de Recenseamento. An off-year survey was completed in 1907 and the censuses of 1940, 1950, and 1960 reported the respective data for the last three years noted above. The 1969 data were originated by the Instituto Brasileiro de Estatística and those for 1974 by FIBGE. The 1920 Establishment surveys were taken on September 1, 1920; the 1940 Establishment surveys on September 1, 1940. The Cr$ 1,000 values for 1920 and 1940 were for the years 1920 and 1939, respectively. The 1950 and 1960 Establishment surveys were taken January 1, 1950, and January 1, 1960, respectively. The Cr$ 1,000 values for 1950 and 1960 were for the years 1949 and 1959, respectively. The 1969 and 1974 Establishment surveys were taken on December 31 of the respective years, and the Cr$ 1,000 values were for the years 1969 and 1974, respectively.

Total value of output, but not by manufacturing industry groups, was available for some years not shown on the table. These included: 1914, Cr$ 996,557; 1925, Cr$ 4,326,070; 1930, 5,906,826; and 1935, 8,438,728. These data were generated by Roberto Simonsen in his A evolução industrial do Brasil, and reported in Anuário estatístico, 1939-40, page 318. The output of small sugar producers (engenhos) was included in the 1907 "food products" category on Table XII-1. Their output was not included in the figures for 1920 and beyond. The 1907 and 1920 industry types were regrouped by the author to conform to 1939 and later industry categories. For 1939 and earlier years the category "chemicals" included plastics/plastic articles, pharmaceuticals/medicines, and perfume/soap/candles.

Table XII-2 shows the value of consumption by Brazilian manufacturing industry groups from 1940 to 1974. The 1940, 1950, and 1960 data were from the Serviço Nacional de Recenseamento, those for 1969 from IBGE and those for 1974 from FIBGE. Establishment figures for 1940, 1950, and 1960 were for January 1 of those years; for 1969 and 1974 these data were for December 31 of the year in question. Sources for 1940 through 1969 reported establishments (Estabs on the table). The 1974 source reported informants (Infrmts on the table). Consumption included the value of all raw materials, packing materials, and fuels and lubricants, but not salaries and wages. Perfume/soap/candles, plastics/plastic articles, and pharmaceuticals/medicines were part of the "chemical" category in 1940. The 1974 data were supplied by 70,859 informants. The numbers of informants for the other years were not supplied by the sources.

Table XII-3 notes the quantum indices of Brazilian industrial production from 1939 to 1975. No origin was given for the 1939-61 data, which appeared in the Fundação Getúlio Vargas's Revista brasileira de economia, março 1962, but the Fundação must have been the source. Werner Baer on page 263 of his Industrialization and Economic Development in Brazil, 1965, also cited this Revista article as the source of his data, which covered the period 1939 to 1961. The Revista, however, only presented data for the years 1947 to 1961.

Table XII-4 reports the output of manufactured goods in Brazil from 1853 to 1976. Stanley Stein in his Brazilian Cotton Manufacture, 1957, page 191, supplied the data on cotton textiles for the period 1853-1905 and for the period 1925-48. His data origins were numerous and included Commissão da tarifa; Borja Castro's "Relatório do segundo grupo" of the Inquérito industrial; O Industrial for June 18, 1881; Archivos da exposição da indústria nacional de 1881; Consul Rickett's Report (1886); Branner's Cotton in the Empire of Brazil; Jornal do Commércio, December 11, 1895; Consul Rhind's Report (1889); Clark's Cotton Goods in Latin America; Garry's Textile Markets of Brazil; CIFTA-Rio Relatório, 1921-22, 1924, 1926, 1927; Indústria textil algodeira; Indústria textil de algodão e da lã; and Anuário estatístico, 1949.

No origin was given by the source (Anuário estatístico, 1939-40) for data for the years between 1911 and 1939 not covered by Stein. Most of the data for 1940, 1941-49, 1950, and some of those for 1960 originated with the Serviço Estatístico da Produção. Other generators of data for these periods were the Sindicatos da Indústria do Papel do Rio de Janeiro e do Estado de São Paulo, the Conselho Nacional de Petróleo, the Serviço de Expansão do Trigo, the Instituto do Açucar e do Álcool, the Secretaria Técnica do Grupo Executivo da Indústria automobilística, the Associação Nacional dos Fabricantes de Papel, the Comissão Executivo de Defesa da Borracha, and the Sindicato da Indústria de Adubos e Colas do Estado de São Paulo.

Gertrude Heare's 1961 Brazil, Information for United States Businessmen was the source for all of the data for 1958 and 1959 and for some of those for 1960 on Table XII-4. Her data origins included the Associaçao Brasileira para o Desenvolvimento das Indústrias de Base (ADIB), the Grupo Executivo da Indústria Mechânica Pesada (GEIMAPE), the Grupo Executivo da Indústria Automobilística (GEIA), the Grupo de Trabalho da Indústria de Material Ferroviário, and the Grupo Executivo da Indústria de Construção Naval (GEICON). The "plastic materials/synthetic resins" data for 1960 were United States Foreign Service estimates, the 1960 "synthetic fibers" data were Brazilian industry source estimates, and the 1960 "pharmaceutical" data were listed by Heare as estimates, but no origins were given for them. No specific sources were given for any of the other Heare data used on Table XII-4.

The data for 1970 and 1971-77 originated with FIBGE, the Sindicato Nacional de Cimento, the Instituto Brasileiro de Siderurgia, the Instituto Brasileiro de Estatística, the Associação Nacional dos Fabricantes do Papel, the Super-intendência da Borracha, the Escritório de Estatística do Ministério da Agricultura, the Conselho Nacional de Petróleo, Petróleo Brasileiro, S.A., the Companhia Pernambucana de Borracha Sintética (COPERBO), the Sindicato da Indústria de Matérias-Primas para Inseticidas e Fertilizantes no Estado de São Paulo, and the Conselho de Desenvolvimento Indus-trial-Grupo Setorial VI.

Other 1970 and 1971-77 data generators included the Superintendência Nacional da Marinha Mercante, the Emprêsa Brasileira de Aeronáutica (EMBRAER), the Instituto de Açucar e do Álcool, the Associação Brasileiro da Indústria de Álcalis e Cloro Derivados, the Campanha Nacional de Álcalis, and the Centro de Informações Econômico-Fiscais.

The 1960 "industrial machinery" output was an estimate of the 1960 capacity of production. The 1958 "agricultural/ highway machinery" output was for firms of five or more employees. The 1960 "synthetic rubber" output was that planned for the year 1960. The 1960 "railway equipment-passenger car" output was a projection of capacity. Output of steel railway passenger cars only began in 1957. Silk output was reported in tons from 1911 to 1938, but in 1956 it was reported in meters. Acetic acid output was reported in liters until 1938 but thereafter it was reported in tons. Bunker oil output was reported in thousands of barrels through 1960, and, thereafter, in tons. Paint and varnish output was listed in tons through 1938 and afterward was reported in thousand liters. Solvent naphtha output was in tons in 1960 but in cubic meters for all later years. Paraffin output was reported in barrels in 1962 and in later years was reported in tons.

Table XII-5 shows the amounts of capital invested in Brazil's manufacturing industries by industry groups from 1907 to 1974. The data for 1907 to 1959 were originated by the censuses, those for 1969 by the Instituto Brasileiro de Estatística, and those for 1974 by IBGE. The explanations of the census data provided in the first paragraph of the text for Chapter XII-1 apply to this table as well. Sources for the years 1907 through 1920 referred to the number of establishments (Estabs on the table), and those for the years 1969 and 1974 referred to informants (Infrmts on the table).

The 1920 census listed capital invested for fourteen separate industry types and one "other industries" category. The industry types were combined by the author to correspond to the smaller number of industry groups used by later censuses. A footnote to the 1920 census table noted that the "other industries" category contained some 35 factories producing goods some of which might well have been included with named industry categories. For example, the 1920 census could have added confetti plants to the paper industry category and aniline dye plants to the chemical industry category, but they were instead lumped in the "other industries" category.

The data for 1907 and 1920 reported "capital employed" (capital empregado) which the author assumed to be the same as the "capital applied" (capital aplicado) category reported by the sources for 1940, 1950, and 1960. Both sets of sources also reported "capital realizado" (capital realized) but these data were not included in the totals for the years shown on Table XII-5. The 1968 and 1971 sources reported "total capital invested" (total inversões de capital) but they did not specify whether this included "capital realized" as well.

Table XII-6 shows the numbers of establishments by employee-size category for Brazil's manufacturing industry groups from 1920 to 1974. The 1920, 1940, 1950, and 1960 data originated with the censuses, those for 1968 with the Instituto Brasileiro de Estatística, and those for 1974 with FIBGE. The 1920 data source reported only production workers (operários), not all employees. This source also reported that 421 plants had no production workers, but these plants were not distinguished by industry group. The 1940 figures were taken on September 1, 1940, the 1950 figures on January 1, 1950, and the 1960 figures on December 31, 1959. The 1950 size categories referred to production workers only, the

1960, 1968, and 1974 size categories to all employees--
administrative, salaried, and production.

Table XII-7 reports the numbers and sales receipts for
categories of retail and wholesale establishments in Brazil
from 1940 to 1970. All data originated with the censuses of
the respective years. For 1940 the numbers of establishments
were those in existence on September 1, 1940, and sales were
for the year 1939. For 1950 the establishment numbers
reported were those present on January 1, 1950, and sales
were for the year 1949. The 1960 establishment numbers were
for January 1, 1960 and sales were for the year 1959. The
1970 establishment data were for December 31, 1970, and sales
were for the year 1970. The 1940 and 1950 sources
distinguish a "mixed retail/wholesale" category but those for
1960 and 1970 did not. Neither did they report the criteria
used to separate this mixed category into retail and
wholesale. Both AN 1965 and AN 1977 reported retail and
wholesale data for 1960. The former source reported a mixed
retail/wholesale group but the latter did not. Their totals
differed slightly: AN 1977 reported a total of 361,503
establishments and AN 1965 reported 361,448 establishments.
AN 1977 also reported Cr$ 5,079,023 more in total sales
receipts than AN 1965. Poor processing of the 1960 census
and later Brazilian agency attempts to rectify this may have
accounted for these discrepancies.

The food/beverages category included alcoholic beverages. Clothing also included textiles, accessories, and
notions. Pharmacies included places selling chemical
products as well. The fuels/lubrication category referred to
places selling fuels and lubricants and included service
stations. Hardware included sanitary apparatus and construction supplies. The autos/vehicle category included all
types of automotive vehicles. General/food establishments
referred to the sale of general merchandise plus food items.
General/nonfood establishments sold general merchandise but
no food items. Furniture included all household furnishings.
Appliances included all kinds of electrical equipment as
well. Stationery establishments included those selling
books. Supermarkets were those establishments selling food
together with domestic and personal items. Primary products
included agricultural products, raw materials of animal,
vegetable, and mineral origin, and animal and vegetable
extracts. Under wholesale the used equipment category
included used industrial equipment. No definition was given
for used articles under retail or used items under mixed
retail/wholesale but the latter probably included some
industrial equipment.

Table XII-8 shows the numbers of establishments and the
monetary receipts for service establishments in Brazil from

1940 to 1970. All data were originated by the censuses of the respective years. For 1940 the numbers of establishments were for September 1, 1940, the receipts for the year 1939. For 1950 establishment and receipt data were for the year 1949, and for 1960 both sets of data were for 1959. All 1970 data were for the year 1970. None of the latter three sources indicated a specific date on which establishments were counted, but presumably they were the same dates on which the retail and wholesale establishments were counted. As was the case for Table XII-7, two sources, AN 1965 and AN 1977, presented slightly conflicting data for 1960. Data in the latter source may have represented an attempt to rectify some of the poorly processed 1960 census data. Nevertheless, because AN 1965 separated hotels with food service from hotels without food service this source was used as the basis for the 1960 data on Table XII-8. For 1950, 1960, and 1970 the barber and beauty shop category may have included a few other types of personal care establishments. Only the 1940 source was explicit in separating out these latter establishments. It reported a total of 45,353 personal service establishments, of which only 119 provided other types of personal care. The remainder were barber and beauty shops.

Table XII-9 presents the numbers and square meterage of building permits in the municípios (counties) of the capitals of Brazil's political subdivisions from 1954 to 1976. The data for 1954 and for 1958 to 1964 originated with the Conselho Nacional de Estatística. Those for 1956 were generated by the Inspectorias Regionais de Estatística Municipal of that agency. The 1966 to 1970 data were originated by the Instituto Brasileiro de Estatística, those for 1972 to 1976 by FIBGE.

For the period 1954 to 1964 the "total permits issued" category and the "area" category included both new construction and additions to existing buildings. For 1966 all data were for new construction only. For the period 1968 to 1976 both new construction and additions to existing buildings were included. For this latter period "total permits issued" minus "permits issued for new construction" equaled "permits issued for additions," and "total area" minus "area of new construction" equaled area of additions. For all years the "area" category included the total square meterage of all floors not just that of the ground floor. The 1954 São Paulo data were for January to November of that year. For 1960 and 1962 the totals included data for Teresina, Piauí, which were collected for only seven months in the former year and only eleven months in the latter year. For 1964, Recife and Rio de Janeiro were the only two municípios of the twenty-six with missing data.

In addition to the nine <u>municípios</u> shown on Table XII-9 by name from 1954 to 1960 sixteen others were also a part of the total in each year from 1954 to 1960. They included Pôrto Velho, Rondônia; Rio Branco, Acre; Manaus, Amazonas; Boa Vista, Roraíma; Macapá, Amapá; São Luis, Maranhão; Teresina, Piauí; Natal, Rio Grande do Norte; João Pessoa, Paraíba; Maceió, Alagoas; Aracaju, Sergipe; Vitória, Espríto Santo; Florianópolis, Santa Catarina; Goiânia, Goiás; and Niterói, Rio de Janeiro. The total became twenty-six for the 1962 data because Brasília, D.F., had come into existence by then. The total remained twenty-six until 1976, by which date Niterói had lost its political function as capital of Rio de Janeiro state to the city of Rio de Janeiro and thus was not included in the Brazilian data.

Table XII-1. Value of Output of Brazilian Manufacturing Industry Groups, 1907-74

	1907 Cr$ 1000	%	1920 Cr$ 1000	%	1930 Cr$ 1000	%	1939 Cr$ 1000	%
Food Products	223,007	30.01	956,853	32.0	-	-	4,927,324	31.5
Chemicals	19,388	2.6	43,939	1.5	-	-	1,424,016	9.1
Metals	38,542	5.2	90,059	3.0	-	-	987,573	6.3
Transportation Equipment	16,798	2.3	38,848	1.3	-	-	463,446	3.0
Textiles	173,519	23.4	806,689	27.0	-	-	3,618,574	23.1
Mechanical Equipment	1,584	.2	10,005	.3	-	-	166,380	1.1
Electrical/Communication Equipment	192	negl.	859	negl.	-	-	143,505	.9
Non-Metallic Minerals	24,110	3.3	81,393	2.7	-	-	584,196	3.7
Paper/Paper Products	5,607	.8	37,234	1.3	-	-	274,551	1.8
Clothing/Shoes/Cloth Articles	61,249	8.3	254,644	8.6	-	-	729,792	4.7
Wood/Lumber	31,451	4.2	124,753	4.2	-	-	440,329	2.8
Plastics/Plastic Articles	-	-	-	-	-	-	-	-
Printing/Publishing	-	-	-	-	-	-	410,877	2.6
Rubber	36	negl.	3,986	.1	-	-	92,030	.6
Furniture	11,760	1.6	39,831	1.3	-	-	251,190	1.6
Pharmaceuticals/Medicines	-	-	24,316	.8	-	-	-	-
Beverages	37,245	5.0	140,701	4.7	-	-	408,410	2.6
Perfume/Soap/Candles	25,036	3.4	80,544	2.7	-	-	-	-
Tobacco	20,318	2.7	106,749	3.6	-	-	279,276	1.8
Leather/Hides	19,539	2.6	69,986	2.3	-	-	295,911	1.9
Other Industries	32,155	4.3	77,787	2.6	-	-	145,629	.9
Total	741,536	100.0	2,989,176	100.0	5,906,826	100.0	15,643,006	100.0

	1949 Cr$ 1000	%	1959 Cr$ 1000	%	1969 Cr$ 1000	%	1974 Cr$ 1000	%
Food Products	34,313,679	31.9	285,151,484	24.3	13,894,607	19.1	83,058,343	15.8
Chemicals	5,565,682	5.2	106,498,558	9.1	8,660,420	11.9	77,247,870	14.7
Metals	8,136,982	7.6	123,894,474	10.5	7,738,142	10.6	74,611,965	14.2
Transportation Equipment	2,476,863	2.3	79,328,017	6.8	6,768,592	9.3	46,827,365	8.9
Textiles	20,025,855	18.6	147,480,649	12.6	7,348,183	10.1	41,038,689	7.8
Mechanical Equipment	1,718,547	1.6	33,614,923	2.9	3,483,560	4.8	38,772,316	7.4
Electrical/Communication Equipment	1,501,530	1.4	45,249,874	3.9	4,166,407	5.7	26,693,519	5.1
Non-Metallic Minerals	4,805,751	4.5	53,396,328	4.5	3,183,490	4.4	18,150,846	3.4
Paper/Paper Products	2,132,270	2.0	35,255,478	3.0	1,884,934	2.6	17,493,033	3.3
Clothing/Shoes/Cloth Articles	4,649,328	4.3	40,206,087	3.4	2,032,967	2.8	17,211,168	3.3
Wood/Lumber	3,634,218	3.4	31,250,238	2.7	1,684,598	2.3	13,053,672	2.5
Plastics/Plastic Articles	214,240	.2	7,757,893	.7	1,097,632	1.5	10,472,575	2.0
Printing/Publishing	3,031,455	2.8	26,916,884	2.3	1,623,177	2.2	10,218,000	1.9
Rubber	1,722,111	1.6	25,524,006	2.2	1,449,656	2.0	8,090,377	1.5
Furniture	1,780,504	1.7	21,736,907	1.8	1,050,270	1.4	7,814,557	1.5
Pharmaceuticals/Medicines	2,077,438	1.9	23,081,836	2.0	1,910,713	2.6	7,697,989	1.4
Beverages	3,397,097	3.2	27,973,804	2.4	1,510,402	2.1	6,902,617	1.3
Perfume/Soap/Candles	1,859,222	1.7	17,973,886	1.5	1,062,175	1.5	5,839,181	1.1
Tobacco	1,474,549	1.4	13,167,472	1.1	825,144	1.1	3,838,254	.7
Leather/Hides	1,629,925	1.5	12,777,618	1.1	490,991	.7	2,617,197	.5
Other Industries	1,316,291	1.2	14,374,771	1.2	917,419	1.3	9,014,029	1.7
Total	107,463,537	100.0	1,172,568,187	100.0	72,783,479	100.0	526,663,562	100.0

Sources: RE 1920E1, pp. XII-XV; RE 1920E1, pp. XVI-XXII; AN 1939-40, p. 1318; AN 1956, p. 119; AN 1963, p. 72; AN 1971, pp. 185-207; AN 1978, p. 448.

Table XII-2. Value of Consumption by Brazilian Manufacturing Industry Groups, 1940-74

	1940		1950		1960		1969		1974	
	Estabs	Cr$ 1000	Estabs	Cr$ 1000	Estabs	Cr$ 1000	Estabs	Cr$ 1000	Infrmts	Cr$ 1000
Food Products	14,905	3,372,525	32,872	24,529,536	33,443	195,816,874	8,649	10,818,888	17,877	60,681,324
Chemicals	1,780	717,512	1,158	3,007,629	1,777	59,564,632	1,467	5,908,662	2,161	53,555,805
Metals	1,460	477,551	2,221	3,631,078	4,764	59,332,315	2,018	4,904,673	6,049	43,198,178
Transportation Equipment	248	248,970	539	1,311,211	2,014	38,238,519	685	4,549,021	1,680	30,246,818
Textiles	2,212	2,140,419	2,941	10,335,815	4,267	80,995,109	1,979	4,714,527	3,864	24,267,311
Mechanical Equipment	327	82,970	762	686,814	1,688	14,694,653	1,204	1,920,594	4,638	18,652,402
Electrical/Communication Equipment	119	83,617	341	714,073	972	24,053,740	659	2,520,068	1,769	14,107,388
Paper/Paper Products	228	170,556	441	1,058,251	766	18,821,078	526	1,196,867	1,209	9,688,162
Clothing/Shoes/Cloth Articles	3,203	417,398	5,076	2,572,440	7,632	20,070,911	2,197	1,332,578	4,960	9,544,108
Non-Metallic Minerals	4,861	228,976	12,750	1,392,395	18,127	17,560,963	5,215	1,618,801	5,594	6,960,683
Wood/Wood Products	3,545	230,773	7,562	1,622,233	11,191	13,713,684	3,696	990,679	6,024	6,366,362
Plastics/Plastic Articles	-	-	104	90,297	291	3,286,022	404	608,514	1,487	5,008,634
Rubber/Rubber Products	65	49,161	119	819,993	301	13,349,541	337	862,567	751	4,309,578
Furniture	2,069	109,956	2,882	743,631	8,140	9,763,892	2,466	662,694	3,521	3,938,608
Printing/Publishing	2,207	176,428	2,749	1,069,614	3,358	10,504,912	1,551	822,862	3,180	3,310,158
Perfume/Soap/Candles	-	-	959	1,108,271	1,070	10,446,404	455	652,176	586	3,179,201
Beverages	1,523	124,475	4,420	1,256,689	3,039	12,332,422	1,569	839,544	1,381	3,163,498
Pharmaceuticals	-	-	547	741,209	506	9,594,386	319	840,442	441	2,516,804
Leather/Hides	1,297	185,257	2,099	1,000,974	2,350	6,867,979	657	349,194	555	1,596,384
Tobacco	178	132,404	252	793,819	278	6,105,585	352	383,411	103	1,563,684
Other	756	66,190	1,370	529,680	2,189	5,677,917	865	452,289	3,029	3,713,324
Total	40,983	9,015,138	82,164	59,035,652	108,163	631,422,538	37,261	46,949,051	70,859	309,550,420

Sources: AN 1956, p. 119; AN 1963, p. 72; AN 1971, pp. 185-297; AN 1978, pp. 447.

277

Table XII-3. Quantum Indices of Production by Brazilian Construction and Manufacturing Industries, 1939–75

	1939	1940	1941	1942	1943	1944	1945	1946	1947	1948	1949	1950	1951	1952	1953
Construction															
Total	51.0	54.0	59.1	55.5	68.3	57.1	67.3	85.6	90.2	93.9	100.0	101.7	115.4	126.0	134.6
Manufacturing															
Total	49.9	51.9	58.4	55.5	61.8	64.8	67.8	77.3	80.3	90.1	100.0	112.7	119.0	125.4	137.1
Non-Met. Mins.	–	–	–	–	–	–	–	–	75.5	91.1	100.0	107.9	113.6	125.3	150.6
Metals	–	–	–	–	–	–	–	–	66.2	83.9	100.0	127.0	139.7	145.8	166.6
Mechanical	–	–	–	–	–	–	–	–	–	–	–	–	–	–	–
Electrical	–	–	–	–	–	–	–	–	–	–	–	–	–	–	–
Trans. Equip.	–	–	–	–	–	–	–	–	–	–	–	–	–	–	–
Paper	–	–	–	–	–	–	–	–	78.9	86.3	100.0	114.5	120.6	120.9	134.6
Rubber	–	–	–	–	–	–	–	–	81.4	87.8	100.0	116.2	127.5	135.4	151.2
Chemicals	–	–	–	–	–	–	–	–	60.8	92.3	100.0	113.1	150.9	137.9	164.4
Textiles	–	–	–	–	–	–	–	–	88.8	93.4	100.0	106.5	102.8	108.5	114.1
Clothing	–	–	–	–	–	–	–	–	–	–	–	–	–	–	–
Food	–	–	–	–	–	–	–	–	80.1	87.9	100.0	111.5	115.6	117.0	124.5
Beverages	–	–	–	–	–	–	–	–	83.0	89.2	100.0	117.7	140.3	127.6	132.6
Tobacco	–	–	–	–	–	–	–	–	81.0	86.2	100.0	114.7	134.5	148.3	154.4

	1954	1955	1956	1957	1958	1959	1960	1961	1962	1963	1964	1965	1966	1967	1968
Construction															
Total	130.5	137.9	156.5	162.7	184.0	–	–	–	–	–	–	–	–	–	–
Manufacturing															
Total	150.0	166.4	176.7	186.5	217.7	245.7	271.8	301.9	100.0	99.7	104.8	99.8	112.1	114.8	133.0
Non-Met. Mins.	180.2	194.1	213.5	212.7	217.5	–	–	–	100.0	99.9	105.6	95.6	104.1	113.0	129.2
Metals	180.0	181.0	210.6	194.1	232.2	–	–	–	100.0	103.4	109.7	105.5	130.3	127.1	150.1
Mechanical	–	100.0	115.0	110.4	119.3	–	–	–	100.0	102.6	104.1	91.5	93.1	88.1	117.2
Electrical	–	100.0	158.9	155.9	261.4	–	–	–	100.0	96.2	105.2	116.4	145.9	159.8	197.5
Trans. Equip.	–	100.0	112.4	248.5	362.9	–	–	–	100.0	89.3	92.4	91.7	113.7	113.9	144.0
Paper	145.1	153.9	167.5	192.3	197.1	–	–	–	100.0	107.8	114.8	112.2	123.1	142.7	149.6
Rubber	172.1	175.7	166.5	167.5	174.4	–	–	–	100.0	100.9	107.6	101.2	128.5	139.0	157.0
Chemicals	183.6	430.0	576.1	587.2	684.7	–	–	–	100.0	103.6	113.8	109.7	126.6	130.9	147.2
Textiles	134.6	141.1	141.2	124.3	166.4	–	–	–	100.0	97.3	101.6	85.2	81.1	79.5	94.9
Clothing	–	100.0	105.1	106.1	129.2	–	–	–	100.0	100.8	113.0	100.7	114.8	108.2	129.5
Food	122.1	146.1	157.3	157.3	172.5	–	–	–	100.0	99.2	100.6	95.8	100.4	107.8	114.4
Beverages	130.8	138.8	131.1	131.1	142.8	–	–	–	100.0	102.0	91.3	99.1	119.0	104.2	108.1
Tobacco	177.8	194.3	206.0	217.2	234.3	–	–	–	100.0	100.5	99.2	94.5	96.9	106.1	119.8

	1969	1970	1971	1972	1973	1974	1975
Manufacturing							
Total	147.4	163.7	111.4	114.1	116.3	107.6	103.7
Non-Met. Mins.	136.9	171.7	104.4	113.7	116.3	114.8	109.0
Metals	171.7	181.8	115.7	115.6	109.4	105.2	109.4
Mechanical	127.1	148.1	124.3	123.5	128.2	111.0	107.4
Electrical	208.3	224.2	107.0	107.0	127.6	118.9	100.5
Trans. Equip.	193.7	225.2	112.9	113.0	109.4	104.3	85.4
Paper	154.8	181.5	109.6	116.3	112.4	110.8	102.7
Rubber	166.3	202.9	112.4	104.1	122.1	108.4	102.9
Chemicals	163.2	192.4	102.5	115.5	108.4	97.7	103.2
Textiles	97.3	97.2	–	–	110.6	106.5	101.2
Clothing	96.4	113.7	–	–	–	–	–
Food	130.2	142.8	–	–	–	–	–
Beverages	128.8	129.9	–	–	–	–	–
Tobacco	128.6	136.7	–	–	–	–	–

Non-Met. Mins. = Non-Metallic Minerals
Trans. Equip. = Transportation Equipment

Sources: Revista Brasileira de Economia,
March, 1962; Baer, p. 263;
AN 1973, p. 204; AN 1975, p. 237.

Table XII-4. Output of Brazilian Manufacturing Industries, 1853-1977

	Output	1911-1919	1920	1921-1929	1930	1931-1939	1940	1941-1949	1950	1951-1959	1960	1961-1969	1970	1971-1977
DURABLE GOODS														
Furniture	000 u	-	-	1547 a	2199	11042 h	-	-	-	-	-	-	-	-
Appliances	000 u	-	-	-	-	-	-	-	-	571500 h	-	-	-	2998322 g
Irons	000 u	-	-	-	-	-	-	-	-	488600 h	-	-	-	-
Radios	000 u	-	-	-	-	-	-	-	-	317600 h	-	-	-	-
Blenders	000 u	-	-	-	-	-	-	-	-	291900 h	-	-	-	-
Refrigerators	000 u	-	-	-	-	-	-	-	-	175100 h	-	-	-	-
Waxers	000 u	-	-	-	-	-	-	-	-	128200 h	-	-	-	2077430 g
Television Sets	000 u	-	-	-	-	-	-	-	-	119200 h	-	-	-	-
Fans	000 u	-	-	-	-	-	-	-	-	50100 h	-	-	-	-
Mixers	000 u	-	-	-	-	-	-	-	-	46400 h	-	-	-	-
Washing Machines	000 u	-	-	-	-	-	-	-	-	39500 h	-	-	-	-
Stoves/Heaters	000 u	-	-	-	-	-	-	-	-	33100 h	-	-	-	-
Vacuum Cleaners	000 u	-	-	-	-	-	-	-	-	-	-	-	-	-
Light Bulbs	mil u	-	-	691 a	215	14155 h	-	-	-	-	-	-	-	-
Batteries	mil u	-	-	29 b	99	148 h	-	-	-	-	-	-	-	-
Musical Instruments														
Records	000 u	116 e	262	-	681	743 h	-	-	-	-	-	-	-	-
String/Wind Instrs.	000 u	-	-	14 f	23	82 h	-	-	-	-	-	-	-	-
Combs	000 u	-	-	875 f	2324	6435 h	-	-	-	-	-	-	-	-
Brushes	000 u	-	-	2423 f	5863	10081 h	-	-	-	-	-	-	-	-
Dusters	000 u	-	-	896 f	581	301 h	-	-	-	-	-	-	-	-
Playing Cards	000 d	358 e	1018	53 f	93	1125 h	-	-	-	-	-	-	-	-
Toys	000 u	-	-	-	20	1652 h	-	-	-	-	-	-	-	-
Hand Tools	tons	7582 f	10830	-	17350	49362 h	-	-	-	-	-	-	-	-
Firearms	000 u	-	-	2 e	4	52 h	-	-	-	-	-	-	-	-
Rifle Balls	tons	-	-	771 a	558	2315 h	-	-	-	-	-	-	-	-
Cartridges	000 u	-	-	146 b	146	648 h	-	-	-	-	-	-	-	-
Cement/Glass/China														
Cement	tons	-	-	13382 f	87160	10363 h	744673	-	1385797	-	4474288	-	8975431	20527954 g
Glass	tons	674 e	2451	-	2303	8920 h	-	-	-	-	-	-	-	-
China	tons	176 e	2754	-	2353	-	-	-	-	-	-	-	-	-
Iron/Steel Products														
Steel Ingots	tons	-	-	4492 d	20985	-	141201	-	768557	-	1843019	-	5390360	9168899 f
Pig Iron Ingots	tons	-	14056	-	35305	-	185570	-	728979	-	1749848	-	4205247	8170228 f
Steel Alloys	tons	-	-	-	-	-	-	-	-	-	33548	-	-	311836 f
Rolled Steel Prods.	tons	-	-	283 e	25895	-	135293	-	623258	-	2769973	-	-	3290429 f
Steel Tubes	tons	-	-	-	-	-	-	-	-	-	93309	-	-	202888 f
Steel Wire	tons	-	-	-	-	-	-	-	-	-	105407	-	-	994803 f
Other I/S Prods.	tons	-	-	-	-	-	-	-	-	-	139620	-	-	2959220 f
Non-Ferrous Metals														
Aluminum Ingots	tons	-	-	-	-	-	-	-	-	-	18175	56069 l	-	-
Arsenic	tons	-	-	-	-	-	-	-	-	-	211	214 l	-	-
Copper	tons	-	-	-	-	-	-	-	-	-	-	3357 l	-	-
Lead	tons	-	-	-	-	-	-	-	-	-	4011	28096 l	-	-
Tin	tons	-	-	-	-	-	-	-	-	-	1332	2509 l	-	-
Gold	kg	-	-	-	-	-	-	-	-	-	3968	5354 l	-	-
Silver	tons	-	-	-	-	-	-	-	-	-	7867	12170 l	-	-

Table XII-4 (continued)

	Output	1951-1959	1960	1961-1969	1970	1971-1977
DURABLE GOODS						
Industrial Machinery						
Lathes & Similars	units	-	3700	-	-	9262 g
Drill Presses	units	-	3030	-	-	-
Saws/Shears	units	-	700	-	-	-
Planers/Slotters	units	-	400	-	-	-
Presses/Rollers/Power Hammers	units	-	2900	-	-	-
Milling Machines	units	-	250	-	-	-
Gearcutters	units	-	900	-	-	-
Diesel Motors (non-vehicular)	units	-	-	-	-	66479 g
Electrical Machinery						
Small Electric Motors	000 u	1500 i	-	-	-	3718 g
Generators	units	8700 i	-	-	-	-
Transformers/Reactors	000 u	24000 i	-	-	-	-
Agricultural/Highway Machinery						
Wheeled Tractors	units	-	37	-	14029	53696 g
Caterpillar Tractors	units	-	-	-	185	6405 g
Micro Tractors	units	-	-	-	409	-
Cultivators	units	-	12500	-	2047	-
Plows	units	-	28800	-	-	-
Reapers	units	-	3300	-	-	-
Harrows	units	-	2500	-	-	-
Pulverizers	units	-	648000	-	-	-
Drills/Seeders	units	-	74196	-	-	-
Threshing Machines	units	-	935	-	927	-
Road Graders	units	-	-	-	-	-
Excavators	units	-	-	-	-	415 g
Motor Vehicles						
Passenger Cars	units	2189 h	37843	-	250289	465657 g
Light/Medium Trucks	units	25713 h	35204	-	37374	⎤ 105588 g
Heavy Trucks	units	5213 h	6495	-	5066	⎦
Cargo/Passenger Vehicles	units	13692 h	34022	-	118514	⎤ 335502 g
Utilitarian (Jeep-types)	units	14322 h	19514	-	5151	⎦
Aircraft	units	-	-	14 g	54	672 g
Railway Equipment						
Passenger Cars	units	-	420	-	-	-
Freight Cars	units	-	7600	-	-	-
Ships	dwt	-	1550	-	88648	585560 f

Table XII-4 (continued)

	Output	1911-1919	1920	1921-1929	1930	1931-1939	1940	1941-1949	1950	1951-1959	1960	1961-1969	1970	1971-1977
NON DURABLE GOODS														
Meat/Meat Products														
Beef	tons							682943 c	955956		1196842		1663587	
Pork	tons							134451 c	121623		164274		290974	
Ham	tons								3692		5992		12021	
Mutton	tons							19566 c	18836		22005		34453	
Goat	tons							10008 c	12012		16981		21963	
Fowl	tons										5822		85661	
Rabbit	tons										8		42	
Bacon	tons								114086		163264		275468	
Sausage	tons								42437		60422		100341	
Lard	tons			48000 e	74000	8000 h			63067		87204		105347	
Extract	tons								198		312		660	
Viscera/Glands	tons			21500 e	23440	33703 h			41089		50923		81487	
Animal Fat	tons			38016 e	43800	51321 h	39546						69380	
Dairy Products														
Whole Milk	tons								161460		363955			
Powdered Milk	tons								7818		39876			
Condensed Milk	tons								18467		18523			
Butter	tons								24513		25318			
Cheese	tons								24073		39455			
Cream	tons								3552		6248			
Processed Seafood														
Fish	tons										56365			
Crustaceans	tons										8580			
Whale	tons										5969			
Mandioca Flour	tons		658115		1040967	1097065 h	675247	1118938 g	1032198					
Wheat Flour	tons						228198		327172					
Milled Wheat Residuals	tons		695262		1144178		893512		1403010					
Sugar	tons										3318719		5069919	8307690 g
Beverages														
Mineral Water	000 ll	181 a	553		7171	15385 h			37806		98293		913181	
Beer	000 ll	68084 a	81853		145610	183812 h						172657 1		
Grape Wine	000 ll	7115 e	13578		32789	56783 h		70154 g						
Cane Wine	000 ll	5086 e	10323		5833	7152 h								
Caxaca	000 ll	94557 g	94410		25327	62335 e		169058 g						
Soft Drinks	000 ll	9669 a	21952			33977 h								
Tobacco Products														
Cigarettes	mil pk	172 a	440			787				54000 h				
Cigars	000 u	113934 a	147145			190653 h				235 h				
Vegetable Oils/Fats														
Castor Oil	tons							8891 a	38455		54381		167270	
Soybean Oil	tons										16632		165717	
Cottonseed Oil	tons							112869 a	64041		92345		146574	
Peanut Oil	tons								21161		63183		131308	
Babacu Oil	tons							6784 a	27895		58175		85472	
Cocoa Butter	tons							4734 d	7957		18489		23765	
Oiticica Oil	tons							18191 a	12277		19555		18107	
Linseed Oil	tons							8883 a	11386		9348		7588	
Corn Oil	tons							832 a	1934		3025		7539	
Olive Oil	000 ll						8412 c							

Table XII-4 (continued)

NON DURABLE GOODS	Output	1911–1919	1920	1921–1929	1930	1931–1939	1940	1941–1949	1950	1951–1959	1960	1961–1969	1970	1971–1977
Vinegar	000 ll	6839 a	18187	-	16891	26695 h	-	-	-	-	-	-	-	-
Textiles														
Cotton (see Addenda)	000 m	378619 a	587187	-	476088	845984 h	840168	1142151 f	-	1252199 f	-	-	-	-
Jute	000 m	49001 a	54863	-	62042	28777 h	-	-	-	-	-	-	-	-
Linen	000 m	302 e	2441	-	89	26663 h	-	-	-	17491 f	-	-	-	-
Wool	000 m	1307 m	3157	-	4932	7652 h	-	-	-	29673 f	-	-	-	-
Reed	000 m	225 f	488	-	258	179 h	-	-	-	-	-	-	-	-
Silk	tons	49 f	49	-	498	4106 h	-	-	-	1359446 f	-	-	-	-
Cloth Articles														
Shirts	000 u	1559 e	7826	-	6425	11275 g	-	-	-	12380 f	-	-	-	-
Pants	000 pr	96 e	977	-	1746	3862 g	-	-	-	-	-	-	-	-
Napkins	000 u	-	1717	-	3129	10522 g	-	-	-	-	-	-	-	-
Blankets	000 u	975 a	3441	-	2903	14806 h	-	-	-	-	-	-	-	-
Sheets	000 u	4695 g	2780	-	5523	21200 h	-	-	-	-	-	-	-	-
Carpets	000 u	-	50	-	85	183 h	-	-	-	-	-	-	-	-
Pijamas	000 u	-	-	111 c	321	637 h	-	-	-	-	-	-	-	-
Curtains	000 u	-	-	146 f	68	914 h	-	-	-	1369 f	-	-	-	-
Suits	000 u	-	-	57 f	485	1960 h	-	-	-	-	-	-	-	-
Sacks	000 u	-	-	-	-	44299 c	-	-	-	-	-	-	-	-
Stockings	000 pr	8866 e	19054	-	28854	56059 h	-	-	-	-	-	-	-	-
Gloves	000 pr	-	-	28 d	66	710 h	-	-	-	-	-	-	-	-
Hats	000 u	18343 a	29950	35693 e	35573	33417 h	-	-	-	-	-	-	-	-
Leather	tons	-	-	-	36804	46988 h	-	-	138524	-	176061	-	241210	-
Cowhide	tons	-	-	-	-	-	-	-	-	-	170228	-	234903	-
Pigskin	tons	-	-	-	-	-	-	-	3551	-	5833	-	6307	-
Hides	tons	-	-	3289 e	3434	3310 h	-	-	-	-	3560	-	5971	-
Sheepskin	tons	-	-	-	-	-	-	-	1696	-	1861	-	1643	-
Goatskin	tons	-	-	-	-	-	-	-	978	-	1369	-	1643	-
Leather Goods														
Suitcases	000 u	-	-	1193 g	382	803 g	-	-	-	-	-	-	-	-
Pocketbooks	000 u	-	-	156 h	70	1784. g	-	-	-	-	-	-	-	-
Portfolios	000 u	-	-	61 h	38	201 g	-	-	-	-	-	-	-	-
Billfolds	000 u	-	-	1103 h	608	1478 g	-	-	-	-	-	-	-	-
Belts	000 u	-	-	963 h	-	2916 g	-	-	-	-	-	-	-	-
Soccer Balls	000 u	-	-	32 h	-	44 g	-	-	-	-	-	-	-	-
Whips	000 u	-	-	324 h	242	364 g	-	-	-	-	-	-	-	-
Reins	000 u	-	-	244 h	146	1722 g	-	-	-	-	-	-	-	-
Saddles	000 u	-	-	151 h	119	157	-	-	-	-	-	-	-	-
Boots/Shoes/Sandals	000 pr	12577 a	19214	-	24784	37259 h	-	-	-	-	53000	-	-	-
Paper/Paper Products	tons	-	-	-	25245	103260 h	-	-	247894	-	474383	-	1498910	2045969 g
Printing Paper	tons	-	-	-	-	-	-	-	65068	-	108521	-	639126	369191 g
Writing Paper	tons	-	-	-	-	-	-	-	33413	-	59641	-	118188	212392 g
Packaging Paper	tons	-	-	-	23543	96009 h	-	-	112158	-	219910	-	509379	966689 g
Industrial Paper	tons	-	-	-	-	-	-	-	15181	-	44088	-	98611	206615 g
Cardboard	tons	-	-	-	-	-	-	-	22074	-	42223	-	133606	291082 g
Alcohol	000 ll	44046 e	120099	-	111018	122683 h	-	-	134935	-	476263	-	625349	1391341 g
Anhydrous	000 ll	-	25690	-	-	-	-	-	-	-	185570	-	233038	1088082 g
Hydrated	000 ll	-	94409	-	-	-	-	-	-	-	287693	-	392311	303259 g

Table XII-4 (continued)

	Output	1911–1919	1920	1921–1929	1930	1931–1939	1940	1941–1949	1950	1951–1959	1960	1961–1969	1970	1971–1977
NON DURABLE GOODS														
Organic Chemicals														
Esters	tons										15460			
Ethers	tons										11000			
Aldehydes	tons										10290			
Fatty Acids/Glycerin	tons										6500			
Acetic Acid	1t/t	5400 f	3500		8700	3900 h					4500			38883 g
Ketones	tons										4170			
Phthalic Acid	tons										1781			
Citric Acid	tons										1450			
Sodium Formate	tons										1141			
Oxalic Acid	tons										900			
Formic Acid	tons										506			
Benzyl Chloride	tons										23			
Essential Oils														
Sassafras	kgs							17000 a			650000			
Japanese Mint	kgs							324000 a			650000			
Rosewood	kgs										570000			
Citriodora Eucalyptus	kgs										135000			
Globulous Eucalyptus	kgs										8000			
Lemongrass	kgs										7000			
Palmrose	kgs										1500			
Citronella	kgs										3000			
Vetyver	kgs										4000			
Lemon	kgs										12000			
Orange	kgs										25000			
Tangerine	kgs										30000			
Geranium	kgs										100			
Eucalyptus Staegerena	kgs										2500			
Petroleum Products														
Gasoline	000 b						166		162		21372		60071	86660 g
Kerosene	000 b						57		52		4031		7887	6425 g
Diesel Oil	000 b						69		151		9910		41692	82657 g
Bunker Oil	000 b/tons						41		89		23575		53079	15745 g
Lubricating Oil	000 b										17666		5120	11503 g
Jet Fuel	000 b										1101			
Stanship	kgs										200			
Lighter Fluid	000 b													321355000 g
Greases	tons										6			
Candles	tons	4184 a	4512		6645	6109 h								
Paint/Varnish														
Water/Alcohol Base	t/000 ll			710 e	1473	5503 h				11800 h				
Oil Base	t/000 ll									17400 h				
Other Paint	t/000 ll			66 e	75	1423 h				23400 h				
Varnish	t/000 ll		609		848	601 h				6200 h				
Matches	mil	525 a		21 g	1076	68773 h			1353620		3252515		8456157	17295000 g
Rubber Products														
Motor Vehicle Tires	units			6 g	2130	58002 h			882906		2274434		5097718	
Motor Vehicle Tubes	units								817118		2694736		3030739	
Bicycle Tires	units								811486		2351836		2566233	
Bicycle Tubes	units													
Raincoats	units	5794 f			9427	73706 h								

Table XII-4 (continued)

NON DURABLE GOODS	Output	1951-1959	1960	1961-1969	1970	1971-1977
Soap						
Laundry Soap	tons	231000 h	-	-	-	-
Toilet Soap	tons	25 h	-	-	-	-
Paste/Powder/Flakes	tons	5000 h	-	-	-	-
Pharmaceuticals						
Penicillin	tril u	-	80	-	-	-
Pure Streptomycin	tons	-	21	-	-	-
Pure Tetracyclin	kgs	-	9400	-	-	-
Pure Aureo-/Achromycin	kgs	-	3900	-	-	-
Pure Terramycin	kgs	-	2000	-	-	-
Pure Sygmamycin	kgs	-	1000	-	-	-
Nystatin	kgs	-	1200	-	-	-
Acetylsalicylic Acid	tons	-	384	-	-	-
Vitamin B1	tons	-	11	-	-	-
Vitamin B2	tons	-	6	-	-	-
Vitamin B12	mil mcg	-	2.9	-	-	-
Insecti-/Fungi-/Herbicides						
Insecticides	tons	39000 h	-	-	-	18566 f
Fungicides	tons	-	-	-	-	7738 f
Herbicides	tons	-	-	-	-	9328 f
Synthetic Rubber	tons	-	-	-	-	1500 f
Coal Tar Chemicals	000 t	-	-	-	71707	152410 f
Asphalt	tons	-	220991	-	702295	909164 f
Road Tar	tons	-	20812	-	-	-
Crude Tar	tons	-	18512	-	-	-
Coal Tar	tons	-	4720	-	-	-
Water Gas Tar	tons	-	2325	-	-	-
Benzol	tons	-	5782	-	-	-
Solvent Naphtha	t/m3	-	520	-	-	-
Crude Naphthalene	tons	-	1540	-	43941	2287479 f
Anthracene	tons	-	540	-	-	-
Creosote Oil	tons	-	2310	-	-	-
Disinfectant Oil	tons	-	891	-	-	-
Pitch	tons	-	2760	-	-	-
Tolul	tons	-	996	-	-	70983 g
Xylol	tons	-	198	-	-	-
Paraffin	b/t	-	-	129508 b	25756	62354 f
Inorganic Chemicals						
Soda Ash	tons	-	20073	-	-	141488 g
Caustic Soda	tons	-	77000	-	-	259000 f
Chlorine	tons	-	58000	-	-	-
Lime	tons	-	1300000	-	-	-
Sulfuric Acid	tons	-	359500	-	-	-
Hydrochloric Acid	tons	-	54700	-	-	-
Nitric Acid	tons	-	78200	-	-	-
Hydroflouric Acid	tons	-	800	-	-	-
Chromic Acid	tons	-	1200	-	-	-
Arsenous Anhydride	tons	-	1500	-	-	-
Zinc Oxide	tons	-	6100	-	-	-
Iron Oxide	tons	-	480	-	-	-
Titanium Oxide	tons	-	1100	-	-	-
Ferrous Oxide	tons	-	2300	-	-	-

	Output	1960	1970	1971-1977
Inorganic Chemicals (continued)				
Ultramarine Blue	tons	1650	-	-
Prussian Blue	tons	565	-	-
Red Lead	tons	1350	-	-
Zinc Yellow	tons	868	-	-
Chromium Pigments	tons	720	-	-
Aluminum Sulfate	tons	51400	-	59699 g
Sodium Sulfate	tons	1820	-	-
Sodium Bisulfate	tons	11500	-	-
Ammonium Sulfate	tons	7370	-	-
Copper Sulfate	tons	3000	-	-
Chromium Sulfate	tons	1100	-	-
Sodium Bichromate	tons	4450	-	-
Sodium Sulfide	tons	8220	-	-
Hydrogen Peroxide	tons	3150	-	-
Carbon Dioxide	tons	10000	-	-
Calcium Chloride	tons	4100	-	-
Potassium Chlorate	tons	3100	-	-
Sodium Phosphate	tons	2400	-	-
Calcium Hypochlorite	tons	3800	-	-
Sodium Hypochlorite	tons	4950	-	-
Ammonia	tons	160000	-	-
Oxygen	m3	29998700	-	-
Nitrogen	m3	16727500	-	-
Hydrogen	m3	450000	-	-
Acetylene	m3	350000	-	-
Freon	tons	1250	-	-
Chemical Fertilizers				
Bicalcic Phosphate	tons	-	2570	1211313 f
Simple Superphosphate (18-20%)	tons	208948	594230	576766 f
Superphosphate (30%)	tons	-	52000	56465 f
Concentrated Superphosphate	tons	-	-	134081 f
Thermophosphate	tons	-	23500	505714 f
Ammonium Phosphates	tons	-	49436	-
Raw Natural Phosphates	tons	74731	141956	-
Milled Natural Phosphates	tons	170249	31012	100239 f
Ammonium Sulfate	tons	7371	7134	38202 f
Nitrocalcic	tons	⌐69564	21790	100015 f
Ammonium Nitrate	tons	⌐	17441	144305 f
Urea	tons	-	-	54983 f
Petrochemicals				
Ethylene	tons	4478	9928	18213 f
Propane	tons	1039	9602	105284 f
Aromatic Residue	tons	75802	2121	-
Liquid Petroleum Gas	tons	246146	687773	1909459 g
Hexane	tons	7940	37711	78734 f
Rubber Solvents	tons	9350	29887	54348 f
Turpentine Solvents	tons	20654	101769	140556 f
Styrene	tons	6000	-	-
Polystyrene	tons	10350	-	-
Carbon Black	tons	1600	-	-
Polyethylene	tons	4500	-	253292 g

Table XII-4 (continued)

NON DURABLE GOODS	Output	1960	1971-1977
Synthetic Fibers			
Filament/Yarn/Monofilament	000 lb	106100	294212 g
High Tenacity Rayon	000 lb	26400	-
Other Viscose/Cupra Rayon	000 lb	29100	-
Acetate/Triacetate	000 lb	10600	-
Non-Cellulose Fibers	000 lb	11100	-
Staple and Tow			
Viscose/Cupra Rayon	000 lb	26600	-
Acetate/Triacetate	000 lb	1300	-
Non-Cellulose Fibers	000 lb	1000	-
Plastic Materials/Synthetic Resins			
Urea Formaldehyde Molding Compounds	tons	6680	-
Phenol Formaldehyde Molding Cmpds.	tons	3410	
Polyvinyl Chloride	tons	13500	160145 g
Monomer Vinyl Acetate	tons	1850	-
Casein Glues	tons	1500	-
Alkyd Resins	tons	1450	-
Melamine Resins	tons	850	-
Maleic Resins	tons	900	-
Polyester Resins	tons	820	-
Ester Gums	tons	375	-
Galalith	tons	240	-
Nylon Molding Powders	tons	635	-

Explanations and Addenda

Key to Nine-Year Date Groupings
a = 1st year
b = 2nd year
c = 3rd year
d = 4th year
e = 5th year
f = 6th year
g = 7th year
h = 8th year
i = 9th year

Abbreviations for Outputs
b = barrels
d = decks
dwt = deadweight tons (metric)
kg = kilograms
ll = liters
lb = pounds (16 ounces)
m = meters
m3 = cubic meters
mcg = micrograms
mil = millions
pk = packs
pr = pairs
t = tons (metric)
tons = metric tons
tril = trillions
u = units

Products With Dual Output Measures
acetic acid: 1916-1938 in liters; 1960 & 1977 in tons
bunker oil: 1940-1970 in barrels; 1977 in 1,000 tons
paint/varnish: 1925-1938 in tons; 1978 in 1,000 liters
solvent naphtha: 1960 in tons; 1970 & 1976 in cubic meters
paraffin: 1962 in barrels; 1970 & 1976 in tons
silk: 1911-1938 in tons; 1956 in meters

Cotton Textile Output in 1,000 Meters
1853	1,210
1866	3,586
1882	22,000
1885	20,595
1905	242,087

Sources: Stein, 1957, p. 191; AN 1939-40, pp. 1,320-1,335; AN 1951, pp. 126-158; AN 1956, pp. 134-157; Heare, 1961, pp. 115-128; AN 1963, pp. 129-158; AN 1972, pp. 206-255; AN 1977, pp. 437-565

Table XII-5. Capital Invested in Brazil's Manufacturing Industries by Industry Group, 1907-74

	1907		1920		1940		1950	
	Estabs	Cr$ 1000	Estabs	Cr$ 1000	Estabs	Cr$ 1000	Estabs	Cr$ 1000
Metals	214	27,547	380	58,720	1,460	871,926	2,221	5,450,868
Food	749	146,182	2,734	366,844	14,905	3,438,286	32,795	9,181,086
Chemicals	153	20,354	134	41,770	1,784	993,405	2,658	4,107,639
Mechanical Equipment	13	1,455	116	5,607	694	391,091	762	727,739
Transportation Equipment	48	10,645	232	19,617	–	–	539	1,083,359
Textiles	202	270,900	1,135	698,251	2,212	3,113,684	2,941	8,904,221
Non-Metallic Minerals	266	27,707	1,823	57,608	4,861	467,100	12,777	3,080,667
Electrical/Communication Equipment	2	56	3	1,050	–	–	341	581,457
Wood/Wood Products	201	14,508	1,190	99,879	5,614	461,648	7,562	1,953,254
Paper/Paper Products	23	6,679	59	29,026	228	304,758	441	1,689,282
Plastics/Plastic Articles	–	–	–	–	–	–	–	–
Beverages	443	37,314	1,093	106,891	1,701	493,446	4,354	1,770,763
Printing/Publishing	–	–	–	–	2,207	354,016	2,749	1,774,613
Clothing/Shoes/Cloth Articles	337	31,656	2,076	105,891	3,218	267,794	5,076	767,203
Rubber/Rubber Products	2	13	14	2,470	65	144,521	119	429,423
Furniture	85	6,033	545	19,790	–	–	2,882	538,269
Pharmaceuticals	–	–	186	10,853	–	–	–	–
Perfume/Soap/Candles	117	17,316	381	49,627	1,297	177,407	2,104	514,894
Leather/Hides	148	12,002	723	44,364	–	–	252	279,437
Tobacco	104	12,951	296	49,858	653	83,489	1,581	696,630
Other	141	22,258	216	47,040	–	–	–	–
Total	3,258	665,576	13,336	1,815,156	40,899	11,564,960	82,154	43,530,804

	1960		1969		1974	
	Estabs	Cr$ 1000	Infrmts	Cr$ 1000	Infrmts	Cr$ 1000
Metals	4,850	45,190,379	1,216	554,833	4,708	5,743,079
Food	33,534	68,416,369	2,951	584,115	10,009	4,745,005
Chemicals	1,774	36,616,661	682	427,178	1,653	4,107,756
Mechanical Equipment	1,692	17,651,169	789	204,350	3,671	3,410,936
Transportation Equipment	2,096	37,875,003	425	494,257	1,365	2,837,427
Textiles	4,272	49,162,447	1,216	373,803	2,729	2,767,566
Non-Metallic Minerals	18,146	24,397,639	1,378	322,588	3,647	2,122,390
Electrical/Communication Equipment	982	14,136,053	461	197,158	1,451	1,363,857
Wood/Wood Products	11,196	13,205,237	1,477	103,186	4,137	1,149,340
Paper/Paper Products	764	10,305,312	309	163,074	971	1,117,111
Plastics/Plastic Articles	295	2,193,183	269	74,243	1,218	882,088
Beverages	3,044	12,771,607	518	110,241	884	796,896
Printing/Publishing	3,389	10,493,171	780	114,076	2,347	784,298
Clothing/Shoes/Cloth Articles	7,639	6,268,585	969	107,292	3,506	693,279
Rubber/Rubber Products	339	6,636,376	200	77,975	614	524,395
Furniture	8,160	5,374,369	911	35,761	2,426	441,738
Pharmaceuticals	504	5,242,255	201	51,586	357	347,665
Perfume/Soap/Candles	1,071	2,772,405	166	41,304	356	193,630
Leather/Hides	2,350	3,667,727	298	19,707	392	151,283
Tobacco	278	2,292,714	69	42,927	66	138,738
Other	2,218	4,099,800	410	38,499	2,005	886,475
Total	108,593	378,768,462	15,695	4,138,158	48,512	35,204,952

Sources: RE 1920E1, pp. XIII-XXII; AN 1948, p. 116; RE 1950C1, p. 18; AN 1966, p. 117; AN 1971, p. 182; AN 1977, p. 428.

Table XII-6. Numbers of Establishments, Total Workers, and Production Workers in Brazilian Manufacturing Industry Groups by Size, 1920-74

1920

		Establishment Size in Total Production Workers									
Number of Establishments	Total	None	1-4	5-9	10-19	20-49	50-99	100-249	250-499	500-999	1000+
Total	13,336	421	6,497	3,181	1,493	920	342	392 ——————		61	29
Textiles	1,211		177 ————		697 ————	78	54		205 ————		
Food	3,969		———— 2,573 ————		1,045 ————	188	77		86		
Metals	509		166 ————		198 ————	82	28		35		
Non-Metallic Minerals	1,590		810 ————		638 ————	94	25		23		
Transportation Equipment	533		358 ————		142 ————	18	6		9		
Clothing/Shoes/Cloth Articles	1,988		1,092 ————		636 ————	151	54		55		
Chemicals	950		571 ————		229 ————	84	34		32		
Furniture	548		207 ————		253 ————	58	18		12		
Leather/Hides	424		236 ————		135 ————	31	13		9		
Construction	533		358 ————		142 ————	18	6		9		
Electric Power Plants	29		14 ————		10 ————	3	–		2		
Luxury Industries	47		16 ————		20 ————	8	2		1		
Number of Production Workers											
Total	275,512	–	15,769	20,357	19,631	27,878	23,585	79,172 ——————		43,063	46,057

1940

	Number of Establishments	Total Workers in Establishments	Total Production Workers in Establishments
Total	40,725	806,734	662,264
Textiles	2,212	233,433	216,477
Food	14,905	173,535	125,736
Metals	1,460	61,338	53,884
Non-Metallic Minerals	4,861	57,416	46,466
Clothing/Shoes/Cloth Articles	3,218	49,317	40,866
Chemicals/Pharmaceuticals	1,610	36,008	27,429
Mechanical Equipment	694	25,624	21,535
Printing/Publishing	2,207	31,617	22,120
Wood/Wood Products	5,614	66,088	50,901
Paper/Paper Products	228	12,318	10,642
Beverages	1,701	29,932	21,751
Rubber/Rubber Products	65	4,524	3,707
Leather/Hides	1,297	14,598	11,587
Other	653	10,971	9,203

Table XII-6 (continued)

1950

Establishment Size in Total Production Workers

Number of Establishments

	Total	None	1-5	6-10	11-20	21-50	51-100	101-250	251-500	500-1000	1000+
Total	82,154	10,815	46,363	10,486	6,749	4,470	1,532	1,060	401	180	98
Textiles	2,941	98	631	499	496	479	225	216	137	100	60
Food	32,975										
Beverages	4,354	6,058	23,835	3,744	2,207	979	246	206	85	28	13
Tobacco	252										
Metals	2,221										
Mechanical Equipment	762										
Electrical/Communication Equipment	341	287	1,317	575	581	567	249	186	68	20	13
Transportation Equipment	539										
Non-Metallic Minerals	12,777	899	8,450	1,843	777	493	177	91	36	8	3
Clothing/Shoes/Cloth Articles	5,076	513	9,990	765	580	452	134	81	11	5	-
Chemicals/Pharmaceuticals	2,658	433	1,127	359	282	238	103	77	30	5	4
Wood/Wood Products	7,562	1,407	5,292	1,748	1,060	687	178	65	-----7-----		-
Furniture	2,882										
Paper/Paper Products	441										
Rubber/Rubber Products	119										
Leather/Hides	2,104	1,120	3,176	953	766	575	220	138	29	-----17-----	
Printing/Publishing	2,749										
Other	1,581										

Total Workers in Establishments

	Total	None	1-5	6-10	11-20	21-50	51-100	101-250	251-500	500-1000	1000+
Total	1,309,614	15,230	156,052	90,431	107,409	156,880	120,276	183,321	154,898	136,366	188,751
Textiles	338,035	119	2,456	4,311	8,176	17,330	17,492	37,234	50,707	75,382	124,828
Food	234,311										
Beverages	39,253	7,805	72,604	28,254	27,456	27,368	18,446	34,821	33,359	21,114	15,345
Tobacco	13,008										
Metals	102,826										
Mechanical Equipment	26,600										
Electrical/Communication Equipment	15,774	483	5,925	5,904	10,657	21,340	19,346	33,981	28,513	14,801	24,432
Transportation Equipment	20,182										
Non-Metallic Minerals	128,928	1,434	28,297	14,975	12,735	16,647	13,787	14,652	14,155	6,799	5,447
Clothing/Shoes/Cloth Articles	76,464	645	10,111	7,193	10,129	16,572	10,468	13,247	4,189	3,910	-
Chemicals/Pharmaceuticals	73,472	593	4,432	3,955	5,773	10,314	8,679	13,475	11,082	4,160	11,009
Wood/Wood Products	68,486	1,988	19,459	16,068	18,289	24,583	13,306	10,415	-----3,180-----		-
Furniture	38,802										
Paper/Paper Products	24,959										
Rubber/Rubber Products	10,861										
Leather/Hides	21,196	2,163	12,768	9,771	14,194	22,726	18,752	25,496	10,981	---- 16,622 ----	
Printing/Publishing	49,367										
Other	27,090										

Total Production Workers in Establishments

	Total	None	1-5	6-10	11-20	21-50	51-100	101-250	251-500	500-1000	1000+
Total	1,095,059	-	99,220	71,116	89,489	134,802	105,541	162,428	137,898	124,328	170,237
Textiles	308,501	-	1,644	3.383	6,837	15,288	15,954	34,632	47,280	70,252	113,231
Food	178,476										
Beverages	28,919	-	44,127	21,470	22,485	22,720	15,418	30,779	29,603	18,572	13,760
Tobacco	11,539										
Metals	89,682										
Mechanical Equipment	22,281										
Electrical/Communication Equipment	13,939	-	3,919	4,674	8,938	18,716	17,361	29,701	23,948	12,635	21,669
Transportation Equipment	15,659										
Non-Metallic Minerals	107,372	-	18,825	12,314	11,131	15,117	12,755	13,234	12,786	6,294	4,916
Clothing/Shoes/Cloth Articles	65,725	-	7,027	5,965	8,812	14,639	9,470	12,230	3,975	3,607	-
Chemicals/Pharmaceuticals	59,060	-	2,627	2,770	4,148	7,853	6,871	11,481	8,995	3,874	10,441
Wood/Wood Products	55,265	-	12,785	12,986	15,662	21,763	12,106	9,588	-----2,953-----		-
Furniture	32,538										
Paper/Paper Products	22,261										
Rubber/Rubber Products	8,861										
Leather/Hides	17,455	-	8,266	7,554	11,516	18,706	15,606	20,783	9,509	----14,163----	
Printing/Publishing	34,766										
Other	22,760										

Table XII- 6 (continued)

1960

				Establishment Size in Total Workers							
Number of Establishments	Total	Unknown	1-4	5-9	10-19	20-49	50-99	100-249	250-499	500-999	1,000+
Total	108,593	1,252	65,442	20,381	9,951	6,398	2,465	1,572	664	307	161
Textiles	4,272	20	1,396	693	703	601	295	232	175	98	59
Food	33,534	380	24,472	5,587	1,579	821	315	233	98	39	10
Metals	4,850	8	2,142	966	696	503	226	180	80	27	22
Non-Metallic Minerals	18,146	605	11,416	3,762	1,291	672	203	125	36	29	7
Transportation Equipment	2,096	3	981	391	265	227	100	72	34	11	12
Electrical/Communication Equipment	982	-	272	157	168	177	86	75	28	13	6
Clothing/Shoes/Cloth Articles	7,639	18	4,149	1,638	864	608	222	107	23	7	3
Chemicals	1,774	13	721	294	272	238	104	76	32	12	12
Mechanical Equipment	1,692	3	501	330	318	298	126	74	22	16	4
Printing/Publishing	3,389	6	1,518	844	512	306	101	63	24	12	3
Wood/Wood Products	11,196	60	6,692	2,273	1,285	661	167	51	6	1	-
Furniture	8,160	16	5,491	1,429	675	381	109	43	12	2	2
Paper/Paper Products	764	6	161	142	160	135	67	60	18	12	3
Beverages	3,044	82	1,746	627	330	145	60	30	13	6	5
Pharmaceuticals	504	-	113	98	100	85	48	32	18	8	2
Plastics/Plastic Articles	295	-	81	60	58	52	27	11	4	1	1
Rubber/Rubber Products	339	-	72	84	61	62	32	15	7	1	5
Leather/Hides	2,350	11	1,638	295	186	125	64	23	6	1	1
Tobacco	278	5	123	47	41	19	17	12	6	6	2
Perfume/Soap/Candles	1,071	10	653	177	112	68	24	18	8	1	-
Other	2,218	6	1,104	487	275	214	72	40	14	4	2
Total Workers in Establishments											
Total	1,753,662	-	150,669	130,397	133,450	194,409	170,202	241,050	231,048	204,102	298,335
Textiles	328,297	-	2,805	4,665	9,260	18,528	20,406	37,404	63,012	67,011	104,846
Food	266,103	-	55,666	34,812	20,555	24,360	22,026	35,974	32,966	25,360	14,384
Metals	174,279	-	4,937	6,246	9,440	15,296	15,393	27,139	27,944	18,794	49,090
Non-Metallic Minerals	163,680	-	27,561	23,340	17,034	20,145	13,712	18,478	12,028	18,677	12,705
Transportation Equipment	81,876	-	2,232	2,571	3,561	6,972	7,034	10,578	12,003	7,771	29,154
Electrical/Communication Equipment	57,904	-	652	1,043	2,298	5,552	6,167	11,891	9,811	9,053	11,437
Clothing/Shoes/Cloth Articles	97,999	-	10,004	10,601	11,654	18,364	15,302	15,690	7,865	4,597	3,922
Chemicals	76,518	-	1,641	1,973	3,721	7,357	7,314	11,831	10,884	7,867	23,930
Mechanical Equipment	62,148	-	1,216	2,257	4,335	9,237	8,798	10,948	7,922	10,356	7,079
Printing/Publishing	60,625	-	3,927	5,622	6,967	9,392	6,851	8,789	8,415	7,455	3,207
Wood/Wood Products	87,822	-	14,952	15,002	17,184	19,590	11,097	7,520	1,926	551	-
Furniture	63,471	-	12,285	9,113	9,162	11,542	7,443	6,191	4,313	1,237	2,185
Paper/Paper Products	40,925	-	428	976	2,239	4,215	4,580	9,572	6,102	7,759	5,054
Beverages	43,880	-	4,226	4,048	4,386	4,411	4,131	4,988	4,204	3,631	9,855
Pharmaceuticals	27,066	-	268	664	1,374	2,727	3,379	4,937	6,166	4,867	2,684
Plastics/Plastic Articles	9,683	-	214	395	804	1,658	1,804	1,651	1,374	541	1,242
Rubber/Rubber Products	20,878	-	193	555	810	2,082	2,316	2,646	2,329	514	9,433
Leather/Hides	24,715	-	3,343	1,873	2,485	4,027	4,514	3,645	1,875	634	2,319
Tobacco	42,922	-	310	303	579	595	1,136	2,113	1,950	3,559	2,624
Perfume/Soap/Candles	14,714	-	1,406	1,152	1,489	2,072	1,733	3,026	2,946	890	-
Other	37,910	-	2,403	3,186	3,753	6,287	5,066	6,039	5,013	2,978	3,185
Total Production Workers in Establishments											
Total	1,390,043	-	79,702	97,530	107,825	163,497	144,068	200,811	189,283	165,210	242,117
Textiles	297,303	-	1,278	3,381	7,817	16,201	18,273	34,310	58,351	62,172	95,520
Food	192,493	-	30,294	25,067	15,650	19,321	17,693	29,224	26,200	17,125	11,919
Metals	146,991	-	2,269	4,512	7,601	12,841	13,319	23,159	23,346	15,951	43,993
Non-Metallic Minerals	131,705	-	15,680	18,662	14,600	17,797	12,232	15,930	10,460	15,689	10,655
Transportation Equipment	60,910	-	1,003	1,801	2,852	5,827	5,891	8,667	9,471	6,000	19,398
Electrical/Communication Equipment	43,998	-	301	721	1,821	4,584	5,067	9,337	8,164	6,666	7,337
Clothing/Shoes/Cloth Articles	82,564	-	5,305	8,175	9,839	16,355	13,916	14,374	7,187	3,965	3,448
Chemicals	54,981	-	837	1,357	2,758	5,661	5,564	9,171	7,454	5,608	16,571
Mechanical Equipment	48,420	-	528	1,600	3,479	7,658	7,286	9,008	6,003	7,659	5,199
Printing/Publishing	42,992	-	2,202	4,197	5,573	7,506	5,415	6,660	5,750	3,970	1,899
Wood/Wood Products	69,640	-	7,523	11,661	14,254	17,346	9,932	6,746	1,647	531	-
Furniture	48,619	-	6,046	6,778	7,664	10,058	6,708	5,437	3,484	837	1,607
Paper/Paper Products	34,237	-	274	756	1,840	3,637	4,019	8,230	4,850	6,735	3,896
Beverages	28,830	-	2,240	2,937	3,306	3,196	2,765	2,779	2,727	2,727	6,153
Pharmaceuticals	13,229	-	106	432	873	1,697	1,946	2,496	2,427	2,273	979
Plastics/Plastic Articles	7,482	-	96	288	653	1,398	1,536	1,259	934	351	967
Rubber/Rubber Products	15,378	-	103	393	640	1,700	1,947	2,238	1,784	288	6,280
Leather/Hides	19,833	-	1,650	1,421	2,007	3,483	4,069	3,301	1,660	597	1,645
Tobacco	10,832	-	168	223	507	499	1,006	1,502	1,504	2,933	2,490
Perfume/Soap/Candles	9,475	-	696	800	1,060	1,473	1,235	1,962	1,582	667	-
Other	30,131	-	1,103	2,368	3,031	5,259	4,249	5,021	4,298	2,646	2,161

289

Table XII-6 (continued)

1968

Number of Establishments	Total	None	1-4	5-9	10-19	20-49	50-99	100-249	250-499	500-999	1,000+
Total	37,016	897	6,788	8,099	7,129	6,911	3,372	2,259	911	442	208
Textiles	2,008	31	59	182	316	484	308	286	170	126	46
Food	8,781	277	2,344	2,823	1,525	894	383	349	138	40	8
Metals	1,971	11	36	209	315	558	359	213	94	44	32
Non-Metallic Minerals	4,318	207	1,351	889	658	654	310	144	58	35	12
Transportation Equipment	692	6	99	80	91	107	92	105	61	29	22
Electrical/Communication Equipment	666	6	30	48	80	160	134	103	57	25	23
Clothing/Shoes/Cloth Articles	2,346	39	324	366	473	604	311	165	44	15	5
Chemicals	1,479	53	223	242	297	310	148	127	44	22	13
Mechanical Equipment	1,197	5	39	125	233	336	223	157	48	20	11
Printing/Publishing	1,562	4	83	323	491	393	133	85	29	14	7
Wood/Wood Products	3,837	88	588	953	1,013	850	250	76	14	3	2
Furniture	2,584	45	472	660	652	499	182	57	11	5	1
Paper/Paper Products	524	6	23	32	58	162	115	89	21	15	3
Beverages	1,582	70	453	461	273	170	70	55	15	10	5
Pharmaceuticals	313	–	19	46	46	70	41	47	27	15	2
Plastics/Plastic Articles	394	3	24	45	85	116	52	43	15	7	4
Rubber/Rubber Products	333	4	26	65	74	67	50	25	12	4	6
Leather/Hides	698	16	160	108	139	159	67	38	10	–	1
Tobacco	374	–	113	186	14	19	14	9	11	7	1
Perfume/Soap/Candles	472	15	124	105	94	68	33	17	13	2	1
Other	855	11	98	151	202	231	97	69	19	4	3
Total Workers in Establishments											
Total	2,026,320	–	18,811	53,965	97,803	214,826	236,012	350,936	316,006	304,633	349,377
Textiles	308,345	–	175	1,278	4,421	15,523	21,873	45 363	59 667	86,350	73,695
Food	239,867	–	6,592	18,525	20,158	27,416	26,608	55,083	47,647	26,926	10,912
Metals	233,533	–	363	1,474	4,447	17,686	25,158	33,931	32,539	30,001	87,934
Non-Metallic Minerals	146,970	–	3,764	5,651	9,198	20,482	21,543	21,542	20,593	23,017	21,180
Transportation Equipment	150,607	–	260	531	1,273	3,268	6,497	16,782	21,860	20,712	79,424
Electrical/Communication Equipment	114,787	–	96	343	1,154	5,289	9,795	16,621	20,304	17,622	43,563
Clothing/Shoes/Cloth Articles	109,389	–	935	2,487	6,583	18,828	21,809	25,528	14,796	11,132	7,291
Chemicals	104,252	–	588	1,658	4,152	9,721	10,270	19,909	14,822	14,954	28,178
Mechanical Equipment	103,617	–	118	912	3,336	10,627	15,855	23,186	16,385	13,818	19,380
Printing/Publishing	74,528	–	276	2,274	6,808	11,853	9,531	12,903	10,489	9,974	10,420
Wood/Wood Products	84,700	–	1,655	6,459	13,792	25,989	17,070	10,862	4,534	2,177	2,162
Furniture	58,122	–	1,320	4,472	8,901	15,149	12,159	8,180	3,472	3,341	1,128
Paper/Paper Products	54,145	–	63	219	857	5,379	8,201	14,235	7,805	10,207	7,179
Beverages	48,549	–	1,032	3,056	3,715	5,206	5,029	8,861	7,413	6,912	10,025
Pharmaceuticals	35,803	–	51	332	634	2,163	2,911	7,296	9,738	10,530	2,148
Plastics/Plastic Articles	30,291	–	65	318	1,172	3,776	3,534	6,137	5,199	4,611	5,479
Rubber/Rubber Products	29,359	–	78	428	1,016	1,976	3,657	3,891	3,907	2,708	11,698
Leather/Hides	23,780	–	370	750	1,849	4,783	4,639	5,801	3,087	–	2,456
Tobacco	16,628	–	415	1,064	202	577	1,029	1,749	3,622	5,761	2,209
Perfume/Soap/Candles	15,946	–	324	709	1,277	1,880	2,164	2,733	4,395	1,369	1,095
Other	43,102	–	271	1,025	2,813	7,255	6,680	10,343	6,432	2,511	5,772
Total Production Workers in Establishments											
Total	1,652,617	–	12,668	40,779	78,781	178,953	197,084	286,347	260,154	248,384	349,377
Textiles	281,038	–	86	856	3,229	13,209	19,322	40,723	55,133	79,905	68,575
Food	187,724	–	4,175	13,384	15,538	21,682	20,641	44,042	38,769	21,371	8,122
Metals	'193,072	–	248	1,112	3,618	14,732	21,260	28,079	27,848	24,844	71,331
Non-Metallic Minerals	125,916	–	2,656	4,558	7,872	18,027	18,914	19,043	16,810	19,793	18,243
Transportation Equipment	121,009	–	191	422	1,018	2,750	5,403	13,931	17,760	16,838	69,696
Electrical/Communication Equipment	89,693	–	65	256	931	4,185	7,976	13,370	15,687	13,758	33,465
Clothing/Shoes/Cloth Articles	95,852	–	638	1,917	5,520	16,435	19,426	22,998	12,856	9,640	6,422
Chemicals	75,765	–	467	1,300	3,188	7,086	7,763	14,281	11,466	10,574	19,640
Mechanical Equipment	79,759	–	80	678	2,719	8,789	13,030	18,145	12,752	10,672	12,894
Printing/Publishing	55,190	–	191	1,749	5,498	9,371	7,409	9,237	7,815	6,710	7,210
Wood/Wood Products	73,812	–	1,160	5,069	11,642	23,195	15,387	9,768	4,139	1,518	1,934
Furniture	48,650	–	922	3,462	7,486	13,080	10,459	6,904	2,965	2,315	1,057
Paper/Paper Products	44,665	–	48	163	700	4,556	7,105	12,007	6,889	7,748	5,449
Beverages	32,452	–	634	2,351	2,864	3,711	3,398	5,379	3,013	4,055	7,047
Pharmaceuticals	18,455	–	31	226	434	1,421	1,549	3,651	4,421	5,606	1,116
Plastics/Plastic Articles	24,862	–	39	237	906	3,182	2,840	5,256	4,588	3,332	4,482
Rubber/Rubber Products	25,016	–	49	305	786	1,518	3,098	3,268	3,411	2,181	10,400
Leather/Hides	20,911	–	272	579	1,557	4,132	4,150	5,176	2,754	–	2,291
Tobacco	13,932	–	287	882	157	471	870	1,289	3,008	5,075	1,893
Perfume/Soap/Candles	10,144	–	228	502	986	1,342	1,539	1,607	2,692	428	820
Other	34,700	–	201	771	2,222	6,079	5,545	8,193	5,378	2,021	4,290

1974

	Total	None	1-4	5-9	10-19	20-49	50-99	100-249	250-499	500-999	1,000+
Number of Establishments											
Total	71,012	1,044	7,198	20,095	15,971	13,616	6,054	4,369	1,700	-----965------	
Total Workers in Establishments											
Total	3,396,769	–	22,832	135,112	218,113	419,147	423,734	678,771	588,732	---910,328----	

Sources: RE 1920E1, pp. LXXX and LXXXIV; RE 1940A4, p. 146; RE 1950A3, pp. 18 and 48-51; RE 1960D1, pp. 21-28; AN 1970, pp. 146-161; AN 1978, p. 401.

Table XII-7. Brazilian Retail and Wholesale Establishments: Numbers and Sales Receipts, 1940-70

	1940			1950		1960		1970	
	Estabs.	Sales		Estabs.	Sales	Estabs.	Sales	Estabs.	Sales
	Number	Estabs. Reporting	Cr$ (000)	Number	Cr$ (000)	Number	Cr$ (000)	Number	Cr$ (000)
Overall Total	185,319	151,953	33,494,682	274,944	178,803,515	361,503	1,234,899,884	628,595	137,684,304
Retail	160,813	130,423	8,088,638	244,241	56,039,971	332,704	566,692,681	587,472	71,157,211
Food/Beverages	105,931	82,996	3,053,668	158,985	21,252,160	209,333	169,953,919	378,386	17,421,510
Clothing	20,037	17,404	1,659,172	29,704	12,250,493	48,349	108,462,447	75,782	9,207,878
Pharmacies	8,218	7,286	417,719	10,527	2,816,878	15,323	31,216,449	19,717	2,981,991
Diverse Articles	2,428	2,098	210,501	3,998	1,354,626	7,142	12,943,372	18,525	2,229,520
Fuels/Lubrication	3,486	2,788	349,073	5,673	2,429,509	7,301	34,037,825	15,511	6,170,809
Hardware	1,638	1,495	207,508	3,604	1,721,438	6,375	25,111,853	15,187	4,701,457
Autos/Vehicles	691	610	606,376	1,948	3,956,925	5,529	73,667,577	14,419	12,223,130
General/Food	12,206	10,618	639,586	20,429	4,674,498	13,868	23,187,313	14,345	1,399,659
Furniture	2,103	1,837	285,974	2,976	1,636,020	7,146	20,921,381	13,036	2,387,787
Appliances	1,265	1,031	365,248	2,025	1,659,892	5,110	41,826,463	9,130	3,932,378
Stationery	1,422	1,241	135,307	1,869	714,944	3,132	8,947,580	7,068	1,311,786
Supermarkets	-	-	-	-	-	-	-	2,936	4,880,651
Used Articles	859	681	46,584	308	48,098	402	348,974	1,719	80,137
General/Non-Food	403	337	111,922	2,193	1,524,446	3,694	16,067,528	1,711	1,228,518
Other/Mal-Defined	126	1	-	2	44	-	-	-	-
Wholesale	11,039	9,113	18,573,757	19,726	97,099,644	28,799	668,207,203	41,123	66,527,093
Food/Beverages	3,843	3,205	5,322,365	6,691	23,784,298	10,389	267,783,422	17,265	25,919,047
Primary Products	4,189	3,297	7,031,259	4,000	29,974,973	6,399	36,246,240	8,126	5,453,212
Hardware	505	445	1,053,243	1,836	7,864,837	2,355	68,588,397	2,949	6,069,803
Appliances	161	144	367,582	1,161	5,131,654	1,493	52,997,020	2,751	5,118,880
Clothing	798	731	2,000,691	1,830	11,409,017	2,324	51,864,224	2,448	2,588,141
Drugs	515	454	814,983	1,291	5,253,331	1,427	39,588,573	1,892	4,197,607
Used Equipment	140	101	23,432	564	182,304	1,000	2,342,253	1,254	298,018
Diverse Articles	258	188	184,319	837	2,215,371	934	11,443,412	1,163	1,050,253
Fuels/Lubrication	259	227	630,981	352	4,403,810	340	67,302,977	880	8,923,602
Paper Products	92	84	265,962	210	823,840	432	12,850,082	787	1,078,628
Autos/Vehicles	49	42	388,128	164	2,291,331	685	33,112,311	774	4,646,910
General/Food	118	102	290,009	490	2,613,354	435	6,812,487	382	578,185
Furniture	50	46	40,404	-	-	322	4,922,939	339	335,138
General/Non-Food	54	47	160,399	300	1,151,524	264	12,352,866	113	269,669
Other/Mal-Defined	8	-	-	-	-	-	-	-	-
Mixed Retail/Wholesale	13,467	12,417	6,832,287	10,977	25,663,900	-	-	-	-
Primary Products	5,615	5,251	711,426	3,326	1,934,893	-	-	-	-
Food/Beverages	3,486	3,199	1,269,687	2,722	4,608,388	-	-	-	-
General/Food	1,026	935	405,135	1,308	2,307,348	-	-	-	-
Clothing	918	839	714,574	1,068	3,892,713	-	-	-	-
Hardware	593	550	712,308	633	3,175,816	-	-	-	-
Drugs	371	340	603,083	356	1,732,902	-	-	-	-
Appliances	323	289	721,423	317	1,852,692	-	-	-	-
Diverse Articles	278	252	196,818	336	742,398	-	-	-	-
Used Items	184	154	25,188	8	5,575	-	-	-	-
Paper Products	170	156	169,605	175	606,809	-	-	-	-
Furniture	169	161	112,754	87	199,029	-	-	-	-
Autos/Vehicles	149	133	350,228	332	2,354,702	-	-	-	-
Fuels/Lubrication	130	115	705,413	69	530,374	-	-	-	-
General/Non-Food	47	43	134,645	240	1,720,261	-	-	-	-
Other/Mal-Defined	8	-	-	-	-	-	-	-	-

Sources: RE 1940A5, pp. 246, 272-274 & 188-291; AN 1965, p. 166; AN 1977, p. 511.

291

Table XII-8. Service Establishments in Brazil: Numbers and Sales Receipts, 1940-70

Services	1940 Estabs. Number	1940 No. of Estabs.	1940 Receipts Cr$ 000	1950 Estabs. Number	1950 Receipts Cr$ 000	1960 Estabs. Number	1960 Receipts Cr$ 000	1970 Estabs. Number	1970 Receipts Cr$ 000
Total	108,529	85,390	2,304,087	136,188	13,639,164	221,450	122,303,688	351,823	12,030,683
Eating/Drinking Places	22,486	16,502	645,395	39,469	4,653,524	74,243	40,265,873	117,923	4,226,384
Personal Services	45,353	36,762	395,967	64,431	2,634,151	74,015	15,615,359	96,432	851,469
Barber/Beauty Shops	19,642	16,127	100,921	25,085	610,651	32,020	5,190,839	50,113	360,571
Tailors/Seamstresses	25,592	20,534	294,028	31,682	1,604,597	32,756	6,988,621	33,916	236,964
Repair/Maintenance Services	22,977	19,057	318,479	—	—	42,971	21,613,317	77,941	1,369,571
Auto Repair	7,263	6,082	138,288	7,291	1,136,575	18,747	14,106,186	34,155	835,510
Commercial Services	4,615	3,404	406,355	9,343	2,511,271	12,175	26,652,830	36,155	3,987,029
Lodging	9,662	7,322	265,998	11,747	1,523,285	13,635	9,710,894	16,099	720,365
With Food Service	9,291	7,037	254,464	10,950	1,253,181	11,444	7,962,806	—	—
Without Food Service	371	285	11,534	797	270,104	2,191	1,748,088	—	—
Entertainment Services	3,436	2,343	271,893	3,907	1,180,358	4,411	8,445,415	7,273	875,865
Radio/Television	76	61	31,175	243	340,845	412	2,621,178	818	452,597

Sources: SI 1940C, p. 52; AN 1965, p. 230; AN 1977, p. 495.

Table XII-9. Building Permits by Square Meterage and Value for the Municípios of Ten Capitals of Brazil's Political Subdivisions, 1954-76

		1954		1956		1958		1960		1962		1964	
		Total Permits Issued	Total Area	Total Permits Issued	Total Area	Total Permits Issued	Total Area	Total Permits Issued	Total Area	Total Permits Issued	Total Area	Total Permits Issued	Total Area
		Number	m²(000)	Number	m²(000)	Number	m²(000)	Number	m²(000)	Number	m²(000)	Number	m²(000)
Total		46,260	8,990	50,620	9,366	43,568	10,522	48,354	10,730	48,107	11,632	25,744	7,910
São Paulo	SP	19,747	3,811	18,140	3,787	16,957	3,892	21,284	4,859	22,985	5,138	14,310	4,461
Rio de Janeiro	RJ	6,217	2,245	8,603	2,059	6,949	2,679	8,156	2,465	7,986	3,383	-	-
Recife	PE	1,961	188	2,046	220	2,692	352	2,843	328	2,799	384	-	-
Belo Horizonte	MG	5,005	627	4,862	500	3,788	565	3,383	561	2,217	635	986	286
Pôrto Alegre	RS	4,418	890	5,040	1,063	4,062	991	2,629	666	2,195	368	1,593	745
Salvador	BA	1,270	199	2,372	338	1,450	317	1,332	313	1,467	222	1,134	358
Fortaleza	CE	851	103	769	164	417	73	1,148	195	846	173	589	203
Curitiba	PR	1,710	280	2,228	343	1,304	306	1,508	386	1,374	346	1,462	386
Belém	PA	718	95	577	61	593	110	669	66	440	59	334	66
Brasília	DF	-	-	-	-	-	-	-	-	390	256	291	70

		Permits Issued		Floor Area			Total Value
		Total	New Const	Total	New Construction Resid.	Non-Resid.	New Const.
		Number	Number	Number	Number	Number	Cr$ 1000
1966							
Total		26,695	26,695	8,463	4,715	3,738	784,630
São Paulo	SP	9,386	9,386	4,192	1,843	2,349	411,469
Rio de Janeiro	RJ	2,959	2,959	840	575	265	104,990
Recife	PE	1,199	1,199	268	201	67	17,936
Belo Horizonte	MG	1,215	1,215	393	283	110	35,731
Pôrto Alegre	RS	1,529	1,529	614	374	240	40,525
Salvador	BA	1,218	1,218	330	215	115	30,360
Fortaleza	CE	1,044	1,044	200	151	49	14,749
Curitiba	PR	1,166	1,166	378	196	182	21,224
Belém	PA	292	292	93	55	38	7,998
Brasília	DF	1,026	1,026	291	161	130	26,064
1968							
Total		68,398	64,358	15,864	10,678	4,859	3,263,762
São Paulo	SP	21,052	20,049	6,073	3,629	2,340	1,246,306
Rio de Janeiro	RJ	6,335	5,904	2,314	1,662	620	602,454
Recife	PE	2,043	1,908	558	420	121	100,867
Belo Horizonte	MG	4,999	4,577	991	713	235	190,211
Pôrto Alegre	RS	3,880	3,276	1,205	907	267	228,778
Salvador	BA	2,233	2,062	615	447	149	146,389
Fortaleza	CE	2,356	2,227	377	227	90	56,212
Curitiba	PR	3,339	3,178	769	534	225	137,089
Belém	PA	701	601	133	90	36	18,003
Brasília	DF	6,103	6,078	1,251	840	407	285,119

Table XII-9 (continued)

1970

Total		63,241	57,976	16,762	10,748	5,571	5,055,046
São Paulo	SP	22,551	21,375	6,935	4,030	2,791	2,284,507
Rio de Janeiro	RJ	8,603	7,804	3,525	2,607	3,398	1,084,899
Recife	PE	1,732	1,320	427	281	115	107,195
Belo Horizonte	MG	1,583	1,074	493	296	143	133,965
Pôrto Alegre	RS	2,608	1,961	891	521	335	250,162
Salvador	BA	2,149	2,046	652	500	141	217,833
Fortaleza	CE	3,787	3,704	433	326	99	97,870
Curitiba	PR	2,560	2,362	749	482	240	199,171
Belém	PA	1,079	978	194	135	50	48,824
Brasília	DF	4,981	4,854	900	578	308	274,594

1972

Total		65,859	60,320	23,151	13,341	9,384	11,028,544
São Paulo	SP	21,813	20,864	12,586	6,955	5,527	6,290,358
Rio de Janeiro	RJ	6,190	5,147	2,738	1,584	1,071	1,534,611
Recife	PE	2,691	2,195	684	398	260	243,266
Belo Horizonte	MG	1,669	1,324	643	347	267	291,440
Pôrto Alegre	RS	2,480	2,087	767	485	249	315,925
Salvador	BA	1,273	1,151	555	382	158	248,164
Fortaleza	CE	2,083	2,008	348	255	84	108,248
Curitiba	PR	1,696	1,520	570	352	204	220,019
Belém	PA	769	737	122	88	28	43,692
Brasília	DF	13,745	13,449	2,017	1,286	714	930,010

1974

Total		62,727	55,457	18,758	10,281	7,932	12,407,727
São Paulo	SP	15,802	14,247	6,259	3,076	3,044	4,530,595
Rio de Janeiro	RJ	8,350	7,591	2,836	1,519	1,248	1,978,513
Recife	PE	2,414	1,911	646	376	238	343,515
Belo Horizonte	MG	3,504	3,006	1,219	733	442	886,582
Pôrto Alegre	RS	2,379	1,927	1,226	711	479	763,809
Salvador	BA	2,203	2,082	809	554	236	441,781
Fortaleza	CE	1,723	1,662	364	207	150	160,881
Curitiba	PR	3,623	3,292	1,132	601	508	713,237
Belém	PA	904	873	83	60	20	31,665
Brasília	DF	9,976	8,579	1,725	1,045	606	1,069,201

1976

Total		74,011	65,307	20,763	12,130	7,894	17,559,541
São Paulo	SP	16,604	15,512	5,018	2,793	2,145	4,382,863
Rio de Janeiro	RJ	6,717	6,031	2,331	1,249	1,015	1,970,033
Recife	PE	1,448	847	468	275	155	374,859
Belo Horizonte	MG	5,683	5,197	2,773	1,732	980	2,508,587
Pôrto Alegre	RS	2,893	2,442	1,675	1,029	610	1,489,858
Salvador	BA	1,871	1,668	1,198	756	401	970,316
Fortaleza	CE	3,206	3,206	753	498	243	560,814
Curitiba	PR	3,362	3,194	997	655	328	883,422
Belém	PA	3,507	3,470	329	246	78	267,664
Brasília	DF	15,629	12,201	2,343	1,008	1,136	1,812,869

Sources: AN 1956, p. 192; AN 1958, p. 171; AN 1965, p. 296; AN 1967, pp. 351-381; AN 1969, pp. 247 & 254; AN 1971, pp. 278 & 285; AN 1975, pp. 280 & 292; AN 1977, pp. 471-480.

Chapter XIII. Ecology, Environment, Recreation and Leisure

For more than four centuries Brazil's vast land, water, and forest resources had been utilized without regard to their degradation or exhaustibility. Conservation, reforestation, and land reclamation were not incorporated into the Brazilian land ethic and, lacking a constituency, were not given a political hearing. By the late nineteenth century, however, the federal government had taken measures to provide water for agriculture to cope with the severe, non-periodic droughts of the northeast interior. Here in the dry scrub and thorn woodland known as the <u>caatinga</u> (see Map I-8, Chapter I) the rainy season, which at best provides for marginal production, fails to develop every few years, forcing a great exodus of rural people who seek refuge in the cities of the coastal northeast and the south of the country.

Little public or private concern, however, was shown for the destruction of the seemingly inexhaustible eastern semideciduous forest (see Map I-8, Chapter I). Nearly all of Brazil's prodigious agricultural output has depended upon those soils which developed under this forest that covered the eastern one-quarter of the country. Most of this resource lay within 500 miles of the Atlantic Ocean and has long been spatially coincident with the bulk of Brazil's population. Outliers of this forest, however, are found beyond Brasilia, more than 1,000 miles inland. By 1970 virtually all of this forest had been cleared for agriculture, for grazing, and, in some parts of Minas Gerais, for the making of charcoal to smelt iron ore. Brazil had reached the end of its easily arable land, which, except in a few parts of São Paulo state, had received little care and input. As a consequence these soils continued to deteriorate with exposure to high heat and humidity. Steep slopes, some up to 30 degrees, were cultivated in open-rowed crops, thus accelerating soil erosion. James,[1] writing in 1969, noted that "instead of an unlimited area, now there was land hunger as pioneers hacked away at the last remnants of forest a thousand miles inland."

In the past decade agriculturists with and without government support have begun to probe the savannas and the selva (tropical rain forest) in attempts to develop new soil bases and to adapt crops to them. In the 1970s the federal government had begun to develop agricultural settlements in the forests of the Amazon basin in the hope that landless farmers from both the humid and dry northeast would be attracted to them.

By 1937 Brazil had established its first national park; by 1960 the census had begun to report a small amount of planted forest land; and by 1980 the federal government had begun to formulate an environmental policy.

Table XIII-1 reports the amount of planted pasture, planted forest, and irrigated land by Brazilian political subdivisions. The 1960 data originated with the Instituto Brasileiro de Estatística and those for 1970 and 1975 were generated by FIBGE. For 1970 the source recorded the national totals for hectares in each of the columns and these agree with similar figures on Table IX-2 (Agriculture). The source, however, rounded each political subdivision's portion of each column and as a consequence the sum of the subdivision figures varies slightly from the national figure in each of the columns.

Planted pasture in 1960 represented 16.4 percent of all pastureland and 8.0 percent of all land in rural establishments. By 1970 these figures had risen to 19.3 and 10.1 percent, respectively. The proportion of land in planted forest showed a reverse trend between 1960 and 1970. In the former year 3.6 percent of all forest lands and 0.83 percent of all lands in rural establishments were in planted forest. By 1970 these figures had fallen to 2.9 and 0.56 percent, respectively. São Paulo led all political subdivisions in 1960 with 21.3 percent of Brazil's planted forest land and in 1970 with 34.8 percent of the nation's forest plantation land.

The proportion of land in all rural establishments under irrigation was 0.18 percent in 1960 and had risen to 2.7 percent in 1970. In 1970 51.2 percent of Brazil's irrigated land was in the state of Rio Grande do Sul, where rice had long been produced in the paddies of the Rio Jacuí valley west of Pôrto Alegre. Some of São Paulo state's irrigated land was also in the form of permanent paddies yielding rice in the Paraíba valley. In the northeastern states the irrigation was in response to the nonperiodic droughts, a condition discussed in detail under Table XIII-2. In the wet and dry savanna climate of Brazil's central plateau, dry upland rice was irrigated through the dry season. In places where water issued from under the cap of this plateau it was channeled to the base of a slope and shot back up the hill over the rice crop by ram pumps installed at intervals in the channels. Irrigation was required even in the Amazon states where water-demanding crops such as bananas had to be carried through the short drier season.

In the 1975 section of Table XIII-1 the source did not specify the definition of wood in the first column. The subtitle of the table in the source referred to the production of <u>madeira</u> <u>em</u> <u>tora</u> (logs, boles, trunks). In the column headings on the same source table, however, the term <u>madeira</u> alone was used indicating that the reference was probably to logs to be sawn into lumber.

Table XIII-2 reports the number and capacity of public and private <u>açudes</u>, or reservoirs, existing in the dry northeast of Brazil for five different years from 1938 through 1978. The 1938 data originated with the Inspetoria Federal de Obras Contra as Sêcas and the later data were generated by this agency's successor, the Departamento Nacional de Obras Contra as Sêcas (DNOCS). The words "Obras Contra as Sêcas" means "works against the droughts." The data for 1938 represent those reservoirs in existence that were built between 1909, the year the Inspetoria began to function, and 1938.

Map I-7 in Chapter I documents how much of Brazil's land area extending from the Amazon basin to within a few miles of the Atlantic Coast is under a savanna climate. This climate is characterized by a winter (May to October) dry season and a summer (November to April) in which nearly all of the annual precipitation, which may reach 60 inches and more, is concentrated. In the interior of the northeastern hump of Brazil, however, these summer rains may occur sporadically or may fail to develop at all. Even sporadic rainfall can bring about a drought because potential evapo-transpiration is so high at these low latitudes (5 to 10 degrees south). In some summers the rainfall pattern might be normal only to be followed by another in which the rains are delayed until April and May during which huge downpours produce massive flooding. Friedrich Friese, reported in James,[2] found that "during the period 1835 to 1935 there were more than fifty years of either drought or flood." The core of this "calamity region" lies in the interior of the states of Ceará, Rio Grande do Norte, Paraíba, and Pernambuco, but parts of the nearby states of Piauí, Alagoas, Sergipe, Minas Gerais, and Bahia are also subject to these capricious droughts. Together these nine states, with the exception of the zone included in the basin of the Rio São Francisco, make up the <u>polígono</u> <u>das</u> <u>sêcas</u>, or the drought polygon to which since 1909 first the Inspetoria then DNOCS have committed resources for the construction of reservoirs (açudes) and irrigation canals.

Table XIII-3 notes the lengths of existing irrigation canals extending from public reservoirs (açudes) in four states of the northeast drought region for 1938, 1945, and 1955. The data were generated by DNOCS.

Table XIII-4 records the numbers of water wells drilled in the nine-state drought polygon of the northeast for the periods 1909-55 and 1956-78. DNOCS originated all the data. No special significance applies to the two time periods presented. The Anuário estatístico do Brasil for 1956 reported well data for the period 1909 to 1955, so this information was kept intact and the remaining information was reported in a bloc for the 1956-78 period. Presumably the wells reported were drilled by DNOCS or under DNOCS supervision although the source does not so specify. Not all wells were drilled to obtain new water supplies. A few drillings were undertaken to make soundings or to clear obstructions from or deepen existing wells, but their numbers were small and they are not distinguished on the table. The Anuários for 1965 and 1967 both reported well data for 1964 but disagreed on the number drilled. The figures in the 1967 Anuário were used on this table. For 1967 the flow of 175 wells was not reported by the source. These wells were dropped from the divisor total when the average flow in liters per hour was calculated.

Table XIII-5 lists Brazil's national and state parks and biological reserves as of 1979 by location, size, and date of creation. The data originated with the Ministério da Agricultura. According to the Anuário for 1979 a national park is an area administered by the federal government that contains one or more ecosystem generally unaltered or little altered by human occupancy, in which animal and vegetable species, geological sites, and habitats are of special scientific, educational, or recreational interest, or in which there occur natural landscapes of great esthetic value. The parks were created to protect and conserve these biologic, geologic, and landscape resources and to impede or eliminate the alteration of these resources.

A national biological reserve is described by the 1979 Anuário as an area created by the public power and administered by it to maintain the area's floral and faunal integrity and natural beauty by prohibiting any land utilization, hunting, capture, or introduction of wild flora or fauna, or any other modification whatsoever, of the environment. These areas are reserved for authorized scientific research.

Table XIII-6 reports the membership, activities, and facilities in Brazilian sports clubs and organizations from 1960 to 1978. The data were originated by the Serviço de Estatística of the Departamento da Educação e Cultura. Small scale soccer is simply soccer played on a field smaller than that used for regular soccer and is known as <u>futebol de salão</u>. For 1978 the figure for Number of Organizations that are professional (378) included 349 organizations that enrolled both professional and amateur athletes. This may also be true of the 1969 figure (380) as well but the source does not so specify. Many professional sports organizations in Brazil are but parts of large sports clubs whose physical plants include facilities for members who wish to participate in amateur sports and other types of recreational and social activities.

Table XIII-7 gives the history of the World Cup final from its inception in 1930 to 1982. Brazil retired the Jules Rimet Cup after winning its third World Cup title in 1974.

<u>References</u>

1. Preston, James, <u>Latin America</u>, 4th ed. (New York: Odyssey Press), 1969, p. 717.

2. James, <u>Latin America</u>, p. 724.

Table XIII-1. Area of Planted Forest, Planted Pasture, and Irrigated
Land, 1960-70, and Production from Planted Forests, 1975,
in Brazil and Its Political Subdivisions

1960	Total Estabs Number	Hectares	Pasture Natural Hectares	Planted Estabs.	Planted Hectares	Forest Natural Hectares	Planted Estabs.	Planted Hectares	Irrigated Land Estabs.	Hectares
Brazil Total	3,337,769	249,862,142	102,272,053	704,219	20,063,333	55,875,299	138,984	2,069,806	35,078	461,550
São Paulo	317,374	19,303,948	5,094,407	80,405	4,777,205	2,339,926	23,844	441,571	3,523	56,072
Rio Grande do Sul	380,201	21,659,406	13,178,558	65,654	361,316	2,060,637	40,472	234,512	9,340	265,556
Paraná	269,146	11,384,934	1,912,081	79,951	781,947	2,839,158	9,613	188,075	617	4,344
Minas Gerais	371,859	38,339,045	21,849,447	89,994	4,095,245	3,252,670	10,601	233,226	2,872	46,992
Santa Catarina	158,268	5,948,950	1,759,987	52,694	233,028	1,744,853	11,898	97,414	5,878	20,499
Rio de Janeiro	51,697	2,976,224	1,206,898	6,091	240,473	527,903	1,282	26,057	1,467	11,773
Pernambuco	259,723	5,924,630	1,780,871	21,704	163,194	1,145,902	3,930	52,728	1,113	6,265
Bahia	381,473	17,666,218	3,313,004	137,403	2,951,147	4,452,127	10,975	160,647	6,826	23,100
Sergipe	65,014	1,469,446	443,533	18,330	291,470	238,165	851	10,851	24	1,057
Goiás	111,015	28,877,314	16,060,502	50,009	3,107,592	4,641,970	3,571	117,178	296	1,145
Espírito Santo	54,795	2,888,667	521,033	17,889	321,623	858,141	1,816	25,296	102	1,233
Rondônia	1,012	303,316	3,096	167	1,599	242,071	33	1,001	1	1
Acre	3,676	9,386,075	10,853	692	9,930	7,709,267	58	343	-	-
Amazonas	48,477	6,398,804	83,035	3,326	40,070	5,611,137	3,699	24,034	4	43
Roraíma	873	869,582	695,378	95	12,485	107,710	1	1	-	-
Pará	83,180	5,253,272	890,417	5,016	102,114	2,636,865	1,732	31,560	10	23
Amapá	1,023	1,242,037	356,330	68	14,442	751,938	32	1,772	-	-
Maranhão	261,865	8,215,613	2,323,264	12,193	150,763	2,068,385	1,882	103,388	32	74
Piauí	87,303	9,106,820	2,542,669	6,584	71,940	2,418,570	1,029	27,460	73	451
Ceará	122,576	10,943,939	3,253,630	7,988	116,844	3,154,658	4,949	140,554	1,566	11,393
Rio Grande do Norte	49,840	3,686,148	1,802,975	2,989	36,910	423,599	998	13,380	362	1,383
Paraíba	117,836	4,070,228	1,809,797	6,534	65,472	427,483	2,988	50,087	296	3,439
Alagoas	62,484	1,907,396	389,903	10,486	149,892	488,178	842	16,439	237	5,610
Mato Grosso	48,104	30,969,873	20,845,685	18,226	1,751,956	5,469,445	1,028	73,806	199	774
Distrito Federal	273	139,378	75,632	92	9,267	15,881	6	131	17	108
Fernando de Noronha	-	-	-	-	-	-	-	-	-	-
Serra do Aimores	22,424	884,098	60,201	9,589	204,806	245,362	705	7,444	16	90
Guanabara	6,258	46,781	8,867	50	603	3,298	149	851	207	125
1970										
Brazil Total	4,924,019	294,145,466	124,406,233	954,773	29,732,296	56,222,957	155,609	1,658,225	104,613	795,815
São Paulo	326,780	20,416,024	5,531,823	82,340	5,931,560	1,849,474	32,312	577,436	12,026	91,463
Rio Grande do Sul	512,303	23,807,180	14,077,981	73,573	557,005	1,725,837	73,276	245,764	25,689	407,496
Paraná	554,488	14,625,530	1,809,429	197,648	2,700,281	2,365,400	12,810	205,163	1,851	9,176
Minas Gerais	454,025	42,009,504	25,991,258	80,329	3,725,330	3,681,574	11,789	271,522	12,218	57,474
Santa Catarina	207,218	7,025,326	2,088,682	69,488	379,303	1,623,220	9,392	128,333	14,148	57,991
Rio de Janeiro	72,390	3,287,812	1,572,186	4,834	151,883	464,029	751	19,088	4,371	25,512
Pernambuco	331,409	6,393,597	2,174,731	29,146	210,832	910,883	1,145	13,103	4,984	19,002
Bahia	541,566	22,260,827	5,163,076	169,518	3,902,529	5,600,551	3,780	41,524	10,662	27,042
Sergipe	95,276	1,743,200	508,361	24,945	508,939	210,933	299	2,488	866	8,639
Goiás	145,115	35,783,038	19,423,118	65,357	4,362,064	4,911,062	907	24,598	732	4,248
Espírito Santo	70,712	3,759,360	1,005,878	23,045	824,097	654,929	985	25,119	1,984	10,169
Rondônia	7,082	1,631,640	82,186	890	41,006	1,070,591	37	446	20	66
Acre	23,102	4,122,085	41,098	795	22,256	3,913,859	60	1,313	-	83,350
Amazonas	85,251	4,475,940	160,913	5,554	81,327	3,470,806	1,809	8,795	210	5,199
Roraíma	1,953	1,594,397	1,125,069	292	21,965	326,031	22	360	4	5
Pará	141,442	10,754,828	2,072,832	12,790	467,849	4,897,922	860	33,955	36	136
Amapá	2,315	603,254	308,247	301	3,368	201,291	20	393	6	13
Maranhão	396,761	10,794,912	2,717,990	28,470	634,787	1,924,083	528	8,620	124	1,820
Piauí	217,886	9,606,731	3,251,161	10,637	101,322	2,684,455	509	6,824	568	1,863
Ceará	245,432	12,104,811	3,970,805	11,630	73,007	3,228,567	1,768	17,120	6,203	25,484
Rio Grande do Norte	103,630	4,571,683	1,878,240	1,817	26,576	971,714	557	4,247	695	5,471
Paraíba	169,667	4,582,831	1,989,030	6,985	67,566	501,820	604	3,738	3,940	13,433
Alagoas	105,160	2,238,523	470,272	15,766	225,585	392,496	287	2,925	2,253	13,218
Mato Grosso	106,104	45,752,567	26,892,613	38,105	4,695,690	8,624,723	728	14,618	379	9,179
Distrito Federal	1,913	170,019	94,123	460	15,740	14,513	122	272	294	1,151
Fernando de Noronha	1	1,600	300	-	-	7	1	2	-	-
Serra do Aimores	-	-	-	-	-	-	-	-	-	-
Guanabara	5,038	28,251	4,831	58	430	2,188	151	462	350	565

1975	Logs Harvested m³	Charcoal Produced tons	Firewood Harvested m³	Black Acacia Bark Harvested tons
Brazil Total	17,937,491	509,968	29,794,651	91,278
São Paulo	11,087,541	94,916	13,803,199	-
Rio Grande do Sul	2,343,890	4,237	11,823,773	90,468
Paraná	1,947,807	135	1,302,905	150
Minas Gerais	1,333,030	410,101	2,105,913	-
Santa Catarina	1,080,971	513	718,648	660
Rio de Janeiro	97,925	-	35,733	-
Pernambuco	45,485	-	420	-
Bahia	842	66	-	-
Sergipe	-	-	300	-
Goiás	-	-	3,760	-

Sources: AN 1967, pp. 89-90; AN 1975, pp. 147-148; AN 1978, p. 380.

Table XIII-2. Public and Private Reservoirs (Açudes) Existing by
Political Subdivisions in the Northeast Drought Region of
Brazil, 1938-78

	Total		Public		Private	
1938	No.	Capacity m^3	No.	Capacity m^3	No.	Capacity m^3
Northeast Drought Polygon	255	2,095,917	119	1,873,942	136	221,975
Ceará	154	1,330,842	40	1,158,051	114	172,791
Paraíba	23	420,453	17	413,308	6	7,145
Pernambuco	9	53,139	8	17,139	1	36,000
Rio Grande do Norte	41	225,915	31	221,792	10	4,123
Bahia	17	49,607	13	48,491	4	1,116
Piauí	8	14,221	8	14,221	-	-
Minas Gerais	-	-	-	-	-	-
Alagoas	-	-	-	-	-	-
Sergipe	3	1,740	2	940	1	800
1945						
Northeast Drought Polygon	358	3,142,695	123	2,657,415	235	485,280
Ceará	234	1,550,263	40	1,158,051	194	392,212
Paraíba	32	1,166,215	18	113,308	14	32,907
Pernambuco	11	56,547	8	17,139	3	39,408
Rio Grande do Norte	47	237,947	31	222,362	16	15,585
Bahia	21	57,499	14	53,131	7	4,368
Piauí	9	68,821	9	68,821	-	-
Minas Gerais	-	-	-	-	-	-
Alagoas	1	3,738	1	3,738	-	-
Sergipe	3	1,665	2	865	1	800
1955						
Northeast Drought Polygon	549	3,744,911	143	2,880,571	406	864,340
Ceará	346	1,877,147	43	1,233,325	303	643,822
Paraíba	56	1,242,146	23	1,160,439	33	81,707
Pernambuco	21	83,897	12	37,639	9	46,258
Rio Grande do Norte	82	395,250	36	320,272	46	74,978
Bahia	27	68,406	14	53,131	13	15,275
Piauí	10	70,321	9	68,821	1	1,500
Minas Gerais	-	-	-	-	-	-
Alagoas	4	6,079	4	6,079	-	-
Sergipe	3	1,665	2	865	1	800
1966						
Northeast Drought Polygon	825	12,353,000	234	11,139,000	591	1,214,000
Ceará	482	7,774,000	54	6,834,000	428	940,000
Paraíba	103	2,534,000	37	2,432,000	66	102,000
Pernambuco	42	746,000	29	695,000	13	51,000
Rio Grande do Norte	106	552,000	43	456,000	63	96,000
Bahia	45	450,000	25	426,000	20	24,000
Piauí	12	173,000	12	173,000	-	-
Minas Gerais	4	79,000	4	79,000	-	-
Alagoas	20	33,000	20	33,000	-	-
Sergipe	11	12,000	10	11,000	1	1,000
1978						
Northeast Drought Polygon	1,104	12,732,000	257	11,997,000	847	1,235,000
Ceará	492	7,561,000	58	6,606,000	434	955,000
Paraíba	127	2,549,000	38	2,445,000	89	104,000
Pernambuco	45	906,000	32	855,000	13	51,000
Rio Grande do Norte	112	701,000	49	605,000	63	96,000
Bahia	50	682,000	30	658,000	20	24,000
Piauí	12	173,000	12	173,000	-	-
Minas Gerais	4	79,000	4	79,000	-	-
Alagoas	164	59,000	23	57,000	121	2,000
Sergipe	98	22,000	11	19,000	87	3,000

Sources: AN 1939-40, p. 15; AN 1956, p. 11; AN 1967, p. 21; AN 1979, p. 59.

301

Table XIII-3. Length of Irrigation Canals from Public Reservoirs (Açudes) by Political Subdivisions in the Northeast Drought Polygon, 1939-55

	1939			1945			1955		
	Total Meters	Main Meters	Branches Meters	Total Meters	Main Meters	Branches Meters	Total Meters	Main Meters	Branches Meters
Northeast Drought Polygon	225,150	78,025	147,125	410,424	100,260	310,164	558,488	198,716	359,772
Ceará	137,598	51,385	86,213	167,548	61,877	105,671	288,761	145,043	143,718
Açude Cedro	58,000	15,000	43,000	58,000	15,000	43,000	58,000	15,000	43,000
Açude Lima Campos	27,458	10,985	16,473	49,068	14,297	34,771	49,068	14,297	34,771
Açude Forquilha	46,040	20,600	25,440	46,040	20,600	25,440	46,040	20,600	25,440
Açude Joaquim Tavora	6,100	4,800	1,300	6,100	4,800	1,300	6,100	4,800	1,300
Açude Santo Antonio de Russas	-	-	-	7,160	6,000	1,160	16,590	6,810	9,780
Açude General Sampaio	-	-	-	1,180	1,180	-	86,293	63,761	22,532
Açude Aires de Sousa	-	-	-	-	-	-	26,670	19,775	6,875
Paraíba	87,552	26,640	60,912	230,207	34,883	195,324	231,288	34,883	196,405
Açude São Goncalo	56,497	14,500	41,997	175,129	19,200	155,929	176,210	19,200	157,010
Açude Condado	31,055	12,140	18,915	55,078	15,683	39,395	55,078	15,683	39,395
Rio Grande do Norte	-	-	-	-	-	-	25,770	15,290	10,480
Açude Itaús	-	-	-	-	-	-	22,800	13,320	9,480
Açude Cruzeta	-	-	-	-	-	-	2,970	1,970	1,000
Pernambuco	-	-	-	12,669	3,500	9,169	12,669	3,500	9,169
Pôsto Agrícola São Francisco	-	-	-	12,669	3,500	9,169	12,669	3,500	9,169

Source: AN 1956, p. 11.

Table XIII-4. Water Wells Drilled in the Drought Polygon of Northeast Brazil by Political Subdivisions, 1909-78

Political Subdivisions		Total Wells Drilled		Wells Brought In		Liters Per Hour	
		Number	Meters	Number	% of Total	Total	Average Per Well
Ceará	1909-1955	1,149	45,464	901	78.4	2,554,576	2,835.3
	1956-1978	2,135	108,183	1,828	85.6	6,485,585	3,547.9
	Total	3,284	153,647	2,729	83.1	9,040,161	3,312.6
Piauí	1909-1955	422	16,484	379	89.8	1,601,918	4,226.7
	1956-1978	2,240	192,532	1,941	90.7	17,259,313	8,892.0
	Total	2,562	209,016	2,320	90.6	18,861,231	8,129.8
Minas Gerais	1909-1955	30	2,128	30	100.0	185,030	6,167.7
	1956-1978	1,784	14,862	1,603	89.9	10,376,956	6,733.9
	Total	1,814	16,990	1,633	90.0	10,561,986	6,723.1
Paraíba	1909-1955	161	9,838	112	69.6	432,576	3,862.3
	1956-1978	1,223	52,053	1,079	87.5	5,665,643	5,250.8
	Total	1,384	61,891	1,191	86.1	6,098,219	5,120.3
Rio Grande do Norte	1909-1955	540	40,784	432	80.0	2,072,891	4,798.4
	1956-1978	703	49,908	611	86.9	3,092,497	5,304.5
	Total	1,243	90,692	1,043	83.9	5,165,388	5,089.1
Bahia	1909-1955	483	19,299	315	65.2	1,166,691	3,703.8
	1956-1978	540	32,822	404	74.8	1,625,683	4,255.7
	Total	1,023	52,121	719	70.3	2,792,374	4,006.3
Pernambuco	1909-1955	286	15,726	207	72.4	1,028,379	4,968.0
	1956-1978	557	30,195	469	84.2	1,552,851	3,521.2
	Total	843	45,921	676	80.2	2,581,230	3,983.4
Sergipe	1909-1955	197	7,200	129	65.5	393,045	3,046.9
	1956-1978	516	24,947	370	71.7	1,449,880	4,154.4
	Total	713	32,147	499	70.0	1,842,925	3,855.5
Alagoas	1909-1955	37	1,599	29	78.4	85,095	2,934.3
	1956-1978	263	12,272	221	84.0	673,090	3,251.6
	Total	300	13,871	250	83.3	758,185	3,212.6
Drought Polygon	1909-1955	3,305	158,522	2,534	76.7	9,520,201	3,757.0
	1956-1978	9,861	517,774	8,526	86.5	4,818,498	5,651.1
	Total	13,166	676,296	11,060	84.0	57,701,699	5,217.2

Sources: AN 1956, p. 12; AN 1957, p. 12; AN 1958, p. 10; AN 1959, p. 20; AN 1961, p. 17; AN 1963, p. 14; AN 1965, p. 17; AN 1967, p. 21; AN 1969, p. 21; AN 1971, p. 22; AN 1972, p. 22; AN 1975, p. 24;

Table XIII-5. National and State Parks and National and State Biological
Reserves in Brazil by Date of Creation, Location, and
Size, 1937-79

	Date of Creation	Location: Political Subdivision	Size In Hectares
National Parks			
Pacaás Novos	1979	RO	764,801
Pico da Neblina	1979	AM	2,200,000
Serra da Capivara	1979	PI	100,000
Amazônia	1974	PA	1,000,000
Araguaia	1973	GO	562,312
Chapada dos Veadeiros	1972	GO	171,924
Emas	1972	GO	170,086
Serra da Bocaina	1972	RJ/SP	100,000
Serra da Canastra	1972	MG	71,525
Tijuca	1967	RJ	3,300
Brasília	1961	DF	28,000
Caparaó	1961	MG/ES	16,194
Monte Pascoal	1961	BA	22,500
São Joaquim	1961	SC	20,000
Sete Cidades	1961	PI	6,221
Sete Quedas	1961	PR	233
Aparados da Serra	1959	RS/SC	10,250
Ubajara	1959	CE	563
Iguaçu	1944	PR	170,086
Serra dos Orgaõs	1939	RJ	4,000
Itatiaia	1937	RJ/MG	11,943
National Biological Reserves			
Atol das Rocas	1979	RN	36,249
Jaru	1979	RO	268,150
Rio Trombetas	1979	PA	1,258,000
Poço das Antas	1974	RJ	5,000
Cará-Cará	1971	MT	61,126
Córrego do Veado	1970	ES	2,400
Nova Lombardia	1970	ES	4,350
Serra Negra	1970	PE	1,100
Sooretana	1943	ES	24,000

Table XIII-5 (continued)

State Parks	Date of Creation	Location: Political Subdivision	Size In Hectares
Jaragua	1977	SP	488
Delta do Jacuí	1976	RS	4,853
Monge	1976	PR	321
Camaquã	1975	RS	7,992
Espinilho	1975	RS	276
Guarapiranga	1975	SP	18,000
Ibitiria	1975	RS	415
Morumbi	1975	PR	76,000
Podocarpus	1975	RS	2,100
Rio Doce	1975	MG	35,973
Serra do Tabuleiro	1975	SC	90,000
Tainhas	1975	RS	4,924
Pedra Branca	1974	RJ	12,500
Jaiba	1973	MG	6,211
Arã	1973	SP	40
Ibitipoca	1973	MG	1,448
Piqueri	1971	SP	980
Desengano	1970	RJ	25,000
Vassununga	1970	SP	1,484
Jacupiranga	1969	SP/PR	150,000
Capital	1968	SP	174
Itacolomi	1967	MG	7,000
Caxambu	1966	MG	968
Turvo	1965	RS	17,491
Campinhos	1962	PR	204
Ilha do Cardoso	1962	SP	22,500
Bauru	1961	SP	287
Morro do Baú	1961	SC	600
Alto Ribeira	1958	SP/PR	35,712
Ilha Bela	1958	SP	27,025
Caraguatatuba	1956	SP	13,769
Espigão Alto	1949	SC/RS	1,431
Nonai	1949	RS	17,498
Vila Velha	1942	PR	3,122
Campos do Jordão	1941	MG/SP	828,630
Caracol	-	RS	100
Guarita	-	RS	1,550
Itapuã	-	RS	1,535
Mendanha	-	RJ	1,400
Rio Vermelho	-	SC	1,100
Serra do Cipó	-	MG	27,600

State Biological Reserves	Date of Creation	Location: Political Subdivision	Size In Hectares
Córrego de São João	1976	MG	255
Ibirapuitã	1976	RS	351
Mestre Álvaro	1976	ES	2,216
Mato Grande	1975	RS	5,161
São Donato	1975	RS	4,392
Scharlau	1975	RS	50
Biológica e Arqueológica de Guaratiba	1974	RJ	1,000
Duas Bocas	1966	ES	3,176
Jequiá	1966	RJ	100
São Carlos	1961	SP	75
Pedra Azul	1960	ES	1,100
Comboio	1953	ES	11,812
Acauã	-	MG	4,000
Aguaí	-	SC	280
Carmo da Mata	-	MG	86
Colônia 31 de Março	-	MG	5,000
Fazenda Cascata	-	MG	62
Fazenda Corunga	-	MG	580
Fazenda Lapinha	-	MG	345
Jacarepaguá	-	RJ	50
Lami	-	RS	71
Mar de Espanha	-	MG/RJ	220
Mata do Ausentes	-	MG	750
Nova Badém	-	MG	246
Sassafrás	-	SC	2,000
São Mateus	-	MG	370
São Sebastião do Paraíso	-	MG	246
Três Marias	-	MG	16,000

Source: AN 1979, p. 44.

Map XIII-1. National Parks and National Biological Reserves in Brazil, 1979

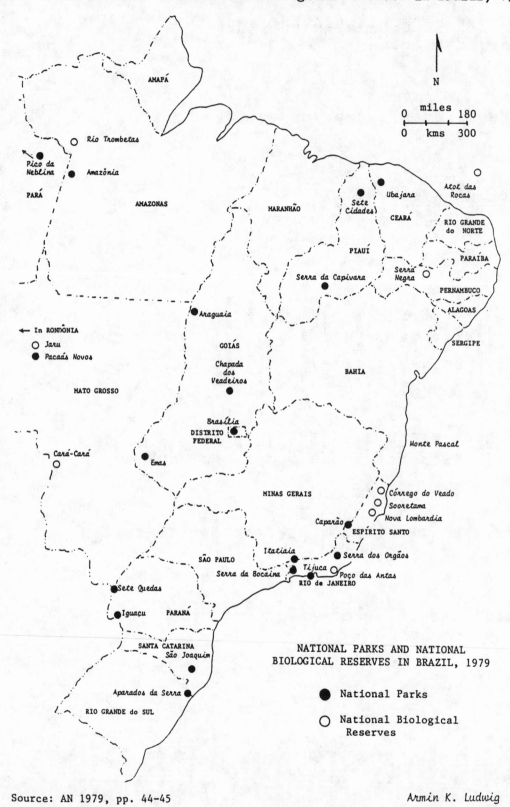

N

miles
0 _____ 180
0   kms   300

AMAPÁ

○ Rio Trombetas

● Pico da Neblina

● Amazônia

PARÁ

AMAZONAS

MARANHÃO

● Sete Cidades

Ubajara

○ Atol das Rocas

CEARÁ

RIO GRANDE do NORTE

PIAUÍ

PARAÍBA

● Serra da Capivara

Serra Negra ○

PERNAMBUCO

ALAGOAS

● Araguaia

SERGIPE

← In RONDÔNIA
○ Jaru
● Pacaás Novos

GOIÁS

BAHIA

● Chapada dos Veadeiros

MATO GROSSO

Brasília
DISTRITO FEDERAL

Monte Pascal

○ Cará-Cará

● Emas

MINAS GERAIS

○ Córrego do Veado
○ Sooretama
○ Nova Lombardia

● Caparão
ESPÍRITO SANTO

● Itatiaia
SÃO PAULO

Serra da Bocaina
● Tijuca ○ Poço das Antas
● Serra dos Orgãos

RIO de JANEIRO

● Sete Quedas

● Iguaçu   PARANÁ

SANTA CATARINA
São Joaquim

● Aparados da Serra

RIO GRANDE do SUL

NATIONAL PARKS AND NATIONAL
BIOLOGICAL RESERVES IN BRAZIL, 1979

● National Parks

○ National Biological
  Reserves

Source: AN 1979, pp. 44-45

Armin K. Ludwig

Table XIII-6. Membership, Activities and Facilities in Brazil's Sports
Clubs and Organizations, 1960-78

	1960	1964	1969	1978
Number of Organizations	8,050	7,677	8,310	7,106
Professional	-	-	380	378
Amateur	-	-	6,130	6,728
Recreational	-	-	3,513	-
Number of Memberships	2,675,813	3,357,325	3,969,979	4,195,822
Athletic Memberships	533,048	649,647	406,725	427,194
Professional Athletes	6,348	8,256	-	6,733
Sports Most Participated In				
Professional	-	-	-	6,733
Soccer	-	-	-	6,714
Golf	-	-	-	8
Auto Racing	-	-	-	8
Boxing	-	-	-	3
Amateur	-	-	-	420,461
Soccer	-	-	-	236,891
Small Scale Soccer	-	-	-	51,374
Swimming	-	-	-	29,873
Volleyball	-	-	-	24,131
Basketball	-	-	-	20,907

	1969			1978		
	Covered & Lighted	Not Covered		Lighted	Not Covered	
		Lighted	Not Lighted		Lighted	Not Lighted
Facilities in Place	2,182	2,613	4,305	2,423	3,410	4,621
Swimming Pools	24	524	360	121	852	734
Olympic	-	-	-	20	225	110
Gymnasiums	318	25	7	346	28	4
Soccer Fields	86	359	2,829	54	401	2,614
Stadiums	-	-	-	18	49	78
Bowling Alleys	-	-	-	457	29	4
Bocci Courts	-	-	-	699	80	34
Basketball Courts				126	503	217
Tennis Courts	338	1,519	830	47	638	218
Volleyball Courts				140	412	304

Sources: AN 1960, p. 313; AN 1967, p. 711; AN 1972, p. 858; AN 1981,
pp. 250-251.

Table XIII-7. History of the World Cup Final Game and National
Standings, 1930-83

Year	Location		Final Game Score		Goal Scorers
1930	Uruguay		Uruguay	4	Dorado, Cea, Iriarte, Castro
			Argentina	2	Peucelle, Stabile
1934	Italy	overtime	Italy	2	Orsi, Schiavio
			Czechoslovakia	1	Puc
1938	France		Italy	4	Coolausi 2, Piola 2
			Hungary	2	Titkos, Sarosi
1942 1946	No World Cup Play				
1950	Brazil		Uruguay	2	Schiaffino, Ghiggia
			Brazil	1	Friaca
1954	Switzerland		West Germany	3	Morlock, Rahn 2
			Hungary	2	Puskas, Czibor
1958	Sweden		Brazil	5	Vava 2, Pele 2, Zagalo
			Sweden	2	Liedholm, Simonsson
1962	Chile		Brazil	3	Amarildo, Zito, Vava
			Czechoslovakia	1	Masopust
1966	England	overtime	England	4	Hurst 3, Peters
			West Germany	2	Haller, Weber
1970	Mexico		Brazil	4	Pelé, Gerson, Jairzinho, Carlos Alberto
			Italy	1	Boninsegna
1974	West Germany		West Germany	2	Breitner, Muller
			Holland	1	Neeskens
1978	Argentina	overtime	Argentina	3	Kempes 2, Bertoni
			Holland	1	Resenbrink
1982	Spain		Italy	3	Rossi, Tardelli, Altobelli
			West Germany	1	Breitner

Standing of the Nations in World Cup Competition, 1983

Championship		Runner-Up		Third Place		Fourth Place	
Brazil	3	Czechoslovakia	2	Brazil	2	Uruguay	2
Italy	3	Hungary	2	Austria	1	Yugoslavia	2
Uruguay	2	Holland	2	Chile	1	Brazil	1
West Germany	2	West Germany	2	France	1	Austria	1
England	1	Brazil	1	Germany	1	Russia	1
Argentina	1	Argentina	1	Poland	1	Spain	1
		Sweden	1	Portugal	1	Sweden	1
		Italy	1	Sweden	1	West Germany	1
				United States	1	Italy	1
				West Germany	1	France	1
				Poland	1		

Sources: Basil Kane, "A History of the World Cup," pp. 62-70, <u>Soccer Digest</u>,
July, 1978; The New York Times, June 25, 1978, Section 5, page 1,
June 26, 1978, page C-1, July 11, Section 5 page 9, July 12, page A-1.

Chapter XIV. External Trade

Table XIV-1 shows the value of Brazil's imports and exports and the trade deficit or surplus for the period 1821 to 1976. The 1821 data originated with the Serviço de Estatística Econômica e Financeira. The 1967 to 1969 data were generated by the Centro de Informações Econômico-Fiscais, and all the remaining data originated with this Centro and the Banco do Brasil's Carteira de Comércio Exterior.

On Table XIV-1 all values were recorded at Brazilian points of ingress or egress (a bordo do Brasil) and all were given in 1,000 cruzeiros (Cr$ 1,000). Figures for 1833 were for the first semester only. Those for 1887 were for the second semester only. The source for 1975 and 1976 (AN 1978) gave exports in both United States dollars and cruzeiros, but gave imports in cruzeiros only. The author calculated the US$ and Cr$ exchange rate on exports and applied it to imports to develop the Cr$ value of imports for 1975 and 1976. The rate was Cr$ 7.93 to the United States dollar in 1975 and Cr$ 10.57 to the United States dollar in 1976. The sharp change on the table between 1966 and 1967 resulted from the introduction of the "new cruzeiro" (NCr$) whose face value was 1/1,000th of the old cruzeiro. The term "new" was subsequently dropped.

Table XIV-2 shows the annual quantum and value of export and import indices from 1939 to 1970. All data were generated by the Laboratório de Estatística of the Conselho Nacional de Estatística. Those data for the period 1939 to 1955 were developed using 1948 as the base year while those for the years 1954 to 1970 were calculated using 1955 as the base year. The quantum data were products of the application of the Lespeyres model and the value data resulted from the use of the Paasche model. For the 1939-55 period 42 export commodities and 180 import commodities were used in the calculation of the indices. The annual aggregate value of export commodities used in these calculations ranged from a high of 96.7 percent of all exports to a low of 70.6 percent. The annual aggregate value of import commodities used ranged from a high of 76.1 percent to a low of 59.7 percent in all imports. For the 1954 to 1970 period a sample of 117 export commodities or commodity groupings was used to calculate the indices. Their aggregate value in any given year was never lower than 79.6 percent of the total value of all exports in that given year. In the same period a sample of 454 import commodities or commodity groupings served as the base for the indices. Their annual total value was never lower than 75.0 percent of the value of all imports.

Table XIV-3 traces the exports of ten of Brazil's major commodities by value and tonnage for ten-year periods and for specific years from 1821 to 1950. Nearly all the data originated with the Serviço de Estatística Econômica e Financeira, but the 1920 and 1930 export tonnages were generated by the Departamento Nacional de Estatística of the Ministério do Trabalho, Indústria e Commércio. All values were in Cr$ 1,000 and represented ten-year summations of exports. The values were established at Brazilian points of egress.

Sugar exports included all types of refined sugar as well as molasses. Tobacco included both leaf (folha) and rope (corda) types. Cotton fibers referred only to the boll (em rama) and not to seeds or linters. Hides and skins included those, both raw and processed, from domestic and wild animals. Rubber included all types such as hevea, sorva, and maçaranduba (see Chapter IX). Erva mate included both raw and processed leaves. Pine lumber included all processed and manufactured forms from the araucaria pine of southern Brazil. For the 1901-10 period the source reported pine exports in numbers of sawn boards (pranchões e tábuas) but since neither the sizes nor weights of these boards were given the table does not present figures for this period.

Table XIV-4 reports significant Brazilian export commodities, other than the ten shown on Table XIV-3, for the period 1920 to 1975. The 1920 and 1930 data were originated by the Departamento Nacional de Estatística of the Ministério do Trabalho, Indústria e Commércio. The 1940 to 1965 data originated with the Serviço de Estatística Econômica e Financeira. Those for 1970 were generated by the Centro de Informações Econômico-Fiscais, and data for 1975 originated with the Banco do Brasil's Carteira do Comércio Exterior. The exports reported on the table are those that were valued at one-half of one percent or more of the nation's total exports for the given year. All export quantities were in metric tons. For most of the years shown on the table sources provided no tonnages for oranges, which were reported by boxes, for bananas, which were reported by stems (cachos), and for leather shoes, which were reported by thousands of pairs. Orange exports by boxes were as follows: 1930,

812,207; 1940, 2,857,791; 1950, 2,416,778 (1950 was the only
year in which the source reported both tonnage and boxes);
1955, 1,313,728; 1960, 3,211,673; 1965, 4,544,167; and 1970,
2,095,490. Banana exports in stems were as follows: 1930,
7,087,353; 1940, 10,247,846; 1950, 7,588,366 (1950 was the
only year in which the source provided both tonnage and
stems); and 1960, 12,697,246. Leather shoe exports totaled
20,391,000 pairs in 1975. Computer exports were reported in
numbers of units, which totaled 10,904 in 1975.

On Table XIV-4 rubber exports were all natural rubber
and included a wide variety of types such as hevea, sorva,
and maçaranduba (see Chapter IX). Only the 1955 source
distinguished Brazil nuts destined for food from those to be
used for oil. For 1960 brans included those from all types
of grains. Tropical wood exports included all nonpine, that
is, nonaraucaria, woods, which in nearly every year from 1920
to 1970 were comprised principally of the imbuia, family
Lauraceas (Phoebe porosa Mez.); jacarandá, subfamily
Papilionacea (Machaerium), and also family Bignoniaceas,
genus Jacaranda; the andiroba, family Meliaceas (Carapa
guianensis Aubl.); and cedar, the name given to several trees
of the families Lauraceas, Meliaceas, and Pinaceas, genuses
Aniba, Cedrela, Larix, and Juniperus. Iron and steel exports
included pig iron, ferro-alloys, and a wide variety of shaped
steel such as bars, rods, plates, tubes, wire, and rails.
Internal combustion engines for 1975 excluded one-cycle
machines. Computers were listed by the 1975 source as
máquinas automáticas de informações (automatic information
machines).

Table XIV-5 reports the values and tonnages of Brazil's
major imports from 1901 to 1975. The data for 1901, 1910,
1940, 1950, and 1960 were originated by the Serviço de
Estatística Econômica e Financeira and those for 1920 and
1930 by the Ministerio da Fazenda. The 1970 and 1975 data
were developed by the Centro de Informações Econômico-
Fiscais. For 1920 the category passenger autos included
trucks as well. Cellulose paste was the raw material base
used in making paper. For all years the major commodity
groupings were those used by the generators of the data.

For 1920 and 1930, automobile imports were given in
units that numbered 9,914 in 1920 and 1,688 in 1930. In 1940
and 1950 they were given in tons and numbered 23,495 and
31,751, respectively. In 1960 the quantity of automobile
imports was given in units numbering 6,130. For 1920 and
1930 coal briquettes were fuel pellets made of compressed
powdered coal. For 1950 trucks/buses/ambulances/etc.,
numbered 15,934. For 1960 no tonnages were given for the
following imports but units were given and are reported here:

agricultural tractors, 14,040 (this category also included Caterpillar type tractors); road graders, 1,106; ships, 33; airplanes, 95; passenger automobiles, 6,130; locomotives, 84; and truck and bus chassis, 12,768. For all years the basic forms of iron, steel, copper, and aluminum consisted primarily of ingots, bars, and rods, and fuel oil consisted principally of diesel oil.

Table XIV-6 shows Brazil's major export trading partners by value of goods for the period 1842/43 to 1976. The table reports every partner that has accounted for one percent or more of Brazil's total exports in any given year since 1842/43. Data for 1842/43 to 1910 were generated by the Diretoria Geral de Estatística and the Serviço de Estatística Econômica e Financeira. The latter also generated the data for 1939 and 1960. The Ministerio da Fazenda originated the data for 1920, 1930, and 1950 and the Banco do Brasil's Carteira do Comércio Exterior originated those for 1970 and 1976. Split dates, for example, 1842/43, are assumed to include only a twelve-month period but the sources did not so specify.

All countries are listed by the names or abbreviations used in 1982 and in most cases they are the popular rather than the formal names. All data for Germany prior to that nation's division in 1945 are reported under West Germany. All data for China prior to the separation of Taiwan in 1950 are reported under China (PRC), the People's Republic of China. From 1903 on exports to Spain included those to the Canary Islands, and for all years exports to Portugal included those to the Madeira and Azores Islands. Only in 1901 did exports to the United Kingdom include those to British possessions as well.

For 1842/43, 1852/53, and 1862/63 exports to Argentina were included with those to Uruguay. For 1842/43 and 1862/63 exports to Paraguay were also included with those to Uruguay. In 1852/53 Paraguay-bound exports were reported separately by the source, but there were none that year. For 1842/43 exports to Chile included those to Peru. From 1852/53 on exports to Peru were listed separately and in the year noted amounted to 4,343 pounds sterling. In no year, however, did exports destined for Peru attain the one percent level necessary to appear on Table XIV-6. Exports to Norway were included with those to Sweden from 1842/43 to 1872/73. In 1901, however, the source indicated no Brazilian exports to either nation.

Table XIV-7 reports Brazil's major import trading partners by value of goods. The table shows every partner that has accounted for one percent or more of Brazil's total imports in any given year since 1842/43. The data origins are the same as those for Table XIV-6. The names of countries were the unofficial ones in use in 1982. Trinidad and Tobago is referred to only as Trinidad. Unlike export data for the previous table import data for this table for 1920 and 1930 did not list European colonies separately. Instead they were grouped by continent as possessions of the mother countries. Consequently, imports to Brazil from, for example, Nigeria could not be distinguished on Table XIV-7.

For 1842/43, 1852/53, and 1862/63 imports from Norway were included with those from Sweden and, as the table indicates, data for the two countries were reported separately in 1872/73. For 1901, however, the source reported imports from Sweden with those of Norway. This rather complicated way of reporting data doubtless stemmed from the growing dominance of Norwegian imports, particularly dried cod, over Swedish imports during this period.

For 1842/43, 1852/53, and 1862/63 imports from Argentina and Paraguay were included with those from Uruguay. There were no imports from Paraguay in 1872/73. From 1901 on, imports from Paraguay were shown separately but did not reach the one percent level necessary to appear on Table XIV-7. For 1842/43 imports from Peru were included with those from Chile. From 1852/53 on, Peru imports were listed separately, but none were reported until 1902. For 1920 and 1930 the source reported Newfoundland imports separately from those of Canada, but they are grouped with Canada's for these and other years on this table. For all years imports from Portugal included those from the Madeira and Azores Islands. Singapore and Malaysia were reported together by the source for 1960 and consequently these two countries are grouped for 1970 and 1976 on this table. Imports from the United States included those from Puerto Rico in 1970 and 1976 and Alaska and Hawaii in 1960.

Table XIV-1. Value of Brazil's Exports, Imports, and Trade Balances, 1821-1978

Date(s)	Exports Cr$ (000)	Imports Cr$ (000)	Surplus/Deficit Cr$ (000)	Date(s)	Exports Cr$ (000)	Imports Cr$ (000)	Surplus/Deficit Cr$ (000)
1821	20,119	21,260	- 1,141	1890	280,665	255,520	+ 25,145
1822	19,754	22,498	- 2,744	1891	439,091	413,680	+ 25,411
1823	20,653	19,420	+ 1,233	1892	618,319	527,104	+ 91,215
1824	19,162	24,061	- 4,899	1893	666,801	546,144	+ 120,657
1825	21,396	22,841	- 1,445	1894	729,455	649,402	+ 80,053
1826	16,599	18,672	- 2,073	1895	790,926	709,018	+ 81,908
1827	24,919	26,894	- 1,975	1896	755,555	743,467	+ 12,088
1828	32,111	31,940	+ 171	1897	824,305	732,173	+ 92,132
1829	33,415	35,531	- 2,116	1898	842,385	792,457	+ 49,928
1830	35,135	42,047	- 6,912	1899	832,082	734,940	+ 97,142
1831	32,431	33,491	- 1,060	1900	850,339	548,939	+ 301,400
1832	31,815	32,146	- 331	1901	860,827	448,353	+ 412,474
1833	20,919	18,165	+ 2,754	1902	735,940	471,114	+ 264,826
1833/34	36,175	36,285	- 110	1903	742,632	486,489	+ 256,143
1834/35	32,992	36,577	- 3,585	1904	776,367	512,588	+ 263,779
1835/36	41,442	41,196	+ 246	1905	685,457	454,995	+ 230,462
1836/37	34,183	45,320	- 11,137	1906	799,670	499,287	+ 300,383
1837/38	33,511	40,757	- 7,246	1907	860,891	644,938	+ 215,953
1838/39	41,598	49,446	- 7,848	1908	705,791	567,272	+ 138,519
1839/40	43,192	52,359	- 9,167	1909	1,016,590	592,876	+ 423,714
1840/41	41,672	57,727	- 16,055	1910	939,413	713,863	+ 225,550
1841/42	39,084	56,041	- 16,957	1911	1,003,925	793,716	+ 210,209
1842/43	41,040	50,640	- 9,600	1912	1,119,737	951,370	+ 168,367
1843/44	43,800	55,289	- 11,489	1913	981,768	1,007,495	- 25,727
1844/45	47,054	55,228	- 8,174	1914	755,747	561,853	+ 193,894
1845/46	53,630	52,194	+ 1,436	1915	1,042,298	582,996	+ 459,302
1846/47	52,449	55,740	- 3,291	1916	1,136,888	810,759	+ 326,129
1847/48	57,926	47,350	+ 10,576	1917	1,192,175	837,738	+ 354,437
1848/49	56,290	51,570	+ 4,720	1918	1,137,100	989,404	+ 147,696
1849/50	55,032	59,165	- 4,133	1919	2,178,719	1,334,259	+ 844,460
1850/51	67,788	76,918	- 9,130	1920	1,752,411	2,090,633	- 338,222
1851/52	66,640	92,860	- 26,220	1921	1,709,722	1,689,839	+ 19,883
1852/53	73,645	87,332	- 13,687	1922	2,332,084	1,652,630	+ 679,454
1853/54	76,843	85,839	- 8,996	1923	3,297,033	2,267,159	+1,029,874
1854/55	90,699	85,171	+ 5,528	1924	3,863,554	2,789,557	+1,073,997
1855/56	94,432	92,779	+ 1,653	1925	4,021,965	3,376,823	+ 645,133
1856/57	114,547	125,227	- 10,680	1926	3,190,557	2,705,553	+ 485,006
1857/58	96,200	130,264	- 34,064	1927	3,644,118	3,273,163	+ 370,995
1858/59	106,782	127,268	- 20,486	1928	3,970,273	3,694,990	+ 275,283
1859/60	112,958	113,028	- 70	1929	3,860,482	3,527,738	+ 332,744
1860/61	123,171	123,720	- 549	1930	2,907,354	2,343,705	+ 563,649
1861/62	120,720	110,531	+ 10,189	1931	3,398,164	1,880,934	+1,517,230
1862/63	122,480	99,163	+ 23,317	1932	2,536,765	1,518,694	+1,018,071
1863/64	131,204	125,700	+ 5,504	1933	2,820,271	2,165,254	+ 655,107
1864/65	141,100	131,800	+ 9,300	1934	3,459,006	2,502,785	+ 956,221
1865/66	157,100	137,800	+ 19,300	1935	4,104,008	3,855,917	+ 248,091
1866/67	156,300	143,200	+ 13,100	1936	4,895,435	4,268,667	+ 626,768
1867/68	185,300	140,600	+ 44,700	1937	5,092,060	5,314,551	- 222,491
1868/69	202,700	166,700	+ 36,000	1938	5,096,890	5,195,570	- 98,680
1869/70	197,100	168,300	+ 28,800	1939	5,615,519	4,993,992	+ 621,527
1870/71	168,000	162,400	+ 5,600	1940	4,960,538	4,964,149	- 3,611
1871/72	190,700	150,300	+ 40,400	1941	6,725,646	5,524,986	+1,200,660
1872/73	214,900	158,500	+ 56,400	1942	7,499,556	4,694,873	+2,804,683
1873/74	189,700	152,800	+ 36,900	1943	8,728,569	6,229,232	+2,499,337
1874/75	208,494	167,549	+ 40,945	1944	10,726,509	8,128,741	+2,598,038
1875/76	183,602	172,149	+ 11,453	1945	12,197,510	8,747,086	+3,450,424
1876/77	195,563	156,886	+ 38,677	1946	18,229,532	13,028,734	+5,200,798
1877/78	186,349	163,517	+ 22,832	1947	21,179,413	22,789,291	-1,609,878
1878/79	204,058	163,505	+ 40,553	1948	21,696,874	20,984,880	+ 711,994
1879/80	222,352	173,645	+ 48,707	1949	20,153,084	20,648,081	- 494,997
1880/81	230,963	179,668	+ 51,295	1950	24,913,487	20,313,429	+4,600,058
1881/82	209,851	182,252	+ 27,599	1951	32,514,265	37,198,345	-4,684,080
1882/83	197,033	190,264	+ 6,769	1952	26,064,993	37,178,622	-1,113,629
1883/84	217,073	202,530	+ 14,543	1953	32,047,276	25,152,079	+6,895,197
1884/85	226,270	178,431	+ 47,839	1954	42,967,571	55,238,775	-2,271,204
1885/86	194,962	197,502	- 2,540	1955	54,521,072	60,225,657	- 5,704,585
1886/87	263,519	297,204	+ 56,315	1956	59,474,292	72,596,808	- 12,123
1887	125,170	103,638	+ 21,532	1957	60,657,129	86,451,541	-25,794,412
1888	206,405	187,488	+ 18,917	1958	63,752,526	103,322,915	-39,570,389
1889	259,095	217,800	+ 41,295	1959	109,449,699	161,284,017	-51,834,318

314

Table XIV-1 (continued)

Date(s)	Exports Cr$ (000)	Imports Cr$ (000)	Surplus/Deficit Cr$ (000)
1960	147,122,627	201,218,687	- 54,096,060
1961	245,150,739	299,357,007	- 54,206,268
1962	307,129,850	511,677,448	- 204,547,598
1963	549,500,904	782,219,819	- 232,718,915
1964	1,177,498	1,242,891	- 65,393
1965	2,214,843	1,929,647	+ 285,196
1966	3,813,340	3,264,773	+ 548,767
1967	4,265,501	4,291,939	- 26,438
1968	6,177,932	6,826,201	- 648,269
1969	9,214,225	8,981,992	+ 232,233
1970	10,844,715	12,903,608	- 2,058,893
1971	15,373,766	19,218,408	- 3,844,642
1972	23,588,417	28,060,426	- 4,472,039
1973	37,827,974	42,851,189	- 5,023,215
1974	53,768,654	94,655,153	- 40,886,499
1975	68,773,057	107,671,765	- 38,898,708
1976	107,105,989	141,842,263	- 34,736,274
1977	167,101,643	181,479,538	- 14,377,895
1978	224,114,456	264,988,521	- 40,874,065

Sources: AN 1956, p. 526; AN 1957, pp. 232-233;
AN 1960, p. 180; AN 1961, p. 222;
AN 1964, p. 158; AN 1967, p. 220;
AN 1976, p. 238; AN 1977, p. 514
AN 1979, p. 496.

Table XIV-2. Brazil's Export and Import Indices by Quantum and Value, 1939-70

	QUANTUM				VALUE			
	Export Base Year = 1948	Import Base Year = 1948	Export Base Year = 1948	Import Base Year = 1948	Export Base Year = 1948	Import Base Year = 1948	Export Base Year = 1948	Import Base Year = 1948
1939	101.6	74.6			74.6	30.7		
1940	81.7	65.5			65.5	37.7		
1941	87.4	65.4			65.4	40.1		
1942	61.4	49.1			49.1	43.6		
1943	62.9	51.3			51.3	48.5		
1944	72.5	65.4			65.4	48.4		
1945	76.1	69.6			69.6	56.8		
1946	100.7	77.5			77.5	72.5		
1947	93.7	115.3			115.3	90.2		
1948	100.0	100.0			100.0	100.0		
1949	90.7	108.0			108.0	91.9		
1950	81.7	131.0			131.0	76.7		
1951	87.2	184.1			184.1	97.4		
1952	67.6	167.0			167.0	105.3		
1953	81.2	137.6			137.6	91.4		
1954	81.6	175.0	87.1	125.5	175.0	150.7	126.1	99.4
1955	85.1	151.0	100.0	100.0	151.0	192.3	100.0	100.0
1956			107.8	97.2			96.6	97.2
1957			99.3	115.9			98.3	98.1
1958			95.6	112.7			91.1	91.9
1959			119.3	123.0			75.4	85.5
1960			119.6	122.7			74.3	91.2
1961			133.1	124.7			73.9	89.6
1962			122.0	125.0			70.1	89.8
1963			142.3	133.9			69.5	84.9
1964			126.7	108.3			79.3	89.1
1965			144.6	94.9			77.3	88.3
1966			164.3	124.6			74.6	91.8
1967			160.9	140.8			72.1	90.1
1968			177.3	170.4			74.4	95.6
1969			210.5	192.2			76.7	89.9
1970			238.2	231.3			80.3	93.8

Sources: AN 1956, p. 237; AN 1963, p. 162; AN 1965, p. 181; AN 1971, p. 292.

Table XIV-3. Ten Major Brazilian Exports by Value and Tonnage, 1821-1975

	1821-1830			1831-1840			1841-1850		
	Cr$ 000	%	Tons	Cr$ 000	%	Tons	Cr$ 000	%	Tons
Total Exports	243,263	100.0	–	348,258	100.0	–	487,977	100.0	–
Coffee Beans	45,308	18.6	190,680	152,429	43.8	584,640	201,469	41.3	1,027,260
Iron Ore	–	–	–	–	–	–	–	–	–
Sugar	78,385	32.2	479,851	83,646	24.0	707,264	130,478	26.7	1,004,043
Cocoa Beans	1,076	.4	11,362	2,093	.6	16,558	4,790	1.0	28,741
Tobacco	5,759	2.4	42,409	6,690	1.9	45,454	8,693	1.8	46,230
Cotton Fibers	48,546	20.0	122,173	38,251	11.0	113,844	36,433	7.4	111,111
Hides/Skins	33,489	13.8	77,619	27,592	7.9	92,425	42,056	8.6	160,688
Rubber	156	.1	329	1,228	.4	2,314	1,913	.4	4,693
Erva Mate	–	–	–	1,718	.5	19,413	4,295	.9	34,165
Total This Group	212,719	87.5	924,423	313,647	90.1	1,581,912	430,127	88.1	2,416,931

	1851-1860			1861-1870			1871-1880		
Total Exports	900,534	100.0	–	1,537,175	100.0	–	1,963,718	100.0	–
Coffee Beans	439,390	48.8	1,575,180	695,352	45.2	1,730,820	1,108,149	56.4	2,180,160
Iron Ore	–	–	–	–	–	–	–	–	–
Sugar	190,708	21.2	1,214,698	185,151	12.0	1,112,762	232,905	11.9	1,685,488
Cocoa Beans	9,191	1.0	35,192	14,182	.9	33,735	24,032	1.2	49,967
Tobacco	23,749	2.6	80,126	46,943	3.1	126,539	67,632	3.4	176,535
Cotton Fibers	55,889	6.2	141,248	282,392	18.4	288,939	186,664	9.5	382,436
Hides/Skins	65,158	7.2	164,841	92,382	6.0	212,394	108,463	5.5	221,936
Rubber	20,140	2.2	19,383	48,943	6.2	37,166	107,904	5.5	60,225
Erva Mate	14,078	1.6	67,347	19,078	1.3	96,169	29,100	1.5	144,235
Total This Group	818,303	90.8	3,298,015	1,384,429	90.1	3,638,524	1,864,849	94.9	4,900,982

	1881-1890			1891-1900			1901		
Total Exports	2,411,006	100.0	–	7,349,258	100.0	–	860,827	100.0	–
Coffee Beans	1,487,532	61.7	3,199,560	4,691,906	63.8	4,469,460	509,598	59.2	885,591
Iron Ore	–	–	–	–	–	–	–	–	–
Sugar	240,201	10.0	2,021,394	416,327	5.7	1,336,202	32,446	3.8	187,166
Cocoa Beans	39,376	1.6	73,627	112,204	1.5	104,460	18,425	2.1	15,682
Tobacco	66,207	2.8	198,831	172,078	2.3	211,812	34,062	4.0	33,471
Cotton Fibers	102,120	4.2	227,778	182,210	2.5	159,002	9,349	1.1	11,765
Hides/Skins	76,869	3.2	180,138	182,210	2.5	246,739	22,661	2.6	23,835
Rubber	185,490	7.7	110,048	1,163,334	15.8	213,755	182,566	21.2	30,241
Erva Mate	27,271	1.1	161,699	104,915	1.4	265,892	19,733	2.3	39,887
Pine Lumber	–	–	–	–	–	–	63	negl.	–
Total This Group	2,225,066	92.3	6,173,075	7,025,184	95.5	7,007,322	828,903	96.3	1,227,638

	1901-1910			1910			1911-1920		
Total Exports	8,123,578	100.0	–	939,413	100.0	–	12,300,768	100.0	–
Coffee Beans	4,179,820	51.5	7,835,912	385,494	41.0	583,425	6,446,402	52.4	7,230,204
Iron Ore	25	negl.	124	6	negl.	9	13	negl.	159
Sugar	101,134	1.2	648,110	10,605	1.1	58,824	392,104	3.2	624,090
Cocoa Beans	227,584	2.8	246,938	20,679	2.2	29,158	454,243	3.7	439,201
Tobacco	200,574	2.5	278,941	24,391	2.6	34,149	318,740	2.6	278,825
Cotton Fibers	172,509	2.1	193,881	13,456	1.5	11,160	243,220	2.0	150,961
Hides/Skins	354,401	4.4	328,171	36,618	3.9	36,755	804,116	6.5	458,175
Rubber	2,268,840	27.9	345,079	376,972	40.1	38,547	1,406,769	11.4	328,755
Erva Mate	228,657	2.8	485,770	29,017	3.1	59,360	374,874	3.1	721,709
Pine Lumber	1,329	negl.	–	150	negl.	–	49,253	.4	481,944
Total This Group	7,734,873	95.2	10,362,926	897,388	95.5	851,387	10,489,734	85.3	10,714,023

Table XIV-3 (continued)

	1920			1921-1930			1930		
	Cr$ 000	%	Tons	Cr$ 000	%	Tons	Cr$ 000	%	Tons
Total Exports	1,752,411	100.0	2,101,380	32,797,147	100.0	-	2,907,354	100.0	2,273,688
Coffee Beans	860,958	49.1	691,487	22,807,258	59.5	8,371,943	1,827,577	62.9	917,305
Iron Ore	2	negl.	17	24	negl.	361	3	negl.	11
Sugar	105,831	6.0	105,149	473,679	1.4	810,032	25,219	.9	84,457
Cocoa Beans	64,450	3.7	54,419	1,043,599	3.2	632,549	91,688	3.2	68,852
Tobacco	42,0051	2.4	31,469	673,540	2.1	336,834	73,798	2.5	37,799
Cotton Fibers	80,697	4.6	24,696	790,364	2.4	227,682	84,602	2.9	30,417
Hides/Skins	110,097	6.3	41,231	1,522,824	4.7	569,299	143,932	4.9	56,673
Rubber	58,350	3.3	23,587	820,437	2.5	202,644	33,584	1.2	14,138
Erva Mate	50,559	2.9	90,686	888,391	2.7	859,146	95,352	3.3	84,846
Pine Lumber	11,545	.7	84,885	163,710	.5	950,296	15,839	.5	85,024
Total This Group	1,384,495	79.0	1,147,626	29,183,826	89.0	12,960,786	2,391,594	82.3	1,379,522

	1931-1940			1940			1941-1950		
Total Exports	41,978,656	100.0	-	4,960,538	100.0	3,236,926	152,050,180	100.0	-
Coffee Beans	21,005,538	50.0	8,801,170	1,589,248	32.0	722,743	65,658,742	43.2	8,289,760
Iron Ore	69,718	.2	1,377,590	16,188	.3	255,553	430,982	.3	3,991,561
Sugar	204,691	.5	401,024	38,696	.8	66,731	1,365,982	.9	686,995
Cocoa Beans	1,727,979	4.1	1,077,134	191,798	3.9	106,799	6,584,988	4.3	1,070,744
Tobacco	636,170	1.5	296,595	44,848	.9	16,812	2,397,712	1.6	299,641
Cotton Fibers	5,994,804	14.3	1,551,182	837,955	16.9	224,265	17,712,287	11.3	1,957,818
Hides/Skins	1,853,280	4.4	496,608	221,758	4.5	51,417	5,300,761	3.5	494,286
Rubber	452,430	1.1	115,536	77,467	1.5	11,835	1,728,649	1.1	123,442
Erva Mate	696,196	1.7	649,622	61,037	1.2	50,520	1,125,949	.7	496,273
Pine Lumber	388,782	.9	1,594,149	67,718	1.4	247,043	4,896,511	3.2	3,904,680
Total This Group	33,029,588	78.7	16,360,610	3,146,713	63.4	1,753,718	106,617,563	70.1	21,315,200

	1950			1955			1960		
Total Exports	24,913,487	100.0	3,819,083	54,521,072	100.0	6,186,066	147,122,678	100.0	106,607,865
Coffee Beans	15,907,569	63.9	890.093	30,366,732	55.7	821,747	59,376,993	40.4	1,009,139
Iron Ore	121,759	.5	890,125	1,231,409	2.3	2,564,551	5,160,266	3.5	9,462,792
Sugar	61,473	.2	23,550	2,254,548	4.1	573,252	10,119,694	6.9	768,741
Cocoa Beans	1,445,797	5.8	131,996	3,694,965	6.8	121,923	5,799,245	3.9	125,457
Tobacco	409,040	1.6	36,367	746,680	1.4	28,209	3,382,496	2.3	31,587
Cotton Fibers	1,936,109	7.8	128,845	5,134,225	9.4	175,706	8,324,623	5.6	95,399
Hides/Skins	584,300	2.3	52,209	395,780	.7	18,415	2,555,039	1.7	27,063
Rubber	41,687	.2	44,494	80,094	.1	3,430	538,745	.4	3,488
Erva Mate	145,948	.6	45,774	643,597	1.2	52,404	1,610,086	1.1	56,130
Pine Lumber	605,276	2.4	499,867	2,109,212	3.9	672,730	7,623,965	5.2	559,073
Total This Group	21,258,958	85.3	2,710,320	46,657,243	85.6	5,032,367	104,491,152	71.0	12,138,869

	1965			1970			1975		
Total Exports	2,214,843,187	100.0	19,681,872	10,884,715	100.0	39,969,585	68,773,057	100.0	92,985,205
Coffee Beans	600,558,199	27.1	808,931	2,610,633	24.0	962,630	6,523,485	9.5	782,160
Iron Ore	190,633,336	8.6	12,731,228	959,735	8.8	28,061,393	7,370,663	10.7	75,521,995
Sugar	103,715,404	4.7	760,009	620,419	5.7	1,126,462	8,859,053	12.9	1,514,588
Cocoa Beans	51,289,593	2.3	91,966	355,372	3.3	119,768	1,776,275	2.6	176,628
Tobacco	45,922,737	2.0	55,299	145,546	1.3	54,468	1,127,358	1.6	98,158
Cotton Fibers	172,706,441	7.8	195,690	700,636	6.4	342,833	801,608	1.2	107,202
Hides/Skins	43,465,161	2.0	49,387	187,129	1.7	52,779	492,148	.7	13,886
Rubber	9,079,833	.4	7,854	20,290	.2	5,306	-	-	-
Erva Mate	12,742,572	.6	41,763	21,939	.2	25,830	79,108	.1	20,807
Pine Lumber	97,433,720	4.4	700,905	330,886	3.0	571,338	554,772	.8	203,746
Total This Group	1,327,546,996	59.9	15,443,032	5,952,585	54.6	31,322,807	27,584,470	40.1	78,439,170

Sources: CEB 1925, pp. 108-146; CEB 1932, pp. 74-95; AN 1956, pp. 526-529; AN 1961, pp. 224-229; An 1967, pp. 225-234; AN 1971, pp. 305-314; AN 1978, pp. 541-549.

Table XIV-4. Other Major Brazilian Exports by Value and Quantity, 1920-75

	Cr$ 000	%	Tons		Cr$ 000	%	Tons
1920				**1960**			
Total Exports	1,752,411	100.0	2,101,380	Total Exports	147,122,627	100.0	10,607,865
Rice	94,158	5.4	134,554	Manganese Ore	5,325,371	3.6	866,318
Frozen/Chilled Beef	63,614	3.6	60,898	Sisal/Agave Fibers	4,001,132	2.7	107,915
Manganese Ore	39,829	2.3	453,737	Carnaúba Wax	3,133,667	2.1	11,080
Lard	22,459	1.3	11,166	Brazil Nuts	2,615,575	1.8	26,394
Brazil Nuts	13,552	.8	9,279	Cocoa Butter	2,458,461	1.7	22,606
Dried Beef (Xarque)	10,213	.6	7,889	Castor Oil	1,786,081	1.2	41,856
				Brans (all types)	1,232,874	.8	125,577
1930				Canned Beef	1,148,482	.8	8,141
Total Exports	2,907,354	100.0	2,273,688	Oranges	1,115,545	.8	-
Frozen/Chilled Beef	136,761	4.7	99,197	Bananas	858,979	.6	-
Rice	25,399	.9	38,341	Alcohol (ethanol)	815,990	.6	71,359
Brazil Nuts	25,002	.9	14,155	Menthol	726,189	.5	346
Carnaúba Wax	23,365	.8	6,711	Tropical Woods	708,896	.5	73,574
Bananas	21,787	.7	-				
Canned Meat	17,307	.6	6,598	**1965**			
Oranges	16,076	.6	-	Total Exports	2,214,843,187	100.0	19,681,872
Chilled/Frozen Viscera	15,282	.5	8,952	Iron & Steel (basic shapes)	78,210,494	3.5	482,355
Dried Beef (Xarque)	9,203	.3	3,646	Manganese Ore	53,521,899	2.4	1,067,763
				Corn	51,016,730	2.3	559,675
1940				Castor Oil	46,828,048	2.1	140,152
Total Exports	4,960,538	100.0	3,236,916	Rice	43,906,124	2.0	236,788
Chilled Beef	226,413	4.6	93,952	Sisal/Agave Fibers	39,583,829	1.8	134,927
Canned Beef	216,567	4.4	46,687	Frozen Beef	36,562,009	1.7	29,782
Carnaúba Wax	169,411	3.4	8,653	Cocoa Butter	24,467,444	1.1	17,197
Castor Beans	119,745	2.4	117,495	Canned Beef	22,200,707	1.0	16,812
Diamonds	81,403	1.6	.05	Raw Wool	21,980,667	1.0	12,319
Cotton Textiles	67,904	1.4	3,959	Brazil Nuts	21,054,440	1.0	19,911
Oranges	57,201	1.2	-	Carnaúba Wax	19,612,830	.9	12,119
Rubber	50,777	1.0	7,399	Tropical Woods	18,947,828	.9	101,659
Cotton Linters	48,883	1.0	39,873	Peanut Bran	14,659,097	.6	115,993
Babaçu Nuts	48,553	1.0	41,187	Rubber	13,503,998	.6	14,110
Cottonseed Cake	46,419	.9	142,604	Oranges	13,353,378	.6	-
Oiticica Oil	43,658	.9	7,235	Soybean Bran	13,130,897	.6	99,052
Cottonseed Oil	42,890	.9	26,311				
Bananas	42,356	.9	-	**1970**			
Raw Wool	32,641	.7	3,613	Total Exports	10,844,715	100.0	39,969,585
Manganese Ore	32,311	.7	222,713	Iron & Steel (basic shapes)	444,886	4.1	769,978
Brazil Nuts	31,502	.6	6,774	Soluble Coffee	193,643	1.8	20,825
				Textiles (all types)	85,867	.8	27,328
1950				Processed Crustaceans	74,666	.7	5,883
Total Exports	24,913,487	100.0	3,819,083	Canned Beef	73,038	.7	16,552
Carnaúba Wax	408,463	1.6	12,758	Sisal	69,989	.6	131,677
Sisal/Agave Fibers	243,958	1.0	46,655	Peanut Bran	68,889	.6	196,499
Oranges	197,156	.8	84,587	Orange Juice	68,523	.6	33,468
Castor Beans	177,474	.7	163,515	Brazil Nuts	62,562	.6	32,267
Cocoa Butter	168,546	.7	9,687	Tropical Woods	58,486	.5	189,742
Bananas	164,920	.7	151,767	Peanuts	55,540	.5	53,473
Cotton Textiles	153,112	.6	1,361				
Cotton Linters	130,267	.5	40,904	**1975**			
				Total Exports	68,773,057	100.0	92,985,205
1955				Soybeans	5,491,259	8.0	3,333,334
Total Exports	54,521,072	100.0	6,186,066	Soybean Cake	3,731,283	5.4	3,133,581
Carnaúba Wax	713,151	1.3	12,466	Soybean Oil	1,231,676	1.8	263,183
Sisal/Agave Fibers	519,781	1.0	80,342	Iron & Steel (basic shapes)	1,083,812	1.6	642,573
Bananas	362,454	.7	-	Leather Shoes	856,035	1.2	-
Brazil Nuts (for food)	287,272	.5	6,088	Soluble Coffee	737,250	1.0	31,359
Brazil Nuts (for oil)	282,907	.5	19,301	Internal Combustion Engines	708,769	1.0	219,584
Tropical Woods	278,088	.5	112,583	Orange Juice Concentrate	661,089	1.0	180,897
Oranges	275,170	.5	-	Cocoa Butter	478,227	.7	21,564
Castor Oil	241,153	.4	24,816	Castor Oil	409,454	.6	91,453
Castor Beans	238,380	.4	61,401	Computers	406,177	.6	-
Soybeans	235,282	.4	51,390				

Sources: CEB 1925, pp. 108-146; CEB 1932, pp. 74-95; AN 1941-45, pp. 262-264; AN 1951, pp. 258-260; AN 1956, pp. 245-248; AN 1961, pp. 224-229; AN 1967, pp. 225-234; AN 1971, pp. 305-315; AN 1978, pp. 541-549.

Table XIV-5. Values and Tonnages of Brazilian Imports by Major Commodity Groups and Specific Commodities, 1901-75

1901	Cr$ 000	%	Tons
Total Imports	448,353	100.0	-
Wheat Flour	31,887	7.1	141,551
Wheat Grain	27,887	6.2	792,986
Coal	16,466	3.7	114,557
Diverse & Other	372,113	83.0	-

1910	Cr$ 000	%	Tons
Total Imports	713,863	100.0	-
Wheat Grain	35,950	5.0	316,313
Coal	35,569	5.0	1,581,719
Wheat Flour	30,612	4.2	158,956
Dried Cod	16,459	2.3	33,841
Kerosene	12,592	1.8	99,530
Iron/Steel Rods/Bars	5,908	.8	37,237
Newsprint	5,014	.7	20,572
Tinplate	4,814	.7	17,589
Passenger Autos	3,477	.5	735
Copper Ingots	2,634	.4	2,439
Lube Oil	2,570	.4	10,168
Aniline Dyes	1,331	.2	286
Auto Accessories	961	.1	206
Gasoline	922	.1	3,369
Cellulose Paste	399	.1	3,504
Diverse & Other	554,651	77.7	-

1920	Cr$ 000	%	Tons
Total Imports	2,090,632	100.0	3,064,330
Manufactured Goods	1,157,528	55.4	825,059
Cotton Textiles	98,523		5,724
Automobiles	52,775		-
Newsprint	41,760		34,702
Tool/Utensils	35,107		13,487
Locomotives	29,841		12,054
Steel Rails	29,487		71,093
Tinplate	29,334		29,776
Barbed Wire	28,505		45,087
Gasoline	27,514		58,500
Wool Textiles	23,690		618
Fuel Oils	21,348		228,651
Automobile Accessories	19,486		4,811
Steel Wire	19,181		25,551
Lighting Equipment	15,959		2,705
Steel Tubes	14,964		17,645
Cutlery	14,924		1,004
Lube Oils	13,816		15,092
Galvanized Steel Sheets	12,082		10,305
Automobile Tires	12,620		1,808
Perfumes	11,260		825
Linen Textiles	11,189		516
Raw Materials	504,730	24.1	1,631,346
Coal	134,402		1,120,575
Jute (raw & processed)	34,464		22,025
Cotton Yarn & Thread	34,263		1,613
Hides/Skins	31,363		1,439
Cement	26,624		172,992
Iron/Steel Ingots	24,144		38,324
Wool Yarn	17,428		670
Rosin	14,602		16,536
Furs (beaver/rabbit, etal)	12,887		222
Silk Yarn	12,636		158
Coal Briquettes	11,796		94,887
Food Products	408,937	19.6	592,198
Wheat Grain	141,068		281,478
Wheat Flour	80,724		109,379
Wines	44,324		36,759
Dried Cod	44,227		29,538
Olive Oil	21,770		4,415
Livestock	19,437	.9	47,897
Cattle	16,585		-

1930	Cr$ 000	%	Tons
Total Imports	2,343,705	100.0	4,733,185
Manufactured Goods	1,229,184	52.5	1,184,510
Gasoline	139,173		279,495
Lighting Equipment	51,683		4,358
Kerosene	46,842		90,465
Fuel Oils	42,198		374,457
Cotton Textiles	31,722		1,338
Lube Oils	27,395		24,561
Steel Rails/Accessories	26,605		54,177
Newsprint	24,537		38,561
Auto Tires/Tubes	24,446		3,226
Tinplate	23,193		24,166
Steel Tubes	21,842		22,491
Sewing Machines	21,384		2,631
Linen Textiles	17,044		719
Wool Textiles	16,201		330
Copper Wire/Cable	14,976		4,634
Caustic Soda	14,396		17,683
Locomotives	13,809		6,822
Auto Accessories	13,737		2,670
Steel Telephone Poles	13,000		11,455
Barbed Wire	12,129		21,538
Automobiles	12,006		-
Electric Transformers	11,803		2,317
Tools/Utensils	11,269		1,417
Food Products	590,697	25.2	979,160
Wheat Grain	264,980		648,240
Wheat Flour	92,142		152,279
Dried Cod	69,005		35,392
Wines	27,588		16,055
Tomatoes	12,775		29,738
Raw Materials	518,723	22.1	2,569,515
Coal	118,526		1,745,826
Cement	47,226		390,593
Jute (raw & processed)	34,776		19,713
Silk Yarn	32,443		439
Wool Yarn	20,407		959
Cellulose Paste	20,234		38,223
Hides/Skins	18,021		351
Cotton Yarn	15,267		957
Copper & Basic Forms	13,863		4,182
Rosin	13,541		18,740
Coal Briquettes	13,224		174,611
Iron/Steel Bars/Rods	12,012		26,252
Livestock/Animal Products	5,101	.2	-

1940	Cr$ 000	%	Tons
Total Imports	4,964,149	100.0	4,336,133
Combustibles/Lube Oils	785,664	15.8	2,371,293
Gasoline	198,370		368,398
Fuel Oil	171,101		694,092
Lube Oils	67,836		44,485
Kerosene	49,348		101,647
Metals/Metal Products	761,108	15.3	354,448
Tinplate	165,191		66,740
Iron/Steel Sheets & Plates	89,770		50,412
Iron/Steel Tubes	72,359		31,716
Steel Rails	70,311		51,649
Copper & Basic Forms	68,441		8,489
Steel Wire	41,035		21,983
Cutlery/Tools/Utensils	37,045		2,845
Iron/Steel Rods	30,831		13,621
Iron/Steel Ingots	27,912		16,079
Food Products	732,971	14.8	958,247
Wheat Grain	471,309		857,937
Dried Cod	45,415		16,021
Apples/Pears/Grapes	40,342		17,331
Machinery/Electrical Machinery	709,481	14.3	40,177
Radio Equipment	54,859		839
Sewing Machines	41,241		1,812
Electric Motors/Generators	27,727		1,517
Transportation Equipment	650,637	13.1	55,010
Automobiles (all types)	312,849		32,086
Auto Accessories	87,796		5,863
Railroad Car/ Accessories	82,522		15,871
Chemicals/Pharmaceuticals	535,971	10.8	263,190
Caustic Soda	48,007		31,515
Aniline Dyes	38,923		544
Cellulose Acetate	28,592		1,796
Chemical Fertilizers	27,670		41,631
Textiles/Fibers	280,722	5.7	28,957
Jute	64,161		22,406
Linen	40,892		674
Wool	39,177		1,338
Cotton	38,974		869
Silk	32,079		197
Paper/Paper Products	81,123	1.6	45,687
Newsprint	63,598		42,816
Diverse & Other	426,472	8.6	219,124

Table XIV-5. (continued)

1950

Item	Cr$ 000	%	Tons
Total Imports	20,313,429	100.0	8,967,894
Machinery/Electrical Machinery	3,691,847	18.2	124,204
Textile Machinery	473,880		15,365
Road Building Machinery	359,608		18,585
Electric Motors/Generators	296,028		6,570
Agricultural Tractors	266,468		13,933
Sewing Machines	187,175		3,815
Radio Equipment	164,898		1,527
Diesel Engines (non-auto)	163,922		5,725
Food Products	3,470,319	17.1	1,430,867
Wheat Grain	2,027,852		1,228,372
Apples/Pears/Grapes	296,693		50,832
Dried Cod	291,035		25,310
Malt	102,293		31,853
Combustibles/Lube Oils	2,960,228	14.6	5,472,172
Gasoline	1,306,117		1,618,008
Fuel Oil	806,255		2,308,688
Coal	327,362		1,082,722
Lube Oils	276,321		115,526
Kerosene	144,116		236,483
Transportation Equipment	2,313,164	11.4	119,037
Truck/Bus Chassis	548,901		15,934
Trucks/Buses/Ambulances/etc.	456,936		28,735
Passenger Cars	407,702		17,575
Auto Accessories/Motors	357,095		8,501
Chemicals/Pharmaceuticals	2,154,501	10.6	739,927
Cellulose Paste	309,167		131,769
Aniline Dyes	193,209		2,054
Antibiotics	127,889		14
Caustic Soda	119,300		65,735
Metals/Metal Products	1,787,449	8.8	359,728
Copper Ingots	195,261		21,259
Tinplate	188,852		48,364
Iron/Steel Tubing	172,502		45,753
Iron/Steel Basic Forms	161,751		48,530
Barbed Wire	168,606		60,578
Steel Wire	124,068		48,001
Lead & Basic Forms	109,573		19,738
Textiles/Fibers	598,317	2.9	14,821
Wool	232,652		3,853
Non-Metallic Minerals & Products	482,053	2.4	529,880
Cement	208,348		404,117
Paper/Paper Products	316,181	1.5	70,571
Newsprint	163,539		60,634
Animals/Animal Products	308,625	1.5	25,378
Animals for Reproduction	157,659		18,518
Diverse & Other	2,230,745	11.0	83,309

1970

Item	Cr$ 000	%	Tons
Total Imports	12,830,326	100.0	28,069,265
Machinery/Electrical Machinery	3,627,407	28.3	216,312
Telephone Equipment	114,516		1,581
Computers	113,590		799
Photoengraving Equipment	69,293		2,606
Ball Bearing Assemblies	68,438		4,586
Harvesters/Combines	65,584		8,052
Chemicals/Pharmaceuticals	2,017,270	15.7	2,943,333
Insecticides/Fungicides	85,913		19,447
Potassium Chlorate	79,363		491,699
Ammonium Sulfate	71,563		697,224
Caustic Soda	71,517		164,185
Coal Tar Dyes	69,016		2,851
Combustibles/Lubricants	1,707,420	13.3	20,020,018
Crude Oil	1,094,986		15,796,648
Coal	186,638		1,998,624
Lube Oils	156,654		420,260
Naphtha	123,358		1,194,515
L P Gas	73,595		376,071
Food Products	1,336,633	10.4	2,514,214
Wheat Grain	584,721		1,969,300
Dried Cod	139,897		47,222
Apples	121,688		108,994
Metals/Metal Products	1,313,946	10.2	698,784
Iron/Steel Basic Forms	571,356		473,657
Iron/Steel Ingots & Bars	43,206		29,563
Aluminum & Basic Forms	100,105		32,552
Copper & Basic Forms	100,104		10,604
Copper Ingots	279,799		42,613
Zinc Ingots & Basic Forms	66,117		43,977
Metal Products	332,547		72,123
Transportation Equipment	914,075	7.1	58,998
Internal Combustion Engines	156,152		10,305
Jet Airplanes	130,208		9
Ships/Ship Accessories	122,035		6,663
Automobile Accessories	73,732		5,975
Aircraft Accessories	69,698		332
Paper/Paper Products	186,290	1.5	216,992
Newsprint	126,742		149,097
Textiles	122,926	1.0	2,370
Synthetic Fabrics	82,795		8,959
Diverse & Other	1,604,359	12.5	1,398,244
Wrist Watches	68,822		–

Table XIV-5 (continued)

1960

	Cr$ 000	%	Tons
Total Imports	201,218,687	100.0	15,609,773
Machinery/Electrical Machinery	40,482,233	20.1	163,482
Agricultural Tractors	811,427		-
Ball Bearings	1,861,864		2,893
Road Graders	1,345,878		-
Laminating Machines	1,068,033		6,716
Combustibles/Lubricants	28,396,654	14.1	11,092,849
Crude Oil	11,263,849		5,683,919
Fuel Oils	6,981,390		2,981,485
Gasoline	4,105,701		890,985
Coal	3,555,808		1,016,632
Lube Oils	1,728,690		212,242
Food Products	25,816,204	12.8	2,268,620
Wheat Grain	14,265,988		2,032,900
Dried Cod	2,322,015		21,270
Malt	1,582,713		49,521
Olive Oil	1,278,828		12,125
Transportation Equipment	25,642,959	12.8	56,731
Automobile Accessories	12,229,192		30,233
Ships	4,204,589		-
Airplanes	2,239,451		5,346
Internal Combustion Engines	1,964,319		
Passenger Autos	1,689,190		-
Locomotives	1,354,262		-
Trucks/Bus Chassis	1,157,258		-
Airplane Accessories	1,077,762		627
Chemicals/Pharmaceuticals	25,367,627	12.6	827,295
Cellulose Paste	2,581,167		8,784
Nitrogen Fertilizer	2,317,659		9,523
Synthetic Rubber	2,138,312		17,418
Caustic Soda	1,765,018		100,620
Aniline Dyes	1,271,011		1,393
Antibiotics	1,097,951		36
Insecticides/Fungicides	1,053,989		13,333
Metal Products	17,138,983	8.5	420,148
Tinplate	3,958,149		85,274
Iron & Steel Sheets & Plates	3,053,991		71,962
Barbed Wire	2,075,135		51,191
Iron & Steel Rods	1,823,324		134,865
Basic Metals	10,644,646	5.3	114,162
Copper Ingots	4,429,239		29,338
Zinc & Basic Forms	1,855,526		30,781
Aluminum & Basic Forms	1,767,335		15,015
Iron & Steel Ingots & Bars	714,346		11,264
Vegetal Products	10,421,332	5.2	144,838
Natural Rubber	4,620,378		24,574
Paper	3,512,533	1.7	190,374
Newsprint	2,603,134		164,491
Diverse & Other	13,795,516	6.9	323,579

1975

	Cr$ 000	%	Tons
Total Imports	13,586,524	100.0	53,055,508
Minerals	3,734,505	27.5	40,843,732
Crude Oil	3,106,618		34,611,037
Coal	192,202		2,735,014
Lube Oils	67,954		318,722
Machinery/Electrical Machinery	3,474,735	25.6	524,862
Agricultural Tractors	141,617		42,008
Caterpillar Tractors	130,620		38,948
Telephone Switching Equipment	122,234		5,805
Metals/Metal Products	1,925,977	14.2	3,327,378
Iron/Steel Ingots & Basic Forms	1,000,361		2,078,022
Copper Ingots	148,915		107,651
Aluminum Ingots & Basic Forms	96,922		91,379
Tinplate	93,984		149,426
Chemicals/Pharmaceuticals	1,623,358	11.9	4,375,244
Naphtha	95,792		862,183
Ammonium Phosphate	93,914		431,747
Superphosphates	83,840		496,989
Chlorate of Phosphate	77,051		884,330
Orthophosphoric Acid	70,336		335,809
Transportation Equipment	739,754	5.4	139,043
Jet Airplanes	126,300		664
Automobile Accessories	119,090		34,169
Vegetable Products	665,122	4.9	2,755,154
Wheat Grain	350,767		2,082,376
Malt	68,508		188,354
Diverse & Other	1,423,073	10.5	1,090,095

Sources: CEB 1925, pp. 19-92; CEB 1932, pp. 18-60;
AN 1941-45, pp. 264-267; AN 1951, pp. 261-264;
AN 1956, pp. 530-533; AN 1961, pp. 230-241;
AN 1971, pp. 317-337; AN 1978, pp. 558-573.

Table XIV-6. Brazil's Major Export Trading Partners by Value of Goods Shipped from Brazil, 1842/43-1976

	1842/43		1852/53		1862/63		1872/73		1901		1910		1920	
	Pound Sterling	%	Pound Sterling	%	Pound Sterling	%	Pound Sterling	%	Pound Sterling	%	Pound Sterling	%	Cr$ 000	%
United States	758,778	18.3	2,649,817	34.3	1,672,277	12.5	6,592,526	29.3	17,462,650	43.0	22,868,529	36.2	725,189	41.4
West Germany	539,176	13.0	407,937	5.3	553,590	4.1	1,716,487	7.6	6,014,842	14.8	7,466,734	11.8	112,301	6.4
Netherlands	24,909	negl	15,773	negl	12,933	negl	97,427	negl	1,978,695	4.9	3,241,896	5.1	52,422	3.0
Japan	–	–	–	–	–	–	–	–	–	negl	670	negl	281	negl
Spain	34,180	negl	68,580	negl	259,094	1.9	169,429	negl	61,981	negl	232,001	negl	11,538	negl
Italy	142,976	3.5	130,988	1.7	62,582	negl	112,849	negl	378,171	negl	434,139	negl	123,122	7.0
U.S.S.R.	12,622	negl	41,262	negl	64,883	negl	35,220	negl	–	–	39,359	negl	–	–
United Kingdom	1,277,736	30.8	2,820,239	36.5	5,068,781	37.9	8,297,863	36.9	5,259,667	12.9	14,581,334	23.1	140,024	8.0
France	275,676	6.7	495,376	6.4	1,692,991	12.7	1,959,585	8.7	4,761,907	11.7	5,310,094	8.4	200,458	11.4
Argentina	–	–	142,646	1.8	–	–	699,911	3.1	907,719	2.2	2,382,457	3.8	120,117	6.9
Yugoslavia	–	–	–	–	–	–	–	–	–	–	–	–	30,208	1.7
Sweden	129,907	3.1	98,069	1.3	257,231	1.9	100,345	negl	–	–	320,896	negl	77,143	4.4
Uruguay	262,048	6.3	116,015	1.5	564,659	4.2	370,014	1.6	477,392	1.2	1,140,245	1.8	–	–
Poland	–	–	–	–	–	–	–	–	–	–	–	–	16,215.	negl
Denmark	84,110	2.0	88,811	1.1	112,450	negl	86,903	negl	–	–	63,767	negl	–	–
Mexico	–	–	–	–	–	–	–	–	–	–	–	–	4,020	negl
Algeria	–	–	–	–	–	–	–	–	–	–	–	–	2,108	negl
Canada	–	–	–	–	–	–	–	–	–	–	77,839	negl	73	negl
Paraguay	–	–	–	–	–	–	729	negl	–	–	10,078	negl	–	–
Venezuela	–	–	–	–	–	–	–	–	–	–	–	–	–	–
Belgium/Luxembourg	106,562	2.6	185,166	2.4	114,422	negl	305,306	1.4	893,793	2.2	1,164,570	1.8	47,794	2.7
Norway	–	–	–	–	–	–	–	–	–	–	63,445	negl	2,286	negl
Hungary	–	–	–	–	–	–	–	–	–	–	–	–	–	–
Bolivia	–	–	–	–	–	–	–	–	–	–	–	–	17	negl
Chile	27,143	negl	46,977	negl	105,326	negl	142,025	negl	–	–	162,857	negl	6,609	negl
East Germany	–	–	–	–	–	–	–	–	–	–	–	–	–	–
Switzerland	–	–	–	–	–	–	–	–	–	–	1	negl	5	negl
Czechoslovakia	–	–	–	–	–	–	–	–	–	–	–	–	–	–
Portugal	344,930	8.3	342,900	4.4	844,249	6.3	1,388,673	6.2	244,549	negl	168,174	negl	35,628	2.0
Hong Kong	–	–	–	–	–	–	–	–	–	–	–	–	–	–
China (PRC)	–	–	–	–	–	–	–	–	–	–	–	–	7	negl
China (Taiwan)	–	–	–	–	–	–	–	–	–	–	–	–	–	–
Total	4,137,591	100.0	7,730,337	100.0	13,382,818	100.0	22,486,257	100.0	40,621,993	100.0	63,091,547	100.0	1,752,411	100.0

Table XIV-6 (continued)

	1930 Cr$ 000	%	1939 Cr$ 000	%	1950 Cr$ 000	%	1960 Cr$ 000	%	1970 Cr$ 000	%	1976 US$ 000	%
United States	1,179,421	40.6	2,030,809	36.2	13,583,772	54.5	57,461,869	39.1	2,485,361	23.0	1,842,943	18.4
West Germany	265,046	9.1	671,849	12.0	335,918	1.3	12,077,445	8.2	989,561	9.1	918,899	9.2
Netherlands	147,847	5.1	214,321	3.8	599,255	2.4	6,478,532	4.4	630,527	5.8	772,863	7.7
Japan	1,531	negl	306,096	5.5	199,375	negl	5,224,033	3.6	646,948	6.0	639,248	6.4
Spain	24,829	negl	15,580	negl	277,484	1.1	2,028,977	1.4	452,120	4.2	441,131	4.4
Italy	125,653	4.3	132,922	2.4	437,016	1.8	3,706,571	2.5	815,966	7.5	419,834	4.2
U.S.S.R.	2,508	negl	—	—	—	—	1,232,925	negl	97,537	negl	411,068	4.1
United Kingdom	237,126	8.2	540,104	9.6	2,077,952	8.3	9,898,636	6.7	544,180	5.0	386,780	3.9
France	266,808	9.2	354,386	6.3	1,174,856	4.7	5,562,250	3.8	406,052	3.8	343,628	3.4
Argentina	199,109	6.8	310,103	5.5	1,402,201	5.6	8,245,383	5.6	798,245	7.4	331,124	3.3
Yugoslavia	2,004	negl	15,845	negl	21,564	negl	766,712	negl	46,607	negl	189,319	1.9
Sweden	57,712	2.0	173,885	3.1	820,119	3.3	3,761,713	2.6	208,578	1.9	185,992	1.9
Uruguay	145,394	5.0	55,371	negl	313,905	1.3	2,852,069	1.9	140,174	1.3	162,559	1.6
Poland	—	—	23,104	negl	29,756	negl	3,703,215	2.5	93,365	negl	156,519	1.6
Denmark	34,931	1.2	86,349	1.5	385,082	1.5	2,317,689	1.6	155,205	1.4	154,274	1.5
Mexico	—	—	1,612	negl	52,149	negl	27,940	negl	93,579	negl	142,184	1.4
Algeria	19,147	negl	26,659	negl	33,239	negl	148,934	negl	115,297	1.1	141,975	1.4
Canada	6,498	negl	18,971	negl	330,474	1.3	1,619,861	1.1	152,666	1.4	136,852	1.4
Paraguay	229	negl	3,558	negl	9,555	negl	145,767	negl	51,322	negl	132,130	1.3
Venezuela	3	negl	2,995	negl	28,766	negl	210,375	negl	37,356	negl	125,195	1.2
Belgium/Luxembourg	91,626	3.2	160,267	2.9	631,747	2.6	3,116,355	2.1	297,816	2.8	122,695	1.2
Norway	5,653	negl	26,780	negl	268,690	1.1	1,749,027	1.2	100,155	negl	107,253	1.1
Hungary	—	—	5,047	negl	7	negl	723,675	negl	56,797	negl	106,566	1.1
Bolivia	13	negl	2,368	negl	2,786	—	108,079	negl	34,957	negl	100,542	1.0
Chile	13,099	negl	22,613	negl	170,671	negl	1,797,639	1.2	96,390	negl	81,844	negl
East Germany	—	—	—	—	—	—	1,176,842	negl	116,317	1.1	78,732	negl
Switzerland	2	negl	34,314	negl	282,570	1.1	597,230	negl	64,829	negl	60,344	negl
Czechoslovakia	—	—	15,211	negl	149,072	negl	2,042,091	1.4	51,439	negl	53,270	negl
Portugal	18,670	negl	34,051	negl	100,453	negl	564,577	negl	58,248	negl	40,422	negl
Hong Kong	8	negl	1,311	negl	1	negl	543,591	negl	149,975	1.4	12,846	negl
China (PRC)	198	negl	168,742	3.0	47,224	negl	80,604	negl	6,207	negl	8,983	negl
China (Taiwan)	—	—	—	—	—	—	—	—	97,501	negl	5,136	negl
Total	2,907,354	100.0	5,615,519	100.0	24,913,487	100.0	147,122,627	100.0	10,825,740	100.0	10,032,926	100.0

Sources: AN 1939-40, pp. 1365-1374; CEB 1919-23, pp. 26-28; CEB 1930-36, pp. 12-13; AN 1939-40, pp. 395-404;
CEB, Resumo Mensal, Jan-dez, 1949-50, pp. 5-6; AN 1961, pp. 221-222; AN 1973, pp. 299-301; AN 1978, pp. 535-537.

Table XIV-7. Brazil's Major Import Trading Partners by Value of Goods Received by Brazil, 1842/43-1976

	1842/43		1852/53		1862/63		1872/73		1901		1910		1920	
	Pound Sterling	%	Pound Sterling	%	Pound Sterling	%	Pound Sterling	%	Pound Sterling	%	Pound Sterling	%	Cr$ 000	%
United States	665,062	11.8	848,335	8.6	662,422	6.1	915,293	5.6	2,659,237	12.4	6,127,582	12.8	880,237	42.1
Saudi Arabia	-	-	-	-	-	-	-	-	-	-	-	-	-	-
Iraq	-	-	-	-	-	-	-	-	-	-	-	-	-	-
West Germany	277,575	4.9	587,273	5.9	589,538	5.5	1,116,816	6.9	2,012,651	9.4	7,607,898	15.9	104,862	5.0
Japan	-	-	-	-	-	-	-	-	-	-	-	-	10,687	negl
Kuwait	-	-	-	-	-	-	-	-	-	-	-	-	-	-
Argentina	87,573	1.6	76,695	negl	64,445	negl	350,841	2.2	2,892,932	13.5	4,071,564	8.5	157,214	7.5
Italy	-	-	-	-	-	-	79,505	negl	816,667	3.8	1,519,965	3.2	50,380	2.4
Iran	-	-	-	-	-	-	-	-	-	-	-	-	-	-
France	679,583	12.1	1,352,055	13.6	2,014,777	18.7	2,380,553	14.7	1,713,060	8.0	4,539,270	9.5	117,381	5.6
United Kingdom	2,739,778	48.7	5,317,007	53.7	5,563,843	51.6	8,416,130	51.9	6,709,338	31.4	13,676,221	28.6	451,673	21.6
Canada	48,701	negl	57,264	negl	-	-	-	-	-	-	233,392	negl	31,670	1.5
Chile	-	-	-	-	-	-	26,884	negl	-	-	59,787	negl	510	negl
Switzerland	-	-	-	-	-	-	-	-	149,883	negl	592,265	1.2	25,395	1.2
Sweden	670	negl	24,232	negl	12,823	negl	28,759	negl	-	-	215,292	negl	26,104	1.2
Netherlands	7,261	negl	9,144	negl	14,358	negl	12,712	negl	129,484	negl	303,701	negl	10,942	negl
Mexico	-	-	-	-	-	-	-	-	-	-	-	-	21,740	1.0
Libya	-	-	-	-	-	-	-	-	-	-	-	-	-	-
Belgium/Luxembourg	71,824	1.3	184,366	1.9	110,477	1.0	384,394	2.4	491,703	2.3	2,163,805	4.5	38,899	1.9
Poland	-	-	-	-	-	-	-	-	-	-	-	-	-	-
Spain	96,062	1.7	85,268	negl	203,308	1.9	270,295	1.7	153,156	negl	450,427	negl	28,499	1.4
Venezuela	-	-	-	-	-	-	-	-	-	-	-	-	-	-
Uruguay	38,0115	6.8	555,612	5.6	728,950	6.8	662,295	4.1	1,394,900	6.5	1,227,055	2.6	27,252	1.3
Nigeria	-	-	-	-	-	-	-	-	-	-	-	-	72	negl
Peru	-	-	-	-	-	-	-	-	-	-	8,704	negl	-	-
Norway	-	-	-	-	-	-	2,605	negl	255,777	1.2	403,230	negl	21,706	1.0
Netherlands Antilles	-	-	-	-	-	-	-	-	-	-	-	-	-	-
Malaysia/Singapore	-	-	-	-	-	-	-	-	-	-	-	-	-	-
Finland	-	-	-	-	-	-	-	-	-	-	-	-	11,501	negl
Denmark	-	-	11,316	negl	7,453	negl	5,939	negl	-	-	86,659	negl	2,220	negl
Portugal	453,167	8.1	658,397	6.6	653,874	6.1	1,302,917	8.0	1,386,820	6.5	2,668,561	5.6	43,212	2.1
Czechoslovakia	-	-	-	-	-	-	-	-	-	-	-	-	2,295	negl
India	-	-	-	-	-	-	-	-	-	-	392,232	negl	18,823	negl
Trinidad/Tobago	-	-	-	-	-	-	-	-	-	-	-	-	-	-
Total	5,622,866	100.0	9,906,953	100.0	10,782,558	100.0	16,210,706	100.0	21,375,256	100.0	47,871,974	100.0	2,090,633	100.0

Table XIV-7 (continued)

	1930 Cr$ 000	1930 %	1939 Cr$ 000	1939 %	1950 Cr$ 000	1950 %	1960 Cr$ 000	1960 %	1970 Cr$ 000	1970 %	1976 US$ 000	1976 %
United States	566,184	24.1	1,672,259	33.4	7,004,546	34.5	67,498,936	33.5	4,156,689	32.2	3,110,902	22.7
Saudi Arabia	-	-	-	-	-	-	2,081,401	1.0	258,605	2.0	1,230,783	9.0
Iraq	-	-	21	negl	5	negl	-	-	215,591	1.7	1,197,384	8.7
West Germany	267,120	11.4	958,234	19.2	352,594	1.7	19,120,793	9.5	1,630,676	12.6	1,190,526	8.7
Japan	5,157	negl	76,074	1.5	24,095	negl	4,621,175	2.3	804,867	6.2	965,978	7.1
Kuwait	-	-	-	-	-	-	2,858,334	1.4	92,874	negl	533,589	3.9
Argentina	312,059	13.3	419,609	8.4	2,031,197	10.0	11,037,353	5.5	773,934	6.0	472,812	3.4
Italy	88,836	3.8	91,408	1.8	264,241	1.3	5,153,891	2.6	398,989	3.1	443,768	3.2
Iran	-	-	57	negl	-	-	-	-	53,686	negl	377,602	2.8
France	118,293	5.0	137,213	2.7	946,112	4.7	10,440,222	5.2	399,590	3.1	374,059	2.7
United Kingdom	452,841	19.3	462,427	9.3	2,505,637	12.3	8,387,563	4.2	733,627	5.7	347,222	2.5
Canada	36,902	1.6	75,188	1.5	233,901	1.3	2,973,077	1.5	322,002	2.5	343,820	2.5
Chile	3,791	negl	29,001	negl	282,253	1.5	1,192,877	negl	161,443	1.3	286,132	2.1
Switzerland	21,171	negl	56,647	1.1	310,298	1.5	2,419,736	1.2	266,142	2.1	268,361	2.0
Sweden	25,158	negl	113,581	2.3	883,358	4.3	4,831,378	2.4	241,572	1.9	258,333	1.9
Netherlands	66,622	2.8	55,632	1.1	465,809	2.3	3,180,813	1.6	225,098	1.7	211,405	1.5
Mexico	35,544	1.5	3,792	negl	18,620	negl	282,332	negl	77,672	negl	202,683	1.5
Libya	-	-	-	-	-	-	-	-	44,700	negl	151,642	1.1
Belgium/Luxembourg	90,800	3.9	209,522	4.2	1,173,028	5.8	3,044,296	1.5	202,037	1.6	148,287	1.1
Poland	20	negl	9,328	negl	12,704	negl	2,622,606	1.3	50,245	negl	124,346	negl
Spain	21,115	negl	3,438	negl	139,424	negl	4,226,321	2.1	146,377	1.1	115,047	negl
Venezuela	37,012	1.6	2	negl	319,968	1.6	11,464,467	5.7	265,891	2.1	109,929	negl
Uruguay	30,748	1.3	43,528	negl	151,615	negl	96,669	negl	52,246	negl	85,407	negl
Nigeria	-	-	2,502	negl	-	-	-	-	130,488	negl	81,509	negl
Peru	26,321	1.1	56,767	1.1	10,553	negl	274,809	negl	46,207	negl	63,997	negl
Norway	24,963	1.1	22,962	negl	263,365	1.3	3,210,425	1.6	101,033	negl	57,342	negl
Netherlands Antilles	-	-	170,727	3.4	1,651,907	8.1	5,976,984	3.0	45,252	negl	45,322	negl
Malaysia/Singapore	-	-	3,921	negl	31,095	negl	3,631,079	1.8	28,732	negl	45,054	negl
Finland	11,599	negl	15,020	negl	112,728	negl	3,317,306	1.6	64,081	negl	40,960	negl
Denmark	11,279	negl	19,970	negl	152,008	negl	4,130,442	2.1	106,527	negl	36,369	negl
Portugal	46,019	2.0	88,735	1.8	129,945	negl	677,443	negl	54,385	negl	22,565	negl
Czechoslovakia	894	negl	16,534	negl	154,164	negl	2,467,910	1.2	45,685	negl	21,461	negl
India	23,052	negl	56,688	1.1	27,331	negl	191,436	negl	1,895	negl	1,858	negl
Trinidad/Tobago	-	-	3,762	negl	315,475	1.6	1,139,322	negl	40,205	negl	339	negl
Total	2,343,705	100.0	4,993,992	100.0	20,313,429	100.0	210,218,687	100.0	12,903,608	100.0	13,726,042	100.0

Sources: AN 1939-40, pp. 1366-1374; CEB 1919-23, pp. 22-24; CEB 1930-36, pp. 8-9; AN 1939-40, pp. 395-404; CEB, Resumo mensal, jan-dez, 1949-50, pp. 5-6; AN 1961, pp. 221-222; AN 1973, pp. 518-520; AN 1978, pp. 552-554.

Chapter XV. Balance of Payments

Table XV-1 reports Brazil's international balance of payments from 1947 to 1978. The data originated with the Super-intendência da Moeda e Crédito and the Banco do Brasil. The category Compensatory Capital Balance is the key to reading this table. This is the capital that flows to compensate a surplus or deficit balance of payments. A positive compensatory flow such as the + US$ 182,000,000 in 1947 goes to make up a balance of payments <u>deficit</u> of US$ 182,000,000. A negative compensatory flow such as the (-) US$ 52,000,000 in 1950 goes as a <u>surplus</u> to pay off past debts because Brazil had a balance of payments in 1950 of +US$ 52,000,000. The Export/Import Balance refers to exports (FOB) minus imports (FOB). The Services Balance is made up of the transfer of nonmonetary gold, and credits and debits for international travel, freight transport, insurance, return on investments, governmental services, and other services. The characteristics of the Gifts and Transferences Balance is not described by the sources with the exception that they note both official (public) and private sectors in this category. The Autonomous Capital Balance is comprised of credits and debits in private investments, reinvestments, loans, mort-gages and amortization categories, and official (public) credits and debits in these same or similar categories. Together with the Errors and Omissions category the balance of all these debits and credits in a given year equals Brazil's balance of payments for that year. The surplus or deficit is brought to zero by Compensatory Capital movements. This category included capital flows from, among other sources, the International Monetary Fund (IMF), the Export/Import Bank, United States banks, the United States Treasury, the Agency for International Development (AID), and European creditors.

Table XV-1. Brazil's International Balance of Payments, 1947-78

In US$ 1,000,000

	1947	1948	1949	1950	1951	1952	1953	1954
Export/Import Balance	+ 130	+ 278	+ 153	+ 425	+ 67	- 286	- 423	+ 150
Services Balance	- 276	- 315	- 271	- 319	- 535	- 421	- 392	- 380
Gifts/Transferences Balance	- 24	- 7	- 3	- 2	- 2	- 2	- 14	- 5
Autonomous Capital Balance	+ 31	- 9	- 35	- 29	+ 56	+ 120	+ 97	+ 22
Private Capital	--	--	--	--	--	--	--	--
Public Capital	--	--	--	--	--	--	--	--
Compensatory Capital Balance	+ 182	+ 24	+ 74	- 52	+ 291	+ 615	- 16	+ 203
Errors/Omissions	- 43	+ 29	+ 82	- 23	+ 123	- 26	- 98	+ 10

	1955	1956	1957	1958	1959	1960	1961	1962
Export/Import Balance	+ 320	+ 436	+ 107	+ 64	+ 72	- 24	+ 111	- 90
Services Balance	- 344	- 418	- 393	- 326	- 373	- 470	- 403	- 406
Gifts/Transferences Balance	- 10	- 11	- 13	- 4	- 10	+ 14	+ 4	+ 38
Autonomous Capital Balance	+ 39	+ 201	+ 290	+ 202	+ 182	+ 52	+ 332	+ 255
Private Capital	--	--	--	--	--	--	+ 300	+ 187
Public Capital	--	--	--	--	--	--	+ 32	+ 68
Compensatory Capital Balance	- 17	- 194	+ 180	+ 253	+ 154	+ 430	- 55	- 343
Errors/Omissions	+ 12	- 314	- 171	- 189	- 25	+ 26	+ 11	- 140

	1963	1964	1965	1966	1967	1968	1969	1970
Export/Import Balance	+ 109	+ 344	+ 655	+ 438	+ 213	+ 26	+ 318	+ 232
Services Balance	- 112	- 305	- 457	- 550	- 567	- 556	- 630	- 815
Gifts/Transferences Balance	+ 39	+ 63	+ 65	+ 79	+ 77	+ 22	+ 31	+ 21
Autonomous Capital Balance	+ 23	+ 92	+ 67	+ 205	+ 63	+ 541	+ 850	+ 1,015
Private Capital	+ 42	+ 67	+ 67	+ 133	+ 84	+ 569	+ 757	--
Public Capital	+ 19	+ 25	0	+ 72	+ 21	+ 28	+ 93	--
Compensatory Capital Balance	+ 279	- 68	- 362	+ 153	+ 245	- 32	- 549	- 545
Errors/Omissions	- 120	- 126	+ 32	- 19	- 31	+ 1	+ 20	+ 92

	1971	1972	1973	1974	1975	1976	1977	1978
Export/Import Balance	- 363	- 244	+ 7	- 4,690	- 3,499	- 2,255	+ 97	- 1,024
Services Balance	- 958	- 1,250	- 1,722	- 2,433	- 3,213	- 3,763	- 4,134	- 4,975
Gifts/Transferences Balance	+ 14	+ 5	+ 27	+ 1	0	+ 1	0	+ 72
Autonomous Capital Balance	+ 1,846	+ 3,492	+ 3,512	+ 6,254	+ 6,161	+ 6,806	+ 5,269	+ 9,439
Private Capital	--	--	--	--	--	--	--	--
Public Capital	--	--	--	--	--	--	--	--
Compensatory Capital Balance	- 530	- 2,439	- 2,179	+ 936	+ 950	- 1,192	- 630	- 3,880
Errors/Omissions	- 9	+ 436	+ 355	+ 68	- 399	+ 403	+ 602	+ 368

Sources: Baer, p. 273; AN 1963, p. 251; AN 1965, p. 291; AN 1967, p. 345; AN 1969, p. 437; AN 1971, p. 488; AN 1973, p. 537; AN 1975, p. 537; AN 1977, p. 628; AN 1979, p. 548.

Chapter XVI. External Public Debt

Brazil's external public debt from 1824 to 1955 is shown on Table XVI-1. All data originated with the Conselho Técnico de Economia e Finanças. The debt total included obligations incurred by federal, state, and município (county) governments. For any given year amortization and interest payments may not constitute the total payments on the debt. The difference between the sum of these two payments and the total payment may include one or both of the following: commissions paid to banks, and, through 1930, payments on a "difference in type" diferença de tipo), a condition not explained by the source. In the amortization column the source noted that "up to 1931 the amounts show the nominal value of the debts retired (títulos resgatados); beginning in 1932, however, the amounts represent the price at which the debts were retired and do not include the amounts of debts acquired in Brazil in national currency."

The implementation of Decree Law No. 6,019 of November 1943 altered the structure of the external national debt in pounds and dollars relative to principal, amortization, and interest. By June 30, 1946, holders of Brazil's debts had to opt for either Plan A or Plan B. Under Plan A the face value of a debt held and the contractual responsibility pertaining to it remained unaltered although the rate of interest and period of amortization could fluctuate. Under Plan B, for which the federal government assumed responsibility, the face value of a debt was reduced by amounts ranging from 20 to 50 percent. To compensate such a reduction a holder received cash in amounts that ranged from 30 to 175 pounds per 1,000 pounds of debt held, or, if in dollars, 75 to 175 dollars per 1,000 dollars of a debt held. A new term of amortization was fixed and a 3 percent interest rate was established. Those holders not opting for either Plan by June 30, 1946, were automatically put on Plan A. The decline in principal owed by Brazil from 1944 to 1946 was in part a result of regular amortization of the debt but also a product of the reduction in face value of debts held by those who opted for Plan B.

Table XVI-2 reports Brazil's external public debt from 1940 to 1975. This table does not supersede XVI-1 but instead elaborates the data for the years common to both tables according to currencies owed. For 1955, AN 1956 reported a debt of 3,582 florins for the states and Distrito Federal while AN 1959 reported this debt as 3,740 florins. The latter source was used on the assumption that time allowed rectification of the error. From 1958 through 1962 some of the sub-federal government levels borrowed abroad under Decree Law No. 6,019 of November 23, 1943, Article No. 2 (in degree 8). The states of Pará and Alagoas incurred debts in pound sterling and the state of Ceará incurred them in United States dollars under this law. The município of Manaus, Amazonas; Belém, Pará; Salvador, Bahia; and Belo Horizonte, Minas Gerais, also incurred pound sterling debts. The sources AN 1967 and AN 1969 reported different external debts for the year 1966. The figure from the latter source was used on the table under the time-allows-rectification principal. For 1975 the federal debt was incurred by autarquias, which are quasi-governmental bodies something like the Tennessee Valley Authority in the United States.

Table XVI-3 notes the registered foreign capital, both invested and reinvested, by industry group and political subdivision in Brazil from 1955 to 1978. Data originators included the Superintendência da Moeda e Crédito (SUMOC), the Carteira do Comércio Exterior (CACEX) of the Banco do Brasil, and the Banco Central do Brasil. From 1970 through 1978 foreign capital registered with one of these agencies included both capital invested and capital reinvested. Prior to 1970 the sources did not specify whether reinvested capital was included in the total. None of the sources defined invested and reinvested capital but reinvestment was usually undertaken with profits from an original foreign investment in Brazil. On Table XVI-3 reinvestment is the difference between Total Investment and Investment. The Public Utilities category included the communication and transportation industries and the production of electrical energy. All post-1970 data excluded loans and financing; sources prior to 1970 did not specify this.

The following outline will be used to explain why the Total Investment figures on Table XVI-3 for the years 1960 through 1966 are suspect and why no other figures are presented for these years. A model (letters are substituted for actual names) of the CACEX calculations of totals for the year 1966 is shown below. It is taken from AN 1967, page 319.

Industry

County of Origin		Basic		Light		States	
A	915	A	311	A	3,603	A(-)	2,041
B	5	B	1,950	B(-)	573	B	47
C	5,072	C	155	C	0	C	1,465
D	94	D	267	D	0	D	4,597
E(-)	2,041	E	0	E	134	T	4,068
F	342	O	0	O(-)	1,779		
G	24	T	2,683 +	T	1,385		
O(-)	343						
T	4,068		= 4,068				

The negative symbols (-) were used by CACEX to represent capital investments registered but not yet applied (efetivado). During this seven-year period, however, these symbols were used as operators rather than notations. For example, if all eight figures under Country of Origin are summed by sign (+) and (-) the total is, indeed, 4,068. This assumes, however, that country "E" by not applying 2,041 actually removed twice that much from the total. First, the 2,041 is not added into the total registered and second, it is subtracted from the total. The same is true for the 343. At the very least the 2,041 and the 343 should be added to the total before being subtracted from it. Again, the system used double counted the negative of a capital sum not applied. Were figures such as a (-) 2,041 and (-) 343 actual unit figures then they could be added back into the total so that all registered capital is thereby recorded. However, each of these figures may, in fact, be the result of the application of a similar bookkeeping system at another level. For example, the (-) 2,041 for Country "E" may be the result of the summing of several blocks of investments among which those blocks not applied are also double-subtracted from the total. Because of this potential confusion the figures are not presented in detail. Nevertheless, to provide some continuity, the author has calculated the Total Investment for each year by adding back into the Total all negative figures by country. These totals must be understood to be only approximations, since, as described above, they may still hide double negative counting.

Table XVI-1. Brazil's External Public Debt and Amortization and Interest Payments in Pound Sterling and Cruzeiros, 1824-1955

	1824	1825	1826	1827	1828	1829	1830	1831	1832
Average Cr$ per Pound Sterling	4.974	4.626	4.967	6.808	7.726	9.746	10.520	9.600	6.832
Loans Made									
Pound Sterling	1,333,300	3,752,900	-	-	-	729,200	-	-	-
Cr$ 1,000	6,632	18,179	-	-	-	7,497	-	-	-
Total Payments on Loans (pounds)	407,334	762,085	290,311	290,310	290,309	682,987	340,846	340,847	340,848
Amortization (pounds)	6,677	33,458	35,131	36,887	38,732	40,668	54,278	56,993	59,842
Interest (pounds)	66,665	371,642	252,304	250,548	248,703	285,227	283,193	280,478	277,629
Principal Remaining (pounds)	1,326,623	5,046,065	5,010,934	4,974,047	4,935,315	5,663,847	5,609,567	5,552,576	5,492,734

	1833	1834	1835	1836	1837	1838	1839	1840	1841
Average Cr$ per Pound Sterling	6.421	6.247	6.614	6.243	8.118	8.384	7.588	7.741	7.836
Loans Made									
Pound Sterling	-	-	-	-	-	-	411,200	-	-
Cr$ 1,000	-	-	-	-	-	-	3,120	-	-
Total Payments on Loans (pounds)	340,845	340,847	340,846	340,846	340,846	340,845	472,637	369,737	369,735
Amortization (pounds)	62,834	65,976	69,274	72,738	76,376	80,193	84,202	96,456	101,279
Interest (pounds)	274,637	271,495	268,197	264,733	261,095	257,278	273,829	269,618	264,795
Principal Remaining (pounds)	5,429,900	5,363,924	5,294,650	5,221,912	5,145,536	5,065,343	5,392,341	5,295,885	5,194,606

	1842	1843	1844	1845	1846	1847	1848	1849	1850
Average Cr$ per Pound Sterling	8.951	9.298	9.298	9.434	8.909	8.571	9.600	9.275	8.347
Loans Made									
Pound Sterling	-	732,600	-	-	-	-	-	-	-
Cr$ 1,000	-	6,812	-	-	-	-	-	-	-
Total Payments on Loans (pounds)	369,734	516,620	429,105	429,107	429,104	429,105	429,106	429,106	429,105
Amortization (pounds)	106,343	111,660	139,395	146,367	153,682	161,369	169,437	177,908	186,805
Interest (pounds)	259,731	291,044	285,462	278,490	271,173	263,488	255,420	246,949	238,052
Principal Remaining (pounds)	5,088,263	5,709,203	5,569,908	5,423,441	5,269,759	5,108,390	4,938,953	4,761,045	4,574,240

	1851	1852	1853	1854	1855	1856	1857	1858	1859
Average Cr$ per Pound Sterling	8.240	8.747	8.421	8.687	8.707	8.707	9.104	9.388	9.572
Loans Made									
Pound Sterling	-	1,040,600	-	-	-	-	-	1,526,500	508,000
Cr$ 1,000	-	9,102	-	-	-	-	-	14,331	4,863
Total Payments on Loans (pounds)	429,106	1,530,790	414,868	414,857	414,857	434,859	414,858	552,601	546,963
Amortization (pounds)	196,143	1,197,142	204,885	215,038	225,706	256,905	248,658	260,994	310,649
Interest	228,714	266,977	205,875	195,712	185,044	173,845	162,092	218,448	230,898
Principal Remaining (pounds)	4,378,097	4,221,555	4,016,670	3,801,632	3,575,926	3,319,021	3,070,363	4,335,869	4,533,220

Table XVI-1. (continued)

	1860	1861	1862	1863	1864	1865	1866	1867	1868
Average Cr$ per Pound Sterling	9.298	9.388	9.056	8.807	8.971	9.599	9.896	10.696	14.117
Loans Made									
Pound Sterling	1,373,000	-	-	3,855,300	-	6,963,600	-	-	-
Cr$ 1,000	12,766	-	-	33,954	-	66,844	-	-	-
Total Payments on Loans (pounds)	834,116	585,672	596,134	1,893,163	570,847	2,732,842	1,051,656	1,050,657	1,051,656
Amortization (pounds)	283,404	323,180	338,768	1,015,967	217,104	227,004	365,022	382,124	400,030
Interest (pounds)	270,573	256,705	251,117	400,395	348,091	686,171	676,222	658,120	641,214
Principal Remaining (pounds)	5,622,816	5,299,636	4,960,868	7,800,201	7,583,097	14,319,693	13,954,671	13,572,547	13,172,517

	1869	1870	1871	1872	1873	1874	1875	1876	1877
Average Cr$ per Pound Sterling	12.757	10.607	9.987	9.600	8.909	9.354	9.153	9.469	9.770
Loans Made									
Pound Sterling	-	-	3,549,600	-	-	-	5,301,200	-	-
Cr$ 1,000	-	-	34,551	-	-	-	48,522	-	-
Total Payments on Loans (pounds)	1,048,656	1,051,657	1,606,923	1,350,551	1,360,548	1,365,551	1,803,802	1,891,435	1,896,430
Amortization (pounds)	415,781	438,413	458,971	603,450	632,139	667,197	693,738	997,154	1,054,250
Interest (pounds)	622,463	602,831	755,253	733,728	715,039	684,981	908,500	875,551	832,455
Principal Remaining (pounds)	12,756,736	12,318,323	15,318,952	14,715,502	14,083,363	13,461,166	18,023,628	17,026,474	15,981,224

	1878	1879	1880	1881	1882	1883	1884	1885	1886
Average Cr$ per Pound Sterling	10.463	10.490	10.463	11.082	11.344	11.130	11.660	12.900	12.843
Loans Made									
Pound Sterling	-	-	-	-	-	4,599,600	-	-	6,431,000
Cr$ 1,000	-	-	-	-	-	51,144	-	-	82,593
Total Payments on Loans (pounds)	1,901,433	1,888,430	1,901,433	1,891,433	1,892,296	2,593,426	1,986,069	1,985,819	2,629,378
Amortization (pounds)	1,105,675	1,145,540	1,213,964	1,262,072	1,323,442	1,281,883	1,336,739	1,401,370	1,466,853
Interest (pounds)	77,030	724,165	668,741	610,633	549,710	692,799	629,942	565,075	818,410
Principal Remaining (pounds)	14,875,549	13,730,009	12,516,045	11,253,973	9,930,531	13,248,248	11,911,509	10,510,139	15,474,286

	1887	1888	1889	1890	1891	1892	1893	1894	1895
Average Cr$ per Pound Sterling	10.690	9.505	9.076	10.630	16.100	19.948	20.701	23.77	24.151
Loans Made									
Pound Sterling	-	7,097,300	19,837,000	-	-	-	3,710,000	-	7,442,000
Cr$ 1,000	-	67,460	180,080	-	-	-	76,801	-	179,732
Total Payments on Loans (pounds)	2,370,056	2,881,523	9,027,570	1,526,631	1,626,593	1,693,518	2,720,432	2,005,859	3,093,919
Amortization (pounds)	1,599,747	1,676,708	8,027,751	207,800	317,940	399,100	402,560	557,920	553,697
Interest (pounds)	747,132	810,938	910,901	1,304,585	1,293,856	1,279,267	1,447,736	1,429,763	1,405,299
Principal Remaining (pounds)	13,874,539	19,295,133	31,104,382	30,896,582	30,578,642	30,179,542	33,486,982	32,929,062	39,817,365

333

Table XVI-1. (continued)

	1896	1897	1898	1899	1900	1901	1902	1903
Average Cr$ per Pound Sterling	26.483	31.093	33.391	32.269	32.269	21.304	20.157	20.078
Loans Made								
Pound Sterling	1,000,000	2,000,000	8,613,717	-	-	18,069,320	-	8,500,000
Cr$ 1,000	26,483	62,186	287,021	-	-	384,949	-	170,663
Total Payments on Loans (pounds)	2,438,934	3,710,123	2,651,996	1,571,245	1,160,056	1,978,188	2,584,449	3,920,188
Amortization (pounds)	614,693	1,742,605	1,573,994	1,196,477	706,637	216,635	227,454	419,558
Interest (pounds)	1,901,957	1,873,716	1,053,455	359,180	443,892	1,296,962	2,331,485	2,828,928
Principal Remaining (pounds)	40,202,672	40,460,067	47,499,790	46,303,313	45,596,676	63,449,361	63,221,907	72,302,349

	1904	1905	1906	1907	1908	1909	1910	1911
Average Cr$ per Pound Sterling	19.794	15.208	14.971	15.917	15.983	15.983	14.927	15.029
Loans Made								
Pound Sterling	2,062,360	6,800,000	10,290,000	5,650,000	23,750,000	43,000,000	18,200,000	9,900,000
Cr$ 1,000	40,822	103,414	154,051	89,931	379,596	68,727	271,671	148,787
Total Payments on Loans (pounds)	3,792,700	4,806,629	5,976,244	7,086,796	14,168,306	9,617,299	12,792,994	14,138,318
Amortization (pounds)	464,931	656,902	657,607	2,060,235	3,396,647	2,214,494	3,624,976	5,975,592
Interest (pounds)	2,967,359	3,167,705	4,148,163	4,689,821	8,235,335	6,850,891	6,415,004	6,899,447
Principal Remaining (pounds)	72,899,778	79,042,876	88,675,269	92,265,034	112,618,387	114,703,893	129,278,917	133,203,325

	1912	1913	1914	1915	1916	1917	1918	1919
Average Cr$ per Pound Sterling	15.000	15.044	16.375	19.272	20.105	18.893	18.618	16.860
Loans Made								
Pound Sterling	4,200,000	19,620,000	18,702,396	3,530,121	1,158,320	-	345,978	2,019,296
Cr$ 1,000	63,000	295,163	306,252	68,032	23,288	-	6,441	34,045
Total Payments on Loans (pounds)	12,333,758	14,997,361	9,453,886	7,593,978	6,953,321	9,618,679	13,477,678	11,109,512
Amortization (pounds)	4,857,947	6,913,417	1,948,405	2,616,939	1,435,255	3,076,345	5,212,892	3,274,720
Interest (pounds)	6,882,351	7,529,170	7,448,674	4,945,091	5,380,406	6,442,488	8,189,594	7,578,684
Principal Remaining (pounds)	132,545,378	145,251,961	162,005,952	162,919,134	162,642,199	159,563,854	154,696,940	153,441,516

	1920	1921	1922	1923	1924	1925	1926	1927
Average Cr$ per Pound Sterling	23.167	28.554	33.994	44.971	40.707	39.485	33.960	41.095
Loans Made								
Pound Sterling	-	20,335,791	17,716,505	-	-	3,082,297	29,245,883	26,621,899
Cr$ 1,000	-	580,668	602,225	-	-	121,704	990,265	1,094,027
Total Payments on Loans (pounds)	10,064,722	10,781,385	11,297,069	11,027,090	10,277,522	10,251,553	15,077,745	15,955,364
Amortization (pounds)	2,087,957	1,302,754	1,706,717	1,935,338	1,758,867	1,782,994	1,773,607	2,889,924
Interest (pounds)	7,889,817	7,356,767	8,017,304	8,988,707	8,411,438	8,284,436	9,491,461	10,295,500
Principal Remaining (pounds)	151,353,559	170,386,596	186,396,384	184,461,046	182,702,179	184,001,482	211,473,758	235,205,733

Table XVI-1. (continued)

	1928	1929	1930	1931	1932	1933	1934	1935
Average Cr$ per Pound Sterling	40.752	40.710	43.992	63.025	48.965	52.965	59.420	58.133
Loans Made								
Pound Sterling	25,292,537	2,876,811	20,000,027	18,359,467	-	-	-	-
Cr$ 1,000	1,030,721	117,115	879,841	1,157,105	-	-	-	-
Total Payments on Loans (pounds)	18,696,458	19,175,323	21,641,950	20,589,993	12,909,828	5,133,875	6,967,903	7,751,864
Amortization (pounds)	4,509,972	5,560,131	6,131,982	8,547,528	7,536,028	1,992,749	2,398,506	1,759,701
Interest (pounds)	12,264,207	13,082,141	13,358,662	11,907,813	5,244,035	3,110,859	4,518,830	5,848,709
Principal Remaining (pounds)	255,988,298	253,304,978	267,173,023	276,984,962	269,448,934	267,448,773	265,039,728	259,802,904

	1936	1937	1938	1939	1940	1941	1942	1943
Average Cr$ per Pound Sterling	57.802	57.056	86.385	75.179	67.220	67.220	67.620	67.620
Loans Made								
Pound Sterling	-	-	-	-	-	-	-	xxx
Cr$ 1,000	-	-	-	-	-	-	-	xxx
Total Payments on Loans (pounds)	7,862,798	8,476,547	-	-	3,131,787	3,981,248	3,987,124	3,886,655
Amortization (pounds)	1,806,781	1,844,895	-	-	518,787	843,978	881,767	806,678
Interest (pounds)	5,918,116	6,497,671	-	-	2,536,859	3,039,867	3,013,496	2,992,885
Principal Remaining (pounds)	253,656,651	243,724,664	243,724,664	243,724,664	242,309,197	240,557,670	232,869,150	227,256,098

	1944	1945	1946	1947	1948	1949	1950	1951
Average Cr$ per Pound Sterling	67.629	67.620	77.225	75.409	75.428	69.879	52.416	52.416
Loans Made								
Pound Sterling	-	-	-	-	-	-	-	-
Cr$ 1,000	-	-	-	-	-	-	-	-
Total Payments on Loans (pounds)	18,797,523	10,775,612	9,191,939	8,367,385	8,206,000	28,687,740	31,872,085	9,279,309
Amortization (pounds)	11,346,860	5,832,789	4,476,838	3,762,758	3,792,580	24,702,003	27,775,583	6,191,407
Interest (pounds)	6,999,948	4,749,783	4,540,080	4,463,796	4,296,770	3,766,720	3,793,632	2,980,260
Principal Remaining (pounds)	187,836,585	174,233,292	161,062,673	155,314,237	146,954,617	117,505,574	107,846,726	98,578,033

	1952	1953	1954	1955
Average Cr$ per Pound Sterling	52.416	52.450	52.573	52.696
Loans Made				
Pound Sterling	-	-	-	-
Cr$ 1,000	-	-	-	-
Total Payments on Loans (pounds)	9,269,973	9,265,089	9,262,193	9,226,883
Amortization (pounds)	6,472,152	6,722,136	6,915,409	7,209,163
Interest (pounds)	2,697,968	2,445,525	2,248,380	1,934,381
Principal Remaining (pounds)	89,752,053	81,376,608	72,229,950	54,405,359

Source: AN 1956, 545-546.

Table XVI-2. The External Public Debt (Principal Owed) of Brazil's
Federal, State and Município Governments by the Specific
Foreign Currencies Involved, 1940-75

	1940	1947	1950	1951	1952	1953	1954	1955
Federal Debt (000's)								
Pounds	102,359	72,660	28,384	25,429	22,271	18,974	15,739	12,562
Dollars	166,853	106,645	88,138	81,956	76,738	70,567	64,132	57,717
Francs - paper	272,909	272,909	37,406	37,406	34,025	32,976	32,976	32,976
Francs - gold	229,186	229,186	25,285	25,285	21,971	20,373	20,373	20,373
States/Distrito Federal Debt (000's)								
Pounds	41,603	24,313	19,486	18,121	15,913	14,752	13,568	12,387
Dollars	146,983	78,795	57,297	50,853	47,403	43,550	39,526	35,826
Francs - paper	225,138	225,138	73,454	73,454	68,759	67,576	67,576	67,576
Florins	6,493	6,428	6,428	6,075	6,037	6,037	6,037	3,740
Município Debt (000's)								
Pounds	8,659	5,001	4,015	3,897	3,765	3,602	3,561	3,492
Dollars	20,830	13,117	8,879	8,069	7,502	6,866	6,262	5,623
Francs - paper	21,520	21,520	4,531	4,531	4,330	4,294	4,294	4,294
Total Debt (000's)								
Pounds	152,621	101,974	51,885	47,447	41,949	37,388	32,886	28,441
Dollars	334,666	198,557	154,134	140,878	131,643	120,983	109,920	99,166
Francs - gold	519,567	519,567	115,391	115,391	107,114	104,846	104,846	104,846
Francs -paper	229,186	229,186	25,285	25,285	21,971	20,373	20,373	20,373
Florins	6,493	6,428	6,428	6,075	6,037	6,037	6,037	3,740

	1956	1957	1958	1959	1960	1961	1962	1963
Federal Debt (000's)								
Pounds	9,641	7,701	6,264	4,802	3,318	1,814	363	-
Dollars	51,124	45,086	38,792	32,218	25,532	19,317	16,892	14,544
Francs - paper	32,976	23,320	22,108	22,122	22,017	-	-	-
Francs - gold	20,373	12,459	11,286	11,312	11,221	-	-	-
States/Distrito Federal Debt (000's)								
Pounds	11,569	10,266	7,888	6,095	5,919	5,720	5,400	5,253
Dollars	32,159	28,410	24,572	20,898	17,623	13,695	12,403	11,198
Francs - paper	67,576	54,384	51,098	50,531	50,096	-	-	-
Florins	3,740	3,740	3,740	117	88	-	-	-
Município Debt (000's)								
Pounds	3,277	2,937	1,440	987	966	943	915	894
Dollars	4,990	4,407	3,808	3,156	2,625	1,987	1,793	1,567
Francs - paper	4,294	3,216	3,050	3,055	3,055	-	-	-
Total Debt (000's)								
Pounds	24,487	20,904	15,592	11,884	10,203	8,477	6,678	6,147
Dollars	88,273	77,903	67,172	56,272	45,780	34,999	31,088	27,309
Francs - gold	104,846	80,920	76,256	75,712	75,168	-	-	-
Francs - paper	20,373	12,459	11,286	11,312	11,221	-	-	-
Florins	3,740	3,740	3,740	117	88	-	-	-

	1964	1965	1966	1967	1968	1969	1970
Federal Debt (000's)							
Pounds	-	-	-	-	-	-	-
Dollars	11,319	9,108	7,080	5,390	-	-	-
Francs - paper	-	-	-	-	-	-	-
Francs - gold	-	-	-	-	-	-	-
States/Distrito Federal Debt (000's)							
Pounds	5,039	4,817	4,589	4,348	3,856	3,593	3,350
Dollars	10,393	9,211	8,100	7,404	6,654	5,559	4,650
Francs - paper	-	-	-	-	-	-	-
Florins	-	-	-	-	-	-	-
Município Debt (000's)							
Pounds	871	850	827	803	779	752	726
Dollars	1,392	1,190	903	553	525	399	328
Francs - paper	-	-	-	-	-	-	-
Total Debt (000's)							
Pounds	5,910	5,667	5,416	5,151	4,635	4,345	4,076
Dollars	23,104	19,509	16,083	13,347	7,179	5,958	4,978
Francs - gold	-	-	-	-	-	-	-
Francs - paper	-	-	-	-	-	-	-
Florins	-	-	-	-	-	-	-

	1971	1972	1973	1974	1975
Federal Debt (000's)					
Pounds	-	-	-	-	714
Dollars	-	-	-	-	-
States/Distrito Federal Debt (000's)					
Pounds	3,097	2,875	2,670	2,483	1,563
Dollars	3,912	3,204	2,507	1,710	1,485
Município Debt (000's)					
Pounds	700	674	651	628	603
Dollars	262	222	188	102	65
Total Debt (000's)					
Pounds	3,797	3,549	3,321	3,111	2,880
Dollars	4,174	3,426	2,695	1,812	1,550

Sources: AN 1956, p. 453; AN 1959, p. 453; AN 1961, p. 441; AN 1963, p. 415; AN 1965, p. 477;
AN 1967, p. 750; AN 1969, p. 682; AN 1971, p. 795; AN 1973, p. 925; AN 1975, p. 771.

Table XVI-3. Investment and Reinvestment of Registered Foreign Capital in Brazil by Countries of Origin, by Brazilian Political Subdivisions, and by Group Recipients of the Registered Capital, 1955-78

	1955	1956	1958	1959	1960	1961	1962	1963	1964	1965	1966	1967	1968
Total Investments (US$ 000)	31,314	87,022	104,176	86,816	85,270	26,464	13,727	9,123	10,164	17,073	8,836	8,681	11,545
Reinvestments	-	-	-	-	-	-	-	-	-	-	-	-	-
Origin Country,Total Investments	-	-	-	-	-	-	-	-	-	-	-	-	-
United States	12,031	36,107	58,858	26,223	-	-	-	-	-	-	-	1,920	7,150
West Germany	7,095	24,531	29,504	16,353	-	-	-	-	-	-	-	3,366	788
Japan	-	-	1,626	6,958	-	-	-	-	-	-	-	434	-
Switzerland	876	2,988	3,674	6,725	-	-	-	-	-	-	-	337	60
United Kingdom	5,118	7,164	1,226	5,528	-	-	-	-	-	-	-	60	58
Canada	504	1,373	1,221	783	-	-	-	-	-	-	-	373	129
France	830	5,746	2,948	6,547	-	-	-	-	-	-	-	-	-
Belgium/Luxembourg	216	401	551	2,172	-	-	-	-	-	-	-	-	-
Panama	-	-	2,191	955	-	-	-	-	-	-	-	-	-
Netherlands	720	1,999	-	6,267	-	-	-	-	-	-	-	1,067	-
Sweden	-	-	298	414	-	-	-	-	-	-	-	224	-
Netherlands Antilles	-	-	538	-	-	-	-	-	-	-	-	-	-
Italy	2,168	3,627	677	4,016	-	-	-	-	-	-	-	300	2,243
Venezuela	-	-	859	2,692	-	-	-	-	-	-	-	-	-
Industry Group,Total Investments	31,314	87,022	104,176	86,816	-	-	-	-	-	-	-	8,681	11,545
Mining	1,622	5,108	-	1,868	-	-	-	-	-	-	-	-	-
Manufacturing	28,447	80,056	104,176	86,816	-	-	-	-	-	-	-	8,681	11,545
Chemicals	2,329	24,542	1,953	6,737	-	-	-	-	-	-	-	5,725	7,309
Transportation Equipment	8,154	15,573	74,943	-	-	-	-	-	-	-	-	-	-
Electrical/Communication Equipment	2,512	7,161	10,649⎱	7,509⎱	-	-	-	-	-	-	-	2,070	2,595⎱
Mechanical	3,192	5,040	⎰	⎰	-	-	-	-	-	-	-	-	1,120⎰
Metals	2,776	5,714	506	3,945	-	-	-	-	-	-	-	-	-
Foods	2,226	2,755	228	669	-	-	-	-	-	-	-	-	-
Pharmaceuticals	899	1,902	1,208	1,725	-	-	-	-	-	-	-	349	-
Rubber	1,336	2,371	1,725	680	-	-	-	-	-	-	-	-	-
Textiles	1,107	7,512	310	285	-	-	-	-	-	-	-	44	60
Paper	120	927	-	-	-	-	-	-	-	-	-	-	-
Non-Metallic Minerals	638	677	3,787	-	-	-	-	-	-	-	-	-	-
Tobacco	-	157	-	-	-	-	-	-	-	-	-	-	-
Wood	85	178	-	-	-	-	-	-	-	-	-	-	-
Apparel	130	130	-	-	-	-	-	-	-	-	-	-	-
Beverages	-	161	-	-	-	-	-	-	-	-	-	-	-
Publishing	-	-	-	-	-	-	-	-	-	-	-	-	-
Public Utilities	1,226	1,273	-	-	-	-	-	-	-	-	-	-	-
Construction	19	-	-	-	-	-	-	-	-	-	-	-	-
Agriculture	-	585	-	-	-	-	-	-	-	-	-	-	-
Services	-	-	-	-	-	-	-	-	-	-	-	-	-
Other	-	-	-	-	-	-	-	-	-	-	-	-	-
Brazil Subdivisions,Total Investments	-	-	93,962	62,369	-	-	-	-	-	-	-	6,051	997
São Paulo	-	-	904	11,240	-	-	-	-	-	-	-	275	-
Rio de Janeiro	-	-	1,990	8,410	-	-	-	-	-	-	-	1,641	325
Guanabara	-	-	4,732	3,758	-	-	-	-	-	-	-	298	127
Minas Gerais	-	-	1,553	30	-	-	-	-	-	-	-	389	100
Rio Grande do Sul	-	-	-	39	-	-	-	-	-	-	-	-	-
Paraná	-	-	234	139	-	-	-	-	-	-	-	-	-
Amapá	-	-	-	170	-	-	-	-	-	-	-	-	-
Pernambuco	-	-	-	155	-	-	-	-	-	-	-	-	-
Rio Grande do Norte	-	-	-	-	-	-	-	-	-	-	-	-	-
Bahia	-	-	238	-	-	-	-	-	-	-	-	-	1,119

Table XVI-3 (continued)

	1969	1970	1971	1972	1973	1974	1975	1976	1977	1978
Total Investments (US$ 000)	3,807	2,347,005	2,911,535	3,404,103	4,579,209	6,027,362	7,303,567	9,005,133	11,228,480	13,740,411
Reinvestments	-	801,353	1,121,920	1,323,175	1,720,586	2,102,236	2,400,740	2,811,238	3,688,514	4,841,995
Origin Country, Total Investments	-	-	-	-	-	-	-	-	-	-
United States	2,301	986,389	1,096,469	1,272,295	1,717,387	2,022,477	2,395,222	2,901,246	3,418,272	3,822,117
West Germany	499	252,780	331,418	372,370	520,776	709,769	871,352	1,118,029	1,533,469	2,096,707
Japan	858	105,066	124,871	192,712	318,260	598,024	841,162	1,005,900	1,203,313	1,403,504
Switzerland	-	132,279	191,855	253,810	357,049	559,621	735,509	980,729	1,202,681	1,331,494
United Kingdom	-	207,815	273,089	280,782	324,477	401,088	430,252	420,674	546,631	744,437
Canada	-	260,303	294,241	305,348	360,152	401,362	410,839	482,032	519,541	697,663
France	-	34,323	129,941	165,111	205,467	241,942	300,066	326,261	429,743	579,145
Belgium/Luxembourg	-	45,594	53,677	58,259	61,127	198,060	245,110	357,044	433,834	508,636
Panama	-	65,951	80,084	98,313	132,003	187,044	217,547	275,176	353,744	376,275
Netherlands	-	-	-	70,320	96,489	153,696	184,952	233,528	306,548	300,489
Sweden	-	39,401	57,731	69,015	73,208	118,903	144,910	220,215	233,015	246,471
Netherlands Antilles	-	58,526	75,173	77,128	113,276	131,902	157,266	191,750	227,901	245,183
Italy	-	32,053	-	-	-	303,474	-	-	-	-
Venezuela	-	-	-	-	-	-	-	-	-	-
Industry Group, Total Investments	3,807	2,347,005	2,911,535	3,404,103	4,579,209	6,027,362	7,303,567	9,005,133	11,228,480	13,740,411
Mining	-	-	26,123	48,175	76,748	121,321	154,427	229,397	256,392	250,979
Manufacturing	3,807	1,590,290	2,383,715	2,802,221	3,526,228	4,514,859	5,572,325	6,885,899	8,587,232	10,593,104
Chemicals	149	382,585	624,480	684,559	814,886	972,715	1,076,187	1,354,494	1,581,556	1,988,517
Transportation Equipment	2,183	340,013	405,539	475,722	672,090	813,412	988,673	1,178,512	1,545,096	1,905,175
Electrical/Communication Equipment	1,335	177,721	261,608	324,954	335,836	424,855	620,035	741,624	968,253	1,194,573
Mechanical	-	73,397	123,699	161,807	234,028	362,659	510,897	728,415	922,462	1,180,811
Metals	-	176,231	213,605	267,046	360,358	453,921	565,539	739,850	950,630	1,164,874
Food	-	105,185	135,443	161,058	191,463	285,587	317,790	385,293	576,694	690,610
Pharmaceuticals	-	95,592	113,436	138,276	197,197	233,774	292,211	390,625	457,823	574,306
Rubber	-	102,994	103,686	114,370	116,346	127,344	170,576	204,295	320,586	371,489
Textiles	-	60,985	69,711	75,003	122,572	193,414	229,836	243,944	277,632	345,685
Paper	-	-	67,867	76,390	88,785	100,191	150,858	195,688	268,576	324,517
Non-Metallic Minerals	-	-	61,613	105,891	124,488	163,750	189,764	214,757	237,795	283,838
Tobacco	-	75,587	112,140	117,626	160,653	190,058	196,635	195,223	102,481	128,759
Wood	-	-	3,965	6,026	18,589	31,753	69,983	85,938	99,669	109,744
Apparel	-	-	11,968	11,339	18,135	23,091	36,205	45,156	60,898	68,731
Beverages	-	-	12,813	17,669	29,658	68,387	34,169	41,408	52,942	61,588
Publishing	-	-	6,924	6,087	10,392	13,408	12,413	15,144	19,615	22,521
Public Utilities	-	131,514	157,390	154,383	190,937	207,701	218,854	229,009	224,548	238,031
Construction	-	-	7,786	-	-	-	-	-	-	-
Agriculture	-	-	20,734	24,394	31,686	43,096	26,415	35,849	51,607	66,476
Services	-	-	276,292	319,493	685,433	1,031,293	1,190,538	1,448,433	1,890,906	2,308,267
Other	-	625,201	39,495	55,437	68,177	109,092	141,008	176,546	217,795	283,554
Brazil Subdivision, Total Investments	-	-	-	-	-	-	-	-	-	-
São Paulo	3,807	-	-	-	-	-	-	-	-	-

Sources: AN 1956, p. 232; AN 1957, p. 218; AN 1961, p. 215; AN 1963, p. 230; AN 1965, p. 269; AN 1967, p. 319; AN 1970, p. 436; AN 1971, p. 445; AN 1972, p. 444; AN 1973, p. 492; AN 1974, p. 526; AN 1975, p. 583; AN 1976, p. 400; AN 1977, p. 750.

Chapter XVII. Tourism

Table XVII-1 shows the origins of tourists visiting Brazil from 1940 to 1978. The data originated with the Departamento Nacional de Imigração, the Superintendência da Política Agrária and the Emprêsa Brasileira de Turismo (EMBRATUR). Almost all of the difference between the "Total" on the first line of the table and the sum total of the "Country Issuing Passport" category is made up of those nationalities which in no year shown on the table comprised as much as one-half percent of the total number of tourists coming to Brazil. (Only tourists of Israeli and Lebanese nationality, even though they never reached one-half percent of any yearly total, are distinguished from this group.) Some small part of this difference between "Total" and the sum of the "Country Issuing Passport" is ascribable to persons of ill-defined nationality or persons without passports. These latter two classes of persons also accounted for some of the differences in any given year between the "Total" and the sum total of the "Continent/Region of Passport Issue" categories. Most of this difference, however, is a result of the way the sources reported the data. From 1940/1944 through 1951 sources reported an "other" category for country of origin, which they did not distribute by continent of origin. As a consequence there is a bloc of unknowns in the "Continent/ Region of Passport Issue" category on the table accounting for the bulk of the difference between this category and the "Total" on the top line.

The 1940/1944 total of 14,755 is for persons who were specified as tourists. A total of 44,347 persons actually entered the country on a temporary basis during this five-year period. Some of these may have been tourists, as well, but the source provided no evidence of this. For the period 1940/1944-1951 the sources reported data for Inglêses (English) but they did not make clear whether Scots, Welsh, and Northern Irish were included in this classification. All post-1951 sources reported tourists as being from the United Kingdom. All German tourists prior to 1945 are reported on the table under West Germany. From 1945 on, tourists from West Germany are reported separately from those of East

Germany. Egypt is included in Africa. From 1964 through 1967, when Syria was joined with Egypt as the United Arab Republic, Syrian tourists were reported by the sources as being from Africa, not from the Middle East. Beginning in 1971 sources included Mexico in North America instead of Central America. In all years the Soviet Union was included in Eastern Europe by the sources. The Anuário estatístico do Brasil, 1972, page 124, has transposed the headings for Egypt and South Africa. This has been rectified on the table.

Table XVII-2 reports the numbers and characteristics of establishments offering overnight lodging in Brazil and in the country's largest cities for 1950, 1961, 1966, 1974, and 1977. The data were originated by the Serviço de Estatística da Educação e Saúde, by IBGE, and by the Orgãos Regionais e Diretoria de Levantamentos Estatísticos of IBGE. For 1950 data for the territory of Rio Branco were for 1949. Twenty-nine of the establishments reported by the source in 1950 were not open for business. For 1961 data for the Distrito Federal (Brasília) were missing. The 1977 results were preliminary. None of the sources provided definitions for the hotel classification scheme.

Table XVII-1. Country and Continent/Region of Passport Issue for Tourists Entering Brazil, 1940-78

	1940-44	1945	1946	1947	1948	1949	1950	1951	1960	1961	1963	1964	1965
Total	14,755	10,354	19,099	21,983	25,153	21,204	23,532	22,773	74,787	82,320	106,446	125,216	102,964
Country Issuing Passport													
Argentina	–	2,721	3,848	4,254	6,169	6,490	7,112	5,292	–	–	31,544	36,038	29,406
Uruguay	5,183	1,898	1,947	1,848	2,332	1,943	3,098	4,335	–	–	19,132	7,088	6,372
United States	5,999	2,378	5,128	5,269	5,573	4,628	4,240	4,732	–	–	16,205	30,792	24,483
West Germany	–	47	149	258	312	417	307	460	–	–	3,919	5,677	4,590
Paraguay	731	172	131	170	341	159	440	202	–	–	5,555	1,806	1,626
Italy	152	153	596	962	1,007	893	2,183	1,086	–	–	3,142	3,437	3,845
France	–	219	911	893	956	560	452	630	–	–	1,957	4,491	3,567
Chile	–	350	548	612	768	775	1,175	1,000	–	–	3,133	4,278	3,244
Portugal	516	122	239	634	637	517	559	551	–	–	1,616	2,745	3,015
Japan	39	–	1	8	2	3	17	19	–	–	704	544	712
United Kingdom	–	427	887	900	995	788	593	600	–	–	1,795	3,830	3,113
Spain	–	278	625	438	620	596	497	460	–	–	1,827	2,170	2,026
Switzerland	144	103	344	330	376	320	319	420	–	–	1,260	2,776	1,845
Canada	–	–	–	–	228	210	100	153	–	–	933	1,519	970
Venezuela	–	–	–	–	–	–	–	–	–	–	1,003	–	–
Bolivia	–	134	126	170	218	88	199	206	–	–	1,689	1,349	872
Mexico	–	–	–	–	–	–	–	–	–	–	1,335	1,626	1,486
Netherlands	–	125	188	172	198	165	116	132	–	–	549	813	780
Peru	–	–	–	–	177	165	119	101	–	–	1,941	3,440	2,938
Sweden	–	–	–	–	–	–	–	–	–	–	501	1,037	761
Belgium	–	34	114	104	190	123	103	148	–	–	346	–	–
Australia	–	–	–	–	–	–	–	–	–	–	118	185	218
South Africa	–	–	–	–	–	–	–	–	–	–	149	289	171
Israel	–	–	–	–	–	–	–	–	–	–	449	656	422
Lebanon	–	15	88	135	146	91	89	90	–	–	370	370	236
Poland	206	76	322	1,193	1,058	271	142	95	–	–	167	140	103
Continent/Region of Passport Issue	12,872	9,352	16,639	19,177	23,387	19,679	22,237	21,092	–	–	104,809	125,118	102,919
South America	5,914	5,275	6,600	7,054	9,828	9,425	12,024	11,035	–	–	65,026	57,349	46,739
Western Europe	812	1,525	4,105	4,793	5,804	4,784	5,423	4,790	–	–	17,798	29,436	25,624
Eastern Europe	108	143	675	1,876	1,725	489	290	220	–	–	477	334	407
North America	5,999	2,378	5,128	5,269	5,801	4,838	4,340	4,885	–	–	17,138	32,311	25,453
Asia	39	–	1	8	2	3	17	19	–	–	887	767	1,026
Central America/Caribbean	–	–	–	–	–	–	–	–	–	–	2,066	2,770	2,240
Middle East	–	31	130	177	227	140	143	143	–	–	1,107	1,624	988
Africa	–	–	–	–	–	–	–	–	–	–	172	320	207
Oceania	–	–	–	–	–	–	–	–	–	–	138	207	235

Table XVII-1 (continued)

	1966	1967	1968	1969	1970	1971	1972	1973	1974	1975	1976	1977	1978
Total	133,487	141,426	136,065	162,191	194,186	287,926	342,941	399,127	480,267	517,967	555,967	634,595	764,152
Country Issuing Passport													
Argentina	25,608	24,194	27,096	32,929	44,658	54,128	56,161	57,818	78,133	78,019	67,440	89,788	130,463
Uruguay	9,974	10,653	11,229	18,036	36,006	37,463	33,320	42,053	45,705	46,637	60,629	73,149	121,997
United States	30,570	37,243	34,473	37,850	30,832	54,248	64,776	79,709	109,469	109,615	94,838	109,317	107,266
West Germany	7,725	7,846	7,836	9,822	10,490	15,808	19,780	24,940	25,647	30,782	34,109	40,012	48,051
Paraguay	2,409	2,056	1,581	4,135	6,596	6,589	7,813	8,073	9,077	8,677	25,308	32,683	36,393
Italy	5,725	6,415	5,657	6,508	7,061	12,585	15,234	18,820	20,775	22,242	25,360	27,749	32,773
France	4,893	5,362	5,410	4,926	5,850	10,673	13,988	17,575	18,240	21,589	28,370	29,975	30,139
Chile	5,251	5,569	5,635	5,798	7,602	6,364	6,281	7,749	10,900	13,431	19,784	24,967	29,567
Portugal	3,294	5,133	4,776	4,621	4,328	8,785	14,482	14,096	16,084	38,485	35,461	23,566	26,024
Japan	1,979	2,107	1,564	1,898	2,177	6,132	8,612	14,837	17,073	15,448	15,474	13,378	22,489
United Kingdom	4,604	4,499	4,259	4,242	5,491	9,105	10,018	11,073	12,455	12,593	16,329	18,175	21,812
Spain	3,220	3,977	3,686	4,679	4,609	7,571	9,294	10,420	12,594	12,805	15,928	19,104	20,520
Switzerland	2,400	2,249	2,188	2,641	2,606	4,218	5,797	8,252	8,104	7,652	10,178	10,852	12,336
Canada	1,715	1,987	1,910	1,941	2,337	4,140	5,876	6,564	8,509	8,252	10,254	12,541	11,902
Venezuela	1,561	2,065	2,099	2,541	2,408	3,320	5,015	5,194	5,678	7,470	12,401	11,247	11,607
Bolivia	2,013	1,917	1,224	888	849	2,772	3,532	3,604	5,792	6,902	8,444	10,497	11,467
Mexico	2,665	2,371	1,742	2,276	2,666	3,513	4,672	5,245	6,049	6,172	7,351	5,975	7,407
Netherlands	1,253	1,358	1,400	1,537	1,432	2,619	3,524	4,865	5,089	6,277	5,124	6,101	6,622
Peru	4,904	3,936	2,415	2,334	2,588	3,584	3,831	4,480	5,114	5,982	6,014	6,017	6,356
Sweden	939	1,042	1,190	1,311	1,415	1,677	2,572	3,088	3,280	3,937	3,946	4,937	5,781
Belgium	646	697	715	758	756	1,316	1,583	2,001	2,103	2,352	2,789	3,741	3,770
Australia	288	393	436	391	499	803	1,128	1,680	1,894	2,095	3,230	3,758	3,767
South Africa	391	250	259	1,620	2,106	3,498	3,552	5,058	6,162	6,573	7,447	6,490	3,282
Israel	924	725	607	682	642	1,080	1,013	1,352	1,531	1,941	1,863	2,375	3,225
Lebanon	994	437	133	79	60	807	911	860	1,200	1,986	1,986	942	1,165
Poland	182	127	89	—									
Continent/Region of Passport Issue	133,340	141,305	135,985	162,119	194,124	276,924	320,318	379,576	457,616	499,443	547,070	622,262	750,517
South America	53,462	51,968	51,611	68,331	102,267	116,681	118,939	133,159	164,370	172,113	206,689	256,147	357,567
Western Europe	36,852	40,839	39,972	44,156	47,560	80,162	103,269	123,322	133,292	167,070	186,840	195,491	220,247
Eastern Europe	726	510	797	—	—	—	—	—	—	—	—	—	—
North America	32,285	39,230	36,383	42,067	35,835	61,901	75,324	91,518	124,027	124,039	112,443	127,833	126,575
Asia	2,529	2,714	1,926	2,371	2,756	8,636	11,475	17,419	20,034	18,436	18,506	19,938	24,986
Central America/Caribbean	4,114	3,566	2,773	1,348	1,491	1,845	2,741	2,944	3,429	3,679	5,285	5,363	5,941
Middle East	2,632	1,760	1,706	1,646	1,484	3,032	3,413	3,742	3,933	4,720	5,517	5,653	6,227
Africa	431	302	343	1,770	2,152	3,661	3,716	5,306	6,339	6,962	8,051	7,581	4,528
Oceania	309	416	474	430	579	1,006	1,441	2,166	2,192	2,424	3,739	4,346	4,446

Sources: AN 1941-45, p. 42; AN 1949, pp. 63-64; AN 1952, pp. 67-68; AN 1961, p. 50; AN 1964, p. 50; AN 1968, p. 105; AN 1969, pp. 112-115; AN 1972, pp. 124-127; AN 1973, pp. 138-141; AN 1975, pp. 110-114; AN 1977, pp. 624-627; AN 1978, pp. 632-635.

Table XVII-2. Numbers and Characteristics of Establishments Offering Overnight Lodging in Brazil and in the Country's Largest Cities, 1950-77

1950

	Brazil	São Paulo	Rio de Janeiro	Recife	Belo Horizonte	Pôrto Alegre	Brasília
Numbers and Types of Establishments	–	–	–	–	–	–	–
Hotels	5,328	178	177	14	57	48	–
de Luxe	–	–	–	–	–	–	–
First Class	–	–	–	–	–	–	–
Second Class	–	–	–	–	–	–	–
Third Class	–	–	–	–	–	–	–
Pensions	–	–	–	–	–	–	–
Motels	–	–	–	–	–	–	–
Other	–	–	–	–	–	–	–
Numbers and Types of Accommodations							
All Establishments	–	–	–	–	–	–	–
Rooms	–	–	–	–	–	–	–
Apartments/Suites	–	–	–	–	–	–	–
Hotels							
Rooms	92,222	–	–	–	–	–	–
Apartments/Suites	12,797	–	–	–	–	–	–
Total Number of Employees	–	–	–	–	–	–	–

1961

	Brazil	São Paulo	Rio de Janeiro	Recife	Belo Horizonte	Pôrto Alegre	Brasília
Numbers and Types of Establishments	12,475	656	175	26	134	87	–
Hotels	–	–	–	–	–	–	–
de Luxe	–	–	–	–	–	–	–
First Class	–	–	–	–	–	–	–
Second Class	–	–	–	–	–	–	–
Second Class	–	–	–	–	–	–	–
Third Class	–	–	–	–	–	–	–
Pensions	–	–	–	–	–	–	–
Motels	–	–	–	–	–	–	–
Other	–	–	–	–	–	–	–
Numbers and Types of Accommodations							
All Establishments	–	–	–	–	–	–	–
Rooms	176,238	11,207	5,004	754	3,629	2,698	–
Apartments/Suites	22,542	3,391	3,496	309	996	735	
Hotels	–	–	–	–	–	–	–
Rooms	–	–	–	–	–	–	–
Apartments/Suites	–	–	–	–	–	–	–
Total Number of Employees	–	–	–	–	–	–	–

1966

	Brazil	São Paulo	Rio de Janeiro	Recife	Belo Horizonte	Pôrto Alegre	Brasília
Numbers and Types of Establishments	12,809	554	166	25	183	82	66
Hotels	7,909	390	156	22	97	54	59
de Luxe	–	–	–	–	–	–	–
First Class	–	–	–	–	–	–	–
Second Class	–	–	–	–	–	–	–
Third Class	–	–	–	–	–	–	–
Pensions	4,361	94	9	2	85	28	4
Motels	–	–	–	–	–	–	–
Others	539	70	1	1	1	–	3
Numbers and Types of Accommodations							
All Establishments	206,191	18,106	9,815	1,109	7,381	3,371	1,953
Rooms	166,444	11,544	3,875	508	5,626	2,397	1,081
Apartments/Suites	39,747	6,562	5,940	601	1,755	1,064	872
Hotels	164,986	15,770	9,658	1,011	6,468	2,919	1,866
Rooms	125,476	9,222	3,763	410	4,713	1,855	994
Apartments/Suites	39,510	6,548	5,922	601	1,755	1,064	872
Total Number of Employees	78,315	5,409	4,978	616	2,411	1,293	1,044

Table XVII-2 (continued)

1974

	Brazil	São Paulo	Rio de Janeiro	Recife	Belo Horizonte	Pôrto Alegre	Brasília
Numbers and Types of Establishments	15,356	548	348	55	211	133	52
Hotels	10,708	-	-	-	-	-	-
de Luxe	66	-	-	-	-	-	-
First Class	320	-	-	-	-	-	-
Second Class	824	-	-	-	-	-	-
Third Class	9,498	-	-	-	-	-	-
Pensions	3,562	-	-	-	-	-	-
Motels	502	-	-	-	-	-	-
Other	584	-	-	-	-	-	-
Numbers and Types of Accommodations							
All Establishments	280,991	18,723	18,468	1,773	6,241	5,051	2,551
Rooms	184,862	8,653	5,774	772	3,786	2,764	588
Apartments/Suites	96,129	10,070	12,694	1,001	2,455	2,287	1,963
Hotels	-	-	-	-	-	-	-
Rooms	-	-	-	-	-	-	-
Apartments/Suites	-	-	-	-	-	-	-
Numbers of Employees by Size Category							
Total Number of Employees	97,167	7,141	8,996	1,031	2,255	2,239	1,599
Employee Size Category							
1-4	28,837	-	-	-	-	-	-
5-9	22,407	-	-	-	-	-	-
10-19	10,522	-	-	-	-	-	-
20-49	10,245	-	-	-	-	-	-
50-99	7,705	-	-	-	-	-	-
100-249	11,729	-	-	-	-	-	-
250+	5,722	-	-	-	-	-	-
Numbers of Establishments by Employee Size Category							
Total Number of Establishments	15,356						
Employee Size Category							
1-4	10,179	-	-	-	-	-	-
5-9	3,785	-	-	-	-	-	-
10-19	825	-	-	-	-	-	-
20-49	354	-	-	-	-	-	-
50-99	116	-	-	-	-	-	-
100-149	82	-	-	-	-	-	-
250+	15	-	-	-	-	-	-
Investments by Types of Establishments (Cr$ 000)							
Total Investment	694,638	41,585	68,228	17,323	4,040	29,321	27,355
Hotels							
de Luxe	193,929	-	-	-	-	-	-
First Class	176,138	-	-	-	-	-	-
Second Class	127,706	-	-	-	-	-	-
Third Class	114,989	-	-	-	-	-	-
Pensions	11,678	-	-	-	-	-	-
Motels	52,018	-	-	-	-	-	-
Other	18,180	-	-	-	-	-	-
Total Income, All Establishments (Cr$ 000)	3,039,723	389,489	519,615	48,741	71,535	90,299	80,860
Numbers of Establishments by Income Category							
0-10 (Cr$ 000)	708	-	-	-	-	-	-
11-49 (Cr$ 000)	6,490	-	-	-	-	-	-
50-99 (Cr$ 000)	3,802	-	-	-	-	-	-
100-199 (Cr$ 000)	2,337	-	-	-	-	-	-
200-499 (Cr$ 000)	1,264	-	-	-	-	-	-
500-999 (Cr$ 000)	355	-	-	-	-	-	-
1000-1999 (Cr$ 000)	183	-	-	-	-	-	-
2000+ (Cr$ 000)	217	-	-	-	-	-	-

Table XVII-2 (continued)

	Brazil	São Paulo	1977 Rio de Janeiro	Recife	Belo Horizonte	Pôrto Alegre	Brasília
Numbers and Types of Establishments	16,807	673	347	48	205	141	59
Hotels	11,095	-	-	-	-	-	-
de Luxe	104	-	-	-	-	-	-
First Class	469	-	-	-	-	-	-
Second Class	949	-	-	-	-	-	-
Third Class	9,573	-	-	-	-	-	-
Pensions	3,462	-	-	-	-	-	-
Motels	787	-	-	-	-	-	-
Other	1,463	-	-	-	-	-	-
Numbers and Types of Accommodations							
All Establishments	322,588	22,600	19,901	1,991	6,498	5,217	3,366
Rooms	188,989	8,694	4,437	569	3,709	2,604	639
Apartments/ Suites	133,599	13,906	15,464	1,422	2,789	2,613	2,727
Hotels	-	-	-	-	-	-	-
Rooms	-	-	-	-	-	-	-
Apartments/Suites	-	-	-	-	-	-	-
Number of Employees by Employee Size Category							
Total Number of Employees	118,288	8,877	11,792	1,495	2,834	2,439	1,950
Employee Size Category							
1-4	30,944	-	-	-	-	-	-
5-9	24,187	-	-	-	-	-	-
10-19	12,590	-	-	-	-	-	-
20-49	14,290	-	-	-	-	-	-
50-99	10,804	-	-	-	-	-	-
100-249	15,680	-	-	-	-	-	-
250+	9,793	-	-	-	-	-	-
Numbers of Establishments by Employee Size Category							
Total Number of Establishments	16,807	-	-	-	-	-	-
Employee Size Category							
1-4	11,041	-	-	-	-	-	-
5-9	4,033	-	-	-	-	-	-
10-19	959	-	-	-	-	-	-
20-49	486	-	-	-	-	-	-
50-99	157	-	-	-	-	-	-
100-249	108	-	-	-	-	-	-
250+	23	-	-	-	-	-	-
Investment by Types of Establishments (Cr$ 000)							
Total Investment	1,956,925	389,502	149,489	118,595	15,915	41,990	42,154
Hotels							
de Luxe	694,299	-	-	-	-	-	-
First Class	663,876	-	-	-	-	-	-
Second Class	283,226	-	-	-	-	-	-
Third Class	201,734	-	-	-	-	-	-
Pensions	19,419	-	-	-	-	-	-
Motels	98,426	-	-	-	-	-	-
Other	40,945	-	-	-	-	-	-
Total Income, All Establishments (Cr$ 000)	9,959,017	1,089,080	1,843,650	174,311	252,112	264,721	281,376
Numbers of Establishments by Income Category							
0-10 (Cr$ 000)	107	-	-	-	-	-	-
11-49 (Cr$ 000)	2,284	-	-	-	-	-	-
50-99 (Cr$ 000)	4,026	-	-	-	-	-	-
100-199 (Cr$ 000)	4,188	-	-	-	-	-	-
200-499 (Cr$ 000)	3,802	-	-	-	-	-	-
500-999 (Cr$ 000)	1,195	-	-	-	-	-	-
1000-1999 (Cr$ 000)	565	-	-	-	-	-	-
2000+ (Cr$ 000)	640	-	-	-	-	-	-

Sources: AN 1952, pp. 492-293; AN 1963, p. 204; AN 1967, pp. 280-282; AN 1979, pp. 481-489.

Chapter XVIII. Government Finance

Taxes have had a relatively short history as major economic factors in Brazil. Barnes[1] notes that, although during the colonial period tax rates on local production were as high as 20 percent (the quinta real, or royal fifth), "the chief sources of colonial revenue were direct exploitation by the crown and the farming of land concessions." Imports were banned. In 1808 when the Portuguese royal court took refuge from Napoleon in Rio de Janeiro "the ban on imports was lifted and customs duties were instituted at a basic rate of 24 percent, reduced to 16 percent on imports from Portugal and to 15 percent on imports from England."[2] The Brazilian Imperial Constitution of 1824 prohibited the provinces (now states) from levying taxes but by 1835 the instrument was amended to allow the provinces to assess taxes not specifically reserved to the empire. Few taxes, however, were not on the reserved list. Under Getúlio Vargas, says Barnes,[3] "the new Constitution promulgated in 1934, reserved the income tax, which had been initiated in 1922, to the federal government and the sales tax to the states. For the first time, municipal governments received an exclusive power to levy taxes." The latter included real property, license, and amusement taxes and a 50 percent share of the state business tax. To prevent overlapping in taxation the Constitution of 1934 was amended to allow a federal tax to prevail over a conflicting state tax.

Chapter XVIII presents the receipts and expenditures of several different levels of Brazilian government. Nearly all the figures are for actual income and actual expenditures. Those figures recording budgeted receipts and expenditures are specifically noted in the text for the appropriate table. Except where noted all figures also include both ordinary and extraordinary income and expenses.

Table XVIII-1 records the actual receipts and expenditures of the Brazilian federal government from 1823 to 1978. The data originated with the Inspetoria Geral de Finanças of the Ministério da Fazenda, the Contadoria Geral da República, the Conselho Técnico de Economica e Finanças, and the <u>Anuário estatístico do Brasil, ano V</u>. Rounding of these figures by different sources reporting the same data (AN 1971 and AN 1972, for example, both report 1970 data) does yield slightly different results depending upon which source was used. The author simply chose the later source in each case on the assumption, often borne out, that the older the data the better the chance that errors in it, whether rounding or data errors, had been corrected. By a decree of October 8, 1828, the fiscal year was changed from the calendar year to the period July 1-June 30. As a consequence, data for 1829 are just for the first semester of that year. In 1888 the fiscal year was changed back to the calendar year. As a consequence of this change the second semester of 1887 was included in the fiscal year 1886-87. The 1960 data include Cr$ 5,197,000, expenditures from previous years.

Table XVIII-2 shows the sources of federal government tax revenue by category from 1937 to 1978. The data originated with the Diretoria das Rendas Aduaneiras, the Contadoria Geral da República, and the Inspetoria-Geral de Finanças of the Ministério da Fazenda. Only the major revenue-producing taxes are shown. Beginning in 1967 the <u>impôsto de consumo</u> (consumption tax) was retitled <u>impôsto sôbre produtos industrializados</u> (tax on industrial products). The income tax is assessed on individuals as well as on corporate entities. Federal stamps must appear on the papers accompanying most business transactions. This is the stamp tax. For most years the bulk of the difference between total revenue and tax-originated revenue was made up of monies borrowed in either foreign or domestic markets.

Table XVIII-3 reports the actual expenditures of the ministries of the Brazilian federal government in five-year increments from 1900 to 1978. The data were originated by the Diretoria Geral de Estatística in its publication <u>Estatística da finanças do Brasil</u>, and by the Serviço de Estatística Economia e Finanças in its report <u>Quadros estatísticos, no. 2</u>. Other origins included the report <u>Balanço geral da união, 1933-34</u>, and the agencies Contadoria Geral da República and Inspetoria Geral de Finanças of the Ministério da Fazenda.

The Labor/Industry and Commerce Ministry existed under that title from 1900 through 1960. In 1961 Industry and Commerce was funded separately as was Labor, to whose title Social Security was added. In 1975 Labor and Social Security were funded separately for the first time. Agriculture was first funded as an independent ministry in 1900. Education and Culture/Public Health was first funded as a ministry in 1930; in 1952 Public Health (later simply Health) was funded

separately from Education and Culture. The title <u>Negócios</u>
<u>Interiores</u> (Interior Affairs) first appeared with the Justice
Ministry title in 1936; the two were separately funded for
the first time in 1968. The Air Force received its first
separate budget in 1941. The Mines and Energy Ministry was
first funded in 1961; the Communications Ministry in 1968.
The Planning and General Coordination Ministry received its
first budget in 1969 and its last in 1974. For the period
1900 to 1923 expenditures included some "gold cruzeiros" (<u>mil</u>
<u>reis</u> <u>ouro</u>) and some "paper cruzeiros" (<u>mil</u> <u>reis</u> <u>papel</u>). The
conversion rates applicable to the data on this table were
given by the source as follows: 1900, 1 gold = 1.800 paper;
1910, 1 gold = 1.687 paper; 1920, 1 gold = 1.2598 paper.

Table XVIII-4 shows the receipts and expenditures of the
states of Brazil from 1897 to 1978. Neither territories nor
the Distrito Federal are included in this table. Among the
data originators are the <u>Quadros estatísticos, no. 2</u> of the
Serviço de Estatística Economia e Finançeira, the <u>Anuário</u>
<u>estatístico do Brasil, ano V</u>, the Contadoria Geral da Repúb-
lica, the Conselho Técnico de Economia e Finanças, and the
Secretaria and Sub-Secretaria de Economia e Finanças of the
Ministério da Fazenda.

For 1897 Espírito Santo, Pernambuco and Rio de Janeiro
expenditures reported were just those fixed and not the total
amount of expenditures, and for the latter two states
receipts were just those budgeted for and not the actual
receipts. For 1899 the source reported only fixed expenditures for Santa Catarina, Paraná, Espírito Santo, Amazonas,
and Pernambuco, and for the latter two states only receipts
budgeted for were reported. Also in 1899 Paraná data were
reported only for the first semester and for this period both
receipts and expenditures were only estimated, although the
source does not indicate by whom. From 1899 to 1928 the
Paraná fiscal year was July 1 to June 30, and in 1929 its
fiscal year covered eighteen months. For 1907 only first
semester receipts and expenditures were reported for
Maranhão. From 1907 through 1924 Pernambuco's fiscal year
was July 1 to June 30; Maranhão had this same fiscal year
from 1908 through 1930 as did Espírito Santo from 1924
through 1928. For 1924 Espírito Santo's fiscal year was
eighteen months long, extending from January 1, 1924, to June
30, 1925. For 1925 Pernambuco's fiscal year was also
eighteen months in length, extending from July 1, 1924, to
December 31, 1925. The 1928 Espírito Santo data and 1930
Maranhão data were each for the second semester only. For
1956 and 1957 the data for Amazonas and Maranhão were for
budgeted (not actual) receipts and expenditures for the years
1957 and 1958, respectively. For 1958 Pará data represented
the balance of 1957, Maranhão's 1959 data the balance of

1958. For 1960 data for Pará, Maranhão, and Piauí were for
budgeted (not actual) receipts and expenditures. For 1964
all Piauí data were missing. No actual expenditure data for
1964, a year of extreme political and administrative chaos,
were reported by any of the sources used for this table. For
1966, 1967, and 1968 all Acre data were missing.

Table XVIII-5 reports the expenditures of all Brazilian
states by functional categories for the period 1914/16 to
1978. Data for Brazilian territories and the Distrito
Federal are not included in this table. The data originated
with the Estatística das finanças do Brasil, 1926, of the
Diretoria Geral de Estatística, the Conselho Técnico de
Economia e Finanças, and the Secretaria and Sub-Secretaria de
Economia e Finanças. The categories were those used by the
sources and they remained relatively constant for the periods
1914/16-1935, 1940-70, and 1975-78. Categories varied considerably, however, in the years between these periods.
Given the five-year sequencing, 1965 data would have been
used on the table, but for that year nearly all the states
reported budgeted and not actual expenditures, so 1966 data
were used instead. The data for the period 1914/16-1935 are
for fixed, and not actual, expenditures. In the year 1930
fixed expenditures amounted to 89.5 percent of actual
expenditures. In 1935 they came to 89.8 percent of actual
outlays. For 1955 the Maranhão "public debt" and "public
services" category were listed by the source in the "other"
category. For 1960 Pará, Maranhão, and Piauí data were for
budgeted, not actual, expenditures. For 1966 all Acre data
were missing and in the same year a Piauí data total was
reported but was not distributed among categories.
Consequently, Piauí was not included in the 1966 data on the
table. For 1975 the Alagoas data were missing. Not every
state in Brazil expended funds in each of the categories
shown. For example, in 1978 nine states had no specific
communications category, three had no development category,
two had no housing category and one had no energy category.

Table XVIII-6 presents the expenditures of all of
Brazil's municípios (counties) for each year from 1907 to
1971. The table does not include the Distrito Federal but
does include municípios in the territories. The data were
originated by the Contadoria Geral da República, the Conselho
Técnico de Economia e Finanças, the Anuário estatístico do
Brasil, ano V, the Inspetoria Geral de Finanças of the
Ministério da Fazenda, and the Sub-Secretaria de Economia e
Finanças. For 1939 the data for Pará municípios were
estimated. For 1965 data for all of the municípios for the
territory of Amapá were missing and data for the município of
the capital city, Manaus, were missing from the Amazonas
data. For 1970 data were missing for the municípios of the

capital cities of Roraíma (Boa Vista) and Ceará (Fortaleza).

Table XVIII-7 shows the receipts and expenditures of the state of São Paulo for the period 1835 to 1978. Origins of the data include reports of the Secretary of Finance of the State of São Paulo, the Quados estatísticos, no. 2 of the Serviço de Estatística Economia e Finançeira, the Conselho Técnico de Economia e Finanças, the Contadoria Geral de República, and the Sub-Secretaria de Economia e Finanças. The Brazilian Year Book, 1909[4] notes that the 1874/75 to 1896 figures "were taken from official publications but do not seem to uniformly include Extraordinary Revenue or Expenditures, and, moreover, debit the whole value of foreign loans to the year in which they were raised at par without reference to the value really drawn for." From 1835/36 to 1890/91 the fiscal year did not correspond to the calendar year, but the Brazilian Year Book, 1909 does not define the fiscal year. The shift to the calendar year after FY 1890/91 doubtless accounted for the large figures for 1892 since the second semester of 1891 was probably added to FY 1892. The 1964 data should probably be considered suspect. AN 1965 reported the 1964 actual expenditures shown on the table, and AN 1966 reported the 1964 actual receipts. The difference between them yields a huge surplus. AN 1965 also reported a budgeted expenditure of Cr$ 627,224,400,000. This was a year of severe inflation and political chaos.

Table XVIII-8 reports the receipts and expenditures of the Old Distrito Federal/State of Guanabara from 1861 to 1974. From 1763 to April 21, 1960, on which date Brasília became the capital of Brazil, the city of Rio de Janeiro was the national capital and for nearly all this period was surrounded by the Distrito Federal, an area roughly 12 by 36 miles in extent. From 1961 through 1974 this Distrito Federal became the state of Guanabara of which the city of Rio de Janeiro was the capital. After 1974 the state of Guanabara was dissolved, the area becoming a part of the state of Rio de Janeiro, and the city of Rio de Janeiro became the capital of Rio de Janeiro, whose previous capital, Niteroi, lost that status. Although the Distrito Federal/ Guanabara state political unit included some rural, indeed pristine, areas for much of its history, the sheer size of the city of Rio's population during most of this period made the Distrito's receipt and expenditure patterns those of an urban area.

Data were originated by the Anuário estatístico do Brasil, ano V, the Contadoria Geral da República, the Conselho Técnico de Economia e Finanças, and the Secretaria and Sub-Secretaria de Economia e Finanças of the Ministério da Fazenda. Data on actual expenditures were not available for the financially and politically chaotic years of 1963 and 1964.

Table XVIII-9 displays the receipts and expenditures for the new Distrito Federal, which included the city of Brasília, from 1961 to 1978. In the early years Brasília was the principal focus of activity in the Distrito Federal and therefore the fiscal data reflected the characteristics of a single new city and its immediate environs. By 1978, however, the fiscal data reflected the characteristics of the functional structures filling the 30-by-60-mile rectangle. Among these structures were rural farming communities, entirely new cities such as Taguatinga, Sobradinho, and Gama and the grafting of urban patterns on preexisting villages like Planaltina. Essentially the new Distrito Federal resembles a small state more than it does a city.

The data originated with the Conselho Técnico de Economia e Finanças, the Contadoria Geral da República, and the Secretaria and Sub-Secretaria de Economia e Finanças. As with many of the other levels of government no actual expenditure data were available for the chaotic years of 1963 and 1964.

References

1. William Sprague Barnes, Taxation in Brazil, World Taxation Series of the International Program in Taxation, Harvard Law School (Boston: Little, Brown, 1957), p. 6.

2. Ibid.

3. Ibid.

4. The Brazilian Year Book, Second Issue--1909, ed. J.P. Wileman (Rio de Janeiro: Office of the Brazilian Year Book), p. 389.

Table XVIII-1. Receipts and Expenditures of the Brazilian Federal Government, 1823-1978

Fiscal Year	Receipts Cr$ 000	Expenditures Cr$ 000	Surplus/Deficit Cr$ 000	Fiscal Year	Receipts Cr$ 000	Expenditures Cr$ 000	Surplus/Deficit Cr$ 000
1823	3,802	4,702	− 900	1901	304,512	334,517	− 30,005
1824	6,029	9,618	− 3,589	1902	343,814	297,721	+ 46,093
1825	4,721	8,358	− 3,637	1903	415,375	363,180	+ 52,195
1826	4,372	9,409	− 5,037	1904	442,770	463,466	− 20,696
1827	6,916	11,842	− 4,926	1905	401,025	374,868	+ 26,157
1828	7,228	10,680	− 3,452	1906	431,685	423,416	+ 8,269
1828/29	9,881	13,911	− 4,030	1907	536,060	522,111	+ 13,849
1829/30	16,531	18,213	− 1,682	1908	441,259	511,013	− 69,754
1830/31	16,779	19,778	− 2,999	1909	449,898	518,288	− 58,390
1831/32	11,796	11,502	+ 294	1910	524,819	623,536	− 98,717
1832/33	16,132	14,263	+ 1,869	1911	653,549	681,913	− 118,364
1833/34	12,472	11,478	+ 994	1912	615,391	789,241	− 173,850
1834/35	14,820	12,908	+ 1,912	1913	654,391	762,945	− 108,554
1835/36	14,135	14,340	− 205	1914	423,252	766,701	− 343,449
1836/37	14,477	13,980	+ 497	1915	404,278	688,522	− 284,244
1837/38	12,672	18,920	− 6,248	1916	477,897	686,558	− 208,661
1838/39	14,971	18,131	− 3,160	1917	537,441	801,447	− 264,006
1839/40	15,948	24,969	− 9,021	1918	618,830	867,162	− 248,332
1840/41	16,311	22,772	− 6,461	1919	625,693	931,579	− 305,886
1841/42	16,319	27,483	− 11,164	1920	922,259	1,226,735	− 304,476
1842/43	18,712	29,165	− 10,453	1921	891,001	1,189,306	− 298,305
1843/44	21,315	25,947	− 4,596	1922	972,179	1,428,261	− 456,082
1844/45	24,805	25,635	− 830	1923	1,258,132	1,569,144	− 311,012
1845/46	26,199	24,464	+ 1,735	1924	1,588,440	1,629,822	− 41,382
1846/47	27,628	26,680	+ 948	1925	1,741,834	1,760,225	− 18,391
1847/48	24,732	26,211	− 1,479	1926	1,647,889	1,867,750	− 219,861
1848/49	26,163	28,289	− 2,126	1927	2,039,506	2,025,959	+ 13,547
1849/50	28,200	28,950	− 750	1928	2,216,513	2,350,107	− 133,594
1850/51	32,697	33,225	− 528	1929	2,201,246	2,422,393	− 221,147
1851/52	37,713	42,755	− 5,042	1930	1,677,952	2,510,544	− 832,592
1852/53	38,103	31,654	+ 6,449	1931	1,752,665	2,046,620	− 293,955
1853/54	34,516	36,234	− 1,718	1932	1,750,790	2,859,668	− 1,108,878
1854/55	35,985	38,740	− 2,755	1933	2,078,476	2,391,813	− 313,337
1855/56	38,634	40,243	− 1,609	1934	2,519,530	3,050,188	− 530,658
1856/57	49,156	40,374	+ 8,782	1935	2,722,693	2,872,001	− 149,308
1857/58	49,747	51,756	− 2,009	1936	3,127,460	3,226,081	− 98,621
1858/59	46,920	52,719	− 5,799	1937	3,462,476	4,143,959	− 681,483
1859/60	43,807	52,606	− 8,799	1938	3,879,768	4,735,434	− 855,666
1860/61	50,052	52,358	− 2,306	1939	4,352,809	4,850,338	− 497,529
1861/62	52,489	53,050	− 561	1940	4,644,813	5,188,986	− 544,173
1862/63	48,342	57,000	− 8,658	1941	4,765,084	5,438,389	− 673,305
1863/64	54,801	56,494	− 1,693	1942	4,987,728	6,343,206	− 1,355,478
1864/65	56,996	83,346	− 26,350	1943	6,010,972	6,512,235	− 501,363
1865/66	58,523	121,856	− 63,333	1944	8,311,049	8,399,164	− 88,115
1866/67	64,777	120,890	− 56,113	1945	9,845,154	10,839,323	− 994,169
1867/68	71,201	165,985	− 94,784	1946	11,569,576	14,202,544	− 2,632,968
1868/69	87,543	150,895	− 63,352	1947	13,853,467	13,393,229	+ 460,238
1869/70	94,847	141,594	− 46,747	1948	15,698,971	15,695,591	+ 3,380
1870/71	95,885	100,074	− 4,189	1949	17,916,540	20,726,713	− 2,810,173
1871/72	102,337	101,581	+ 756	1950	19,372,788	23,669,854	− 4,297,066
1872/73	110,713	121,874	− 11,161	1951	27,428,004	24,609,329	+ 2,818,675
1873/74	102,652	121,481	− 18,829	1952	30,739,617	28,460,745	+ 2,278,872
1874/75	104,707	125,855	− 21,148	1953	37,057,229	39,925,491	− 2,868,262
1875/76	100,718	126,780	− 26,062	1954	46,539,009	49,250,117	− 2,711,108
1876/77	98,970	135,801	− 36,831	1955	55,670,936	63,286,949	− 7,616,013
1877/78	109,221	151,492	− 42,271	1956	74,082,539	107,028,203	− 32,945,664
1878/79	111,802	181,469	− 69,667	1957	85,788,466	118,711,591	− 32,923,125
1879/80	120,393	150,134	− 29,741	1958	117,816,368	148,478,452	− 30,662,084
1880/81	128,364	138,583	− 10,219	1959	157,826,693	184,273,251	− 26,446,558
1881/82	130,456	139,471	− 9,015	1960	233,012,566	264,636,262	− 31,623,696
1882/83	129,698	152,958	− 23,260	1961	317,454,000	419,914,000	− 102,460,000
1883/84	132,593	154,257	− 21,664	1962	511,828,000	726,694,000	− 214,866,000
1884/85	121,974	158,496	− 36,522	1963	953,054,000	1,277,577,000	− 324,523,000
1885/86	126,883	153,623	− 26,740	1964	2,010,623,000	2,770,714,000	− 128,618,000
1886/87	218,763	227,045	− 8,282	1965	3,593,921,000	4,414,920,000	− 820,999,000
1888	150,726	147,451	+ 3,275	1966	6,007,010,000	6,138,559,000	− 131,549,000
1889	160,840	186,165	− 25,325	1967	7,384,437,000	8,172,972,000	+ 788,535,000
1890	195,253	220,646	− 25,393	1968	11,785,505	11,542,898	+ 242,607
1891	228,945	220,592	+ 8,353	1969	19,683,563	18,651,502	+ 1,032,061
1892	227,608	279,281	− 51,673	1970	29,819,965	28,115,660	+ 1,704,305
1893	259,851	300,631	− 40,780	1971	27,051,574	26,142,517	+ 909,057
1894	265,057	372,751	− 107,694	1972	39,419,929	38,198,339	+ 1,221,590
1895	307,755	344,767	− 37,012	1973	52,725,872	50,766,874	+ 1,958,998
1896	346,213	368,921	− 22,708	1974	75,663,458	71,749,814	+ 3,913,644
1897	303,411	379,336	− 75,925	1975	100,590,849	103,838,692	− 3,247,843
1898	324,053	668,113	− 344,060	1976	172,372,127	168,181,101	+ 4,191,026
1899	320,837	295,363	+ 25,474	1977	252,605,448	247,466,754	+ 5,138,694
1900	307,915	433,555	− 125,640	1978	357,704,780	356,000,370	+ 1,704,410

Sources: AN 1956, p. 541; AN 1958, p. 442; AN 1961, pp. 403, 418, 421 & 430; AN 1965, p. 463; AN 1967, p. 733; AN 1969, p. 662; AN 1971, pp. 778 & 786; AN 1972, p. 880; AN 1976, pp. 712 & 722; AN 1977, pp. 727 & 730; AN 1979, pp. 745 & 748.

Table XVIII-2. Tax Sources of Brazilian Federal Revenue, 1937-78

	1937	1938	1939	1940	1941	1942
Total Revenue (Cr$ 000)	3,462,476	3,879,768	4,352,809	4,664,813	4,765,084	4,987,728
Taxes (Cr$ 000)	2,309,079	2,430,188	2,655,010	2,725,018	3,119,294	3,348,284
Consumption/Industrial Products	667,074	853,666	1,029,688	1,053,747	1,185,495	1,253,612
Income	232,391	287,312	323,547	410,603	537,082	988,336
Import	1,173,413	1,052,512	1,031,197	977,514	1,058,775	674,220
Stamp	227,856	229,265	263,194	283,044	337,942	431,945

	1943	1944	1945	1946	1947	1948
Total Revenue (Cr$ 000)	6,010,972	8,311,049	9,845,154	11,589,576	13,853,467	15,698,971
Taxes (Cr$000)	4,226,592	5,631,423	7,080,404	9,366,880	11,667,479	12,150,220
Consumption/Industrial Products	1,553,577	1,947,127	2,332,166	4,008,862	4,462,971	4,854,257
Income	1,497,547	2,037,506	2,349,784	2,751,221	3,901,808	4,194,997
Import	596,467	902,439	1,026,039	1,404,033	1,876,437	1,650,271
Stamp	579,901	742,657	865,602	1,194,444	1,423,888	1,448,358

	1949	1950	1951	1952	1953	1954
Total Revenue (Cr$ 000)	17,916,540	19,372,788	27,428,004	30,739,617	37,057,229	43,051,984
Taxes (Cr$ 000)	13,716,361	15,590,011	21,876,404	24,804,465	27,626,950	37,010,950
Consumption/Industrial Products	5,639,157	6,409,818	8,216,025	9,123,573	10,774,509	14,541,579
Income	4,784,809	5,581,581	8,104,401	9,993,994	11,639,053	15,339,971
Import	1,700,532	1,694,871	2,801,194	2,588,572	1,384,678	2,280,825
Stamp	1,589,130	1,900,428	2,705,521	3,091,984	3,821,681	4,840,209

	1955	1956	1957	1958	1959	1960
Total Revenue (Cr$ 000)	52,474,865	66,563,465	80,428,469	117,816,368	157,826,693	233,013,000
Taxes (Cr$ 000)	48,367,955	61,033,646	72,936,460	101,997,727	140,181,955	196,899,000
Consumption/Industrial Products	17,429,472	22,988,188	30,480,988	39,518,090	53,817,280	83,515,000
Income	19,258,772	24,519,199	24,018,169	31,856,296	46,381,578	62,229,000
Import	2,248,862	1,979,100	2,763,605	12,925,477	19,113,829	22,032,000
Stamp	6,444,756	8,187,113	9,486,907	12,068,528	17,867,448	25,469,000
Electrical Energy	843,513	1,064,331	1,196,655	1,387,419	1,485,128	1,699,000

	1961	1962	1963	1964	1965	1966
Total Revenue (Cr$ 000)	317,454,000	511,828,000	953,054,000	2,010,624	3,593,921	6,007,010
Taxes (Cr$ 000)	282,584,000	444,125,000	845,759,000	1,707,615	3,002,928	4,731,650
Consumption/Industrial Products	122,690,000	204,239,000	408,065,000	880,002	1,307,530	2,214,959
Income	83,697,000	115,567,000	242,947,000	482,415	1,022,621	1,339,405
Import	35,716,000	58,405,000	86,810,000	124,401	208,512	415,769
Stamp	36,054,000	60,717,000	91,790,000	188,008	347,685	538,778
Electrical Energy	1,914,000	2,167,000	11,937,000	32,619	97,137	193,584

	1967	1968	1969	1970	1971	1972
Total Revenue (Cr$ 000)	7,384,437	11,785,505	19,683,563	29,819,965	27,051,574	39,419,929
Taxes (Cr$ 000)	4,898,144	9,860,113	14,164,679	18,187,512	24,235,016	34,820,842
Consumption/Industrial Products	2,840,336	5,075,408	6,751,439	8,505,530	11,412,589	14,889,049
Income	1,549,689	2,173,134	3,763,746	4,897,074	6,503,158	9,980,908
Petroleum	-	1,597,257	2,288,771	2,852,535	3,669,874	4,573,056
Import	369,779	815,732	1,077,961	1,329,844	1,805,873	2,635,950
Stamp	-	-	-	-	-	-
Electrical Energy	104,901	-	233,317	449,622	603,490	1,073,660
Financial Operations	-	-	-	-	-	1,328,197

	1973	1974	1975	1976	1977	1978
Total Revenue (Cr$ 000)	52,725,872	75,663,458	100,590,849	172,372,127	252,605,448	357,704,780
Taxes (Cr$ 000)	46,074,333	66,172,735	87,426,816	144,743,012	205,696,431	282,472,526
Consumption/Industrial Products	19,853,652	27,911,741	34,404,022	50,953,490	69,410,706	96,891,888
Income	12,802,838	19,339,689	26,312,086	41,413,664	70,918,905	92,417,732
Petroleum	5,556,280	6,671,977	8,255,414	24,070,978	29,662,862	41,066,522
Import	3,816,971	6,803,540	9,610,210	15,069,601	17,132,861	23,018,317
Stamp	-	-	-	-	-	-
Electrical Energy	1,543,425	1,975,263	2,721,473	4,179,537	5,583,997	9,384,321
Financial Operations	2,018,947	2,784,422	4,010,444	6,898,869	8,797,211	13,164,659

Sources: AN 1939-40, pp. 507, 517, 519 & 522; AN 1941-45, p. 485; AN 1952, p. 502; AN 1953, p. 423; AN 1956, p. 400; AN 1958, p. 446; AN 1961, p. 420; AN 1963, p. 404; AN 1964, p. 365; AN 1965, p. 464; AN 1967, p. 734; AN 1969, p. 663; AN 1972, p. 884; AN 1975, p. 890; AN 1976, p. 719; AN 1979, p. 745.

Table XVIII-3. Expenditures by Ministries of the Brazilian Federal Government, 1900–1978

Ministry	1900 Cr$ 000	1905 Cr$ 000	1910 Cr$ 000	1915 Cr$ 000	1920 Cr$ 000	1925 Cr$ 000	1930 Cr$ 000	1935 Cr$ 000	1940 Cr$ 000
Total Expenditures	433,555	374,868	623,536	688,522	1,226,735	1,760,225	2,510,544	2,872,001	5,188,986
Treasury	241,838	175,983	246,386	290,056	238,883	563,559	890,407	1,159,396	1,234,019
Military	74,237	80,278	129,422	122,577	204,036	408,798	483,798	713,311	1,244,129
Army	46,650	52,061	69,226	77,933	132,236	306,381	302,690	519,430	882,361
Navy	27,587	28,217	60,196	44,644	71,800	102,047	181,108	193,881	361,768
Air Force	–	–	–	–	–	–	–	–	–
Transportation & Public Works	91,900	79,804	172,156	207,805	493,125	520,721	576,385	574,523	1,297,358
Education & Culture	–	–	–	–	–	–	10,326	144,995	309,786
Health	–	–	–	–	–	–	–	–	–
Mines & Energy	–	–	–	–	–	–	–	–	–
Interior	23,040	34,701	48,898	47,602	75,191	130,525	201,059	132,917	167,810
Justice	–	–	20,899	13,777	42,373	50,192	78,063	67,834	126,728
Agriculture	–	–	–	–	–	–	–	–	–
Communications	–	–	–	–	–	–	–	–	–
Foreign Relations	2,540	4,102	5,775	6,662	9,917	26,360	37,832	60,935	77,933
Social Security	–	–	–	–	–	–	820	18,090	86,199
Labor	–	–	–	–	–	–	–	–	–
Industry & Commerce	–	–	–	–	–	–	–	–	–
Planning & General Coordination	–	–	–	–	–	–	–	–	–

Ministry	1945 Cr$ 000	1950 Cr$ 000	1955 Cr$ 000	1960 Cr$ 000	1965 Cr$ 000	1970 Cr$ 000	1975 Cr$ 000	1978 Cr$ 000
Total Expenditures	10,839,323	23,669,854	63,286,949	264,636,262	4,414,920,000	28,225,660	103,838,692	356,000,370
Treasury	3,474,051	4,575,930	14,369,082	84,298,326	1,328,900,341	13,864,043	1,530,139	7,272,523
Military	2,853,354	6,339,378	17,842,439	54,792,433	921,081,417	5,172,001	13,259,052	40,858,237
Army	1,615,043	3,005,917	8,300,153	27,178,173	460,786,683	2,598,115	6,090,237	17,588,894
Navy	618,354	1,635,622	5,027,695	13,616,695	223,766,174	1,328,036	3,611,633	11,881,855
Air Force	619,957	1,697,839	4,514,591	13,997,565	236,528,560	1,245,850	3,557,282	11,387,488
Transportation & Public Works	1,403,612	3,726,045	14,092,470	57,135,271	903,650,653	3,876,702	7,036,386	18,361,497
Education & Culture	551,035	2,497,474	3,600,137	18,029,687	396,424,538	1,337,094	5,262,058	23,739,801
Health	–	–	2,603,290	10,459,527	117,996,869	1,313,138	1,170,351	6,458,594
Mines & Energy	–	–	–	–	142,664,993	920,747	632,989	2,298,987
Interior	477,794	1,011,949	2,705,434	8,200,410	102,569,548	808,507	1,558,461	5,444,600
Justice	298,807	1,066,354	3,158,698	10,272,282	124,133,817	127,727	494,044	1,686,724
Agriculture	–	–	–	–	–	340,716	950,658	7,178,356
Communication	110,858	176,782	398,584	2,345,339	13,386,518	330,405	825,271	1,669,712
Foreign Relations	–	–	–	–	–	195,363	550,501	2,134,613
Social Security	574,897	760,186	1,491,987	3,156,559	86,637,881	181,050	564,328	11,947,158
Labor	–	–	–	–	–	30,101	409,944	2,532,470
Industry & Commerce	–	–	–	–	–	119,024	80,644	903,335
Planning & General Coordination	–	–	–	–	6,916,945	–	–	–

Sources: AN 1939-40, p. 1411; AN 1951, p. 496; AN 1952, p. 435; AN 1956, p. 411; AN 1961, p. 430; AN 1971, p. 786; AN 1979, p. 748.

Table XVIII-4. Receipts and Expenditures of the States of Brazil, 1897-1978

Fiscal Year	Receipts Cr$ 000	Expenditures Cr$ 000	Surplus/Deficit Cr$ 000	Fiscal Year	Receipts Cr$ 000	Expenditures Cr$ 000	Surplus/Deficit Cr$ 000
1897	173,967	195,871	- 21,904	1938	1,860,317	2,122,287	- 261,970
1898	155,945	180,377	- 24,432	1939	2,191,701	2,387,630	- 195,929
1899	172,895	191,798	- 18,903	1940	2,295,118	2,579,363	- 284,245
1900	162,057	188,339	- 26,282	1941	2,684,467	2,803,022	- 118,555
1901	148,695	168,709	- 20,014	1942	2,950,836	3,104,944	- 154,108
1902	134,719	148,776	- 14,057	1943	3,759,163	3,548,559	+ 210,604
1903	139,818	155,045	- 15,227	1944	4,749,492	4,575,794	+ 173,698
1904	155,946	148,200	+ 7,746	1945	5,426,470	6,007,615	- 581,145
1905	170,008	228,456	- 58,448	1946	6,859,928	7,187,500	- 327,572
1906	168,571	182,623	- 14,052	1947	7,560,662	8,761,012	- 1,200,350
1907	179,438	192,852	- 13,414	1948	9,411,947	10,545,559	- 1,133,612
1908	157,626	192,730	- 35,104	1949	11,373,976	12,565,831	- 1,191,855
1909	189,696	199,544	- 9,848	1950	13,457,072	15,761,630	- 2,304,558
1910	193,900	228,319	- 34,419	1951	19,221,101	20,563,422	- 1,342,321
1911	200,260	226,776	- 26,516	1952	21,113,879	26,022,239	- 4,908,360
1912	238,244	259,692	- 21,448	1953	25,179,964	30,470,256	- 5,290,292
1913	228,982	291,142	- 62,160	1954	32,995,255	38,331,781	- 5,336,526
1914	201,936	266,286	- 64,350	1955	40,873,995	44,425,238	- 3,551,243
1915	243,268	251,107	- 7,839	1956	54,957,751	54,836,302	+ 121,449
1916	258,074	258,948	- 874	1957	71,523,915	75,171,254	- 3,647,339
1917	278,068	282,780	- 4,712	1958	83,974,293	92,012,490	- 8,038,197
1918	281,544	309,959	- 28,415	1959	127,244,706	128,299,767	- 1,055,061
1919	345,981	336,410	+ 9,571	1960	185,204,764	192,159,996	- 6,955,232
1920	432,298	438,264	- 5,966	1961	307,489,763	316,001,930	- 8,512,167
1921	432,220	446,612	- 14,392	1962	491,510,628	525,670,397	- 34,159,769
1922	462,489	512,404	- 49,915	1963	844,781,000	927,939,000	- 83,158,000
1923	619,814	662,971	- 43,157	1964	1,889,286,566	—	—
1924	755,903	768,132	- 12,229	1965	3,164,872	3,804,635	- 639,763
1925	944,796	972,134	- 27,338	1966	4,629,888	5,124,760	- 494,872
1926	903,872	1,143,557	- 239,685	1967	6,488,437	7,260,810	- 772,373
1927	1,018,893	1,303,607	- 284,714	1968	10,420,763	10,587,998	- 167,235
1928	1,103,405	1,274,855	- 171,450	1969	14,572,938	15,037,195	- 464,257
1929	1,264,641	1,536,090	- 271,449	1970	19,099,071	19,332,506	- 233,435
1930	1,016,208	1,484,174	- 467,966	1971	24,090,167	23,505,725	+ 584,442
1931	1,154,504	1,451,315	- 296,811	1972	30,956,379	31,484,629	- 528,250
1932	1,141,552	1,398,965	- 257,413	1973	41,772,143	42,135,077	- 362,934
1933	1,132,718	1,282,214	- 159,496	1974	59,399,516	60,435,898	- 1,135,382
1934	1,250,599	1,569,676	- 319,077	1975	88,913,813	88,233,727	+ 680,086
1935	1,623,793	1,758,624	- 134,831	1976	126,698,533	128,206,013	- 1,507,480
1936	1,814,325	1,887,296	- 72,971	1977	181,788,207	185,257,794	- 3,469,587
1937	1,819,013	2,059,186	- 240,173	1978	284,757,976	288,221,034	- 3,463,058

Sources: AN 1939-40, p. 412; AN 1950, p. 540; AN 1958, p. 442; AN 1961, pp. 433 & 435; AN 1962, p. 346;
AN 1963, pp. 409-410; AN 1966, pp. 504 & 516; AN 1967, pp. 745-746; AN 1968, pp. 562-563;
AN 1969, pp. 677 & 679; AN 1971, pp. 790 & 792; AN 1972, pp. 901 & 908; AN 1973, pp. 874 & 882-883;
AN 1975, pp. 911 & 920; AN 1977, pp. 739 & 743.

Table XVIII-5. Expenditures of All Brazilian States by Functional Categories, 1914/16-78

	Average 1914/16 Cr$ 000	Average 1917/19 Cr$ 000	Average 1923/25 Cr$ 000	1930 Cr$ 000	1935 Cr$ 000	1940 Cr$ 000
Total	258,780	309,717	598,108	1,327,697	1,580,066	2,930,698
General Administration	13,612	14,596	21,520	87,571	75,965	392,078
Financial Administration	15,021	18,937	27,497	52,017	53,901	141,636
Public Safety	45,767	54,873	95,800	172,017	193,235	327,801
Education	36,307	42,897	79,002	198,405	214,357	333,510
Social Welfare	-	-	-			-
Public Health	-	-	-	57,570	73,846	167,617
Development	-	-	-	65,470	80,847	122,090
Industrial	-	-	-	-	-	507,059
Public Debt	48,483	56,640	113,296	266,019	271,661	436,079
Public Services	-	-	-	-	-	265,928
Transportation/Public Works	14,332	20,643	48,723	332,252	436,255	-
Natural Resources/Agriculture	-	-	-	-	-	-
Energy	-	-	-	-	-	-
Justice	12,379	14,046	21,453	37,709	43,559	-
Other	72,879	87,085	190,817	58,667	136,440	236,900

	Average 1945 Cr$ 000	Average 1950 Cr$ 000	Average 1955 Cr$ 000	1960 Cr$ 000	1966 Cr$ 000	1970 Cr$ 000
Total	6,007,614	15,761,630	44,425,238	221,616,592	5,124,760	18,866,567
General Administration	640,174	1,224,315	4,198,195	31,660,532	1,449,517	4.401,046
Financial Administration	214,780	663,614	1,848,688	8,240,490	-	1,736,422
Public Safety	612,075	1,768,686	4,327,253	18,047,188	-	1,692,087
Education	657,176	2,538,682	6,687,202	32,158,332	867,093	3,327,056
Social Welfare	-	-	-	-	589,970	1,589,487
Public Health	369,024	1,255,482	3,571,599	14,756,620	318,869	921,796
Development	427,714	869,215	2,107,945	15,524,336	-	-
Industrial	1,141,105	2,521,680	4,859,855	19,594,545	359,043	365,820
Public Debt	715,620	1,515,936	6,908,779	7,330,545	-	-
Public Services	821,389	1,881,232	3,967,465	25,215,844	229,900	1,519,487
Transportation/Public Works	-	-	-	-	569,283	2,244,537
Natural Resources/Agriculture	-	-	-	-	150,221	824,623
Energy	-	-	-	-	209,825	-
Justice	-	-	-	-	-	-
Other	409,057	1,522,788	6,948,257	49,088,160	-	253,196

	1975 Cr$ 000	1978 Cr$ 000
Total	88,233,727	288,221,034
Legislative	901,026	3,121,504
Judiciary	1,539,748	10,027,452
Administration/Planning	23,994,829	76,108,121
Agriculture Supply & Organization	2,201,634	7,211,169
Communications	146,833	338,293
Public Safety	6,964,940	23,125,729
Regional Development	2,725,177	10,490,468
Education/Culture	17,124,171	55,345,569
Energy/Mineral Resources	4,205,882	10,139,752
Housing/Urban Development	624,701	3,020,482
Industry/Commerce/Services	3,059,950	6,631,299
Justice	1,392,812	-
Physical/Mental Health	6,330,635	20,020,207
Labor/Social Welfare	5,468,163	26,305,815
Transportation	10,958,514	36,335,354
Other	594,712	-

Sources: AN 1939-40, p. 1417; AN 1948, p. 500; AN 1952, p. 525; AN 1953, p. 453; AN 1956, pp. 418 & 542-543; AN 1961, p. 435; AN 1968, p. 564; AN 1973, p. 883; AN 1976, p. 748; AN 1979, p. 765.

Table XVIII-6. Receipts and Expenditures of the Municípios (Counties) of Brazil, 1907-71

Fiscal Year	Receipts Cr$ 000	Expenditures Cr$ 000	Surplus/Deficit Cr$ 000	Fiscal Year	Receipts Cr$ 000	Expenditures Cr$ 000	Surplus/Deficit Cr$ 000
1907	71,538	73,542	− 2,004	1939	860,210	912,196	− 51,982
1908	99,346	95,742	+ 3,874	1940	936,558	921,747	+ 14,811
1909	97,501	97,788	− 287	1941	1,105,276	982,752	+ 32,524
1910	112,518	103,178	− 9,440	1942	1,064,615	1,097,492	− 32,877
1911	107,698	105,992	− 1,706	1943	1,164,203	1,123,280	+ 40,923
1912	116,092	107,629	+ 8,463	1944	1,320,025	1,335,236	− 15,211
1913	92,961	99,934	− 6,973	1945	1,442,822	1,596,472	− 153,650
1914	95,464	99,364	− 3,900	1946	1,722,848	1,806,864	− 84,016
1915	99,590	106,629	− 7,039	1947	2,235,269	2,347,157	− 111,888
1916	101,290	105,521	− 4,231	1948	2,821,655	2,899,060	− 77,405
1917	106,392	107,049	− 657	1949	3,753,916	4,053,703	− 299,787
1918	111,569	112,643	− 1,074	1950	4,794,286	5,195,758	− 401,472
1919	120,103	151,704	− 31,601	1951	5,582,008	5,870,360	− 288,352
1920	135,986	139,416	− 3,430	1952	6,672,300	7,268,965	− 596,665
1921	149,169	162,999	− 13,830	1953	8,785,174	8,831,521	− 46,347
1922	161,206	176,060	− 14,854	1954	10,152,056	10,727,539	− 120,483
1923	192,213	220,134	− 27,921	1955	12,979,168	13,515,385	− 536,217
1924	216,109	233,747	− 17,638	1956	17,053,107	17,534,688	− 481,581
1925	269,538	277,013	− 7,475	1957	22,847,918	23,981,367	− 1,133,449
1926	296,041	302,454	− 6,413	1958	27,050,185	28,538,869	− 1,488,684
1927	334,398	357,384	− 22,986	1959	34,104,307	34,083,829	+ 20,478
1928	383,199	421,559	− 38,360	1960	44,992,050	46,019,147	− 1,027,097
1929	424,415	463,023	− 38,608	1961	62,025,124	63,573,662	− 1,548,538
1930	386,384	416,175	− 47,791	1962	94,292,083	100,392,347	− 6,100,264
1931	412,952	409,282	+ 3,670	1963	124,483,602	—	—
1932	396,528	404,947	− 8,419	1964	268,986,487	—	—
1933	419,360	432,907	− 13,547	1965	635,265	672,622	− 37,357
1934	437,234	431,466	+ 5,768	1966	1,069,070	1,138,920	− 69,850
1935	450,620	437,640	+ 12,980	1967	2,024,987	1,972,544	+ 52,443
1936	607,448	605,396	+ 2,152	1968	3,227,101	3,277,972	− 50,871
1937	672,752	672,552	+ 200	1969	3,972,651	4,127,470	− 154,819
1938	751,559	745,867	+ 5,692	1970	4,868,847	4,970,189	− 101,342
				1971	6,248,370	6,314,791	− 66,421

Sources: AN 1956, p. 540; AN 1958, pp. 499 & 506; AN 1961, p. 499 & 506; AN 1962, p. 350; AN 1963, p. 403;
AN 1964, p. 372; AN 1965, p. 463; AN 1966, p. 519; AN 1968, pp. 567-568; AN 1969, pp. 680-681;
AN 1972, p. 880; AN 1973, p. 850; AN 1975, pp. 943 & 950.

Table XVIII-7. Receipts and Expenditures of the State of São Paulo, 1835-1978

Fiscal Year	Receipts Cr$ 000	Expenditures Cr$ 000	Surplus/Deficit Cr$ 000		Fiscal Year	Receipts Cr$ 000	Expenditures Cr$ 000	Surplus/Deficit Cr$ 000	
1835/36	293	171	+	122	1908	42,693	67,989	-	25,296
1836/37	338	208	+	130	1909	56,660	67,758	-	11,098
1837/38	436	286	+	150	1910	43,281	65,852	-	22,571
1838/39	316	307	+	9	1911	63,946	83,860	-	19,914
1839/40	431	412	+	19	1912	75,641	96,643	-	21,002
1840/41	326	203	+	123	1913	76,008	107,738	-	31,730
1841/42	405	679	-	274	1914	65,711	100,160	-	34,449
1842/43	293	363	-	70	1915	79,316	93,697	-	14,381
1843/44	327	271	+	56	1916	79,248	86,444	-	7,196
1844/45	409	587	-	178	1917	82,556	97,794	-	15,238
1845/46	574	586	-	12	1918	75,642	103,388	-	27,746
1846/47	706	615	+	91	1919	94,474	110,902	-	16,428
1847/48	572	503	-	69	1920	175,679	174,665	+	1,014
1848/49	432	452	-	20	1921	160,580	177,977	-	17,397
1849/50	458	524	-	66	1922	157,019	204,888	-	47,869
1850/51	490	504	-	14	1923	202,722	233,135	-	30,413
1851/52	587	599	-	12	1924	227,020	278,656	-	51,636
1852/53	716	614	+	102	1925	353,271	406,687	-	53,416
1853/54	840	707	+	133	1926	352,584	511,230	-	158,646
1854/55	798	981	-	183	1927	404,044	594,808	-	190,764
1855/56	971	1,069	-	98	1928	408,424	523,802	-	115,378
1856/57	1,014	852	+	162	1929	438,460	618,436	-	179,976
1857/58	992	1,087	-	95	1930	400,204	616,197	-	215,993
1858/59	1,038	1,089	-	511	1931	429,571	662,906	-	233,335
1859/60	1,123	911	+	212	1932	382,424	662,669	-	280,245
1860/61	1,299	942	+	357	1933	432,283	593,139	-	160,856
1861/62	1,310	1,051	+	259	1934	475,919	656,967	-	181,048
1862/63	1,090	1,058	+	32	1935	657,142	745,583	-	88,441
1863/64	969	2,028	-	1,059	1936	703,590	747,458	-	43,868
1864/65	1,205	1,125	+	80	1937	680,693	816,722	-	136,029
1865/66	1,173	1,287	-	114	1938	626,682	787,906	-	161,224
1866/67	1,205	1,078	+	127	1939	843,231	1,035,386	-	192,155
1867/68	1,594	1,185	+	409	1940	878,204	1,108,174	-	229,970
1868/69	2,205	1,265	+	760	1941	1,095,055	1,199,562	-	104,507
1869/70	1,605	1,463	+	142	1942	1,164,732	1,245,652	-	80,920
1870/71	1,420	2,225	-	805	1943	1,554,371	1,477,219	+	77,152
1871/72	1,597	1,962	-	365	1944	2,052,365	1,993,125	+	59,240
1872/73	1,955	2,005	-	50	1945	2,428,109	2,793,419	-	365,310
1873/74	2,829	2,695	+	134	1946	3,069,909	3,210,055	-	140,146
1874/75	2,476	3,257	-	781	1947	3,147,485	3,780,554	-	633,069
1875/76	2,506	2,952	-	446	1948	3,818,852	4,636,396	-	817,544
1876/77	2,071	4,076	-	2,005	1949	5,794,560	6,023,380	-	228,820
1877/78	3,323	2,702	+	621	1950	5,966,324	7,778,463	-	1,812,139
1878/79	3,762	3,037	+	635	1951	9,132,128	10,753,350	-	1,621,222
1879/80	3,768	3,066	+	702	1952	9,884,966	14,337,874	-	4,452,908
1880/81	3,521	3,426	+	95	1953	11,917,046	16,630,478	-	4,713,432
1881/82	4,015	3,745	+	270	1954	16,061,822	21,836,567	-	5,774,745
1882/83	3,625	3,789	-	164	1955	20,185,608	23,252,753	-	3,067,145
1883/84	3,786	3,792	-	6	1956	28,682,796	28,168,253	+	514,543
1884/85	4,397	4,325	+	72	1957	36,854,807	36,631,504	+	223,303
1885/86	3,802	4,481	-	679	1958	42,505,754	46,901,230	-	4,395,476
1886/87	5,701	5,462	+	239	1959	68,406,342	68,332,897	+	73,445
1887/88	3,826	7,827	-	4,001	1960	95,163,181	95,162,210	+	971
1888/89	6,869	9,531	-	2,662	1961	138,695,357	138,695,778	-	421
1889/90	19,123	16,106	+	3,017	1962	226,946,704	238,376,395	-	11,429,691
1890/91	23,318	18,377	+	4,941	1963	357,390,560	420,721,473	-	63,330,913
1892	60,401	44,845	+	15,556	1964	823,788,324	529,501,040	+	294,287,284
1893	34,534	-			1965	1,313,147	1,753,477	-	440,330
1894	45,465	42,428	+	3,037	1966	2,048,531	2,309,371	-	260,840
1895	55,538	50,108	+	5,430	1967	3,061,750	3,442,933	-	381,183
1896	57,329	51,832	+	5,497	1968	4,712,758	4,712,552	+	206
1897	48,571	57,455	-	8,884	1969	7,025,594	7,025,506	+	88
1898	42,280	54,146	-	11,866	1970	8,951,929	8,939,024	-	12,905
1899	43,114	36,749	+	6,365	1971	10,459,127	10,575,746	-	116,619
1900	42,651	36,298	+	6,353	1972	13,703,246	13,838,553	-	135,307
1901	45,685	45,692	-	7	1973	18,362,840	18,538,834	-	175,994
1902	37,649	40,913	-	3,264	1974	25,871,645	26,107,538	-	235,893
1903	34,127	40,743	-	6,616	1975	37,946,282	38,301,692	-	355,410
1904	42,604	35,873	+	6,731	1976	52,641,414	53,147,109	-	505,695
1905	67,347	111,861	-	44,514	1977	72,271,623	72,952,416	+	680,793
1906	58,993	61,615	-	2,622	1978	109,254,215	112,580,352	-	3,326,137
1907	52,178	68,570	-	16,392					

Sources: BYB 1909, pp. 407-408; AN 1939-40, p. 1414; AN 1950, p. 502; AN 1951, pp. 514 & 516; AN 1953, pp. 450-451; AN 1954, pp. 494 & 497; AN 1958, p. 462 & 467; AN 1961, pp. 433 & 435; AN 1962, p. 347; AN 1963, pp. 403 & 409-410; AN 1964, pp. 320 & 369; AN 1965, pp. 473-474; AN 1966, p. 516; AN 1967, pp. 745-746; AN 1968, pp. 562 & 564; AN 1969, pp. 677-678; AN 1971, pp. 790-791; AN 1972, pp. 901 & 908; AN 1973, pp. 874 & 918; AN 1975, pp. 911 & 918; AN 1977, pp. 739 & 743; AN 1979, pp. 760 & 765-766.

Table XVIII-8. Receipts and Expenditures for Old Distrito Federal/State
of Guanabara Surrounding the City of Rio de Janeiro,
1861-1974

Fiscal Year	Receipts Cr$ 000	Expenditures Cr$ 000	Surplus/Deficit Cr$ 000	Fiscal Year	Receipts Cr$ 000	Expenditures Cr$ 000	Surplus/Deficit Cr$ 000
1861	575	507	+ 68	1918	44,946	48,206	- 3,260
1862	596	606	- 10	1919	51,013	65,499	- 14,486
1863	628	673	- 45	1920	57,625	67,677	- 10,052
1864	608	595	+ 13	1921	65,579	84,148	- 18,569
1865	609	621	- 12	1922	72,249	101,109	- 28,860
1866	724	723	+ 1	1923	93,951	137,470	- 43,519
1867	734	747	- 13	1924	109,017	114,747	- 5,730
1868	670	664	+ 6	1925	123,612	143,989	- 20,377
1869	694	620	+ 74	1926	128,666	129,834	- 1,168
1870	735	800	- 65	1927	151,380	156,951	- 5,571
1871	802	816	- 14	1928	167,565	232,770	- 65,205
1872	898	881	+ 17	1929	176,391	246,226	- 66,835
1873	899	906	- 7	1930	195,617	232,606	- 36,989
1874	1,232	1,242	- 10	1931	183,019	253,165	- 70,146
1875	1,011	1,011	0	1932	182,840	180,336	+ 2,504
1876	1,057	1,059	- 2	1933	208,649	191,560	+ 17,089
1877	1,275	1,275	0	1934	247,260	257,070	- 9,810
1878	1,060	1,059	+ 1	1935	256,853	256,361	+ 492
1879	1,287	1,282	+ 5	1936	286,726	251,723	+ 35,003
1880	1,142	1,149	- 7	1937	316,388	275,701	+ 40,687
1881	1,182	1,153	+ 29	1938	378,742	349,373	+ 29,369
1882	1,496	1,496	0	1939	404,143	399,652	+ 4,491
1883	1,321	1,351	- 30	1940	423,379	463,386	- 40,007
1884	1,651	1,631	+ 20	1941	505,078	489,611	+ 15,467
1885	1,636	1,478	+ 158	1942	655,128	621,026	+ 34,102
1886	1,477	1,471	+ 6	1943	885,477	799,860	+ 85,617
1887	1,350	1,532	- 182	1944	1,016,396	915,514	+ 100,882
1888	1,625	1,627	- 2	1945	953,470	1,034,639	- 81,169
1889	2,282	2,275	+ 7	1946	1,395,973	1,388,511	+ 7,462
1890	8,591	6,171	+ 2,420	1947	1,407,152	1,655,206	- 248,054
1891	3,675	4,836	- 1,161	1948	1,781,094	1,829,725	- 48,631
1892	17,180	18,257	- 1,077	1949	2,548,593	2,284,445	+ 264,148
1893	16,727	15,901	+ 371	1950	2,918,096	2,778,137	+ 139,959
1894	17,029	16,939	+ 90	1951	3,684,094	3,772,327	- 88,233
1895	25,877	26,910	- 1,033	1952	3,987,818	4,755,325	- 767,507
1896	33,511	33,532	- 21	1953	5,296,626	5,423,485	- 126,859
1897	19,703	19,117	+ 586	1954	6,211,144	6,451,379	- 240,235
1898	18,323	18,936	- 613	1955	7,657,650	8,428,184	- 770,534
1899	23,485	23,419	+ 66	1956	10,161,242	11,478,629	- 1,317,387
1900	25,348	24,909	+ 439	1957	12,100,719	11,586,044	+ 514,675
1901	20,679	21,180	- 501	1958	16,302,068	18,025,297	- 1,723,229
1902	26,265	25,678	+ 587	1959	18,504,314	20,885,084	- 2,380,770
1903	30,773	31,379	- 600	1960	26,249,276	29,456,596	- 3,207,320
1904	28,302	28,218	+ 84	1961	33,748,882	37,150,383	- 3,401,501
1905	31,396	31,360	+ 36	1962	65,239,247	66,124,354	- 885,107
1906	48,437	48,133	+ 304	1963	112,467,518	-	-
1907	27,215	32,438	- 5,223	1964	240,209,682	-	-
1908	39,161	38,932	+ 229	1965	384,903	439,991	- 55,088
1909	53,724	53,304	+ 420	1966	523,756	563,529	- 39,773
1910	50,852	50,291	+ 561	1967	789,165	848,993	- 59,828
1911	39,632	38,793	+ 839	1968	1,251,911	1,302,917	- 51,006
1912	47,812	47,781	+ 31	1969	1,791,017	1,824,773	- 33,756
1913	41,108	47,136	- 6,028	1970	2,119,260	2,284,065	- 164,805
1914	38,036	39,617	- 1,581	1971	2,745,024	2,613,801	+ 131,223
1915	40,740	44,144	- 3,404	1972	3,143,052	3,162,850	- 19,798
1916	41,769	46,500	- 4,731	1973	4,029,250	3,898,874	+ 130,376
1917	41,029	45,907	- 4,878	1974	5,411,251	5,714,916	- 303,665

Sources: BYB 1909, p. 398; AN 1958, pp. 462 & 467; AN 1961, pp. 433 & 435; AN 1963, pp. 346-347, 403 & 410;
AN 1965, p. 463; AN 1966, p. 516; AN 1967, p. 745; AN 1968, pp. 562-563; AN 1969, pp. 677-678;
AN 1971, pp. 790-791; AN 1972, pp. 901 & 908; AN 1972, pp. 874 & 883; AN 1975, pp. 911 & 918.

Table XVIII-9. Receipts and Expenditures for the New Distrito Federal
Surrounding the city of Brasília, 1961-78

Fiscal Year	Receipts Cr$ 000	Expenditures Cr$ 000	Surplus/Deficit Cr $ 000
1961	414,588	901,400	- 479,812
1962	1,212,527	1,143,758	+ 68,769
1963	3,926,459	-	-
1964	24,183,313	-	-
1965	51,361	46,140	+ 5,221
1966	148,596	143,571	+ 5,025
1967	364,505	366,387	- 1,882
1968	318,724	338,864	- 20,140
1969	417,360	408,412	+ 8,948
1970	465,108	465,939	- 831
1971	530,992	548,552	- 17,560
1972	716,896	698,073	+ 18,823
1973	1,021,957	1,008,237	+ 13,720
1974	1,322,331	1,342,119	- 19,788
1975	1,843,256	1,882,393	- 39,137
1976	2,961,268	2,982,749	- 21,481
1977	4,174,426	4,162,655	+ 11,771
1978	6,569,417	6,583,931	- 14,514

Sources: AN 1962, pp. 346-347; AN 1963, p. 403; AN 1965, p. 463;
AN 1966, p. 516; AN 1967, p. 745; AN 1968, p. 562;
AN 1969, pp. 677-678; AN 1971, p. 790-791; AN 1972, pp. 901 & 908;
AN 1973, pp. 874 & 883; AN 1975, pp. 911 & 918;
AN 1977, pp. 739 & 743; AN 1979, pp. 760 & 765-66.

Chapter XIX. Economic Development Planning

Table XIX-1 reports chronologically those entities created by the federal government which were intended to play roles in national, sectoral or regional economic development from 1933 to 1979. Government-owned companies which took over existing systems are not included in this table except where specifically noted.

Major National and Sectoral Entities

The term "economic development" was not part of the Brazilian lexicon when the government set up the Sugar and Alcohol Institute (Instituto de Açucar e do Álcool--IAA) in 1933. The Institute, one of the earliest of a genre dealing with agricultural commodities, "was an important policy making body, fixing prices, regulating production and controlling exports for the growing sugar industry," according to Heare.[1] The Institute was given responsibility for Brazil's gasohol program, which began in 1931 (see Chapter X). Robock[2] reaches back to 1934 to report "that a first effort at government planning was attempted through the creation of the Federal Foreign Trade Council," but he provides no description of its charges or accomplishments. In 1936 the venerable Bank of Brazil added an Agricultural and Industrial Credit Branch to provide capital to these two sectors of the economy. By 1971 this unit had been renamed the General and Rural Credit Branch. In 1938, the National Petroleum Council was established to control all phases of petroleum exploration, production, processing, and marketing in Brazil. Petrobrás later (1953) assumed control of exploration and production. In 1938 to support his Estado Novo (New State), Getúlio Vargas, who by now was virtual dictator of Brazil, established the Administrative Department of Public Service (Departamento Administrativo de Serviço Público--DASP). Daland[3] writes that "DASP represented the rational 'scientific', central instrument of administrative control as envisioned in the scientific management movement. . . ." and that "it was staffed by a new generation of technicians in public administration and planning." In 1939 DASP prepared the First Five Year Plan, 1939-43 (Plano Qüinqüenal de Obras e Reaparelhamento da Defesa Nacional), which turned out to be nothing more than a list of capital expenditures. The Brazilian federal budget included the following expenditures for this Plan: 1940, Cr$ 559,350,000; and 1942, Cr$ 595,193,000.[4] In 1940 the National Salt Institute (Instituto Nacional do Sal) was created to plan for domestic production of Alkalis such as caustic soda and soda ash in order to reduce Brazil's dependence upon foreign sources of these basic industrial raw materials.

In 1942 the Brazilian government hired a group of American specialists, mostly engineers, headed by Charles S. Taub to study the country's industrial development potential. The group's ten-year plan, calling for an investment of four billion United States dollars, was kept secret for years, then dropped altogether when Vargas left office in 1946.

Between 1942 and 1945 World War II cut Brazil off from suppliers of many of its basic industrial needs. In response to this the federal government created five major new economic entities. In 1942 the Rio Doce Valley Company (Companhia do Vale do Rio Doce--CVRD) was formed for the production and subsequent export of iron ore from the Itabira district in Minas Gerais state. The ore was carried by the Vitória a Minas railroad to the port of Vitória, Espírito Santo. The mines, the railroad and the port's ore handling facilities all predated the government purchase but were upgraded and mechanized with the aid of US$ 37 million in credits from the Export-Import Bank. In 1943 the government's National Steel Company (Companhia Siderúrgica Nacional--CSN) built the Guilherme Guinle steel works at Volta Redonda, Rio de Janeiro state, with the aid of an Ex-Im Bank loan. Also in 1943 the National Salt Institute's earlier studies led to the formation of the National Alkali Company (Companhia Nacional de Álcalis) with a capital of US$ 2.5 million. The Salt Institute owned the majority of shares in the Companhia, which chose Cabo Frio, Rio de Janeiro state, as the site for its solvay-process plant to produce soda ash and caustic soda.[5] Capitalization and loan problems delayed construction of the plant until the mid-1950s.[6] In 1943 the National Motors Company (Fábrica Nacional de Motores--FNM) was organized to produce airplane motors in a plant near the city of Rio de Janeiro. Only about twenty airplane engines were assembled from parts imported from the United States and for the next five years the plant was virtually idle until an Italian firm contracted to assemble automobile motors and truck chassis.[7] By 1960 FNM, under Alfa Romeo licensing arrangements, was producing diesel trucks and passenger cars, the contents of which by weight were, respectively, 84 and 64 percent of Brazilian manufacture. FNM is the only automobile company in Brazil to be publicly owned. In 1944 the government set up the Special Steel Company of Itabira (Companhia Aços Especiais de Itabira--ACESITA) at Acesita, Minas Gerais, to produce special alloy steels.

In 1943 the Vargas administration set up the Cooperative Credit Foundation. In 1951 this Foundation became the National Bank for Credit to Cooperatives (Banco Nacional de Crédito Cooperativo--BNCC) whose activities have included the granting of loans to both producer and consumer cooperatives in the agricultural, horticultural, fishing, animal, and agro-industrial sectors.

In 1943 Morris L. Cooke led the American Technical Mission to Brazil. The Americans, sponsored by the semi-official Getúlio Vargas Foundation, also had a counterpart group of Brazilian technicians. The Mission studied production, transportation, fuel, petroleum, energy, textiles, minerals, chemicals, education, and the development of the São Francisco Valley. The results, notes Daland,[8] were along the lines of research findings and did not constitute a plan. No costs were supplied for those proposals that were offered. The report was kept secret until released by the United States government in 1948.

In 1943 Vargas developed a Second Five Year Plan for the years 1944-48 (Plano de Obras e Equipamentos e dá Outras Providências), which did contain a few suggestions for its implementation. As with Vargas's First Five Year Plan no records of the accomplishments of the Second Five Year Plan are available. The Brazilian federal budget did record the following Second Five Year Plan expenditures: 1944, Cr$ 948,502,000; 1945, Cr$ 989,446,000; and 1946 Cr$ 872,213,000.[9]

In 1948 President Dutra's government requested American planning aid and the ensuing Joint Brazil-United States Technical Commission prepared a report emphasizing the broad problems of the Brazilian economy. Although the report was not a plan per se some of its recommendations such as those dealing with the physical and administrative restructuring of the railroad system were carried out.[10]

Beginning in 1946, under President Dutra, DASP and São Paulo state technicians began to prepare the SALTE Plan to cover the years 1949-53. The Plan's emphases were expressed in the acronym SALTE, which stood for health (Saúde), food supply (Alimentação), transportation (Transporte), and electrical energy (Energia elétrica). In 1949 Congress appropriated Cr$ 1,900,000,000 to SALTE, only Cr$ 37,500,000 of which remained for the next fiscal year.[11] The Ministry of Finance disbursed these funds, but the sources for this chapter do not indicate on what the Ministry spent the money. Baer[12] notes that SALTE really did not extend past the first year owing to implementation and financing difficulties. Congress did not officially recognize the Plan until 1950, at which time its life was shifted to 1950-54. Proposed funding for the five-year life of SALTE was as follows: health, Cr$ 2,620 million plus US$ 141 million; food supply, Cr$ 3,700 million plus US$ 200 million; transportation, Cr$ 8,030 million plus US$ 433 million; electrical energy, Cr$ 10,672 million plus US$ 577 million; and interest, Cr$ 700 million plus US$ 38 million. Confusion of roles and functions marked the SALTE era, but by 1951 Vargas had turned it into an office assigning SALTE funds to government agencies eligible to receive them under the Plan. Daland[13] comments that this setting of priorities was a step forward for Brazilian planning mechanisms.

In 1952 the Brazilian Coffee Institute (Instituto Brasileiro do Café--IBC) was organized to replace the Old National Coffee Department, the sale of whose stock was to help fund SALTE.[14] The Department's main function was to buy up coffee surpluses in order to maintain price levels. IBC's program, on the other hand, was sectorally developmental in nature and included among other things, according to Heare,[15] a long-range program to renew old coffee plantings, improvement of the quality of the coffee being produced, and encouraging a domestic soluble coffee industry by providing it with green coffee at market prices and "guaranteeing the right to purchase fixed percentages of soluble coffee for four years that would liquidate plant investments." The latter policy was suspended in 1961 for further study.

In 1953 Petrobrás (Petróleo Brasileiro S.A.), a government-controlled stock company, was set up to monopolize the prospecting for and development of petroleum, other fluid hydrocarbon and natural gas resources. With the exception of refineries extant on or authorized by June 30, 1953, and pipeline and tanker facilities in operation by October 31, 1953, Petrobrás's monopoly covered the refining of domestic or imported petroleum, the ocean transportation of petroleum and petroleum products produced in the country as well as pipeline transportation of crude oil, its derivatives, and natural gas of any origin.[16] All these functions were removed from the National Petroleum Council which now had only policy-making and supervisory functions.[17]

In 1953 the Executive Commission for the National Coal Plan (Comissão Executivo do Plano do Carvão Nacional--CEPCAN) was created to promote coal production, to stabilize the marketing of coal, and to encourage construction of thermoelectric power plants.[18]

Beginning in 1951, under President Vargas, the Joint Brazil-United States Economic Development Commission set in motion a sequence of events that led to important planning and development results. The Commission was, notes Daland,[19] "to render the necessary technical assistance so as to speed the preparation of applications for loans for development projects which would be submitted to United States and international lending agencies." The theory: public funds invested to eliminate bottlenecks in the transport and energy infrastructure will stimulate private investment in many sectors once the bottlenecks are broken. The plan that resulted from the Commission's work had the rather unwieldy title "Plan for Retooling and Stimulating the National Economy." To implement it the National Bank for Economic development (BNDE) was created on June 20, 1952. The Bank in turn formed another Commission, the Mixed Group, Economic Commission for Latin America-National Economic Development Bank (Grupo Misto CEPAL-BNDE). This commission was to provide a development strategy for the economy for the period 1955-62. For Brazilian planning mechanisms, however, its role was crucial since, writes Dickenson,[20] "its report followed the current thinking of CEPAL: that in order to overcome conditions of underdevelopment the State must participate in development; that this participation should be within the framework of declared planning; but that at the same time participation by private enterprise should be encouraged."

In 1956 President Kubitschek's Program of Targets (Programa de Metas) was established based on the work of CEPAL-BNDE and the Joint Commission of 1951-55. Also in 1956 Kubitschek created the Council for Development to administer and implement the program. The program covered the period 1956-60 and followed the Joint Commission's principals by bringing the federal government directly into the development process. During the life of the Program of Targets Executive Groups (Grupos Executivos--GEs) were set up and given responsibility for the development of specific industries as well as general sectors of the economy.[21] A group was established for each of the following areas: automobiles, with tractors added in 1959 (GEIA); naval construction (GEICON, which became GEIN in 1961); computers (GEACE); heavy machinery (GEIMAPE); modernization of agriculture (GEMAG); assistance to medium and small industries (GEAMPE); metal-working (GEIMET); agricultural and road machinery (GEIMAR); and motion pictures (GEICINE).

The proposed cost of targets was Cr$ 338 billion plus US$ 2.318 billion. It was not a comprehensive program but gave priority to sectors of the economy. Thirty targets were established, ten in basic industry and the remainder in energy, transportation, education and food supply. This "growing point" approach, as Dickenson[22] describes it, was "of great importance in shaping the structure and distribution of Brazilian industry." During the five years only the cellulose production target was reached but measurable progress was made in the steel, cement, alkali, automobile, and shipbuilding industries. In addition, highways, hydro-electric dams and power grids and the new national capital, Brasília, were put in place.

Under the Program of Targets three new steel plants were constructed by government companies in all of which BNDE was an important shareholder and in two of which foreign capital was invested directly. In 1958 the company called Minas Gerais Steel Mill (Usina Siderúrgica de Minas Gerais-- USIMINAS) capitalized at Cr$ 4 billion had begun construction of its iron and steel plant at Coronel Fabriciano, Minas Gerais, near Belo Horizonte. Forty percent of USIMINAS's capital was provided by a consortium of Japanese steel firms. In 1959 the Vitoria Iron and Steel Company (Companhia Ferro e Aço de Vitória--Aço Vitória) began to build its new iron and steel complex near Vitória, Espírito Santo. Forty percent of Aco's capital was owned by a West German steel firm. In 1959 the Piaçaguera Steel Company (Companhia Siderúrgica Piaça- guera--COSIPA), capitalized at Cr$ 12 billion, initiated construction of its iron and steel plant at Piaçaguera, São Paulo, at tidewater near the port city of Santos. In addition to the federal government's majority holdings much of the rest of COSIPA's capital was held by the state of São Paulo, the state-controlled Bank of São Paulo and by private interests.[23]

In 1956 the federal government set up National Cold Storage, Inc. (Frigoríficos Nacionais, S.A.--FRINASA), whose charge was to build and operate cold storage warehouses and cold storage shipping facilities for all modes of trans- portation.[24] In 1958 the Brazilian Tourism Commission (Comissão Brasileira de Turismo--COMBRATUR) was established for the purpose of encouraging tourism, particularly foreign tourism with its hard currencies, in Brazil.[25] A decade later the Brazilian Tourist Corporation (Emprêsa Brasileira de Turismo--EMBRATUR) had taken over these functions. By 1968 special tax incentives such as those applicable to SUDENE and SUDAM (see Major Regional Entities) had become available to individuals and corporations investing in EMBRATUR-approved projects.

In 1961 the Council for the Development of the Fishing Industry (Conselho de Desenvolvimento da Pesca--CODEPE) was created to establish policy and plan for the development of the Brazilian fishing industry.[26] Its tasks included the construction of ports, shipyards, cold storage plants and processing plants, and arranging tax exemptions and technical and financial assistance for vessel construction and the establishment of fishing firms. A decade later the Superintendency for the Development of the Fishing Industry (Superintendência do Desenvolvimento da Pesca--SUDEPE) was performing these functions. By 1968 SUDEPE-approved projects were receiving investments from special tax incentives, which were also applicable to EMBRATUR, SUDENE, and SUDAM (see Major Regional Entities).

In 1961 the Brazilian National Electric Company (Emprêsa Centrais Elétricas Brasileiras--Eletrobrás) was established with a mandate to "make studies and formulate programs in the electric power field and construct, own and operate generating plants, transmission lines and distribution facilities."[27]

In 1961 President Jânio Quadros set up the National Planning Commission (COPLAN) to absorb Kubitschek's Council for Development. Quadros resigned the presidency in August 1961, and the caretaker cabinet established seven objectives to be implemented by COPLAN. Daland[28] lists these as a 7.5 percent annual increase in the Gross National Product, full employment, reduction of income inequality, price stabilization, reduction of regional inequalities, improved balance of payments, and structural corrections in the economy. COPLAN was to implement these goals using tax reform, development programs, and domestic and foreign investment, and to do so set up plans at three different levels: an emergency plan, a five year plan and a twenty year plan.

In 1963, under the Goulart administration, Celso Furtado produced the Three Year Plan (Plano Trienal) to cover the period 1963-65. Because of the political and economic turmoil that culminated in the revolution of April 1964, Dickenson[29] notes that the plan "was abandoned before its completion but its approach was broader than that of its predecessors adding health, resources survey and institutional reform to the main sectors of the Program of Targets. Trienal sought an increase of 7 percent in the Gross National Product and 11 percent in industrial production. The latter did increase by 11.3 percent a year between 1956 and 1961 but had fallen to less than one percent per year in 1963." Probably owing to Furtado's experience with regional planning in the Northeast (see Major Regional Entities), Plano Trienal "acknowledged a need for regional planning within the development process. . . ."[30]

In 1964 the new government under President Castello Branco instituted the Plan for Government Economic Action (Plano de Açao Econômico do Govêrno--PAEG) to cover the period 1964-66. The plan's principal goals were to control inflation, improve balance of payments, restore economic growth and introduce administrative reform. Robock[31] points out that "the decision to stimulate the expansion of exports and the adoption of incentives and administrative reforms represented a major policy shift for Brazil. . . ." President Goulart's tight restrictions on profit remittances by foreign-owned companies were repealed. In 1964 under PAEG the National Housing Bank (Banco Nacional de Habitação--BNH) was set up to finance a massive housing program in the country.

In 1965 the Ten Year Plan (Plano Decanal) was developed under Castello Branco, and its five-year investment program served as a basis for the Strategic Program for Development (Programa Estratégico de Desenvolvimento), which was created by the Costa e Silva administration to cover the period 1968-70. The program, says Dickenson,[32] "combined a broad economic strategy with detailed sectoral and regional policies. Its aims were a 6 percent growth rate over the period, improvements in income levels and social conditions and an increase in labour absorption from 2.6 percent per annum to 3.5 percent by 1975." Basic industries such as metal, chemical, and engineering were to receive 10 percent of the proposed investment. "During the Plan period," writes Dickenson,[33] Brazil was described as experiencing an economic miracle unique among developing countries, with a 9.5 percent increase in the Gross National Product and an 11 percent increase in industrial production.

In 1966 under Law No. 5106 and in 1970 under Decree Law No. 1134, federal income tax exemptions were granted individuals and corporations for investments in and maintenance of existing forests, and for reforestation.

In 1970 under President Medici the national objectives and sectoral strategies for the next decade were laid out in the document called "Goals and Bases for Government Action" (Metas e bases para a ação de govêrno). The document's long-range goal was to make Brazil a developed country by the year 2000, but its shorter-range goals included increasing the annual rate of economic growth to 10 percent, increasing per capita income levels, generating new jobs and expanding exports.[34] The document envisioned a larger role for the private sector and for foreign capital. A 51 percent increase in industrial output was projected for the years from 1969 through 1973. "The proposals," says Dickenson,[35] "encouraged 15 broad fields of action. In manufacturing the principal areas of action were steel, non-ferrous metals, chemicals, fertilizers, plastics, electrical and mechanical engineering." Regional programs were incorporated into the proposal (see PIN in the Major Regional Entities section).

In 1972 under President Medici National Development Plan I (I Plano Nacional de Desenvolvimento--PND I) was developed. It covered the period 1972-74 and incorporated the objectives of the "Goals and Bases" document. PND I goals included a per capita income of US$ 500 by 1974, an annual growth rate in the Gross National Product of 8 to 10 percent, an increase of 13 percent in the economically active population and an increase of 46 percent in industrial output between 1970 and 1974.[36] Plan I proposed a broad sectoral approach to social, economic, and regional development. As in earlier plans, however, specific targets were set, in this case in industries producing steel, cement, and fertilizer. In addition, support was given to higher technology industries such as those producing electronics, aeronautical, and chemical products, which could either enter the export market or support traditional industries at home. The regional components of PND I are discussed in the Regional Entities section.

In the three years 1972-74 with the plan in full effect the Gross Domestic Product (GDP) increased by 10.4, 11.4, and 9.6 percent, respectively. Per capita GDP increased by more than 6.5 percent in each year. Industrial output rose by 11 percent in 1970 and 1971 and by 13.8 percent in 1972. Because of the OPEC-created oil crisis and Brazil's reliance on imports for two-thirds of its oil, Plan I notwithstanding, the nation's industrial output and GDP both declined in 1974 and 1975.

In 1975 under President Geisel National Development Plan II (II Plano Nacional de Desenvolvimento--PND II) was developed to cover the period 1975-79. To a great extent it re-ordered or downscaled some of the PDN I goals and projects.[37] Emphasis was on basic industries in capital goods, electronics, and raw materials to produce for export and to substitute for imports since Brazil's foreign exchange was depleted after paying its oil bill. The focus was on steel, nonferrous metals, petrochemicals, fertilizers/pesticides, paper, cellulose, cement, nonmetallic minerals, and raw materials for the pharmaceutical industry. Development of hydroelectric resources was to be stimulated in order to provide electric energy for smelting metals. Continued emphasis on technologically sophisticated industries was encouraged. Plan II envisioned the reduction of regional imbalances in industrial development. Its regional components are detailed in the Major Regional Entities section.

Major Regional Entities

The Northeast

The year 1909 marked the federal government's earliest formal administrative attempt to deal with a regional problem. In that year the National Inspectorate for Works Against the Droughts (Inspetoria Nacional de Obras Contra as Sêcas-- INOCS) was established to deal with the nonperiodic droughts (sêcas) that affect the interior of the northeast part of the country. Robock[38] reports that written records of sêcas go back to 1614 and that the Brazilian government officially recognized them as a national problem as the result of the severe drought of 1877. INOCS's charge was "to build railroads and roads, drill wells, construct reservoirs and undertake 'other works whose utility against the effects of the droughts has been demonstrated.'"[39] For the results of some of these works see Chapter XIII. In 1945 INOCS became DNOCS, the National Department for Works Against the Droughts (Departamento Nacional de Obras Contra as Sêcas). The new Constitution of 1946 earmarked 1 percent of annual federal tax revenues as a special emergency relief fund for Northeast droughts. Works of one or the other agency were in place for most of the severe pre-1960 droughts of this century, which occurred in 1900, 1915, 1919-20, 1931-32, 1951-52, and 1958. They were, however, of little use. The destruction of crops and livestock and the mass exodus of people continued to mark each drought. The hydraulic approach provided no solutions to drought engendered problems.

In 1952 the federal government set up the Bank of the Northeast (Banco do Nordeste do Brasil--BNB), headquartered in Fortaleza, Ceará, to provide loans and technical assistance to economically viable development projects. The BNB, which almost immediately became a model for efficiency and accomplishment, represented a shift away from the welfare/public works approach to the Northeast's problems and a step toward broader regional planning.

In response to the severe drought that began in 1958 in the interior northeast, in April 1959 the federal government created the Council for the Development of the Northeast (Conselho de Desenvolvimento do Nordeste--CODENO). By the end of the year the Council had become the Superintendency for the Development of the Northeast (Superintendência do Desenvolvimento do Nordeste--SUDENE) with a broad mandate to change the economic and social structure of both the humid coastal zone and the dry interior of the Northeast. Baer[40] reports that "SUDENE was to direct and coordinate all activities of the federal government in the region." He notes that the basic aims of the agency in its initial as well as all subsequent plans included (1) increased industrial investment through special tax incentives to create urban employment; (2) in the humid coastal belt, an increase in productivity of the sugar economy and the establishment of family-size farm units producing staple foods; (3) in the semiarid zone, an ecologically sound increase in productivity; (4) integration of the humid agricultural frontier lands of southern Bahia and of Maranhão into the Northeast's economy; and (5) a program of road construction to open these frontiers and to link the Northeast with Amazônia and thereby encourage northeasterners to migrate to new lands. SUDENE developed four different plans in the 1960s and 1970s and Baer[41] points out that the accomplishments of each fell well below these original goals. The agrarian structure was little changed. The special tax incentives, which allowed a firm to use 50 percent of its federal tax bill for investment in the region, did bring in many industries, but most were located in just two places, Salvador and Recife, and generated relatively little employment. SUDENE's weak response to the severe 1970 drought triggered direct federal action through such plans as PIN and PROTERRA which are described in the Amazonia section.

The São Francisco Valley

In 1945 the federal government set up the São Francisco Hydroelectric Company (Companhia Hidroelétrica do São Francisco—CHESF), whose principal charge was to develop the one million kilowatt potential of Paulo Afonso Falls on the São Francisco River between the states of Alagoas and Bahia. By 1954 the Paulo Afonso complex was generating 120,000 kilowatts and plans were laid for additional capacity.[42] Robock[43] points out that the "preoccupation with engineering weakened CHESF's attention to the market side of the problem," and that "The distribution systems in Recife and Salvador, owned by subsidiaries of the American and Foreign Power Company, lagged because of the general difficulty faced by foreign utilities in raising capital and uncertainties about expropriation." Robock's[44] praise for CHESF is, however, unstinting when he comments that it "deserves special attention because it stands in sharp contrast to previous federal projects in the Northeast. It demonstrated that a federal agency could operate efficiently, effectively and honestly."

In 1946 the new Constitution provided that for twenty years 1 percent of federal tax revenues be used for the economic development of the São Francisco River and its tributaries. To administer these funds, in 1948 the government created the São Francisco Valley Commission (Comissão do

Vale do Rio São Francisco--CVSF). Its charges included stream regulation and water control, river and port improvement, provision of river navigation equipment, irrigation, drainage, roads, airfields, communication facilities, municipal water and sewer installations, and hydroelectric projects.[45] The inclusion of a wide range of interrelated programs in a natural resource region made CVSF unique among Brazilian agencies up to that time. Pursuing what CVSF itself called "a great policy of small services," the Commission soon became, according to Robock,[46] the instrument of certain political groups, demonstrated little initiative and imagination, and had little contact with DNOCS, which shared a part of the São Francisco Valley. When, in 1956, President Kubitschek decided to proceed with the huge multi-purpose Três Marias dam on the São Francisco River in Minas Gerais he bypassed CVSF to work with the state-owned Minas Gerais Power Company.[47] In 1971 the federal government set up PROVALE to accelerate the agricultural development of the empty areas around the São Francisco River, but by 1978 Baer[48] found that few of the program's objectives had been reached.

Amazonia

In 1942 the Rubber Credit Bank (Banco de Crédito de Borracha) was set up to stimulate production of Amazon rubber to replace Far East supplies cut off by World War II. In 1950 the institution became the Credit Bank of Amazonia (Banco de Crédito da Amazônia--BCA) with a somewhat broader mandate. In 1966 the BCA was abolished and replaced by the Bank of Amazonia (Banco da Amazônia, S.A.--BASA), a true regional development bank modeled on the Bank of the Northeast. In 1946, Article 199 of the new Constitution, according to Mahar,[48] "provided for the establishment of a development program for Amazônia to be financed through a 3 percent share of total federal tax revenues for a period of twenty consecutive years." In 1953 Congress acted upon this article and created the Plan for Economic Improvement of Amazônia and the agency to administer it, the Superintendency of the Plan for Economic Improvement of Amazonia (Superintendência do Plano de Valorização da Amazônia--SPVEA). The Plan was to provide an array of services and public works in the agriculture, mineral, and industrial sectors and to elevate the social and economic well-being of Amazônia's population. SPVEA's area of responsibility was ultimately defined as the "legal Amazon," which included Amapá, Acre, Roraíma, Rondônia, Amazonas, Pará, Mato Grosso north of the 16th parallel, Goiás north of the 13th parallel, and Maranhão west of the 44th meridian. SPVEA's First Five Year Plan was created to cover the period 1955-59. Mahar[49] writes that it emphasized communications, modernization of river fleets and port facilities, credit to the agricultural and industrial sectors, improvement of hospitals and clinics and water and sewer systems, and agricultural self-sufficiency in food-stuffs. The plan's implementation was hindered, says Mahar,[50] by its own defects and by administrative abuses, but by the early 1960s it had overseen completion of the Belém-Brasília highway and modernization of Belém's port facilities, and had financed several major industries, most in or near Belém. Nevertheless, by 1964 SPVEA's new superintendent described it as "a failed and disorganized institution, incapable of performing its duties as the region's socio-economic agency."[51]

In 1966 under Castello Branco's administration Operation Amazônia was passed by Congress. The new law provided the basic orientation of a new Amazônia policy which, Mahar[52] notes, included establishing "development poles" and stable self-sustaining population groups (especially in frontier areas), encouraging immigration, providing incentives to private capital, developing infrastructure, and doing research on natural resource potentials. In 1966 to implement this program the Superintendency for Amazonia Development (Superintendência do Desenvolvimento da Amazônia--SUDAM) was set up to replace SPVEA. SUDAM established a five-year plan covering the period 1967-71, which gave highest priority to development of the highway system. This activity not only served as the basis for further development but also served what Mahar[53] calls "the geopolitical imperative of human occupation," both of which were overriding objectives of SUDAM. Crops, livestock, and industry were given the next highest priorities in the Five Year Plan. The major weakness in the plan's implementation was SUDAM's reliance on other government agencies for funds and administrative cooperation. Only 12 percent of the plan's total resources came from SUDAM's own budget.

Also in 1966 Congress passed legislation that, as Mahar[54] puts it, "widened the scope of fiscal (tax) legislation incentives." This phrase suggests that there existed earlier, similar legislation relative to Amazonia but he makes no reference to it. The 1966 law allowed firms judged to be in the development interest of Amazonia to be exempt from federal income tax until 1982. In 1966 the Bank of Amazonia (BASA) was created (see earlier paragraph in Amazonia section) and firms were allowed income tax credits up to 75 percent of the value of BASA stock they held. In addition they were able to exempt 50 percent of their total tax bill when these savings were invested in agriculture, livestock, industry, and basic services in projects approved by SUDAM.

In 1967 the Manaus Free Trade Zone (Zona Franca de Manaus--ZFM) was established. Firms locating in the Zone were exempt from import and export duties and the federal manufacturers sales tax. Mahar[55] explains that all goods exported from the Zone to a Brazilian market were free of this sales tax but that goods with a foreign-import content were subject to import duties (upon entering Brazil from the ZFM) at a rate reduced in proportion to the value added in the Zone. The Zone represented a fiscal attempt to create a development pole for central Amazonia.

In 1970, probably in response to the severe drought of that year in the Northeast, President Medici established the National Integration Program (Programa de Integração Nacional--PIN) to cover the period 1971-74. It was a major regional centerpiece of the First National Development Plan, or PND I. In 1972 its duration was extended to 1978. This program of direct federal involvement in regional development included the construction of the Trans-Amazon highway to connect Amazonia to the Northeast, the development of an irrigation plan for the Northeast, the construction of an east-west highway along the northern bank of the Amazon River and the construction of a north-south highway from Cuiabá, Mato Grosso to Santarém, Pará, on the Amazon River.[56] In addition to receiving funds from other sources, PIN received 30 percent of Amazonia's special tax incentive fund.

In 1971 President Medici created the Land Distribution Program--PROTERRA to facilitate land acquisition, improve rural labor conditions, and promote productivity in both Amazonia and the Northeast during the period 1971-74. It, like PIN, was an important part of the First National Development Plan. The PROTERRA funds came from federal allocations, from PIN, and from a 20 percent share of special tax incentives, and were applied, according to Mahar,[57] to the purchase or appropriation of large landholdings for resale to holders of small and medium farms, to supply credit, to finance agroindustry, to subsidize modern agricultural inputs, to support agricultural export prices, and to supervise lands in the public domain.

In 1972 the First Amazon Development Plan (Plano de Desenvolvimento da Amazônia I--PDAM I) was developed by SUDAM as a part of the First National Development Plan. It abandoned the Five Year Plan and concentrated on surveying the regional economy and programming federal initiatives for the period 1972-74.[58] Livestock and modern agricultural development received the highest priorities.

In 1974 the federal government decreed the existence of the Program of Amazonian Agricultural, Ranching, and Agromineral Growth Poles (Programa de Pólos Agropecuários e Agrominerals da Amazônia--POLAMAZONIA) and charged it with the creation of fifteen "growth poles" selected on the basis of their perceived comparative advantages in various productive sectors.[59] POLAMAZONIA's goal was to create an infrastructure that would encourage investments in private enterprises. In a joint venture with the Rio Doce Valley Company, POLAMAZONIA was to develop the infrastructure around the iron ore reserves, estimated at 18 billion tons, in the Serra do Carajás, Pará.

In 1975 the Second Amazon Development Plan (Plano de Desenvolvimento da Amazonia II--PDAM II) was created as a regional complement to the Second National Development Plan. Covering the years 1975-79, it concentrated on certain key sectors such as mining, lumbering, livestock, modern agriculture, and tourism, all of which had, as Mahar[60] describes it, "a high potential to either generate foreign exchange through exportations or conserve it through substitution of imports." The plan recognized that livestock projects ought to be located in the savanna vegetation and not in the tropical forest regions, thus slowing the "grassification" of the Amazon forest.

The Southwest

In 1956 the Superintendency for Planning the Economic Improvement of the Southwest Frontier Region of the Country (Superintendência do Plano de Valorização Econômica da Região Fronteira Sudoeste do Pais) was created to work in cooperation with the states of this region. Heare[61] reports that its development plans covered the fields of electric power, transportation, communication, health, education, and production. In 1967 the agency became the Superintendency for Development of the Southwest Frontier, or SUDESUL, whose area of responsibility included 791 municípios (counties) in four states: 279 in Paraná; 237 in Rio Grande do Sul; 194 in Santa Catarina; and 84 in Mato Grosso.

The Center West

In 1943 the Vargas administration organized the Central Brazil Foundation (Fundação Brasil Central--FBC). Its charge, according to Wythe,[62] was to aid Brazil's "march to the west" (marcha para oeste) by planning the colonization of the plateaus of southern Goiás and Mato Grosso states near the headwaters of the Xingú and Araguaia rivers. In its early years FBC built roads across the Triangulo Mineiro (the panhandle of Minas Gerais state) and southern Goiás, and laid out the town of Aragarças, on the Araguaia River in Goiás nearly 300 miles due west of present-day Brasília.

In 1956 President Kubitschek spurred the creation of the government-owned Company for Urbanizing the New Capital (Companhia Urbanizadora da Nova Capital--NOVACAP). Article 4 of the Transitory Provisions of the 1946 Constitution called for the transfer of the federal capital to the central plateau (**planalto** **central**) of Brazil. Kubitschek made "build Brasília" a major theme of his winning campaign. In the meantime others were at work. In 1955 a federal commission carved a 30-by-60-mile quadrangle out of Goiás state to be the new Distrito Federal.[63] NOVACAP was charged with virtually every aspect of construction of a huge urban and rural complex that included the new cities of Brasília, Taguatinga, Sobradinho, Gama, and all their supporting infrastructure, as well as rural settlement nuclei in the more remote parts of the savanna-covered Distrito Federal. In 1957 NOVACAP estimated Brasília's cost to be Cr$ 170 million but in 1962 Sir William Holford, one of the judges for the selection of the city's urban plan, estimated that Brasília cost Cr$ 336 billion.[64] By 1980 the Distrito Federal was home to more than one million people. Rarely has a Brazilian planning agency been able to point to such a conspicuous accomplishment.

Table XIX-2 reports the funds expended by major national, sectoral, and regional development entities from 1950 to 1978. The data on Special Tax Incentives originated with the Centro de Informações Econômico-Fiscais and the Coordenação do Sistema de Informações Econômico-Fiscais. All other data originated with the respective development entities. Nearly all sources published figures for several years running and later sources often reported figures for a given year that differed from those of that year published by an earlier source. In all cases the latest source was used for this table on the assumption that time allowed for rectification of errors.

The "Approval" column for the National Bank for Economic Development (BNDE) refers to BNDE collaborations with various economic entities, which were approved for funding by BNDE. These entities included the following special funds: AID/BNDE (Agency for International Development/BNDE); the Fund for Development of Productivity (Fundo de Desenvolvimento da Produtividade--FUNDPRO); the Scientific and Technical Development Fund (Fundo de Desenvolvimento Técnico-científico--FUNTEC); the Small and Middle-Sized Business Financial Fund (Fundo de Financiamento a Pequena e Média Emprêsas--FIPEME); the Fund for Acquisition of Industrial Equipment and Machinery (Fundo de Financiamento para Aquisição de Máquinas e Equipamentos Industriais--FINAME); and the Fund to Finance Program and Project Studies

(Fundo de Financiamento de Estudos de Projetos e Programas--FINEP). Funding in United States dollars by BNDE included the granting of monies in the name of BNDE itself, as well as in the name of the National Treasury, and for the operations of FIPEME (see above). BNDE funds granted to FIPEME and FINAME and to regional and state development banks private enterprises were the intended beneficiaries of these monies. The public sector included all federal government organs and firms with a government majority ownership, most of which were in the steel, petroleum, transportation, electric power, and warehousing sectors.

For 1967 Alagoas Special Tax Incentive data were missing. For 1970 the Special Tax Incentives for SUDENE included those for Pesca-Sudene (the fishing development organization under SUDENE's aegis) and Turismo-Sudene (the tourism development organization under SUDENE). These Incentives for SUDAM included those for both Pesca-Sudam and Turismo-Sudam. By 1971 the Agricultural and Industrial Credit Branch of the Banco do Brasil had been renamed the General and Rural Credit Branch and in 1974 this branch began to report loans to firms in the comercial (retail and wholesale) sector. Prior to 1972 the Special Tax Incentives for Forestation were governed by Law 5,106/66, but in 1972 the sources began reporting Incentives that were governed by Decree Law 1,134/170. Both laws have remained in force and their figures are combined on Table XIX-2.

References

1. Gertrude E. Heare, Brazil: Information for United States Businessmen (Washington, D.C.: United States Department of Commerce, Bureau of International Programs, 1961), p. 80.

2. Stefan H. Robock, Brazil: A Study in Development Progress (Lexington, Mass.: Lexington Books, 1975), p. 25.

3. Robert T. Daland, Brazilian Planning, Development Politics and Administration (Chapel Hill: University of North Carolina Press, 1967), p. 16.

4. Anuário Estatístico do Brasil, 1952, p. 504.

5. George Wythe, Royce A. Wight, and Harold M. Midkiff, Brazil: An Expanding Economy (New York: Twentieth Century Fund, 1949), p. 164.

6. Heare, Brazil, p. 26.

7. Wythe, <u>Brazil</u>, p. 225.

8. Daland, <u>Brazilian</u>, p. 27.

9. Anuário, p. 504.

10. Daland, <u>Brazilian</u>, p. 32.

11. Ibid., p. 29.

12. Werner Baer, <u>The Brazilian Economy: Its Growth and De-</u><u>velopment</u> (Columbus, Ohio: Grid Publishing, 1979), p. 73.

13. Daland, <u>Brazilian</u>, p. 31.

14. Wythe, <u>Brazil</u>, p. 15.

15. Heare, <u>Brazil</u>, p. 82.

16. Ibid., p. 105.

17. Ibid., p. 25

18. Heare, <u>Brazil</u>, p. 23.

19. Daland, <u>Brazilian</u>, p. 32.

20. John Dickenson, <u>Brazil</u>, Studies in Industrial Geography (Folkestone, England: Wm. Dawson & Sons, and Boulder, Colo.: Westview Press, 1978).

21. Heare, <u>Brazil</u>, pp. 22-24.

22. Dickenson, <u>Brazil</u>, p. 17.

23. Heare, <u>Brazil</u>, p. 120.

24. Ibid., p. 27.

25. Ibid., p. 131.

26. Ibid., p. 93.

27. Ibid., p. 109.

28. Daland, <u>Brazilian</u>, p. 40.

29. Dickenson, <u>Brazil</u>, p. 17.

30. Ibid., p. 18.

31. Robock (1975), p. 31.

32. Dickenson, <u>Brazil</u>, p. 18.

33. Ibid., p. 19.

34. Ibid.

35. Ibid.

36. Ibid., p. 20.

37. Ibid.

38. Stefan H. Robock, <u>Brazil's Developing Northeast: A Study of Regional Planning and Foreign Aid</u> (Washington, D.C.: Brookings Institution, 1963), p. 69.

39. Ibid., p. 75.

40. Baer, <u>Brazilian</u>, p. 204.

41. Ibid.

42. Robert F. Mehl, "The Metallurgical Industry of Brazil," in <u>Brazilian Technical Studies</u>, Prepared for the Joint Brazil-United States Economic Development Commission (Washington, D.C.: Institute of Inter-American Affairs, Foreign Operations Office, 1954), p. 331.

43. Robock (1963), p. 85.

44. Ibid., p. 86.

45. Ibid., p. 82.

46. Ibid., p. 83.

47. Baer, <u>Brazilian</u>, p. 205.

48. Dennis J. Mahar, <u>Frontier Development Policy in Brazil: A Study of Amazônia</u> (New York: Frederick A. Praeger, 1979), p. 6.

49. Ibid., p. 8.

50. Ibid., p. 10.

51. Ibid.

52. Ibid., p. 11.

53. Ibid., p. 14.

54. Ibid., p. 12.

55. Ibid., p. 13.

56. Ibid., p. 18.

57. Ibid., p. 19.

58. Ibid., p. 20.

59. Ibid., p. 27.

60. Ibid.

61. Heare, Brazil, p. 24.

62. Wythe, Brazil, p. 234.

63. Armin K. Ludwig, Brasília's First Decade: A Study of Its Urban Morphology and Urban Support Systems (Amherst: University of Massachusetts, International Area Studies Program, Program in Latin American Studies, Occasional Paper Series No. 11, 1980), pp. 2, 10.

64. Ibid., p. 42.

Table XIX-1. Entities Created by the Brazilian Federal Government with Roles in National, Sectoral, and Regional Economic Development, 1909-79

Major National/Sectoral Entities

Date(s) of Creation or Existence	Titles of Entities and Their Acronyms	Presidential Administration
1933	Sugar and Alcohol Institute (IAA)	Vargas
1934	Federal Foreign Trade Council	Vargas
1936	Bank of Brazil Agricultural and Industrial Credit Branch	Vargas
1938	National Petroleum Council	Vargas
1938	Administrative Department for Public Service (DASP)	Vargas
1939-1943	First Five Year Plan	Vargas
1940	National Salt Institute	Vargas
1942	Taub Mission Ten Year Plan	Vargas
1942-1945	Federal Government Responses to World War II	Vargas
1942	Rio Doce Valley Company (CVRD)	Vargas
1943	National Steel Company (CSN)	Vargas
1943	National Alkali Company	Vargas
1943	National Motors Company (FNM)	Vargas
1944	Special Steels Company of Itabira (ACESITA)	Vargas
1943	Cooke Mission	Vargas
1943	Cooperative Credit Fund	Vargas
1951	National Bank for Credit to Cooperatives (BNCC)	Vargas
1944-1946	National Security Council Commission on Economic Planning	Vargas
1944-1948	Second Five Year Plan	Vargas
1948	Joint United States-Brazil Technical Commission	Dutra
1949-1953	SALTE Plan	Dutra
1952	Brazilian Coffee Institute	Vargas
1953	Brazilian Petroleum, Inc. (Petrobrás)	Vargas
1953	Executive Commission for the National Coal Plan (CEPCAN)	Vargas
1951-1953	Joint Brazil-United States Economic Development Commission	Vargas
1952	Plan for Re-tooling and Stimulating the National Economy	Vargas
1952	National Bank for Economic Development (BNDE)	Vargas
1953	CEDAL-BNDE Commission Development Strategy for 1955-1962	Vargas
1956-1960	Council for Development	Kubitschek
1956-1960	Program of Targets	Kubitschek
1956-1961	Executive Groups	Kubitschek
1956	National Cold Storage, Inc. (FRINASA)	Kubitschek
1958	Brazilian Tourism Commission (COMBRATUR)/Brazilian Tourist Corp. (EMBRATUR)	Kubitschek
1958	Minas Gerais Steel Mill (USIMINAS)	Kubitschek
1959	Piãcaguera Steel Company (COSIPA)	Kubitschek
1959	Vitória Iron and Steel Company (Aço Vitória)	Kubitschek
1961	Council for the Development of the Fishing Industry (CODEPE)/ Superintendency for the Development of the Fishing Industry (SUDEPE)	Quadros
1961	Brazilian National Electric Company (Electrobrás)	Quadros
1961-1963	National Planning Commission Plans (COPLAN)	Quadros
1963-1964	Three Year Plan (Plano Trienal)	Goulart
1964-1966	Plan for Government Economic Action (PAEG)	Castello Branco
1964	National Housing Bank (BNH)	Castello Branco
1965-1975	Ten Year Plan (Plano Decanal)	Castello Branco
1966	Tax Incentives for Reforestation	Castello Branco
1968-1970	Strategic Program for Development	Costa e Silva
1970	Goals and Bases for Government Action, National Objectives and Sectoral Strategies	Medici
1970	Tax Incentives for Reforestation	Médici
1972-1974	National Development Plan I (PND I)	Médici
1975-1979	National Development Plan II (PND II)	Geisel

Table XIX-1 (continued)

<u>Major Regional Entities</u>

Date(s) of Creation or Existence	Titles of Entities and Their Acronyms	Presidential Administration
The Northeast		
1909-1945	National Inspectorate for Works Against the Droughts (INOCS)	Peçanha
1945	National Department for Works Against the Droughts (DNOCS)	Vargas
1952	Bank of the Northeast (BNB)	Vargas
1959	Council for the Development of the Northeast (CODENO)	Kubitschek
1959	Superintendency for the Development of the Northeast (SUDENE)	Kubitschek
1959	Special Tax Incentives	Kubitschek
São Francisco Valley		
1945	São Francisco Hydroelectric Company (CHESF)	Vargas
1946	Constitution of 1946	Dutra
1948	São Francisco Valley Company (CVSP)	Dutra
1971	PROVALE	Medici
Amazonia		
1942-1966	Rubber Credit Bank/Credit Bank of Amazonia	Vargas
1946	Constitution of 1946	Dutra
1953-1964	Superintendency of the Plan for Economic Improvement of Amazonia (SPVEA)	Vargas
1965	Operation Amazonia	Castello Branco
1966	Superintendency for Amazonia Development (SUDAM)	Castello Branco
1966	Special Tax Incentives	Castello Branco
1967-1971	SUDAM First Five Year Plan	Castello Branco
1966	Bank of Amazonia (BASA)	Castello Branco
1967	Manaus Free Trade Zone (ZFM)	Castello Branco
1970	National Integration Program (PIN)	Médici
1970	Special Tax Incentives	Médici
1971	Land Distribution Program (PROTERRA)	Médici
1971	Special Tax Incentives	Médici
1972-1974	SUDAM First Amazon Development Plan (PDAM I)	Médici
1974	Program of Amazonian Agricultural, Ranching and Agromineral Growth Poles (POLAMAZONIA)	Médici
1975	SUDAM Second Amazon Development Plan (PDAM II)	Geisel
The Southwest		
1956-1966	Superintendency for Planning the Economic Improvement of the Southwest Frontier Region of the Country	Kubitschek
1967	Superintendency for Development of the Southwest Frontier (SUDESUL)	Castello Branco
The Center West		
1943	Central Brazil Foundation (FBC)	Vargas
1956	Company for Urbanizing the New Capital (NOVACAP)	Kubitschek

Sources: Daland, pp. 16, 27, 28, 29, 31, 32, 35, 38, 39 & 40; Dickenson, pp. 15, 19 & 21; Heare, pp. 17, 18, 23, 24, 25, 26, 27, 80, 81, 93, 98, 105, 106, 118, 120, 122, 125 & 131; Robock (1963), pp. 38, 75, 82, 84 & 93; Robock (1975), pp. 25, 32 & 34; Wythe, pp. 126, 164, 172, 225 & 273; Baer (1979), p. 205; Mahar, pp. 6, 10, 12, 13, 14, 17, 19, 20, 26 & 27.

Table XIX-2. Funds Expended by Major National, Sectoral, and Regional Development Entities in Brazil, 1950-78

Dates of Existence	Entity	Currency	Type of Movement	1950	1951	1952	1953	1954	1955	1956	1957	1958	1959	1960	1961	1962	1963	1964
1936-date	Bank of Brazil, Agricultural and Industrial Credit Branch	Cr$ 000	Loan	5,035,929	7,831,863	12,674,095	11,622,621	15,328,258	15,864,309	21,759,538	30,693,999	33,266,312	46,713,606	67,178,000	96,045,000	194,977,000	284,956,000	665,438,000
	Agriculture	Cr$ 000	Loan	3,056,916	3,994,346	5,576,387	6,193,749	8,383,731	8,387,467	12,199,454	18,110,229	2,027,815	30,571,716	39,676,000	56,717,000	111,584,000	168,112,000	418,271,000
	Ranching	Cr$ 000	Loan	825,722	1,419,800	2,006,682	1,959,000	2,762,442	2,414,009	3,124,323	4,361,435	5,213,266	6,451,076	11,386,000	11,741,000	30,283,000	25,929,000	62,011,000
	Industry	Cr$ 000	Loan	897,990	1,960,641	3,938,999	2,397,432	2,841,591	3,350,377	4,434,510	7,117,738	6,498,354	7,366,000	10,664,000	18,582,000	33,834,000	49,137,000	104,176,000
1951-date	National Bank for Credit to Cooperatives (BNCC)	Cr$ 000	Loan	-	171,180	202,855	388,331	334,139	452,967	566,552	1,049,523	1,175,803	1,934,876	1,819,125	2,152,293	3,562,111	4,263,163	15,321,632
1952-date	National Bank for Economic Development (BNDE)																	
	Total in Cruzeiros	Cr$ 000	Approval	-	-	1,181,000	1,485,700	2,997,800	2,592,600	6,722,800	8,700,800	12,232,400	10,816,400	14,912,100	25,473,300	26,196,100	43,722,300	103,641,000
	Public Sector	Cr$ 000	Approval	-	-	1,181,000	1,322,500	2,708,600	1,999,500	6,409,600	6,854,200	10,675,700	7,134,800	13,682,400	23,048,800	25,041,700	39,766,500	97,599,800
	Private Sector	Cr$ 000	Approval	-	-	-	163,200	289,200	593,100	313,200	1,846,600	1,647,700	3,681,600	1,229,700	2,424,500	1,154,400	3,955,800	6,041,200
	Total in Dollars	US$ 000	Approval	-	-	-	2,178	7,133	20,672	48,954	89,865	209,983	156,291	50,169	62,836	67,533	10,755	2,481
	Public Sector	US$ 000	Approval	-	-	-	-	6,566	14,614	46,220	58,610	187,862	156,291	5,629	62,836	25,160	8,755	2,481
	Private Sector	US$ 000	Approval	-	-	-	2,178	567	6,058	2,734	31,255	22,121	6,720	44,540	-	42,373	2,000	-

Table XIX-2 (continued)

Existence	Entity	Currency	Type of Movement	1965	1966	1967	1968	1969	1970	1971
1936-date	Bank of Brazil, Agricultural and Industrial Credit Branch	Cr$ 000	Loan	767,492,000	1,306,492	1,903,565	2,897,519	3,838,883	5,456,368	8,184,077
	Agriculture	Cr$ 000	Loan	475,189,000	868,372	1,293,490	1,824,441	2,403,221	3,523,696	5,082,591
	Ranching	Cr$ 000	Loan	64,690,000	186,021	285,666	459,070	629,060	782,385	1,423,549
	Industrial	Cr$ 000	Loan	142,345,000	211,117	316,885	604,229	789,494	1,150,287	1,677,937
1951-date	National Bank for Credit to Cooperatives (BNCC)	Cr$ 000	Loan	47,560,318	74,127,842	104,063	165,223	203,147	167,040	208,191
1952-date	National Bank for Economic Development (BNDE)									
	Total in Cruzeiros	Cr$ 000	Approval	356,029,200	531,253,800	752,687	990,389	1,348,795	1,864,560	3,217,590
	Public Sector	Cr$ 000	Approval	239,920,400	308,818,700	493,262	453,970	541,346	645,752	1,095,554
	Private Sector	Cr$ 000	Approval	116,108,800	222,435,100	259,425	536,419	807,449	1,218,808	2,122,036
	Total in Dollars	US$ 000	Approval	55,423	44,268	44,442	89,666	111,821	93,200	98,831
	Public Sector	US$ 000	Approval	41,778	4,641	8,889	58,457	92,404	12,986	65,665
	Private Sector	US$ 000	Approval	13,645	39,267	35,553	31,209	19,417	80,214	33,166
1966-date	Special Tax Incentives	Cr$ 000	Investment	-	-	-	722,582	1,111,411	1,749,414	2,439,654
	Northeast (SUDENE)	Cr$ 000	Investment	-	-	-	465,862	626,572	939,685	1,046,442
	Amazonia (SUDAM)	Cr$ 000	Investment	-	-	-	164,919	260,225	383,761	475,142
	Fishing (SUDEPE)	Cr$ 000	Investment	-	-	-	44,192	138,714	233,995	227,439
	Tourism (EMBRATUR)	Cr$ 000	Investment	-	-	-	36,018	44,590	68,030	93,526
	Forestation	Cr$ 000	Investment	-	-	-	11,591	41,310	114,835	416,462

Existence	Entity	Currency	Type of Movement	1972	1973	1974	1975	1976	1977	1978
1936-date	Bank of Brazil, Agricultural and Industrial Credit Branch	Cr$ 000	Loan	13,569,585	19,671,372	37,282,959	72,123,667	100,344,502	138,129,744	201,012,711
	Agriculture	Cr$ 000	Loan	8,229,803	12,267,710	21,376,465	41,101,011	63,120,227	90,879,385	121,937,679
	Ranching	Cr$ 000	Loan	2,052,617	3,512,127	5,038,719	12,522,374	16,027,981	14,208,562	26,992,278
	Industry	Cr$ 000	Loan	3,807,325	3,891,535	10,867,775	15,500,292	21,196,294	33,041,707	52,382,754
1951-date	National Bank for Credit to Cooperatives (BNCC)	Cr$ 000	Loan	280,859	332,375	693,389	1,711,232	3,114,014	4,403,735	6,864,530
1952-date	National Bank for Economic Development (BNDE)									
	Total in Cruzeiros	Cr$ 000	Approval	4,869,950	7,508,078	20,340,838	37,743,082	68,436,104	45,637,458	167,816,572
	Public Sector	Cr$ 000	Approval	1,062,625	1,032,279	6,815,388	8,555,905	13,158,936	9,503,946	21,874,728
	Private	Cr$ 000	Approval	3,807,325	6,475,799	13,525,450	29,187,177	55,277,168	36,133,512	145,941,844
	Total in Dollars	US$ 000	Approval	92,043	65,156	354,522	430,983	575,438	453,731	617,825
	Public Sector	US$ 000	Approval	72,166	2,585	29,250	249,744	17,925	13,171	75,000
	Private Sector	US$ 000	Approval	19,877	62,571	325,272	181,239	557,513	440,560	542,825
1966-date	Special Tax Incentives	Cr$ 000	Investment	3,599,424	5,096,461	8,107,219	5,275,020	6,793,937	33,608,002	-
	Northeast (SUDENE)	Cr$ 000	Investment	813,726	1,153,032	1,697,227	2,647,317	2,631,353	5,473,946	-
	Amazonia (SUDAM)	Cr$ 000	Investment	308,096	388,785	664,095	833,223	876,527	2,168,222	-
	Fishing (SUDEPE)	Cr$ 000	Investment	101,564	99,165	89,567	102,289	91,267	145,230	-
	Tourism (EMBRATUR)	Cr$ 000	Investment	55,023	70,032	157,455	123,958	179,691	232,365	-
	Forestation	Cr$ 000	Investment	395,569	558,029	904,250	1,359,074	2,695,171	6,254,074	-
	PROTERRA	Cr$ 000	Investment	1,003,620	892,375	1,436,140	⌐	257,465	5,713,586	-
	Program of National Integration (PIN)	Cr$ 000	Investment	616,725	1,336,883	2,166,354	⌐	-	8,570,426	-

Sources: AN 1954, p. 380; AN 1955, P. 410; AN 1956, pp. 222, 228; AN 1957, pp. 207-209; AN 1958, p. 205; AN 1959, p. 228; AN 1960, pp. 168, 173; AN 1961, pp. 202, 209; AN 1962, pp. 147-148, 151; AN 1963, pp. 244-246; AN 1964, pp. 240-242; AN 1965, pp. 284-285; AN 1966, pp. 276-277, 280-281; AN 1967, pp. 331-334; AN 1968, pp. 381-382, 386; AN 1969, pp. 420-423, 425, 473, 672; AN 1970, pp. 458-465, 468, 471-472; AN 1971, pp. 473-475, 784; AN 1972, p. 892; AN 1973, pp. 515-518, 521, 523, 860; AN 1974, pp. 562-565, 568, 571, 864; AN 1975, pp. 608, 616, 897; AN 1976, pp. 423-425, 428, 430, 725; AN 1977, pp. 733,773, 777,780; AN 1978, pp. 794; AN 1979, pp. 753, 796, 798, 800, 803.

Chapter XX. National and Public Security

Table XX-1 reports national and public security personnel by sex and the budgets of security organizations from 1872 to 1977. The data originated with the censuses of 1872, 1900, 1920, 1940, 1950, 1960, and 1970, with the Serviço de Estatística Demografica, Moral e Política, with the Relatório, anos 1916, 1917 and 1929 of the Departamento Geral da Estatística, and with the Anuário estatístico do Brasil, anos I, II and V.

All data for all years except the census years noted above originated with surveys taken at places of work. Most of the data for the census years were originated by census-takers at the respondent's place of residence with the exception of the 1950 non-Armed Forces data, which were from place of work surveys. The year 1950 was the only one in which the two data origins overlapped. The disparity between them was considerable owing to a combination of differing criteria and definitions as to who was or was not in a given job category and to the number of persons missed in the residential surveys of the censuses. For example, in 1950 the work survey reported 50,183 Military Police and the census (residential survey), 44,929. Fire protection personnel numbered 4,676 in the work survey and 3,756 in the census (residential survey). In the 1950 census persons giving their military ranks were listed on the "Occupation" table but those giving their branches of service were on the "Principal Activity" table. The former numbered 162,971, the latter 163,425. In the dicennial censuses military police were not listed as part of the military but only as part of National Defense/National Security. On Table XX-1 they are listed separately from all other organizations.

For 1935, Military Police personnel were reported by the source as those in "effective state" (41,617) and those in "complete state" (39,770). The difference was not explained but "effective state" figures were used for this and all subsequent years for which the two states were given. The 1935 personnel data for Paraíba, Pernambuco, Rio Grande do Norte, and Rio Grande do Sul were for 1934. For Fire personnel in 1935 and 1937 in Pará, only the city of Belém fire company was reported; in Rio de Janeiro only the fire companies in Petrópolis anad Niterói were reported; in Rio Grande do Sul only Pôrto Alegre and Pelotas companies were reported; in São Paulo only São Paulo (city), Santos, Ribeirão Prêto and Campinas companies were reported; and in Santa Catarina a volunteer company in Joinville was not reported. For 1942 all Civil Guard figures were only for the municípios of the state capitals plus the Distrito Federal. For 1946 the Military Police personnel for Pará and Piauí included Firemen, and the Military Police personnel for São Paulo state were for 1945. For 1946 all Civil Guard figures were only for municípios of the state capitals plus the Distrito Federal, and included Territorial Guards in the territories. Civil Guard personnel for 1946 for Espírito Santo included Special Police personnel and for Sergipe they included Transit Police personnel. The 1946 São Paulo data were for 1945. Although for 1946 the source combined Civil Guard and Transit Police budgets, for Goiás only the Civil Guard budget was reported and the budget for Natal, Rio Grande do Norte, was missing.

For 1947 São Paulo Military Police and Civil Guard data were for 1945. Civil Guard figures for 1947 were for the municípios of the state capitals plus the Distrito Federal. The Fire Protection budgets for the cities of Manaus, Amazonas; São Luis, Maranhão, and Teresina, Piauí, were included with those of the Military Police. For 1948 all Civil Guard figures were for municípios of state capitals plus the Distrito Federal. Civil Guard personnel included Territorial Guards in the territories. The 1948 Bahia Civil Guard data were for 1947. Distrito Federal data on Transit Police were missing. Military Police data for Rio Grande do Norte were for 1947.

For 1949 all Civil Guard figures were for the municípios of the state capitals plus the Distrito Federal. Military Police personnel figures included Fire companies in Alagoas and the cities of São Paulo and Santos in São Paulo state. Civil Guard personnel included Territorial Guards. All Civil Guard data for the Distrito Federal were missing. In the state of Pará and in the city of Curitiba, Paraná, Transit Police budget figures were included with those of the Civil Guard, but for Niterói, Rio de Janeiro state, they were included in the Public Security budget and do not appear as part of the total on Table XX-1.

For 1950 all Civil Guard figures were for the municípios of state capitals plus the Distrito Federal. These figures included Territorial Police in the territories. São Luis, Maranhão, and Distrito Federal figures were for 1949 and all

Civil Guard personnel reported for Florianópolis, Santa Catarina, were privately maintained. The Civil Guard budget for Natal, Rio Grande do Norte, included Transit Police. The Transit Police budget for Niterói, Rio de Janeiro state, was included with the Public Security budget and is not reported as part of the total shown on this table. Military Police figures for Rio Grande do Norte, Mato Grosso, Maranhão, and the Distrito Federal were for 1949. Fire data for Rio de Janeiro state were for 1949. Fire personnel in Santos, São Paulo state, and in Cruz Alta, Livramento & Passo Fundo in Rio Grande do Sul state, were paid by the Military Police and on Table XX-1 are included in that budget.

For 1952 São Paulo budget data were only for the city of São Paulo. Budget data for Pernambuco were missing. For 1954 the sources reported no Transit Police budget for Rondônia (which had one policeman) and Amapá (which had four). In Rio Grande do Norte there were 87 Transit Police and the Cr$ 70,000 budget was for personnel only. This money was for two persons under Transit Police aegis; the rest of the Transit Police were paid by the Civil Guard.

For 1955 in Sergipe and Mato Grasso the Civil Guard did Transit Police duty. For 1956 this same pattern held. Also in 1956 no Civil Guard or Territorial Police were reported in the territories or in Santa Catarina state. In Rio de Janeiro state Civil Guard duties were assumed by the Guarda Nocturna Municipal (Nighttime Municipal Guard). Civil Guard figures for Amazonas, Pará, Maranhão, Ceará, Alagoas, Sergipe, Bahia, Mato Grosso, Espírito Santo, and Paraná were only for the municípios of the state capitals. In Alagoas, Transit Police budget and personnel figures were included in Civil Guard figures.

For 1957 Civil Guard figures for Pará, Maranhão, Ceará, Alagoas, Sergipe, Bahia, Minas Gerais, Espírito Santo, and Paraná were only for the municípios of the state capitals. In Santa Catarina Civil Guard functions were handled by the Força Pública and in Rio de Janeiro state by the Municipal Guard. The Civil Guard budget for Pernambuco was for the year 1956. For 1958 Civil Guard personnel and budget for Rio Branco were for 1957; Pernambuco data were for 1956. Civil Guard figures for Pará, Maranhão, Ceará, Alagoas, Sergipe, Bahia, and Espírito Santo were only for the municípios of the state capitals. In Santa Catarina the Força Pública did the Civil Guard's job and it was done in Rio de Janeiro state by the Municipal Guard. The Fire Protection personnel total for 1958 included Mato Grosso's figure that was for 1957.

For 1962 Sergipe Transit Police duties were carried out by other agencies. For 1963 Civil Guard in Guanabara reported 1,872 personnel but no budget. São Paulo state listed 76 Transit Police but no budget, the Distrito Federal listed 94 but no budget, and Alagoas listed 49 whose budget was included with that of the Guarda Civil. All data for Niterói, capital of Rio de Janeiro state, were missing. For 1964 the Civil Guard and Transit Police Budgets of Amazonas were for 1963, and for 1965 for Amazonas these budgets were missing altogether. For 1967 the Maranhão budgets for the Civil Guard and Transit Police were for 1966.

For 1968 the Amazonas Civil Guard budget was for 1967 and Transit Police budgets for Pará, Paraíba, Bahia, and Espírito Santo were all for 1967. The 1968 Transit Police budgets for Acre and Amazonas were for personnel only. Together they amounted to Cr$ 146,165 and covered 95 persons. For the Distrito Federal the Transit Police budget of Cr$ 2,591,129 was all committed to the 93 personnel. For 1969 the Civil Guard personnel data were for 1968. The Transit Police budget for Pará, covering 82 personnel, was missing. Civil Guard deputy totals for Amazonas were for the year 1968. Transit Police Deputies were missing from the personnel of the Military Police/Public Forces for Guanabara state. For 1971 Paraíba's Transit Police budget was for 1969. The Mato Grasso Transit Police budget, covering 46 Police, were missing. The Public Security Forces, first reported in 1971, had both Military Police/Public Forces Deputies and other deputies as well. For convenience all of them are reported on Table XX-1 under the Civil Guard Deputies. The Civil Guard may have been absorbed by these services but the sources did not so specify. For 1972 the Bahia and Minas Gerais Transit Police budgets were for 1971.

Table XX-1. Public and National Security Personnel by Sex, and Budgets of Organizations, 1872-1977

	1872	1900	1908	1912	1917	1920	1924
Personnel							
Armed Forces	49,419	31,945	-	-	-	56,145	-
Officers	-	-	-	-	-	6,723	-
Non-Commissioned Officers	-	-	-	-	-	⎤ 49,422	-
Enlisted Personnel	-	-	-	-	-	⎦	
Army	27,716	-	-	-	-	49,920	-
Officers	-	-	-	-	-	4,376	-
Non-Commissioned Officers/ Enlisted Personnel	-	-	-	-	-	38,544	-
Navy	21,703	-	-	-	-	13,225	-
Officers	-	-	-	-	-	2,347	-
Non-Commissioned Officers/ Enlisted Personnel	-	-	-	-	-	10,878	-
Air Force	-	-	-	-	-	-	-
Officers	-	-	-	-	-	-	-
Non-Commissioned Officers/ Enlisted Personnel	-	-	-	-	-	-	-
Public Security Services							
Military Police	-	-	23,707	24,774	28,744 ⎤		35,263
Civil Guard	-	-	-	-			..
Civil Guard Deputies From:							
Military Police/Public Forces	-	-	-	-			-
Other	-	-	-	-	-	30,564	..
Transit Police							
Transit Police Deputies From							
Military Police/Public Forces	-	-	-	-			-
Other	-	-	-	-	⎦		-
Fire Protection Companies	-	-	-	-	-	1,654	-

	1928	1933	1935	1936	1937	1940 Total	1940 Male
Personnel							
Armed Forces	-	-	-	-	-	103,009	102,362
Officers	-	-	-	-	-	-	-
Non-Commissioned Officers	-	-	-	-	-	-	-
Enlisted Personnel	-	-	-	-	-	-	-
Army	-	-	-	80,145	-	79,103	78,662
Officers	-	-	-	5,161	-	-	-
Non-Commissioned Officers/ Enlisted Personnel	-	-	-	74,984	-	-	-
Navy	-	-	-	18,184	-	21,424	21,391
Officers	-	-	-	2,470	-	-	-
Non-Commissioned Officers/ Enlisted Personnel	-	-	-	15,714	-	-	-
Air Force	-	-	-	-	-	2,482	2,349
Officers	-	-	-	-	-	-	-
Non-Commissioned Officers/ Enlisted Personnel	-	-	-	-	-	-	-
Public Security Services	-	-	-	-	-	-	-
Military Police	37,767	37,349	41,617	-	45,684	40,832	40,713 ⎤
Civil Guard	-	-	8,481	-	8,855		
Civil Guard Deputies From:							
Military Police/Public Forces	-	-	-	-	-		
Other	-	-	-	-	-	16,875	16,591
Transit Police	-	-	1,491	-	2,304		
Transit Police Deputies From:							
Military Police/Public Forces	-	-	-	-	-		
Other	-	-	-	-	-	⎦	
Fire Protection Companies	-	-	3,411	-	3,384	3,738	3,730

Table XX-1 (continued)

Personnel	1942	1946	1947	1948	1949	1950 Total	1950 Male	1952
Personnel								
Armed Forces	-	-	-	-	-	162,971	160,175	-
Officers	-	-	-	-	-	-	-	-
Non-Commissioned Officers	-	-	-	-	-	-	-	-
Enlisted Personnel	-	-	-	-	-	-	-	-
Army	-	-	-	-	-	99,137	97,538	-
Officers	-	-	-	-	-	-	-	-
Non-Commissioned Officers/ Enlisted Personnel	-	-	-	-	-	-	-	-
Navy	-	-	-	-	-	31,808	31,533	-
Officers	-	-	-	-	-	-	-	-
Non-Commissioned Officers/ Enlisted Personnel	-	-	-	-	-	-	-	-
Air Force	-	-	-	-	-	32,026	31,004	-
Officers	-	-	-	-	-	-	-	-
Non-Commissioned Officers/ Enlisted Personnel	-	-	-	-	-	-	-	-
Public Security Services								
Military Police	48,812	47,782	46,258	38,116	48,550	50,183	-	-
Civil Guard	8,862	10,966	11,921	12,645	12,617	13,275		14,326
Civil Guard Deputies From:								
Military Police/Public Forces	-	-	-	-	-	-	-	-
Other	-	-	-	-	-	-	-	-
Transit Police	2,124	2,201	2,475	3,427	3,391	2,598		
Transit Police Deputies From:								
MilitaryPolice/Public Forces	-	-	-	-	-	-	-	-
Other	-	-	-	-	-	-	-	-
Fire Protection Companies	4,048	4,220	4,268	4,561	4,561	4,676	-	5,049
Budgets (Cr$ 000)								
Military Police	233,381	373,941	481,211	463,817	773,396	848,258	-	-
For Personnel	188,491	318,836	425,599	421,942	699,065	754,447	-	-
Civil Guard	76,702	72,205	92,648	96,203	142,737	159,007	-	284,024
For Personnel	71,758	64,202	83,658	89,381	134,889	148,579	-	269,574
Transit Police	-				48,548	43,557	-	-
For Personnel					41,237	39,032	-	-
Fire Protection	24,864	54,590	60,337	68,041	67,030	89,645	-	100,207
For Personnel	18,636	46,534	53,511	51,693	49,157	69,683	-	75,116

Personnel	1953	1954	1955	1956	1957	1958	1960 Total	1960 Male
Personnel								
Armed Forces	-	-	-	-	-	-	218,903	213,734
Officers	-	-	-	-	-	-	-	-
Non-Commissioned Officers	-	-	-	-	-	-	-	-
Enlisted Personnel	-	-	-	-	-	-	-	-
Army	-	-	-	-	-	-	130,033	127,377
Officers	-	-	-	-	-	-	-	-
Non-Commissioned Officers/ Enlisted Personnel	-	-	-	-	-	-	-	-
Navy	-	-	-	-	-	-	49,422	48,487
Officers	-	-	-	-	-	-	-	-
Non-Commissioned Officers/ Enlisted Personnel	-	-	-	-	-	-	-	-
Air Force	-	-	-	-	-	-	39,448	37,870
Officers	-	-	-	-	-	-	-	-
Non-Commissioned Officers/ Enlisted Personnel	-	-	-	-	-	-	-	-
Public Security Services	-	-	-	-	-	-	-	-
Military Police	-	-	-	-	-	-	68,327	67,494
Civil Guard	14,450	15,271	16,838	18,455	20,058	19,099		
Civil Guard Deputies From:								
Military Police/Public Forces	-	-	-	-	-	6,611		
Other	-	-	-	-	-	4,093	49,587	48,420
Transit Police	4,562	4,059	4,402	4,634	5,122	3,810		
Transit Police Deputies From:								
Military Police/Public Forces	-	-	-	-	-	2,268		
Other	-	-	-	-	-	3,519		
Budgets (Cr$ 000)								
Military Police	-	-	-	-	-	-	-	-
For Personnel	-	-	-	-	-	-	-	-
Civil Guard	297,888	411,825	623,292	811,079	798,760	1,209,862	-	-
For Personnel	281,902	389,875	599,520	757,062	752,074	1,138,049	-	-
Transit Police	93,801	116,142	139,275	277,240	295,132	316,235	-	-
For Personnel	77,121	97,051	113,842	235,229	245,434	262,500	-	-
Fire Protection	-	-	-	-	-	-	-	-
For Personnel	-	-	-	-	-	-	-	-

Table XX-1 (continued)

Personnel	1962	1963	1964	1965	1966	1967
Armed Forces						
Officers	–	–	–	–	–	–
Non-Commissioned Officers	–	–	–	–	–	–
Enlisted Personnel	–	–	–	–	–	–
Army						
Officers	–	–	–	–	–	–
Non-Commissioned Officers/						
Enlisted Personnel	–	–	–	–	–	–
Navy						
Officers	–	–	–	–	–	–
Non-Commissioned Officers/						
Enlisted Personnel	–	–	–	–	–	–
Air Force						
Officers	–	–	–	–	–	–
Non-Commissioned Officers/						
Enlisted Personnel	–	–	–	–	–	–
Public Security Services						
Military Police	–	–	–	–	–	–
Civil Guard	22,688	22,354	22,228	24,118	21,326	21,265
Civil Guard Deputies From:						
Military Police/Public Forces	8,594	9,655	19,275	35,639	44,648	37,554
Other	7,554	8,177	9,015	10,871	15,156	15,829
Transit Police	4,802	4,415	4,412	5,554	5,656	5,036
Transit Police Deputies From:						
Military Police/Public Forces	2,935	3,992	3,716	3,685	3,945	4,547
Other	3,901	3,462	3,738	2,412	5,994	7,948
Fire Protection Companies	–	–	–	–	17,727	–
Budgets (Cr$ 000)						
Military Police	–	–	–	–	–	–
For Personnel						
Civil Guard	4,927,397	9,554,316	23,945,512	48,489,584	57,748,597	83,868,536
For Personnel	4,561,488	9,149,817	23,071,445	43,214,984	55,091,216	81,870,411
Transit Police	716,308	1,318,816	5,203,420	9,452,890	8,413,543	13,377,942
For Personnel	629,284	781,211	3,046,133	7,090,533	8,413,543	10,159,075
Fire Protection	–	–	–	–	–	–
For Personnel						

Table XX-1 (continued)

Personnel	1968	1969	1970 Total	1970 Male	1971	1972	1974	1977
Armed Forces	-	-	253,708	247,151	-	-	-	-
Officers	-	-	-	-	-	-	-	-
Non-Commissioned Officers	-	-	-	-	-	-	-	-
Enlisted Personnel	-	-	-	-	-	-	-	-
Army	-	-	155,663	151,952	-	-	-	-
Officers	-	-	-	-	-	-	-	-
Non-Commissioned Officers/	-	-	-	-	-	-	-	-
Enlisted Personnel	-	-	-	-	-	-	-	-
Navy	-	-	49,296	48,273	-	-	-	-
Officers	-	-	-	-	-	-	-	-
Non-Commissioned Officers/	-	-	-	-	-	-	-	-
Enlisted Personnel	-	-	-	-	-	-	-	-
Air Force	-	-	48,749	46,926	-	-	-	-
Officers	-	-	-	-	-	-	-	-
Non-Commissioned Officers/	-	-	-	-	-	-	-	-
Enlisted Personnel	-	-	-	-	-	-	-	-
Public Security Services	-	-	-	-	55,224	-	-	-
Military Police	-	-	149,100	148,425	-	-	-	-
Civil Guard	22,227	24,327	-	-	-	-	-	-
Civil Guard Deputies From:								
Military Police/Public Forces	40,049	29,625	-	-	106,529	-	-	-
Other	16,048	11,565	75,410	73,157	17,549	-	-	-
Transit Police	4,959	4,140	-	-	5,118	5,421	-	-
Transit Police Deputies From:								
Military Police/Public Forces	3,390	2,902	-	-	6,329	7,026	-	-
Other	7,654	5,159	-	-	1,786	2,060	-	-
Fire Protection Companies	14,794	17,794	10,779	10,767	-	17,551	18,811	27,818
Budgets (Cr$ 000)								
Military Police	-	-	-	-	-	-	-	-
For Personnel	122,073,343	321,674	-	-	725,960	-	-	-
Civil Guard	-	-	-	-	-	-	-	-
For Personnel	112,231,503	309,534	-	-	632,743	-	-	-
Transit Police	-	-	-	-	-	-	-	-
For Personnel	34,912,935	29,843	-	-	63,776	81,913	-	-
Fire Protection	-	-	-	-	-	-	-	-
For Personnel	26,147,014	17,160	-	-	39,531	43,924	-	-

Sources: RE 1920D5, pp. VII-XIII; AN 1939-1940, pp. 1,427 and 1,280-1,284;
AN 1937, pp. 811-813, 815, 829-830; RE 1940A1, p. 40; AN 1941-1945, pp. 515-516;
AN 1947, pp. 520-521; AN 1948, pp. 535-536; AN 1949, pp. 628-629; AN 1950, pp. 541-542;
RE 1950 A1, pp. 25 and 44; AN 1951, pp. 551-552; AN 1954, pp. 530-532;
AN 1955, pp. 605-606; AN 1956, pp. 461-462; AN 1957, pp. 526-527; AN 1958, pp. 520-521;
AN 1959, pp. 459-461; AN 1960, pp. 399-400; RE 1960A1, p. 53; AN 1964, pp. 375-376;
AN 1965, pp. 478-481; AN 1966, pp. 522-524; AN 1967, pp. 751-753; AN 1968, pp. 573-576;
AN 1969, pp. 684-688; AN 1970, pp. 742-746; RE 1970A1, p. 79; AN 1972, pp. 953-957;
AN 1973, pp. 927-928; AN 1974, pp. 921-924; AN 1976, p. 772; AN 1979, p. 279.

Chapter XXI. Criminal and Civil Justice

Table XXI-1 reports the numbers of appeals made to and accepted by the Brazilian Supreme Court and the numbers and types of decisions handed down and published by the Court from 1934 to 1978. The Court itself (Supremo Tribunal Federal) and the Secretariat of the Court (Secretaria do Supremo Tribunal Federal) were listed as the originators of all the data from 1938 to 1978. The 1937 data originated with the Serviço de Estatística Demografia, Moral e Política. No origins were given by the sources for the 1934/35 and 1936 data but a footnote in AN 1937, page 201, indicated that most of the 1935 data originated with the Diário da justiça of February 3, 1937.

Almost every Anuário source reported data for the three latest years for which data were available. In a given Anuário data for the earliest of the three years reported was often different than data for that same year reported in an earlier Anuário owing to rectification of errors. Table XXI-1 reports the rectified data for every year. No explanation was given by the sources why in some years "Appeals Accepted" and "Decisions Handed Down" exceeded "Appeals Made," but it may reflect a backlog from the previous session.

Among the categories of Decisions Published by the Brazilian Supreme Court Special Appeals is the closest translation of Recursos extraordinários. Habeas Corpus needs no translation. Reconsideration of Decision seems to be the best translation of the term Agravo de instrumento. The Pequeno diccionário brasileira da língua portuguêsa, page 39, defines a legal agravo as "a judicial appeal, admissible only under very narrow legal constructs, that permits the judge in certain cases to review a previous decision of his and either reformulate it or sustain it before sending it to the appropriate tribunal." Guarantee of a Fundamental Right is the term suggested by Delta Sue Best of the Drake University Law School, Des Moines, Iowa, to translate Mandado de segurança. The Pequeno diccionário. . . ., page 760, defines it as "a constitutional guarantee to protect individual rights, which rights are readily recognizable and whose existence requires no demonstration but which are not helped by habeas corpus, against illegality or abuse of power whatever the authority that engages in these practices." Appeals is the direct translation of apelações. Extradition needs no translation.

For 1952, 1953, and 1954 under Decisions Published the sources did not specify whether Guarantee of a Fundamental Right was criminal or civil. For 1978 the total of Decisions Published (3,755) included thirty-nine undistributed by category of law.

Table XXI-2 covers the period 1934 to 1977 and shows the numbers of persons arrested and held by crime, and by crime for which convicted, the prison population at the beginning of a year, the numbers convicted and sentenced during a year, and the prison population at the end of a year. No origins were given by the sources for the 1934 data but 1943 and 1946 data originated with the Sistema Regional e Serviço de Inquérito da Secretaria Geral do IBGE. Data for 1947 and 1948 were generated by the Serviço de Estatística Demografia, Moral e Política and Instituto Brasileiro de Geografia e Estatística. Data for all subsequent years were generated by the Serviço alone.

For all years the "Persons Leaving Prison During Year" included those leaving by discharge, death, and escape. For 1934 "Homicide" included "Attempted Homicide" as well. The 1934 prison population was that as of June 30, 1934; all subsequent prison populations were those as of December 31 of the year in question. For 1946, data for the state of Bahia included no women, the São Paulo data were for 1944, and the Pará, Paraíba, Minas Gerais, and Distrito Federal data were for 1945. For 1947 the São Paulo data were still for 1944, the Pará data for 1945, and the Alagoas and Sergipe data were for 1946. For 1948 data for Rio Grande do Norte and Bahia were for 1947.

For 1950 Mato Grosso data were for 1949. The Brazil totals for 1950 did not include all persons convicted and sentenced; some were awaiting transfer to a penitentiary. For 1954 the prison population at the end of the year (15,322) included five persons whose crimes were not available. Paraná figures included only those for the capital, Curitiba, and Pôrto Alegre was missing from the Rio Grande do Sul figures. For 1959 Acre data were missing for "Persons Arrested and Held." For 1957 the total of "Persons Arrested and Held" did not include data from the cities of Teresina, Piauí; Salvador, Bahia; Natal, Rio Grande do Norte; and Goiânia, Goiás. The "Prison Population End of Year"

category included full counts from all states and territories
but from only one prison (Dr. Lemos Brito) in the Distrito
Federal. For 1959 Acre data were missing from "Persons
Arrested and Held." For 1960 Guanabara data for "Persons
Arrested and Held" were missing. The "Prison Population End
of Year" total (22,135) included 615 persons whose crimes
were not known to the source. For 1961 Guanabara and
Distrito Federal (Brasília) data were missing for "Persons
Arrested and Held."

For 1962 Bahia data were missing for all categories on
Table XXI-2. For 1963 Distrito Federal (Brasília) data were
missing from the category "Persons Arrested and Held," and
Guanabara data were missing from the category "Prison
Population End of Year." For 1965 Guanabara data were
missing from "Persons Arrested and Held." Guanabara data
were also missing from the 1966, 1967, 1968, 1969, 1971, and
1972 "Persons Arrested and Held" categories. Also for 1971,
in all categories but "Prison Population End of Year," data
for Pernambuco and Paraná were missing. The "Persons
Convicted and Sentenced during Year" total for 1971 (34,558)
included 614 escapees recaptured. For 1972 Guanabara data
for "Persons Arrested and Held" were missing and the "Persons
Convicted and Sentenced" total (27,784) included 847
escapees. The 1972 São Paulo and Mato Grosso "Persons
Convicted and Sentenced" data were preliminary. For 1973 the
"Persons Convicted and Sentenced" total (28, 229) included
839 recaptured escapees, and the "Prison Population End of
Year" (32,875) included 302 persons not distributed by crime.
For 1974 the "Persons Convicted and Sentenced" (28,059),
"Transferees" (+411), "Persons Leaving Prison during Year"
(20,832), and "Prison Population End of Year" (28,403) did
not include figures from the old state of Guanabara. This
last figure (28,403) included 241 São Paulo prisoners who
were not distributed by crime. For 1975 the total "Persons
Convicted and Sentenced" (24,382) included 3,261 prisoners in
Rio de Janeiro state and 73 in Pernambuco who were not
distributed by crime. The "Prison Population End of Year"
(37,071) included 7,395 prisoners in Rio de Janeiro state, 90
in Paraná, 260 in Pernambuco, and 399 in São Paulo state, all
of whom were not distributed by crime. For 1976 "Persons
Arrested and Held" data were missing for Rondônia, Piauí,
Alagoas, Santa Catarina, and Goiás, and for the same category
in 1977 data for Piauí and Goiás were missing. Also for 1977
"Persons Convicted and Sentenced" (27,154) included 5,566
prisoners in Rio de Janeiro state not distributed by crime,
and "Prison Population End of Year" (37,251) included 7,709
prisoners in Rio de Janeiro state not distributed by crime.

Table XXI-3 reports the sex and educational level
attained among persons arrested and held, and the sex,

educational attainment level, and length of sentences imposed for persons convicted and sentenced during the year in question, and for persons in prison at the end of the year in question. The data origins are the same as those for Table XXI-2. For 1934 the "Prison Population End of Year" and "Sentences Imposed" data were for June 30, 1934. The 1934 "Sentences Imposed" total (5,269) did not include 943 prisoners whose lengths of sentences were not available. For each of the years 1943, 1946, 1947, 1948, 1949, and 1950, because of missing information, the "First Time Offenders" and "Repeat Offenders" categories do not sum to the "Prison Population End of Year" total. For 1947 the São Paulo data were for 1944, Pará data for 1945, and Sergipe data for 1946. For 1948 the Bahia data were for 1947.

For 1954 the male plus the implicit female category cannot sum to the total "Prison Population End of Year" because the sex of the prisoner was not known in five cases. The data for Rio Grande do Sul did not include the city of Pôrto Alegre. A total of 2,796 prisoners was missing from the "First Time Offenders" and "Repeat Offenders" categories: 1,362 from São Paulo; 1,322 from Rio de Janeiro; 77 from Rio Grande do Sul; and 35 from Ceará. For 1956 the Distrito Federal data reported only the Central Penitentiary and no other institutions. For 1957 the total of "Persons Arrested and Held" did not include data from the cities of Teresina, Piauí; Salvador, Bahia; Natal, Rio Grande do Norte; and Goiânia, Goiás. For 1958 Guanabara data were missing from "Persons Arrested and Held." For 1959 Acre and Guanabara data were missing from "Persons Arrested and Held," and Guanabara data were missing from "Prison Population End of Year." For 1966 Guanabara data were missing from "Persons Arrested and Held." The 1966 "Prison Population End of Year" included 615 persons whose sex was not known. For 1961 Guanabara and Distrito Federal (Brasília) data were missing from "Persons Arrested and Held." For 1962 Bahia data were missing from all categories on Table XXI-3. For 1963 Distrito Federal (Brasília) data were missing from "Persons Arrested and Held," and Guanabara data were missing from "Prison Population End of Year." For the years 1965 through 1972 Guanabara data were missing from "Persons Arrested and Held." For 1967 and 1968 under "Persons Convicted and Sentenced During Year" the two next-to-last age categories were listed by the sources as 20-26 and 26-30 years. They are reported on the table in the 20-25 and 25-30-year categories, respectively.

For 1971 the total "Persons Convicted and Sentenced during Year" (33,997) included 419 persons sent to mental hospitals without the term of sentence being specified by the source. No 1971 Pernambuco or Paraná data occurred in

"Persons Convicted during Year" or in "Prison Population End of Year." Also for 1971 Guanabara data were missing for "Persons Arrested and Held." For 1973 the "Prison Population End of Year" (32,875) included 302 prisoners whose Sex, Educational Level, First Time Offender, and Repeat Offender statuses were not known. For 1974 the large numbers of "Persons Arrested and Held" who were in the "Beyond Elementary" educational level probably reflected the roundup of suspected urban terrorists, many of whom were college educated. The 1974 total of 20,845 "Persons Convicted and Sentenced during Year" included 438 held for security reasons with no length of term specified. The 1974 "Prison Population End of Year" (28,283) included 3,156 persons held for security reasons with no length of term specified. The "Prison Population End of Year" (28,483) included 241 São Paulo prisoners whose Sex, Educational Level, First Time Offender, and Repeat Offender statuses were not known. For 1975 "Persons Convicted and Sentenced during Year" (24,382) included 172 persons held for security reasons with no length of term specified, and 3,261 persons in Rio de Janeiro state whose Sex, Educational Level, and Length of Term statuses were unknown. The 1975 "Prison Population End of Year" total (37,071) included 90 prisoners from Paraná, 399 from São Paulo, and 7,395 from Rio de Janeiro who were not distributed by Length of Term. Another 1,956 prisoners held for security reasons with specified terms were also not distributed by length of term. For the 1975 "Prison Population End of Year" the male and female columns referring to Sex and Educational Level were reversed in the source, Table 20, AN 1978, page 301.

For 1976 data for Rondônia, Piauí, Alagoas, Santa Catarina, and Goiás were missing from "Persons Arrested and Held." For 1977 data for Piauí and Goiás were missing from "Persons Arrested and Held." The total of "Persons Convicted and Sentenced during Year" (27,154) included 5,566 persons from Rio de Janeiro state for whom no Sex, Educational Level, First Time Offender, or Repeat Offender information was available. Also in the "Persons Convicted and Sentenced during Year" category the Length of Sentence total (21,232) included 5,566 persons from Rio de Janeiro and 356 from Paraíba for whom no lengths of sentences were available. The "Prison Population End of Year" total (37,251) included 7,709 persons from Rio de Janeiro state for whom no Sex, Educational Level, First Time Offender, and Repeat Offender information was known to the source. In this same category, Length of Sentence (37,251) included 7,709 persons from Rio de Janeiro state for whom no length of sentence was known.

Table XXI-4 reports the numbers, sex distinctions, capacities, and budgets for Brazil's penal institutions from

1922 to 1977. The data for 1922 and 1937 originated with the Relatório, ano 1922 of the Diretoria Geral de Estatística, and the Anuário estatístico do Brasil, ano IV. Data for 1950 to 1954 were developed by the Serviço de Estatística Demografica, Moral e Política, and those for 1957 and 1977 were generated by the Divisão de Estatística de Secretaria-Geral of the Ministério da Justiça.

For 1959 all Acre data were missing. In 1969 penal institutions totaled 4,464 and included penitentiaries, custodial and treatment centers, penal and agricultural colonies, presídios (there were twelve of these), jails (cadeias and xadrezes), and establishments for minors. In 1972 penal institutions included only presídios (there were 2,878 of these), penal, and medico-penal institutions and totaled only 3,453 in number. The changes in nomenclature, and very possibly administration, suggest a prison reorganization with a stronger role for the military since a presidio is a military prison. For 1973 the "Expenditure" total, Cr$ 173,714,000 included Cr$ 360,000 for Pernambuco and Cr$ 1,907,000 for Rio de Janeiro state, for which the distribution of Inmates, Administration, Rent/Upkeep, and Other was not known. For 1975 and 1977 the number of cells included not only cubicles (cubículos) but also group living spaces (salões). For 1977 figures for Amapá were missing from "Expenditures."

Table XXI-1. Appeals Made to and Accepted by the Brazilian Supreme
Court, Decisions Handed Down by Civil/Criminal Category,
and Decisions Published by Type of Case or Branch of Law,
1934-78

	1934	1935	1936	1937	1938	1939	1940	1941	1942	1943	1944	1945
Appeals Made	1,410	1,501	1,869	1,886	1,175	1,564	2,389	2,629	2,496	2,480	2,565	2,722
Appeals Accepted	1,368	1,473	1,869	-	-	-	-	-	-	-	-	-
Decisions Handed Down	2,348	1,214	1,413	1,360	2,234	1,590	1,807	2,265	2,447	2,355	2,321	1,860
Civil	-	-	-	-	1,761	1,075	1,455	1,852	2,105	1,997	1,930	1,418
Criminal	-	-	-	-	473	515	352	413	342	358	391	442
Decisions Published	-	-	-	-	1,672	1,314	1,469	2,105	2,238	2,110	2,001	1,801
Special Appeals (Civil)	-	-	-	-	243	250	419	824	994	997	1,006	843
Habeas Corpus	-	-	-	-	806	555	640	885	714	641	552	529
Reconsideration of Decisions (Civil)	-	-	-	-	56	88	31	31	11	13	17	14
Guarantees of Fundamental Rights (Criminal)	-	-	-	-	-	-	-	-	-	-	-	-
Guarantees of Fundamental Rights (Civil)	-	-	-	-	-	-	-	-	-	-	-	-
Appeals (Civil)	-	-	-	-	345	284	262	263	375	271	247	194
Extradition	-	-	-	-	3	8	2	2	2	2	-	3

	1946	1947	1948	1949	1950	1951	1952	1953	1954	1955	1956	1957
Appeals Made	2,415	2,782	2,729	3,335	3,091	3,286	3,956	4,903	4,710	5,015	6,556	6,597
Appeals Accepted	-	-	-	-	-	-	-	-	4,710	4,686	6,379	6,126
Decisions Handed Down	1,819	2,565	2,988	3,269	3,299	2,917	4,197	4,464	3,933	4,146	4,940	6,174
Civil	1,394	1,933	2,168	2,445	2,511	2,251	3,174	3,334	3,290	3,448	4,046	5,180
Criminal	425	632	820	824	788	666	1,023	1,130	643	698	894	994
Decisions Published	1,251	1,992	2,079	2,758	3,393	2,216	2,476	3,385	4,474	3,730	3,794	5,251
Special Appeals (Civil)	475	1,402	1,399	1,887	2,376	1,432	1,512	2,364	2,809	2,519	2,371	3,215
Habeas Corpus	505	329	248	354	412	448	454	460	845	471	549	820
Reconsideration of Decisions (Civil)	19	78	67	133	270	143	-	-	-	-	-	-
Guarantees of Fundamental Rights (Criminal)	-	-	-	-	-	-	227	319	394	408	560	900
Guarantees of Fundamental Rights (Civil)	-	-	-	-	-	-	-	-	-	-	-	-
Appeals (Civil)	159	82	56	35	21	4	4	6	6	6	2	2
Extradition	2	2	5	4	5	4	2	7	23	3	7	8

Table XXI-1 (continued)

	1958	1959	1960	1961	1962	1963	1964	1965	1966	1967	1968
Appeals Made	7,114	6,470	6,506	6,751	7,705	8,216	8,960	8,556	7,378	7,614	8,612
Appeals Accepted	7,816	7,440	5,972	6,682	7,628	8,737	8,526	13,929	7,489	7,644	8,778
Decisions Handed Down	7,301	8,360	5,645	6,886	7,436	6,880	7,849	6,241	7,931	9,933	9,898
Civil	6,246	7,238	4,737	6,021	6,468	6,021	6,652	5,130	6,780	6,617	8,178
Criminal	1,055	1,122	908	865	968	859	1,197	1,111	1,151	1,316	1,720
Decisions Published	6,400	7,980	4,422	7,000	7,317	7,316	7,511	5,204	6,611	6,479	6,731
Special Appeals (Civil)	4,036	4,675	2,351	3,421	2,936	2,987	2,538	1,815	2,402	2,379	2,309
Habeas Corpus	—	—	—	—	664	775	984	1,007	733	1,093	1,377
Reconsideration of Decisions (Civil)	747	1,639	1,213	1,914	1,974	1,845	1,974	1,075	1,338	863	814
Guarantees of Fundamental Rights (Criminal)	—	—	—	—	—	—	—	—	—	—	—
Guarantees of Fundamental Rights (Civil)	1,036	1,241	621	866	1,408	1,399	1,551	981	1,594	1,015	989
Appeals (Civil)	6	3	3	4	1	5	14	27	19	13	7
Extradition	5	9	1	8	10	7	1	3	5	4	6

	1969	1970	1971	1972	1973	1974	1975	1976	1977	1978
Appeals Made	8,023	6,367	—	6,692	7,298	7,854	9,324	6,935	6,313	7,815
Appeals Accepted	10,308	6,716	—	6,523	8,049	7,986	9,083	7,565	7,947	8,848
Decisions Handed Down	9,954	6,486	6,407	5,372	6,848	6,682	8,029	6,558	7,017	7,819
Civil	8,754	—	5,370	—	—	—	—	—	—	—
Criminal	1,200	1,112	1,037	1,151	1,201	1,304	1,054	1,007	930	1,029
Decisions Published	5,848	3,328	3,265	3,926	4,340	—	3,945	3,433	3,611	3,755
Special Appeals (Civil)	2,799	1,579	—	—	—	—	—	—	—	—
Habeas Corpus	1,283	1,003	—	—	—	—	—	—	—	—
Reconsideration of Decisions (Civil)	182	25	—	—	—	—	—	—	—	—
Guarantees of Fundamental Rights (Criminal)	—	—	—	—	—	—	—	—	—	—
Guarantees of Fundamental Rights (Civil)	354	58	—	—	—	—	—	—	—	—
Appeals (Civil)	2	—	—	—	—	—	—	—	—	—
Extradition	12	5	—	—	—	—	—	—	—	—
Trial	—	—	288	1,189	1,548	—	1,505	1,596	2,140	1,810
Penal	—	—	948	1,102	757	—	461	510	136	581
Civil	—	—	609	441	798	—	516	469	461	425
Tax	—	—	372	400	503	—	589	346	339	414
Administrative	—	—	339	242	480	—	371	240	318	152
Labor/Social Welfare	—	—	542	363	87	—	64	101	99	121
Commercial	—	—	89	50	29	—	297	83	43	118
Constitutional	—	—	46	93	71	—	73	52	43	68
International	—	—	32	46	67	—	69	36	32	17
Industrial	—	—	—	—	—	—	—	—	—	10

Sources: AN 1939-1940, p. 1,289; AN 1948, pp. 540-541; AN 1950, p. 547; AN 1953, p. 477; AN 1954, p. 533;
AN 1956, pp. 466-467; AN 1957, p. 827; AN 1959, 469-470; AN 1960, p. 409; AN 1961, p. 452; AN 1962, p. 360;
AN 1963, p. 418; AN 1964, p. 379; AN 1965 p. 483; AN 1966, p. 526; AN 1967, p. 691; AN 1968, p. 570;
AN 1970, p. 749; AN 1971, pp. 804-805; AN 1972, p. 961; AN 1973, pp. 931-932;
AN 1974, p. 927; AN 1975, p. 973, AN 1976, pp. 774-775; AN 1979, pp. 268-269.

Table XXI-2. Persons Arrested and Held by Crime; Prison Population at
the Beginning of a Year, Numbers Convicted and Sentenced
during a Year, and Prison Population at the End of a Year
All by Crime for Which Convicted, 1934-77

	1934	1943	1946	1947	1948	1949	1950	1954	1955	1956	1957
Persons Arrested and Held	-	-	-	-	-	-	-	-	-	-	-
Prison Population Beginning of Year	-	8,132	7,687	7,805	6,752	9,005	9,176	-	-	-	-
Persons Convicted and Sentenced During Year	-	-	-	9,740	10,535	7,413	6,647	-	-	-	-
Transferees In/Out of System (Balance)	-	-	-	-	-	(-) 94	-	-	-	-	-
Persons Leaving Prison During Year	-	-	-	9,099	9,446	6,459	6,877	-	-	-	-
Prison Population End of Year	6,212	8,347	7,490	8,446	7,841	9,865	8,946	15,322	16,278	18,714	18,561
Crime											
Homicide	3,832	4,336	2,996	3,143	2,514	2,806	2,305	1,009	5,506	6,429	6,188
Burglary	391	1,172	1,329	1,966	2,044	2,757	2,683	3,689	4,214	5,099	4,744
Robbery	645	772	347	579	419	409	564	967	787	1,163	1,345
Drug Use/Traffic	-	-	-	-	-	-	-	-	-	-	-
Assault	238	625	492	745	822	965	716	1,681	1,572	1,656	1,686
Fraud	-	89	53	84	89	154	184	404	418	423	503
Attempted Homicide	-	133	143	89	52	99	117	448	648	546	506
Rape	279	58	186	192	264	366	279	512	537	615	607
Theft	79	185	135	139	152	232	176	293	226	326	287
Statutory Rape	-	147	178	195	266	249	226	565	515	518	528
Indecent Behavior	-	70	51	85	80	126	92	199	197	216	191
Counterfeiting	-	11	17	25	30	41	43	149	54	78	101
Other	748	609	1,563	1,204	1,109	1,661	1,561	1,401	1,604	1,645	1,875

	1958	1959	1960	1961	1962	1963	1964	1965	1966	1967	1968
Persons Arrested and Held	31,951	31,376	32,763	28,095	29,785	30,295	40,864	39,157	39,915	41,000	47,770
Prison Population Beginning of Year	-	-	-	-	-	-	-	-	-	-	26,161
Persons Convicted and Sentenced During Year	-	-	-	-	-	-	-	-	-	-	25,540
Transferees In/Out of Prison	-	-	-	-	-	-	-	-	-	-	(-) 6,815
Persons Leaving Prison During Year	-	-	-	-	-	-	-	-	-	-	17,365
Prison Population End of Year	19,046	22,033	22,135	21,047	19,771	16,183	23,385	24,219	22,534	24,767	27,521
Crime											
Homicide	6,253	6,721	6,585	6,223	6,354	5,898	6,658	6,894	6,493	6,838	7,783
Burglary	4,775	5,408	5,575	5,055	4,837	3,874	6,301	6,539	5,319	6,609	7,061
Robbery	1,528	1,421	1,544	1,365	1,433	937	1,800	1,005	1,701	1,976	1,954
Drug Use/Traffic	-	-	-	649	517	188	724	1,905	980	1,251	1,328
Assault	1,723	1,981	1,952	1,948	1,682	1,547	2,067	6,539	1,773	1,886	2,123
Fraud	506	656	648	523	531	327	691	787	663	743	782
Attempted Homicide	507	674	579	615	719	585	624	635	694	723	735
Rape	565	655	596	627	525	477	523	619	561	596	682
Theft	325	415	345	279	281	290	304	288	384	397	362
Statutory Rape	438	640	579	584	500	517	600	655	527	520	597
Indecent Behavior	194	218	207	208	184	172	212	218	227	225	295
Counterfeiting	103	132	103	73	50	45	63	46	23	31	226
Other	2,129	3,112	2,807	5,056	2,158	1,326	2,818	2,966	3,189	3,341	4,045

Table XXI-2 (continued)

	1969	1971	1972	1973	1974	1975	1976	1977
Persons Arrested and Held	52,436	46,268	47,605	60,703	55,733	86,380	100,030	124,305
Charge								
Burglary	-	-	-	-	9,923	13,435	15,048	18,183
Assault	-	-	-	-	7,996	11,690	12,457	13,174
Vagrancy	-	-	-	-	3,999	7,565	7,961	11,444
Homicide	-	-	-	-	7,491	7,556	7,070	8,052
Drug Use/Traffic	-	-	-	-	4,467	4,334	6,112	7,355
Robbery	-	-	-	-	4,649	5,932	5,394	7,167
Attempted Homicide	-	-	-	-	3,482	3,807	4,024	4,428
Fraud	-	-	-	-	1,439	2,815	2,789	3,024
Gambling	-	-	-	-	1,148	2,060	2,554	2,615
Carrying Arms	-	-	-	-	1,528	1,530	2,371	2,603
Rape	-	-	-	-	1,104	1,318	1,448	1,704
Smuggling	-	-	-	-	265	341	392	393
Extortion	-	-	-	-	212	267	312	375
Prostitution	-	-	-	-	188	196	223	268
Embezzling	-	-	-	-	107	128	152	172
Other	-	-	-	-	7,735	23,406	31,723	43,328
Prison Population Beginning	26,535	25,128	30,787	31,649	28,059	35,266	-	35,275
of Year								
Persons Convicted and	26,579	34,558	27,784	28,229	20,845	24,382	-	27,154
Sentenced During Year								
Crime								
Burglary	-	7,174	-	-	4,976	5,113	-	4,698
Robbery	-	2,776	-	-	3,365	2,360	-	4,206
Homicide	-	4,474	-	-	3,427	3,346	-	3,554
Assault	-	2,735	-	-	2,110	2,616	-	2,215
Drug Use/Traffic	-	2,446	-	-	1,599	1,897	-	1,831
Attempted Homicide	-	1,152	-	-	812	861	-	875
Fraud	-	1,094	-	-	722	1,043	-	792
Rape	-	662	-	-	532	508	-	594
Statutory Rape	-	977	-	-	400	447	-	300
Theft	-	366	-	-	176	471	-	268
Indecent Behavior	-	651	-	-	157	153	-	112
Counterfeiting	-	22	-	-	19	16	-	28
Other	-	10,029	-	-	2,607	2,217	-	2,115
Transferees In/Out of	(+) 6,484	(-) 9,382	-	-	(+) 411	(-) 1,420	-	(-) 2,148
System (Balance)								
Persons Leaving Prison	18,092	22,837	27,888	27,003	20,832	3,997	-	23,030
During Year								
Prison Population End of Year	28,538	27,467	30,683	32,875	28,483	37,071	-	37,251
Crime								
Homicide	7,441	8,912	7,837	7,631	7,506	6,966	-	6,872
Burglarly	7,061	6,468	7,013	7,280	6,157	6,402	-	6,749
Robbery	2,235	2,528	3,421	4,645	4,282	4,630	-	6,731
Drug Use/Traffic	1,755	1,550	2,135	2,389	1,611	1,993	-	1,948
Assault	2,063	1,908	2,112	2,403	2,029	2,233	-	1,622
Fraud	959	773	1,289	1,097	917	962	-	955
Attempted Homicide	807	1,041	1,194	1,205	966	864	-	856
Rape	733	663	774	836	838	704	-	810
Theft	392	457	755	557	571	774	-	737
Statutory Rape	713	815	676	698	492	426	-	309
Indecent Behavior	289	602	210	209	160	162	-	144
Counterfeiting	43	26	16	48	25	18	-	23
Other	4,047	3,724	3,251	3,575	2,688	2,771	-	1,786

Sources: AN 1937, p. 819; AN 1941-1945, p. 517; AN 1947, p. 522; AN 1948, pp. 538-539;
AN 1949, pp. 632-632; AN1950, pp. 544-546; AN 1952, p. 560; AN 1956, p. 463;
AN 1957, p. 528; AN 1959, p. 522; AN 1959, pp. 463-365; AN 1960, pp, 402-404;
AN 1961, pp. 445-447; AN 1962, pp. 354-365; AN 1963, pp. 420 and 423-424;
AN 1964, pp. 581 and 584-585; AN 1965, pp. 485 and 488-489;
AN 1966, pp. 528 and 531-532; AN 1967, pp. 758 and 762-763; AN 1968, p 581;
AN 1969, pp. 693 and 697-698; AN 1970, pp. 754-756; AN 1971, pp. 806 and 810-812;
AN 1973, pp. 933, 935, 937 and 939; AN 1974, pp. 929 and 932-934;
AN 1975, pp. 974 & 977-979; AN 1977, pp. 274, 278, 279, and 281;
AN 1978, pp. 294 and 298-299; AN 1979, pp. 271, 272, 274, 275 and 277.

Table XXI-3. Sex and Educational Level of Persons Arrested and Held, and Sex, Educational Level, and Length of Sentences Imposed for Persons Convicted and Sentenced During the Year, and Persons in Prisons at the End of the Year, 1934-77

	1934	1943	1946	1947	1948	1949	1950	1954	1955	1956
Persons Arrested and Held	-	-	-	-	-	-	-	-	-	-
Male	-	-	-	-	-	-	-	-	-	-
Educational Level	-	-	-	-	-	-	-	-	-	-
Persons Convicted and Sentenced During Year	-	-	-	-	-	-	-	-	-	-
Male	-	-	-	-	-	-	-	-	-	-
Educational Level	-	-	-	-	-	-	-	-	-	-
Sentences Imposed	-	-	-	-	-	-	-	-	-	-
First Time Offenders	-	-	-	-	-	-	-	-	-	-
Repeat Offenders	-	-	-	-	-	-	-	-	-	-
Prison Population End of Year	6,212	8,347	7,490	8,446	7,841	9,865	8,946	15,322	16,276	18,714
Male	-	8,200	7,361	8,243	7,663	-	8,674	14,851	15,704	18,089
Educational Level										
None	-	3,833	2,711	3,544	4,377	-	3,791	6,155	5,903	6,704
Elementary	-	4,045 }	3,141 }	4,667 }	6,464 }	-	4,882 }	9,130 }	10,373 }	12,010 }
Beyond Elementary	-					-				
Unknown	-	469	1,638	235	-	-	-	37	-	-
Sentences Imposed	5,269	-	-	-	-	-	-	-	-	-
0-6 Months	} 122	-	-	-	-	-	-	-	-	-
6 Months-1 Year		-	-	-	-	-	-	-	-	-
1-2 Years	} 875	-	-	-	-	-	-	-	-	-
2-4 Years		-	-	-	-	-	-	-	-	-
4-6 Years	982	-	-	-	-	-	-	-	-	-
6-8 Years	} 1,266	-	-	-	-	-	-	-	-	-
8-10 Years		-	-	-	-	-	-	-	-	-
10-12 Years	} 1,304	-	-	-	-	-	-	-	-	-
12-16 Years		-	-	-	-	-	-	-	-	-
16-20 Years		-	-	-	-	-	-	-	-	-
20-25 Years		-	-	-	-	-	-	-	-	-
25-30 Years	} 720	-	-	-	-	-	-	-	-	-
30 + Years	-	-	-	-	-	-	-	-	-	-
First Time Offenders	-	5,314	5,098	6,956	6,321	-	6,270	9,955	13,728	13,856
Repeat Offenders	-	1,060	1,319	1,255	1,278	-	856	2,571	2,548	3,658

	1957	1958	1959	1960	1961	1962	1963	1964	1965	1966
Persons Arrested and Held	32,139	31,951	31,376	32,763	28,095	29,785	30,295	40,864	39,157	39,915
Male	30,829	30,438	30,046	31,187	26,649	28,258	28,804	39,081	37,411	38,305
Educational Level										
None	11,256	11,332	10,853	10,155	9,932	9,927	10,046	11,040	11,040	11,021
Elementary	20,485	19,998	17,405	19,272	15,965	16,352	17,349	23,020	22,757	22,481
Beyond Elementary	398	549	3,118	520	437	585	476	908	911	1,155
Unknown	-	72	-	2,816	1,761	2,921	2,424	5,896	4,449	5,238
Persons Convicted and Sentenced During Year	-	-	-	-	-	-	-	-	-	-
Male	-	-	-	-	-	-	-	-	-	-
Educational Level	-	-	-	-	-	-	-	-	-	-
Sentences Imposed	-	-	-	-	-	-	-	-	9,119	-
0-6 Months	-	-	-	-	-	-	-	-	1,482	-
6 Months-1 Year	-	-	-	-	-	-	-	-	1,519	-
1-2 Years	-	-	-	-	-	-	-	-	1,738	-
2-4 Years	-	-	-	-	-	-	-	-	1,879	-
4-6 Years	-	-	-	-	-	-	-	-	951	-
6-8 Years	-	-	-	-	-	-	-	-	558	-
8-10 Years	-	-	-	-	-	-	-	-	293	-
10-12 Years	-	-	-	-	-	-	-	-	203	-
12-16 Years	-	-	-	-	-	-	-	-	229	-
16-20 Years	-	-	-	-	-	-	-	-	131	-
20-25 Years	-	-	-	-	-	-	-	-	81	-
25-30 Years	-	-	-	-	-	-	-	-	55	-
30 + Years	-	-	-	-	-	-	-	-	-	-
First Time Offenders	-	-	-	-	-	-	-	-	-	-
Repeat Offenders	-	-	-	-	-	-	-	-	-	-
Prison Population End of Year	18,561	19,046	22,033	22,135	21,047	19,771	16,183	23,385	24,219	-
Male	17,938	18,404	21,482	20,252	20,359	19,129	15,612	22,791	23,514	-
Educational Level										
None	6,495	12,543	7,868	6,556	7,250	7,025	6,419	7,339	7,746	-
Elementary	12,023	6,503 }	12,705	13,388	12,854	12,004	9,173	15,027	15,263	-
Beyond Elementary	43		439	302	500	362	297	635	893	-
Unknown	-	-	1,021	1,889	443	380	294	384	317	-
Sentences Imposed	-	-	-	-	-	-	-	-	-	-
First Time Offenders	14,998	13,992	16,661	15,285	16,457	15,675	12,833	17,427	18,380	17,828
Repeat Offenders	2,563	5,054	5,372	5,620	4,590	4,090	3,350	5,958	5,839	4,706

Table XXI-3 (continued)

	1967	1968	1969	1971	1972	1973	1974	1975	1976	1977
Persons Arrested and Held	41,000	47,770	52,436	46,268	47,605	60,703	55,733	86,380	100,030	124,305
Male	39,276	45,150	49,786	43,789	45,056	57,223	52,561	79,172	89,744	112,972
Educational Level										
None	10,604	12,617	13,077	9,669	10,579	3,480	3,172	7,208	10,286	11,333
Elementary	24,479	25,734	26,083	28,357	28,688	34,859	9,659	48,564	59,749	72,307
Beyond Elementary	834	862	1,430	2,229	3,763	3,816	30,624	6,981	7,241	9,073
Unknown	5,083	8,557	11,846	6,013	4,575	8,812	3,788	15,414	17,598	23,489
Persons Convicted and Sentenced During Year	–	25,540	26,579	34,558	27,784	28,229	20,845	24,382	–	27,154
Male	–	–	–	33,673	–	–	20,187	20,319	–	20,893
Educational Level										
None	–	–	–	7,747	–	–	3,783	4,135	–	3,610
Elementary	–	–	–	20,659	–	–	14,459	11,908	–	13,662
Beyond Elementary	–	–	–	4,839	–	–	2,093	3,732	–	3,111
Unknown	–	–	–	1,313	–	–	510	1,346	–	1,205
Sentences Imposed	11,512	12,929	15,524	33,997	–	–	20,407	20,949	–	21,232
0-6 Months	1,821	2,169	3,216	8,349	–	–	2,774	3,702	–	4,808
6 Months-1 Year	2,216	2,417	2,754	4,840	–	–	3,891	3,460	–	3,174
1-2 Years	2,380	2,826	3,251	5,255	–	–	3,411	3,503	–	3,233
2-4 Years	2,166	2,398	2,879	4,924	–	–	3,040	3,231	–	3,575
4-6 Years	1,169	1,251	1,396	3,162	–	–	3,024	2,735	–	2,565
6-8 Years	625	576	702	1,992	–	–	1,397	1,441	–	1,316
8-10 Years	347	358	434	1,193	–	–	768	813	–	775
10-12 Years	228	212	266	907	–	–	636	574	–	496
12-16 Years	252	256	298	987	–	–	577	611	–	567
16-20 Years	152	151	156	693	–	–	463	387	–	363
20-25 Years	102	82	94	413	–	–	218	230	–	166
25-30 Years	59	233	78	296	–	–	111	132	–	118
30 + Years	–	–	–	547	–	–	97	130	–	76
First Time Offenders	–	–	–	22,204	–	–	15,251	16,163	–	16,409
Repeat Offenders	–	–	–	12,354	–	–	5,594	4,958	–	5,179
Prison Population End of Year	24,767	27,521	28,538	27,467	30,683	32,875	28,483	37,071	–	37,251
Male	24,141	26,750	27,726	26,710	29,683	31,668	27,479	27,941	–	28,915
Educational Level										
None	7,772	9,041	8,661	6,483	6,368	6,967	6,254	6,326	–	5,731
Elementary	15,718	17,096	18,171	16,668	17,001	21,982	19,062	17,417	–	18,412
Beyond Elementary	701	927	1,244	2,671	5,914	2,638	1,942	4,141	–	4,102
Unknown	576	457	462	1,645	1,400	986	984	1,303	–	1,297
Sentences Imposed	–	–	–	–	–	–	25,327	27,231	–	29,067
0-6 Months	–	–	–	–	–	–	1,034	1,347	–	1,523
6 Months-1 Year	–	–	–	–	–	–	2,628	2,018	–	1,987
1-2 Years	–	–	–	–	–	–	3,360	3,226	–	3,039
2-4 Years	–	–	–	–	–	–	4,129	4,155	–	4,325
4-6 Years	–	–	–	–	–	–	4,525	4,464	–	4,866
6-8 Years	–	–	–	–	–	–	2,392	2,963	–	3,247
8-10 Years	–	–	–	–	–	–	1,649	1,937	–	2,276
10-12 Years	–	–	–	–	–	–	1,523	1,780	–	1,890
12-16 Years	–	–	–	–	–	–	1,690	2,139	–	2,119
16-20 Years	–	–	–	–	–	–	1,117	1,265	–	1,366
20-25 Years	–	–	–	–	–	–	616	792	–	816
25-30 Years	–	–	–	–	–	–	378	517	–	665
30 + Years	–	–	–	–	–	–	286	628	–	948
First Time Offenders	18,495	20,694	22,116	19,817	21,940	23,515	20,735	21,131	–	–
Repeat Offenders	6,272	6,827	6,422	7,650	8,743	9,058	7,507	8,056	–	–

Sources; AN 1937, p. 820; AN 1941-45, p. 597; AN 1946, p. 522; AN 1948, pp. 538-39; AN 1949, p. 631; AN 1950, p. 544; AN 1952, p. 560; AN 1956, p. 463; AN 1957, p. 528; AN 1960, pp. 402 & 404; AN 1961, pp. 445 & 447; AN 1962, pp. 354 & 356; AN 1963, pp. 420 & 423; AN 1964, pp. 581 & 584-85; AN 1965, pp. 485 & 488; AN 1966, pp. 528 & 531; AN 1967, pp. 758-59 & 762; AN 1969, pp. 693-94 & 697; AN 1970, pp. 750-51 & 755; AN 1971, pp. 806-11; AN 1973, pp. 933, 938 & 940; AN 1974, pp. 929 & 932-34; AN 1975, pp. 974 & 979; AN 1977, pp. 274 & 280-81; AN 1978, pp. 294 & 300-01; AN 1979, p. 271 & 275-77.

Table XXI-4. Penal Institutions: Number, Sex Distinctions, Inmate Capacities, and Expenditures, 1922-77

	1922	1937	1950	1954	1956	1957	1958	1959	1960	1961	1962	1963
Total Number of Institutions	1,328	1,503	3,466	4,059	5,434	4,321	4,162	4,162	4,188	4,188	3,736	3,842

	1964	1965	1966	1969	1972	1973	1974	1975	1977
Total Number of Institutions	4,201	4,350	4,464	4,464	3,453	3,445	3,496	3,550	3,343
Federal	–	–	–	–	27	32	–	–	–
State	–	–	–	–	3,426	3,413	–	–	–
For Males	–	–	–	–	220	224	226	203	234
For Females	–	–	–	–	16	16	16	20	23
Unisex	–	–	–	–	3,217	3,205	3,254	3,327	2,086
Number of Cells	–	–	–	–	24,747	24,548	24,806	24,875	26,119
Square Meters	–	–	–	–	388,702	344,803	–	–	–
No. of Insts. By Capacity									
Inmate Capacity									
1–10	2,997	3,141	3,252	3,252	–	–	–	–	–
11–20	726	734	735	735	–	–	–	–	–
21–50	358	350	350	350	–	–	–	–	–
51–100	58	64	65	65	–	–	–	–	–
101–200	25	19	19	19	–	–	–	–	–
201–500	25	28	29	29	–	–	–	–	–
501–2500	12	14	14	14	–	–	–	–	–
Expenditures (Cr$ 000)	–	–	–	–	–	173,714	229,570	319,937	672,882
For Inmates	–	–	–	–	–	94,855	130,893	185,691	362,025
For Administration	–	–	–	–	–	73,216	92,577	129,513	257,343
For Rent/Upkeep	–	–	–	–	–	3,376	6,100	4,377	10,982
Undistributed/Other	–	–	–	–	–	–	–	–	42,532

Sources: AN 1939-1940, p. 1,428; AN 1952, p. 559; AN 1956, p. 462; AN 1958, p. 521; AN 1959, p. 402; AN 1960, p. 401; AN 1961, p. 444; AN 1962, p. 353; AN 1963, p. 417; AN 1964, p. 378; AN 1965, p. 482; AN 1966, p. 525; AN 1967, pp. 754-755; AN 1971, p. 802; AN 1974, p. 931; AN 1975, pp. 976-981; AN 1977, p. 277; AN 1978, p. 277; AN 1979, p. 273.

Chapter XXII. Politics and Government

Table XXII-1 reports the numbers of public employees by sex from 1872 to 1970. The dicennial censuses were the originators of the data. In Brazil "authorities" (autarquias) are quasi-governmental agencies much like the Tennessee Valley Authority in the United States. All other categories on the table include federal, state, and municipal levels of government. For 1872 "Judicial" included "judges" and "officials of justice," neither of which group was classed by the census as "public employees" but as "jurists." The table assumes them to be public employees. For 1900 the census lists "administration" among the professions. Since private administrative positions were probably few in number in Brazil in 1900, and very likely did not total 45,710, all of these positions are put in the public sector. For 1920 "public administration" was listed as such, but the category may have included legislators as well. Judicial employees were probably reported in the "judicial professions" category in the 1920 census. But because this category included lawyers in private practice, as well as public employees, such as judges, it is not reported on the table for 1920.

Table XXII-2 shows the number of federal positions and employees from 1936 to 1966 and the numbers by federal agencies in 1960. The source gives no origin for the 1936 data. The 1939 data originated with the Serviço de Estatística Demografica, Moral e Política and the Sistema Regional e Secção de Sistematização da Secretaria Geral do IBGE. The data for 1953 were generated by the Comissão do Plano de Classificação de Cargos and those for 1958 by the Censo do Servidor Público Federal of October 15, 1958. Data for 1960 and 1962 originated with the Departamento Administrativo do Serviço Público (DASP).

For 1939 the figures included "ordinary" (ordinário) personnel who appear to have held regular positions and "extraordinary" (extraordinário) personnel, the largest bloc of which is made up of laborers. For 1953 another 1,553 employees were listed in an "other" category not shown on Table XXII-2. This category included the Special Commission on Frontier Belts, the Commission on Rehabilitation of Armed Forces Personnel, the São Francisco Valley Commission (CVSF), the Council on Immigration and Colonization, the National Economic Council, the National Petroleum Council, the Administrative Department for Public Services (DASP), and the Staff of the President of the Republic. For 1958 the source, AN 1961, page 414, reported a total of 246,582 employees, 13,950 of whom were state and municipal employees in Alàgoas, Mato Grosso, and Goiás and therefore not on the federal payroll. Subtracting them brings the total to 232,632 federal employees, 3,210 of whose sex was not known. They were subtracted from the 232,632 total to make the male/female distinction meaningful. For 1960 the "Positions" and "Employees" categories include both "positions" (<u>cargos</u>) and "functions" (<u>funções</u>), the definitions of which were not given. For 1966 the total of 700,031 federal employees included 1,832 federal public servants outside the country.

Table XXII-3 notes the registered voters and votes cast in Brazilian elections from 1933 to 1978. The origin of all these data was the Secretaria do Tribunal Superior Eleitoral. Iguaçu and Ponta Porã were federalized zones in south Brazil along the border with Argentina set up during World War II in response to the latter nation's pro-Axis political stance. The AN 1956, page 469, notes that in the period 1945-54 the Regional Tribunals reported a cancellation of only 400,000 registered voters when the decline from deaths alone was estimated to be 1,800,000. Owing to this slow removal of names from the voting rolls the percentage of registered voters actually casting votes remained very low in this period, 83.1 in the 1945 federal election; 70.7 in the 1947 state elections; 68.5 in the 1947/48 municipal elections; 72.1 in the 1950 federal/state/municipal elections; and 65.2 in the 1954 federal/state/municipal elections. The 1947 "state" election in Guanabara, which was the Distrito Federal at that time, was for the <u>Câmara</u> <u>dos</u> <u>vereadores</u> (city council). The votes in the 1965 state elections were missing for Pará, and votes in the 1972 municipal elections were missing from São Paulo and Acre. Up to 1966 Fernando de Noronha votes were reported with those of Guanabara state (the old Distrito Federal).

Table XXII-4 lists the rulers of Brazil from 1549 to 1889. The source did not indicate the origins of the data. For the first thirty years after Brazil's discovery in 1500 few Portuguese came to settle. Beginning in 1532 the land was divided into the first of what became twelve captaincies, which amounted to land grants from the king for the purpose of agricultural settlements. By 1549 the crown required a surrogate in Brazil and Tomé de Sousa was named the first governor-general. In 1570, after the death of Mem de Sá, Dom Sebastião, king of Portugal, divided Brazil into two parts. Luis de Brito Almeida was appointed to govern the northern part and Antônio de Salema the southern. In 1580, upon the death of Lourenço da Veiga, Cosmé Rangel assumed office illegally for a year. He was replaced by a junta in 1581, and two years later, in view of the junta's ineptness, Manuel Teles Barreto was named governor-general. In 1587 when Barreto died the two-man junta of Barreiros and Barros succeeded him. On June 13, 1621, Phillip III of Portugal and IV of Spain (the nations were ruled as one from 1580 to 1640) created the state of Maranhão which extended from Cabo São Roque, at the "hump" of Brazil, along the north coast to the Rio Oiapoque, Brazil's present boundary with Cayenne (French Guiana). Beginning with Furtado in 1621 all subsequent governors-general noted on the table ruled only the state of Brazil; the state of Maranhão had its own government. In 1624 d'Eca became Brazil's governor-general upon Albuquerque's death. In 1641 a triumvirate assumed power upon Mascarenhas's death. In 1675 after the death of Mendonça a triumvirate assumed power. Although Albuquerque e Sousa is listed by the source as the first viceroy in 1714, two of the governors-general had actually held that title, Dom Jorge de Mascarenhas in 1640 and Dom Vasco Mascarenhas in 1663. In 1719 a triumvirate served upon the death of Faro e Sousa. Another triumvirate ruled upon the return to Portugal of Meneses de Ataide in 1754. In 1760 a triumvirate was nominated to rule upon the death of the Marquis of Lavradio but the Crown confirmed only de Andrada and Brito e Alvim. In 1808 after Napoleon's invasion of Portugal the Portuguese court, led by Dona Maria I, queen of Portugal and the Algarve, and Dom João, regent and prince of Brazil, was transported to Rio de Janeiro, Brazil. During the reign of Dom João, prince of Brazil, Brazil became the functional center of the Portuguese Empire and was formally raised to equal status with Portugal as part of the "United Kingdom of Portugal and of Brazil and the Algarve." In 1816 upon the death of Dona Maria I, the prince of Brazil ascended the throne under the name of Dom João VI. In 1821 Brazil was elevated to the status of a kingdom. In 1831 a three-member provisional regency ruled during the minority of the emperor of Brazil, Dom Pedro II. This was followed shortly by the creation of a permanent three-member regency to serve during the minority of Emperor Dom Pedro II. In 1835 Feijó became regent during the minority of Dom Pedro II, and he was followed in 1837 by Araújo Lima. In 1871 the Imperial Princess Dona Isabel became regent while Dom Pedro II traveled in Europe. In 1876 and again in 1888 when Dom Pedro went to Europe for health reasons Dona Isabel served as regent.

Table XXII-5 shows the holders of the offices of president and vice-president of Brazil and the number of votes each obtained as candidates for these offices from 1889 to 1979. All the data originated with the Secretaria do Tribunal Superior Eleitoral. Candidates for president in Brazil run on tickets separate from vice-presidential candidates. For the sake of easier identification with the table all names used in the text that follows are the sequential last names of the men who held these offices. These individuals, however, were not always known in Brazil by these names. For example, Presidente José de Morais Barros was popularly known as Prudente de Morais, and Venceslau Brás Pereira Gomes and Juscelino Kubitschek de Oliveira were known popularly only by their first two names. The legal terms of presidential office have varied in Brazil. Until 1930 it was four years, from 1946 to 1977 it was five years, and since 1977 it has been six years.

In 1889 Fonseca served as head of the provisional government. In 1891 Vice-president Peixoto became president when Fonseca resigned. In 1896 Vice-president Pereira acted as president during Barros's illness. In 1900 Silva acted as president when Salles was out of the country. In 1903 Pena was substituted for Brandão in a special election on June 17, and was installed as vice-president on that date. In 1909 Pena died on January 4, and Peçanha served out Pena's term. In 1917 Vice-president Araújo acted as president when Gomes was out of the country. In 1918 Alves was unable to assume the presidency for health reasons and Vice-president Ribeiro served in Alves's stead until new elections could be held in 1919. In 1920 Ribeiro died on July 1. Paiva replaced him on the vice-presidential ballot, was elected on September 6, 1920, and installed on November 10 of that year. In 1922 Araújo was elected vice-president but died before his installation. Coimbra was elected to replace Araújo on August 20, 1922, and was installed on November 11 of that year.

In 1930, on October 24, Sousa was deposed by the military before his term expired in order to prevent his inaugurating Albuquerque who had beaten Vargas in the elections of March 1, 1930. Fragoso became head of a three-man Provisional Military Governing Junta that included General João de Deus Mena Barreto and Rear Admiral José Isaias de Noronha. In November 1930 Vargas became head of the Provisional Government and in 1934 he became president under the terms of the Constitution of 1934. In 1937 Vargas was indirectly elected president under Article 175 of his own Constitution of 1937. In 1945, after Vargas was forced out of office, Linhares, president of the Supreme Court, served as president. In 1946 Ramos was elected vice-president indirectly by the Constituent Assembly. In 1954 Vargas committed suicide on August 24, and Café Filho assumed the presidency. In 1955 Luz, President of the Chamber of Deputies, acted as president during Café Filho's illness. Also in 1955 Ramos, vice-president of the Senate, served as president in the president's absence. In 1960 Mazzilli, president of the Chamber of Deputies, acted as president while Kubitschek was abroad. In 1961 Quadros resigned the presidency on August 8. Later in 1961 Mazzilli acted as president for Vice-president Goulart, who was abroad when Quadros resigned and thus was unable to assume the presidency immediately. Again in 1961 Mazzilli acted as president when Goulart was abroad.

On April 1, 1964 Goulart, fled the country during a confrontation with the military and Mazzilli acted as president. The office was declared open by Congress on April 2. Castello Branco and Alkmim were elected by Congress on April 11, 1964, under the Institutional Act of April 9, and were installed April 15, 1964. Branco was to finish Goulart's term but Congress added fourteen more months, extending his term to March 15, 1967. In 1967 Costa e Silva and Aleixo were elected under the Second Institutional Act of October 27, 1965, and Article 5 of the Third Institutional Act of February 5, 1966, and were installed on March 15, 1967. In 1969 Costa e Silva was incapacitated by a stroke on August 31. To replace Costa e Silva, Medici and Grünewald were elected by Congress under the Sixteenth Institutional Act of October 14, 1969, and the Complementary Act Number 73 of October 15, 1969, and took office on October 30, 1969. In 1974 Geisel and dos Santos were elected in accord with Article 74 of the Constitution of October 17, 1969, by the Electoral College, whose composition and functions were regulated by Complementary Law Number 15 of August 13, 1973, and were installed on March 15, 1974. In 1979 Figueiredo and Mendonça were elected by the Electoral College and took office under the same codes as Geisel and dos Santos (above) but the Complementary Law Number 15 was altered by Decree-Law 1,539 of April 14, 1977, and Constitutional Amendment Number 8 of April 14, 1977, which set the presidential and vice-presidential terms at six years.

413

Table XXII-1. Numbers of Public Employees by Sex, 1872-1970

	1872		1900		1920		1940	
	Total	Male	Total	Male	Total	Male	Total	Male
Total	13,297	13,297	45,710	39,845	95,709	94,487	222,349	201,317
Administrative	10,710	10,710	45,710	39,845	95,709	94,487	199,588	181,133
Federal	-	-	-	-	46,904	45,476	63,212	56,754
State	-	-	-	-	29,390	28,255	53,142	46,072
Municipal	-	-	-	-	19,415	20,756	83,234	78,307
Judicial	2,587	2,587	-	-	-	-	7,902	7,363
Legislative	-	-	-	-	-	-	-	-
Authorities	-	-	-	-	-	-	5,617	4,729
Other	-	-	-	-	-	-	9,242	8,092

	1950		1960		1970	
	Total	Male	Total	Male	Total	Male
Total	260,767	220,636	363,669	290,447	633,490	483,762
Administrative	192,101	160,844	192,674	152,859	372,015	286,572
Federal	48,617	38,341	47,124	34,656	107,988	80,081
State	68,383	56,391	79,618	61,255	113,907	79,070
Municipal	75,101	66,112	65,932	56,948	150,120	127,421
Judicial	29,879	24,571	48,615	37,944	75,678	55,154
Legislative	3,833	2,955	15,197	10,919	12,072	8,484
Authorities	31,210	28,807	18,336	15,030	12,909	10,669
Other	3,744	3,459	88,847	73,695	160,816	122,883

Sources: RE 1920D4, pp. VIII-XIII; RE 1940A2, p. 40; RE 1950A1, p. 35; RE 1960A1, p. 53; AN 1970, p. 79.

Table XXII-2. Numbers of Federal Positions and Employees from 1936 to 1966 and the Numbers by Federal Agencies in 1960

	1936		1939		1953	1958	
	Positions	Employees	Positions	Employees	Employees	Employees	Male
Total	-	-	-	-	-	229,422	182,235
Ministries and Organs	-	-	-	-	-	-	-
Ministries	106,099	57,460	129,221	105,606	178,857	-	-
Transport and Public Works	64,849	21,006	69,069	63,225	73,254	-	-
Agriculture	3,578	2,531	9,320	7,844	11,646	-	-
Treasury	12,469	11,059	13,379	8,690	15,076	-	-
Aeronautics	-	-	-	-	12,674	-	-
War	5,462	4,912	9,712	6,752	14,233	-	-
Health	⎱7,683	⎱6,760	⎱13,034	⎱9,236	⎱21,170	-	-
Education	⎰	⎰	⎰	⎰	⎰	-	-
Navy	4,377	4,111	5,712	3,222	11,695	-	-
Justice and Interior	1,056	850	6,480	4,592	14,782	-	-
Labor, Industry and Commerce	6,173	5,839	1,867	1,534	3,845	-	-
Foreign Relations	452	392	648	511	482	-	-

	1960		1962	1966
	Positions	Employees	Employees	Employees
Total	415,824	345,565	360,032	700,031
Ministries and Organs	273,645	231,504	212,606	-
Ministries	270,408	228,942	-	-
Transportation and Public Works	101,172	79,882	-	-
Agriculture	26,227	24,826	-	-
Treasury	26,034	19,868	-	-
Aeronautics	20,005	17,353	-	-
War	19,564	17,492	-	-
Health	19,517	18,998	-	-
Education	18,411	15,691	-	-
Navy	17,184	14,566	-	-
Justice and Interior	14,561	13,249	-	-
Labor, Industry and Commerce	6,818	6,232	-	-
Foreign Relations	915	785	-	-
Organs	3,237	2,562	-	-
São Francisco Valley Commission (CVSF)	989	835	-	-
Administrative Department for Public Service (DASP	809	639	-	-
Agency for Planning and Economic Development of Amazonia (SPVEA)	498	361	-	-
National Petroleum Council (Petrobrás)	332	207	-	-
National Economic Council	161	117	-	-
Technical Office, University of Brasil	114	114	-	-
Armed Forces Chief of Staff	108	89	-	-
Coordinating Council on Supply	71	65	-	-
National Council on Waters and Electrical Energy	54	43	-	-
Secretary of the President	29	20	-	-
Commission on Rehabilitation of Armed Forces Personnel	25	25	-	-
National Development Council	20	20	-	-
Executive Commission, National Coal Plan	18	18	-	-
Executive Commission, Warehouses and Silos	9	9	-	-
Authorities (By Ministry or Parent Entity)	142,179	114,061	109,253	-
Labor, Industry and Commerce	62,740	51,712	-	-
Industrial Workers Retirement and Pensions Institute (IAPI)	17,927	11,763	-	-
Transport Workers Retirement and Pensions Institute (IAPETC)	11,142	10,793	-	-
Retail Workers Retirement and Pensions Institute (IAPC)	11,049	10,415	-	-
State Employees Retirement and Pensions Institute (IAPE)	8,359	7,131	-	-
Railroad and Public Service Workers Retirement and Pensions Institute (IAPFSP)	5,419	4,614	-	-
Maritime Workers Retirement and Pensions Institute (IAPM)	2,820	2,365	-	-
Social Welfare Food Service	2,520	1,638	-	-
Bank Workers Retirement and Pensions Institute (IAPB)	1,997	1,750	-	-
National Institute of Pine Lumber	951	902	-	-
Julia Kubitschek Hospital	271	116	-	-
Brazilian Salt Institute	156	107	-	-
Federal and Regional Council on Engineering and Architecture	95	89	-	-
Federal and Regional Council on Accounting	34	29		

Table XXII-2 (continued)

	1960		1962	1966
	Positions	Employees	Employees	Employees
Authorities (continued)				
Transportation and Public Works	37,370	29,806	-	-
National Highway Department (DNER)	16,922	11,681	-	-
Port Authority of Rio de Janeiro	9,449	7,357	-	-
Loide Brasileiro (government-owned ship line)	7,711	7,711	-	-
Navigation Service of Amazonia and the Port of Pará	2,111	2,032	-	-
Navigation Service of the Plata Basin	750	598	-	-
Merchant Marine Commission	427	427	-	-
Education and Culture	17,826	11,201	32,173	-
Universities	17,826	11,201	-	-
Minas Gerais	4,505	2,974	-	-
Paraná	2,830	1,332	-	-
Rio Grande do Sul	2,485	1,457	-	-
Recife	2,453	1,887	-	-
Bahia	2,432	1,454	-	-
Ceará	1,412	676	-	-
Brasil	742	731	-	-
Rural of Pernambuco	509	332	-	-
Pará	458	358	-	-
Treasury	14,661	14,061	-	-
Federal Savings Banks	14,661	14,061	-	-
Guanabara	3,073	3,073	-	-
São Paulo	2,802	2,802	-	-
Minas Gerais	858	858	-	-
Rio Grande do Sul	656	656	-	-
Paraná	579	579	-	-
Distrito Federal (Brasília)	552	258	-	-
Rio de Janeiro	464	464	-	-
Bahia	266	266	-	-
Pernambuco	249	249	-	-
Santa Catarina	126	126	-	-
Pará	113	113	-	-
Ceará	94	94	-	-
Paraíba	89	89	-	-
Espírito Santo	82	82	-	-
Amazonas	49	49	-	-
Alagoas	48	48	-	-
Mato Grosso	43	43	-	-
Maranhão	31	31	-	-
Piauí	28	28	-	-
Goiás	25	22	-	-
Rio Grande do Norte	24	24	-	-
Sergipe	21	21	-	-
Brazilian Coffee Institute (IBC)	4,313	4,010	-	-
Executive Council for Federal Savings Banks	76	76	-	-
Presidency of the Republic	7,755	5,828	-	-
Brazilian Institute of Geography and Statistics (IBGE)	5,908	4,215	-	-
National Council of Statistics (CNE)	4,838	3,581	-	-
National Council of Geography (CNG)	1,070	634	-	-
Institute of Sugar and Alcohol (IAA)	1,612	1,445	-	-
National Research Council	122	85	-	-
Brazilian Institute for Documentation and Bibliography	66	36	-	-
National Institute for Research on Amazonia	47	47	-	-
Agriculture	1,827	1,453	-	-
National Institute of Immigration and Colonization (INIC)	746	625	-	-
Rural Social Service	460	310	-	-
National Bank for Credit to Cooperatives	346	274	-	-
Credit Bank for Fishing	143	118	-	-
National Mate Institute	132	126	-	-

Sources: AN 1937, p. 779; AN 1939-1940, pp. 1,231-1,253; AN 1954, p. 463; AN 1961, p. 414; AN 1962, pp. 335-336; AN 1965, p. 462; An 1967, p. 732.

Table XXII-3. Voters Registered and Votes Cast by Political Subdivisions in Brazilian Elections, 1933-78

	1933 Constitutional Convention Delegates Voters Registered	1934 Federal/State Legislators Voters Registered	1945 Federal Voters Registered	1945 Federal Votes Cast	1947 State Voters Registered	1947 State Votes Cast	1947 Municipal Voters Registered	1947 Municipal Votes Cast	1948 Municipal Voters Registered	1948 Municipal Votes Cast	1950 Federal/State Municipal Voters Registered	1950 Federal/State Municipal Votes Cast	1954 Federal/State Municipal Voters Registered	1954 Federal/State Municipal Votes Cast
Total	1,466,700	2,659,171	7,459,859	6,200,805	7,710,504	5,454,111	7,400,415	5,091,836	625,991	405,899	11,449,532	8,254,989	15,104,604	9,890,475
São Paulo	299,074	534,487	1,688,598	1,395,670	1,601,283	1,149,049	1,683,963	1,193,469	—	—	2,043,840	1,502,841	2,757,309	1,929,731
Rio de Janeiro	69,522	158,574	383,100	324,717	404,472	280,384	460,532	324,030	—	—	631,872	449,644	911,081	563,867
Guanabara	84,892	136,085	549,353	496,771	589,972	441,086	—	—	—	—	837,427	607,831	965,481	695,472
Minas Gerais	311,374	530,654	1,231,251	1,014,064	1,276,286	876,224	1,572,192	1,125,363	—	—	1,936,741	1,330,626	2,366,606	1,542,684
Rio Grande do Sul	231,194	327,264	753,232	625,840	788,659	558,747	842,538	568,858	—	—	987,236	719,336	1,212,792	837,755
Paraná	34,844	64,208	229,672	195,768	239,801	146,489	267,977	181,416	—	—	372,796	274,474	609,838	417,920
Bahia	91,118	185,483	440,621	357,621	477,535	328,230	586,829	381,064	—	—	859,626	609,696	1,090,000	679,607
Pernambuco	69,318	122,849	321,736	269,955	340,788	245,962	357,514	233,152	—	—	452,545	404,189	837,377	459,573
Ceará	30,748	75,509	369,550	291,739	383,442	280,527	457,064	301,668	—	—	683,465	475,464	683,465	553,966
Santa Catarina	36,187	88,839	248,086	216,817	261,182	186,290	292,683	217,515	196,985	121,671	367,695	279,731	474,379	328,295
Goiás	16,114	33,691	103,079	83,012	116,657	81,739	138,294	93,108	—	—	217,892	151,072	363,728	225,406
Pará	28,990	46,774	159,395	123,474	177,601	123,790	221,776	157,453	—	—	277,692	194,987	345,588	188,721
Paraíba	29,664	51,452	175,634	150,396	195,946	153,992	150,271	79,771	—	—	346,141	265,125	439,460	249,817
Maranhão	12,432	45,658	109,101	75,497	130,379	81,444	139,954	101,342	—	—	262,295	158,690	403,586	201,497
Espírito Santo	29,731	51,944	122,281	107,161	126,585	94,558	—	—	166,619	119,146	180,607	130,565	261,969	180,255
Piauí	10,462	40,959	132,957	113,831	139,957	111,404	—	—	165,984	106,273	220,073	166,303	292,583	189,119
Rio Grande do Norte	18,959	47,402	131,560	107,273	159,310	118,430	—	—	96,403	58,809	243,231	175,867	324,309	190,333
Alagoas	23,742	34,730	82,068	67,959	87,166	57,640	80,642	46,782	—	—	146,182	99,927	195,016	121,505
Mato Grosso	8,788	21,888	59,121	45,839	74,417	44,305	—	—	—	—	132,037	87,194	182,743	110,391
Mato Grosso do Sul	—	—	—	—	—	—	—	—	—	—	—	—	—	—
Sergipe	23,460	45,657	97,089	81,328	101,578	69,063	106,531	63,902	—	—	147,144	102,532	218,847	128,476
Amazonas	4,389	9,884	31,948	23,966	37,488	24,828	41,655	22,943	—	—	75,367	47,964	121,565	68,502
Rondônia	—	—	2,902	2,114	—	—	—	—	—	—	5,181	3,814	11,283	7,244
Acre	1,958	5,130	6,895	5,522	—	—	—	—	—	—	12,284	9,264	18,421	12,678
Amapá	—	—	3,365	2,720	—	—	—	—	—	—	6,737	5,169	9,982	4,248
Roraima	—	—	673	504	—	—	—	—	—	—	3,506	2,684	7,196	3,413
D. F. (Brasília)	—	—	—	—	—	—	—	—	—	—	—	—	—	—
Iguaçu	—	—	16,733	13,451	—	—	—	—	—	—	—	—	—	—
Ponta Porã	—	—	10,351	7,796	—	—	—	—	—	—	—	—	—	—
Fernando de Noronha	—	—	—	—	—	—	—	—	—	—	—	—	—	—

Brazil: A Handbook of Historical Statistics

Table XXII-3 (continued)

	1955 Federal/State Voters Registered	1955 Votes Cast	1958 Fed./State Munic. Voters Registered	1958 Votes Cast	1960 Fed./State Munic. Voters Registered	1960 Votes Cast	1962 Fed./State Munic. Voters Registered	1962 Votes Cast	1963 Federal Referendum Voters Registered	1965 State Voters Registered	1965 Votes Cast	1966 Fed./State Munic. Voters Registered	1966 Votes Cast
Total	15,243,246	9,097,014	13,780,244	12,678,997	15,543,332	12,586,354	18,528,847	14,747,221	12,286,175	8,591,064	6,574,226	22,387,251	17,285,556
São Paulo	2,784,717	1,962,285	2,855,751	2,702,012	3,412,611	3,040,669	3,822,235	3,303,350	3,038,145			4,901,494	4,079,811
Rio de Janeiro	842,988	485,430	790,546	729,781	827,338	686,872	1,115,176	903,857	811,365			1,323,799	1,025,437
Guanabara	992,459	693,336	977,839	927,582	1,099,490	1,000,385	1,198,588	1,022,217	1,047,359	1,380,412	1,176,014	1,497,401	1,284,646
Minas Gerais	2,458,361	1,308,335	2,026,003	1,888,027	2,151,283	1,728,455	2,565,505	2,067,555	1,599,539	2,726,140	1,880,694	3,067,453	2,307,578
Rio Grande do Sul	1,319,170	903,408	1,274,344	1,214,094	1,409,310	1,263,451	1,561,162	1,353,697	1,222,234			1,927,796	1,578,515
Paraná	672,645	454,140	684,881	625,854	885,418	723,609	1,100,637	814,842	725,482	1,437,801	1,016,572	1,476,143	1,136,123
Bahia	1,093,808	498,277	920,249	826,087	943,317	584,878	1,206,453	886,163	569,185			1,394,598	961,226
Pernambuco	873,070	460,864	614,537	549,670	676,179	483,606	851,398	607,695	444,520			999,651	708,407
Ceará	509,085	383,052	656,716	569,064	668,703	436,124	853,282	634,942	421,025			926,431	658,846
Santa Catarina	493,928	351,443	524,109	494,052	581,358	524,047	638,527	555,305	478,476	756,300	651,320	787,719	667,117
Goiás	363,728	163,662	326,976	291,409	407,667	318,280	510,135	343,710	266,460	552,348	384,351	649,320	462,202
Pará	373,125	197,266	271,374	232,506	324,511	232,632	421,531	275,117	157,593			478,683	293,668
Paraíba	447,598	239,763	291,120	262,228	353,371	286,312	405,407	309,702	210,165	456,938	344,997	553,055	413,247
Maranhão	426,046	158,842	278,094	223,955	384,327	235,049	497,436	319,559	258,967	405,549	247,156	292,443	233,060
Espírito Santo	249,194	164,247	233,053	221,045	235,056	194,509	307,009	248,586	214,739			377,884	280,513
Piauí	304,472	134,558	232,368	211,348	244,262	132,333	315,158	230,264	141,006			346,029	239,374
Rio Grande do Norte	294,870	154,778	229,523	196,011	278,087	225,588	322,107	250,283	200,843	375,416	281,125	398,571	295,884
Alagoas	189,977	106,984	134,959	124,609	154,621	123,976	192,223	145,103	105,651	203,071	143,967	224,957	160,379
Mato Grosso	194,151	103,186	144,004	153,851	203,984	156,077	263,002	189,508	135,539	297,089	203,649	318,441	212,892
Mato Grosso do Sul													
Sergipe	200,900	98,730	145,303	123,737	150,095	94,666	192,503	141,899	92,823			218,194	148,617
Amazonas	119,771	51,880	88,712	78,565	91,929	63,462	137,317	103,563	63,071			160,747	92,506
Rondônia	6,995	5,781	8,126	7,395	8,339	5,595	12,759	9,462	8,027			16,049	8,514
Acre	17,284	9,034	14,941	13,619	14,941	11,357	19,544	14,835	12,165			27,309	20,334
Amapá	9,229	5,016	7,718	6,869	7,875	7,279	13,666	10,751	9,555			16,340	11,719
Roraima	5,675	2,717	5,998	5,627	5,696	4,301	6,087	4,656	3,604			6,744	4,941
D. F. (Brasília)	—	—	—	—	23,564	21,842	—	—	48,637			—	—
Iguaçu	—	—	—	—								—	—
Ponta Porã	—	—	—	—								—	—
Fernando de Noronha	—	—	—	—								—	—

Table XXII-3 (continued)

	1968 Municipal	1969 Municipal	1970 Federal/State Municipal		1972 Municipal		1974 Federal/State		1976 Municipal		1978 Federal/State	
	Registered	Registered	Registered	Cast	Registered	Cast	Registered	Cast	Registered	Cast	Registered	Cast
Total	24,903,261	25,741,173	28,966,114	22,435,521	32,873,297	—	35,810,715	28,982,400	42,218,102	34,993,422	46,030,464	37,629,180
São Paulo	5,723,706	5,978,523	6,548,835	5,400,898	7,252,851	—	8,024,599	7,117,868	9,338,615	8,314,575	10,241,247	9,095,452
Rio de Janeiro	1,378,290	1,421,045	1,600,467	1,275,728	1,868,802	—	2,001,475	1,680,060	4,737,996	4,108,429	5,141,852	4,494,128
Guanabara	1,602,415	1,668,260	1,779,112	1,531,238	1,936,191	1,505,537	2,212,705	1,928,541	—	—	—	—
Minas Gerais	3,222,455	3,288,109	3,769,687	2,829,149	4,191,172	3,294,881	4,478,350	3,461,137	5,229,944	4,268,276	5,400,733	4,460,145
Rio Grande do Sul	2,207,784	2,255,835	2,402,204	2,031,032	2,634,562	2,303,915	2,893,152	2,579,767	3,307,185	2,953,767	3,541,669	3,129,585
Paraná	1,889,726	1,887,411	2,074,356	1,606,437	2,446,046	1,861,916	2,692,609	2,129,125	3,244,187	2,546,510	3,565,871	2,639,050
Bahia	1,428,182	1,472,507	1,953,576	1,362,073	2,260,997	1,508,771	2,424,529	1,587,999	2,852,716	2,158,167	3,219,772	2,238,573
Pernambuco	1,197,901	1,235,855	1,316,539	896,923	1,462,692	1,060,451	1,600,677	1,215,789	1,857,704	1,425,043	2,018,686	1,527,005
Ceará	961,024	997,247	1,238,161	882,686	1,365,152	962,850	1,373,670	1,060,428	1,762,636	1,395,348	1,924,702	1,524,412
Santa Catarina	896,413	914,801	1,050,006	906,020	1,203,344	1,016,386	1,332,895	1,152,167	1,537,172	1,337,262	1,654,723	1,428,137
Goiás	672,850	750,892	890,022	642,006	1,003,452	745,015	1,134,785	866,126	1,391,792	1,091,993	1,574,718	1,167,010
Pará	512,897	536,386	596,838	370,753	682,442	472,040	753,339	550,960	975,789	710,338	1,037,099	792,758
Paraíba	623,736	643,615	630,584	476,069	751,582	549,689	834,429	640,089	964,111	746,132	1,012,967	768,566
Maranhão	329,911	350,580	470,731	351,850	628,642	459,205	675,393	465,740	914,744	697,386	1,077,915	758,306
Espírito Santo	424,429	452,687	494,947	352,239	556,019	412,386	577,474	449,000	670,595	560,979	727,735	612,740
Piauí	336,329	330,636	458,922	349,083	562,253	416,131	598,187	441,238	700,660	562,795	755,544	598,253
Rio Grande do Norte	382,078	396,443	442,516	342,401	515,530	402,026	565,625	445,630	654,090	525,526	719,213	564,932
Alagoas	242,593	251,217	274,933	208,652	332,242	251,824	376,318	292,325	475,670	380,094	520,294	412,086
Mato Grosso	325,337	339,088	370,843	271,835	491,870	369,962	579,728	418,328	769,005	571,774	372,332	273,931
Mato Grosso do Sul	—	—	—	—	—	—	—	—	—	—	523,059	378,876
Sergipe	214,962	221,500	252,505	167,677	234,259	189,846	270,234	221,404	317,715	261,857	352,650	285,667
Amazonas	178,234	178,234	265,281	122,162	234,250	131,232	276,523	173,663	330,264	238,901	389,325	281,399
Rondônia	14,273	14,916	15,734	8,744	20,783	12,521	32,699	26,296	54,691	40,777	93,920	74,928
Acre	24,071	24,295	40,104	29,713	39,937	—	58,318	46,691	72,812	56,638	92,795	70,270
Amapá	16,262	17,383	21,423	15,246	24,313	15,889	29,619	20,837	39,908	28,312	44,229	33,941
Roraima	6,092	6,452	7,788	4,907	7,659	6,015	12,323	8,185	18,101	12,543	27,414	19,030
D.F. (Brasília)	91,180	107,125	—	—	166,255	—	—	—	—	—	—	—
Iguaçu	—	—	—	—	—	—	—	—	—	—	—	—
Ponta Porã	—	—	—	—	—	—	—	—	—	—	—	—
Fernando de Noronha	131	131	—	—	—	—	—	—	—	—	—	—

Sources: AN 1956, pp. 468–469; AN 1979, pp. 293–294.

Table XXII-4. Rulers of Brazil, 1549-1889

From	To	Governors-General (1549-1714)
1- 7-1549	5- 1-1553	Tomé de Sousa
5- 1-1553	7-23 1556	Dom Duarte da Costa
7-23-1556	3- 7 1570	Mem de Sá
3- 7-1570	12-10 1572	Luis de Brito e Almeida Antônio de Salema
12-10-1572	4-12-1577	Luís de Brito e Almeida
4-12-1577	6-17 1580	Lourenço da Veiga
6-17-1580	5- 9 1583	Cosme Rangel
5- 9-1583	5- 9 1587	Manuel Telles Barreto
5- 9-1587	6- 9 1591	Dom Antônio Barreiros Cristóvão de Barros
6- 9-1591	4- 1 1602	Dom Francisco de Sousa
4- 1-1602	8-22 1608	Diogo Botelho
8-22-1608	8-22 1612	Diogo de Meneses e Sequeira
8-22-1612	1- 1 1617	Gaspar de Sousa
1- 1-1617	10-12 1621	Dom Luís de Sousa
10-12-1621	7-26 1624	Diogo de Mendonça Furtado
7-26-1624	9-24 1624	Matias de Albuquerque
9-24-1624	12- 3 1624	Francisco Nunes Marinho d'Eca
12- 3-1624	12-28 1626	Dom Francisco de Moura Rolim
12-28-1626	12-11 1635	Diogo Luis de Oliveira
12-11-1635	1-23-1639	Dom Pedro da Silva de S. Paio
1-23-1639	10-21 1639	Dom Fernando Mascarenhas, Count of Tôrre
10-21-1639	5-26 1640	Dom Vasco Mascarenhas, Count of Óbidos
5-26-1640	4-16 1641	Dom Jorge Mascarenhas, Marquis of Montalvão, First Viceroy of Brazil
4-16-1641	7-14 1642	Bishop Dom Pedro da Silva de S. Paio Luís Barbalho Bezerra High Steward Lourenço Brito Correia
7-14-1642	12-26 1647	Antônio Teles da Silva
12-26-1647	3-10 1650	Antônio Teles de Meneses, Count of Vila Pouca de Aguilar
3-10-1650	12-14 1654	General João Rodrigues de Vasconcellos e Sousa, Count of Castello-Melhor
12-14-1654	6-20 1657	Dom Jerônimo de Ataide, Count of Atouguia
6-20-1657	7-21 1663	General Francisco Barreto
7-21-1663	6-13 1667	Dom Vasco Mascarenhas, Count of Óbidos, Second Viceroy of Brazil
6-13-1667	5- 8 1671	Alexandre de Sousa Freire
5- 8-1671	11-26 1675	Afonso Furtado de Castro de Mendonca, Viscount of Barbacena
11-26-1675	3-15 1678	Judge Agostinho de Azevedo Monteiro Álvaro de Azevedo Antônio Guedes Brito
3-15-1678	5-23 1682	Roque da Costa Barreto
5-23-1682	6- 4 1684	Antônio de Sousa de Meneses
6- 4-1684	6- 4 1687	Dom Antônio Luís de Sousa Telo Meneses, Marquis of Minas
6- 4-1687	10-24 1688	Matias da Cunha
10-24-1688	10- 8 1690	Dom Fr. Manual da Ressureição
10- 8-1690	5-22 1694	Antônio Luiz Gonçalves da Câmara Coutinho
5-22-1694	7- 3 1702	Dom João Lencastro
7- 3-1702	9- 8 1708	Dom Rodrigo da Costa
9- 8-1708	5- 3 1710	Luís César de Meneses
5- 3-1710	10-14 1711	Dom Lourenço de Almara
10-14-1711	6-11 1714	Pedro de Vasconcellos de Sousa

Table XXII-4 (continued)

From	To	Viceroys (1714-1808)
11-14-1714	8-21-1718	Dom Pedro Antônio de Noronha Abuquerque e Sousa, Marquis of Angeja
8-21-1718	10-13-1719	Dom Sancho de Faro e Sousa, Count of Vimeiro
10-14-1719	11-23-1720	Dom Sebastião Monteiro da Vide
		Judge Caetano de Brito e Figueiredo
		João de Araújo e Azevedo
11-23-1720	5-11-1735	Vasco Fernandes César de Meneses, Count of Sabugosa
5-11-1735	12-17-1749	André de Melo e Castro, Count of Galveias
12-17-1749	8-17-1754	Dom Luiz Pedro Peregrino de Carvalho Meneses e Ataide, Count of Atouguia
8-17-1754	12-23-1755	Archbishop Dom José Botelho de Matos
		Manuel Antônio da Cunha Soto Maior
		Coronel Lourenço Monteiro
12-23-1755	1- 9-1760	Dom Marcos de Noronha, 6th Count of Arcos
1- 9-1760	7- 4-1760	Dom Antônio d'Almeida Soares e Portugal, 3rd Count of Avintes and 1st Count of Lavradio
7- 4-1760	6-27-1763	Tomás Rubi de Barros Barreto, Chancellor
		José Carvalho de Andrada, Chancellor
		Coronel Gonçalo Xavier de Brito e Alvim
		Dom Frei Manuel de Santa Inés
6-27-1763	8-31-1767	Dom Antônio Alvares da Cunha, Count of Cunha
11-17-1767	11- 4-1769	Dom Antônio Rolim de Moura, Count of Azambuja
11- 4-1769	4-30-1778	Dom Luís de Almeida Portugal Soares de Alarcão Eça e Melo Silva e Mascarenhas, Second Marquis of Lavradio
4-30-1778	5- 9-1790	Luiz de Vasconcellos e Souza
5- 9-1790	10-14-1801	Dom José Luiz de Castro, 2nd Count of Rezende
10-14-1801	10-14-1806	Dom Fernando José de Portugal e Castro, Count and Marquis of Aguiar
10-14-1806	1-22-1808	Dom Marcos de Noronha e Brito, 8th Count of Arcos

		State of Brazil in the Kingdom of Portugal and Algarve (1808-1815)
1-22-1808	3-20-1815	Dom João, Prince of Brazil

		United Kingdom of Portugal and of Brazil and Algarve (1815-1821)
12-15-1815	4-26-1821	Dom João, Prince Regent
3-20-1816	4-26-1821	Dom João VI, King of the United Kingdom of Portugal and of Brazil and Algarve

		Kingdom of Brazil (1821-1822)
4-26-1821	9- 7-1822	Dom Pedro, Prince Royal, Regent of the Kingdom of Brazil

		First Empire of Brazil (1822-1831)
9- 7-1822	4- 7-1831	Dom Pedro I, Emperor of Brazil

		Second Empire of Brazil (1831-1889)
4- 7-1831	6-17-1831	José Joaquim Carneiro de Campos, Senator and Marquis of Caravelas
		Nicolau Pereira de Campos Vergueiro, Senator
		General Francisco Lima e Silva
6-17-1831	10-12-1835	José da Costa Carvalho, Deputy, later Viscount and Marquis of Monte Alegre
		João Bráulio Muniz, Deputy
		Francisco Lima e Silva, General
10-12-1835	9-19-1837	Padre Diogo Antônio Feijó
9-19-1837	7-23-1840	Pedro de Araújo Lima, later Viscount and Marquis of Olinda
7-23-1840	3-25-1871	Dom Pedro II, Emperor of Brazil, declared of age
8-25-1871	3-30-1872	The Imperial Princess, Dona Isabel
3-31-1872	3-25-1876	Dom Pedro II, Emperor of Brazil
3-26-1876	9-26-1877	The Imperial Princess, Dona Isabel
9-27-1877	6-29-1888	Dom Pedro II, Emperor of Brazil
6-30-1888	8-22-1888	The Imperial Princess, Dona Isabel
8-23-1888	11-15-1889	Dom Pedro II, Emperor of Brazil

Source: Brazil, 1966, pp. 17-22.

Table XXII-5. Holders of the Office of President and Vice-President of Brazil and the Numbers of Votes Obtained as Candidates For These Offices, 11-15-1889/3-15-1979

Term Served From	Term Served To	President	Votes Received	Vice President	Votes Received
11-15-1889	11-23-1891	Manuel Deodoro da Fonseca	-	Floriano Peixoto	-
11-23-1891	11-15-1894	Floriano Peixoto	-	---	-
11-15-1894	11-10-1896	Prudente José de Morais Barros	276,583	Manuel Vitorino Pereira	249,638
11-10-1896	3-4-1897	Manuel Vitorino Pereiro	-	---	-
3-4-1897	11-15-1898	Prudente José de Morais Barros	-	Manuel Vitorina Pereira	-
11-15-1898	10-17-1900	Manuel Ferraz de Campos Salles	420,286	Francisco de Assis Rosa e Silva	412,074
10-17-1900	11-8-1900	Francisco de Assis Rosa e Silva	-	---	-
11-8-1900	12-15-1902	Manuel Ferraz de Campos Salles	-	Francisco de Assis Rosa e Silva	563,734
12-15-1902	11-15-1906	Francisco de Paula Rodrigues Alves	592,039	Francisco Silviano de Almeida Brandão	652,247
				Afonso Augusto Moreira Pena	272,529
11-15-1906	6-14-1909	Afonso Augusto Moreira Pena	288,185	Nilo Peçanha	-
6-14-1909	11-15-1910	Nilo Peçanha	-	---	-
11-15-1910	11-15-1914	Hermes Rodrigues da Fonseca	403,867	Venceslau Brás Pereira Gomes	406,012
11-15-1914	9-8-1917	Venceslau Brás Pereira Gomes	532,107	Urbano Santos da Costa Araújo	556,127
9-8-1917	10-9-1917	Urbano Santos da Costa Araújo	-	---	-
10-9-1917	11-15-1918	Venceslau Brás Pereira Gomes	-	Urbano Santos de Costa Araújo	-
---	---	Francisco de Paulo Rodrigues Alves	386,467	Delfim Moreira da Costa Ribeiro	382,491
11-15-1918	7-28-1919	Delfim Moreira da Costa Ribeiro	-	---	-
7-28-1919	11-15-1922	Epitácio da Silva Pessoa	386,373	Delfim Moreira da Costa Ribeiro	191,842
11-15-1922	11-15-1926	Artur da Silva Bernardes	466,877	Urbano Santos da Costa Araújo	477,595
				Estácio de Albuquerque Coimbra	303,496
11-15-1926	10-24-1930	Washington Luís Pereira de Sousa	688,528	Fernando de Melo Viana	685,754
---	---	Júlio Prestes de Albuquerque	1,091,709	Vital Henrique Batista Soares	1,079,360
10-24-1930	11-3-1930	Augusto Tasso Fragosa	-	---	-
11-3-1930	10-29-1945	Getúlio Dorneles Vargas	-	---	-
10-29-1945	1-31-1946	José Linhares	-	---	-
1-31-1946	1-31-1951	Eurico Gaspar Dutra	3,251,507	Nereu Ramos	-
1-31-1951	8-24-1954	Getúlio Dorneles Vargas	3,849,040	João Café Filho	2,520,790
8-24-1954	11-9-1955	João Café Filho	-	---	-
11-9-1955	11-11-1955	Carlos Coimbra da Luz	-	---	-
11-11-1955	1-31-1956	Nereu de Oliveira Ramos	-	---	-
1-31-1956	8-5-1960	Juscelino Kubitschek de Oliveira	3,077,411	João Belchoir Marques Goulart	3,591,409
8-5-1960	8-11-1960	Ranieri Mazzilli	-	---	-
8-11-1960	1-31-1961	Juscelino Kubitschek de Oliveira	-	---	-
1-31-1961	8-25-1961	Jânio da Silva Quadros	5,636,623	João Belchoir Marques Goulart	4,547,010
8-25-1961	9-7-1961	Ranieri Mazzilli	-	---	-
9-7-1961	4-21-1963	João Belchoir Marques Goulart	-	---	-
4-21-1963	4-29-1963	Ranieri Mazzilli	-	---	-
4-29-1963	4-1-1964	João Belchoir Marques Goulart	-	---	-
4-1-1964	4-15-1964	Ranieri Mazzilli	-	---	-
4-15-1964	3-15-1967	Humberto de Alencar Castello Branco	-	José Maria Alkmim	-
3-15-1967	10-30-1969	Arthur da Costa e Silva	-	Pedro Aleixo	-
10-30-1969	3-15-1974	Emílio Garrastazu Médici	-	Augusto Hamann Rademaker Grünewald	-
3-15-1974	3-15-1979	Ernesto Geisel	-	Adalberto Pereira dos Santos	-
3-15-1979		João Baptista de Oliveira Figueiredo	-	Antônio Aureliano Chaves de Mendonça	-

Sources: Brazil, 1966, pp. 31-32; AN 1979, p. 295.

Chapter XXIII. Banking, Finance, Insurance, Money Supply and Exchange Rates

Table XXIII-1 reports the numbers of banking and financial institutions in Brazil from 1954 to 1978. Data originated with the Banco Central do Brasil, the Emprêsa Pública Caixa Econômica Federal, the Conselho Superior das Caixas Econômicas Federais, and the Serviço de Estatística Economia e Financeira. By 1972 in addition to the Banco do Brasil, in which the federal government owned a majority of the stock, three other federally-owned banks had been created: the Banco do Nordeste (BNB) in 1952; the Banco da Amazônia, S.A. (BASA), in 1966; and the Banco de Roraíma in 1972. The bank totals on the table include small branch offices (pôstos de serviços). The numbers of branches of the Banco do Brasil do not include that bank's overseas branches. Credit companies included investment societies (sociedades de investimento). According to informants in the American consulate in Rio de Janeiro, a sociedade corretora and a sociedade distribuidora are both brokerage organizations, but the latter handles a greater diversity of paper. When numbers for a given year varied among the different sources figures were taken from the latest source.

Table XXIII-2 describes the money supply, gold reserves, transactions, and accounts of banks and of the federal savings institutions, and the national check flows from 1822 to 1978. The data were originated by the Caixa Economica Federal, the Conselho Superior das Caixas Econômicas Federais, the Emprêsa Pública Caixa Econômica Federal, the Contadoria Geral da República, the Serviço de Estatística Econômica e Financeiras, the Superintendência da Moeda e Crédito, the Centro de Informações Econômico-Fiscais and Caixa de Amortização (both of the Banco do Brasil), and the Conselho Técnico de Economia e Finanças. All figures on the table are for December 31 of the year in question except where noted in the text. The category Official Banks includes federal, state, and development banks. The Serviço de Estatística Economia e Financeira (SEEF) calculated banking figures differently from the Banco do Brasil. Because the Banco's figures did not cover the years and the areas that the SEEF figures did, the latter were used on this table. All Loans included loans in current accounts, mortgages, and discounted paper (stocks and bonds). All Deposits included demand, short-term, and middle-term deposits, although the sources did not specify the length of terms. On the table Gold Reserve figures were rounded to conform to the year-end totals. The Money Supply section may be read this way: Money Issued (-) Savings (=) Money in Circulation (+) Money on Deposit (=) the Money Supply. The sources specify that from 1949 to 1978 Gold Reserves included both monetary and exchange reserves. The sources do not specify the makeup of the pre-1949 Gold Reserves. The makeup of the "Other Credits, Properties, Securities" category and of the "Other Demand Accounts, Special Obligations" category, both of which were reported only for the period 1968-76, was not specified thereby making it impossible to classify the pre-1968 figures on this same basis. For 1949, 1950, and 1951 both total Loans and Loans of the Banco do Brasil included data for foreign correspondent banks of the Exchange Branch of the Banco do Brasil. For these same years both total Deposits and Deposits of the Banco do Brasil included accounts of the Exchange Branch of the Banco do Brasil plus obligatory deposits required of the Banco do Brasil and foreign banks by Decree No. 24,038 of March 26, 1934. For 1952, 1953, and 1954 the Money Issued category on the table does not include Cr$ 2 million issued by the Caixa de Estabilização, which became extinct in 1955. For 1953 the Federal Savings Banks Balance total incorporated only the first semester for the state of Mato Grosso, and for 1953, 1954, and 1955 this balance excluded stocks and bonds as well as compensatory accounts. For 1960 Federal Savings Banks Loans and Deposits were as of June 30, 1960, for Espírito Santo Rio de Janeiro and Mato Grosso, and as of December 31, 1959, for Santa Catarina. For 1962 Federal Savings Banks Loans for Rio de Janeiro, Santa Catarina, and Mato Grosso were for the first semester only.

For 1963 Federal Savings Banks Loans for Mato Grosso and the Distrito Federal were for the first semester only as were the Deposits for Maranhão, Alagoas, and the Distrito Federal. For 1966 Federal Savings Banks Loans and Deposits for Espírito Santo were missing. For 1968 the source (AN 1969, page 438) reported Federal Savings Banks Loans and Deposits in new cruzeiro units. These should have been reported in thousand new cruzeiro units. For the period 1968 to 1976 all figures reported were for domestic banks only and did not include figures for foreign banks. For 1975, 1976, and 1977 savings to monetary authorities (these were governmental) had already been subtracted from Money Issued before Savings (these were public) were reported. For 1977 and 1978 the accounting systems used by the sources were changed thereby destroying continuity with earlier figures.

Table XXIII-3 reports the numbers of cruzeiros required to purchase one unit of a foreign currency from 1824 to 1978. Data origins include the Banco do Brasil's Relatórios, 1900-1927, Werner Baer, 1965, and the Câmara Sindical de Bôlsas de Valores of Rio de Janeiro. Unless otherwise specified all quotations for the period 1963 to 1978 were annual averages on the free market. The official rate for United States dollars underwent an adjustment within the year 1953 so that the 25.82 rate for 1954 actually applied to the later months of 1953 as well. Similar intrayear dollar adjustments also took place in 1954, 1957, and 1958. Pound sterling intrayear adjustments were made in 1953, 1954, 1955, and 1957; and in 1958 two intrayear adjustments were made. For 1959, 1960, and 1961 the source, AN 1962, page 134, confused the Uruguayan and Swiss rates but these are corrected on this table. For 1965 the sources rounded the rates to whole numbers. Beginning in 1966 the cruzeiro rates were reported in new cruzeiros (NCr$), worth 1,000 old cruzeiros. For 1966 the Italian lira is reported on the table as .00 new cruzeiros. This currency was actually valued at 4.00 old cruzeiros but could not be reported at 1/1,000th of this value.

Table XXIII-1. Numbers and Types of Brazil's Banking and Financial Institutions, 1938-78

	1938	1939	1940	1941	1942	1943	1944	1945	1946	1947	1948
Banks/Banking Houses											
Main Banks	261	277	354	512	548	625	663	509	477	444	426
Branches	678	741	1,006	1,134	1,380	1,556	1,796	1,565	1,634	1,783	1,855
Federal Banks	1	1	1	1	1	1	1	1	1	1	1
Bank of Brazil	1	1	1	1	1	1	1	1	1	1	1
Branches	-	-	-	-	-	-	-	-	-	-	-
Other	-	-	-	-	-	-	-	-	-	-	-
State Banks	-	-	-	-	-	-	-	-	-	-	-
Branches	-	-	-	-	-	-	-	-	-	-	-
Private Banks	-	-	-	-	-	-	-	-	-	-	-
Branches	-	-	-	-	-	-	-	-	-	-	-
Foreign Banks	⎤79	⎤78	⎤80	⎤80	⎤80	⎤44	⎤39	⎤39	⎤36	⎤42	⎤42
Branches	⎦	⎦	⎦	⎦	⎦	⎦	⎦	⎦	⎦	⎦	⎦
Federal Savings Banks	-	-	-	-	-	-	-	-	-	-	-
Branches	-	-	-	-	-	-	-	-	-	-	-
Other Financial Institutions	-	-	-	-	-	-	-	-	-	-	-

	1949	1950	1951	1952	1953	1954	1955	1956	1957	1958	1959
Banks/Banking Houses											
Main Banks	418	413	405	408	394	384	366	360	357	345	343
Branches	2,012	2,183	2,280	2,619	2,909	2,909	3,672	3,897	4,271	4,512	4,792
Federal Banks	1	1	1	2	2	2	2	2	2	2	2
Bank of Brazil	1	1	1	1	1	1	1	1	1	1	1
Branches	-	-	-	-	-	-	-	-	-	-	-
Other	-	-	-	-	-	-	-	-	-	-	-
State Banks	-	-	-	-	-	-	-	-	-	-	-
Branches	-	-	-	-	-	-	-	-	-	-	-
Private Banks	-	-	-	-	-	-	-	-	-	-	-
Branches	-	-	-	-	-	-	-	-	-	-	-
Foreign Banks	⎤42	⎤42	⎤43	⎤43	⎤44	⎤37	⎤35	⎤35	⎤35	⎤36	⎤39
Branches	⎦	⎦	⎦	⎦	⎦	⎦	⎦	⎦	⎦	⎦	⎦
Federal Savings Banks	-	-	1	1	1	1	1	1	1	1	1
Branches	-	-	378	416	429	448	455	459	467	478	483
Other Financial Institutions	-	-	-	-	-	-	-	-	-	-	-

	1960	1961	1962	1963	1964	1965	1966	1967	1968	1969
Banks/Banking Houses										
Main Banks	338	332	332	326	328	320	297	249	217	192
Branches	5,010	4,949	5,561	5,967	6,389	6,789	7,110	7,357	7,587	7,656
Federal Banks	2	2	2	2	2	2	3	3	3	3
Bank of Brazil	1	1	1	1	1	1	1	1	1	1
Branches	-	-	-	-	-	-	-	-	661	684
Other	-	-	-	-	-	-	-	-	-	-
State Banks	-	-	-	-	-	-	-	-	-	-
Branches	-	-	-	-	-	-	-	-	-	-
Private Banks	-	-	-	-	-	-	-	-	-	-
Branches	-	-	-	-	-	-	-	-	-	-
Foreign Banks	⎤41	⎤43	⎤44	⎤44	⎤44	⎤45	⎤46	⎤42	⎤42	⎤42
Branches	⎦	⎦	⎦	⎦	⎦	⎦	⎦	⎦	⎦	⎦
Federal Savings Banks	1	1	1	1	1	1	1	1	1	1
Branches	526	561	595	595	595	595	645	517	534	539
Other Financial Institutions	-	-	-	-	-	-	-	-	-	-

	1970	1971	1972	1973	1974	1975	1976	1977	1978
Banks/Banking Houses									
Main Banks	172	145	128	115	109	106	106	107	107
Branches	7,682	7,679	7,903	7,931	8,320	8,544	8,895	9,722	10,222
Federal Banks	3	3	4	4	4	4	4	4	4
Bank of Brazil	1	1	1	1	1	1	1	1	1
Branches	699	730	781	793	969	962	1,064	1,227	1,235
Other	2	2	3	3	3	3	3	3	3
Branches	135	136	140	141	149	148	151	154	228
State Banks	25	25	24	24	24	24	23	23	23
Branches	1,307	1,315	1,343	1,457	1,673	1,745	1,865	1,992	2,176
Private Banks	144	117	92	79	72	69	69	70	68
Branches	5,541	5,498	5,605	5,506	5,495	5,655	5,779	6,312	6,546
Foreign Banks	-	-	8	8	9	9	10	10	12
Branches	-	-	34	34	34	34	36	37	37
Federal Savings Banks	1	1	1	1	1	1	1	1	1
Branches	528	532	522	608	609	610	609	609	736
Other Financial Institutions	-	-	1,753	1,728	1,702	1,667	1,686	1,642	1,570
State Savings Banks	-	-	5	5	5	5	5	5	5
Investment Banks	-	-	44	45	41	40	39	39	39
Finance/Investment Companies	-	-	157	152	150	142	135	126	119
Federal Development Banks	-	-	3	3	3	3	3	3	3
State Development Banks	-	-	10	10	11	12	12	13	13
Savings/Loan Associations	-	-	34	36	36	36	36	36	36
Real Estate Credit Societies	-	-	46	44	46	42	40	40	40
Brokerage Firms (distribuidoras)	-	-	568	569	567	552	527	509	477
Brokerage Houses (corretoras)	-	-	417	414	396	380	362	327	280
Stock Exchange	-	-	16	16	17	16	15	15	12
Insurance Companies	-	-	126	110	100	98	96	96	95
Credit Cooperatives	-	-	327	324	329	334	349	360	367
Other	-	-	-	-	-	7	67	73	74

Sources: AN 1952, p. 405; AN 1953, p. 374; AN 1955, p. 406; AN 1956, pp. 216 & 226; AN 1957, pp. 200 & 210; AN 1959, p. 226; AN 1960, p. 171; AN 1961, pp. 190 & 207; AN 1962, pp. 136 & 149; AN 1964, pp. 228 & 248; AN 1965, p. 292; AN 1967, pp. 321 & 346; AN 1968, pp. 369 & 398; AN 1969, pp. 404-438; AN 1970, pp. 376, 450 & 489; AN 1972, pp. 365, 449 & 488; AN 1976, pp. 398, 404, 410, 412, 415-416, 420 & 443-444; AN 1977, p. 756; AN 1978, p. 802; AN 1978, p. 788.

Table XXIII-2. Brazilian Money Supply, Gold Reserves, and Accounts and Transactions of Banking and Financial Institutions, 1822-1978

	1822	1823	1824	1825	1826	1827	1828	1829	1830	1831	1832	1833
Money Supply (Cr$ 000)												
Money Issued	9,171	9,994	11,391	11,941	13,391	21,575	21,356	20,507	20,350	20,350	20,350	20,350

	1834	1835	1836	1837	1838	1839	1840	1841	1842	1843	1844	1845
Money Supply (Cr$ 000)												
Money Issued	20,350	30,703	30,703	30,703	39,476	39,476	39,531	40,496	44,015	46,754	48,593	51,023

	1846	1847	1848	1849	1850	1851	1852	1853	1854	1855	1856	1857
Money Supply (Cr$ 000)												
Money Issued	51,618	50,281	49,317	48,679	48,032	47,997	50,315	52,262	62,224	67,756	85,821	95,216

	1858	1859	1860	1861	1862	1863	1864	1865	1866	1867	1868
Money Supply (Cr$ 000)											
Money Issued	92,569	95,837	87,990	82,012	79,064	81,723	99,544	100,649	112,864	117,161	124,686

	1869	1870	1871	1872	1873	1874	1875	1876	1877	1878
Money Supply (Cr$ 000)										
Money Issued	183,225	192,527	191,806	188,807	185,011	183,095	181,869	179,423	179,348	208,934

	1879	1880	1881	1882	1883	1884	1885	1886	1887	1888
Money Supply (Cr$ 000)										
Money Issued	216,913	215,678	212,285	212,240	210,997	209,626	207,861	213,583	202,292	205,288

	1889	1890	1891	1892	1893	1894	1895	1896	1897	1898	1899	1900	1901	1902	1903
Money Supply (Cr$ 000000)															
Money Issued	211	298	448	524	632	712	678	712	780	780	734	700	680	676	675

	1904	1905	1906	1907	1908	1909	1910	1911	1912	1913	1914	1915	1916
Money Supply (Cr$ 000000)													
Money Issued	674	669	702	744	724	854	925	982	1,004	897	980	1,077	1,217
Savings	-	-	-	-	-	-	-	-	201	214	312	341	340
Banks/Banking Houses													
Balance End of Year (Cr$ 000000)	-	-	-	-	-	-	-	-	2,726	3,230	3,400	3,609	4,032
Loans	-	-	-	-	-	-	-	-	634	731	654	632	794
Deposits	-	-	-	-	-	-	-	-	701	728	650	713	925

	1917	1918	1919	1920	1921	1922	1923	1924	1925	1926	1927
Money Supply (Cr$ 000000)											
Money Issued	1,484	1,700	1,748	1,848	2,098	2,366	2,649	2,964	2,707	2,589	3,005
Savings	387	492	571	839	859	705	703	688	682	626	819
Banks/Banking Houses											
Balance End of Year (Cr$ 000000)	4,528	5,912	8,110	9,792	11,303	12,770	14,616	16,089	15,898	16,585	20,735
Loans	966	1,367	1,800	2,102	2,900	3,093	3,873	4,037	3,865	3,765	4,955
Deposits	1,066	1,559	1,908	2,220	3,075	3,425	3,609	3,830	3,661	3,790	4,930

	1928	1929	1930	1931	1932	1933	1934	1935	1936	1937	1938
Money Supply (Cr$ 000000)											
Money Issued	3,379	3,394	2,842	2,942	3,238	3,037	3,157	3,612	4,050	4,550	4,825
Savings	1,045	1,269	896	925	1,029	801	775	760	761	1,064	1,246
Money In Circulation	-	-	-	-	-	-	-	-	-	-	-
Money on Deposit	-	-	-	-	-	-	-	-	-	-	-
Gold Reserves (kilograms)											
Beginning of Year	-	-	-	-	-	-	325	6,683	14,846	21,793	28,120
Domestic Purchases	-	-	-	-	-	325	6,358	8,163	6,947	6,327	6,739
Foreign Purchases	-	-	-	-	-	-	-	-	-	-	-
Foreign Sales/Deliveries	-	-	-	-	-	-	-	-	-	-	6,046
Banks/Banking Houses											
Balance End of Year (Cr$ 000000)	24,800	26,328	26,422	26,394	28,721	28,989	30,080	31,981	33,169	35,122	39,873
Loans	6,009	6,076	5,961	5,893	6,697	6,880	7,406	7,753	7,718	8,599	9,942
Official Banks	-	-	-	-	-	-	-	-	-	-	-
Bank of Brazil	-	-	-	-	-	-	-	-	-	-	-
Private Banks	-	-	-	-	-	-	-	-	-	-	-
Foreign Banks	-	-	-	-	-	-	-	-	-	1,560	1,580
Other Credits, Property Securities	-	-	-	-	-	-	-	-	-	-	-
Official Banks	-	-	-	-	-	-	-	-	-	-	-
Bank of Brazil	-	-	-	-	-	-	-	-	-	-	-
Private Banks	-	-	-	-	-	-	-	-	-	-	-
Foreign Banks	-	-	-	-	-	-	-	-	-	-	-
Deposits	5,882	5,925	5,731	5,962	6,843	6,344	7,419	7,767	8,332	8,812	11,665
Official Banks	-	-	-	-	-	-	-	-	-	-	-
Bank of Brazil	-	-	-	-	-	-	-	-	-	-	-
Private Banks	-	-	-	-	-	-	-	-	-	-	-
Foreign Banks	-	-	-	-	-	-	-	-	-	1,757	1,912
Other Demand Accounts, Special Obligations	-	-	-	-	-	-	-	-	-	-	-
Official Banks	-	-	-	-	-	-	-	-	-	-	-
Bank of Brazil	-	-	-	-	-	-	-	-	-	-	-
Private Banks	-	-	-	-	-	-	-	-	-	-	-
Foreign Banks	-	-	-	-	-	-	-	-	-	-	-
Federal Savings Banks (Cr$ 000000)											
Balance End of Year	-	-	-	-	-	-	-	-	-	-	-
Loans	-	-	-	-	-	-	-	-	-	-	-
Deposits	-	-	-	-	-	-	-	-	1,790	1,559	1,339

427

Table XXIII-2 (continued)

	1939	1940	1941	1942	1943	1944	1945	1946	1947	1948
Money Supply (Cr$ 000000)								45,?52	47,067	50,239
Money Issued	4,971	5,185	6,647	8,238	10,981	14,462	17,535	20,494	20,399	21,696
Savings	1,117	1,091	1,337	2,108	2,439	2,800	3,214	3,674	3,517	3,962
Money in Circulation	-	-	-	-	-	-	-	16,820	16,882	17,734
Money on Deposit	-	-	-	-	-	-	-	28,942	30,185	32,505
Gold Reserves (kilograms)										
Beginning of Year	28,813	35,122	45,025	62,103	102,043	225,659	292,529	314,600	314,881	314,881
Domestic Purchases	7,856	8,221	7,321	7,125	4,951	4,546	2,965	557	-	37
Foreign Purchases	1,167	1,699	9,762	32,817	118,667	62,325	22,363	9,015	-	-
Foreign Sales/Deliveries	2,714	17	5	2	2	1	3,257	9,291	-	33,312
Banks/Banking Houses										
Balance End of Year (Cr$ 000000)	42,002	44,852	59,594	69,547	99,648	142,174	167,871	187,123	203,866	223,999
Loans	11,282	12,837	15,894	18,206	28,757	40,107	43,860	45,276	46,539	51,309
Official Banks	-	-	-	-	-	-	-	-	-	-
Bank of Brazil	-	-	-	-	-	-	-	-	14,525	16,234
Private Banks	-								-	-
Foreign Banks	1,728	-	-	-	-	-	-	-	3,377	3,111
Other Credits, Property, Securities	-	-	-	-	-	-	-	-	-	-
Official Banks	-	-	-	-	-	-	-	-	-	-
Bank of Brazil	-	-	-	-	-	-	-	-	-	-
Private Banks	-	-	-	-	-	-	-	-	-	-
Foreign Banks	-	-	-	-	-	-	-	-	-	-
Deposits	12,523	13,664	16,532	21,541	31,570	39,703	45,286	48,768	51,809	52,218
Official Banks	-	-	-	-	-	-	-	-	-	-
Bank of Brazil	-	-	-	-	-	-	-	-	17,136	19,140
Private Banks	-								-	-
Foreign Banks	2,138	-	-	-	-	-	-	-	4,005	4,345
Other Demand Accounts, Obligations	-	-	-	-	-	-	-	-	-	-
Official Banks	-	-	-	-	-	-	-	-	-	-
Bank of Brazil	-	-	-	-	-	-	-	-	-	-
Private Banks	-	-	-	-	-	-	-	-	-	-
Foreign Banks	-	-	-	-	-	-	-	-	-	-
Check Flows										
Numbers of Checks (000)	2,080	2,215	2,626	2,660	3,349	4,096	4,802	5,509	5,672	6,152
Values of Checks (000000)	34,331	35,444	47,577	57,392	87,673	114,142	129,850	165,816	184,272	204,128
Federal Savings Banks										
Balance End of Year (Cr$ 000000)	-	2,497	2,707	3,028	3,723	4,781	5,704	7,287	8,507	8,822
Loans	-	1,371	1,500	1,566	1,580	2,025	2,679	4,117	5,339	6,121
Deposits	-	2,349	2,530	2,843	3,524	4,447	5,306	6,765	7,898	7,997

	1949	1950	1951	1952	1953	1954	1955	1956
Money Supply (Cr$ 000000)	58,376	78,260	90,693	104,155	124,070	151,482	177,923	217,283
Money Issued	24,045	31,205	35,319	39,280	47,002	59,039	69,340	80,819
Savings	4,684	6,064	6,858	7,747	9,134	10,074	12,240	13,361
Money in Circulation	19,361	25,141	28,461	31,533	37,868	48,965	57,100	67,458
Money on Deposit	39,015	53,119	62,232	72,622	86,202	102,517	120,823	149,825
Gold Reserves (kilograms)								
Beginning of Year	281,606	282,035	282,858	283,707	284,545	285,282	286,023	286,681
Domestic Purchases	679	823	841	846	737	741	658	835
Foreign Purchases	-	-	265	17,950	166	209	395	647
Foreign Sales/Deliveries	250	-	257	17,958	166	209	395	644
Banks/Banking Houses								
Balance End of Year (Cr$ 000000)	246,948	308,488	365,867	489,078	601,642	772,709	868,508	1,008,508
Loans	61,974	87,455	105,624	58,117	159,287	203,373	224,115	286,332
Official Banks	-	-	-	-	-	-	-	-
Bank of Brazil	21,186	33,482	41,784	55,189	74,846	103,648	113,426	153,277
Private Banks	-	-	-	-	-	-	-	-
Foreign Banks	3,539	4,791	5,177	5,307	6,367	6,139	6,374	7,704
Other Credits, Property, Securities	-	-	-	-	-	-	-	-
Official Banks	-	-	-	-	-	-	-	-
Bank of Brazil	-	-	-	-	-	-	-	-
Private Banks	-	-	-	-	-	-	-	-
Foreign Banks	-	-	-	-	-	-	-	-
Deposits	64,026	84,800	104,258	128,161	146,098	177,089	209,950	260,193
Official Banks	-	-	-	-	-	-	-	-
Bank of Brazil	18,741	24,371	35,125	50,952	57,148	71,835	87,777	112,480
Private Banks	-	-	-	-	-	-	-	-
Foreign Banks	4,575	6,145	6,229	8,185	8,022	6,754	8,050	8,938
Other Demand Accounts, Special Obligations	-	-	-	-	-	-	-	-
Official Banks	-	-	-	-	-	-	-	-
Bank of Brazil	-	-	-	-	-	-	-	-
Private Banks	-	-	-	-	-	-	-	-
Foreign Banks	-	-	-	-	-	-	-	-
Check Flows								
Numbers of Checks (000)	7,053	8,147	9,732	10,689	11,929	14,403	16,440	20,789
Values of Checks (Cr$ 000000)	244,445	321,871	443,568	486,143	565,579	775,210	936,879	1,299,679
Federal Savings Banks								
Balance End of Year (Cr$ 000000)	9,976	11,362	13,380	14,971	17,820	20,397	24,615	27,614
Loans	6,978	8,096	9,436	10,767	12,639	14,870	18,633	22,042
Deposits	9,127	10,506	12,377	13,731	16,883	19,374	22,661	25,554

Table XXIII-2 (continued)

	1957	1958	1959	1960	1961	1962	1963
Money Supply Cr$ 000000)	290,939	353,138	500,572	692,032	1,041,842	1,698,874	2,792,183
Money Issued	96,575	119,814	154,621	206,140	313,858	508,780	888,768
Savings	15,298	20,083	27,596	36,786	58,084	111,737	204,943
Money in Circulation	81,277	99,731	127,025	169,354	255,774	397,043	683,825
Money on Deposit	209,662	253,407	373,547	522,678	786,068	1,301,831	2,108,358
Gold Reserves (kilograms)							
Beginning of Year	287,519	287,857	289,015	290,257	255,195	253,200	244,784
Domestic Purchases	342	1,158	1,242	1,246	1,496	674	–
Foreign Purchases	25,157	881	1,292	1,345	–	2,814	11,353
Foreign Sales/Deliveries	25,161	881	1,292	37,653	3,491	11,904	2,529
Banks/Banking Houses							
Balance End of Year (Cr$ 000000)	1,228,393	1,703,836	2,164,614	3,144,084	5,090,311	8,651,142	14,059,891
Loans	371,879	419,159	504,225	776,104	1,277,766	2,214,553	3,575,711
Official Banks	–	–	–	–	–	–	–
Bank of Brazil	204,945	217,928	231,553	385,686	765,118	1,424,126	2,329,748
Private Banks	–	–	–	–	–	–	–
Foreign Banks	8,734	11,678	14,912	20,167	24,343	34,309	57,827
Other Credits, Property, Securities	–	–	–	–	–	–	–
Official Banks	–	–	–	–	–	–	–
Bank of Brazil	–	–	–	–	–	–	–
Private Banks	–	–	–	∴	–	–	–
Foreign Banks	–	–	–	–	–	–	–
Deposits	348,076	377,831	529,610	753,826	1,183,433	2,195,303	3,447,994
Official Banks	–	–	–	–	–	–	–
Bank of Brazil	147,704	135,955	177,233	268,228	517,439	1,101,285	1,654,666
Private Banks	–	–	–	–	–	–	–
Foreign Banks	11,887	14,352	18,414	23,524	33,513	53,872	92,715
Other Demand Accounts, Special Obligations	–	–	–	–	–	–	–
Official Banks	–	–	–	–	–	–	–
Bank of Brazil	–	–	–	–	–	–	–
Private Banks	–	–	–	–	–	–	–
Foreign Banks	–	–	–	–	–	–	–
Check Flows							
Numbers of Checks (Cr$ 000)	24,544	30,310	34,857	44,780	59,191	78,465	97,591
Values of Checks (Cr$ 000000)	1,638,724	2,347,970	3,307,777	4,916,915	7,491,021	12,480,492	22,340,046
Federal Savings Banks							
Balance End of Year	33,672	39,301	44,752	54,524	72,194	112,361	173,426
Loans	25,583	31,419	34,649	40,634	48,185	72,308	108,443
Deposits	30,949	36,305	40,981	48,847	63,271	96,262	143,742

	1964	1965	1966	1967	1968	1969	1970	1971
Money Supply (Cr$ 000000)	5,190,709	9,104,056	10,470	14,931	21,382	28,350	35,920	47,160
Money Issued	1,483,765	2,174,781	2,741	3,458	4,970	6,213	7,638	9.498
Savings	327,986	444,879	398	514	890	823	918	943
Money in Circulation	1,155,779	1,729,902	2,343	2,944	4,080	5,390	6,720	8,555
Money on Deposit	4,034,930	7,374,154	8,127	11,987	17,302	22,960	29,200	38,605
Gold Reserves (kilograms)								
Beginning of Year	253,608	81,001	55,795	40,174	40,154	40,154	40,154	40,154
Domestic Purchases	–	595	–	2	–	–	–	–
Foreign Purchases	3,614	4,434	2,457	743	333	–	–	1,014
Foreign Sales/Deliveries	176,221	30,235	18,078	765	333	–	–	–
Banks/Banking Houses								
Balance End of Year (Cr$ 000000)	31,444,504	31,461,049	38,139	57,942	83,710	113,521	170,973	273,744
Loans	8,221,459	14,270,682	11,608	17,278	23,838	32,850	44,164	62,168
Official Banks	–	–	–	–	14,921	20,662	27,998	37,829
Bank of Brazil	5,936,233	4,379,689	6,411	8,654	10,227	13,726	18,434	25,263
Private Banks	–	–	–	–	8,917	12,188	16,166	24,339
Foreign Banks	96,924	185,350	180	238	–	–	–	–
Other Credits, Property, Securities	–	–	–	–	33,440	44,733	69,359	87,079
Official Banks	–	–	–	–	19,452	27,651	41,013	51,973
Bank of Brazil	–	–	–	–	13,184	19,822	29,108	31,633
Private Banks	–	–	–	–	13,988	17,082	28,346	32,106
Foreign Banks	–	–	–	–	–	–	–	–
Deposits	7,902,032	16,091,206	14,403	19,405	27,427	33,227	42,186	56,539
Official Banks	–	–	–	–	14,843	18,757	23,679	30,566
Bank of Brazil	4,684,096	6,075,530	7,334	8,415	10,339	13,097	16,263	21,336
Private Banks	–	–	–	–	12,584	14,470	18,489	25,973
Foreign Banks	158,231	256,524	276	343	–	–	–	–
Other Demand Accounts, Special Obligations	–	–	–	–	28,962	42,349	67,521	83,749
Official Banks	–	–	–	–	17868	26,937	41,063	52,944
Bank of Brazil	–	–	–	–	11,481	18,201	27,699	30,282
Private Banks	–	–	–	–	11,094	15,412	26,458	30,805
Foreign Banks	–	–	–	–	–	–	–	–
Check Flows								
Numbers of Checks (000)	120,766	140,520	165,779	178,617	230,014	265,544	316,998	380,070
Values of Checks (000000)	47,048,399	80,431,728	128,223	178,387	298,663	433,600	593,362	903,683
Federal Savings Banks								
Balance End of Year (Cr$ 000000)	510,993	–	1,866	–	–	–	–	–
Loans	148,608	–	496	771	1,398	1,966	3,112	4,803
Deposits	242,801	–	487	898	1,002	1,365	2,367	3,281

Table XXIII-2 (continued)

	1972	1973	1974	1975	1976	1977	1978
Money Supply (Cr$ 000000)	61,550	90,490	120,788	172,433	236,506	325,243	462,655
Money Issued	12,718	18,384	23,199	34,111	50,017	69,966	101,744
Savings	1,171	1,957	2,392	3,080	3,824	4,761	7,671
Money In Circulation	11,547	16,427	20,807	31,031	46,193	65,205	94,073
Money on Deposit	50,003	74,063	99,981	141,402	190,313	260,038	368,582
Gold Reserves (kilograms)							
Beginning of Year	41,168	41,253	41,274	41,274	41,274	41,274	47,130
Domestic Purchases	-	} 21	-	-	-	5,856	-
Foreign Purchases	85		-	-	-	-	-
Foreign Sales/Deliveries	-	-	-	-	-	-	-
Banks/Banking Houses							
Balance End of Year (Cr$ 000000)	449,626	767,727	1,888,776	3,213,390	5,294,969	-	-
Loans	84,964	119,709	190,673	303,573	476,976	-	-
Official Banks	49,716	71,506	122,546	200,524	328,045	-	-
Bank of Brazil	31,756	44,281	80,266	140,303	222,825	-	-
Private Banks	35,248	48,203	68,127	103,049	148,932	-	-
Foreign Banks	-	-	-	-	-	-	-
Other Credits, Property, Securities	119,374	204,609	1,019,722	1,474,037	2,341,955	-	-
Official Banks	68,230	92,883	876,170	1,228,848	2,030,907	-	-
Bank of Brazil	45,035	58,445	-	-	-	-	-
Private Banks	51,144	111,726	143,552	245,189	311,048	-	-
Foreign Banks	-	-	-	-	-	-	-
Deposits	75,052	104,329	197,892	277,903	375,840	-	-
Official Banks	36,657	52,868	132,440	182,205	234,967	-	-
Bank of Brazil	23,278	33,478	52,822	71,957	79,005	-	-
Private Banks	38,395	51,461	65,452	95,698	131,873	-	-
Foreign Banks	-	-	-	-	-	-	-
Other Demand Accounts, Special Obligations	122,104	210,015	999,941	1,478,879	2,414,467	-	-
Official Banks	73,022	100,060	852,988	1,225,651	2,081,919	-	-
Bank of Brazil	46,032	59,243	-	-	-	-	-
Private Banks	49,082	109,955	146,953	253,228	232,549	-	-
Foreign Banks	-	-	-	-	-	-	-
Check Flows							
Numbers of Checks (000)	432,361	505,777	575,851	618,574	803,167	-	-
Values of Checks (Cr$ 000000)	1,434,761	2,413,610	3,549,527	7,382,008	20,079,867	-	-
Federal Savings Banks							
Balance End of Year (Cr$ 000000)	-	-				-	-
Loans	7,255	11,672	21,080	43,022	115,561	-	-
Deposits	5,742	9,482	18,028	33,502	99,371	-	-

Sources: AN 1950, pp. 234, 382; AN 1952, pp. 266-267; AN 1953, pp. 258-259, 375;
AN 1956, pp. 216-220, 225-228, 515-516, 518, 524-525; AN 1957, pp. 185, 201-203, 214, 210-211;
AN 1960, pp. 140, 156-159, 171, 175; AN 1961, pp. 173-174,208,211; AN 1962, pp. 129, 136-139, 150, 152;
AN 1963, pp. 233-234, 249; AN 1964, pp. 224, 228-232, 245, 248-249; AN 1965, pp. 267, 271-275, 292-293;
AN 1966, pp. 258, 262, 266, 287-288; AN 1967, pp. 317, 321-324, 343, 346, 370-371, 398; AN 1968, p. 379;
AN 1969, pp. 400, 404-409, 432, 438; AN 1970, pp. 434, 441-445, 479; AN 1971, pp. 443, 452-455, 485, 489;
AN 1972, pp. 442, 450, 457-462, 484, 488; AN 1973, pp. 533, 538, 552; AN 1974, pp. 525, 545-547, 581, 585-586;
AN 1975, pp. 590-592, 603-604, 625; AN 1976, pp. 398-399, 404, 410, 412, 415-416, 420, 430, 443-444;
AN 1978, pp. 764, 777-779, 781, 802; AN 1979, p. 781.

Table XXIII-3. Exchange Rates: The Number of Cruzeiros Required to Purchase One Unit of Foreign Currency, 1824-1978

United Kingdom — Official Rate (Pound), 1824–1919

Year	Rate	Year	Rate	Year	Rate	Year	Rate
1824	4.97	1840	7.74	1856	8.71	1872	8.71
1825	4.63	1841	7.84	1857	9.10	1873	8.91
1826	4.97	1842	8.95	1858	9.39	1874	9.35
1827	6.81	1843	9.30	1859	9.57	1875	9.15
1828	7.73	1844	9.30	1860	9.30	1876	9.47
1829	9.75	1845	9.43	1861	9.39	1877	9.77
1830	10.52	1846	8.91	1862	9.06	1878	10.46
1831	9.60	1847	8.57	1863	8.81	1879	10.49
1832	6.83	1848	9.60	1864	8.97	1880	10.46
1833	6.42	1849	9.28	1865	9.60	1881	11.08
1834	6.25	1850	8.35	1866	9.90	1882	11.34
1835	6.61	1851	8.24	1867	10.70	1883	11.13
1836	6.24	1852	8.75	1868	14.12	1884	11.60
1837	8.12	1853	8.42	1869	12.76	1885	12.90
1838	8.38	1854	8.69	1870	10.61	1886	12.84
1839	7.59	1855	8.71	1871	9.99	1887	10.69

Year	Rate	Year	Rate
1888	9.51	1904	19.79
1889	9.08	1905	15.21
1890	10.63	1906	14.97
1891	16.10	1907	15.92
1892	19.95	1908	15.98
1893	20.70	1909	15.98
1894	23.78	1910	14.93
1895	24.15	1911	15.03
1896	26.48	1912	15.00
1897	31.09	1913	15.04
1898	33.39	1914	16.38
1899	32.27	1915	19.27
1900	32.27	1916	20.11
1901	21.30	1917	18.89
1902	20.16	1918	18.62
1903	20.08	1919	16.86

1920–1935

	1920	1921	1922	1923	1924	1925	1926	1927	1928	1929	1930	1931	1932	1933	1934	1935
United Kingdom Free Market (Pound)	23.17	28.55	33.99	44.97	40.71	–	–	–	–	39.49	33.96	41.10	49.40	53.76	44.55	85.10
Official Rate (Pound)	–	–	–	–	–	–	–	–	–	–	–	–	40.75	40.71	44.00	57.94
United States Free Market (Dollar)	–	–	–	–	–	–	–	–	–	–	–	–	–	–	9.24	17.37
Official Rate (Dollar)	–	–	–	–	–	–	–	–	–	–	–	–	–	–	–	11.80

1936–1951

	1936	1937	1938	1939	1940	1941	1942	1943	1944	1945	1946	1947	1948	1949	1950	1951
United Kingdom Free Market (Pound)	86.02	79.43	86.39	85.56	76.38	–	–	–	–	–	–	–	–	–	–	–
Official Rate (Pound)	57.58	56.80	–	75.18	62.15	79.86	79.58	79.58	79.32	78.90	78.28	75.41	75.42	69.68	52.42	52.42
United States Free Market (Dollar)	17.31	16.07	17.62	19.53	18.80	–	–	–	–	–	–	–	–	–	–	–
Official Rate (Dollar)	11.62	11.37	–	16.90	16.61	19.72	19.64	19.58	19.50	19.42	19.42	18.73	18.72	18.72	18.72	18.72
Belgium (Franc)	–	–	.60	.67	.68	–	–	–	–	–	.44	.43	.43	.41	.38	.38
Canada (Dollar)	–	–	17.55	18.36	18.29	18.26	17.92	17.78	18.61	18.37	18.40	18.13	18.40	18.13	16.95	18.16
Denmark (Krone)	–	–	3.90	3.95	3.85	–	–	3.97	3.93	3.90	3.90	3.70	3.90	3.70	2.74	2.74
France (Franc)	–	–	.51	.49	.42	.35	–	.44	.17	.16	.09	.07	.54	.07	.04	.05
Germany (Mark)	–	–	7.11	7.92	7.79	7.93	–	6.03	6.05	6.03	6.03	–	–	5.73	5.73	5.73
Italy (Lira)	–	–	.93	1.00	1.00	1.02	1.14	1.04	.85	.54	.04	.04	.04	.04	1.04	.03
Japan (Yen)	–	–	5.09	5.00	4.67	4.66	4.65	4.42	4.42	4.42	4.42	4.66	4.67	4.42	4.42	–
Netherlands (Florin)	–	–	9.68	10.03	10.54	–	–	–	10.48	10.51	10.48	6.91	7.06	6.78	4.91	4.92
Portugal (Escudo)	–	–	.82	.78	.75	.80	.81	.80	.79	.77	.76	.73	.76	.73	.66	.66
Sweden (Krone)	–	–	4.49	4.64	4.74	4.72	4.72	4.72	5.04	5.21	5.04	4.59	5.21	4.59	3.62	3.62
Switzerland (Franc)	–	–	4.05	4.32	4.49	4.70	4.67	4.67	4.56	4.40	4.38	4.37	4.38	4.37	4.37	4.35

431

Table XXIII-3 (continued)

			1952	1953	1954	1955	1956	1957	1958	1959	1960	1961	1962	1963	1964	1965
United Kingdom	Pound	Free Market	-	117.75	169.81	203.12	203.17	206.76	370.87	434.56	542.28	772.45	1060.58	1562.64	3625.03	5428.
		Official Rate	52.42	52.45	72.05	94.57	-	-	-	-	-	-	-	-	-	-
United States	Dollar	Free Market	-	43.32	62.18	73.54	73.59	75.67	130.06	159.83	189.90	278.66	390.52	577.65	1293.42	1904.
		Official Rate	18.72	18.72	25.82	33.82	-	-	-	-	-	-	-	-	-	-
Belgium	Franc		.38	.81	1.14	1.42	1.36	1.48	2.56	3.32	3.82	5.46	7.10	12.05	27.02	41.
Canada	Dollar		19.05	42.59	64.75	76.02	74.89	77.41	134.58	159.79	196.56	264.02	372.27	554.97	1286.63	1829.
Denmark	Krone		2.74	5.65	6.91	8.79	8.96	9.16	16.49	21.81	26.90	38.01	52.08	78.58	168.74	265.
France	Franc		.05	.12	.15	.20	.19	.20	.30	.32	38.66	58.77	84.20	114.80	289.06	384.
Germany	Mark		-	-	-	16.73	17.51	18.28	31.59	38.56	45.51	70.02	95.15	141.72	336.98	484.
Italy	Lira		.03	-	-	.11	.12	.12	.21	.25	.31	.44	.64	.94	2.06	3.
Japan	Yen		-	-	-	-	-	-	-	-	-	-	-	-	-	-
Netherlands	Florin		4.92	11.68	-	17.48	19.46	20.62	35.15	47.56	50.27	76.73	104.51	159.74	289.69	524.
Portugal	Escudo		.66	1.51	2.16	2.62	2.58	2.57	4.49	5.41	6.67	9.67	13.38	20.09	41.75	67.
Sweden	Krone		3.62	7.20	10.06	12.36	12.76	13.26	24.39	30.54	37.02	37.02	77.14	113.73	287.15	370.
Switzerland	Franc		4.36	9.92	14.23	17.68	17.22	17.58	28.63	35.60	44.05	63.31	85.53	136.48	311.78	462.

			1966	1967	1968	1969	1970	1971	1972	1973	1974	1975	1976	1977	1978
United Kingdom	Pound	Free Market	6.19	7.356	8.138	9.842	11.060	14.434	14.639	14.493	17.580	18.498	21.258	30.840	42.702
		Official Rate	-	-	-	-	-	-	-	-	-	-	-	-	-
United States	Dollar	Free Market	2.21	2.686	3.470	4.114	4.616	5.635	6.215	6.160	7.435	9.070	12.345	16.050	20.920
		Official Rate	-	-	-	-	-	-	-	-	-	-	-	-	-
Belgium	Franc		.04	.054	.068	.081	.092	.126	.141	.151	.207	.231	.346	.496	.728
Canada	Dollar		2.05	2.443	3.254	3.902	4.483	5.660	6.268	6.276	7.547	8.970	12.346	14.840	17.705
Denmark	Krone		.32	.382	.442	.555	.616	.802	.911	1.001	1.329	1.479	2.157	2.812	4.132
France	Franc		.45	.532	.687	.783	.827	1.444	1.655	1.926	1.687	2.042	2.501	3.444	5.022
Germany	Mark		.55	.673	.872	1.076	1.267	1.739	1.946	2.314	3.123	3.483	5.264	7.685	11.507
Italy	Lira		.00	.004	.006	.006	.013	.001	.011	.010	.016	.014	.014	.018	.025
Japan	Yen		-	-	.009	.011	.013	.018	.021	.022	.025	.030	.042	.067	.108
Netherlands	Florin		.61	.743	.920	1.122	1.276	1.741	1.930	2.214	2.996	3.399	5.053	7.105	10.654
Portugal	Escudo		.07	.095	.120	.144	.163	.212	.234	.245	.310	.339	.406	.411	.454
Sweden	Krone		.43	.521	.648	.780	.883	1.159	1.315	1.368	1.844	2.059	3.015	3.468	4.895
Switzerland	Franc		.51	.623	.811	.955	1.071	1.444	1.655	1.926	2.981	3.479	5.076	8.057	12.940

Sources: AN 1956, pp. 521, 545-46; Baer 1965, pp. 271-72; AN 1959, p. 199; AN 1960, p. 147; AN 1962, p. 134; AN 1965, p. 268; AN 1966, p. 259; AN 1967, p. 318; AN 1970, p. 435; AN 1972, p. 443; AN 1975, p. 583; AN 1977, p. 749; AN 1979, p. 781.

Chapter XXIV. Stocks, Insurance and Corporate Formation

Table XXIV-1 notes the volumes and types of transactions on Brazilian stock exchanges from 1938 to 1978. The data originated with the Banco do Brasil, the Bôlsas de Valores (stock markets) of Rio de Janeiro, Recife, Paraná, Vitória, and Santos, the Bôlsa Oficial de Valores (stock market) of São Paulo, and the Câmara Sindical dos Corretores of the Bôlsa de Fundos Públicos do Rio de Janeiro. All Private Securities figures included rights (direitos) as well, which conferred upon the purchaser the right to acquire new issues of a given stock. The total volume recorded for a stock market included securities sold in various ways, the most prevalent being in the common (comum) manner which made up nearly all sales. On the table, Government Securities and Private Securities categories included only common sales. The difference between the total volume of sales for a given stock market and all common sales (the latter equaled all Government Securities plus all Private Securities sold in that market) was made up of sales in the term, auction or judicial manner. The Government Securities category is made up of external debt securities and internal debt securities. Only the internal debt securities are shown on the table. For some years, in addition to federal, state, and municipal bonds, treasury notes were also sold in the Government Securities category. These are not shown on the table. Up to 1955 the County category in Government Securities included the Distrito Federal, but the sources do not specify whether this holds after 1955.

Table XXIV-2 records capital issues in Brazil from 1951 to 1978. The figures are for capital floated by public, public/private, and private corporations. All data were generated by the Fundação Getúlio Vargas. The Chemicals category includes pharmaceuticals. The Transportation Equipment category is made up solely of the automobile industry. The figures for 1952 are only for the Distrito Federal (Rio de Janeiro) and São Paulo state, which together, says the source, accounted for 70 percent of the Brazil total. For 1954 the total Industry figure included 4 billion cruzeiros relative to the incorporation of Petrobrás. Prior to 1959

Mining was included by the sources as a part of an "other industry" category and thereby cannot be shown separately but only as a part of the Industry total. The same was true of Construction prior to 1957. For many of the years prior to 1973 the categories from Agriculture to Services fail to sum to the annual total because categories such as "diverse" and "other" are not shown on the table. Rounding errors prevent the categories from Agriculture to Services from summing to the Brazil total for the years 1973 to 1977.

Table XXIV-3 shows the numbers of private insurance companies and cooperatives in Brazil and the numbers of policies in force together with coverage, premium costs, and claims paid from 1938 to 1978. The data originated with the Serviço de Estatística de Previdência e Trabalho, the Instituto de Resseguros do Brasil, the Instituto de Previdência e Assistência do Servidores do Estado (IPASE), and Federal de Seguros, S.A. Although new cruzeiros (one NCr$ equaled 1,000 old cruzeiros) did not come into use until 1967 the sources for insurance data began applying this revaluation retro-actively in order to reduce the size of the numbers reported. This table does the same. Sources for nearly every year specify that their data do not include insurance figures for the Federal Government Welfare and Administration departments. Since no major "humps" appear in the data for the years in which sources provide no such specification, data for these years can be assumed to exclude these departments. The same pattern holds for the National Agricultural Insurance Company (Companhia Nacional de Seguros Agrícola).

For 1941 Work Accidents in the Premiums and Claims categories excluded data for one company. For 1942 the Premiums and Claims categories excluded data for German and Italian companies during the months they operated. For 1944 one company's data were missing from the Life category. For 1945 data for one company were missing from the Premium category for Fire, Auto, Transportation, Personal Accident, and Work Accidents, and from the Claims category for these same types of insurance except Work Accidents. Also for 1945 data from two companies were missing for Life insurance in both the Premiums and Claims categories. For 1950 the Numbers of Companies excluded data from five Brazilian firms in process of liquidation, and data for Life insurance in both the Premium and Claims categories were missing for one company in liquidation. For 1951 data were missing from one Brazilian company; for 1953 from one company; for 1955 from four companies; and for 1956 from one company. For 1956 one company's data were missing from Work Accidents in the Premiums and Claims categories. For 1959 and 1960 data were missing from one company in these same categories. For 1964 data were missing from one company and one cooperative. For 1965 data for two companies were missing. For 1966, 1967, and 1969 the data from five companies were missing. In 1968 obligatory vehicular liability went into effect, accounting for the large 1967 to 1968 jump in Liability figures on the table. The 1969 count of companies and data excluded five companies and all accident cooperatives, the latter of which were made extinct by Law 3/6/67 and had their functions transferred to the Department of Welfare and Social Assistance for Federal Government Employees (IPASE). For 1969 and earlier years the Liability category in the sources had no subdivisions. For 1970 and later all subdivisions of liability listed by the sources were summed into the Liability category on this table. For 1970 one company's data were missing and the Claims category excluded two insurers. Beginning in 1971 the total number of companies was reduced by the number founded and incorporated by existing firms in the course of their usual operations. For 1971 and 1972, however, the insurance company totals (138 and 109, respectively) each included thirteen companies that sent in separate balance sheets in spite of their being parts of other companies.

Table XXIV-1. Volume and Types of Transactions on Brazilian Stock
Exchanges, 1937-78

	1937	1938	1939	1940	1941	1942	1943
Brazil (Cr$ 000)	710,000	738,410	797,474	933,526	1,167,453	1,305,753	1,748,928
Government Securities	-	643,665	671,969	761,830	934,357	913,491	1,089,252
Federal	-	283,663	276,035	317,610	407,283	324,410	366,429
State	-	286,456	301,742	341,038	431,711	461,658	590,604
County (Município)	-	73,546	94,192	103,182	95,363	127,423	132,219
Private Securities	-	94,795	125,505	171,696	233,096	392,262	659,676
Rio de Janeiro (Cr$ 000)	444,926	452,820	508,382	582,426	778,966	747,427	1,017,633
Government Securities	357,882	414,795	436,933	505,986	635,354	594,504	647,655
Federal	209,857	269,815	249,924	303,402	356,636	297,257	334,911
State	115,478	128,447	174,678	156,084	223,470	209,723	240,822
County (Município)	3,159	15,532	12,331	40,851	32,093	83,189	68,392
Private Securities	31,204	32,008	55,124	68,537	131,823	141,905	351,387
Stocks	18,179	20,911	42,477	39,081	97,497	106,393	314,010
Debentures	11,078	8,036	11,089	29,455	34,024	34,786	36,711
Mortgage Notes	15	2	-	1	302	726	666
São Paulo (Cr$ 000)	248,000	271,131	274,179	329,884	353,600	495,663	672,073
Government Securities	-	212,023	-	-	-	-	-
Federal	-	9,618	-	-	-	-	-
State	-	169,608	-	-	-	-	-
County (Município)	-	32,797	-	-	-	-	-
Private Securities	-	59,108	-	-	-	-	-
Stocks	-	58,575	-	67,314	53,068	64,338	192,489
Debentures	-	533	-	-	-	-	-
Mortgage Notes	-	-	-	-	-	-	-
Recife (Cr$ 000)	3,000	1,997	2,405	2,204	2,465	7,488	4,055
Paraná (Cr$ 000)	-	-	-	-	-	-	-
Pôrto Alegre (Cr$ 000)	14,000	12,383	12,113	20,753	31,433	55,117	55,164
Vitória (Cr$ 000)	-	129	395	892	989	58	3
Santos (Cr$ 000)	-	-	-	-	-	-	7,694

	1944	1945	1946	1947	1948	1949	1950
Brazil (Cr$ 000)	1,613,193	1,848,592	2,002,867	1,623,843	1,884,457	2,189,407	2,587,643
Government Securities	1,047,613	1,315,103	1,501,213	948,184	1,217,832	1,595,832	1,745,260
Federal	524,919	816,755	1,087,404	585,697	406,265	387,898	567,800
State	422,059	434,887	340,743	312,670	775,455	1,169,347	1,131,299
County (Município)	100,635	63,461	73,066	49,817	36,112	38,527	46,161
Private Securities	565,580	533,489	501,654	675,659	666,625	591,635	842,383
Rio de Janeiro (Cr$ 000)	952,823	994,830	1,068,609	816,411	626,837	621,425	1,040,315
Government Securities	653,499	715,582	840,838	488,596	349,269	388,786	685,555
Federal	447,433	562,559	690,070	367,438	257,586	265,234	418,041
State	183,210	137,173	140,992	109,873	86,811	114,139	254,061
County (Município)	20,409	14,518	9,638	10,981	3,386	8,993	10,023
Private Securities	281,186	267,651	208,845	308,225	262,178	220,219	340,229
Stocks	243,717	242,074	185,628	268,391	238,631	198,727	322,534
Debentures	36,950	23,741	21,539	16,684	15,644	18,290	12,656
Mortgage Notes	519	1,836	1,678	23,150	7,903	3,657	5,039
São Paulo (Cr$ 000)	594,545	797,661	843,050	758,453	1,193,782	1,498,443	1,451,325
Government Securities	-	555,970	591,317	422,611	829,890	1,173,487	1,013,340
Federal	-	238,167	353,161	195,439	128,565	106,006	119,546
State	-	296,577	200,225	199,524	681,565	1,051,063	876,759
County (Município)	-	21,226	37,931	23,590	16,951	13,838	15,155
Private Securities	-	241,690	251,733	335,842	363,892	324,956	437,985
Stocks	210,076	199,478	214,268	320,331	326,137	308,916	430,081
Debentures	-	42,212	35,996	15,049	36,521	14,137	7,169
Mortgage Notes	-	-	1,469	462	1,234	1,903	735
Recife (Cr$ 000)	19,848	9,712	15,777	15,478	16,522	17,966	22,299
Paraná (Cr$ 000)	-	-	-	-	-	-	-
Pôrto Alegre (Cr$ 000)	38,283	39,182	59,191	27,143	37,390	42,223	53,965
Vitória (Cr$ 000)	-	-	-	-	-	-	-
Santos (Cr$ 000)	7,207	6,240	9,926	7,350	19,739	13,831	19,656

Table XXIV-1 (continued)

	1951	1952	1953	1954	1955	1956	1957
Brazil (Cr$ 000)	2,855,509	2,488,548	4,034,471	5,925,056	5,087,949	6,083,343	5,388,655
Government Securities	1,764,345	1,378,954	1,889,831	3,464,365	2,274,705	1,828,849	2,275,558
Federal	494,037	561,093	554,543	673,216	543,912	59,694	676,765
State	1,224,490	756,635	1,286,575	2,729,681	1,676,348	1,139,668	1,123,878
County (Município)	45,818	61,226	48,713	61,468	54,448	98,507	474,915
Private Securities	1,091,164	1,109,594	2,144,640	2,460,691	2,813,244	4,254,634	3,113,097
Rio de Janeiro (Cr$ 000)	1,041,725	1,082,787	1,858,362	1,486,842	1,477,079	1,689,007	1,790,038
Government Securities	506,197	589,312	585,473	618,734	544,251	595,652	792,986
Federal	351,633	395,519	415,312	463,871	399,748	450,943	530,418
State	142,100	186,339	164,314	151,795	143,148	143,962	261,561
County (Município)	10,232	6,429	5,538	2,947	1,345	691	939
Private Securities	517,018	460,320	1,246,128	833,301	897,754	1,008,353	967,577
Stocks	490,008	44,192	1,227,357	815,003	835,270	976,690	941,014
Debentures	21,207	13,583	11,990	15,059	60,663	22,160	14,849
Mortgage Notes	5,803	2,545	6,781	3,239	1,831	9,503	11,714
São Paulo (Cr$ 000)	1,728,332	1,253,255	2,056,504	4,299,645	3,497,538	4,134,533	3,236,520
Government Securities	1,222,665	705,439	1,243,110	2,771,942	1,691,142	1,195,110	1,431,430
Federal	120,554	125,601	107,215	174,751	121,361	118,285	111,151
State	1,085,007	544,172	1,110,874	2,554,631	1,532,566	1,036,066	1,011,604
County (Município)	17,034	32,606	25,021	42,560	37,215	40,759	304,372
Private Securities	505,667	547,815	813,394	1,527,703	1,806,396	2,939,423	1,805,090
Stocks	495,820	532,112	798,816	1,444,379	1,781,284	2,889,356	1,778,457
Debentures	8,265	12,314	9,296	7,469	14,609	7,073	9,966
Mortgage Notes	782	498	56	48	–	–	573
Recife (Cr$ 000)	32,552	50,990	30,709	37,322	37,059	147,350	–
Paraná (Cr$ 000)	–	–	–	–	–	–	–
Pôrto Alegre (Cr$ 000)	39,069	81,860	71,266	80,181	72,325	75,218	–
Vitória (Cr$ 000)	–	–	–	–	–	2,319	–
Santos (Cr$ 000)	17,630	21,066	19,601	21,066	19,601	43,578	–

	1958	1959	1960	1961	1962	1963	1964
Brazil (Cr$ 000)	8,009,279	9,211,926	18,728,000	42,297,000	104,284,000	177,545,000	502,298,000
Government Securities	4,210,462	3,917,695	4,087,000	4,127,000	25,801,000	33,189,000	204,435,000
Federal	1,365,253	647,823	1,380,000	1,335,000	22,022,000	27,537,000	197,893,000
State	1,073,059	1,346,349	1,521,000	1,599,000	2,995,000	4,692,000	5,503,000
County (Município)	1,772,150	1,923,523	1,186,000	1,193,000	784,000	960,000	1,039,000
Private Securities	3,798,817	5,294,231	14,641,000	38,170,000	78,483,000	144,356,000	297,863,000
Rio de Janeiro	3,434,358	3,040,150	5,334,389	8,080,088	22,207,683	84,725,809	134,959,496
Government Securities	1,563,750	810,998	1,272,499	1,197,661	2,003,793	3,304,661	3,974,902
Federal	424,921	513,435	814,437	840,600	1,565,732	1,144,172	2,641,849
State	314,298	297,177	294,679	356,924	437,926	715,321	952,494
County (Município)	1,682	386	543	137	135	33	5
Private Securities	1,846,790	2,187,938	3,961,345	6,840,561	19,863,413	81,036,214	130,401,790
Stocks	1,800,977	2,092,989	3,851,201	6,755,510	19,347,252	58,160,980	77,150,299
Debentures	17,387	50,687	78,608	57,388	481,844	619,503	1,375
Mortgage Notes	28,426	44,262	30,470	24,213	34,097	36,102	193
São Paulo (Cr$ 000)	4,129,375	5,785,687	12,021,141	31,885,717	74,258,197	104,266,448	327,335
Government Securities	2,604,424	3,044,603	2,566,716	2,745,516	3,996,589	19,146,135	9,244
Federal	95,212	104,117	273,056	474,244	1,390,071	1,399,843	766
State	954,593	1,238,467	1,044,008	1,079,267	1,822,659	2,872,709	3,472
County (Município)	1,554,619	1,702,019	1,249,652	1,192,005	783,859	955,858	1,038
Private Securities	1,524,951	2,741,084	9,454,425	29,140,201	70,261,608	85,120,313	318,091
Stocks	1,493,936	2,630,417	6,299,996	5,505,806	14,529,226	27,290,484	35,363
Debentures	21,702	42,618	69,331	6,346	328,903	3,711	871
Mortgage Notes	5	81	–	–	–	–	–
Recife (Cr$ 000)	–	–	–	–	–	–	3,445
Paraná (Cr$ 000)	–	–	–	–	2,360,163	2,565,051	7,704
Pôrto Alegre (Cr$ 000)	–	–	–	–	–	–	–
Vitória (Cr$ 000)	–	–	–	–	–	–	–
Santos (Cr$ 000)	–	–	–	–	–	–	–

Table XXIV-1 (continued)

	1965	1966	1967	1968	1969	1970	1971
Brazil (Cr$ 000)	-	-	-	-	-	-	-
Government Securities	-	-	-	-	-	-	-
Federal	-	-	-	-	-	-	-
State	-	-	-	-	-	-	-
County (Município)	-	-	-	-	-	-	-
Private Securities	-	-	-	-	-	-	-
Rio de Janeiro (Cr$ 000)	373,690,825	356,116	227,483	258,640	1,608,499	3,037,791	1,378,791
Government Securities	29,941,936	21,881	10,544	8,069	35,795	14,325	908
Federal	25,514,454	19,803	7,858	4,460	35,687	13,310	41
State	3,514,736	2,018	2,686	3,609	108	1,015	867
County (Município)	4	-	-	-	-	-	-
Private Securities	340,921,073	334,235	216,939	250,190	1,571,216	3,020,779	13,783,882
Stocks	122,319,980	100,352	175,643	249,458	1,550,171	2,928,105	13,768,448
Debentures	8,424	4,633	202	64	830	1,894	12,868
Mortgages	282	210	412	450	1,063		
São Paulo (Cr$ 000)	540,827	514,639	313,890	352,950	1,058,837	1,798,692	11,543,397
Government Securities	29,764	56,256	38,167	136,637	175,231	178,006	125,069
Federal	17,479	48,791	18,164	86,941	87,608	49,925	13,703
State	10,925	4,189	1,096	350	7	-	-
County (Município)	1,360	3,276	18,907	49,346	87,616	128,081	11,366
Private Securities	511,064	458,383	275,723	216,312	883,605	1,620,687	11,418,327
Stocks	69,695	51,174	94,123	163,265	821,443	1,577,292	11,198,714
Debentures	12,737	8,408	824	450	3,144	11,253	174,624
Mortgage Notes	-	-	-	-	-		
Recife (Cr$ 000)	4,505	8,555	9,134	23,633	53,572	19,874	53,759
Paraná (Cr$ 000)	20,168	27,458	4,352	6,228	5,536	7,484	70,950
Pôrto Alegre (Cr$ 000)	-	-	-	-	-	-	-
Vitória (Cr$ 000)	-	-	-	-	-	-	-
Santos (Cr$ 000)	-	-	-	-	-	-	-

	1972	1973	1974	1975	1976	1977	1978
Brazil (Cr$ 000)	-	-	-	-	-	-	-
Government Securities	-	-	-	-	-	-	-
Federal	-	-	-	-	-	-	-
State	-	-	-	-	-	-	-
County (Município)	-	-	-	-	-	-	-
Private Securities	-	-	-	-	-	-	-
Rio de Janeiro (Cr$ 000)	7,703,057	6,930,617	6,481,789	15,679,818	17,017,335	22,956,738	29,326,734
Government Securities	152	5	1	46	113	-	705
Federal	56	4	1	46	113	-	705
State	96	1	-	-	-	-	-
County (Município)	-	-	-	-	-	-	-
Private Securities	7,702,905	6,930,512	6,481,788	15,679,772	17,017,222	18,591,137	23,790,650
Stocks	7,685,284	6,921,416	6,472,977	15,667,238	17,003,063	18,558,264	23,355,250
Debentures	} 16,728	} 8,871	} 7,869	} 12,199	} 12,265	} 2,032	} 3,351
Mortgage Notes							
São Paulo (Cr$ 000)	10,412,370	11,238,383	7,184,497	11,160,396	11,194,061	14,907,931	24,060,225
Government Securities	93,824	27,754	7,148	133	99	9	-
Federal	4,470	3,057	3,221	40	37	9	-
State	-	-	-	-	-	-	-
County (Município)	89,354	24,697	3,927	93	62	-	-
Private Securities	10,318,516	11,210,638	7,177,349	11,160,213	11,193,962	14,907,922	24,060,225
Stocks	9,755,828	10,058,149	6,405,030	11,085,468	9,353,264	14,774,859	23,804,689
Debentures	25,606	38,367	57,200	66,700	40,812	30,134	38,204
Mortgage Notes	-	-	-	-	-	-	-
Recife (Cr$ 000)	35,723	15,615	24,364	46,852	76,433	151,157	113,884
Paraná (Cr$ 000)	15,929	112,696	32,793	36,638	48,475	78,811	144,568
Pôrto Alegre (Cr$ 000)	-	-	-	-	-	-	-
Vitória (Cr$ 000)	-	-	-	-	-	-	-
Santos (Cr$ 000)	-	-	-	-	-	-	-

Sources: AN 1939-40, pp. 373-74; AN 1941-45, pp. 221 & 223; AN 1947, pp. 244-45; AN 1948, p. 231;
AN 1949, p. 278; AN 1951, pp. 260 & 263; AN 1953, pp. 243 & 246; AN 1956, pp. 208, 213 & 523;
AN 1957, pp. 191-92 & 197; AN 1960, pp. 143 & 153; AN 1961, p. 182; AN 1962, p. 135;
AN 1965, pp. 269-70; AN 1966, p. 261; AN 1967, p. 320; AN 1969, p. 403; AN 1970, p. 437;
AN 1971, p. 447-48; AN 1973, p. 494; AN 1975, pp. 586-87; AN 1977, p. 754; AN 1979, p. 786.

Table XXIV-2. Capital Issues in Brazil, 1951-78

	1951	1952	1953	1954	1955	1956	1957	1958	1959	1960
Total (Cr$ 000,000)	10,996	16,053	16,815	28,442	31,454	85,958	61,677	56,783	116,964	143,194
New Companies	2,004	2,166	2,642	7,347	5,226	5,878	6,682	7,671	·9,465	21,772
Increase in Existing Capital	8,992	13,887	14,173	21,095	26,228	80,080	53,995	49,112	107,449	121,422
For Reserves	-	-	-	-	-	-	6,598	3,942	15,723	19,232
For Corporate Improvements	-	-	-	-	-	-	8,749	300	13,422	14,616
For Cash Subscription	-	-	-	-	-	-	31,303	37,639	65,235	71,526
Agriculture	-	-	-	-	-	-	-	-	487	6,377
Mining	-	-	-	-	-	-	-	-	-	-
Industry	6,554	9,153	9,984	17,809	15,972	54,422	34,451	34,763	66,779	70,423
Metals	-	-	-	-	-	-	8,848	3,182	11,479	9,457
Chemicals	-	-	-	-	-	-	4,606	3,467	5,730	4,954
Textiles	-	-	-	-	-	-	2,224	1,417	2,597	5,793
Food	-	-	-	-	-	-	3,381	3,070	4,594	7,353
Transportation Equipment	-	-	-	-	-	-	1,262	8,776	9,127	4,723
Electrical/Communication Equipment	-	-	-	-	-	-	1,502	2,076	2,415	2,137
Mechanical Industries	-	-	-	-	-	-	-	-	-	-
Petroleum	-	-	-	-	-	-	4,058	4,015	13,881	14,671
Construction	-	-	-	-	-	-	1,288	1,117	2,210	2,953
Public Utilities/Transport	633	944	771	774	3,386	3,818	6,096	3,128	12,378	16,125
Retail/Wholesale	2,448	3,229	2,632	4,948	7,102	16,584	9,876	9,043	18,888	21,570
Finance	553	1,263	1,354	1,399	838	3,479	2,395	2,581	7,668	7,892
Transportation/Communication	-	-	-	-	-	-	-	-	-	-
Services	-	-	-	-	-	-	-	-	-	-

	1961	1962	1963	1964	1965	1966	1967	1968	1969
Total (Cr$ 000,000)	178,755	340,650	565,257	2,280,512	6,291,234	6,057,705	9,527	12,899	23,564
New Companies	15,042	34,379	39,378	77,306	111,287	124,946	492	872	1,049
Increase in Existing Capital	163,713	306,271	525,879	2,203,206	6,179,947	5,932,759	9,035	12,027	22,515
For Reserves	33,329	50,795	82,363	130,096	434,849	966,323	957	1,318	8,642
For Corporate Improvements	30,107	31,195	134,761	1,483,409	4,026,349	2,768,310	5,171	5,129	7,063
For Cash Subscriptions	77,169	175,574	242,203	377,193	1,133,827	1,664,502	2,429	3,911	5,070
Agriculture	-	-	-	-	-	-	-	-	-
Mining	5,445	8,509	7,950	65,182	72,200	98,469	144	209	229
Industry	90,621	185,862	274,327	1,253,613	3,692,407	2,951,002	5,455	5,687	11,167
Metals	14,698	53,487	76,036	245,705	829,457	380,058	1,164	997	1,829
Chemicals	12,777	10,749	19,855	146,459	353,921	279,110	515	582	1,300
Textiles	10,938	15,987	30,729	147,261	366,221	242,051	219	326	791
Food	12,727	23,104	38,757	188,999	605,663	397,218	577	699	1,234
Transportation Equipment	5,040	17,674	17,611	72,903	151,270	116,257	106	351	696
Electrical/Communication Equipment	5,289	6,870	7,543	37,932	146,882	132,797	180	290	418
Mechanical Industries	-	-	-	-	-	-	-	-	-
Petroleum	1,845	13,897	4,103	87,431	89,569	339,701	1,131	645	816
Construction	4,812	9,881	14,913	98,088	180,538	114,656	210	383	678
Public Utilities/Transport	21,984	29,818	112,579	217,372	1,038,292	1,927,480	1,924	4,148	4,503
Retail/Wholesale	26,396	51,962	74,233	256,075	657,421	275,262	302	791	2,307
Finance	13,146	24,064	34,892	193,183	2,222,574	313,508	624	847	2,543
Transportation/Communication	-	-	-	-	-	-	-	-	-
Services	-	-	-	-	-	-	-	-	-

	1970	1971	1972	1973	1974	1975	1976	1977	1978
Total (Cr$ 000,000)	21,910	32,102	35,829	53,963	60,821	99,950	137,752	182,068	259,942
New Companies	1,213	3,047	2,710	4,835	2,976	4,595	3,379	1,169	3,772
Increase in Existing Capital	20,696	29,055	33,119	49,128	57,845	95,355	134,373	180,899	256,170
For Reserves	·6,797	5,398	9,825	14,414	22,951	34,529	51,107	63,830	90,884
For Corporate Improvements	6,556	7,340	7,222	11,273	7,844	18,376	39,588	47,546	70,516
For Cash Subscription	5,600	14,006	12,815	16,452	21,062	31,635	34,326	48,127	71,016
Agriculture	-	-	-	1,341	1,596	3,403	2,922	3,121	4,577
Mining	458	1,011	1,977	2,035	1,815	2,156	1,465	1,796	1,999
Industry	10,053	14,357	14,976	20,212	28,886	48,272	77,803	106,184	146,096
Metals	2,879	3,932	2,665	3,376	4,590	8,673	13,512	14,165	27,289
Chemicals	997	1,505	1,246	3,667	6,008	8,497	8,735	14,836	25,736
Textiles	967	348	1,135	1,683	1,911	3,445	8,560	13,541	21,567
Food	1,239	2,066	2,092	2,772	2,919	4,795	8,845	13,921	10,987
Transportation Equipment	313	518	932	1,217	1,372	1,052	960	1,412	2,912
Electrical/Communication Equipment	572	656	877	953	1,395	2,746	5,045	5,044	3,415
Mechanical Industries	-	-	-	-	1,374	1,818	3,052	4,649	5,990
Petroleum	718	1,393	2,053	-	-	-	-	-	-
Construction	807	1,219	1,361	2,777	2,909	6,374	9,973	13,385	15,898
Public Utilities/Transport	4,987	7,936	8,432	5,813	6,961	13,440	15,901	16,138	22,007
Retail/Wholesale	2,520	2,572	3,223	2,978	3,762	6,016	11,776	10,628	10,781
Finance	1,585	3,119	3,593	7,544	6,943	8,668	8,621	9,788	25,487
Transportation/Communication	-	-	-	8,173	3,944	7,109	3,118	2,152	8,497
Services	-	-	-	3,089	4,004	4,511	6,172	18,877	24,600

Sources: AN 1956, p. 207; AN 1957, p. 190; AN 1960, p. 148; AN 1962, p. 134; AN 1965, p. 269; AN 1967, p. 319; AN 1969, p. 402; AN 1971, p. 445; AN 1973, p. 492; AN 1974, p. 526; AN 1975, p. 583; AN 1976, p. 400; AN 1977, p. 750; AN 1978, p. 766; AN 1979, p. 782.

Table XXIV-3. Insurance Companies in Brazil: Numbers of Companies and Policies, Coverage and Premium Costs, and Claims Paid, 1938-78

	1938	1939	1940	1941	1942	1943	1944	1945	1946	1947
Numbers Of Companies	100	106	111	112	106	110	121	132	141	149
Foreign	33	33	33	33	25	25	25	25	25	25
Premiums Collected (Cr$ 000)	376,330	379,698	392,120	468,535	733,066	990,351	1,037,979	1,224,880	1,614,739	1,858,029
Fire	124,108	106,725	121,274	147,909	172,700	239,667	310,941	376,938	448,227	515,124
Personal Accidents	7,046	8,301	9,141	10,700	12,580	16,421	20,708	27,901	43,920	48,638
Transport	33,827	30,394	36,210	50,691	87,217	117,711	174,250	214,179	281,204	283,921
Life	127,182	144,186	131,989	147,247	157,487	217,331	237,035	299,352	426,021	503,399
Liability	2,381	1,587	1,890	2,335	1,929	2,514	2,675	4,166	5,468	10,306
Personal Injury	-	-	-	-	-	-	-	-	-	-
Marine	1,604	5,201	2,680	4,877	6,670	9,140	10,382	10,172	9,698	8,391
Automobile	8,849	9,446	10,577	12,760	9,075	8,580	12,067	18,926	37,825	63,236
Work Accidents	61,522	72,932	77,143	90,059	105,245	132,930	178,877	238,014	318,631	370,545
Aeronautical	-	-	-	-	-	34	10,456	15,700	26,492	36,808
Claims Paid (Cr$ 000)	107,663	123,251	134,714	157,730	210,026	345,901	348,958	406,967	594,683	623,286
Fire	35,526	39,786	36,785	41,053	36,161	52,970	77,111	102,609	145,552	168,765
Personal Accidents	1,592	1,614	3,376	4,515	3,332	4,063	3,594	3,844	5,710	10,034
Transport	13,482	12,254	14,109	17,202	36,437	59,292	86,779	122,196	176,283	127,073
Life	19,768	24,598	30,663	33,915	35,238	47,223	49,038	53,422	81,360	97,962
Liability	288	343	612	466	836	400	905	1,323	1,615	3,148
Personal Injury	-	-	-	-	-	-	-	-	-	-
Marine	328	1,504	1,528	5,711	4,318	2,212	5,561	7,665	5,064	6,973
Automobile	4,636	5,365	5,333	6,311	5,142	3,639	5,158	7,696	19,472	34,920
Work Accidents	31,864	37,670	42,000	48,058	55,640	66,205	83,582	95,491	135,480	154,319
Aeronautical	-	-	-	-	-	-	-	9,670	19,543	15,529

	1948	1949	1950	1951	1952	1953	1954	1955	1956
Numbers of Companies	151	149	152	153	152	154	154	159	172
Foreign	25	26	28	28	28	28	28	28	30
Premiums Collected (Cr$ 000)	2,210,017	2,508,709	3,252,976	3,258,399	3,931,685	4,360,909	5,519,242	6,836,774	8,836,170
Fire	566,505	673,170	717,127	898,580	1,186,224	-	-	-	2,604,379
Personal Accidents	60,989	80,979	92,958	123,669	159,884	-	-	-	289,151
Transport	288,028	290,943	316,672	434,556	410,488	-	-	-	909,127
Life	728,973	839,064	386,858	882,997	1,023,706	-	-	-	2,130,079
Liability	18,507	29,758	50,233	51,504	78,870	-	-	-	195,368
Personal Injury	-	-	-	-	-	-	-	-	-
Marine	9,410	10,347	19,830	35,999	46,037	-	-	-	85,184
Automobile	93,924	97,704	116,724	180,607	239,788	-	-	-	2,604,379
Work Accidents	388,555	429,991	481,478	559,117	666,238	-	-	-	1,645,398
Aeronautical	34,160	31,176	32,176	40,644	45,878	-	-	-	76,169
Claims Paid (Cr$ 000)	697,639	752,025	772,129	1,004,793	1,266,583	1,440,986	2,040,490	2,138,448	2,361,575
Fire	202,799	151,553	153,933	227,651	273,516	-	-	-	551,191
Personal Accidents	12,376	12,723	18,914	27,050	34,529	-	-	-	76,928
Transport	126,002	97,923	96,025	151,017	207,755	-	-	-	346,170
Life	107,249	204,175	185,850	185,626	235,853	-	-	-	641,221
Liability	6,874	6,658	9,918	17,076	24,485	-	-	-	78,115
Personal Injury	-	-	-	-	-	-	-	-	-
Marine	6,505	3,907	4,032	18,626	17,570	-	-	-	47,477
Automobile	54,287	58,881	63,048	94,586	273,516	-	-	-	265,896
Work Accidents	166,437	195,777	220,048	259,029	307,604	-	-	-	537,227
Aeronautical	9,702	10,863	13,281	15,607	13,604	-	-	-	36,605

	1957	1958	1959	1960	1961	1962	1963	1964
Numbers of Companies	177	184	188	193	193	193	192	195
Foreign	30	33	35	35	35	35	35	35
Premiums Collected (Cr$ 000)	10,767,804	13,775,014	18,770,228	24,946,392	36,043,934	59,677,465	99,551,157	187,816
Fire	3,038,388	3,770,964	4,979,802	6,482,203	8,817,389	13,389,393	24,965,488	43,619
Personal Accidents	369,183	465,964	677,389	943,808	1,316,279	1,941,762	3,515,379	6,325
Transport	941,655	1,903,360	1,415,059	1,897,468	2,546,813	3,747,803	5,822,737	11,438
Life	2,595,110	3,304,051	3,953,885	5,016,642	6,017,788	9,285,904	13,956,777	24,636
Liability	252,314	363,902	514,353	665,877	1,165,183	1,913,537	2,833,959	5,020
Personal Injury	-	-	-	-	-	-	-	-
Marine	84,009	110,910	128,738	173,202	266,614	1,149,969	1,983,836	2,259
Automobile	626,700	942,918	1,317,876	1,979,284	2,785,804	5,039,589	10,237,400	21,650
Work Accidents	2,442,879	3,038,373	4,689,561	6,182,105	9,857,037	14,799,193	26,265,027	53,904
Aeronautical	98,789	141,657	335,324	423,231	933,425	2,105,043	3,696,937	5,112
Claims Paid (Cr$ 000)	3,778,146	5,117,052	6,521,601	8,931,423	13,234,079	22,476,340	37,022,567	62,540
Fire	542,122	918,924	759,226	1,045,370	1,646,052	2,222,989	3,114,874	6,142
Personal Accidents	120,002	137,889	157,840	247,949	291,416	475,379	910,826	1,286
Transport	328,549	323,027	425,380	641,893	815,950	1,692,244	1,758,109	2,925
Life	919,266	1,264,876	1,527,750	2,076,091	2,686,790	3,881,921	5,932,277	10,685
Liability	99,002	136,136	168,611	244,953	391,213	541,381	885,023	1,609
Personal Injury	-	-	-	-	-	-	-	-
Marine	59,037	116,516	73,000	60,611	161,013	218,637	909,556	1,074
Automobile	343,382	466,502	749,778	1,124,934	1,672,152	2,964,855	5,478,521	10,412
Work Accidents	1,208,597	1,616,397	2,377,001	2,986,908	4,792,878	7,462,935	12,267,614	22,910
Aeronautical	92,274	48,126	77,832	234,476	303,641	2,201,121	4,298,675	2,284

440

Table XXIV-3 (continued)

	1965	1966	1967	1968	1969	1970	1971	1972
Numbers of Companies	201	205	204	197	184	185	159	138
Foreign	35	35	35	34	29	29	21	18
Premiums Collected (Cr$ 000)	295,274	405,846	550,862	916,556	1,203,613	1,674,718	2,136,937	3,166,347
Fire	69,867	95,840	125,669	184,667	280,445	400,486	518,536	768,473
Personal Accounts	12,091	19,198	31,253	45,667	66,015	112,224	153,555	234,803
Transport	16,352	23,152	28,281	41,747	64,003	86,360	151,143	234,083
Life	41,908	63,851	96,692	130,666	195,090	298,237	393,460	532,024
Liability	5,996	6,405	8,110	41,737	198,803	211,828	263,957	317,678
Personal Injury	-	-	-	-	-	-	-	-
Marine	2,446	4,089	7,164	11,966	17,761	23,210	31,318	75,473
Auto	35,305	46,080	75,643	110,786	211,472	361,144	417,604	657,198
Work Accidents	89,553	116,478	141,125	115,732	47,722	6,096	516	261
Aeronautical	3,775	16,035	6,457	9,827	13,462	16,207	17,737	38,969
Claims Paid (Cr$ 000)	110,213	156,922	221,025	364,310	569,346	723,536	1,122,425	1,390,896
Fire	10,756	15,099	22,779	36,080	86,237	81,658	211,553	187,966
Personal Accidents	1,952	3,991	6,734	10,659	14,494	25,499	45,968	68,337
Transport	4,940	7,597	10,533	20,183	25,319	32,190	50,568	87,006
Life	17,909	30,915	48,682	67,473	96,742	134,893	206,103	280,6P3
Liability	2,090	2,775	3,913	36,526	93,937	108,985	127,554	159,662
Personal Injury	-	-	-	-	-	-	-	-
Marine	4,024	1,998	3,075	6,231	10,957	14,275	36,023	30,974
Automobile	17,315	23,477	39,371	74,892	140,747	244,170	308,514	381,816
Work Accidents	42,537	59,461	71,704	91,481	58,540	27,100	18,105	24,732
Aeronautical	3,485	2,320	4,035	7,176	11,137	9,573	9,148	23,075

	1973	1974	1975	1976	1978	1979
Numbers of Companies	109	100	98	96	95	95
Foreign	14	7	6	6	6	5
Premiums Collected (Cr$ 000)	4,519,834	7,057,978	10,324,609	16,452,946	25,007,108	38,662,524
Fire	1,096,959	1,824,012	2,736,720	3,998,775	6,216,879	9,141,456
Personal Accident	351,169	515,078	768,187	1,153,026	1,777,019	2,659,565
Transport	339,329	683,136	918,559	1,320,759	1,777,700	2,566,916
Life	798,942	1,141,708	1,661,002	2,417,111	3,675,583	5,737,048
Liability	424,281	519,284	651,978	834,893	1,229,787	1,890,433
Personal Injury	-	-	-	1,413,252	2,173,785	3,019,689
Marine	114,035	202,990	269,364	397,219	668,905	973,384
Automobile	841,600	1,204,428	1,880,436	2,514,410	3,582,374	6,372,224
Work Accidents	-	-	142	17	8	-
Aeronautical	57,605	102,895	169,497	236,866	314,181	420,531
Claims Paid (Cr$ 000)	1,903,141	3,033,623	4,267,018	5,913,333	9,538,014	15,492,031
Fire	277,628	480,734	670,497	95,771	1,409,112	2,163,570
Personal Accidents	112,097	154,917	214,635	314,910	432,321	674,683
Transport	161,546	328,031	497,613	390,662	507,450	736,382
Life	404,574	576,154	776,199	1,068,354	1,604,773	2,436,110
Liability	195,793	274,308	372,116	497,222	744,652	1,033,695
Personal Injury	-	-	18	122,339	617,578	960.001
Marine	44,832	74,668	90,295	175,742	313,325	366,451
Automobile	458,067	728,286	1,092,193	1,505,128	2,257,638	4,194,289
Work Accidents	-	-	21,266	25,145	38,210	33,833
Aeronautical	45,892	73,282	71,927	118,129	190,230	203,286
Numbers of Policies Contracted	14,216,801	9,162,793	16,251,934	13,011,404	14,860,359	16,307,255
Fire	845,256	941,204	1,058,104	1,024,924	1,112,940	1,231,400
Personal Accidents	477,035	428,345	698,906	912,977	909,987	1,225,019
Transport	981,162	1,090,379	1,162,420	1,155,980	799,341	1,006,095
Life	3,260,865	3,519,677	9,886,557	2,530,611	3,365,527	1,905,337
Liability	2,654,286	2,283,769	2,458,869	1,010,591	915,781	1,367,421
Personal Injury	-	-	-	5,101,050	6,337,858	7,356,650
Marine	2,264	2,844	4,290	8,714	8,463	31,808
Automobile	682,468	706,560	750,246	958,944	1,117,243	1,494,136
Work Accidents	-	-	-	-	-	-
Aeronautical	4,571	5,856	5,858	6,612	8,295	8,918
Coverage (Cr$ 000)	1,121,286,463	1,683,191,033	4,836,045,926	3,518,136,055	7,685,571,680	9,590,335,827
Fire	364,003,031	613,448,645	810,702,970	1,075,072,160	1,877,184,966	2,898,560,791
Personal Accidents	187,009,559	304,211,640	516,004,007	559,235,853	1,535,335,627	1,907,200,519
Transport	219,608,706	315,522,536	427,341,963	617,159,002	880,337,571	1,530,754,165
Life	104,532,356	149,811,033	2,548,973,554	425,382,056	1,145,602,466	808,663,652
Liability	135,519,693	163,182,395	299,421,953	372,739,197	615,306,765	701,140,617
Personal Injury	-	-	-	110,074,233	286,036,129	369,417,837
Marine	7,229,598	8,694,029	16,453,004	60,648,320	111,851,699	173,028,619
Automobile	24,154,870	23,347,149	37,300,982	57,393,554	179,573,780	170,830,051
Work Accidents	-	-	-	-	-	-
Aeronautical	6,419,187	11,454,652	13,417,603	31,745,526	37,207,188	72,308,745

Sources: AN 1947, pp. 388, 393; AN 1948, p. 385; AN 1949, pp. 455, 460-461; AN 1952, p. 399; AN 1955, p. 404; AN 1956, pp. 324-325; AN 1957, pp. 334-335; AN 1960, pp. 272-273; AN 1961, p. 34; AN 1963, p. 203; AN 1965, p. 229; AN 1967, p. 272; AN 1969, p. 351; AN 1970, pp. 368-369; AN 1971, pp. 376-377; AN 1973, pp. 397-399; AN 1974, pp. 422-424; AN 1976, pp. 321-323; AN 1977, p. 687; AN 1979, p. 684.

Chapter XXV. Living Costs, Retail and Wholesale Prices and Price Indices

Table XXV-1 reports wholesale prices of various foodstuffs in the Rio de Janeiro market. The figures are annual averages of weekly price quotations. The data were originated by the Bôlsa de Mercadorias do Rio de Janeiro and the <u>Anuário estatístico do Distrito Federal, ano vi, 1938</u>. Figures in the Animals category were supplied by the Santa Cruz Slaughterhouse in Rio de Janeiro. Mascavo sugar is unrefined and of very poor quality. The names of cities and states following a commodity indicate its place of origin. Salt, Norte refers to salt from the north, most of which was and is produced in Rio Grande do Norte state. Salt, Cabo Frio refers to the coastal town in the state of Rio de Janeiro east of the city of Rio de Janeiro.

Table XXV-2 shows Brazilian wholesale price indices from 1944 to 1979. The Fundação Getúlio Vargas originated all the data. For the period 1944-60 the year 1948 was the base year and its index equaled 100. For 1961-64 the year 1953 equaled 100. For 1965-77 the 1965-67 average equaled 100. For 1976-78, the base year of 1977 equaled 100. Prior to 1965 the sources did not distinguish Domestic and World Market categories. For 1965 all indices were rounded. For 1966 the indices for Industrial Products and its sub-categories were rounded. Petroleum Products prices entered into the calculation of the Chemicals index.

Table XXV-3 reports the cost of living indices for Rio de Janeiro from 1912 to 1960, for Rio de Janeiro, São Paulo, and Pôrto Alegre from 1939 to 1966, and for the <u>municípios</u> (counties) of the twenty-six federal, state, and territorial capital cities during the period 1944-66. Data for the first two groups were originated by the Serviço de Estatística Economia e Financeira of the Ministerio da Fazenda, by the Fundação Getúlio Vargas, and by the Prefeitura Municipal de São Paulo, Capital. Data for the twenty-six <u>municípios</u> were developed by the Serviço de Estatística da Previdência e Trabalho. For the twenty-six <u>municípios</u> expenditures taken into account included food, housing, clothing, hygiene, transportation, and utilities. The average for all of Brazil in 1948 was 100. Each annual index was the arithmetic average of twelve monthly indices.

Table XXV-4 shows actual household and personal expenditures and indices of such expenditures by families in Rio de Janeiro and São Paulo from 1912 to 1978. The source did not give the geographic basis for either place but it is assumed to be the <u>município</u> in which each city is located. The data originated with the Instituto de Pesquisas Econômicas da Universidade de São Paulo (in a later entry this originator was listed as the Instituto de Pesquisas Econômicas de São Paulo), the Divisão de Estatística e Documentação Social da Prefeitura de São Paulo, and the Fundação Getúlio Vargas. Each annual index was the arithmetic average of twelve monthly indices. For the São Paulo modal family, each previous December had an index of 100, so the rise in prices was for the given year only. For the Rio de Janeiro Lower and Middle Class Family category, the base of 100 is the 1965-67 average for each category. For these Families the 1976, 1977, and 1978 indices were presented by the source only on a monthly basis. These monthly figures were summed by the author and divided by twelve to obtain the annual average indices that would conform longitudinally.

Table XXV-5 reports annual average retail food prices in cruzeiros for the period 1961-75. The data originated with the Diretoria de Levantamentos Estatísticos of IBGE. Each index is an average of the average annual prices observed in eighty-seven Brazilian cities by the National Prices Survey (Inquérito nacional de preços). Canned and bulk lard are reported on the table; packaged lard is not. In 1969 the source reported bulk and packaged lard together as bulk lard. From 1961 to 1966 Canned Lard was reported by the sources in 2 kilogram cans. Prior to 1967 coffee was listed by the sources as roasted and powdered (cafe torrado em pó) but from 1967 on as ground (moído).

Table XXV-1. Annual Averages of Weekly Price Quotations in Cruzeiros for Selected Foods in the Rio de Janeiro Wholesale Market, 1893-1937

	Unit	1893	1894	1895	1896	1897	1898	1899	1900	1901	1902
Animals											
Cows											
Maximum	1 kg.	.800	.800	.800	1.000	.900	1.040	1.000	1.000	.900	.800
Minimum	1 kg.	.790	.770	.700	.560	.700	.900	.900	.800.	.700	.450
Swine											
Maximum	1 kg.	1.860	1.350	1.800	1.300	1.300	1.400	1.400	1.400	1.600	1.400
Minimum	1 kg.	1.000	1.350	1.500	.800	1.200	1.200	.800	.800	1.200	.700

	Unit	1903	1904	1905	1906	1907	1908	1909	1910	1911	1912
Animals											
Cows											
Maximum	1 kg.	.800	.520	.600	.800	.640	.700	.620	.620	.670	.800
Minimum	1 kg.	.500	.370	.420	.400	.400	.480	.450	.350	.400	.460
Swine											
Maximum	1 kg.	1.300	.900	1.000	1.400	1.500	1.200	1.100	1.100	1.300	1.200
Minimum	1 kg.	.600	.500	.500	.800	.900	.600	.600	.600	.700	.700

	Unit	1913	1914	1915	1916	1917	1918	1919	1920	1921
Animals										
Cows										
Maximum	1 kg.	.800	.740	.760	.820	1.010	1.200	1.200	1.200	1.200
Minimum	1 kg.	.520	.560	.400	.430	.600	.840	.760	.920	.960
Swine										
Maximum	1 kg.	1.600	1.800	1.400	1.400	1.400	1.550	1.600	2.100	2.800
Minimum	1 kg.	.900	.700	.750	.900	1.000	1.100	1.200	1.400	1.500
Sugar, white crystal	60 kgs.	22.620	18.900	25.860	-	38.700	49.980	51.660	62.860	41.700
Sugar, yellow crystal	60 kgs.	17.940	16.740	21.600	-	31.680	41.760	44.640	54.120	34.800
Sugar, mascavo	60 kgs.	12,360	12.900	17.520	-	21.720	29.400	35.040	43.800	24.120
Rice, brilhado #1	60 kgs.	-	-	-	-	-	49.878	-	-	-
Rice, brilhado #2	60 kgs.	-	-	-	-	-	44.444	-	-	-
Rice, especial	60 kgs.	-	-	-	-	-	40.470	-	-	-
Olive Oil	1 liter	-	-	-	-	-	-	-	-	-
Lard, Itajaí SC	1 kg.	1.313	1.182	1.119	-	1.597	2.140	1.926	1.864	1.853
Lard, Pôrto Alegre, RS	1 kg.	1.261	1.220	1.167	-	1.716	-	1.951	1.920	1.902
Potatoes, MG & SP	1 kg.	-	.181	-	-	-	.297	-	-	-
Potatoes, RS	1 kg.	-	-	-	-	-	.337	-	-	-
Coffee, type 7	10 kgs.	6.080	4.560	4.760	-	5.500	6.075	12.200	9.360	10.600
Onions	1 kg.	-	.364	.432	-	.286	-	.522	-	-
Dried Beef (xarque) RS	1 kg.	1.004	-	-	-	-	1.583	-	-	-
Dried Beef (xarque) MG & SP	1 kg.	-	-	-	-	-	1.424	-	-	-
Mandioca Flour, especial	50 kgs.	19.697	8.100	10.050	-	20.650	22.170	17.650	15.150	14.100
Mandioca Flour, fina	50 kgs.	18.238	7.150	9.550	-	19.750	24.034	16.000	13.850	13.300
Mandioca Flour, grossa	50 kgs.	11.935	4.850	7.950	-	12.750	17.262	12.050	11.000	10.650
Wheat Flour, first class	44 kgs.	24.192	-	-	-	-	29.553	-	-	-
Wheat Flour, second class	44 kgs.	23.187	-	-	-	-	28.600	-	-	-
Wheat Flour, third class	44 kgs.	22.192	-	-	-	-	-	-	-	-
Black Beans, superior/good	60 kgs.	24.150	21.420	23.850	-	20.040	26.903	25.200	27.720	29.940
Butter, MG and RJ	1 kg.	3.159	2.079	2.491	2.496	3.704	3.718	5.877	5.075	4.808
Corn, yellow	60 kgs.	7.891	6.960	7.320	-	7.500	10.915	12.900	14.280	14.160
Salt, Norte	60 kgs.	5.905	5.340	4.500	-	8.760	10.801	9.420	8.880	9.240
Salt, Cabo Frio	60 kgs.	4.243	4.200	3.660	-	8.040	10.246	8.820	7.080	6.480
Bacon, common	1 kg.	1.108	1.015	.867	-	1.087	1.192	1.252	1.391	1.514
Bacon, smoked	1 kg.	-	-	-	-	-	1.872	-	-	-

Table XXV-1 (continued)

	Unit	1922	1923	1924	1925	1926	1927	1928	1929
Animals									
Cows									
	1 kg.	1.080	1.300	1.540	1.600	1.500	1.500	1.560	1.700
Maximum	1 kg.	.620	.700	1.000	1.300	1.080	1.000	1.000	1.220
Minimum									
Swine									
	1 kg.	2.100	2.400	3.600	6.000	4.000	3.400	3.300	3.800
Maximum	1 kg.	1.500	1.400	1.000	2.800	2.400	2.600	2.500	2.700
Minimum	60 kgs.	34.500	73.800	75.600	58.260	54.600	51.835	67.221	52.347
Sugar, white crystal	60 kgs.	22.500	59.580	65.580	50.460	47.460	43.042	57.237	45.783
Sugar, yellow crystal	60 kgs.	20.640	49.500	60.300	44.400	33.200	32.885	44.146	38.500
Sugar, mascavo	60 kgs.	-	56.323	-	-	-	73.000	84.969	90.954
Rice, brilhado #1	60 kgs.	-	46.250	-	-	-	63.354	74.198	80.731
Rice, brilhado #2	60 kgs.	-	48.312	-	-	-	64.000	77.458	81.427
Rice, especial	1 liter	-	-	-	-	-	-	6.729	6.723
Olive Oil	1 kg.	1.841	2.202	3.204	4.833	3.300	-	2.720	2.884
Lard, Itajaí SC	1 kg.	1.912	2.190	3.375	4.979	3.508	3.163	2.740	2.786
Lard, Pôrto Alegre RS	1 kg.	-	.531	-	-	-	.576	.632	.693
Potatoes, MG & SP	1 kg.	-	.493	-	-	-	.510	.457	.604
Coffee, type 7	10 kg.	15.280	20.614	29,290	31.750	24.380	23.243	26.810	24.519
Onions	1 kg.	-	-	-	-	-	-	.685	1.518
Dried Beef (xarque) RS	1 kg.	-	1.567	-	-	-	2.056	2.283	2.761
Dried Beef (xarque) MG & SP	1 kg.	-	1.480	-	-	-	2.800	2.219	2.521
Mandioca Flour, especial	50 kgs.	17.450	21.407	29.800	39.300	24.000	20.583	18.810	19.190
Mandioca Flour, fina	50 kgs.	16.350	19.920	27.500	34.900	21.300	17.729	16.865	17.497
Mandioca Flour, grossa	50 kgs.	13.200	15.017	21.350	26.550	16.250	13.286	12.408	12.094
Wheat Flour, 1st class	44 kgs.	-	38.366	-	-	-	43.313	39.375	36.000
Wheat Flour, 2nd class	44 kgs.	-	36.568	-	-	-	41.396	37.375	34.000
Wheat Flour, 3rd class	44 kgs.	-	37.086	-	-	-	40.125	36.375	33.000
Black Beans superior/good	60 kgs.	30.720	31.946	62.040	75.300	33.600	39.333	51.562	47.908
Butter, MG & RJ	1 kg.	5.629	6.430	7.481	6.645	7.895	7.537	6.877	6.609
Corn, yellow	60 kgs.	14.760	14.858	27.120	26.520	18.240	-	24.285	13.394
Salt, Norte	60 kgs.	8.400	8.741	12.780	17.400	17.460	12.979	13.000	9.719
Salt, Cabo Frio	60 kgs.	5.580	6,293	10.140	12.840	12.420	12.000	11.711	8.177
Bacon, common	1 kg.	1.401	1.440	2.302	3.645	2.520	2.349	2.197	2.489
Bacon, smoked	1 kg.	-	-	2.142	-	-	3.500	3.326	3.292

	Unit	1930	1931	1932	1933	1934	1935	1936	1937
Animals									
Cows									
Maximum	1 kg.	1.640	1.410	1.260	1.173	1.220	1.260	1.460	1.700
Minimum	1 kg.	1.180	1.000	1.010	.940	.951	.924	1.080	1.260
Swine									
Maximum	1 kg.	3.400	3.000	2.940	2.200	3.400	2.791	3.200	3.500
Minimum	1 kg.	2.700	2.257	2.034	1.846	2.040	2.208	2.712	2.500
Sugar, white crystal	60 kgs.	28.385	36.135	37.513	44.549	50.792	50.124	49.577	64.108
Sugar, yellow crystal	60 kgs.	25.136	32.583	33.042	43.224	46.733	46.822	48.417	59.889
Sugar, mascavo	60 kgs.	21.931	28.219	28.292	31.765	46.920	39.608	32.217	45.277
Rice, brilhado #1	60 kgs.	78.073	62.880	65.785	68.948	71.744	65.787	84.617	-
Rice, brilhado #2	60 kgs.	66.114	54.111	59.184	61.507	65.125	58.235	78.592	-
Rice, especial	60 kgs.	63.427	49.719	58.792	63.812	66.044	59.639	-	-
Olive Oil	1 liter	5.779	7.131	6.764	6.702	6.367	6.750	6.750	-
Lard, Itajaí SC	1 kg.	2.898	2.975	2.645	1.872	2.119	3.101	3.816	4.218
Lard, Pôrto Alegre RS	1 kg.	2.838	2.902	2.592	1.892	2.105	3.112	3.795	4.179
Potatoes, MG & SP	1 kg	.538	.559	.513	.711	.594	.703	.857	-
Potatoes, RS	1 kg.	.496	.412	.398	.639	.509	.593	.812	-
Coffee, type 7	10 kgs.	13.719	12.067	12.100	9.800	14.667	11.533	13.567	11.739
Onions	1 kg.	1.030	.672	.690	.893	.818	.609	1.010	.884
Dried Beef (xarque) RS	1 kg.	2.817	2.405	2.293	1.776	1.912	1.940	2.521	2.730
Dried Beef (xarque) MG & SP	1 kg.	2.660	2.313	1.092	1.850	1.846	1.907	2.356	2.721
Mandioca Flour, especial	50 kgs.	20.606	20.948	25.417	-	-	-	29.600	34.118
Mandioca Flour, fina	50 kgs.	18.932	19.904	22.606	19.436	14.930	16.921	24.359	32.340
Mandioca Flour, grossa	50 kgs.	13.244	14.669	16.487	13.064	11.328	11.885	-	22.980
Wheat Flour, first class	44 kgs.	37.791	34.542	36.000	34.111	35.113	37.675	47.308	55.855
Wheat Flour, second class	44 kgs.	35.791	32.542	34.250	33.111	34.113	36.604	46.308	54.400
Wheat Flour, third class	44 kgs.	34.791	31.400	34.000	34.111	33.111	35.450	45.308	51.417
Black Beans, superior/good	60 kgs.	25.427	20.972	33.264	27.430	25.478	21.187	37.006	36.181
Butter, MG & RJ	1 kg.	6.316	5.613	5.445	5.437	5.392	4.509	6.208	7.908
Corn, yellow	60 kgs.	17.329	15.487	17.091	13.773	16.520	14.902	19.733	19.997
Salt, Norte	60 kgs.	8.489	8.637	9.100	9.100	8.767	8.700	11.675	17.100
Salt, Cabo Frio	60 kgs.	7.500	7.637	8.100	8.100	6.733	6.500	9.510	15.000
Bacon, common	1 kg.	2.347	2.481	2.268	1.777	1.754	2.290	3.100	3.190
Bacon, smoked	1 kg.	2.829	2.965	2.994	2.335	2.393	2.580	3.872	4.350

Source: AN 1939-1940, pp. 1,382-1,383.

Table XXV-2. Brazilian Wholesale Price Indices, 1944-79

	1944	1945	1946	1947	1948	1949	1950	1951	1952	1953	1954	1955	1956	1957	1958	1959	1960	[1953]	1961
Domestic Market																			
Raw Materials	57	68	78	86	100	113	136	165	185	211	273	306	356	389	429	581	771	100	504
Food	52	65	73	85	100	112	130	149	177	206	264	296	347	383	406	544	732	100	475
Construction Materials	93	88	100	110	100	114	125	153	156	183	239	245	321	383	488	647	735	100	576
World Market																			
Agricultural Products	51	63	75	85	100	113	137	166	189	214	276	311	330	371	417	574	751	100	489
Industrial Products	83	90	101	99	100	105	109	129	139	160	211	240	298	349	408	587	724	100	644
Chemicals	79	77	83	89	100	96	106	119	128	146	198	241	302	305	400	584	780	100	714
Petroleum Products	96	95	89	92	100	106	107	111	117	146	174	245	284	416	502	780	862	100	991
Metals	87	80	87	96	100	113	118	140	143	209	262	300	382	401	579	831	882	100	548
Leather/Shoes	67	74	94	96	100	103	107	129	140	156	204	242	305	353	367	573	943	100	760
Cloth/Textiles	79	90	111	98	100	103	119	131	144	153	225	250	296	344	400	533	732	100	730
Leather/Hides	–	–	–	–	–	–	–	–	–	–	–	–	–	–	–	–	–	–	–
Cloth/Clothing/Shoes	–	–	–	–	–	–	–	–	–	–	–	–	–	–	–	–	–	–	–

	1962	1963	1964	1965	1966	1967	1968	1969	1970	1971	1972	1973	1974	1975	1976	1977	[1977]	1978	1979
Domestic Market																			
Raw Materials	798	1,536	2,631	72	101	128	157	187	223	271	319	368	475	607	852	1,198	100	139	216
Food	762	1,265	2,554	73	102	125	152	179	215	249	285	328	445	584	785	1,054	100	129	197
Construction Materials	824	1,645	2,709	68	103	129	150	185	228	293	352	406	520	668	986	1,414	100	148	233
World Market																			
Agricultural Products	785	1,295	2,583	71	98	131	177	210	247	283	340	413	554	687	956	1,316	100	137	226
Industrial Products	933	1,711	3,137	74	101	126	156	188	229	276	327	381	492	627	898	1,280	100	138	215
Chemicals	1,128	2,365	5,359	72	102	127	149	181	233	292	357	425	550	682	1,085	1,622	100	142	223
Petroleum Products	1,292	2,291	4,534	75	100	125	163	196	229	269	312	358	463	599	818	1,139	100	135	211
Metals	850	1,654	2,939	85	91	124	125	173	200	234	281	319	495	673	941	1,357	100	133	210
Leather/Shoes	1,100	1,735	2,795	80	100	120	155	195	225	276	350	401	641	881	1,398	2,112	100	133	223
Cloth/Textiles	1,036	1,872	3,253	78	101	121	158	195	245	280	316	369	513	659	874	1,149	100	129	194
Leather/Hides	–	–	–	69	104	128	149	184	252	317	452	663	679	721	1,132	1,572	100	144	318
Cloth/Clothing/Shoes	–	–	–	74	100	126	168	180	210	249	290	339	383	418	595	792	100	129	186

Sources: AN 1959, pp. 267-68 & 280; AN 1961, p. 256; AN 1965, p. 218; AN 1970, p. 218; AN 1974, p. 359; AN 1970, p. 402; AN 1978, p. 656; AN 1979, p. 655.

Table XXV-3. Cost of Living Indices for Rio de Janeiro, 1912-60, for Three Brazilian Cities, 1939-60, and for Twenty-six Brazilian Cities, 1944-66

	1912	1913	1914	1915	1916	1917	1918	1919	1920	1921	1922	1923	1924	1925
Rio de Janeiro GB	28.7	29.1	29.1	31.7	34.0	37.4	42.0	43.4	47.7	49.1	53.1	59.1	69.1	73.7

	1926	1927	1928	1929	1930	1931	1932	1933	1934	1935	1936	1937	1938
Rio de Janeiro GB	76.0	78.0	76.9	76.3	69.4	66.9	67.1	66.6	71.7	76.3	86.9	93.4	97.4

	1939	1940	1941	1942	1943	1944	1945	1946	1947	1948	1949	1950	1951	1952
Rio de Janeiro GB	100.0	104.2	115.5	128.6	142.6	160.1	186.4	217.4	264.8	273.7	285.9	312.2	349.8	410.3
Three Cities														
Rio de Janeiro GB	21	22	25	27	30	34	40	46	56	58	61	67	75	87
São Paulo SP	14	15	17	19	22	30	37	42	54	59	58	62	67	82
Pôrto Alegre RS	-	-	-	-	-	-	-	-	-	62	68	73	80	89
Twenty Six Cities														
Rio de Janeiro GB	-	-	-	-	-	-	-	-	-	122	132	145	175	213
Pôrto Velho RO	-	-	-	-	-	-	-	-	-	137	149	158	181	209
Rio Branco AC	-	-	-	-	-	-	-	-	--	141	148	155	164	181
Manaus AM	-	-	-	-	-	-	-	-	-	134	145	148	158	193
Boa Vista RR	-	-	-	-	-	-	-	-	-	136	150	157	186	196
Belém PA	-	-	-	-	-	-	-	-	-	122	139	141	156	176
Macapá AP	-	-	-	-	-	-	-	-	-	109	115	119	131	147
São Luis MA	-	-	-	-	-	-	-	-	-	118	142	155	174	174
Teresina PI	-	-	-	-	-	-	-	-	-	88	101	111	142	149
Fortaleza CE	-	-	-	-	-	-	-	-	-	125	132	140	165	185
Natal RN	-	-	-	-	-	-	-	-	-	117	126	135	146	168
João Pessoa PB	-	-	-	-	-	-	-	-	-	116	129	143	165	179
Recife PE	-	-	-	-	-	-	-	-	-	115	135	141	166	188
Maceió AL	-	-	-	-	-	-	-	-	-	108	135	135	156	182
Aracaju SE	-	-	-	-	-	-	-	-	-	97	110	123	131	153
Salvador BA	-	-	-	-	-	-	-	-	-	122	139	149	168	184
Belo Horizonte MG	-	-	-	-	-	-	-	-	-	118	125	127	137	163
Vitória ES	-	-	-	-	-	-	-	-	-	105	113	118	131	160
Niterói RJ	-	-	-	-	-	-	-	-	-	121	129	137	144	191
São Paulo	-	-	-	-	-	-	-	-	-	136	138	143	161	197
Curitiba PR	-	-	-	-	-	-	-	-	-	116	121	139	152	165
Florianópolis SC	-	-	-	-	-	-	-	-	-	99	100	108	113	130
Pôrto Alegre RS	-	-	-	-	-	-	-	-	-	101	106	114	116	128
Cuiabá MT	-	-	-	-	-	-	-	-	-	113	124	138	145	176
Goiânia GO	-	-	-	-	-	-	-	-	-	102	107	117	135	174
Brasília DF	-	-	-	-	-	-	-	-	-	-	-	-	-	-

	1953	1954	1955	1956	1957	1958	1959	1960	1961	1962	1963	1964	1965	1966
Rio de Janeiro GB	469.5	574.6	707.5	855.4	994.8	1140.4	1586.9	2053.5	-	-	-	-	-	-
Three Cities														
Rio de Janeiro GB	100	122	151	182	212	243	338	437	-	-	-	-	-	-
São Paulo SP	100	118	141	173	206	237	325	439	-	-	-	-	-	-
Pôrto Alegre RS	100	149	179	216	242	267	328	431	-	-	-	-	-	-
Twenty Six Cities														
Rio de Janeiro GB	240	286	345	428	518	603	784	1,033	1,353	1,992	3,425	6,213	10,982	14,936
Pôrto Velho RO	229	288	322	365	453	518	665	854	1,350	1,913	3,013	5,244	8,860	11,075
Rio Branco AC	206	265	298	298	503	571	750	943	1,426	2,104	3,495	6,969	12,253	16,296
Manaus AM	213	271	327	327	521	613	707	874	1,279	1,826	3,111	5,143	9,359	12,728
Boa Vista RR	196	231	273	273	419	568	681	919	1,463	2,276	3,656	6,021	9,156	11,994
Belém PA	202	245	314	409	468	526	774	1026	1,338	1,984	3,434	5,916	9,690	13,178
Macapá AP	177	203	239	239	433	543	681	920	1,286	1,916	3,175	5,062	8,891	10,936
São Luis MA	194	245	291	361	484	618	764	997	1,356	1,902	3,248	5,272	9,573	13,211
Teresina PI	156	199	216	290	356	464	588	717	996	1,486	2,495	4,215	7,805	10,303
Fortaleza CE	203	233	270	333	396	482	642	705	931	1,483	2,427	3,952	7,057	9,174
Natal RN	193	223	251	311	397	458	577	738	921	1,386	2,185	3,671	7,408	9,779
João Pessoa PB	199	249	289	372	460	556	711	870	1,221	1,949	3,141	5,279	9,627	12,419
Recife PE	204	239	278	324	421	484	631	820	1,058	1,644	2,528	4,600	7,934	11,187
Maceió AL	194	217	250	250	382	494	607	783	1,050	1,715	2,875	5,089	8,958	11,377
Aracaju SE	178	213	272	345	414	500	663	824	1,193	1,840	3,078	5,236	8,571	10,628
Salvador BA	201	246	319	404	482	589	763	1,059	1,461	2,344	3,615	6,029	10,507	15,130
Belo Horizonte MG	210	259	337	409	480	488	650	806	1,040	2,632	2,722	4,647	7,707	10,636
Vitória ES	185	226	258	315	410	451	602	746	945	1,426	2,370	4,103	6,750	9,383
Niterói, RJ	217	247	309	362	418	464	606	771	1,008	1,503	2,556	4,787	8,194	10,980
São Paulo SP	233	274	326	418	494	570	788	1,068	1,474	2,198	3,661	5,993	10,355	14,808
Curitiba PR	198	240	287	352	410	484	654	808	1,124	1,759	2,990	5,130	8,480	11,957
Florianópolis SC	152	186	224	273	349	382	509	653	842	1,319	2,256	3,978	6,949	9,451
Pôrto Alegre RS	139	175	237	337	389	453	583	728	933	1,329	2,206	3,787	6,660	9,834
Cuiabá MT	222	253	300	371	433	448	635	813	1,075	1,760	3,018	5,394	8,735	12,666
Goiânia, GO	214	262	301	343	431	510	681	946	1,371	2,094	3,512	5,677	9,617	10,579
Brasília DF	-	-	-	-	-	-	-	504	637	917	1,464	2,506	4,044	6,753

Sources: Baer 1965, pp. 300-301; AN 1956, pp. 294-298; AN 1958, pp. 287-290; AN 1960, pp. 220-222; AN 1963, pp. 266-267; AN 1964, pp. 262-263; AN 1967, pp. 417-419.

Table XXV-4. Normal Expenditures in Cruzeiros of a Middle Class Family of Seven in the City of Rio de Janeiro, 1912-39; Cost of Living Indices for a Skilled Factory Worker in the City of São Paulo, 1952-70; and for a Family at the Modal Income Level in the Municipio of São Paulo, 1972-77, and for Lower and Middle Class Families in the Municipio of Rio de Janeiro, 1970-78

Rio de Janeiro Lower Class Family of Seven

	1912	1913	1914	1915	1916	1917	1918	1919	1920	1921	1922	1923	1924	1926	1926
Total (Cr$)	691.1	705.8	706.3	766.5	823.1	906.8	1,018.1	1,051.5	1,157.4	1,185.9	1,299.6	1,433.0	1,671.2	1,785.9	1,836.6
Rent	200.0	200.0	200.0	210.0	210.0	220.0	240.0	260.0	300.0	300.0	350.0	400.0	500.0	550.0	610.0
Food	302.7	321.7	318.4	346.7	347.5	420.1	464.3	484.4	515.4	542.1	541.6	611.6	739.5	766.2	714.5
Clothing	50.0	50.0	50.0	55.0	60.0	65.0	70.0	75.0	100.0	100.0	100.0	110.0	120.0	140.0	160.0
Utilities	68.4	64.1	67.9	77.8	99.6	120.7	160.8	142.1	142.0	133.8	178.0	166.4	151.7	154.7	164.1
Servants	40.0	40.0	40.0	45.0	45.0	45.0	50.0	55.0	55.0	60.0	70.0	75.0	80.0	90.0	100.0
Furnishings/Utensils	30.0	30.0	30.0	32.0	34.0	36.0	38.0	40.0	45.0	50.0	60.0	70.0	80.0	85.0	88.0

Rio de Janeiro Middle Class Family of Seven

	1927	1928	1929	1930	1931	1932	1933	1934	1935	1936	1937	1938	1939
Total	1,888.8	1,858.2	1,843.6	1,676.2	1,616.4	1,621.6	1,608.1	1,735.3	1,828.3	2,099.5	2,260.0	2,358.8	2,415.8
Rent	610.0	610.0	610.0	550.0	500.0	480.0	460.0	500.0	500.0	600.0	620.0	635.0	650.0
Food	737.9	741.6	732.9	648.6	614.4	639.9	646.6	715.8	747.1	846.0	935.1	934.0	953.3
Clothing	160.0	160.0	160.0	144.0	140.0	140.0	140.0	190.0	235.0	250.0	250.0	259.5	260.5
Utilities	165.9	133.6	127.7	128.6	162.0	161.7	161.5	127.0	126.2	126.8	126.8	126.8	126.8
Servants	120.0	120.0	120.0	120.0	120.0	120.0	120.0	120.0	120.0	139.2	170.8	186.7	200.0
Furnishings/Utensils	95.0	93.0	93.0	85.0	80.0	80.0	80.0	82.5	100.0	137.5	157.5	216.8	225.2

São Paulo Skilled Worker

	1951	1952	1953	1954	1955	1956	1957	1958	1959	1960	1961	1962	1963	1964	1965	1966	1967	1968	1969	1970
Total	100	123	150	177	212	258	308	355	488	657	908	1,386	2,404	4,495	7,269	10,659	13,810	17,152	21,138	25,171
Food	100	129	174	208	247	305	341	383	552	797	1,073	1,694	2,817	5,533	8,306	12,298	15,173	18,316	22,861	26,802
Housing	100	123	133	140	173	209	258	319	403	458	643	948	1,760	2,962	5,168	7,697	10,337	12,815	14,676	16,526
Clothing	100	112	122	156	193	229	269	299	380	505	743	1,121	2,018	3,536	6,015	8,217	10,645	14,128	17,576	20,302
Fuel	100	121	123	158	186	208	262	346	528	673	879	1,304	2,547	4,666	8,094	11,767	16,885	20,343	24,322	26,762
Health	100	108	135	175	184	240	322	344	371	555	749	1,046	1,787	3,490	6,214	8,535	12,527	15,985	21,855	28,642
Personal Items	100	113	137	180	233	267	350	392	555	767	976	1,425	2,505	5,167	10,415	14,458	18,786	26,444	33,936	48,010
House Cleaning/Maintenance	100	107	126	178	201	247	293	327	505	733	870	1,125	2,014	4,197	6,796	9,470	11,124	13,049	14,758	18,787
Furniture	100	125	132	183	223	251	480	562	815	846	1,045	1,598	2,822	5,322	8,913	11,779	16,737	21,410	26,709	32,595
Transportation	100	100	115	162	191	299	353	393	510	817	1,331	1,902	3,474	5,396	9,512	15,938	20,607	25,907	31,527	36,565
Diverse	100	133	144	157	175	196	241	278	381	529	855	1,258	2,128	4,081	6,897	9,992	15,696	20,620	27,375	37,616

Rio de Janeiro Lower/Middle Class Family

	1970	1971	1972	1973	1974	1975	1976	1977	1978
Total	238	286	333	375	479	618	877	1,260	1,747
Food	218	267	314	360	492	617	879	1,282	1,801
Clothing	220	257	289	309	348	397	509	703	853
Housing	303	354	390	421	499	692	1,092	1,590	2,202
Household Items	215	249	271	296	374	455	604	870	1,192
Health	247	300	352	392	479	633	853	1,245	1,725
Personal Services	260	314	381	438	541	734	1,041	1,477	2,018
Public Services	254	315	392	443	526	718	966	1,292	1,853

São Paulo Modal Family

	1971	1972	1973	1974	1975	1976	1977
Total	116	114	114	133	129	138	141
Food	121	117	117	137	126	138	139
Personal Items	115	115	115	131	127	133	157
Education	116	127	127	135	127	129	146
Housing	115	108	108	127	132	137	139
Health	122	116	116	125	142	146	134
Transportation	111	110	110	146	132	147	139
Clothing	109	106	106	122	129	147	136

Sources: AN 1939-1940, p. 1,384; AN 1961, p. 286; AN 1969, p. 339; AN 1973, p. 376; AN 1974, p. 402; AN 1975, p. 376; AN 1976, p. 296; AN 1979, p. 652.

Table XXV-5. Brazil's Annual Average Retail Food Prices in Cruzeiros, 1961-75

Food	Units	1961	1962	1963	1964	1965	1966	1967	1968	1969	1970	1971	1972	1973	1974	1975
Squash	Kg	-	-	-	-	-	-	.30	.34	.42	.54	.65	.80	1.17	1.74	2.31
Sugar, Refined	Kg	30.2	48.4	99	203	.31	.35	.47	.57	.69	.85	1.02	1.17	1.32	1.69	2.22
Sugar, Crystal	Kg	24.8	41.2	84	180	.24	.28	.37	.45	.58	.68	.82	.98	1.18	1.51	1.97
Sweet Mandioca	Kg	-	22.5	38	61	.11	.16	.24	.24	.34	.43	.53	.70	.93	1.29	1.74
Garlic	Kg	-	380.9	752	855	.98	2.33	4.42	5.50	4.56	4.31	7.18	10.14	12.87	13.52	18.49
Rice, Needle	Kg	38.1	87.8	173	252	.29	.48	.72	.79	.89	.99	1.36	1.84	2.03	3.16	4.79
Rice, Big Yellow	Kg	-	-	-	-	-	-	.78	.89	1.04	1.16	1.62	2.13	2.33	3.56	5.36
Rice, Blue Rose	Kg	-	-	-	-	-	-	.63	.70	.76	.86	1.18	1.56	1.68	2.76	4.19
Rice, Japanese	Kg	33.9	76.1	151	218	.26	.44	.64	.70	.77	.85	1.19	1.63	1.79	2.90	4.36
Olive Oil	Kg	-	450.3	1,036	1,870	2.99	2.38	3.75	4.22	4.71	5.30	6.18	6.87	8.82	13.44	19.52
Dried Cod (Bacalhau)	Kg	-	-	-	-	-	-	3.87	4.50	5.09	6.18	8.48	10.72	14.18	22.71	29.76
Bananas, d'Agua	Dozen	-	31.1	51	117	.16	.20	.26	.33	.44	.58	.70	.82	1.20	1.81	2.61
Bananas, Prata	Dozen	-	-	-	-	-	-	.32	.40	.53	.66	.87	1.06	1.42	2.02	2.83
Lard, Bulk	Kg	-	187.5	346	954	1.44	1.39	1.77	1.91	2.77	2.88	3.31	4.53	4.49	10.84	10.14
Lard, Canned	Kg	332.7	370.2	672	1,965	3.03	3.02	1.93	2.13	2.99	3.33	3.77	5.31	5.22	11.49	12.04
Potatoes, White	Kg	26.8	55.0	83	124	.24	.49	.43	.41	.73	.78	.87	1.18	2.21	2.33	2.66
Coffee, Roasted/Ground	Kg	60.9	57.8	95	182	.25	.40	.40	.91	1.47	1.97	3.61	6.39	8.22	10.95	17.14
Beef, First Class	Kg	148.8	229.9	386	670	1.08	1.95	2.41	2.62	2.96	4.00	5.29	6.54	9.43	13.86	16.03
Beef, Second Class	Kg							1.49	1.71	2.02	2.83	3.81	4.78	6.75	8.37	10.40
Pork	Kg	-	-	-	-	-	-	2.19	2.43	2.96	3.83	4.81	6.27	8.87	13.70	14.94
Dried Meat (Xarque)	Kg	185.1	302.1	493	936	1.57	2.46	3.05	3.22	3.69	4.95	6.71	8.30	12.19	17.75	19.55
Onions	Kg	-	122.0	89	459	.43	.59	.58	.87	.84	.88	1.60	1.77	3.35	2.56	3.91
Flour, Mandioca	Kg	22.2	56.7	73	88	.15	.25	.36	.40	.44	.61	.91	1.09	1.18	1.62	2.56
Flour, Wheat	Kg	-	65.9	126	224	.39	.50	.61	.77	.90	1.13	1.32	1.47	1.76	2.27	2.42
Beans, Sulfur	Kg	-	115.7	152	228	.35	.69	.67	.83	1.43	1.67	1.83	2.09	4.63	4.44	5.47
Beans, Little Mulatto	Kg	37.4	112.4	132	180	.30	.60	.51	.61	1.23	1.33	1.52	1.68	4.16	3.59	4.61
Beans, Common Black	Kg	33.9	90.3	130	172	.24	.53	.55	.55	.94	1.54	1.57	1.59	3.56	3.96	3.76
Beans, Black Little Uberaba	Kg	-	-	-	-	-	-	.65	.67	1.18	1.87	2.03	2.13	4.48	5.08	5.16
Corn Meal	Kg	-	45.1	56	107	.18	.24	.33	.35	.44	.61	.72	.89	1.11	1.60	2.12
Chicken, Live	Kg	-	-	-	-	-	-	2.11	2.24	2.53	3.11	3.77	4.44	5.80	8.10	9.32
Chicken, Pressed	Kg	-	-	-	-	-	-	2.46	2.72	3.06	3.82	4.39	4.99	6.52	8.40	9.55
Goiaba Jelly	Kg	-	111.0	227	380	.64	.84	1.09	1.31	1.55	1.93	2.48	2.79	3.18	4.37	5.30
Cocoa Butter	Kg	-	177.3	352	910	1.29	1.41	1.62	2.04	2.38	2.73	3.52	3.93	4.46	8.68	10.00
Oranges	Dozen	-	-	-	-	-	-	.64	.76	1.14	1.34	1.41	1.78	2.34	3.23	3.32
Milk, Condensed Canned	400 Gr	-	83.0	135	270	.49	.63	.84	.95	1.16	1.38	1.70	2.01	2.34	3.43	4.76
Milk, Powdered Canned	454 Gr	158.3	234.4	375	701	1.16	1.53	2.04	2.29	2.87	3.20	3.80	4.44	5.23	7.42	10.23
Milk, Whole	Liter	23.9	38.5	66	117	.19	.28	.36	.41	.49	.58	.69	.81	.98	1.43	2.03
Macaroni, Without Eggs	Kg	-	88.0	168	316	.51	.65	.81	1.00	1.17	1.46	1.72	2.03	2.59	3.64	4.25
Pasta, of Semolina	Kg	-	-	-	-	-	-	1.10	1.37	1.66	2.13	2.54	2.97	3.74	5.28	6.19
Butter, Salted Bulk	Kg	321.4	408.4	679	1,562	2.32	3.05	3.71	4.60	5.73	5.80	8.86	10.15	10.47	15.64	20.21
Butter, Salted Canned	Kg	358.8	452.8	751	1,806	2.60	3.32	4.04	5.16	6.80	6.78	9.44	10.70	10.83	16.71	21.70
Margarine	Kg	-	-	-	-	-	-	2.36	2.75	3.32	3.56	4.32	4.89	5.16	8.79	11.52
Corn, Kernels	Kg	14.2	28.9	34	71	.11	.15	.22	.22	.29	.38	.45	.56	.73	1.04	1.62
Cottonseed Oil, Canned	Kg	148.5	164.5	283	861	1.19	1.44	1.53	1.82	2.22	2.58	3.39	3.52	3.68	6.79	7.98
Peanut Oil, Canned	Kg	-	174.2	298	970	1.28	1.54	1.63	1.96	2.44	2.84	3.66	3.96	4.20	7.20	9.35
Corn Oil, Canned	Kg	-	-	-	-	-	-	2.35	2.74	3.14	3.70	4.49	5.03	5.31	8.07	11.58
Soybean Oil, Canned	Kg	-	-	-	-	-	-	1.59	1.87	2.28	2.61	3.31	3.34	3.50	6.46	7.64
Eggs, Chicken	Dozen	-	138.6	227	357	.66	.89	1.12	1.33	1.61	1.92	2.22	2.42	3.28	4.31	4.99
Bread, Common Salt	Kg	54.4	77.9	146	256	.43	.56	.76	1.03	1.22	1.51	1.81	2.06	2.43	3.25	4.10
Fish, Fresh	Kg	-	-	-	-	-	-	1.68	1.91	2.26	2.74	3.36	4.23	6.19	8.79	10.66
Cheese, Prata (Silver)	Kg	-	411.2	680	1,371	2.16	3.20	3.72	4.59	5.53	6.23	8.14	9.35	12.52	18.52	23.88
Salt, Refined	Kg	-	30.9	63	114	.25	.28	.29	.31	.38	.42	.47	.53	.65	.99	1.33
Tomatoes	Kg	-	69.0	120	195	.36	.45	.54	.67	.98	.90	1.24	1.58	2.13	2.78	3.55
Bacon	Kg	-	183.5	346	854	1.34	1.33	1.73	1.91	2.70	3.09	3.55	4.98	5.75	10.94	11.18

Sources: AN 1963, pp. 198-99; AN 1965, p. 221; AN 1967, p. 267; AN 1970, p. 362; AN 1972, 353; AN 1975, p. 449; AN 1976, p. 303.

Chapter XXVI. National Accounts

Table XXVI-1 reports the structure of Brazil's Gross Domestic Product (GDP) and capital transactions from 1939 to 1979. Rounding errors account for the failure of a few totals to equal the sum of the parts of a category. The structure of the table follows that presented in the <u>United Nations Yearbook of Accounts Statistics, 1982</u>, which publication was also the source of the data for the years 1960, 1965, and 1970-79. The Instituto Brasileiro de Economia of the Fundação Getúlio Vargas originated the data for these and all other years. Based on these data for all other years the author calculated the figures to fill in the United Nations-modeled table. The Gross Domestic Product (GDP) data by activity for 1961-64 were calculated from the U.N. Yearbook noted above. It gave the percentage of GDP by activity. After summing the percentages the author assumed (although the sources did not specify) that the differences between this sum and the total GDP was the Net of (-) Bank Service, (+) Import Duties, (+) Value Added Tax, (+) Other Adjustments. For 1969 the Increase in Stocks category was included in the category Private Final Consumption Expenditures.

The following sources and methods were used in the <u>Yearbook</u> to establish the four major statistics shown on Table XXVI-1. They are taken verbatim from page 131 of that source:

a) Gross Domestic Product. The main approach used to estimate GDP is the income approach but the production approach is also used.

b) Expenditures on the Gross Domestic Product. The expenditure approach is used to estimate government final consumption expenditure increase in stocks and exports and imports of goods and services. A combination of the commodity-flow method and the expenditure approach is used to estimate gross fixed capital formation, whereas private final consumption expenditure is taken as a residual. Government consumption expenditure is estimated by the Center of Fiscal

Studies, based on information from government budgetary and accounting statements. Bench-mark estimates on production and imports of capital goods have been prepared for 1949, 1959, and 1970 based on industrial censuses and foreign trade statistics. These estimates are extrapolated by an index of material purchases and adjusted for business mark-ups and value added. For urban construction, bench-mark estimates are obtained from the industrial censuses held in 1950, 1960, and 1970. The bench-mark estimates are extrapolated by the use of an indicator made up of data on consumption of construction materials and wholesale prices. Bench-mark estimates for rural construction are based on the censuses of agriculture in 1940 and 1950 and the demographic censuses of 1950, 1960, and 1970. Extrapolation is done by the estimated growth of rural population and a general price index. Data on exports and imports of goods and services are prepared by the Central Bank. To calculate constant prices, government consumption expenditure is deflated by the implicit price index of gross domestic product, whereas value added of private consumption expenditure is calculated as a residual. Gross fixed capital formation of the base-year is extrapolated by different volume indexes. The value of 1970 exports of goods is extrapolated by a quantum index. In order to include the value of exports of services, the obtained value is expanded by the ratio of total goods to export of goods.

c) Cost Structure of the Gross Domestic Product. Estimates for wages and salaries are based on the demographic and economic censuses carried out usually at 10-year intervals. Four noncensus years social security data are used as estimators. Operating surplus is calculated as a residual. Depreciation is estimated for all years at 5 percent of the gross domestic product. Estimates of indirect taxes and subsidies are obtained from the federal, state, and municipal budgets and balance sheets.

d) Gross Domestic Product by Kind of Economic Activity. The table of GDP (in the UN *Yearbook*) by kind of economic activity is prepared in net factor values. Depreciation and indirect taxes net of subsidies are estimated as aggregates only. Combinations of the income approach and the production approach are used to estimate the value added of all industries except the agricultural sector, for which only the production approach is used. Factor income data are not available for this sector. The censuses of 1949, 1959, and 1970 provide agricultural bench-mark data. For the years after 1959 estimates of gross product are made by using value indexes. The rates of intermediate consumption found in 1959 and 1970 censuses have been interpolated and extrapolated to apply to other years. For mining and quarrying, manufacturing and construction the census data for 1949, 1959, and 1970 are used as bench marks. For mining and manufacturing, value indexes for the most important products are used as estimators for the years after 1970. For the estimation of the value of construction after 1970, indicators based on construction inputs are used in the calculation of value added, data from the demographic censuses and business income tax files are also used. Bench-mark estimates for the trade sector are based on the censuses of commerce taken in 1950, 1960, and 1970. Small units are covered by the industrial or demographic census. For the transport sector, data are provided by the authorities of air transport, railways and maritime transport. For road transportation, special surveys of freight and passenger transport enterprises are held every second year. Data on self-employed carriers are estimated through data from the demographic census. The censuses taken in 1950 and 1970 provide the basis for bench-mark estimates for the financial institutions. Estimates for other years are based on accounts data from various sources. Rent estimation is based on the demographic censuses of 1950, 1960, and 1970 and includes imputed rents for owner-occupied dwellings. For noncensus years the main indicator is the series of property tax revenues. For the community, social and personal services, government data are obtained from official budgetary and accounting statements. Constant prices for the agricultural sector are obtained through extrapolating the value added of 1970 by quantity indexes of output for each of the three subsectors: farming, livestock production and forestry. For mining and quarrying, a quantity index of output based on the production data for the three most important mineral products is applied to the value added of 1970. Value added in manufacturing is extrapolated by a quantity index of ouput based on production data for approximately 400 products. Value added of construction is extrapolated by an index based on the production of principal materials used in the sector. For the trade sector, value added is extrapolated by a quantity index of output. Value added in the transport sector is extrapolated by various output indicators. For financing, insurance, real estate and business services, value added is deflated by the cost of living index. Value added in public administration and defense is deflated by the implicit price index of gross domestic product, whereas value added in other private services is deflated by the cost of living index.

Table XXVI-2 shows the relations among Brazil's national account aggregates from 1947 to 1979. The data originated with the United Nation's <u>Yearbook of Accounts Statistics, 1982,</u> from which the model for this table was taken, and by the Instituto Brasileiro de Economia of the Fundação Getúlio

Vargas. The data shown represent the latest published rectifications for the years in question. Data for 1969, however, are listed as preliminary even in the latest <u>Anuário</u> reporting them. As in the previous table the author utilized both <u>Anuário</u> and U.N. <u>Yearbook</u> data to frame out the United Nations-model table, then calculated the missing statistics from them.

Table XXVI-1. The Structure of Brazil's Gross Domestic Product (GDP) and Capital Transactions, 1939–79

	1939	1948	1955	1959	1960	1961	1962	1963	1964	1965	1966	1967	1968	1969
Expenditure on the GDP in Current Prices (Cr$ 000000)														
General Government Final Consumption Expenditure	—	—	—	249	367	538	835	1,952	2,920	4,226	6,251	8,486	11,428	15,468
Private Final Consumption Expenditure	—	—	—	1,332	1,913	2,748	4,530	8,154	15,596	24,886	38,837	52,199	71,788	95,606
Gross Capital Formation	—	—	—	427	507	788	1,343	2,232	4,294	6,764	8,187	10,848	17,347	21,949
Increase in Stocks	—	—	—	60	41	91	162	134	490	1,360	(–) 12	524	712	—
Gross Fixed Capital Formation	—	—	—	368	467	697	1,181	2,099	3,804	5,405	8,199	10,324	16,635	21,949
Exports of Goods and Services	—	—	—	134	167	278	339	1,156	1,721	3,246	4,074	4,738	6,867	10,144
Less: Imports of Goods and Services	—	—	—	153	203	300	446	1,207	1,476	2,305	3,626	4,786	7,551	10,050
Gross Domestic Product	—	—	—	1,989	2,751	4,052	6,601	11,927	23,055	36,818	53,723	71,485	99,871	133,117
Expenditure on the GDP in Constant (1970) Prices (Cr$ 000000)														
General Government Final Consumption Expenditure	—	—	—	—	—	—	—	—	—	14,856	—	—	—	—
Private Final Consumption Expenditure	—	—	—	—	—	—	—	—	—	95,102	—	—	—	—
Gross Capital Formation	—	—	—	—	—	—	—	—	—	32,243	—	—	—	—
Increase in Stocks	—	—	—	—	—	—	—	—	—	4,931	—	—	—	—
Gross Fixed Capital Formation	—	—	—	—	—	—	—	—	—	27,312	—	—	—	—
Exports of Goods and Services	—	—	—	—	—	—	—	—	—	8,446	—	—	—	—
Less: Imports of Goods and Services	—	—	—	—	—	—	—	—	—	6,711	—	—	—	—
Gross Domestic Product	—	—	—	—	—	—	—	—	—	143,936	—	—	—	—
GDP By Kind of Activity in Current Prices (Cr$ 000000)														
Agriculture, Hunting, Forestry, Fishing	10	46	167	—	508	729	1,254	2,028	4,158	6,708	8,186	11,153	13,873	17,771
Mining and Quarrying				—	10					89				
Manufacturing	8	36	162	—	483	729	1,188	2,385	4,185	6,297	11,652	15,197	22,299	30,552
Electricity, Gas, Water				—	39	90	132	119	462	633				
Construction				—	33	40	66	119	231	341				
Transport, Storage, Communication	3	12	42	—	145	243	396	716	1,155	1,998	2,557	3,647	4,604	5,859
Wholesale & Retail Trade, Restaurants, Hotels	8	31	109	—	338	486	792	1,551	2,541	4,059	5,658	7,412	10,273	13,540
Finance, Insurance, Real Estate, Business Services				—	220					3,126				
Community, Social, Personal Services	11	42	185	—	470	1,094	1,782	3,220	6,237	6,896	14,852	20,563	27,231	35,961
Subtotal: Net Domestic Product in Factor Values	40	166	665	—	2,246	3,411	5,610	10,138	18,942	30,147	42,905	57,972	78,281	103,683
Net of: (–) Bank Service, (+) Import Duties, (+) Value Added Tax, (+) Other Adjustments	—	—	—	—	505	641	991	1,789	4,113	6,671	10,818	13,513	21,590	29,434
Gross Domestic Product	—	—	—	1,989	2,751	4,052	6,601	11,927	23,055	36,818	53,723	71,485	99,871	133,117
Cost Components of the GDP in Current Prices (Cr$ 000000)														
Net Indirect Taxes	—	—	—	275	373	471	742	1,319	2,828	4,850	8,159	9,980	16,654	22,843
Indirect Taxes Paid	—	—	—	294	397	520	829	1,525	3,214	5,538	8,859	10,921	17,762	24,088
Less: Subsidies Paid	—	—	—	19	24	49	87	206	386	688	700	941	1,108	1,245
Consumption of Fixed Capital	—	—	—	99	137	201	327	593	1,145	1,820	2,659	3,533	4,945	6,591
Compensation of Employees Paid By Resident Producers	—	—	—	1,420	752	3,061	5,030	9,083	17,013	10,951	36,255	50,584	78,272	103,683
Net Operating Surplus	—	—	—		1,489					19,197				
Gross Domestic Product	—	—	—	1,989	2,751	4,052	6,601	11,927	23,055	36,818	53,723	71,485	99,871	133,117

Table XXVI-1 (continued)

	1970	1971	1972	1973	1974	1975	1976	1977	1978	1979
Expenditure on the GDP in Current Prices (Cr$ 000000)										
General Government Final Consumption Expenditure	21,176	27,536	35,485	47,899	65,455	99,354	157,434	220,840	326,521	553,695
Private Final Consumption Expenditure	138,980	183,676	240,523	320,259	468,671	694,337	1,071,712	1,601,776	2,442,519	4,108,048
Gross Capital Formation	48,961	70,080	92,663	136,121	227,283	-	-	-	-	-
Increase in Stocks	2,571	6,772	9,407	21,420	52,913	-	-	-	-	-
Gross Fixed Capital Formation	46,390	63,309	83,256	114,701	174,370	255,903	370,164	515,878	766,688	1,244,678
Exports of Goods and Services	13,660	16,679	25,203	40,152	57,174	74,815	114,593	180,623	242,101	431,639
Less: Imports of Goods and Services	14,476	21,164	30,706	46,123	99,064	115,029	153,632	197,193	285,216	555,950
Gross Domestic Product	208,301	276,808	363,167	498,307	719,519	1,009,380	1,560,271	2,321,924	3,492,613	5,872,110
Expenditure on the GDP in Constant (1970) Prices (Cr$ 000000)										
General Government Final Consumption Expenditure	21,176	23,475	25,770	28,872	29,998	34,307	38,314	37,802	39,397	42,945
Private Final Consumption Expenditure	138,980	157,339	174,171	191,747	208,029	232,706	253,927	266,540	283,551	305,265
Gross Capital Formation	48,961	59,566	67,226	82,791	105,914	-	-	-	-	-
Increase in Stocks	2,571	5,619	6,588	12,874	24,628	-	-	-	-	-
Gross Fixed Capital Formation	46,390	53,947	60,638	69,917	81,266	92,576	95,683	95,074	102,442	106,716
Export of Goods and Services	13,660	13,647	18,174	23,005	19,264	20,849	23,361	27,186	26,503	26,549
Less: Imports of Goods and Services	14,476	18,022	21,632	26,045	33,465	31,950	31,553	29,164	30,500	33,004
Gross Domestic Product	208,301	236,005	263,709	300,370	329,740	348,487	379,732	397,438	421,392	448,472
GDP By Kind of Activity in Current Prices (Cr$ 000000)										
Agriculture, Hunting, Forestry, Fishing	17,127	23,973	30,560	44,271	65,657	87,821	137,703	236,849	320,671	529,555
Mining and Quarrying	1,327	1,470	2,219	2,871	7,420	11,361	15,271	19,327	25,511	41,881
Manufacturing	45,802	62,154	83,870	118,820	179,255	251,935	380,304	453,838	797,627	1,331,202
Electricity, Gas, Water	3,575	4,775	6,737	8,630	11,925	18,168	26,467	40,095	58,126	100,982
Construction	9,934	12,555	16,649	22,944	34,988	47,398	70,684	108,890	163,997	279,379
Transport, Storage, Communications	8,740	11,236	15,004	21,040	29,682	42,620	66,833	97,738	149,339	244,260
Wholesale & Retail Trade, Restaurants, Hotels	26,283	35,367	46,571	64,710	95,819	132,829	201,289	296,735	430,056	715,803
Finance, Insurance, Real Estats, Business Services	23,131	31,827	40,490	54,076	73,006	114,488	189,697	287,418	525,187	899,717
Community, Social, Personal Services	31,310	40,795	51,356	65,083	89,004	127,366	195,146	279,242	428,191	718,702
Subtotal: Net Domestic Product in Factor Values	167,229	224,423	293,366	402,444	586,756	833,985	1,283,394	1,910,132	2,898,705	4,861,481
Net of: (-) Bank Service, (+) Import Duties, (+) Value Added Tax, (+) Other Adjustments	41,072	52,385	69,802	95,863	132,763	175,394	276,871	411,792	593,908	920,629
Gross Domestic Product	208,301	276,808	363,167	498,307	719,519	1,009,380	1,560,271	2,321,924	3,492,613	5,782,210
Cost Components of the GDP in Current Prices (Cr$ 000000)										
Net Indirect Taxes	30,755	38,675	51,819	71,185	97,117	125,655	200,143	297,771	423,566	639,819
Indirect Taxes Paid	31,895	40,412	53,858	73,452	102,039	133,357	210,843	314,269	453,654	674,266
Less: Subsidies Paid	1,140	1,737	2,039	2,267	4,922	7,703	10,700	16,498	30,088	34,447
Consumption of Fixed Capital	10,317	13,710	17,983	24,678	35,647	49,740	76,729	114,021	170,342	280,811
Compensation of Employees Paid By Resident Producers	78,006	104,877	140,546	186,874	264,656	392,042	1,283,399	1,910,132	2,889,705	6,702,740
Net Operating Surplus	89,222	119,547	152,820	215,570	322,100	441,943				
Gross Domestic Product	208,301	276,808	363,167	498,307	719,519	1,009,380	1,560,271	2,321,924	3,492,613	5,782,110

Sources: AN 1970, pp. 500-509; AN 1972, pp. 510-511; AN 1973, p. 569; UN 1982, pp. 106, 131-133.

Table XXVI-2. Relations among Brazil's National Account Aggregates, 1947-79

	1947	1948	1949	1950	1951	1952	1953	1954	1955	1956	1957	1958	1959
Gross Domestic Product (Cr$ 000,000)	164	187	234	253	306	351	429	556	661	843	1,007	1,458	1,990
Plus: Net Factor Income From Abroad	(-) 1	(-) 2	(-) 2	(-) 2	(-) 2	(-) 1	(-) 4	(-) 5	(-) 6	(-) 7	(-) 7	(-) 10	(-) 15
Equals: Gross National Product	163	185	232	251	304	350	425	551	655	836	1,000	1,448	1,975
Less: Consumption of Fixed Capital	8	9	12	13	15	18	21	28	35	44	53	72	103
Equals: National Income at Market Prices	155	176	220	238	289	332	404	523	620	792	947	1,375	1,872
Less: Direct Taxes Paid to Supranational Organizations	-	-	-	-	-	-	-	-	-	-	-	-	-
Plus: Net Current Transfers Received From Abroad	-	-	-	-	-	-	-	-	-	-	-	-	-
Equals: National Disposable Income at Market Prices	-	-	-	-	-	-	-	-	-	-	-	-	-
Less: Final Consumption	141	156	202	220	255	291	367	445	582	749	907	1,210	1,701
Equals: Net Saving	14	20	18	18	34	41	37	78	38	43	40	165	171
Less: Brazil's Surplus on Current Transactions	-	-	(-) 2	-	-	-	-	-	(+) 1	(-) 1	(+) 14	(+) 18	(+) 33
Equals: Net Capital Formation	-	-	16	-	-	-	-	-	39	42	54	183	204

	1960	1961	1962	1963	1964	1965	1966	1967	1968	1969	1970
Gross Domestic Product (Cr$ 000,000)	2,751	4,052	6,601	11,927	23,055	36,818	53,723	71,485	99,871	133,117	208,301
Plus: Net Factor Income From Abroad	(-) 22	(-) 24	(-) 62	(-) 52	(-) 151	(-) 394	(-) 507	(-) 787	(-) 913	(-) 1,234	(-) 1,842
Equals: Gross National Product	2,729	4,028	6,539	11,875	22,904	36,424	53,216	70,698	98,958	131,883	206,459
Less: Consumption of Fixed Capital	136	201	327	593	1,145	1,820	2,659	3,533	4,945	6,591	10,317
Equals: National Income at Market Prices	2,592	3,827	6,212	11,282	21,759	34,604	50,557	67,165	94,013	125,292	196,142
Less: Direct Taxes Paid to Supranational Organizations	-	-	-	-	-	-	-	-	-	-	-
Plus: Net Current Transfers Received From Abroad	-	-	-	-	-	-	-	-	-	-	-
Equals: National Disposable Income at Market Prices	-	-	-	-	-	-	-	-	-	-	-
Less: Final Consumption	2,279	3,286	5,366	9,747	18,516	29,113	45,088	60,685	83,216	111,074	160,156
Equals: Net Saving	313	541	846	1,535	3,243	5,491	5,469	6,480	10,797	14,218	35,986
Less: Brazil's Surplus on Current Transactions	(+) 58	(+) 46	(+) 170	(+) 122	(-) 94	(-) 547	(+) 59	(+) 835	(+) 1,606	(+) 1,140	(+) 2,658
Equals: Net Capital Formation	371	587	1,017	1,657	3,149	4,944	5,528	7,315	12,403	15,358	38,644

	1971	1972	1973	1974	1975	1976	1977	1978	1979
Gross Domestic Product (Cr$ 000,000)	276,808	363,167	498,307	719,519	1,009,380	1,560,271	2,321,924	3,492,613	5,782,110
Plus: Net Factor Income From Abroad	(-) 2,459	(-) 3,311	(-) 4,469	(-) 6,183	(-) 14,016	(-) 24,827	(-) 40,217	(-) 83,835	(-) 162,704
Equals: Gross National Product	274,349	359,856	493,838	713,336	995,364	1,535,444	2,281,707	3,408,778	5,619,406
Less: Consumption of Fixed Capital	13,710	17,983	24,678	35,647	49,740	76,729	114,021	170,342	280,811
Equals: National Income at Market Prices	260,639	341,874	469,161	677,690	945,624	1,458,715	2,167,686	3,238,436	5,338,595
Less: Direct Taxes Paid to Supranational Organizations	-	-	-	-	-	-	-	-	-
Plus: Net Current Transfers Received From Abroad	-	-	-	-	-	-	-	-	-
Equals: National Disposable Income at Market Prices	-	-	-	-	-	-	-	-	-
Less: Final Consumption	211,212	276,008	368,157	534,126	793,691	1,229,146	1,822,616	2,769,040	4,661,743
Equals: Net Saving	49,427	65,867	101,003	143,564	151,933	229,570	345,071	469,396	676,852
Less: Brazil's Surplus on Current Transactions	-	-	-	-	-	-	-	-	-
Equals: Net Capital Formation	56,371	74,680	111,443	191,637	-	-	-	-	-

Sources: AN 1962, pp. 195 & 199; AN 1967, p. 420; AN 1969, p. 458; AN 1973, pp. 562-63; AN 1974, pp. 606-08; UN 1982, p. 133.

Index

462

Index

military
    expenditures, 355
    personnel, 387
    police, 387-90
    schools, 111
milk, production, 207
Milne, Lorus and Margery, 186
Minas Gerais, 16, 18, 22-24, 47, 49-58, 84, 109-10, 164,
    167-68, 193-94, 202-04, 206-07, 209-11, 221, 225,
    242, 245, 248-49, 251-53, 255, 257, 267-68, 293,
    300-01, 303-06, 337, 417-19
mineral water, 220-21
minerals, 215, 220-22
minerals, price and quantum indices, 222
minifúndios, 101
minimum wage, 149, 164
minor employees, 161-62
Misericórdia Order (Portugal), 76
molluscs, production, 213-14
Momsen, Richard, 28
money supply, 423-24, 427-30
Moroccans, 105-06
mortality rates, 86
motels, 343-45
motor vehicles, 234, 253
motor vehicles, output, 280
mules, 206
musical instruments, output, 279

Natal, Rio Grande do Norte, 15, 17-18, 55, 84, 164, 254,
    262-64, 267, 448
Napoleon, 5
national account aggregates, 453-54
National Bank for Credit to Cooperatives, 385-86
National Bank for Economic Development, 385-86
national economic development agencies and entities,
    363-71
National Housing Bank, 42
national parks, 296
national security, 387-90
natural gas
    consumption, 228
    production, 216, 223
natural population increase, 83
Neblina Peak, 20
necatoriasis, 92-93
neoplasms, malignant/non-malignant causes of death, 86
nervous system diseases, causes of death, 86
Netherlands/Dutch, 104, 323-26, 337-38, 341-42, 431-32
Netherlands Antilles, 325-26, 337-38

palm Hearts, 186, 208-09
palm fiber and oil, 187
pampa-like grasses, 9, 13
Pan American Union Library, 3
Panama/Panamanians, 106, 337-38
panthers (onças), 188
paper products, output, 276-78, 282
Pará, 15, 18, 23-24, 47-58, 84, 109-10, 164, 202-03,
     209-12, 214, 221, 254, 257, 259, 262-64, 267-68,
     293, 300, 304, 306, 417-19
Paraguaçu, royal captaincy, 17
Paraguay/Paraguayans, 18, 104-06, 323-24, 241-42
Paraíba, 15, 17-18, 49, 52, 54, 56-58, 84, 109-10, 164,
     167-68, 202-03, 206, 209-10, 254, 257, 262-64, 267,
     300-03, 417-19
Paraíba River, 21
Paraná, 16, 18, 22-24, 47-49, 51-58, 84, 109-10, 164-66,
     193-94, 202-04, 206-07, 209-10, 221, 225, 242, 250,
     252, 255, 257, 261-64, 267-68, 293, 300, 304-06,
     337, 417-19, 436-38
Paraná pine, 12
Paraná River, 25
Paranaguá, Paraná, 259, 262-64
parasitic disease, causes of death, 86
parks, map, 306
parks, national and state, 298, 304-05
passenger cars, railroad, 242
passengers
     air, 256
     railroad, 242
passports, 339
pasture, irrigated/planted, 296, 300
payments, balance of, 327
peaches, 200, 203
peanuts, 198, 202
pears, 200, 204
Pearse, Andrew, 101
peccary hides, 189
Pedroso, Dr. Odair, 76
Pelotas, Rio Grande do Sul, 18, 262-64
penal institutions, 399-400, 407
pension funds, 173-75, 343-45
pepper, black, 199, 203
Pentecostalism, 37
pequi (fruit), 187, 208-09
perfume, output, 276-77
Pernambuco, 15, 17-18, 23-24, 47, 49, 52, 54, 54-58, 84,
     109-10, 164, 167-68, 193-94, 202-04, 206, 209-11,
     214, 221, 225, 249, 252-54, 258-64, 267-68, 293,
     300-04, 306, 337, 417-19, 436-38
persimmons, 200, 204

Indian, pre-1500, 39-41, 66
major political subdivisions, 27-31, 47-54
metropolitan, 33-34, 56
minor civil divisions, 31-35
rural, 32, 34-36, 57-59
sex, 36, 59-64
slave, 30, 54-60
underenumeration, 73
urban/urbanized areas, 32, 34-36, 56-59
Pôrto Alegre, Rio Grande do Sul, 15, 18-19, 22-25, 49,
52, 55-56, 84, 164, 255-56, 259, 262-64, 267-68,
293, 436-38, 448
Pôrto Nacional, Goiás, 23-24
Pôrto Seguro land grant, 17
Pôrto Velho, Rondônia, 15, 18, 164, 254, 267, 448
ports, characteristics, facilities, tonnages, 238, 259,
262-64
Portugal/Portuguese, 38, 76, 103-06, 308, 323-26,
341-42, 431-32
Portugal-Algarve Kingdom, 421
Portuguese
Empire, 6
royal court, 32
Portuguese crown
weak bureaucracy in Brazil, 1
colonization schemes in Brazil, 5
post-secondary institutions, 120, 122-24
postal system, 238-39, 265
potatoes, sweet/white, 198, 202-03
pound stirling, British, 431-32
precipitation, 23-24
pregnancy diseases, causes of death, 86
presidents of Brazil/votes received, 422
price indices, agriculture, 185, 205
price indices, minerals, 215, 222
prices, food, retail/wholesale, 443-47, 450
primary energy, sources/consumption, 228
primary schools, 120-21
printing and publishing, output, 276-77
prison expenditures, 407
prison population, characteristics, 396-400, 403-06
processed seafood, output, 281
professional athletes, 307
prostheticians, 91
Protestants, 65
psychiatric cases, by type admitted to hospitals, 95
psychoses, 95
public administrator schools, 111
public debt, external, 329-30
public employees, 409
public health measures, World War II, 35
public security, 387-91, 394

479

DATE DUE

MAR 1

A313 0526259 1